Tea Cultures of Europe: Heritage and Hospitality

Tea Cultures of Europe: Heritage and Hospitality

Arts & Venues | Teaware & Samovars |
Culinary & Ceremonies

Edited by
Hartwig Bohne

DE GRUYTER

ISBN 978-3-11-075842-9
e-ISBN (PDF) 978-3-11-075857-3
e-ISBN (EPUB) 978-3-11-075871-9

Library of Congress Control Number: 2023952386

Bibliographic information published by the Deutsche Nationalbibliothek
The Deutsche Nationalbibliothek lists this publication in the Deutsche Nationalbibliografie; detailed bibliographic data are available on the internet at http://dnb.dnb.de.

© 2024 Walter de Gruyter GmbH, Berlin/Boston
Cover image: Kempinski Hotel Taschenbergpalais Dresden
Typesetting: Integra Software Services Pvt. Ltd.
Printing and binding: CPI books GmbH, Leck

www.degruyter.com

Acknowledgements and Preface

This book combines two major passions: one for the fascinating world of hospitality and the second for the warmth and strength of black tea, preferably Assam. Therefore, it was my pleasure to connect the nicest elements from both parts, the backgrounds of tea culture and hospitality experiences, national or regional differences and similarities, and also European secrets about tea utensils, teahouses and tea ceremonies.

This is the first book about a European cultural approach to tea embraced by hospitality and should make the readers familiar with the fascinating world of European tea traditions and habits, connecting people for whom tea plays an important cultural role. In regions where tea is used to create a trustful atmosphere for social or business gatherings, people now realise the value of tea and its supplements, and it is for this reason that in East Frisia and Türkiye/Azerbaijan the regional tea cultures have been listed by UNESCO as intangible world heritage.

Therefore, this is a helpful guide for tea lovers, a practical knowledge base for lecturers, researchers and students as well as an interesting story book for hotel guests and entrepreneurs.

> Serving tea shows a taste for the finest, because tea is sociable and polite, it is stimulating and humble. (John Galsworthy)

A special thank you is offered to my family, who supported and challenged me. As especially my parents have been drinking black tea nearly every day, their positive impact on my taste for this clear and reliable beverage is obvious. In addition, I would like to thank my special tea related colleagues and friends all over the world, especially Dr. Annette Kappert-White and Mrs Lysbeth Vink in The Netherlands as well as Dr. Irena Weber in Slovenia. When we founded the European Tea Culture Research Circle in 2021, we used the pandemic to meet and virtually drink tea and discuss different tea culture related projects and research tasks in Europe. We laughed a lot, but we also talked seriously, and tea was the anchor for joint articles and future projects. In addition, Mrs Lee Jolliffe from Canada played an important role in introducing me to the working group of international tea tourism. This worldwide tea network has become a lovely community of passionate tea drinkers, researchers and ambassadors of this wonderful beverage.

> While there is tea, there is hope. (Arthur Pinero)

I also would like to thank all my contributors, from academia or the industry, from the North or the South, West or East of Europe – or beyond. In addition, the support of Mary Douglas (Kamm Teapot Foundation, Statesville/USA), Kerstin Fahrenson-Baaten (Silbersuite, Schweitenkirchen/Germany) and Katja Steiner (SATS Translation Services, Tengen/Germany) was very helpful for pictures and questions regarding teapots and kettles made from different materials.

https://doi.org/10.1515/9783110758573-202

It was my dream and hope to create a book presenting the variety of tea cultures in Europe connecting hospitality and guest orientation. And, illustrating this with more than 500 pages and about 100 figures, tables and pictures, this first book about the European approach of consuming and celebrating tea is an impressive piece of evidence for hundreds of years of history and culture of trading, producing, preparing and ennobling tea, of the development of tea events, tea spaces and specific table-ware, as well as of entrepreneurial spirit and diverse European links of the arts and tea, lifestyle and tea-related heritage.

This book project would not have been realised without the massive support of three extraordinary students, Ms. Carina Pardek, Mr. Moritz Ey, and Mr. Alexandros Sakellariou, who worked hard in order to manage the variety of contributions, the pictures and graphs as well as the challenging formalities.

Thank you all very much and, now, enjoy reading while drinking a wonderful cup of tea!

Prof. Dr. Hartwig Bohne
Berlin
May 2024

Tea Master Joel Belouet

Foreword: Passion for tea in luxury hotels

With a first focus on hospitality, my career started many years ago, more precisely in 1967 in Orleans, France. After gathering experience from many places, my path took me to Germany, where in 1974 I joined the Hotel Vier Jahreszeiten Kempinski in Munich. Being part of the bar team, I shortly became one of the loved personalities who served big names such as Queen Silvia of Sweden, Jacques Chirac, Aga Khan and many others. Slowly the art of tea gathered my whole attention, and passionately I shared this with several guests. Dedicating my time to discover everything there is to know about tea, my journey began. Traveling to Sri Lanka, where I received a "Tea Master Gold" certification, during an intense study in the origin, fabrication, preparation and storage of tea as well as how to correctly savour the aromas, the information I was seeking was discovered (see Figure 1).

Figure 1: Tea Master Joel Belouet.
Source: Hotel Vier Jahreszeiten Kempinski Munich

I have shared with my guests from the Hotel Vier Jahreszeiten Kempinski Munich my experience of over 45 years of preparing, serving, and enjoying tea. Recommending a guest the perfect tea is a delicate and attentive matter. The tea sort needs to fit the guests' mood. Only in this way can the guest enjoy a classic afternoon tea. Regarding my personal preferences, Earl Grey tea with scones, clotted cream, and orange mar-

https://doi.org/10.1515/9783110758573-203

malade must be the favourite. And if you might ask, lemon is poison to tea. And for a sweet tea flavour, white rock candy is recommended, but not normal white sugar, and definitely not any kind of (artificial) sweetener.

Pursuing further, even though I have met well-known figures from politics, business, and Hollywood sectors, I would always miss the discussions and exchanges with the regular guests. The trust put in me has always filled me with pride. The lobby of the hotel might be the largest tearoom of Munich, where 30 different varieties of tea can be enjoyed. From black to green, from herbal to fruit, everything can be found. Nevertheless, from a professional perspective, fruit or herbal tea cannot be counted as tea; we might better call it "infusion."

After nearly 50 years of service dedicated to tea in the lobby of the Hotel Vier Jahreszeiten Kempinski Munich, I am still passionate about tea, tea service, and watching guests enjoying tea. Tea makes people calm and friendly, they relax and seize the day – more than with other beverages. Therefore, it is my pleasure to see this book about European tea culture and hospitality, combining these two distinctive elements that mean so much to me, and finally being part of such an amazing project. I am happy to see the varieties of tea cultures in different parts of Europe, the links between tea, signature products, and food pairings as well as impressive tea venues or tea related artworks.

Again, I feel confirmed in my conviction that tea is much more than only a beverage; it should be seen as an enriching cultural heritage connecting people and offering space for peace and harmony. Following this approach, this book will be profitable for all tea related or interested readers, such as lecturers, students, and tea lovers, as well as all people involved in tea culture in hospitality.

Tea Master Joel Belouet

Foreword: It's all about tea: ceremonial enjoyment, successful entrepreneurship, and cultural pride

My first experience of tea in a food service context was at Teatime, my teashop in London which I opened in 1983 with two friends and managed for six years. When we opened the tearoom, friends and colleagues told us that we were wasting our time and money since no one went out for tea any more. How was it then that an impressively large group of people was waiting outside the shop while we put the finishing touches to the art deco interior? Within minutes of declaring ourselves open for business, every seat was filled. Older customers told us how they had missed going out for a proper cup of tea and that they were determined to go home and unpack from the attic or spare room the teapots they had used in the past, the favourite cups and saucers they had hidden away as mugs had become more fashionable. Younger guests found the entire experience somewhat quirky and old fashioned but also rather charming and so they too indulged in the traditional finger sandwiches, the warm scones with jam and clotted cream, and slices of the cakes I baked each morning. What visitors seem to have missed was the ceremonial aspect of British tea drinking and Afternoon Tea and, as time went by, we attracted people of all ages, from different countries, famous actors and rock stars as well as friends, locals and neighbours. Teatime's theatrical style was certainly an attraction but what really drew customers to the shop again and again was the time-honoured ritual of being seated at a table covered with a hand embroidered floral table cloth, perusing the menu which offered not just Afternoon Tea but all the traditional foods we had grown up with – toasted muffins and crumpets, hot buttered teacakes and scones. Our guests loved the choices they were offered – different breads for the sandwiches, a selection of jams, and a variety of teas. Everything we offered sprang from our own childhood memories so that we could share our traditional tea rituals and our love of tea times past.

But, just because the British are known around the world for their Afternoon Tea 'ceremony', it does not mean that every other country must copy our way of serving and drinking tea. Tearoom owners and hotel tea lounge managers around Europe should have a real desire to make their tea service a perfect example of their particular way of tea and should highlight and honour local traditions and rituals. Clever ideas, focused marketing, special offers during traditional seasonal occasions such as St Valentine's Day, Easter, Mothers' Day, Midsummer, Christmas, can attract new guests and loyal regulars. And at the heart of each location's tea service there must be a deep-

https://doi.org/10.1515/9783110758573-204

seated determination to give every single customer a special experience so that they too understand more about local rituals, traditional foods and the value of tea in the culture of each country. The menu should include a selection of teas to suit local tastes and traditions and can even include teas now being grown in that country. The foods offered should be made to local traditional recipes, using local ingredients. The service must be friendly and courteous and always delivered with a genuine warm smile. The brewing and serving of tea must ensure that each and every cup is perfect – brewed using the correct quantities of tea and water, the optimum water temperature, the correct steep time, and the leaves separated from the liquor. Each and every member of staff must understand the importance of and take pride in all those multilayered aspects of tea and tea drinking. And we should all remember that at times it's good to turn the clock back and pause to value and enjoy the simple traditions and ceremonies of the past instead of running helter skelter into the ever increasing speed of modern life. Settling around the tea table, wherever we are, creates a tranquil interlude during which we feel calm and soothed by the tea, the setting and the awareness of tea's timeless power to remind us of its importance through history and still today.

Jane Pettigrew/UK Tea Academy

Contents

A European views on tea

B Approaching tea cultures and hospitality

F Experiencing the islands of tea

G Exploring tea by the sea

H Discovering tea by land

I Hospitalitea in Europe: Tea culture and hospitality heritage

List of figures

https://doi.org/10.1515/9783110758573-206

List of tables

https://doi.org/10.1515/9783110758573-207

List of contributors

Arnaud Bachelin, originally from the Bourgogne region, has been operating his tearoom and tea shop "théritoires" in Paris since 2016. As a studied archaeologist, he became a tea expert with passion for Chinese tea, culinary arts and tea culture and heritage. He has contributed to the development of tea in prestigious salons by leading tea workshops and signing tea cards. His tea business in the French capital, and his books about French culinary arts are a perfect match to his passion for renovation historic monuments.

Carol Bailleul (1968) is a confident businesswoman and manager with her own tea company since early 2013. She combines various types of tea activities: organising tea tastings and tea workshops, advising restaurants and hosting afternoon tea parties. She works very hard to achieve her goals. Sitting still and doing nothing are not her cup of tea. She quickly converts ideas into actions and usually works simultaneously on several projects. In recent years she has been studying the British Afternoon Tea as a tea sommelier. That's why she was apprenticed to an English tea historian, studied Afternoon Tea Etiquette and read many books on this theme. She published her own book on this quintessential British ceremony in May 2019 called *Afternoon Tea or High Tea?* in Dutch and English.

Samuel Bartoš acquired work experience in several hotel and gastronomy establishments in Slovakia, France, and Italy. His main focus is connected with beverage gastronomy, especially wine, beer, and tea culture and its influence on culture and regional development.

Bernhard Bauer has a PhD in cultural anthropology from the University of Vienna. He was living in the Caucasus from 2018 to 2020 and has been responsible for implementing various consultancy projects related to tourism and gastronomy in the region until today. Since 2018 Bernhard has been strategically collaborating with the Italian based non-profit association Slow Food, focusing on the development of culinary tourism destinations, products and experiences. He is working as an independent consultant for tourism development and does research about the commodification of culture and the creative economy. Bernhard has been collaborating with UNESCO, UNWTO, the World Bank and other international donors in more than 30 countries from the Caribbean to the Maldives and the Philippines.

Hartwig Bohne has gained than 25 years of experience in the international hospitality industry based on which he was appointed Professor of International Hotel Management in 2018. His teaching and research foci are hotel development, people management and European tea culture. He finished his apprenticeship as a hotel expert at the Kempinski Hotel Taschenbergpalais Dresden and graduated from University Trier and EM Strasbourg Business School (Grande École) in business administration, tourism and international management. In addition, he worked at the Kempinski Hotel President Wilson in Geneva, at the German Hotel Association (IHA), for a member of Germany's federal parliament (Deutscher Bundestag) as well as at the Kempinski Hotels head office. He has published several articles and books about hospitality, people management and tea cultures. Teaching and researching about tea culture for many years, he founded the "European Tea Culture Research Circle" in 2021 and took the chair of the "Working Group of International Tea Tourism" in October 2022. Since January 2024 he has been acting as founding president of the European Tea Culture Institute, located in Berlin/Germany (www.teaculture-europe.org).

Maria Teresa Borges Tiago is Assistant Professor at the University of Azores and an invited professor at NOVA Information Management School (NOVA IMS). She has a Ph.D. in International Marketing and teaches marketing and hospitality management courses. She is a Research Fellow at the Centre of Applied Economics Studies of the Atlantic – the University of the Azores and Advance/CSG, ISEG – Lisbon University. Her main research interests include digital marketing, consumer behaviour, and tourism. She has published articles in peer-reviewed scientific international journals such as *Journal of Business Research, Tourism Review,* and

https://doi.org/10.1515/9783110758573-208

International Journal of Hospitality Management and Tourism Management and belongs to the editorial board of tourism and hospitality journals.

Lyudmila Britenkova is the chief paleographer of the department for scientific reference at the State Archive of the Tula region. More than 25 years she has been studying the history of the Russian samovar and Tula samovar production. Since 2014, she has been the curator of the museum of samovars and spirit kettles, the private collection of M. M. Borshchev. She has done a number of scientific researches and articles dedicated to the samovar and the culture of tea drinking in Russia. She is also the author of the book about Tula samovars, published in Russia in 2009.

Felix Bröcker completed his B.A. in film studies and philosophy at Gutenberg-University in Mainz followed by an M.A. in curatorial studies at the Goethe-University and Städelschule in Frankfurt after working as a trained chef for eight years. Felix assisted artistic performances of several artists, e.g., Paul McCarthy, Rirkrit Tiravanija and Peter Kubelka. He implements gastronomic projects at the interface of art, culture and science, has worked as gastronomic consultant, as head of a food lab and is a Ph.D. fellow at the University of Art and Design in Offenbach observing visual staging strategies of food. He currently works for the Max Rubner-Institute (MRI) on a project about the social dimension of sustainable nutrition. Since 2024, also member of the board of the European Tea Culture Institute (www.teaculture-europe.org).

Duarte Nuno Chaves has a Ph.D. in Art History from the University of Évora. As a fellow of the Regional Fund for Science and Technology of the Government of the Azores, he carried out a post-doctoral project (2017–2020) entitled "Religiosity and collective memory in the context of cultural tourism." He has been a researcher at the CHAM-Centro de Humanidades since 2010, in which he held the position of coordinator of the research group "Art, History and Heritage" and deputy director of the nucleus of this centre at the University of the Azores. As coordinator, author, and co-author, he is responsible for editing and participating in the writing of several books, articles, and chapters, dealing with issues related to the insular space of Macaronesia, particularly in the fields of History, Identity, Religiosity, Traditions, and Gastronomy.

Ann Teresa Conway has been lecturing with the School of Tourism and Hospitality Management in Technological University Dublin in marketing, management, and business studies since graduating with an MPhil in Consumer Behaviour and Tourism Marketing from the Dublin Institute of Technology in 1999. Ann also holds a PG Certificate in Teaching (2002), a PG Diploma Teaching (2003), and a MA in Teaching (2004), following research into the phenomenon of attrition and retention rates in the BA Hospitality Management programme. Ann is currently Chair of this programme.

Ann obtained her EdD from the University of Sheffield, (2015) with her thesis on the effects of change on culture and identities through a case study of a higher educational institution undergoing transition. Ann has also worked in the Irish hospitality sector, was sales and marketing representative with Fáilte Ireland and market researcher with the Tourism Research Centre.

Susana Goulart Costa is an Associate Professor at the University of the Azores and a researcher at the CHAM Centre for the Humanities, an inter-University research unit of the Faculty of Social and Human Sciences, NOVA University of Lisbon, and of the University of the Azores, funded by the Foundation for Science and Technology. She teaches in the areas of history and cultural heritage, areas where she investigates with a particular emphasis on heritage management, landscapes, and cultural tourism. She was a member of the UNESCO Culture Pilot Project in Portugal in 2030 and was the Regional Director of Culture in the Azores, Portugal, between 2018 and 2020. She is a member of the International Center for the Conservación del Patrimonio (CICOP), and Director of the Department of History, Philosophy, and Arts of the University of the Azores since 2018.

Belinda Davenport is the owner of Davenports Tea Room, an award-winning quintessential English tearoom based in Cheshire, UK. Belinda started her career in hospitality with her family boating business at the early age of 12. After studying at Bournemouth University, she embarked on her career as a travel agent, then travel and tourism lecturer. In 2006, after completing a master's degree in Tourism Management, she opened a tearoom with her husband, which eventually specialised in afternoon teas. With an inquisitive mind, and a passion for tea and history, Belinda has developed the business and her skills to achieve a tearoom recognised in the UK by *Britain magazine* (2023), *The Times* (2023) and *The Tea Guild* (2013) as one of the top tea places in the UK. She is a contributory author of *The Handbook of Tourism* (Routledge) and member of the European Speciality Tea Tourism forum as well as member of the board of the European Tea Culture Institute (www.teaculture-europe.org).

Lavinia Eifler M.A. studied German Studies, History and European Ethnology at the University of Bamberg and Comparative Cultural Science at the University of Regensburg. Her master thesis explored contemporary consumption of sugar and the perception of sugar as a drug. She worked as a research assistant at the chair of Comparative Cultural Science at the University of Regensburg from 2018 to 2021. Her research focuses on contemporary and historical consumption and perception of food and nutrition.

Robin Emmerson as curator of decorative art at Norwich Castle Museum found himself curating a collection of over 600 English teapots dating from 1700 to about 1800. He therefore bought another 2000 teapots dating from 1780 to 1850, and persuaded Twinings, the oldest company of tea blenders in Europe (founded 1706), to pay for a gallery and a catalog, *British Teapots and Tea Drinking 1700–1850* (Her Majesty's Stationery Office, 1992). Robin went on to become Curator of the Department of Decorative Art at National Museums Liverpool and, after retirement in 2010, Chairman of the Northern Ceramic Society.

Kateryna Fedosova is an Associate Professor at the Department of Hotel and Restaurant Business of the Odesa National University of Technology (ONTU), Odesa, Ukraine. She has been working in the field of Hotel and restaurant business and marketing for more than 10 years and is also a founder of the consulting company where they assist in developing launching and promoting Ukrainian restaurants. At her university she used to teach courses in restaurant management, information and communication technology in the hotel and restaurant business, culinary arts and a number of others in the field of hospitality and tourism. Unfortunately, due to the Russian war against Ukraine, the ONTU is providing contionously its studiy programmes only online.

Vahid Ghasemi, Ph.D., is Assistant Professor at Universidade Europeia in Lisbon, Portugal, and integrated research member in CEFAGE (Évora, Portugal). His research areas include marketing, destination management, luxury tourism, and tourist behaviour. He has published papers in several tourism and hospitality journals such as *Journal of Destination Marketing and Management*, *Tourism Analysis*, *Anatolia*, and *European Journal of Tourism Research* among others. He received the Emerald Literati Award 2020 for the Outstanding Author Contribution.

Jan Hán is the vice-rector for science, research and international relationships at University College Prague. His research is focused on the topics of hospitality marketing management, hospitality processes modelling and simulation, culinary heritage, wine, and tea culture. He is the manager of several research projects and the author of research publications and innovative applications. He cooperates with leading universities in Europe and Asia.

Kateřina Havelková applies the experience gained while working abroad in hotel and gastronomy establishments in her projects. She focuses on the topics of mixology, coffee and tea culture, wine, and beverage gastronomy in general. Since 2024, treasurer and member of the board of the European Tea Culture Institute (www.teaculture-europe.org).

Christian Hincheldey was born into the world of tea in 1969 in Scandinavia's oldest tea family. Being fifth generation in the family-owned business, he and his sister followed in their forefathers' footsteps of tea merchants in the old 188-year-old family business. Christian was trained as a tea-sommelier in Hamburg, Germany, in the early nineties and has studied tea all over the world through numerous travels, such as in South East Asia. Christian holds a Master of Arts in international business communication.

Gunther Hirschfelder studied history, European Ethnology and agricultural science at the university in Bonn, Germany. He received his PhD in 1992 from the University of Trier. Hirschfelder's thesis looked at historic trade relations of Cologne in the late Middle Ages. After holding a research position in Manchester he has since worked at the University of Bonn. His habilitation thesis treated the historical consumption of alcoholic drinks at the beginning of the industrial age. Having worked as a lecturer in Mainz and Bonn, he has been professor for Comparative Cultural Science at the University of Regensburg since 2010. Hirschfelder focuses on food, nutrition, and agricultural processes from a historical and contemporary perspective. Next to his research and teaching activities at the University of Regensburg, he is member of various public committees focusing on food and nutrition in today's and tomorrow's Europe.

Lee Jolliffe is a Visiting Scholar, Mah Fah Luang University, Thailand. She has published extensively on tea tourism, including through the editorship of *Tea and tourism: Tourists, transitions and transformations* (2007) and as lead editor for the *Routledge handbook of tea tourism* (2022). While researching tea tourism she visited tea gardens and estates in many countries, completing a Japanese Tea Master Course in Japan through the Global Japanese Tea Association and the World Tea Tours Darjeeling Immersion programme in India.

Annette Kappert-White PhD is currently an Associate Academic and Online Course Developer for the University of Derby. She has worked extensively in higher education and in the hospitality industry, facilitating her penchant for applied learning. Her research interests include food and cultural heritage, food and gender and visual and narrative research methods. She is currently researching the historical significance and traditions of the Dutch tea industry. Since 2021, committed to the European Tea Culture Research Circle, and since 2024 also member of the board of the European Tea Culture Institute (www.teaculture-europe.org).

Ute Kemmerling studied history and literature at the FernUniversität in Hagen. Since 2015 she has been working in the department Geschichte Europas in der Welt (Global History of Europe) at the FernUniversität in Hagen. The research focus is on modern history of Asia, the history of knowledge, the cultural transfer research, and local colonialism in the German Empire. In her master's thesis, Ute Kemmerling addressed the colonial handling of tropical diseases on tea plantations in Assam. Pursuing her Ph.D., her dissertation topic deals with the Muslim pilgrimage site of Ajmer in northwestern India under the colonial British administration and the accompanying interactions, power structures, and negotiation processes (1818–1947).

Nicole Klauß born in 1969, she studied Romance languages and literature, journalism and art history. She completed wine training at the German Wine and Sommelier School, and now works as a Mindful Sommelière and advises restaurateurs, develops alcohol-free drinks, and organizes tastings and workshops on the topic of alcohol-free food accompaniment with a clear focus on tea. She is a freelance food writer and author of "Die neue Trinkkultur – Speisen perfekt begleiten ohne Alkohol" (The new drinking culture – perfect food accompaniment without alcohol) and gives lectures on pairings and alcohol-free drinks. The Swiss food magazine *Salz & Pfeffer* regularly publishes her alcohol-free column, "Ausgetrunken." In 2023, she published "Alkoholfrei" (at Verlag) and in 2024 she became treasurer of the European Tea Culture Institute (www.teaculture-europe.org).

Hanne Klöver is a German journalist, filmmaker, and book author. She studied German language and literature with a focus on Low German, English and Dutch at the Georg-August-University in Göttingen. Since the early 1990s she has worked as a journalist for print, radio, and television. She has written features, reports, and documentaries for Radio Bremen, Deutschlandradio, and Norddeutscher Rundfunk. Her main topics include reports on the Low German language and literature, the cooking and eating culture of Northern Germany, the regional history of East Friesland and of the Oldenburg region, nature and environmental topics as well as travel reports. She also deals with aspects of women's history. Her book publications include "Tee in Ostfriesland", "Spurensuche im Saterland", "Ostfriesland kocht", and "Barßel damals". A publication with the working title "Teeland Ostfriesland – Eine ostfriesische Teereise" is in preparation. Her awards include "Oostfreeske Tuffel" (awarded by the association Onno e.V. – the East Frisian network for ecology, region and future) and "Keerlke" (the East Frisian "Oscar" is awarded by the association Ostfreeske Taal).

Monika Kostera is a Polish sociologist. She is Professor Ordinaria in Management in Poland, holding a titular professorship in economics (2004) and the humanities (2017). She has authored and edited over 50 books in Polish and English and a number of articles published in journals including *Organization Studies*, *Journal of Organizational Behavior*, and *British Journal of Management*. Her current research interests include the imagination and organising, desalination of work, organisational ethnography, and organisational and archetypes.

Martin Krieger is professor for Northern European History at the University Kiel, Germany. His special field of interest is the history of the Northern European countries. He has extensively published on the former Danish colonies in India, on the history of natural science between Northern Europe and India, and on cultural exchange within the Baltic Sea area as well as between the Baltic Sea Area and the world. Furthermore, he has studied the history of tea and coffee as global consumer goods with a focus on early modern times. In 2022, he published the volume *Nathaniel Wallich. Global Botany in Nineteenth Century India* (Manohar Publishers-Routledge).

Gabriella Lombardi in 2010 founded Chà Tea Atelier, the first tea shop in Milan with a tearoom specialised in high-quality loose-leaf teas and flavoured and herbal teas (http://www.chateaatelier.it/). Gabriella Lombardi is the first tea sommelier in Europe certified by the Tea and Herbal Association of Canada. She is involved in educational programs for consumers and professionals and consultancy to restaurants, hotels, and spas for tea and food pairing, menu design, and cooking with tea. Following her passion, was the author of the book *Tea sommelier*, a book about tea and tea culture, tea and food pairing, and cooking with tea, published in four languages and sold worldwide. In several international conferences and tea forums aimed at professionals in the sector, Gabriella was a speaker about the latest trends in tea and food pairing in Italy and Europe, and an international judge, e.g., at the World Tea Forum: Korea – October 2013; World Tea Championship: Korea – September 2014; Mount Emei International Tea Culture Exhibition: Sichuan, China – April 2016; first International Green Tea Conference, Shengzhou, Zhejiang, China – March 2019; and fourth Annual International Tea Conference (online) – Yibin, Sichuan, China – May 2021. In addition, she is the President of the Protea Academy Association and national coordinator for the Tea Masters Cup competition in Italy.

Andreas N. Ludwig is Senior Lecturer at the Chair of International Relations, Catholic University Eichstaett-Ingolstadt (Germany), and Adjunct Lecturer for European Integration at the Carinthia University of Applied Sciences (Austria). His research, teaching, and publications focus on Austrian, British, and German foreign policy, European integration, and new approaches in IR theory, especially complexity thinking and memory. Ludwig holds a Ph.D. in International Relations from KU, German-French Master's degrees in political science from KU and Sciences Po Rennes (France), and a Master's degree in international history from the University of Strasbourg (France).

Maksym Malyhin is a tea maker and project manager of Zhornina Tea Plantation (Ukraine, Transcarpathia, Mukachevo), tea expert and consultant, as well as Tea Master Cup National Judge, Ukraine.

Gihan Mauris with a childhood spent standing on tea chests in factories alongside his father, Gihan's love and knowledge for the tea industry began at a young age. This early exposure instilled in him a deep passion for this artisan product, surpassing his actual years in the business. Through extensive studies and travels to tea-producing countries such as Sri Lanka, Japan, India, Taiwan, South Korea, China, and Germany, he has honed his expertise in tea. While his father, a renowned tea pioneer in Sweden, imparted much of his knowledge, there were certain aspects that could only be learned through firsthand experience. The competitive nature of the tea business constantly challenges him to expand his understanding of this multifaceted product. His goal is to introduce tea in innovative ways, enlightening customers about its diverse varieties, flavours, aromas, and health benefits. He eagerly anticipates the opportunity to continue this pursuit and make a meaningful impact in the world of tea.

Detta Melia is a lecturer in hospitality management with Technological University Dublin, City Campus, in the School of Tourism and Hospitality Management, lecturing on a diverse range of modules and has completed a Doctorate with Loughborough University in the UK in January 2009. Her doctorate research "Towards Performance Measurement in Hotels: An Incremental Approach," focused on small and medium-sized independently owned hotels in Ireland. She has a wide range of industrial experience in hospitality and tourism including business consultancy. She continues her research and has a number of publications and conference papers which are available online and in the TUDublin ARROW Library. The most recent include *The future of hospitality education: Trends and drivers for change* and the *Growth of resort hotels in Ireland*. A further paper, "Food tourism: Cases from food tourism providers networks," was presented at the EuroCHRIE Conference 2022. Dr. Melia is currently a judge for the Good Food Ireland awards and one of the Vice Presidents of the European Tea Culture Institute (www.teaculture-europe.org).

Stefan Nungesser is professor and programme manager for hotel management at the Carinthian University of Applied Sciences, School of Management. Before moving to Austria in 2011, he was a senior consultant at TREUGAST Solutions Group in Munich. In addition to consulting small and medium-sized hotels, he prepared feasibility studies for hotel projects at home and abroad. As head of the TREUGAST International Institute, he co-edited numerous industry-specific publications and conducted market research projects. Elsewhere, he has also worked as a trainer for part-time continuing education since 2005. Her professional focus, as book author, consultant, and trainer, lies in strategic and operational hotel and gastronomy management, especially in classic and digital marketing, sales, service quality, and (digitalised) service processes, as well as increasingly in people management in the tourism, hotel, and gastronomy sector.

Carina Pardek comes from Romania and is a researcher at the Fraunhofer Institute for Industrial Engineering in Stuttgart, Germany. She works in the FutureHotel Innovation Network, research project that focuses on the potential emerging technologies have on the hotel industry. With a background in hospitality, Carina is a graduate of the SRH Berlin Universiy of Applies Sciences, with a bachelor degree's in International Hotel Management. She discovered her passion for research and writing during her studies, and followed a carrier that combines both. As a former student of Prof. Dr. Hartwig Bohne, her love for tea and the hotel industry has been developed over the course of three and a half years of studies.

Bernard Ricolleau Based on a deep interest in the world of protocol and tradition, Bernard Ricolleau started his career at the Hôtel de Matignon in Paris in the service of the Prime Minister. Trained as a maître d'hôtel, he had the opportunity to work in numerous luxury hotels in France and abroad. His understanding of service excellence is his guideline for teaching and research in food and beverage operations as essentials of his professional life working passionately as a Maître d'hôtel at the Institut LYFE (ex Institut Paul Bocuse) in Ecully. Consequently, the gourmet representations of French and foreign traditions as well as a special interest in cheese, wine, but also coffee and tea, have become real passions.

Marion Roehmer is a historian and classical archeologist, and currently research fellow at the Department of Prehistorical Archaeology at Bonn University; she is also director of several museum research projects concerning the objects of drinking culture in Renaissance and early modern times. She is an executive board member of *Internationaler Arbeitskreis Keramikforschung*, with research activities and publications in the field of international historical ceramics. For ten years she was director of the East Frisian Tea-Museum at Norden. Up until now she is calles upon as an expert on tea culture and early Thuringian porcelain. She has publicated widely on tea culture in East Frisia, the history of coffee in Germany, and medieval and modern drinking and serving vessels in their historical and cultural contexts.

Henrik Scander is a lecturer and has a PhD in Culinary Arts and Meal Science, in the field of food and drink combinations. He wrote his thesis on food and beverages in combination based on cultural habits and nutritional contribution. The focus was on combining qualitative and quantitative methodology to see how and why food and beverage combinations are consumed and what they lead to. Henrik thus highlights the "good" combination from a health perspective and a pleasure perspective. In 2011, Henrik finished his master's degree in Culinary Art and hospitality Science, in which his essay focused on the tacit knowledge and craft of sabrering Champagne. Henrik has been employed as lecturer since 2008 at Campus Grythyttan, Örebro University. Henrik has worked primarily on the development of craft for the sommelier and how it can be linked to scientific perspectives, as well as wine tasting with a special focus on wine, tea, and coffee. Before his employment at the University, he completed the bachelor programme at Grythyttan for Sommeliers. He has also worked in the restaurant business since the 1990s. Henrik has held positions as a sommelier in Sweden and in France and has served on the board of the Swedish Sommelier Association. Since 2021, committed to the European Tea Culture Research Circle, since 2024, Vice President of the European Tea Culture Institute (www.teaculture-europe.org).

Markus Schuckert is Professor and Department Chair of Hospitality Management (HMGT) at the Peter T. Paul College of Business and Economics. His core industry experience is from aviation and tourism on international level. As an entrepreneur, Markus established a tourism and hospitality related consulting firm for market research, product development, and change management in Europe. As researcher, Markus specializes in digital marketing, travel technology, and strategic management for hospitality and tourism. Markus contributes to top journals in the field, international conferences, industry meetings, consulting, and edits books for education and industry. As an educator, Markus delivers related subjects at business schools across the globe. Caring for the next generation of industry leaders, he supervises postgraduate students in Europe, America and Asia. Markus works at the edge of contemporary teaching technology to enhance learning experience, integrating new methods and techniques into courses and seminars on-campus and online. Prior joining UNH, Markus held academic positions in the U.S., Hong Kong, Switzerland, Austria, and Germany.

Gundega Silniece is the founder of the TEA TEA ME app, which is a platform for tea tourism, education, and events. Gundega is a board member of the European Specialty Tea Association and is responsible for the international development of tourism, hospitality, and sustainability in the organisation. She is one of the international judges at the Tea Master Cup and a member of the executive board of the Latvian Tea Association.

Isabell Stern lives in Klagenfurt/Austria and completed her Bachelor in Business Management and Master in Business Development Management at the Carinthian University of Applied Sciences (CUAS). As a staff member at CUAS, she is part of the modularisation team for the curriculum and jointly responsible for quality management in the further study development. Due to her professional background in tourism and the hotel industry, she is also involved in various tourism projects that deal with issues of employee recruitment and training, workplace attractiveness, and the attractiveness of Carinthia as a tourism destination in general. Her areas of activity in these projects include the organisation and coordination, evaluation, and preparation of data, coordination and information exchange with clients and employees as well as the design and implementation of workshops.

Flávio Tiago is Regional Director of Science and Technology in the Azores Government. He has been a Professor at the University of the Azores since 2006. He holds a Ph.D. in Economics and Business Sciences from the University of the Azores and completed his aggregation at ISEG. He is a researcher at ISEG's ADVANCE centre and CEEAplA Azores. Additionally, he served as chairman of the founding board of directors of NONAGON Science and Technology Park. He has promoted and participated in several studies and projects in private and public organisations and has publications in leading international journals.

Virginia Utermohlen Lovelace MD explores the aromas of teas, how they come about, and how these aromas interact in the mouth, nose, and brain. As faculty member of the Division of Nutritional Sciences at Cornell University, Ithaca, New York, she has earned numerous teaching awards, including the State University of New York's Chancellor's Award for Excellence in Teaching. Retirement saw her focus on bringing the science behind our sensory perceptions of tea to audiences both professional and amateur. Most recently she joined Jason McDonald and Timothy Gipson of The Great Mississippi Tea Company to create workshops on how to grow and process tea for delicious aroma development. Her books on tea are: A Nerd Contemplates the Japanese Tea Ceremony, *Three Basic Teas & How to Enjoy Them, Tea: a Nerd's Eye View*, and *A Nerd's Tea Lab*. The "Scents of Tea" kit that she created with Scott Svihula won a Best of Tea Award at World Tea Expo 2020.

Lysbeth Vink is a lecturer at Hotelschool The Hague, The Netherlands. She received her bachelor's and master's degrees in Hotel and F&B Management. She has a research interest in tea and the cultural heritage of tea. She has written papers on the cultural heritage of tea in The Netherlands and the art of tea in the hospitality industry. She is an internationally certified tea sommelier with a great interest in the culture behind a cup of tea. Since 2021, committed to the European Tea Culture Research Circle, since 2024, Vice President of the European Tea Culture Institute (www.teaculture-europe.org).

Irena Weber, sociologist and anthropologist, is an assistant professor of social sciences and humanities in tourism at the Faculty of tourism studies Turistica, University of Primorska. She is the Head of the Department of Cultural Tourism. She received her Ph.D. the Faculty of Arts, University of Ljubljana (Department of Sociology of Culture). She conducted postgraduate research with a British Council Grant at SOAS, University of London, Department of Anthropology. In 2015, she was a visiting scholar at San Diego State University (USA) (Department of Geography). Her research interests include anthropology and sociology of tourism, specifically Mediterranean, cultural heritage, anthropology of space, food and culinary tourism, film, and literary tourism, qualitative methodology, childhood studies, and art. Her research interest in tea is focused mainly on representations of tea in diverse forms of art, Asian tea ceremonies, the ethnography of contemporary teahouses, and tea ware design. Since 2021, committed to the European Tea Culture Research Circle, since 2024, also member of the board of the European Tea Culture Institute (www.teaculture-europe.org).

Petra Werner studied history and geosciences with a focus on art history, ethnology, and monument preservation at the University of Bamberg from 1982 to 1990 where she received her master's degree.

Since then, she has been employed at the Porzellanikon State Museum of Porcelain in Hohenberg an der Eger / Selb. There, she is the chief curator and head of the department of art and cultural history of porcelain. In addition, she served as archivist to the Rosenthal AG from 1992 to 2009.

Katrina Wild is the creative associate of the TEA TEA ME app. She is responsible for social media, article writing, presentations, networking, and innovative ideas on how to progress forward. Her focus is the cultural anthropology of tea and its elements within contexts of various corners of the world, as well as agriculture and the production of tea as she has completed an internship at Kyoto Obubu Tea Farms in Japan in 2022. In researching tea, Katrina has been and continues to explore Europe, Africa, and Asia via direct long-term expeditionary immersion within tea and its cultural landscapes.

Allan L. Winther teaches as an Associate Professor in hospitality and hosting and has a degree as MSc in Biology. He has been teaching since 2014 at University College Lillebaelt in Odense, Denmark. Before that, he worked in the experience industry, mainly aquariums, as a biologist and ranger for more than 17 years. He is researching in hosting and has presented papers at many EUROChrie conferences.

Assoc. Prof. Dr. Gülsün Yildirim has B.A. degree in Tourism Management from Adnan Menderes University and ELT (English Language Teaching) from Pamukkale University. After graduating from B.A. she attained her M.A degree from Eskişehir Osmangazi University in Tourism Management and her Ph.D. degree from Selcuk University/Gazi University in Tourism Management. She worked as a tour guide for three years. She also worked as a lecturer in Ardesen Vocational School of Recep Tayyip Erdogan University between 2012 and 2019. She has been working as Associate Professor in the department of Gastronomy and Culinary Arts in the Tourism Faculty of Recep Tayyip Erdoğan University. Her research interests are rural tourism, agritourism, sustainable tourism, tourism marketing, and gastronomy. She is editor of a publication entitled "Cases on Tour Guide Practices for Alternative Tourism," published by IGI Global. Her works have appeared in book chapters released by Routledge. She has written book chapters on tea culture and tea tourism in works published by Routledge and Peter Lang Publishing House.

A European views on tea

European Tea culture shows the variety of traditions and venues, regional customs and preferences, entrepreneurial innovations and geographical dimensions – from the Azores to Georgia, from Sweden to Italy.

Hartwig Bohne

A.1 European views on tea

Almost everywhere in the world, tea is enjoyed in different variations. There are different occasions when tea is drunk and over the years individual tea cultures have emerged. But what is meant by "tea culture"? And, are there any European specifics?

When family and friends get together, offering tea is an important social ritual. It is simply the epitome of hospitality to share a glass of tea with one's guests. This tradition is a hospitable expression of warmth and cordiality, which creates a pleasant atmosphere. Additionally, tea forms a part of food and beverage services in hospitality settings offering hospitality experiences. In particular, tea ceremonies can symbolise pride of a population, a social anchor or a certain understanding of ritualising drinks. Furthermore, tea and food pairings as well as tea events or signature tea products can be profitable for hospitality operations. In addition, international hotel chains as well as family-owned hotels embracing national and regional tea traditions can deliver on the authentic beverage services that visitors expect to receive at local destinations (Bohne & Jolliffe, 2021). Tea culture also affects the design and decoration of hotel facilities as well as tableware or utensils. And, tea in the arts is an expression of lifestyle and different national tea cultures reflect the European way of adapting tastes and traditions to this beverage, mainly produced in Asia and Africa.

With this book, deep insights into the world of tea traditions in Europe will be offered as well as different types of artworks are explained in order to get an entire picture of the wide interpretation of tea culture in Europe. The focus is on tea, made from the Camellia sinensis plant. Consequently, any infusions of fruits or herbs or roibosh are only partially mentioned. As every good beverage, tea needs time to develop, to enrich the atmosphere, and to give joy to the consumers. Tea culture also needs time to impress people and to take them on the journey celebrating a beverage influenced by hundreds of years of harvesting, trading, ennobling, and making a cup of tea a fine element of a special moment.

In addition, tea in Europe is much more than a beverage with Chinese origin. There are several tea plantations, with the oldest in operation found on the Azores, but also in Georgia where a long tradition of harvesting tea can be seen. And, tea consumption can be differentiated between a daily beverage and an essential ingredient of a ceremonial event – both types can be found in Europe, too. As an appetising perspective, Figure A.1.1 shows the locations of tea plantations, the top four tea consuming countries/regions in Europe, and the UNESCO listed and world record awarded regions/countries. Enjoy your cuppa!

https://doi.org/10.1515/9783110758573-001

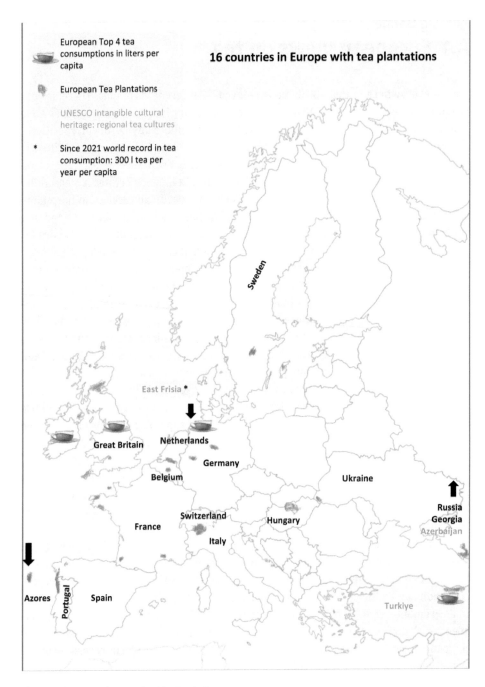

Figure A.1.1: Tea culture and cultivation in Europe.
Source: Author

B Approaching tea cultures and hospitality

Tea and Hospitality can be seen as two sides of one medal – symbolising warmth and cosiness, security and feeling at home.

Bernard Ricolleau, Hartwig Bohne and Lysbeth Vink

B.1 Exploring Thea sinensis – sorts, origin, and history

Introduction

It is all about tea. After water, tea is the second most consumed drink in the world. Tea offers a significant variety of sorts, producing countries as well as consumption habits. In addition, the pure sorts of tea are blended and/or mixed with flavours, coincidently like the famous Early Grey or with a clear selling proposition like lemongrass green tea (Krekel, 2013).

In order to get familiar with tea, its value and history, the botanical basics, and traditional rituals have to be seen as essentials, for economic roots and opportunities of this beverage.

Historical development

The success story of tea began in 2737 BC, in China, when the emperor Shennong was boiling water under a tree and coincidently some tea leaves fall into his pot of boiling water. He tasted it and he was surprised about the refreshing taste and effect. As he also liked the colour and the fragrance, he was happy to find this new beverage. The tree was a wild tea plant: tea was born (Gaylard, 2021).

Culturally, and socially, the Chinese dynasties had enormous influence on the consumption habits, on the connection between art and tea, but as well as on the awareness of tea.

During the Han Dynasty (206 BC–220 AD) tea was drunk only by the royal family (Su, Fang, & Yin, 2014) and later on during the Tang Dynasty (618–907) monks from China, Japan, and Korea used the tea leaves to concentrate during their meditation and started planting them around the cloisters. Tea evolved into a more popular use, going beyond pharmacopoeia to become a refined part of everyday life and with a positive impact on health. The main preparation was based on steaming and crushing, while the tea was also spiced with orange peel, peppermint or cloves (Pettigrew, 2001; Freeman & d'Offay (2018).

But, also for painters, potters, and poets tea became an interesting topic and purpose to meet in teahouses, using this environment for artistic inspiration. One of them, Lu Yu (723–804), wrote the first treatise on tea, Cha Jing or Classic of Tea, a poetic work in which he described the nature of the plant and codified the method of preparation and tasting of the drink. He wrote, "the same order and harmony are found in the serving of tea as in everything else" (Ellis et al., 2015).

https://doi.org/10.1515/9783110758573-002

In Tibet, tea was not used as loose tea, but made in the form of compressed bricks, which were roasted before being ground into powder and mixed with boiling water. Some ingredients were added, including salt, spices, rancid butter, etc. This is still how tea is consumed in Tibet (Gaylard, 2021).

During the Song dynasty (960–1279) the use of tea was elaborated further and the requirements became higher. The teas consumed were increasingly refined and ceramics took on a determining role in the world surrounding tea. The leaves were pulverised with a grinder to obtain a very fine powder, to which simmering water was added. The mixture was then beaten into a froth with a bamboo whisk. Alongside this rite, reserved for the court, a wider consumption was developing, affecting other social circles. The first loose teas appeared, which were easy to produce in large quantities and could thus satisfy a growing popular demand (Hincheldey, 2011; Rohrsen, 2022).

The Japanese monk Eisai, who went to China to study chan Buddhism (in Japanese: zen), explored powdered green tea and brought it to Japan. This drink, called matcha, was originally associated with the ritual of Zen monasteries where it was served on various occasions, such as the offering to the Buddha, or to keep monks awake during long meditation sessions. The close relations established between the ruling Japanese military class and these temples promoted the spread of tea in the Shogunal milieu in the fourteenth century. Originally consumed for its medicinal virtues, it becomes a pretext for refined meetings (Gaylard, 2021).

The term "tea ceremony" is a Western adaptation of the Japanese term chanoyu which literally means "hot water for tea," with the simplicity of these words not implying any notion of ceremony. The word chanoyu was used in Japan as early as the ninth century, but it took on the meaning known to it only in the second half of the fifteenth century, once the rules governing the first meetings of tea were defined. Its extension became widespread in the early seventeenth century after the great tea master of the Momoyama period, Sen no Rikyū (1522–1591), had imposed his style at these meetings (Universalis, 2023).

The Yuan-Dynasty from 1368 to 1644 was dominated by Mongolians, who conquered China but who had a rather low interest in the Chinese tea culture. Therefore, the development of tea habits stagnated until the next period (Gaylard, 2021)

In fact, the Ming dynasty (1368–1644) brought back much energy and interest in tea and tea culture. It was not attractive any more, manufacturing the compressed tea, and tea began to be consumed in its present form, infused in a vessel. This way of drinking tea had an influence on the objects and accessories used for its preparation. It was the beginning of earthenware and porcelain services. In addition, poets and artists used that era to focus on tea and arts, writing books, and creating artworks related to tea (Lombardi, 2013).

The following period, the Quing Dynasty (1644–1911), was the export period of tea. The product of China became more democratic and found a new economic boom with the export of tea. In addition, Chinese cultural impact (colours, paintings, porcelain) became more and more attractive for the people in tea importing countries, e.g., the

"Chinoiserie"-painted tea porcelain was born. In 1606, the first tea from Indonesia arrived in Amsterdam, the first known shipment of tea to be registered in a European port (Lombardi, 2013).

The East India Company, a Dutch company, maintained regular relations with the Far East at this time and, despite the foundation of the East India Company, its British competitor, in 1615, retained a monopoly on the tea trade until the late 1660s. English and Dutch emigrants took tea with them to the New World, where it would play a decisive role in the history of the United States. The product was subject to heavy taxes and in 1773 the colonists of Boston decided to boycott imports. On December 16, they threw the cargo of a ship anchored in the port into the sea. This was the Boston Tea Party, which led to reprisals by the English authorities against the inhabitants of Massachusetts, thus setting off the mechanisms that would lead to the War of Independence. In the nineteenth century, China was no longer able to satisfy the ever-increasing Western consumption of tea and the British began to develop tea cultivation in other countries around 1830 (Temming, 1983; Hincheldey, 2011).

At that time, the tea plantations in India, Ceylon, and Kenya (British colonies at that time) became more important to fulfil the required quantity of tea in Europe. In addition, tea porcelain, also called tea china, was developed and a special type of ship, called "tea clipper" was used to bring the tea from India to Europe (Gaylard, 2021).

In Western Europe, the tea consumption habits (e.g., preference for strong black tea, biscuits, sweetening, milk, using China) follow this British heritage and the tea arrived by ship. Meanwhile in Eastern Europe, the tea habits (e.g., using glass and samovars, smoky teas, very sweet) are more influenced by the trading via Russia and Tibet. The tea was brought by caravans via the ancient tea horse road.

As a result of the different trade routes, two main sources for differentiating the name of tea emerged: following the Amoy dialect in the southern Chinese province of Fujian (té), this term reached Western Europe via Dutch traders and was gradually transferred from Dutch (thee) into English (tea), French (thé), Spanish (té) and German (Tee). This version also became established in Scandinavia and the western Mediterranean region. As the term "cha" was derived from the word "chàh" in the province of Guangzhou (Canton), and also in the city of Macau, which was primarily used by Portuguese traders, this expression was transferred to the Portuguese language, but also to the eastern Mediterranean and above all in countries that were supplied with tea via overland trade routes, e.g. Albania, Serbia, Slovenia and the Czech Republic. A few countries adapted the Latin term "herbis thea": Poland, Ukraine, Lithuania and Belarus refer to this, e.g. tea is called "Herbata" in Poland (Rohrsen, 2022).

Botanical background

In 1753, the Swedish botanist Carl von Linné documented firstly a plant called "Thea sinensis". Later, in 1887 a new categorisation as "Camellia sinensis" was initiated by the German botanist Carl Ernst Otto Kuntze, which has been used till today. This plant can be differentiated in four varieties with slightly different types of leaves, required growing conditions and the regions to be found, while the "China-Bush" and the "Assam-Bush" are the most used plants for tea plantations worldwide (Krieger, 2021; see Table B.1.1).

Table B.1.1: Varieties of Camellia sinensis.

Camellia sinensis			
Camellia sinensis var. sinensis (**"China-Bush"**)	*Camellia sinensis var. assamica* (**"Assam-Bush"**)	*Camellia sinensis var. dehungensis*	*Camellia sinensis var. pubilimba*
Mostly to be found in the south of China	**Mostly to be found in Birma, India (Assam), Bangladesh and, also in the south of China**	Mostly to be found in the south of Yunnan region/ China	Mostly to be found in the southeast of China

Tea plants are growing primarily in subtropical and humid regions, e.g., Thailand, South Korea, China, Japan, Laos, Myanmar, Vietnam, but also in Kenya and parts of Latin America – **in the "tea belt" between 43rd degree north latitude and 30th degree south latitude**

Source: Author, in accordance with Rohrsen (2022)

Differentiation of taste – one plant, six sorts of tea

The plant *Camellia sinensis* can be treated differently to get six main types of tea: black, green, white, Oolong, yellow and Pu-Erh-Tea. In addition, the naming can also change due to the colour of the tea's infusion; the tea which is usually called "black tea" out of China is named "red tea" within China, Oolong Tea can also be found as "blue green tea" and the Pu-Erh-Tea is called "black tea" in China.

As with wine, there are many different varieties (known as cultivars for tea). The differences in terroir and cultivation methods will result in teas of different quality levels while the six colours of tea come from their oxidation and/or fermentation (see Table B.1.2).

First category: Teas without fermentation/oxidation or very light fermentation.

Green, yellow and white teas are not supposed to be fermented. Therefore, their taste is much lighter as the taste of fermented (=black) teas. This original type of tea (green) is still very popular in China, Taiwan and Japan. After plucking, the leaves of the tea plant are often withered and then heated very quickly to a high temperature (drying), in order to destroy the enzymes and thus prevent any possibility of oxidation. Afterwards, they are rolled and dried several times (rolling). The Chinese method of drying uses copper basins placed over a fire, while the Japanese use steam drying.

Table B.1.2: Different treatments of Camellia sinensis.

Fresh leaves plucked sorted and checked for interfering objects					
Withering	Withering	Withering	Sun Withering Afterwards Indoor withering	Withering	Withering
Pan-Firing (Panning) (China) or steaming (Japan) The term for this is "killing the greens"	Pan-Firing		Bruising		Pan-firing
Rolling or shaping	Sweating	Drying	Pan-Firing	**Orthodox Rolling** OR Crush Tear Curl CTC	Orthodox rolling
Drying and sorting	Wrapped in wooden boxes, afterwards drying and sorting		Ball forming drying and sorting	Oxidation Drying, sorting	**Drying and compressing, ageing** OR Wet heaping, drying, sorting
No fermentation	No fermentation	Light fermentation due to 2–3 days of withering	Partial fermentation	Full fermentation	Half fermented and treated with special microorganisms and fungi, stored in cakes or bricks
Pan-fired or steamed				**Orthodox** or CTC	**Sheng** or Shou/ripe
GREEN TEA	**YELLOW TEA**	**WHITE TEA**	**OOLONG TEA**	**BLACK TEA**	**PU ERH TEA**

Source: Author, based on Hincheldey (2009); Gaylard (2021); Bowles (2021); Battle (2017)

Japanese green tea should be prepared with boiled water at 60 degrees Celsius and Chinese green with water at 70 degrees Celsius (Rohrsen, 2022).

Sun-dried green teas have a light green appearance, while pan-fired green teas have a much darker green appearance. The Japanese steamed green teas have a very bright green appearance.

A yellow tea is a Chinese green tea that has undergone a post-enzymatic fermentation phase. High quality green teas are sometimes also called yellow tea. After roasting and rolling, the leaves covered with a damp cloth are piled up in small heaps for about two hours. Meanwhile the flavour of chocolate and coffee is arising. Afterwards the drying process starts on a wooden fire at 150 degrees Celsius (Rohrsen, 2022).

White teas are the least processed teas. Only budsets (immature leaves, shoots, or tips) are harvested to produce white tea. It goes through a minimal withering process, then dried, ideally sun-dried. The original classical definition of white tea could only be produced from special cultivars in certain regions of China (Gold & Stern, 2010).

Second category: Partially to fully fermented/oxidated, with a stronger taste and darker colour – Oolong, Black and Pu-Erh tea. The uncompleted oxidation is giving the Oolong tea the characterising colour of its infusion, therefore it is also called "blue-green tea". It is a popular tea in Asia, where it is commonly served in restaurants. Oolong is traditionally made from whole leaves and is low in caffeine. The type of Oolong depends on the stage of its oxidation, with 12% meaning the tea gets a rather green taste (Chinese method) or up to 70% leading to an almost black tea (Formosa method). For a typical black tea the leaves have to be processed for complete oxidation. These teas are the result of a manufacturing process developed by the British in India in the mid-nineteenth century. The British were inspired by Chinese methods, which they largely rationalised and simplified, introducing in particular the use of machines (grinders, dryers, sieves, etc.), whereas the Chinese continued to prepare teas by hand (Rohrsen, 2022).

Based on the name of a small village in the region of Yunnan, the Pu-Erh tea is a post-fermented tea, also called "black tea" in China because of the very dark colour of its infusion. Most of these earth bounded teas are still coming from Yunnan and have undergone a different non-enzymatic oxidation than black teas. For this, two different processes can be used. Traditionally, post-fermented teas are obtained from tea leaves that are roasted to stop enzymatic oxidation, then compressed and finally stored for a long period during which a complex process of non-enzymatic oxidation and fermentation takes place. This type of tea is named "raw". The second option is a quicker process by roasting, keeping the tea very humid (compost-like atmosphere) and consequently allowing the accelerated post-fermentation. Often, this tea is compressed and named "cooked". Those post-fermented teas have the particularity of improving with time; their age is thus an essential element of their price. They have a very particular taste: earthy, reminiscent of leather, damp leaves or mushrooms. The infusion is particularly pungent in young teas (especially for the "cooked" ones); it softens and becomes richer with age (Battle, 2017).

Conclusion

Tea is based on a long Chinese history that has also been influenced by European botanists and the trading traditions of the Netherlands, Portugal and Britain. As a result of different treatments, six different basic flavours emerge, and at the same time a multitude of possibilities for blending and flavouring. A beverage full of impressive history, cultural density and healthy effects, and an impressive example of adaptability and intercultural exchange, it is consequently open for use in various hospitality services in hotels and restaurants.

References

Battle, W. (2017). *The world tea encyclopedia*. Matador.

Ellis, M., et al. (2015). *Empire of tea*. Reaktion Books.

Freeman, M., & d'Offay, T. (2018). *The life of tea*. Mitchell Beazley.

Frembgen, J. (2014). *Tausend Tassen Tee*. Lambert Schneider.

Gaylard. L. (2021). *Das Teebuch*. Penguin Random House.

Gold, C., & Stern, L. (2010). *Culinary tea: More than 150 recipes steeped in tradition from around the world*. Running Press Adult.

Hincheldey, C. (2009) *Tea from leaf to elixir*. N.T. Production & Divine Tea.

Krekel, S. (2013). *Tea*. Umschau-Verlag.

Krieger, M. (2021). *Geschichte des tees. Anbau, handel und globale genusskulturen*. Böhlau Verlag.

Lombardi, G. (2013). *Tee-Sommelier*. Whitestar.

Parker Bowles, T. (2021). *Time for tea*. HarperCollins Publishers.

Pettigrew, J. (2001). *A social story of tea*. National Trust Enterprises.

Rohrsen, P. (2022). *Das Buch zum Tee*. C.H. Beck.

Su, Y., Fang, X., & Yin, J. (2014). Impact of climate change on fluctuations of grain harvests in China from the Western Han dynasty to the five dynasties (206 BC–960 AD). *Science China Earth Sciences*, 57, 1701–1712.

Temming, R. (1983). *Vom Geheimnis des Tees*. Harenberg.

Markus Schuckert
B.2 The magic of tea and hospitality

Relationship between tea and hospitality: An introduction

Tea and hospitality have a long-standing relationship in many cultures around the world. Tea has been used as a symbol of hospitality and a means of welcoming guests for centuries. The act of offering tea to guests is considered a gesture of warmth, generosity, and friendship.

In various cultures, such as China, Japan, India, and the Middle East, tea ceremonies or rituals are often performed as a way of showing hospitality. These ceremonies involve the preparation, serving, and consumption of tea in a deliberate and ceremonial manner. The host takes great care in serving the tea, and the guest is expected to appreciate and enjoy the experience.

Tea is often offered to guests upon their arrival to make them feel welcome and comfortable. It provides an opportunity for people to connect, engage in conversation, and establish bonds. In many cultures, serving tea is seen as a way of expressing respect, honor, and a willingness to take care of others.

The act of sharing tea can create a sense of community and foster social interaction. It is often accompanied by the sharing of stories, laughter, and meaningful conversations. Offering tea can also be a way to show gratitude or apologise for any inconvenience caused to the guests.

Overall, tea and hospitality are closely intertwined, as tea serves as a symbol of welcome, friendship, and a shared experience. It promotes a sense of warmth, relaxation, and connection between people, making it an integral part of many hospitality traditions and customs.

Hospitality in Europe

European hospitality refers to the cultural norms and practices related to providing warm, welcoming, and gracious treatment to guests and visitors in European countries. While hospitality customs can vary across different regions and countries in Europe, there are some common characteristics that are often associated with European hospitality:

– Warmth and friendliness: Europeans are generally known for their warm and friendly approach towards guests. It is common for hosts to greet visitors with a genuine smile, offer assistance, and make them feel comfortable and at ease.

https://doi.org/10.1515/9783110758573-003

- Generosity and hospitality: European hospitality often involves offering guests food, beverages, and sometimes accommodations. Sharing a meal or a drink together is seen as an important part of the hospitality experience. Europeans take pride in their culinary traditions and often go out of their way to provide guests with a delightful gastronomic experience.
- Attention to detail: European hospitality often emphasises attention to detail in ensuring guest satisfaction. Whether it's providing comfortable accommodations, offering personalised recommendations, or catering to individual needs, hosts strive to create a memorable experience by paying attention to the small details.
- Cultural exchange: European hospitality often fosters cultural exchange and dialogue. Hosts may share insights about their local customs, traditions, and landmarks, and may be interested in learning about the guests' background and experiences. This exchange can lead to a deeper appreciation and understanding of different cultures.
- Respect for privacy: while European hospitality is known for its warmth and generosity, hosts also respect guests' privacy. They understand the importance of providing space and time for guests to relax and unwind without intruding on their personal boundaries.
- Etiquette and politeness: Europeans generally value etiquette and politeness in social interactions. Hosts are likely to be polite, use formal greetings and expressions, and demonstrate good manners. This extends to respecting cultural norms and customs, such as removing shoes at the entrance or observing dress codes. Table B.2.1 shows the contribution of European hoteliers to this development.

Table B.2.1: Contribution of European Hoteliers to hospitality heritage.

Hospitality Entrepreneur	Contribution
Adlon, Lorenz (1849–1921), Germany	Born in Mainz, he operated several gastronomy businesses very successfully before building the famous Hotel Adlon in Berlin, directly at the Brandenburg Gate, in 1907. This property was seen as the "unofficial residence" of the German emperor, Wilhelm II, who preferred its comforts to the drafty halls of the Imperial Palace. Today, the Hotel Adlon is again an icon of luxury at the same place and a brand for luxury goods and gastronomic operations.
D'Oyly Carte, Richard (1844–1901) (The Savoy family), UK	Opened Savoy Hotel London (1889). Stands for innovation and elegance.
Escoffier, Auguste (1846–1935), France	As a French chef and culinary innovator he made significant contributions to the development of modern gastronomy. Although not a hotelier himself he worked with influential hoteliers (Ritz), shaping the culinary standards of luxury hotels.

Table B.2.1 (continued)

Hospitality Entrepreneur	Contribution
Kempinski, Berthold (1843–1910), Germany	Started successfully his business with a wine shop and several restaurants before founding Kempinski Hotels 1897 in Berlin, Germany as Luxury focused multi-unit company.
Kracht, Friedrich (–1875), Germany	Friedrich Kracht bought the well-known "Hotel Ernst" in Cologne in 1871. As a German resident in Belgium, he had to move from Brussels to Cologne as a result of the Franco-Prussian War. Four years after acquiring the Cologne hotel, Friedrich Kracht died. His wife and son Carl continued to run the hotel and founded a company owning and operating several luxury hotels in Europe till today.
Nagelmackers, Georges (1845–1905), Belgium	Founded the Compagnie Internationale des Wagons-Lits et des Grands Express Européens, introducing luxury sleeping cars on trains and established related hotels (Hotel Terminus, Paris and Hotel Astoria, Brussels).
Palumbo, Raffaele (1853–1923), Italy	Owned and operated the Grand Hotel Excelsior Vittoria in Sorrento, Italy. Established in 1834, it became synonymous with refined hospitality, dedication to exceptional service and prime location, as prototype of a Mediterranean luxury hotel.
Ritz, César (1850–1918), Switzerland	Established the Ritz Hotels in London and Paris. As Swiss hotelier, Ritz became synonymous with elegance and high standards in the hospitality industry. He inspired Édouard Nignon (owner Carlton Hotel, Cannes, France), Edoardo Nettis (owner Hotel Danieli, Venice, Italy).
Sacher, Eduard (1843–1892), Austria	Eduard Sacher was an Austrian hotelier and restaurateur who built the famous Hotel Sacher in Vienna in 1876 and gave the "Sachertorte", invented by his father Franz Sacher, its present form.
Steigenberger, Albert (1889–1958), Germany	Founded in Germany 1930, Steigenberger Hotels & Resorts blueprinted modern multi property hotel business operations.

Source: Author

Tea ceremony and the element etiquette in European hospitality

Tea ceremonies or rituals have a rich history and cultural significance. The Chinese tea ceremony, known as "Gongfu Cha," is an elaborate and highly formalised practice that emphasises the preparation, serving, and appreciation of tea. In a traditional Chinese tea ceremony, the host meticulously selects tea leaves, usually of high quality, and prepares them using specific techniques to extract the best flavours and aromas. The ceremony is often conducted in a calm and serene setting, such as a teahouse or a peaceful garden. Chinese tea ceremonies vary in style and intricacy across different regions and traditions. Each ceremony reflects the unique cultural values, aesthetics, and philosophies associated with tea. However, the essence of all Chinese tea ceremonies lies in the reverence for tea, the art of preparation, and the shared experience of enjoying this beloved beverage.

Tea ceremonies or rituals in Japan are deeply rooted in the country's history, aesthetics, and cultural traditions. The Japanese tea ceremony, known as "Chado" or "Sado," is a highly ritualised and meditative practice that centres around the preparation and serving of matcha, powdered green tea. The Japanese tea ceremony is deeply influenced by Zen Buddhism and embodies principles such as wabi-sabi (appreciation of imperfection and transience) and ichi-go ichi-e (the idea that each meeting is unique and should be treasured). It is a profound cultural practice that goes beyond the mere act of drinking tea, serving as a means of self-reflection, connection, and the pursuit of inner peace. It's important to note that there are various styles and schools of Japanese tea ceremony, each with its unique interpretations and practices. However, the core principles of harmony, respect, and mindfulness remain integral to all tea ceremonies in Japan.

Tea ceremonies or rituals in India are not as formalised or structured as those in China or Japan. However, tea holds a significant place in Indian culture, and the act of serving and sharing tea is considered a gesture of hospitality and warmth. India is known for its diverse tea traditions and the popularity of chai, a spiced milk tea that is a staple beverage for many Indians. Tea holds a special place in the daily lives of many Indians. It is seen as a comforting and energising beverage, bringing people together and providing moments of respite in the midst of busy schedules. While India may not have a formalised tea ceremony like in other cultures, the act of preparing and sharing tea plays a vital role in fostering connections, building relationships, and expressing hospitality.

Tea ceremonies or rituals in the Middle East, particularly in countries such as Turkey, Iran, and some Arab nations, have their own unique customs and traditions. Tea, typically black tea, holds great importance in Middle Eastern culture and is a symbol of hospitality and friendship. Tea is often served in small glasses, and the preparation and serving process is steeped in tradition. Tea ceremonies in the Middle East reflect the region's rich cultural traditions and the importance placed on community and social connections. The preparation and serving of tea are done with care and attention, creating an atmosphere of warmth and conviviality. Whether enjoyed at home, in a teahouse, or in public spaces, Middle Eastern tea ceremonies are a cherished part of the region's social fabric.

Tea ceremonies or rituals in England are most associated with the tradition of afternoon tea, a cultural practice that dates back to the nineteenth century. While not as formalised as some of the ceremonies in other cultures, afternoon tea in England is a leisurely affair centred around enjoying a pot of tea accompanied by a selection of sandwiches, scones, and pastries. Afternoon tea in England is often seen as a social event, providing an opportunity for friends, family, or colleagues to come together and enjoy a pleasant afternoon. It is a time to relax, indulge in delectable treats, and appreciate the art of tea and conversation. While the practice of afternoon tea is widely recognised in England, it is also common to find tea being enjoyed throughout the day in households and workplaces, typically accompanied by a simple biscuit or cake. Tea is deeply ingrained in English culture as a comforting beverage and a symbol of hospitality and camaraderie (see Table B.2.2).

Table B.2.2: The Role of Hospitality and Tea by Cultural Origin.

Cultural Origin	Description of Hospitality
China	Throughout the tea ceremony, etiquette and respect play crucial roles. The host demonstrates a high level of hospitality by focusing on the guests' needs, ensuring they feel comfortable and attended to. The guests, in turn, show appreciation for the tea and the host's efforts.
Japan	Throughout the tea ceremony, there is a strong emphasis on mindfulness, harmony, and respect. The host strives to create a serene and meditative environment, allowing the participants to appreciate the beauty of simplicity and find tranquility in the present moment.
India	Tea holds a special place in the daily lives of many Indians. It is seen as a comforting and energising beverage, bringing people together and providing moments of respite in the midst of busy schedules. While India may not have a formalised tea ceremony like in other cultures, the act of preparing and sharing tea plays a vital role in fostering connections, building relationships, and expressing hospitality.
Middle East	Tea ceremonies in the Middle East reflect the region's rich cultural traditions and the importance placed on community and social connections. The preparation and serving of tea are done with care and attention, creating an atmosphere of warmth and conviviality. Whether enjoyed at home, in a teahouse, or in public spaces, Middle Eastern tea ceremonies are a cherished part of the region's social fabric.
British	While not as rigid as in the past, there is still a sense of etiquette associated with afternoon tea. It is customary to hold the teacup with the pinky finger down, to use the saucer to catch any drips, and to stir the tea in a gentle back-and-forth motion. Guests are encouraged to engage in polite conversation and enjoy the food and tea at a leisurely pace.

Source: Author

An extended view on hospitality and tea

In non-traditional tea countries where tea may not have a long-standing cultural history or specific ceremonial practices, the consumption of tea tends to vary and adapt to local customs and preferences. Here are some general observations about tea ceremonies or rituals in such countries:

– Informal tea gatherings: in non-traditional tea countries, tea consumption often takes place in informal settings like homes, cafes, or workplaces. People may gather casually over a cup of tea to socialise, catch up with friends, or take a break from daily activities. These gatherings are more relaxed and flexible, focusing on conversation and relaxation rather than formal rituals.

– Personalised tea preparations: tea is often prepared according to individual preferences rather than following specific ceremonial procedures. People may use tea bags, tea leaves, or instant tea mixes, depending on their convenience and taste. There is a wide variety of tea flavours available, including herbal infusions, fruit infusions, and flavoured blends.

– Accompaniments and snacks: tea in non-traditional tea countries may be enjoyed with a range of accompanying snacks or pastries that suit local culinary traditions. These can include biscuits, cakes, sandwiches, or other savoury treats that complement the tea-drinking experience.

– On-the-go tea culture: in some countries, tea is consumed on-the-go as a quick pick-me-up. This is commonly seen in the form of takeaway tea cups or ready-to-drink bottled teas that can be purchased at cafes, convenience stores, or vending machines. The focus is on convenience and portability.

– Fusion tea practices: in non-traditional tea countries, innovative and fusion tea practices may emerge. This can involve incorporating local ingredients, spices, or cultural influences into tea preparations: for example, adding milk or condensed milk to tea, creating unique tea blends, or experimenting with iced tea variations.

– Health and wellness focus: in recent years, there has been a growing interest in tea's health benefits and herbal infusions. People in non-traditional tea countries may explore tea as part of their wellness routines, seeking out herbal infusions or blends known for their medicinal properties or relaxation effects.

It's important to note that tea ceremonies and rituals can evolve and adapt over time as tea gains popularity in different cultures. Non-traditional tea countries often exhibit their own unique tea-drinking customs, influenced by local preferences, lifestyles, and cultural practices. These customs may be more flexible, diverse, and accommodating to individual tastes and preferences.

Conclusion: Socio-psychological traits behind tea and hospitality

Tea and hospitality have a strong socio-psychological link, as the act of serving and sharing tea is deeply rooted in cultural practices and social interactions across many societies, and related to individuals' emotions, well-being, and interpersonal relationships. Figure B.2.1 introduces an overview of the various aspects.

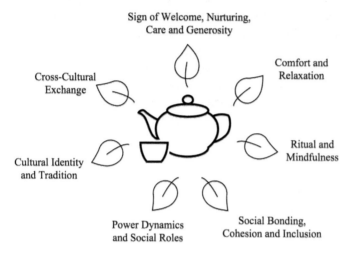

Figure B.2.1: Socio-psychological Aspects of Tea and Hospitality.
Source: Author

Sign of welcome, nurturing, care and generosity: offering tea is seen as a gesture of welcome and hospitality and express the hosts' desire to create a warm, caring, and inviting environment for their guests. It signifies concern for well-being and comfort and creates a sense of reciprocity, fostering a positive social atmosphere where individuals feel valued and cared for, in both the giver and the receiver.

Comfort and relaxation: tea can create a soothing and calming effect on individuals, helping to alleviate stress, promote mindfulness, and provide a sense of comfort.

Ritual and mindfulness: the preparation and consumption aspect in tea ceremonies and rituals shift focus, require attention, and create mindfulness, supporting a sense of presence and staying in the moment.

Social bonding, cohesion and inclusion: whether in formal ceremonies or casual settings, the sharing aspect creates an opportunity for social bonding, conversation, and social ties, while the act of serving tea to guests creates a sense of inclusion and belonging.

Power dynamics and social roles: hosts, typically taking the role of the server, assume a position of authority, responsibility, and care for others, while guests, in turn, may reciprocate by expressing gratitude, appreciation, and respect. Both dynamics shape hierarchies and reinforce social norms.

Cultural identity and tradition: tea-related practices that are specific to one's culture contribute to a sense of pride, connection to heritage, and continuity with the past, strengthening a sense of belonging, identity reinforcement, and maintain a sense of continuity with the past.

Cross-cultural exchange: as a product, tea has a long history of being traded and shared across cultures, leading to the exchange of ideas, customs, and traditions. Drinking tea stands for (intercultural) communication and understanding, facilitating the exploration and appreciation of diverse perspectives.

The sociology behind tea and hospitality highlights how tea ceremonies and the act of serving tea are not merely about the beverage itself but encompass broader social and cultural dynamics. Tea becomes a medium through which social connections are formed, traditions are preserved, and individuals experience a sense of belonging and care within their communities.

The psychological aspects of tea and hospitality demonstrate the potential for these practices to enhance well-being, foster social connections, and contribute to positive emotional experiences. Whether it's the sensory pleasure of tea, the act of sharing with others, or the cultural significance, tea and hospitality have the capacity to positively impact individuals' psychological states and interpersonal relationships.

References

Chen, S.H., Huang, J., & Tham, A. (2021). A systematic literature review of coffee and tea tourism. *International Journal of Culture, Tourism and Hospitality Research, 15*(3), 290–311.

Jolliffe, L. (2006). Tea and hospitality: more than a cuppa. *International Journal of Contemporary Hospitality Management, 18*(2), 164–68.

Jolliffe, L. (Ed.). (2007). *Tea and tourism: Tourists, traditions and transformations* (Vol. 11). Channel View Publications.

Jolliffe, L., Aslam, M.S.M., Khaokhrueamuang, A., & Chen, L.H. (Eds.). (2022). *Routledge handbook of tea tourism*. Taylor & Francis.

Munns, E.A. (2021). *Steeped in culture: Tea tourism in Japan* (Doctoral dissertation, Austin College).

Murray, A., & Johnsen, S. (2011). Community hospitality initiatives: 'Make a cup of tea first, ask questions later'. *Psychodynamic Practice, 17*(3), 325–29.

Sato, Y., & Parry, M.E. (2015). The influence of the Japanese tea ceremony on Japanese restaurant hospitality. *Journal of Consumer Marketing*.

Su, M.M., Wall, G., & Wang, Y. (2019). Integrating tea and tourism: a sustainable livelihoods approach. *Journal of Sustainable Tourism, 27*(10), 1591–608.

Zhou, Q., Zhu, K., Kang, L., & Dávid, L.D. (2023). Tea culture tourism perception: A study on the harmony of importance and performance. *Sustainability, 15*(3), 2838.

Ute Kemmerling
B.3 Thirst and power – Assam as the Empire's tea garden

Introduction

Tea is one of the most popular beverages in the world today. China and India each produce about one third of the world's tea harvest. In addition, tea is mainly grown in Kenya, Sri Lanka, and Vietnam for worldwide export. From the seventeenth century, the consumption of tea in Europe, and especially in England, increased steadily, as tea had become a fashionable drink across all social classes. With the conquest of Assam in the early nineteenth century, the British colonial government and entrepreneurs saw an opportunity to produce tea on a large scale in their own empire, while also allowing them to become independent of imports from China. Therefore, the tea trade in Assam required a completely new infrastructure in order to be able to export the high yields at all. The trade routes, the rail network, and shipping were successively expanded by the British colonial government as the tea trade became established. Tea from Assam – and later from other tea-growing regions such as Darjeeling and Ceylon (Sri Lanka) – became the dominant trade commodity. This is reflected in expressions for tea such as "green gold" and shows the economically important role that tea cultivation played in British India. In addition, this immense boom also required a large labour force, which was recruited from all over British India and partly from China. However, the hygienic conditions on the newly established tea plantations were in part devastating and provided breeding grounds for contagious and often fatal diseases, as will be pointed out further on.

From Asia to Europe

In 1610, the first cargo of tea from the Japanese island of Hirado was unloaded in the port of Amsterdam. In Japan, as in China, the use of tea as a beverage was known from the late sixth century. As a result of the increasing European maritime trade, which had gradually spread to Southeast Asia from the sixteenth century, traders discovered tea as a consumer product for the European market. For a century, the Dutch trading company VOC (Vereenigde Oostindische Compagnie) dominated the tea trade until it was replaced by the British East India Company. China had become the main supplier of tea, whose export was solely handled by the English trading company until 1833. In the following decades, tea became increasingly popular as a hot beverage in Europe, initiating the success story of tea up to the present day. In the Netherlands and England, especially from the eighteenth century, tea developed into a fashionable drink and spread from there to the various regions of the world. Everyday tea traditions developed and found their way

https://doi.org/10.1515/9783110758573-004

into various societies. In total, the hot beverage was successively cultivated in more than 45 countries worldwide. Due to the steadily increasing demand in Europe and beyond, tea production had to be increased significantly. Accordingly, the East India Company looked for suitable areas for tea cultivation in addition to China, especially in India. Like sugar and coffee, tea was to become a cash crop, an agricultural product that was cultivated to generate profits. Assam was seen as a suitable region for this, as wild tea plants had been discovered there at the beginning of the nineteenth century, meaning that tea was indigenous (Rohrsen, 2013, p. 31; Baruah, 2020, pp. 12–14, 43).

The conquest of Assam

The conquest of Assam by the East India Company and the discovery of the tea plant located on the north-eastern edge of British India, made Assam an important region in England's colonial pride, although it was one of the later conquests of the British colonial power. In the eighteenth century, the then ruling Ahom Empire, which had maintained its independence since the thirteenth century, came between the expansionist ambitions of the East India Company and the Burmese Konbaung dynasty. Before the occupation by the British, trade was conducted with neighbouring Tibet. Silk, rice, iron, lacquer and pearls were exchanged for rock salt, wool, horses and gold dust. In addition to trade with Tibet, trade with Bengal was also conducted to a limited extent; in particular, one's own goods were exchanged mainly for salt. In 1822, the Burmese King Bagyidaw took over the rule of Assam, which had been weakened by internal power struggles. The country had been severely devastated due to war and the population massively oppressed. The East India Company took the devastation of Assam as an opportunity to intervene for humanitarian reasons but securing its own border areas and economic interests in Assam likely also played a decisive role. The First Anglo-Burmese War began in 1824 and ended in 1826. With the Treaty of Yandabo of February 24, 1826, the new province of Assam became part of the British Empire. There was hardly any administrative structure left and the economy was in ruins, as the original trade centres had been destroyed. Large parts of present-day Bangladesh and the areas bordering the Brahmaputra River came under British rule. Assam found itself administratively part of the Presidency of Bengal from 1826 until it became an independent province of British India in 1874. In central India, as well as among the British colonisers, Assam was characterised by its geographical remoteness and referred to as a wasteland, since much of the land was covered by dense jungle and was accessible only by isolated trade routes or by river. Thus, the reclaimed region initially showed little economic potential for the East India Company and was seen more as a transit point for trade with Burma and Tibet (Goswami, 2012, pp. 26, 158–159; Sharma, 2011, p. 3; see Figure B.3.1).

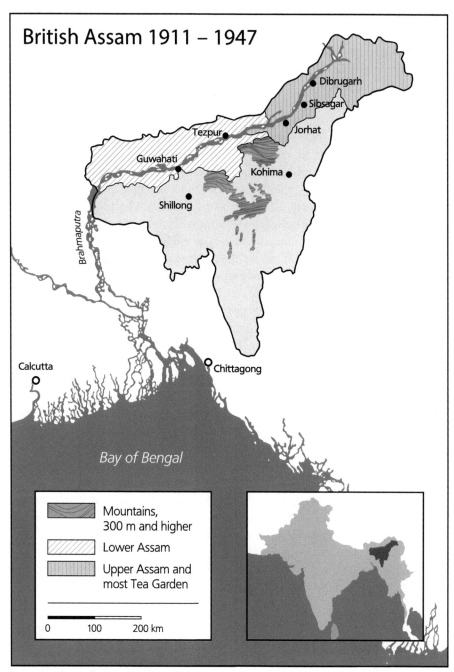

Layout: Ute Kemmerling / Graphic: Mike Glüsing

Figure B.3.1: Map of British India and Assam 1911–1947.
Source: Layout Ute Kemmerling; Graphic Mike Glüsing

Discoveries

China held a monopoly position in global tea production until the nineteenth century. Ship Captains of the East India Company, an English trading company increasingly active in India and East Asia, also brought tea seeds to India from their voyages to China in the late eighteenth century. In 1788, the English naturalist and botanist Joseph Banks (1743–1820) expressed to the East India Company the idea of growing tea beyond China. To Banks, India seemed like an ideal cultivation area. In fact, however, wild tea plants were found in Assam itself. The discovery of the Assamese tea plant (lat. Camellia sinensis var. assamica) in 1823 is attributed to British Major Robert Bruce, who was in Assam for trading purposes. The local people brewed a drink from the leaves, which was probably used for medical purposes. Charles Alexander Bruce sent some tea plants to the head of the East India Company in Assam, David Scott, who gave them to the director of the Botanical Garden in Calcutta, Dr. Nathaniel Wallich. The Bruce brothers had pointed out the discovery of Assamese tea early on but failed to gain scientific and commercial recognition for the discovery at that time. A decade later, it was Lieutenant Andrew Charlton, an officer in a British battalion stationed in Assam, who, based on his agrarian expertise, identified the indigenous tea plant as such. He documented that the indigenous people boiled the leaves, crushed it into a ball, and then dried it in the sun. Charlton sent seeds and leaves to the newly formed Tea Committee. Because of the British colonial government's strong interest in establishing tea in Assam, the Governor General of India, Lord William Bentick (r. 1828–1835), had constituted a Tea Committee in 1834. The committee was headed by Nathaniel Wallich, director of the Calcutta Botanical Garden. Charlton reported that the plant was growing wild everywhere. In December 1834, the Tea Committee made public the discovery of the wild tea plant, which now made Assam especially valuable to the agricultural and commercial future of British India. As tea was growing in Assam, it was assumed that Chinese tea could also be planted in the region. Cultivating wild autochthonous tea on a large scale was not initially part of these plans. In 1836, a scientific delegation led by Nathaniel Wallich was established on behalf of the East India Company to develop a strategy for tea cultivation in British India. Major General Francis Jenkins, a member of the Agricultural Society of Great Britain, proposed to Lord Bentinck and his council that they seek cultivation of the tea plant by European companies in the future.

Uncertainties of trade

The uncertainty of trade relations with China, as well as the profitability of the tea trade, encouraged this move. Jenkin's recommendations set the stage for European companies to invest in Assam. They began with a few tests regarding the suitability of the Assamese tea plant for large-scale cultivation. However, Chinese tea, as it was known, was to be transferred to Assam as well. The Tea Committee sent their secretary, G.J. Gordon, to China because he had good contacts there. Gordon was to find out information about the cultivation and production of tea. This was not an easy task, as the Chinese guarded their knowledge of tea preparation like the apple of their eye, since they were well aware that almost the entire tea production for worldwide trade was produced in their country. In the period from 1835 to 1836, 20,000 tea seeds arrived in Assam from China, half of which became unusable during transport due to poor storage or vermin. With the help of recruited Chinese planters, cultivation was tested in various areas of British India, including Madras in the southeast, Mysore in the southwest, and Saharanpur in the northeast, in addition to Assam. While in the south the cultivation of seedlings was unsuccessful because the climate was too dry and too hot, in Assam modest results were seen with the Chinese tea plant. At the same time, however, it was found that the indigenous tea plant, which had been grown with Bruce's first seedlings from the Assamese jungle, thrived much better. It was not until years later that the view was taken that the indigenous tea plant was quite competitive if special attention was paid in regard to the care of the plants. Charles Bruce was put in charge of experimental tea cultivation. Initially, the company continued to grow Chinese tea plants in the tea gardens of Assam. Until 1855, tea seeds from China were used almost exclusively for new plantings in Assam. In addition, experiments with hybrids between the Assamese and Chinese tea plants took place on the plantations. In the following years, the British successively learned tea cultivation and made themselves independent of the expertise of Chinese planters. In addition, it became apparent that the China-Assam hybrid plant was not as well suited to the Assam environment as initially thought. In the 1870s, British planters even referred to the hybrid tea plant as "plague." Instead, the Assamese plant species was now cultivated on a large scale, so that the Chinese tea plant was also used less and less (Antrobus, 1957, pp. 30–34; Sharma, 2011, pp. 30, 71; Baruah, 2020, p. 71).

The first Empire-tea on the world market

After the annexation of Assam, and especially in the context of the successive tea exports, the lack of transport routes and infrastructure was a problem. Roads that still existed during Ahom rule had been destroyed to warfare. The region was mostly covered by jungle that stretched for hundreds of kilometres across the country. The land was covered by large forests and, in certain areas, by kharga grass that reached a height of ten to fifteen feet and was marked only by occasional paths to the detached rice fields. For tea cultivation, forest was preferred to grass jungle and cleared on a large scale (Ukers, 1935, p. 156). The favoured means of transport on land were elephants or water boats (see Figure B.3.2).

Figure B.3.2: The beginning of tea export. Men loading tea on a boat in Assam.
Source: Bourne & Shepherd A. (The photo was taken around 1903)

Rivers and streams, especially the Brahmaputra River, which arises in Tibet and crosses Assam, particularly characterise the country. In some places the Brahmaputra River was two miles wide. The river was the main artery of communication and remained the most important link connecting Assam with the rest of British India until the early twentieth century. Especially in the early days of tea exports, it was difficult to transport tea from the cultivating regions to the markets in Calcutta. In the early 1830s, a boat from Guwahati in northern Assam to Calcutta took about six to seven weeks. In 1834, the first paddle steamer was used to cover the distance of about 1,000 miles, and by 1836 there were already four steamers covering the distance in four to 15 days, depending on the distance. Tea was brought via tributaries to the Brahmaputra, where it was then transferred to the steamers. In 1891, with the support of the British government, the Assam Bengal Railway was established to connect the districts where tea was produced with the Brahmaputra. The first railroad line was opened at Jorhat in the northern Surma Valley for a direct connection with Chittagong. The transportation of tea remained cumbersome during this period. To get the tea to the railroad line, it was transported by trucks or oxcarts for several miles. The roads in Assam were unpaved and covered with dust or mud depending on the season. At times, during the rainy season, roads were impassable in many places. For the further distance to the port of Calcutta, the existing sections of the railroad were used, as well as the steamboats on the Brahmaputra River (Ukers, 1935, p. 403; Goswami, 2012, p. 184).

Reputation of Assam tea

The first tea plantations, which were more like experiments in terms of climate, soil conditions, and tea varieties, initially produced low yields. But at the end of 1838, the first 12 boxes were shipped by the merchant ship "Calcutta" to the London Directorate to have Assamese tea evaluated for its quality. Until that time, only tea from China was known in Great Britain. With a comprehensive examination of the quality, it was decided at this time whether there would be a commercial future for Indian tea. Samples were distributed to traders, private individuals, and scientific institutions. The "Assam Tea" with the strong tart taste was favourably reviewed and created considerable success among merchants and consumers alike as the first tea from the British Empire. Eight boxes of tea, totaling 350 pounds, were sold at auction in the early months of 1839, fetching record prices. Twenty times the usual price for Chinese tea was achieved, which Sharma interprets to mean that "the British consumer was receptive to Empire tea" (Sharma 2011, p. 32). At the Great Exhibition in London in 1851, visitors could visit the Crystal Palace, where medal-winning teas from the gardens of Assam were on display. In no other country in Europe did tea find such fertile ground as in Great Britain. As late as the seventeenth century, the beverage was associated with the aristocracy and nobility and was an expensive product at the time. With additional production regions, tea now became affordable for ordinary people. The fact that tea spread exponentially to all levels of society over the next few centuries was also due to the tea culture that emerged, which is so strikingly evident in Great Britain to this day. The wife of the Seventh Duke of Bedford, Anna (1788–1861), had a particular influence on the emerging habit, although she was not the inventor but a passionate follower of this tradition. Finding the time from lunch to dinner too long, it became customary serving tea and cakes in the middle of the afternoon, a practice that apparently found favour first in aristocratic homes. From the upper classes, "high tea" (tea was served with cakes, pastries, and savoury sandwiches) spread to ordinary households, where it triggered an enthusiasm for tea among the middle classes and working classes and the rituals associated with it. Home teatime was celebrated with Chinese porcelain and other special accessories, and teahouses became increasingly popular in public life. Drinking tea became a central social event, changing the rhythm of the day and thus having a significant impact on the culture of British society (Sharma, 2011, p. 31; Baruah, 2020, p. 74; Krieger, 2021, p. 201; Macfarlane, 2004, pp. 83, 93; see Figure B.3.3).

Figure B.3.3: Advertising for tea from the Empire. Victorian Handbill of 1899.
Source: Ukers 1935, II., p. 298

Economic establishment of the tea trade in the nineteenth century

Increasing demand

Thus, the demand for tea grew considerably in Great Britain. Accordingly, the positive outcome of the auction in London for tea from India was the signal for entrepreneurs and investors from the metropolis. The following decades showed that the province of Assam was developing into an economically important region for the British Empire. As early as the 1830s, the East India Company, with the support of the Tea Committee, had advertised attractive terms for European applicants. The terms did not directly exclude Indian competitors, but the demands of the initial capital ensured that, with few exceptions, European applicants qualified. In 1839, businessmen got together in London and formed the Assam Company. In that same year, merchants in Bengal united to form the Bengal Tea Association. The two companies merged to form the Assam Company, making it the first private tea company to operate in Assam. In 1840, most of the tea gardens of the East India Company were transferred to the Assam Company. For the next fifty years, the Assam Company remained the major British tea producer. In Calcutta, the first tea auction took place in 1841. It involved 130 boxes of tea from the first British-Indian tea growing area in Assam (Sharma, 2002; Baruah, 2020; see Figure B.3.4).

Figure B.3.4: Imperial architectur that symbolises success. Company office of James Finlay Muir & Co. LTD., Calcutta, founded 1870.
Source: Ukers 1935, II., p. 140

From the 1850s onwards, production showed much greater success, and tea gardens were now increasingly created in northern Assam. A first tea garden with purely indigenous tea plants was established in 1855. By 1859, the Tea Company owned a total of 4000 acres of tea growing land in Assam, with a yield that year of 760,000 pounds (Gait 1933, p. 407). In China, tea had been grown by peasants. In Assam, large-scale plantation farming was to be implemented from the beginning with modern planning and organisation. New tea gardens were started in all areas of Assam, in the swampy lowlands as well as on the plateau on both sides of the Brahmaputra River, which was coupled with the adventurous speculative appetite of investors and government officials. Their hope was for high commercial profit in tea production. The East India Company made land available for new tea plantations regardless of its suitability, and clearing was undertaken on a large scale. In many cases, however, the tea plantations that had been hastily established had to be abandoned again due to bad investments. In 1865–66 the tea market collapsed, as in the meantime investors from all walks of life but without know-how wanted to participate in the boom of the tea business. The market re-regulated itself with fewer companies. During this period, the question of how to lucratively sell Indian tea on the domestic market also arose. In the last third of the nineteenth century, tea from the British Empire began to be promoted intensively. In 1881, the first Tea Store with pure Indian teas opened in London. In 1887, Queen Victoria celebrated her fiftieth anniversary on the throne, which was also marked by countless exhibitions and events. Many institutions found that their own history was linked to the Queen's reign – including the tea industry in British India. Gripped by jubilee fever, the year 1887 was declared the fiftieth anniversary of the tea industry in Assam, since the first Indian tea had reached England in 1837. The fact that the date did not quite correspond to the actual circumstances was overlooked; the tea jubilee was more a celebration of the global context. In the following decades, tea production increased significantly and became one of the most lucrative agricultural sectors in British India. In 1885, Assam produced 53.5 million pounds of tea, and by 1901 134 million pounds of tea. In 1922, production increased further to 237 million pounds of tea. The main tea growing areas were in the Brahmaputra Valley, Cachar and Sylhet in the centre of the country. In 1866, 96% of tea was imported into England from China and only 4% from Assam's tea gardens. By 1886, 38% was imported from Assam. By the turn of the century, certain retailers and importers had become major brands in Britain, such as Lipton, Twinings, Brooke Bond, and Mazawattee. Tea production grew steadily until the 1920s, despite the global recession of 1920 and 1921. Assam remained the largest single producer. By 1931, however, tea prices had fallen to an all-time low. The Indian Tea Association reacted with panic, reporting that many gardens were closing, and thousands of workers were out of work. The Association demanded that the import tariff be reduced, but the English government did not comply. Out of desperation, growers initiated a massive public relations campaign to attract consumers to British Empire tea. The "Drink Empire Tea" campaign tied in with the "buy British" movement that had peaked in the 1930s. Trade and consumer advertising, posters, radio broadcasts and public lectures to the citizens, retailers and local authorities called for drinking only tea from the British Empire. The campaign also had a political impact; the import duty on Indian tea was reduced (Rappaport, 2017, pp. 113, 163–178, 237, 244–251; Gait, 1933, pp. 408–409).

With the successful establishment of tea production, the province of Assam had changed significantly. The British colonial power dominated the country and dictated the complete transformation of Assam. The jungle on the edge of British India gave way to a large imperial Tea Garden and was shaped by ideological doctrine to improve agriculture. Knowledge from botanical gardens with regard to tea cultivation was inevitably linked to capital. Progressive capitalism formed the fulcrum of British Indian socioeconomic policy (Sharma, 2011, p. 3; see Figure B.3.5).

Figure B.3.5: 1930s modern Advertising for Empire Tea.
Source: Ukers (1935 II., p. 306)

Tea industry, coolies and diseases

The workers were of high importance for the tea production. Workers cleared and tilled the land, planted, and tended the young tea trees. In the spring time, the new leaves were picked and taken from the tea gardens to the nearby factory, where the leaves were sorted and processed. In those early years of tea production, everything was manual labour, so it took many hands to keep tea production going. However, it was the procurement of cheap labour that turned out to be one of the biggest problems in the global plantation industry and just as much in the tea gardens of Assam. Attempts to recruit sufficient labour from nearby areas failed. The recruitment of Chinese tea workers and members of the Kachari ethnic group from southern Assam failed after a short time because they could not be integrated into the disciplinary regime of the tea plantations. The Assam Company was forced to recruit workers from Bengal starting in 1853 and was dependent on the help of the British colonial government. After 1820, labour was more in demand than ever as a result of the globalisation push. A recruitment of Indians began in all plantation regions of European colonial empires (Varma, 2017, pp. 35–36; Kemmerling, 2021, p. 23).

The indenture or contract system included various pieces of legislation governing the recruitment of workers, the costs and terms of contracts, and regulations governing worker safety. The Workmen's Breach of Contract Act (Act XIII) of 1859 was the first legislative measure of a whole package of laws. The Act included economic as well as extra-economic compulsions to perform labour and was not abolished in some provinces of British India until the 1930s. Since the abolition of slavery in the British Empire in the 1830s, Indian workers based in the Central and East Indies were recruited for the world's sugar plantations. The recruitment of labourers to Assam was organised through labour agencies based in Calcutta. In 1864 the government concept of labour recruitment was expanded. The indenture system became a key mechanism for the plantation economy in Assam, making tea gardens a lucrative business. Workers, known as coolies, were recruited from various parts of British India for the tea gardens. The term "coolie" (English term) comes from the Hindi word "kuli" (wages), which was used to refer to labourers from the Indian Ocean region. The recruited workers were contractually bound to the owners of the tea plantations for several years. The prospect of a piece of land at the end of the contract period drove the workers to the tea gardens (Varma, 2017, pp. 48–49; Gait, 1963, p. 413; Mann, 2005, p. 231; Sharma, 2011, p. 73; Dey, 2018, p. 121; Kemmerling, 2021, p. 23).

Living conditions and wages were extremely meager. There were rules for employers, such as maximum working hours for coolies of nine hours, six days a week, and the construction of a hospital on each plantation. However, these rules were often not followed. A constitutive element of the indenture system was also the construction of railroads and the development of Assam via regular steamboat traffic on the Brahmaputra River (Kemmerling, 2021, p. 24; see Figure B.3.6).

Overall, many epidemic diseases were present in British India in the nineteenth and twentieth centuries, exacerbated by poor hygiene conditions, many of which were found in the tea gardens. Cholera and malaria appeared throughout the subcontinent and were treated with new hygienic concepts and quinine. In the last third of the nineteenth century, an unknown disease also appeared, particularly in the tea gardens of Assam. In the first decades of its perception, the disease was thought to be a severe form of malaria. In the regions of Assam and Bengal, the rate of infection, especially at the end of the nineteenth century, was higher than in any other region of India. The disease, called kala-azar (black disease) in Hindi, occurred in intervals. The indigenous people of the region called the disease sarkari bimari, the British government disease. The peculiarity of the kala-azar disease was that it simultaneously occurred with the cultivation of tea in Assam and accordingly broke out many times in the tea plantations. Up to the time of the discovery, or rather perception of this disease in 1869, similar initial symptoms were recognised as malaria, but the British physicians agreed that this disease was incomparably more dangerous for humans. The disease is transmitted by a sand fly and, without treatment, led to death within a very short time due to organ failure and anemia. Tea workers were particularly affected by febrile illness, which was subsumed as "jungle fever" until the 1890s. For

Figure B.3.6: Immigrant tea workers. Women sorting tea in Assam.
Source: Bourne & Shepherd (The photo was taken around 1903)

decades, people were at a loss as to what kind of disease it was. Accordingly, no medicines could be developed to treat the disease. In 1885, the medical journal *Indian Medical Gazette* noted that kala-azar had claimed as many lives as cholera in India (Indian Medical Gazette, 1885, pp. 83–84).

For the British colonial power and for the tea plantation owners, the epidemic disease in India became a problem. The expanding plantation economy of Assam with its extremely poor hygienic conditions and the migratory movements of contract workers supported a rapid spread of this disease. At intervals of 15 to 20 years, the epidemic persisted for about three to four years. During colonial rule, Assam suffered several such epidemics, which resulted in entire areas being depopulated. However, a high death rate of workers also resulted in reduced tea production. Since Assam tea gardens were of particular importance to the economy of British India, an epidemic policy was developed to combine medical knowledge, colonial ordinances, and commercial interests. The high production demands of the tea industry were directly related to the huge demand for labour. While in 1876 about 34,000 workers were distributed among the various tea gardens, 1895 showed a total labour force of over

500,000 workers. The overall mortality rate in Assam's tea gardens averaged over 30% between 1876 and 1895. The particularly high mortality rate and the fact that the disease could not be casually classified for a long time also presented medical science with a particular challenge. Misconceptions meant that kala-azar remained untreatable for decades. Individual researchers took a particularly close look at kala-azar and conducted on-site research with long-term studies in the Assamese tea gardens. From the beginning, that is, with the registration of the first cases of the disease in 1869, medical research was linked to the economic and political interests of the region. The colonial government and medical research showed an interdependent relationship. By the end of the nineteenth century, the colonial economy had emerged as the highest priority in an imperial age. The newly established tea industry, which had quickly become one of the main economic sectors in British India, helped dictate the approach to kala-azar (Kemmerling, 2021, pp. 4, 25–28, 52, 83; Dutta, 2005, p. 16). This is also expressed in an article published in the newspaper Homeward Mail from India, China, and the East in 1913. According to the text, Assam was often described in the press as the "Cinderella Province of India". The province had a very bad reputation among the British because of its wild nature and many deadly diseases such as malaria, black fever and kala-azar. These diseases cost many workers their lives, with the result that tea garden owners had to pay a high price to keep the tea industry going. The province of Assam, however, was on a good path: "And but for the unfortunate vicissitudes through which it has passed there is every reason to believe that it would now have been probably one of the richest portions of the Indian Empire" (Homeward Mail from India, China, and The East, 1913, p. 838).

Initially, the government had not considered itself responsible for legislating health policies in the tea gardens. However, the high number of deaths in the gardens forced the colonial government to enact a law in 1882 with sanitary measures for agents, planters, and coolies to follow. Among the most important measures enacted was that doctors should be present at the collection points for contract labourers. Workers who were obviously ill were required to burn their clothes. Drinking water was to be provided on the steamships to Assam, as well as adequate sanitary facilities, separated for men and women. In addition, the new law ordered that diseases and death rates be registered from then on. In the same year, the first long-term surveys were conducted in the tea gardens in order to develop further measures to contain the disease. However, the first government measures failed because the regulations were not followed with government control in the tea gardens. By 1892, any kind of febrile illness had been grouped together. It was not until 1893 that specific investigations into kala-azar were undertaken. The Indian Tea Association supported the investigation in the tea gardens. One of the first scientists to study kala-azar intensively in Assam was the British epidemiologist Leonard Rogers, who traveled to Nowgong in 1896. But even he could not decipher the cause of the disease. Only after many long-term studies in the tea gardens and examinations in the laboratories by various scientists, who also conducted research beyond England and India, did the Englishmen William Boog Leishman and Charles Donovan finally discover the pathogen in 1903 through modern examination techniques of bacteriology. With the decoding of the pathogen, however, the disease was no less frightening, nor was the route of infection known (Kemmerling, 2021, pp. 31–33, 42). Because the disease was a "disaster" for the tea industry, as the physician Charles McCombie Young wrote in his report on kala-azar, drastic measures were carried out. The expulsion of infected people was legalised. McCombie stated in his report that ignorance still prevailed regarding the means of transmission of kala-azar, so that "these methods were necessarily empirical" (McCombie Young, 1924, pp. 21, 42).

In the early 1920s, special hospitals and the first medicines were tested. Treatment facilities were provided in all areas of Assam and attended to by assistants and doctors from the Indian Medical Service. As a result of widespread treatment, the mortality rate declined significantly. Although more than 1.1 million people became infected with kala-azar in the years between 1931 and 1940, the colonial government's budget for comprehensive measures to control this disease and, moreover, to conduct deeper research on it, remained small. Treatment facilities were provided in all infected areas of Assam and were attended by more than a hundred surgical sub-assistants and doctors from each local authority. As a result of this widespread treatment, the mortality rate markedly declined. The measures taken to contain the disease severely limited the scope of action for the population and the immigrant tea workers. They had no influence on the decisions made by the colonial government and the medical staff of the Indian Medical Service. In this context, research prioritised practical measures to contain the epidemic and took little account of the diseased people themselves (Kemmerling, 2021, pp. 57–59, 83; Dutta, 2005, p. 21).

The end of Empire tea

After India's independence in 1947, the tea industry was not entirely in European hands, but British entrepreneurs and planters had dominated the market. For centuries, the British Empire had been a player in global trade; with independence, a new chapter emerged for the tea industry. This was particularly affected by the division of the subcontinent into India and Pakistan. The eastern part of Bengal and the Assamese region of Sylhet became the eastern part of Pakistan (Bangladesh since 1971) because of the Muslim majority in the population. The new borders cut through cultures, natural areas, and also economic regions. The old trade routes between Assam, Calcutta and Chittagong were no longer easily passable. Road, rail, and river routes were blocked or made unsafe. Investors were very reluctant to invest because of these new circumstances. The Indian tea industry was slow to change, with most plantations initially remaining in British hands. Only slowly did tea in British India evolve from an imperial to a global commodity. India's world market share fell from 40% to

33% in the 1950s and 1960s. But in the decades that followed, the tea industry underwent a massive restructuring. After an initial stagnation in tea production, Indian capital, local expertise, and government control in many areas saw a resurgence in production, but the power of European-based international corporations also resumed its influence on the Indian tea trade. In India itself, consumption of tea has grown successively since independence, even overtaking the United Kingdom as the largest market for tea. In 1960, the Indian Central Tea Board launched a major campaign in the UK to improve and modernise the image of Indian tea. In the years that followed, the Indian government promoted British and Indian private companies with the goal of reintroducing Indian tea to the global market. India sent trade missions around the world, such as to Cairo, Khartoum, Tehran and Hong Kong, and held exhibitions in New York, Seattle, Paris and Stockholm. It reflected the desire of politicians and businessmen to end dependence on Britain and other Western countries.

Assam today

Assam has maintained its position as the largest tea growing region in India over the centuries. Today, about 2,000 tea gardens are found in Assam and both black and green tea are produced. More than 52% of India's total tea production comes from Assam. The total production in India in 2020 was nearly 126 million tons of tea. The main consumers of Indian tea are especially Russia, Germany (East Frisian tea consists of at least half of Assam tea), Poland, the United Arab Emirates, Iran, Pakistan and Bangladesh. It is interesting to note that the share of small Indian tea growers is steadily increasing. They account for about 35% of tea production in Assam. In India, as in Great Britain and other countries of the world, tea has taken a central place in the culture. While tea is prepared differently depending on the region, the Hindi word "chai" has become its synonym in India (Rappaport, 2017; Baruah, 2020; Tea Board India und Ministry of Commerce and Industry).

References

Anonymous. (1855). The 'Kala-Azar' or black death of the Garo Hills. *Indian Medical Gazette, 20*(3), 83–84.
Anonymous. (1913). The Administration of Assam. In *Homeward Mail from India, China and The East*, p. 838.
Antrobus, H.A. (1957). *A history of the Assam Company 1839–1953*. T. and A. Constable.
Baruah, P. (2020). *History of tea. The beginning and development of Indian tea*. EBH Publishers.
Bourne, S. & Shepherd, A. (n.d.). Assamese men in costume loading tea onto bamboo boats. Wikimedia. Retrieved October 10, 2023, from https://upload.wikimedia.org/wikipedia/commons/5/53/Assamese_men_in_costume_loading_tea_onto_bamboo_boats_by_Bourne_%26_Shepherd.jpg

Bourne, S. & Shepherd, B. (n.d.). Assamese women in costume sorting tea. Wikipedia. Retrieved October 10, 2023, from https://upload.wikimedia.org/wikipedia/commons/a/a2/Assamese_women_in_costume%2C_sorting_tea_by_Bourne_%26_Shepherd.jpg

Dey, A. (2018). *Tea environments and plantation culture*. Cambridge University press.

Dutta, A.K. (2005). Kala-Azar in Assam. British medical intervention and people's response. In A.K. Bagchi & K. Sonan, *Maladies, preventives and curatives: debates in public health in India* (pp. 15–31). Tulika Books.

Gait, E. (1933). *A history of Assam*. Thacker Spink and Co.

Goswami, Priyam (2012). The history of Assam: from Yandabo to partition, 1826–1947, Orient Black Swan.

Homeward Mail from India, China and the East (1913) N.N. The Administration of Assam (July 7th).

Indian Medical Gazette (1885). N.N. The 'Kala-Azar' or black death of the Garo Hills 20 (3), pp. 83–84.

Kemmerling, U. (2021). Die "Entdeckung" der Tropenkrankheit Kala-Azar in Britisch-Indien. Interkulturelle Begegnung, Forschung und Transformation medizinischen Wissens, unpublished MA Thesis. Hagen. (will be published 2024 under the title: Medizinisches Wissen und koloniale Macht. Die Entdeckung der Tropenkrankheit Kala-Azar in Britisch-Indien, Hagen University Press).

Krieger, M. (2021). *Geschichte des Tees. Anbau, Handel und globale Genusskulturen*. Böhlau Verlag.

Macfarlane, A., & Macfarlane, I. (2004). *Green gold. The empire of tea*. Ebury press.

Mann, M. (2005). *Geschichte Indiens. Vom 18. bis zum 21. Jahrhundert*. Schöningh.

McCombie Young, T.C. (1924). *Kala-Azar in Assam. An account of the preventive operations. 1910 to 1923 and notes on the epidemiology of the disease in Assam and India*. H.K. Lewis and Co.

Rappaport, E. (2017). *A thirst for empire. How tea shaped the modern world*. Princeton University Press.

Rohrsen, P. (2013). *Der Tee. Anbau, Sorten. Geschichte*. Beck Verlag.

Sharma, J. (2002). *An European tea 'garden' and an Indian 'frontier': the discovery of Assam*. Cambridge University press.

Sharma, J. (2011). *Empire's garden. Assam and the making of India*. Duke University press.

Tea Board India and Ministry of Commerce and Industry, Government of India. (n.d.). Retrieved October 11, 2023, from https://www.teaboard.gov.in

Ukers, W.H. (1935). *All about tea, Vol. II*. Kingsport press.

Varma, N. (2017). *Coolies of capitalism. Work in global and historical perspective*. De Gruyter.

Martin Krieger
B.4 Tea – from luxury product to everyday comfort

Introduction

Tea presently ranks among the most important global beverages consumed in more or less every country of the world. It is easily available, can be obtained at a reasonable price and may be deemed a "great and invaluable comfort of life," as coined by nineteenth-century Danish botanist Nathaniel Wallich. Tea consumption has not only heavily shaped our drinking-habits, but simultaneously our material culture, and still offers today a distinct perspective of perceiving the cultures and enigmas of East Asia. It can constitute a quick early morning-cuppa as well as an elaborate five o'clock-experience in one of the leading hotels of Europe, North America or elsewhere. However, and wherever it is enjoyed, we apparently know almost everything about it. For more than two centuries, botanists have studied the physiognomy of *Camellia sinensis*, economists have debated the economic sense (or non-sense) of trading in this commodity, while tea-sommeliers delve into the flavours, taste, and secrets of a remarkable beverage deeper than ever before (Krieger, 2022).

A closer look into the historical records, however, leaves the impression that blank spaces within about two millennia of tea-history still remain. In some instances, myth and "real" history are hardly separated from each other, while in other cases sources are missing. Sometimes, the proper questions have not been addressed to the sources yet. Furthermore, rather simple sounding questions prove tricky to answer. How did the Europeans learn about tea and why did they start consuming it? How was an initially highly expensive luxury product converted into an article of mass-consumption?

This contribution tries to outline the major developments of early tea-history between Asia and Europe from the sixteenth to the outset of the eighteenth century. At first, it will study the observations of the early European missionaries, merchants, soldiers, and surgeons, who came across one of the most remarkable beverages between China, Japan, and the island of Java. Furthermore, it intends to reconstruct the media and contents of the transfer of tea-knowledge from those areas to Europe and how European scholars dealt with these materials. Finally, it will try to identify how tea as a commodity first reached Europe and why it was converted into an object of mass-consumption from the 1730s. Only an investigation of the early history of tea in Europe can offer a broader insight into the causes of the enormous success with which tea consumption spread and still spreads across the modern world.

https://doi.org/10.1515/9783110758573-005

Early observers in East- and Southeast-Asia

During the 1630s, the German intellectual and traveller Adam Olearius (1599–1671) visited the Persian capital Isfahan. Olearius served as secretary of an embassy despatched by the North German Duke of Schleswig-Holstein-Gottorf to Persia intending to establish trading between both territories. Even if the practical results of that enterprise were meagre, Olearius extensively studied the social, economic, political, and cultural life of his hosts and later published a seminal travel-account. This voluminous study came out in various editions and was in 1662 and 1669 published in English under the title "The voyages a travells of the ambassadors, sent by Frederick, Duke of Holstein, to the Great Duke of Muscovy and the King of Persia." The author reports that he had encountered some kind of tea-stalls during his stay in Isfahan and "that the Persians are great frequenters of the Taverns or Tipling-Houses, which they call Tzai Chattai Chane, in regard there they may have The, or Cha, which the Usbeques Tartars bring thither from Chattai." He furthermore noted that the use of such a remarkable drink would cure diseases of the stomach, lung, and liver and simultaneously would purify the blood. However, the North German traveller left it to the phantasy of the reader to guess if he himself tasted the drink at all (Olearius, 1662).

Olearius' text renders the impression that tea drinking was quite common in places distant from its areas of production and that it must have constituted a trading commodity in the Indian Ocean region some time before its dried leaves reached Europe. That this observation does not only apply to Olearius' times but already to the sixteenth century transpires from the report of the Persian merchant Hajji Mohammed who noted down that "Chai Catai" had many friends in his home country already then. It was along the shores of the Indian Ocean and its surrounding seas where Europeans encountered that beverage for the very first time. Jesuit missionaries as well as Portuguese, Dutch, English or German merchants and soldiers tasted it right on the spot and reported their experiences and knowledge back to Europe. We may assume that the breeding ground for tea consumption in the West was prepared by sixteenth- and seventeenth-century Europeans residing in or travelling through Asia. They informed those left at home not only about the drink itself, but also about the plant which yielded such remarkable leaves, the modes of preparation, and health-benefits attributed to it (Krieger, 2021).

That tea increasingly gained importance as a trading-commodity within the intra-Asiatic trading-networks from the sixteenth century resulted from significant developments in China, the largest producer before Japan. Ming-China witnessed striking innovations in the proceeding of tea, which raised its attraction elsewhere. This notably applies to the increasing importance of loose leaf-tea in contrast to the declining production of the traditional teacakes. The former was much cheaper to produce and much easier to be prepared by the consumer. Loose leaves just needed to be briefly soaked in warm water and then entirely covered with boiling water in a suitable pot. The beverage was then poured into small cups, while the leaves remained in the pot.

In addition to this, black tea simultaneously gained importance as an export-commodity, while green tea remained the most popular variety in East Asia itself. When the Europeans came to know tea, they first and foremost encountered green and black leaf tea, the latter becoming the most common sort in the West until this day. However, nobody in Europe knew that the green and the black varieties were produced from one and the same plant (Benn, 2015).

The earliest information to be recorded by a European on that drink originated from Japan and not from China, the former being more accessible to foreigners during the sixteenth century. Its visitors from Portugal or other countries commonly stayed here for many years if they ever returned home at all. The only opportunity to transfer knowledge and information back to their places of origin was by sending letters or producing text-manuscripts for later publication. Compared to the huge East Asian writing on the plant and its beverage, any European compilation, however, remained cursory at that period.

In 1546, the Portuguese merchant Jorge Alvares reported on tea the very first time. Alvares had lived for some years in the Japanese town Kagoshima and came to know that the locals used to drink hot water, which was flavoured by distinct herbs during wintertime. Cold water was never consumed. Some years later, Louis de Almeida (1525–1583), merchant, surgeon and later missionary, wrote on tea as well. After having joined the Jesuits, de Almeida did not only establish a hospital in Japan but set off for extensive travels across the country. He encountered tea gardens and – of even greater importance – was invited to join tea ceremonies. De Almeida was probably the first European who came to know that *camellia sinensis* was not just any drink, but a social beverage to be consumed within a highly formalised ceremony (Chanoyu) (Cooper as cited in Varley, 1998).

It was recognised by the Jesuits soon after that any foreigner familiar with Chanoyu would gain social access to the Japanese elites more easily. A comprehensive manuscript chiefly on the Japanese tea ceremony was compiled by João Rodrigues (1561–1633) – the "Arte del Cha." Formal tea-drinking was finally adopted by the Jesuits themselves. Their Roman headquarters instructed them to maintain tidy rooms in their Japanese outstations with all utensils necessary for arranging a ceremony for their local guests.

Cultivation and consumption in China were delved into deeper only during the seventeenth century. The prominent Jesuit father Matteo Ricci (1552–1610), later to become astronomer at the imperial court of Beijing, studied tea in some detail in his published diary. In comparison with Japan, the tea ceremony was obviously of lesser importance in China; it was not described by Ricci in much detail (Hsia, 2010).

While Portuguese merchants and Jesuit missionaries were the first to render an obviously tiny European readership familiar with tea, it was the servants of the Dutch East India Company (VOC) who gained an even deeper insight into the issue and established comprehensive knowledge as a precondition for its later trading to Europe. The VOC as an early-modern joint-stock company was the most successful enterprise venturing to trade with the Indian Ocean area around the Cape of Good Hope from about 1600. It dethroned the erstwhile powerful Portuguese Estado da India and made Amsterdam the most eminent emporium for trading with the East. As a precondition for continuity in Asia-trade, the VOC established a number of fortified settlements along the shores of the Indian Ocean. Former Batavia on the island Java, today's Indonesian capital Jakarta became the headquarters of the Dutch maritime enterprise from 1619. Batavia emerged into a virtual European-Asian metropolis with a European quarter and a fortress at its heart. From its very beginnings, Batavia proved to be highly attractive to Chinese immigrants, who came here with their families in ever growing numbers to settle in their own Chinese quarter. Here not only merchants but hookers and workmen were to be met, while vegetables for sale on the local markets were produced in their gardens. The Chinese migrants brought their language, traditions, and consumer habits along with them – among the latter also tea-connoisseurship (Schmitt et al., 1988).

The Chinese quarter of Batavia thus offered an abundance of opportunities to learn about traditional tea drinking at home in East Asia. While most of the European visitors to that presumably lively and colourful part of the city never left any trace of their observations and adventures, quite a large number of written testimonies nevertheless survives. German residents of Batavia, having entered VOC-services in increasing numbers in the wake of the Thirty-Years-War, seem to have been particularly eager to write down what they saw and heard. Some of their texts were later published. Those Germans either served as soldiers in the VOC, like Johann Jacob Saar (1625–1664) from Nuremberg, Caspar Schmalkalden (1616–1673) from Thuringia or Johann von der Behr (c. 1615–c. 1692) from Leipzig, or as highly educated surgeons like Andreas Cleyer (1634–c. 1697) from Kassel. Their texts constitute a substantial share of all documents recording the consumption of tea in Dutch Batavia, and an early image of tea-drinking in Asia developing in Europe during the seventeenth century was thus significantly shaped by them.

Saar, for instance, noted that the Chinese were "busy people, active in any kind of selling and buying, and skilled workmen." During his visits to their quarter, he necessarily came across an unknown drink from "a herb tea, which grows in China. They boil it and drink it very hot, accompanied by all kinds of sweets." Schmalkalden proves to be more detailed than Saar by not only focusing on its consumption but also its health-benefits:

> They often drink a beverage made from an herb called Chia in their language or more commonly Thé. It is very healthy, and thus consumed by the Dutch themselves as well. This water particularly proves to be beneficial against a dull mood. You can enjoy it when you are drunken – it will raise your appetite then and improve your stomach. Those who regularly have it, will never be concerned about consumption or gout. (Saar, 1672)

Schmalkalden does not only record the fact that Europeans drank tea as well, but that it was supposed to be immensely beneficial for one's health. Next to the benefits mentioned by him, Johan von der Behr additionally contends that "it increases memory and raises your mind." The consumption of tea mixed with arrack and sugar, known as punch ever since, is recorded by Christoph Langhans from Breslau/Wroclaw (Langhans, 1705). We may contend that most qualities attributed to tea later in Europe itself were borrowed from Chinese and Japanese by VOC-employees. An additional investigation of early English company-records might yield corresponding results from Bantam on Java or Indian Madras as well as Surat (Langhans, 1705).

Some VOC-servants gained an even deeper insight – those who served as company-representatives on the tiny, artificial island of Deshima off Japanese Nagasaki. Here, the Dutch East India Company maintained a trading-settlement, which was almost entirely secluded from its indigenous environment (Schmitt et al., 1988). However, now and then the head of the trading-post, accompanied by a small group of other Europeans, was dispatched to an embassy in the imperial Japanese court while, on other occasions, a VOC-surgeon was called to attend a sick Japanese person. It was notably the well-educated VOC-surgeons who cast an eye on the natural treasures and products of the country during their rare journeys and reported on their observations. In contrast to the Europeans in Batavia, they not only witnessed the consumption of tea, but also its cultivation in the countryside (Schmitt et al., 1988).

The surgeon Willem ten Rhijne (1647–1700) was the first to investigate *camellia sinensis* from a botanical perspective. Ten Rhijne had studied medicine in Franeker as well as Leiden and subsequently entered the service of the Dutch East India Company. He was sent to Deshima, where he was commissioned to cultivate European medical plants. Even if he apparently did not succeed in this matter, he nevertheless extensively studied the local flora and published his botanical hunts in several publications such as in his "Excerpta ex observationibus suis Japonicis Physicis &c. de Fructis Thee" edited by Jakob Breyne in Gdansk/Danzig (ten Rhijne, 1678).

Andreas Cleyer followed in his footsteps and reported on the tea-plant in a number of letters he sent to Europe. These letters offered the material for further publications in Europe itself by others, such as "De Herba Thée" by Christian Mentzel (1622–1701) from Berlin. First and foremost, Engelbert Kaempfer (1651–1716) from German Lemgo is to be mentioned as one of the most eminent VOC-surgeons on Deshima. Kaempfer initially had left Europe with a Swedish embassy to Persia but continued his travels through Asia on his own account, later entering an appointment in the VOC. Between 1690 and 1692, he served as a surgeon on Deshima to submit several scholarly studies after his return to Europe. His "Amoenitates exoticae" comprises, among other subjects, the hitherto most extensive and elaborate investigation on tea. Here he did not only study its natural history but also its social aspects in Japan: while the highest qualities were devoted to the imperial court, even poor people did not go without at least a tumbler prepared from a meagre quality (Kaempfer, 1779).

Early tea-knowledge in Europe

The early texts on the beverage originating from those men on the spot left deep traces among the intellectual debate in Europe itself. Against the backdrop of seventeenth-century so-called "Scientific Revolution," knowledge from Japan or China was eagerly absorbed by medical scholars in Amsterdam, Leiden, Copenhagen or elsewhere (Shapin, 1996). It is no wonder that interest in the new plant was most intense in the hub of European-Asian enterprise – in the Netherlands. As early as 1652, Claes Pieterszoon (1693–1674), commonly known through his lectures in anatomy as Dr. Tulp, published his seminal "Observationes Medicae," incorporating the small treatise on "Herba Thé." This text is apparently the oldest study on tea by an intellectual, who has never been to Asia himself (Tulp, 1739).

Tulp's treatise was read throughout Europe and inspired the Danish baroque intellectual Ole Worm (1588–1654), chiefly known for his archaeological studies, to conduct an experiment. Somehow, he came in possession of samples of green and black tea, which he soaked in warm water. While the black tea remained fragmentary and brittle, the green tea-pieces unfolded themselves into more or less intact leaves. In times without proper printed images or even herbarium specimens, this experiment offered a unique opportunity to study the structure of the leaves with their serrated edge. In his posthumously published "Museum Wormianum" the first tea-leave ever shown in print was subsequently published (Worm, 1665).

The intellectual tea-debate gained impetus by the early studies of Tulp, Worm, and others, with the same health-benefits being discussed among the Chinese ever since. Later, the debate joined a more general scientific discourse promoted by celebrities such as Gottfried Wilhelm Leibniz (1646–1716) with his deep interest in China. An increasing number of texts, some illustrated with ever-improving images of the tea-plant in its natural environment, with blossoms and seeds, came out in print. During the 1680s, no less than 21 academic publications on tea (some of them simultaneously dealing with coffee, chocolate, or tobacco) were brought to light. Mere medical interest was subsequently supplemented in them by discussing supposed moral virtues of tea or probable damages caused by excessive drinking (Li & Poser, 2000).

The first cup of tea in Europe

Without any doubt, the academic debate would not have been so intense without increasing quantities of tea being imported to Europe. It is not recorded when the very first sample of *camellia sinensis* reached Europe, by whom it was prepared, and how it tasted. It is likely that this remarkable incident occurred in the Netherlands sometime during the 1630s. It may be presumed that tea's good reputation as a remedy against a number of diseases heightened its acceptance – even if the first sip was bitter and strange. The hitherto unknown caffeine was stimulating, and tea leaves boiled with water proved to be a healthier drink than cold water directly drawn from a river or canal.

Moreover, the new, exotic consumer article brought about an entirely new material culture. Kettles for boiling water, pots, and cups were needed, as well as bottles for storing the leaves in a dry environment, sugar bowls, sugar tongs, spoons, milk cans and bowls for rinsing the cups in water, because strainers were still not in use for that purpose. The pot was kept on a metal warmer, and the cups were served on trays. Many of those items were directly imported from East Asia – over the course of time, they were imitated by upcoming porcelain factories or metal workshops in Europe itself (North, 2003).

The consumption of tea spread from the Netherlands across the Channel to England as well as across the North Sea ports to North Germany, Scandinavia, and the Baltic Sea area. France became addicted to tea at the outset, but later shifted to coffee. The more distant a place was situated from the seaports, the less chance it had to be supplied with the costly leaves of *camellia sinensis*. Quite the exception was Russia, where the new drink came overland through China and Siberia in growing quantities.

The spreading of tea was not just a geographical but even more so a social development. A higher social rank and a thicker purse rendered it more likely to get in contact with it. The initially immensely expensive beverage constituted an ideal indicator of wealth and power and thus served as a means of displaying prestige, probably even more than coffee. It is reported that the British East India Company once presented King Charles II with two pounds of tea to raise his attention to the company's trading. In another instance, the leaves were compared with Catharine of Braganza in a poem and thus virtually ennobled themselves: "the best of queens, and the best of herbs." The French king Louis XIV supposedly ordered to have them prepared in golden pots (Rappaport, 2017).

Even if such stories – or maybe myths – spread across the courts of Europe, tea was to a lesser degree a royal drink, but it was much more cherished by the wealthy merchant elites, who first encountered that rare commodity from the East in the port towns. They might have heard of the beverage from their counterparts in Batavia or Deshima, and now and then a small quantity of leaves reached their hands as a mere curiosity. Later, the VOC itself brought even larger amounts back home and let them sell off at their auctions in the Netherlands. During the seventeenth century, tea merchants emerged, such as *Jan Jacob Voute & Sons* in Amsterdam. By the mid-eighteenth century no less than fifty tea shops existed in the town of Leiden. Here, tea could not just be purchased, but freshly brewed and tasted (Krieger, 2009).

It is reported that the first tea-room of London was established by a homecomer from Asia around 1650. The unknown man had supposedly been the servant of a VOC-employer, got married and finally opened a tea room, which, according to a temporary source made him rich. This success is said to have served as a model, and many similar houses offering tea as well as coffee were established by others. Regardless of whether this story is true, it is for sure that tea was offered in the early coffee-houses of London such as in so-called "Sultan's head" in 1658. Surprisingly, England remained a country of coffee-lovers for two more generations until it became a tea-connoisseurs paradise (N.N., 1690; Herbert, 1956).

About the same time the beverage was readily available at "Sultan's head" it could be drunk in Hamburg as well as in Copenhagen. From those Northern trading-emporia its consumption spread across the country and was to be met, for instance, in the Danish town of Ålborg during the latter half of the seventeenth century. Sometime later, teacups were recorded in probate inventories in Polish towns bordering the Baltic (Hoff, 2015).

From luxury-product to every-day pleasure

The earliest tea-arrivals in Amsterdam did not come directly from China, but were purchased by the Dutch East India Company in Batavia. A never ceasing traffic in junks from China supplied the colonial metropolis of Java with almost any commodity from Canton, Amoi, and other Chinese ports. It was the Dutch VOC-merchants who sent smaller quantities of *Camellia sinensis*, which they had tasted in the tea-stalls of Batavia themselves, back home. As early as 1637, the directors of the VOC in Amsterdam subsequently ordered any vessel to return from Asian waters and bring along a small portion of Chinese or Japanese tea. However, the shipments remained negligible in contrast to the ever-growing dispatches of spices and later textiles to reach Europe. It seemed to be quite a lot, such as when the ship "Pouleran" carried about 650 kg in 1678, while 50–150 kg per vessel were the norm (Krieger, 2009).

The English East India Company (EIC) felt even less inclined to ship that exotic commodity from Bantam on Java or even from Indian Madras. Some 110 kg were carried to England altogether in 1669. As late as 1685, the English company started systematically placing orders as: "[. . .] we would have you send us yearly five or six canisters of the very best and freshest tea." At home the new beverage slowly gained acceptance, not least due to the increasing number of printed texts on the plant. Prices remained high, which finally induced the EIC to attempt to send ships directly to China in 1697 (Chaudhuri, 1978).

A major obstacle for shipping to Europe directly from China was the restrictive trading policy of the Chinese imperial court in the wake of the transfer of power from the Ming- to the Manchu-dynasty. Despite the early English attempts to reach some ports in the South, foreign overseas trade remained forbidden, with extensive traffic in junks to Southeast Asia being not more than tolerated. The situation changed in 1713, when the imperial court, driven by its ever-increasing demand for silver, legalised direct trading to Europe. At the same time, any commercial exchange with the Europeans was restricted to the town of Canton near today's Hong Kong. Four years later, the EIC sent its first ships to Canton to be followed by vessels from the Austrian Netherlands, France, Denmark, Sweden, and Hamburg. Even though large quantities still reached Batavia on Asian junks, the VOC initially felt no motivation to enter the field as well and continued to do its purchases on Java. In the long term, this policy proved to be disadvantageous to the Dutch, because prices were usually higher in Batavia than in Canton, and the quality deteriorated by reloading in the Dutch entrepôt. Only in 1728 did the VOC finally change its mind and sent the "Coxhorn" as the first Dutch intercontinental enterprise from the Netherlands directly to Canton (Glamann, 1958; Furber 1976).

Trading in tea via Canton was strongly monopolised. This did not only apply to the European chartered trading-companies with their monopolies, but to the Chinese side as well. A local guild, the so-called Co Hong, was the only institution to be permitted to enter commercial contacts with the Europeans. The Co Hong did not only sell tea to the trading-companies, but it likewise rented out factory-premises at the waterfront of Canton. Here, the Europeans resided during the trading-season, while they returned to Europe afterwards or stayed in nearby Portuguese Macao for the remaining year. Only in later times did European head-merchants, the supercargoes, sometimes remain there during off-season for procuring cheaper tea-supplies. To some degree, this system proved to be of advantage to the Europeans, because the costly construction of a fortress and the maintenance of European troops, which was necessary in Southeast Asia or in India, could be avoided (Ptak, 1994).

The growing attraction of the tea market in Canton led to the fact that Japanese teas hardly played a role any more for the European Asia-trade. From the 1730s onwards, ever increasing amounts of tea left Canton for the European ports. While the EIC exported 143 tons of tea during 1720/21, the quantity rose to about 700 t in 1729/30, further significantly increasing during subsequent decades. A suitable ballast for the East Indiamen was porcelain, which simultaneously flooded the European luxury markets (Chaudhuri, 1978).

Political developments heavily influenced the European tea-market in the wake of the War of Spanish Succession. In 1715, an Ostende-Company had gained trading privileges from the authorities of the Habsburg-Netherlands. For some time, the Ostenders constituted a substantial competition for the Dutch and the British, until their company was suspended by the imperial Austrian court in exchange for the acceptance of the new Austrian law of succession by the West European powers. Financial capital left the Southern Netherlands to find investment with the Swedish and Danish Asiatic companies likewise trading in tea (Gent, 1996).

A taste for quality

The sorts of tea transported to Europe in the age of the Northwest European trading-companies significantly differed from the qualities of today. They were generally of much inferior quality, which did not only result from lower grades packed in China, but simultaneously from its transport-conditions in a humid, warm environment to Europe for more than half a year. In contrast to China with its enormous consumption of green teas, most tea reaching Europe was oxidated, in our terms "black" or of the Oolong-type. While China itself boasted an immense range of different qualities and regions of origin – already during the Ming-period more than 50 sorts were counted among the better qualities – only very few sorts ever reached the European markets during the heyday of company-trading.

Bohea was the most simple, coarse, and cheap black sort, which constituted from one third to more than half of the entire amounts annually brought to Europe. Already in Batavia it was known that *bohea* was of an inferior quality and was hardly consumed by the Chinese themselves. It was blamed for its stringent and bitter taste. Despite it being the cheapest sort, it nevertheless flooded eighteenth-century European markets and only disappeared from the pricelist from around the 1850s (Bremen, StAB).

Black *kongou* was of a more even character, but like *bohea* constituted the harvest of larger, elder leaves, however, without the many fragments and dust to be found within *bohea*. Its infusion was lighter and dispersed a gentler fragrance, but it simultaneously was twice as expensive as the former. Even better than *kongou* were *souchong*, which hardly played any role in Europe, and *pekoe*. The latter was deemed to be the finest and costliest black sorts available. It was fabricated from younger leaves and contained more tips. Since its price was twice as much as that of *kongou*, consumption was small and only about 2% of all imports to Europe were *pekoe* throughout the eighteenth century (Krieger, 2009).

At the beginning, green tea was of almost the same importance as the black sorts, but its exports significantly declined from the 1730s. The basic green sort was *songlo* or *thea viridis*, which was similarly coarse and simple like the *bohea*, but was more expensive. The higher green qualities *hyson* and *bing* only played a small or entirely insignificant role (N.N., 1836).

Only from the latter half of the nineteenth century were new and better sorts or even brands cherished among the Western consumers, and they still play a major role today. Even if most Europeans enjoyed tea of an inferior quality, the new beverage penetrated among almost every house of Western and Northern Europe during the eighteenth century. At the end of the century, one was tempted to remark, "Now the tea kettle has lost the power of astonishing" (Berg et al., 2015).

Conclusion

It took about one century for tea to be converted from a curiosity and luxury product into an object of mass consumption. At the outset, the first dispatches of this beverage reached the Western world more or less by random, and shortly after the Dutch and English East India companies systematically started ordering smaller quantities. Only the opening of the Chinese export market to European East Indiamen offered the opportunity for more extensive trade, and finally for a price reduction for consumers. However, as shown here, a prehistory of tea-drinking in Europe exists. The first European connoisseurs were offered their first cup during a tea-ceremony in Japan, at the imperial court of China or within the bazars of the Chinese quarter of Batavia. It was the VOC-surgeons on Deshima who conducted the first botanical studies, and it was sailors and soldiers from various European countries who first wrote back home about their culinary experiences. All these men and a few women learned that tea could be consumed with milk and sugar – and that a sweet side dish enhanced enjoyment. Even today we still use tea leaves and not the fragments of tea cakes, a heritage of seventeenth-century colonial experience.

Next to the physical encounter, the transfer of knowledge was of similar importance. Without the knowledge that tea was healthy and made the drunkards sober again – published in numerous academic and popular texts – the beverage would certainly have been less attractive. Resulting from falling prices and an increasing knowledge, entire societies became virtually addicted to tea (however, others to coffee). And only few ever asked if it made sense to export tons and tons of silver annually for the import of such a perishable good.

References

Benn, J.A. (2015). *Tea in China. A religious and cultural history*. University of Hawaii Press.

Chaudhuri, K.N. (1978). *The trading world of Asia and the English East India Company, 1660–1760*. Cambridge University Press.

Cooper, M. (1998). The early Europeans and tea. In Paul Varley & Isao Kumakura (Eds.), *Tea in Japan. Essays on the history of Chanoyu*. University of Hawaii Press.

Furber, H. (1978). *Rival empires of trade in the Orient, 1600–1800*. University of Minnesota Press.

Glamann, K. (1958). *Dutch-Asiatic Trade 1620–1740*. Martinus Nijhoff.

Hoff, A. (2015). *Den Danske Tehistorie*. Wormianum.

Hsia, R.P. (2010). *A Jesuit in the forbidden city. Matteo Ricci 1552–1610*. Oxford University Press.

Kaempfer, E. (1779). *Geschichte des Japanischen Thees, appendix to: ibid., Geschichte und Beschreibung von Japan*, vol. 2. Meyersche Buchhandlung.

Krieger, M. (2009). *Tee. Eine Kulturgeschichte*. Böhlau.

Krieger, M. (2021). *Geschichte des Tees. Anbau, Handel und globale Genusskulturen*. Böhlau.

Krieger, M. (2022). *Nathaniel Wallich. Global botany in nineteenth-century India*. Manohar Publishers.

Langhans, C. (1705). *Neue Ost-Indische Reise, worinnen umständlich beschrieben werden unterschiedene Küsten und Inseln in Ost-Indien, auf welche die holländische geoctroirte Compagnie zu handeln pfleget*. Michael Rohrlachs seel. Wittib und Erben.

N.N. (1690). *Caffe- und The-Logia, oder kurtze Anzeigung und Beschreibung dieser Geträncke*.

North, M. (2003). *Genuss und Glück des Lebens. Kulturkonsum im Zeitalter der Aufklärung*. Böhlau.

Olearius, A. (1662). *The voyages and travels of the ambassadors, sent by Frederick, Duke of Holstein, to the Great Duke of Muscovy and the King of Persia, first edition*. Thomas Dring and John Starkey.

Parmentier, J. (1996). *Tea time in Flanders. The maritime trade between the southern Netherlands and China in the 18th century*. Ludion Press.

Ptak, R. (1994). Die Rolle der Chinesen, Portugiesen und Holländer im Teehandel zwischen China und Südostasien (ca. 1600–1750). *Jahrbuch für Wirtschaftsgeschichte, 1*.

Rappaport, E. (2017), *A thirst for empire. How tea shaped the modern world*. Princeton University Press.

Ricci, M. (1953). *China in the sixteenth century. The journals of Matthew Ricci, 1583–1610*. Translated from the Latin by Louis J. Gallagher. Cambridge University Press.

Saar, J.J. (1672). *Ost-Indianische Funfzehn-Jährige Kriegs-Dienste und Wahrhafftige Beschreibung was sich . . . von Anno Christi 1644 biß Anno Christi 1659 . . . begeben habe*. Tauber Felßecker.

Schmalkalden, C. (1983). *Die wundersamen Reisen des Caspar Schmalkalden nach West- und Ostindien*, ed. by Wolfgang Joost, 2nd. ed. Edition Leipzig.

Schmitt, E., Schleich, Th., & Beck, Th. (Eds.) (1988). *Kaufleute als Kolonialherren. Die Handelswelt der Niederländer vom Kap der Guten Hoffnung bis Nagasaki 1600–1800*. Buchner.

Shapin, S. (1996). *The scientific revolution*. University of Chicago Press.

Ten Rhijne, W. (1678). Excerpta ex observationibus suis Japonicis Physicis &c. de Fructis Thee. In Jakob Breyne, *Icones Exoticarum aliarumque Minus Cognitarum Plantarum in Centuria Prima descriptarum Plantae Exoticae*.

Tulp, N. (1739). Herba Thé. *Observationes Medicae*.

Twining, S.H. (1956). *The House of Twining, 1706–1956*. R. Twining.

Von der Behr, J. (1668). *Diarium, oder Tage-Buch über dasjenige, so sich Zeit einer neunjährigen Reise . . . zugetragen*. Spaltholtz.

Worm, O. (1665). *Museum Wormianum. Seu Historica Rerum Rariorum*. Elsevier.

Gunther Hirschfelder and Lavinia Eifler

B.5 More than a beverage – appropriation, prevalence and cultural meaning of tea in everyday culture

Introduction

The history of tea, its cultivation, production, trade, and consumption habits are linked to historical and contemporary globalisation patterns, political conflicts, social issues, and changes in the attribution of cultural value. Starting in ancient China, tea was cherished as medicine. Over the centuries, the bitter leaves were seasoned, and tea became more popular as a daily beverage. With Europeans travelling to China and Japan since the fifteenth century, tea was written about in travel reports and finally introduced to Europe where it was abandoned at first for its bitter taste, but soon after became an appreciated beverage.

This article will illustrate the origins of tea cultivation and consumption in China and Japan, before historically contextualising tea consumption, prevalence and appropriation in Europe, focussing on political, social and medical attributions as well as the underlying argumentative patterns. After providing historical background, we will discuss contemporary forms of tea consumption, with a focus on product ranges, ingredients, consumption habits, advertising and marketing, which helps to perceive the shift in political, medical and social influences and their effects on food culture. How is tea linked to civilisational progress and the development of drug consumption? Which impact did tea have on historical and contemporary Britishness and associated stereotypes? Is tea simultaneously a symbol of self-identification and othering? Why do German rappers launch their own brands of iced tea? What's the secret behind bubble tea? Why do people in the North of Germany drink more tea, than people located in the South? These questions and many more will be answered, for tea is central to cultural and national identity formation. Ultimately, this paper will argue that tea is more than a beverage. It is a symbol of status and daily pleasure, it speaks of traditions and represents modern lifestyle, and, due to its versatility, it serves as an indicator for social change and cultural appropriation – it's more than a beverage!

Consumption habits and availabilities

The consumption of goods is one of the requirements for the development of civilisation and a basic pattern of human action. Consumption generates progress, trade and cultural exchange. The reasons for people's food choices, how, when and with whom

https://doi.org/10.1515/9783110758573-006

they drink and eat, are subject to various factors, such as individual taste, economic situation, environmental conditions, social milieu, or psychological patterns. Consumption – and its rejection – is a way to express identity by attributing meaning to objects that are understood by others (Beck, 2003). Affiliation with social groups, expression of lifestyle, or personal satisfaction can (seemingly) be accomplished by consumption of the appropriate goods. Historically, opportunities were strongly limited by financial means and availability. Contemporary affluent societies offer a wider spectrum of objects that represent lifestyle and identity.

However, tea as a product comes with certain limitations, one of which is its transitory nature. Unlike objects manufactured for long-term use, tea is not bought to be conserved and passed on to the next generation, but for "best-before" consumption and enrichment of daily life, which includes a considerably short time span between purchase and disposal. Furthermore, nowadays being mostly drunk for enjoyment and enrichment, tea is classified as semi-luxury food, having stimulating effects on mind and body. Due to the aspect of stimulation, semi-luxury food is often linked to addictive substances. The distinction between semi-luxury food, addictive substance and medical remedy depends on temporal, cultural, regional, religious, educational and social circumstances. Quite often, one commodity contains all these interpretations at the same time and loses some of them as time passes (Merki, 2003). Tea, therefore, is an optimal example to show this process.

For consumers today, tea is available at all prices and quality levels. Various tastes, natural or aromatised, are offered in the range between specialised shops and discount supermarkets. Historically speaking, this was not always the case, when first introduced to European audiences in the seventeenth century, tea was a luxury good only affordable for ruling elites. Using tea as an example, this paper will outline the history of a product that developed from a luxury item to an affordable commodity.

Regardless of the wide range of its monetary value, the preparation of tea as a beverage seems rather straightforward. The drink consists of leaves from a tea plant (or surrogates) and water. The tealeaves are either boiled in the liquid or the hot liquid is poured over the leaves, then left to stand for a certain amount of time before the beverage is sifted. Seeming simple, this procedure varied widely across time and place. The basic principle – cooking plants in fluids – is very old; since the beginning of humankind, humans used the plants in their environment as food, medication, or drugs. Early on, they also discovered the healing effects of certain plants – tea is only one of them.

European culture looks back on over 400 years of tea consumption – a long time to acculturate and reshape. Therefore, and following Beck's argument that "Consumption brings about culture, and culture circulates through consumption. Even more, culture emerges through consumption – turning consumers themselves into producers" (Beck, 2003, p. 46),[1] this paper will show that drinking tea is more than an action performed in everyday life, it is a cultural artefact and symbol. Consequently, this paper will highlight political, social, and medical attributions as well as their argumentative basis. In a final step, contemporary forms of tea consumption will be observed, in order to briefly comment on the most recent developments in the history of tea culture. To contextualise the papers' interest in the socio-cultural developments of European tea culture, a quick look at the origins of tea cultivation and consumption in ancient China will be provided, before the discussion will focus on the beverages' consumption, prevalence and appropriation in Europe.

History and origins of consumption and inherent cultural meanings

Originally indigenous to China, the tea bush was first cultivated on small family farms from 220 AD. A few centuries later, tea consumption had spread, and production took now place on broad plantations under command of the Chinese imperial dynasty, which raised the first tea tax about 780 AD. Quickly, Chinese producers and customers discovered that the taste of the final product varied, depending on the quality of the leaves and the water. Whereas the water was often locally sourced, the leaves were prepared for transport and sale by being cured and pressed into "tea cakes", from which small pieces were broken off to be dashed with boiling water. As the demand for tea of the highest quality rose among customers, so did the degree of expertise demanded of tea producing professionals. Between 600 and 900 AD, the position of tea master became a profession in itself, and as such it included detailed knowledge about the quality of plants and water, how to use proper dishes, and how to develop the necessary virtuosity required for enacting the highly ritualised ceremony that was performed for guests in noble houses and at the imperial court (Ellis et al., 2015; Menninger, 2004). During the twelfth century AD, the invention of heat-resistant and tasteless porcelain enriched drinking tea, as it was now possible to concentrate on the tea's taste excluding the possible taste of other drinking vessels. Tea and porcelain formed a symbiosis, which lasts until the present day. As time passed, so did the developments in the production, preparation, and consumption of tea: during the thirteenth century pressed tea cakes were superseded by trading dried loose leaves, and processing of the raw plant was refined until green tea, as we know it today, was created in the thirteenth and fourteen century. Between the fourteenth and seventeenth

---

1 The quote was translated by the author, see the original text: „Konsum stiftet Kultur, und Kultur zirkuliert durch Konsum. Mehr noch: sie entsteht durch Konsum – was den Konsumenten zum gleichsam sich selbst kreierenden Produzenten erhebt." (Beck, 2003, p. 46)

century the fermentation of green tea enabled the creation of black tea. Both green and black teas were refined by adding leaves of other plants: lotus, rose, jasmine and orange blossoms. Moreover, drinking tea was not a pleasure restricted to members of the upper class. From the tenth century public teahouses were established and quickly became centres of social interaction and exchange, where tea was served while entertainment was provided. As time passed, the innovative progress made in producing, trading, preparing and finally enjoying a cup of tea resulted in the emergence of a distinct pattern of cultural practice that affected everyday life across social barriers and spatial boundaries, but also found expression in specialised and highly exclusive rituals performed within the upper classes – not just in China. In fact, tea, and the cultural practice associated with its consumption, slowly but steadily travelled along trading routes from China to Japan, Persia, India, Mongolia, Indonesia and the Philippines, before it finally reached Europe (Menninger, 2004; Ellis et al., 2015).

It is a fact based on anthropological evidence that humans have always had a sweet tooth (Hirschfelder, 2018). So how could a drink as bitter as the original tea spread so widely? The story of the beverage begins with the initial use of the plant for medical purpose. The plant was valued for its stimulating and diuretic effects, as well as its preventive and calming properties. Soon, however, tea was consumed not only in reference to specific illnesses but became a daily remedy due to its overall benefits linked to human health. Nowadays, the classification of tea as an addictive substance, due to the caffeine it contains, may raise concerns. Historically, however, most semi-luxury goods were classified as "drugs", albeit without today's negative connotation (Merki, 2003). Historically speaking, the consumption of stimulating substances and the use of drugs is often closely linked to the development of humankind. Archaeologic relics dating back to Palaeolithic Age indicate the consumption of plant juices having intoxicating and psychedelic effects (Hirschfelder, 2005).

Those substances were consumed therapeutically (and possibly for so-called mind-expanding effects), for example during religious and spiritual ceremonies, when coping with everyday life, or simply for enjoyment. Regardless of the various potential reasons for those early forms of drug consumption, the use of such substances for medical purpose remains uncontested (Hirschfelder, 2007). Considering these facts, it is hardly surprising that tea gained such popularity over a relatively short time span, since it is similar to medicinal and stimulating substances used before. However, since the chemical process of dissolving tannins into caffeine, which can then be absorbed into the bloodstream, requires a substantial amount of time, the consumption of tea is also associated with waiting and the passing of time. Therefore, unlike coffee, drinking tea is often associated with rest and repose – a ritual rather than a quick fix. This ritualistic element of tea consumption links its past and present.

A new chapter – prevalence in Europe

The prevalence of tea in Europe is closely linked to and unthinkable without institutional medicine. Back in the fifteenth century, scholarly European travellers discovered the beverage and sent reports about tea to their home countries. At first, it was assumed that Chinese people were extraordinarily healthy thanks to their tea consumption. Despite this, a certain degree of scepticism remained, since European equivalents to the bitter taste, the dark colour and the custom to drink it as a hot beverage did not exist. In the end, however, the advantages and positive effects of tea outweighed European scepticism. The Portuguese Jesuit João Rodrigues (1561–1633), who lived in China and Japan, outlined the almost miraculous effects of this unknown medicine:

> Both the Chinese and Japanese attribute various properties to cha. It aids digestion, expels drowsiness, and relieves headaches; it brings down fever, eases the heart, and relieves melancholy; it is conducive to chastity because it cools the kidneys, and it flushes out excess body fluids, thus bringing relief to pain caused by the stone. As a result of these healthy properties, plague and pestilence are seldom experienced in China and Japan, despite the densely populated nature of these two countries. (Cooper, 1989, pp. 101–133, cited in Menninger, 2009, p. 123)

Those effects described by Rodrigues and other travellers were in line with European early modern medical believes. Following humoral theory, physicians aimed to balance the four humours (blood, phlegm, black, and yellow bile) to heal their patients, or at least ease the afflictions. This system of medicine was still in practice when the first documented shipment of tea arrived in Amsterdam in 1610 AD. It took some time until the hot beverage was accepted by physicians and patients, due to its bitter taste. Drinking habits of the time mainly saw the consumption of wine and diluted beer, as drinking unprocessed water often resulted in illness (Hirschfelder, 2005).

However, after gaining momentum as a remedy against a variety of ailments, tea's positive effects overweighed superstitions and doubts, and medical treatises about tea and details of use, such as the advice of sipping it slowly to avoid oral burns, spread. Those publications were written in accessible language and aimed to promote the medical application of tea. The previously condemned bitter taste was now believed to chase worms out of the body, and phlegm diluting effects were attributed to the beverage. Tea was prescribed as a remedy for heart complaints, kidney stones, gout, lung disease and period pain, to list but a few examples. The effects were also believed to be useful for the human brain, as tea was said to help avoid strokes and relieve headaches and migraines.

Furthermore, drinking tea was understood to positively affect dental hygiene, as its consumption was said to prevent caries. Unsurprisingly, tea became very popular within a rather short time, which resulted in a substantial increase of tea imports. In 1669, 222 pounds of tea were imported, and in 1690 the British East India Company already shipped 38,390 pounds of tea to European harbours (Menninger, 2004). Tea was welcome as a cure in plague-ridden Europe.

As European demands for tea increased significantly, tea production in China expanded accordingly. Tea had become an important commodity, affecting the relationship between European trading nations, price fluctuation and different trading systems. In China, tea was traded primarily for silver, but in the nineteenth century a new medium of exchange became lucrative: opium. Having colonised India, the British gained access to cheap opium, which could be traded for tea – with enormous profits. More and more opium reached China and addiction rates rose dangerously. The Chinese imperial dynasty's attempt to stop the import of opium culminated in two Opium Wars (1839–1842 and 1856–1860), in which the British Empire was ultimately victorious. From now on, China's position as an equal in the tea trade weakened. Additionally, the Indian tea plant (Camellia sinensis var. assamica) was discovered and successfully cultivated within the British colonies. The British Empire thus dominated the tea market and due to colonisation it became possible to cheaply produce tea at the cost of exploitation of native peoples and nature (Menninger, 2004). Tea being a colonial good, just like coffee, tobacco, chocolate, or sugar, shifted the distribution of power within the global economic system. As more and more tea was imported and profit was made, taxation escalated. Alas, with the help of acts of subterfuge, such as smuggling, tea consumption changed once again:

> It was the dealers in contraband tea who made Scotland a nation of tea drinkers in the 1760s, and who were responsible for the establishment of distribution networks that ran through the coastal regions into country's heartland. It was smugglers who supplied tea to the provincial margins of Great Britain, establishing illicit routes to distribute tea imported from China through the European rivals to the East India Company. It was they who were responsible for undermining the perception of tea drinking as a practice of the city's modish middling sorts. Above all, it was they who drove down the market prices for tea, and who thus brought the commodity within the reach of provincial working families. (Ellis et al. 2015, pp. 177–178)

In early modern times, new consumer cultures emerged, interpreting consumption in an individualistic, affirmative, enriching way. Beforehand, luxury goods and the consumption beyond one's basic needs was associated with temptation and therefore condemned for moral and religious reasons (Beck, 2003).

As tea was democratised and became accessible to many rather than just a few, the luxurious product was redefined as a commodity. In combination with porcelain, tea culture was adapted into and reshaped by regional customs and specific milieus. This includes the labelling of other plants but the tea bush as "tea". As shown, original tea leaves were extremely expensive over a long period of time, however the habit of drinking a hot beverage for medicinal or other reasons spread. The solution was to use other, regional plants.

Beyond the medicinal use, tea consumption evolved into a social event. Sweetened with sugar that was imported from overseas, tea was enjoyed in social scenarios, served to guests at home, or while visiting the local coffee house, which also offered coffee and hot chocolate to its guests. Just like in China, coffee houses were spaces of social interaction, cultural performances, as well as intellectual and political exchange. One of the earliest European coffee houses was located in Oxford, England, opening its doors in 1650. Many others followed, *Caffè Florian* in Venice, established in 1720, and *Lloyd'Coffeehouse*, established in London 1688, to name but a few. Soon coffee houses could be found in every large city, quickly spreading into smaller towns too (Deutscher Kaffeeverband). Prevalence took far longer in rural areas, where tea was sold by itinerant traders and on local markets until the second half of the nineteenth century. Establishing itself as a part of daily life, tea influenced the European food system. In vast parts of Europe, a soup made of beer and bread was typical for breakfast. Introducing tea and coffee instead opened new opportunities to traders and consumers, and gradually the beer soup was replaced by tea and coffee, served with bread and pastries, depending on the respective financial budget (Menninger, 2004). Equally, depending on the economy of a household, sets of porcelain were purchased, either as a simple commodity or especially manufactured in China according to the customers wishes. In 1707, the first European porcelain manufactory was set up in Meissen, a town in Germany close to Dresden, and competed with Chinese manufactures. In the form of Chinoiserie, European artists and craftsmen imitated Chinese and Eastern Asian motives in art, architecture, music and so on in the seventeenth and eighteenth century, thus creating longlasting stereotypes of Asian culture (Bischoff, 2005). Unique examples of Chinoiserie porcelain, teapots and tea cups, were created by porcelain painters in Augsburg at the beginning of the eighteenth century by ennobling Meissen porcelain with paintings in gold and iron red (see figure B.5.1).

Figure B.5.1: Teapot and tea cups ("Koppchen") with chinoiserie.
Note: Teapot and tea cups ("Koppchen") with Chinoiserie by Martin Engelbrecht (1725), painting in gold and iron red.
Phographer: Lenz Mayer
Source: Kunstsammlungen und Museen Augsburg, Maximilianmuseum

Anti-tea movement

Being a luxury good that symbolised status and prestige at first, tea slowly made its way from mansions to middle- and lower-class households. However, the history of tea culture also shows that changes do not always happen smoothly. While the beverage was promoted by physicians as a cure for a multitude of ailments, an anti-tea movement formed that classified tea as a dangerous substance.

To provide proof for their concerns, physicians and former tea consumers reported negative effects they had experienced, like nervousness, tremors, discomfort, hysteria and anxiety. More worryingly though was the suspicion that tea caused infertility. Furthermore, the positive effect of dissolving phlegm was now interpreted in a negative way, in that the consumption of tea lead to exsiccation and emaciation (Menninger, 2004). Simon Pauli, Professor of Botanicas and physician from Germany in service of the Danish royal family, published a series of papers warning against the consumption of tobacco, coffee and tea. About the latter, he wrote:

> It is, therefore, the Duty of every European to join in engaging the Legislature to put a Stop to this epidemical Evil, and prohibit the Abuse, not only of Tea, but also of Tobacco, since both of these, and Coffee, as I have before shewn, so enervate the European Men, that they become incapable of propagating their Species. (Pauli, 1746, p. 163, cited Fraund, 2010, p. 51)

The threat of – especially male – infertility was more than an individual concern, as it affected the future of the entire nation. Following such publications on the danger of tea consumption, the drink was deemed improper and officially considered dangerous. As a result, numerous regional acts and regulations concerning tea consumption were published. In 1768, for example, Frederick William II, King of Prussia, declared that in the princedom Minden only persons having a medical certificate were permitted to buy and drink tea (Menninger, 2004). One should be aware, though, that in many cases such regulations were only superficially concerned with citizens' health issues. Since coffee houses were places to meet and potentially exchange political ideas – including oppositional or radical opinions – in a rather informal setting, state authorities often felt threatened by such gathering places. The prohibition of stimulating beverages such as tea, coffee and hot chocolate resulted in coffee house closures and thus the lack of assembly places. Thus, tea consumption regulations sometimes had a hidden agenda, and served as an instrument of governmental control to oppress oppositional thoughts. On a sociocultural level, however, the ruling elites continued to uphold tea as a prestige product of "symbolic capital" that not everybody was allowed to consume (Bourdieu, 2020).

As the population grew, however, and the supposedly negative effects of tea failed to appear, the voices of medical critics of tea consumptions slowly grew less prominent. Nonetheless, the concerns about the influence and effects of this beverage did not entirely disappear. Instead, they resurfaced in a new disguise, as can be observed in the case of Great Britain. With the expansion of global trade due to the transatlantic expansion in the fifteenth century and the trade with Asia, more foreign cultural identities stepped into European awareness. Opening to unknown nations, people and customs often cause a contrary reaction in the home country. National identity and self-images are discussed most widely, when influences from outside grow. Tea as an imported product from China differing a lot in culture, religion, political system and so on, did not only cause enthusiasm, but also neophobia and othering processes. The acculturation of drinking tea in England led to a negatively connotated stereotypical image of China projected onto tea by its opponents. One feared that by drinking tea, stereotypical Chinese attributes, like small body size and a feminine presence, could affect British consumers and endanger their masculinity. Xenophobia and misogyny went hand in hand. On top of it all tea consumption was declared unpatriotic, for leaves and herbs also grew on the British Isles.

Tea supporters on the other hand devised the opposite. China being a cultural role model, this should be imitated concerning architecture, literature and the arts – in the form of *Chinoiserie* – and of course tea consumption. In this view tea had caused the blooming of Chinese culture and prevented illness, profligacy and wars. Even more, drinking tea being a non-alcoholic, stimulating beverage, was used by the temperance movement. Tea held big potential, as it was an alternative to beer and hard liquors during working hour breaks. Therefore, it structured daily routines and brought safety to industrialised factories in the nineteenth century (Fraund, 2010).

In spite of such binary points of view the acculturation of tea in Great Britain – and the rest of Europe – wasn't to stop. Instead, the former controversial tea became a British national symbol. What had happened? Passing tea consumptions from one generation to the next, the alterity discourses fell increasingly silent, and people got used to tea coming from abroad. Also, after the Opium Wars mentioned above, most of the tea consumed in Great Britain was planted in India, which, being part of the Commonwealth, did not seem as foreign: "Tea functioned in Victorian Britain as a powerful signifier of national identity, a shared taste that unites all people – metaphorically if not actually – across a series of social divides" (Ellis et al., 2015, p. 227). Tea was increasingly understood as a British product, and still is today.

Before heading to contemporary tea culture, we will take a glimpse on tea culture in Russian and Islamic culture. Tea was first introduced to what was later to become Russia due to caravan trading routes from Mongolia. As in Europe, tea was a status symbol and only accessible for urban aristocracy over centuries. The democratisation of tea didn't start until the nineteenth century and lasts up to the present day. Drinking black tea prepared in a samovar is prevalent in the post socialistic world and part of daily cultural habits (Schütz, 1986). In areas influenced by Islamic culture, drinking tea also symbolises tradition. As a social practice the habit signifies hospitality and holds a high position in everyday life, as it is a non-alcoholic drink. Exemplary is the term "whisky marocain" for sweetened mint tea in Moroccan culture. In contexts of growing migration and refuge processes, food culture being highly symbolic of cultural origin is brought to Europe. Eating habits are culturally transmitted and picked up by social milieu. They grant emotional security, especially when coping with traumatic experiences and crisis (Hirschfelder & Pollmer, 2018). Drinking tea, therefore, could open doors for integration and affiliation, as the beverage is compatible with and part of various food cultures all over the world.

Contemporary European tea culture

Historically, black and green tea was a symbol for status and prestige, for disregarded and imitated foreign culture; it was leverage in political conflicts and is closely linked to colonial history in Asia. So how about the present day? Do people still drink tea? And if so, why and in which form?

In Germany, consumers drunk about 47 billion cups of tea in 2019. Tea surrogates (40.000t volume, being 67% of total consumption), like fruit and herbal infusions, prevail black and green tea (19.200t volume, being 33% of total consumption). Black tea clearly predominates green tea, with 73% to 27% of consumption (Teereport, 2020). Tea is mostly bought in food retail markets, with only 12.4% bought in specialised tea shops. This signifies that tea is a product mainly purchased at the same time as other groceries. A minority of consumers visit specialised shops, which offer tea at a higher price level, but also of higher quality (Teereport, 2021). As mentioned above, the prevalence of food culture depends on various aspects. In Germany, tea is an excellent example to show this. While in the South of Germany tea is consumed in ordinary volumes, in a region in the North, called Eastern Frisia, tea consumption is outstandingly high. For comparison, in 2019, 222 litres of black and green tea were drunk per person in Ireland, 177 litres per person in Great Britain, both of which are known for their tea culture and high level of tea consumption. Eastern Frisia outnumbers them both with 300 litres per person, which globally marks the highest tea consumption per person (Teereport, 2020). The geographic location of Eastern Frisia near to Amsterdam, where the first shipload of tea reached Europe in 1610, explains these high levels of tea consumption. The Netherlands was a big player in historical tea trade and constant supply was possible in Eastern Frisia. Therefore, tea was integrated in local culture and is part of Eastern Frisia's local identity up to the present day, including a ritualised tea ceremony, teahouses and patterned dishes (Ostfriesische Landschaft, 2021) like cups, saucers and pots. Since 2016, Eastern Frisia's tea culture is listed in the National List for Intangible Cultural Heritage of Germany (Deutsche UNESCO Kommission), while in 2022 the tea cultures in Türkiye and Azerbaijan have also been awarded.

Contemporary consumption leads to another question. Where does tea come from today? India is still the biggest supplier for black tea, followed by Kenia. In India, over 80% of tea production is consumed within the country; Kenia, on the other hand, exports over 90%. For green tea, China is the leading supplier, but again most of the tea is produced for domestic sales (Teereport, 2020). Tea production has expanded to South America as well, and maté tea is gaining ground in Europe due to the higher caffeine level and exotic taste. The main suppliers are Brasilia, Argentina and Paraguay (Teereport, 2021).

Tea and lifestyle

Early twenty-first century societies can be described as plural, prosperous and lifestyle orientated in vast parts of Western Europe. Clothes, food and drink, habits and objects are used to express lifestyle, social milieu and more:

> Due to an increasing globalisation of food systems, traditional food patterns seemed to be on the decline in the last third of the 20th century. In the early 21st century, food and eating habits play an important role regarding the representation of self. (Hirschfelder et al., 2020, p. 19)

An excellent example to highlight the fast-moving nature of cultural attribution concerning international food trends is bubble tea in Germany. Bubble tea, also known as pearl milk tea or boba tea, is a beverage based on green or black tea that originated in Taiwan in the 1980s. It mostly consists of heavily sweetened tea, milk, and tapioca balls, which pop open dissolving flavoured fluid when chewed. From the start the target group for bubble tea were children and teenagers. Following a global trend, the first store offering bubble tea in Germany was established in 2010 and caused a nationwide hype, which ended only two years later. What had happened? A study conducted by a German university postulated the theory of cancer-causing ingredients in bubble tea and classified it as dangerous. The hype ended, though the concerns could not be proofed. In 2020, the hype revived due to the social media app TikTok where users in other countries started generating short clips showing bubble tea in every possible colour and flavour. Bubble tea is considered as hip and trendy, it is marked as an exotic product due to the fruity flavours, symbolising global lifestyle. The consumption can be described as a multisensorial event, as there is no comparable product containing tapioca balls. The negatively connotated artificially aromatised bubbles were replaced by "bobas" filled with yoghurt- or fruit-filling (Bronewski, 2021; Miller, 2021). The colourful drink, sometimes offered in sustainable cups with paper straws, is compatible with current food trends. As a takeaway product it fits into mobile consuming patterns. During the Covid-19 pandemic takeaways became even more important, especially for young people, as meeting friends inside was oftentimes not allowed and alternatives in open, public spaces had to be found. Being offered in organic, vegan, lactose- and sugar-free versions, bubble tea can be consumed without regrets concerning the individually chosen nutritional style. And as those nutritional styles are often imitated from social media influencers, it is no surprise that bubble tea was very present on Instagram and the like during the Pandemic.[2]

On social media channels, lifestyle is mainly promoted and expressed through consumption. Using the range of influencers can therefore be a lucrative way to place a product. Messmer, a German tea company, launched "Cold Tea" in 2020, winking at Japanese Mizudashi: by leaving tea in cold water for several hours the aroma dissolves slowly and fewer bitter compounds are released. Like mentioned above, this way of preparation is linked to the slow-food-movement and awareness. "Cold Tea" does not contain black or green tea and is drinkable after only 30 seconds. It can be classified as a lifestyle product, with taste and easy preparation seeming to be central. Referring to "Do-It-Yourself"-culture, instead of buying a drink, consumers put the tea bag in cold water, wait for 30 seconds, shake the bottle – Messmer also offers a special bottle for the product – and enjoy a sugar-free drink low in calories. For promotion, Messmer collaborated with German travel Influencer "venividiwander" (17,900 subscribers on Instagram[3]) and successfully addressed young, sportive and health-conscious women as a target group (OMR magazine, 2020).

Tea and health

Being in good health is a trend at least since individual fitness became fashionable in the 1980s and is linked to capability, commonly classified as desirable. People track their body functions, visit fitness centres, detox themselves, hoping for the desired effect. The Covid-19 Pandemic even reinforced this trend, as human health is endangered, and a pandemic situation was new, especially for young people. As has been argued, tea historically started its career because of its positive effects on health. Getting integrated into daily life and consumption, its status as a remedy faded, but drinking tea was still related to being healthy and specialised tea products were offered, which are mostly still found today. The product assortment of Bad Heilbrunner, a German producer of medicinal tea, shows the wide range: pregnancy, blood pressure, digestion, nervosity, cold and associated symptoms, urinary tract, and vitality (Bad Heilbrunner, Website).

Since the 1960s and 70s another attribution was added to tea being drunk for health reasons. The hippie movement, which had formed in the late 1960s in San Francisco and spread to Europe shortly after, opened up to a spiritual way of thinking about health, that pills prescribed by academic medicine should not heal people, but rather a natural lifestyle. Followers of the hippie culture travelled to Asia and attrib-

---

2 See for example more than two and a half million posts "#bubbletea" on Instagram: https://www.instagram.com/explore/tags/bubbletea/ (November 9, 2021).
3 See https://www.instagram.com/venividiwander/ (November 9, 2021).

uted an esoteric and mystic meaning to tea. Up to the present day, tea is linked to health, awareness and eastern philosophy. In supermarkets a big assortment of tea is offered linked to yoga, esoterism and Ayurveda.

The meaning of tea as a universal remedy of early modern time is not relevant anymore. Instead, awareness of individual health and wellbeing is attributed to the beverage, promising relaxing and calming effects on body and mind in combination with refreshment and strengthening.

Tea as a non-alcoholic alternative

Having a similarly stimulating effect, tea and coffee have always been in competition. The prevalence of coffee outnumbers tea easily. But new trends are coming up, like maté tea, high in caffeine, mentioned above. Among students, the brand "Club Mate" offering maté as a sweetened ready-to-drink product enjoys cult status in particular. Back in the 1990s hackers from Berlin discovered the accomplished combination of sugar and caffeine in the beverage. Slowly, "Club Mate", which was invented in Germany in 1998, spread within the country, and is now sold internationally (Club Mate). The producers bank on buzz marketing; as a result "Club Mate" was only known within certain social milieus, for a long time being an insider tip. The drink contains less sugar than caffeinated soft drinks and is considered healthy due to maté tea as main ingredient. Being sold in reusable glass bottles and produced in Germany, "Club Mate" is easily integrated into a sustainable lifestyle.

Next to "Club Mate", tea is very successful in the form of iced tea and attracted attention in 2021 as three German rappers launched their own brands. Why did they do so? Iced tea is the most popular drink among teenagers, because it is a non-alcoholic alternative to lemonades and other soft drinks and considered "healthy" as tea is the main ingredient. Start-ups discovered iced tea as a profitable product some years ago, as it is compatible with most food trends and can be produced in vegan, gluten-free, sugar-free, and sustainable variations. Globally, the market for bottled ready-to-drink tea grows:

> RTD tea's growth [. . .] will continue its upwards steady trend following increasing consumer preference for ready-to-drink and healthier-for-you beverages and innovations surrounding flavours (new tea varieties, exotic flavour and ingredient infusions), formats (new delivery methods beyond traditional bottles and cans) and styles (unsweetened, slightly sweetened, fresh brewed, all natural, organic, high in polyphenols, probiotics, or antioxidants, etc), and as manufacturers focus on expanding their global footprints. (TC Trade Journal, 2018)

The popularity opens a vast market opportunity and teenagers hold increasing purchasing power. Additionally, rap music is especially popular among young people. In 2021 HaftBefehl, Shirin David and Capital Bra used this combination of market opportunity plus their own range and launched iced tea brands, which can partly be purchased in grocery stores. The rapper HaftBefehl relied on Cannabis flavour mixed with green tea and low sugar levels. His "HafTea" is promoted as a healthy and relaxing drink to chill out, due to Cannabis terpenes. Though the Cannabis based ingredients are legal and low-dosed, the overtone using the reputation Cannabis has within the "gangsta rap" scene is a marketing strategy. Shirin David's "DirTea" is advertised with the slogan "stay safe, drink DirTea" referring to the hygienic surface, as the top of the aluminium can is covered in extra foil. The brand title "DirTea" is pronounced like the word "dirty," creating a wordplay. The drink addresses customers appreciating heavily sweetened and artificially aromatised iced tea, which turned out a success.[4] Capital Bra had already launched a frozen convenience pizza and expanded his product line with iced tea, called "BraTee." The commercial humorously presents the drink in an exotic vacation scene as spare time enjoyment.[5]

Conclusion

After more than 400 years of consumption, tea is still part of everyday food habits in Europe. The positive connotations and attributions concerning human health outlived the negative ones. Today´s science is able to explain how tea operates within the human body in molecular detail and how it helps to support individual health. Nevertheless, tea is not only drunk for reasons related to a healthy body. It symbolises tradition, as shown by British and Eastern Frisian examples, and modernity, in the form of novel products. Due to its combinability with other products, tea can easily be included in modern nutritional philosophies – with tea as the basic ingredient vegan, gluten-, lactose- and sugar-free, sustainable products can be brought up. Even more, tea being halal, kosher and non-alcoholic, it's compatible with various religious and regional food cultures. Tea companies managed to stay on top of the game, launching new product types fitting current demands. In a globalised world, tea is a trendsetting beverage – an ending of tea consumption isn't to be seen any time soon.

The attribution of being prestigious "symbolic capital" changed due to mass production. Surely, tea still is available at very high price and quality levels, but nevertheless it is a common consumer product. But even tea of low price and quality level symbolises enrichment of everyday life. During the Covid-19 pandemic tea consumption has increased further (Teereport, 2021). The reasons are as various as ever, but clearly drinking tea seems to have a certain meaning and positive, calming, and warming effect during troubling times.

---

4 See Shirin David's official release video on YouTube: https://www.youtube.com/watch?v=GGYm qEnrRDk (November 9, 2021).
5 See Capital Bra's official commercial on YouTube: https://www.youtube.com/watch?v=CvCAhZgl1M8 (November 9, 2021).

References

Bad Heilbrunner Website. (n.d.). Arznei- und Kräutertee – für Ihr Wohlbefinden und Ihre Bedürfnisse. Retrieved January 23, 2024, from https://bad-heilbrunner.de/produktvielfalt/

Beck, R. (2003). Luxus oder Decencies? Zur Konsumgeschichte der Frühneuzeit als Beginn der Moderne. In R. Reith & T. Meyer (Eds.), *"Luxus und Konsum" – eine historische Annäherung* (pp. 29–46). Waxmann.

Bischoff, C. (2005). *Chinoiserie*. Enzyklopädie der Neuzeit, Bd. 2 (column 713–717).

Bourdieu, P. (2020). *Die feinen Unterschiede. Kritik der gesellschaftlichen Urteilskraft*, 27th edition. Suhrkamp.

Bronewski, G. (2021, July 11). Trendgetränk 2021. *Die unerwartete Rückkehr des verrufenen Bubble Teas*. Retrieved January 23, 2024, from https://www.welt.de/icon/essen-und-trinken/article232333883/Der-Bubble-Tea-ist-zurueck-aber-galt-das-Getraenk-nicht-als-krebserregend.html

Club Mate Website. (n.d.). Club-Mate International. Retrieved January 23, 2024, from https://www.club-mate.de/international/

Deutscher Kaffeeverband. Die Geschichte des Kaffees. (n.d.). Retrieved January 23, 2024, from https://www.kaffeeverband.de/de/kaffeewissen/geschichte#

Deutscher Tee und Kräutertee Verband. (2020). Tee Report 2020. Tee verbindet. Wann immer, wo auch immer. Retrieved January 23, 2024, from https://www.teeverband.de/files/bilder/Presse/Marktzahlen/TeeReport_2020_ES.pdf

Deutscher Tee und Kräutertee Verband. (2021). Tee Report 2021. Tee setzt positive Zeichen. Retrieved January 23, 2024, from https://www.teeverband.de/files/bilder/Presse/Marktzahlen/Teereport_2021_ES.pdf

Deutsche UNESCO-Kommission. Bundesweites Verzeichnis Immaterielles Kulturerbe. (n.d.). Ostfriesische Teekultur. Retrieved January 23, 2024, from https://www.unesco.de/kultur-und-natur/immaterielles-kulturerbe/immaterielles-kulturerbe-deutschland/ostfriesischer-tee

Ellis, M., Coulton, R., & Mauger, M. (2015). *Empire of tea. The Asian leaf that conquered the world*. Reaktion Books.

Fraund, T. (2010). *Die kulturelle Bedeutung von Tee im Großbritannien des 18. Jahrhunderts: self-fashioning, Kollektivsymbol und nationale britische Identität*. Wissenschaftlicher Verlag Trier.

Hirschfelder, G. (2005). *Europäische Esskultur. Geschichte der Ernährung von der Steinzeit bis heute*. Campus.

Hirschfelder, G. (2007). Rausch und Sucht in der Vormoderne. Zwischen kulturellem Zwang und individueller Freiheit. In S. Matthiesen & R. Rosenzweig (Eds.), *Von Sinnen. Traum und Trance, Rausch und Rage aus Sicht der Hirnforschung* (pp. 196–218). Mentis.

Hirschfelder, G., & Pollmer, P. (2018). *Ernährung und Esskultur: Kulturwissenschaftliche Perspektiven – Nutrition and eating habits: Cultural aspects*. Aktuelle Ernährungsmedizin.

Hirschfelder, G. (2018). Zucker: Kulturgeschichte und Konsumstruktur eines umstrittenen Lebensmittels. *Aktuelle Ernährungsmedizin 3*, Supl.1), 3–7.

Hirschfelder, G., Pollmer, P., & Schuller, N. (2020). Western food cultures and traditions. In S. Braun, C. Zübert, D. Argyropoulos, H. Casado & F. Javier (Eds.), *Nutritional and health aspects of traditional and ethnic foods (nutritional and health aspects of food in Western Europe)* (pp. 19–39). Academic Press.

Kunstsammlungen und Museen Augsburg, Maximilianmuseum. (2023). Teapot and tea cups ("Koppchen") with chinoiserie by Martin Engelbrecht (1725). Picture made by Lenz Mayer.

Menninger, A. (2004). *Genuss im kulturellen Wandel. Tabak, Kaffee, Tee und Schokolade in Europa* (16.–19. Jahrhundert). Franz Steiner Verlag.

Menninger, A. (2009). Tabak, Kaffee, Tee und Schokolade in Wissenskulturen der Frühen Neuzeit. *Zeitenblicke*, 8. urn:nbn:de:0009-9-21278.

Merki, C.M. (2003). Zwischen Luxus und Notwendigkeit. Genußmittel. In R. Reith & T. Meyer (Eds.), *"Luxus und Konsum" – eine historische Annäherung* (pp. 83–95). Waxmann.

Miller, X. (2021, March 21). Bubble Tea. Es blubbert wieder. Süddeutsche Zeitung. Retrieved January 23, 2024, from https://www.sueddeutsche.de/panorama/bubble-tea-kultgetraenk-rueckkehr-1.5271700

OMR magazine. (2020). Wie Meßmer mit Cold Tea und digitalem Marketing die Generation Instagram umwirbt. Retrieved January 23, 2024, from https://omr.com/de/messmer-cold-tea-sponsored-post/

Ostfriesische Landschaft. (2021). Tee – Ostfrieslands flüssiges Gold. Kulturkalender 2021. Retrieved January 23, 2024, from https://www.ostfriesland.travel/fileadmin/ostfriesland/PDF/OL_Kulturkalender_2021_ Sonderteil_Tee.pdf

Reith, R. (2003). "Luxus und Konsum" – eine historische Annäherung. In R. Reith & T. Meyer (Eds.), *"Luxus und Konsum" – eine historische Annäherung* (pp. 9–27). Waxmann.

Schütz, J. (1986). *Russlands Samowar und russischer Tee: kulturgeschichtlicher Aufriss*. Osteuropainstitut Regensburg-Passau.

Tea & Coffee Trade Journal. (2018, December 7). Global RTD Tea Consumption Shows Steady Growth in 2018. Retrieved January 23, 2024, from https://www.teaandcoffee.net/blog/20692/global-rtd-tea-consumption-shows-steady-growth-in-2018/

C Culinary embracing tea

Tea is more than just a hot beverage, it is an ingredient for baking, cooking, chocolate, and cocktails, and can be offered as an element for non-alcoholic food pairing, as well as the key for a ceremonial delight.

Virginia Utermohlen Lovelace

C.1 Hosting tea and wine – Similarities of guest service excellence

Should we move tea into settings where wine is traditionally served? The answer is clearly "yes!" As Broecker in this volume notes (see Chapter C.4):

> This elaborated tea service is not limited to the end of the menu. Still rather new is the idea of serving tea as a beverage with food in Western high cuisine. Tea is an ideal beverage for a non-alcoholic menu accompaniment. For some restaurants, a pure tea accompaniment is a matter of course alongside wine.

In the Western world, fine dining instantly invokes the thoughtful pairing of fine wines with the food. In order to successfully introduce tea into the wine and fine dining world, and to develop pairings that work simultaneously for wine and tea, it is important to understand the parallels and the differences between the flavour experiences of teas and wines.

To start, we need to take four important points into consideration:

The first is that no two people (except perhaps identical twins) experience the same flavours from a tea or a wine. Our genetic differences as well as our life experiences and health all influence what we are capable of experiencing in a beverage. So, a pairing that may work well for one person may not work as well for another.

The second is that wine has alcohol whereas tea does not. It may seem that I am simply stating the obvious, but the situation is more complex. Alcohol itself is experienced differently by different people: some people feel alcohol's burn more strongly than others, and some people may experience alcohol's bitterness more strongly than others. Both burn and bitterness are potentially aversive; for an individual diner, aversive experiences may dominate the perception of a wine, making the experience of other flavours in a wine or its accompanying food weaker, thus defeating the purpose of a pairing.

Third, while teas may not burn the way a wine might, teas can be quite bitter and also astringent, so it may be worthwhile to seek out parallels for pairing according to the bitterness and astringency of a wine. Importantly, sweetness in a food will bring out bitterness and astringency in both wine and tea.

Fourth, wine is significantly more acidic than tea. The pH of wines ranges between three and four whereas water at about pH 6.5 is best for brewing tea. The result is that wines will taste significantly more sour than tea – in fact sourness is an undesirable trait in tea, with the possible exception of the fermented teas, yellow tea and

https://doi.org/10.1515/9783110758573-007

puer. Sourness will also affect the perception of pairings: the sweeter the food the more sour the wine will taste and vice versa.

Given these considerations, let us proceed to parallels between wines and teas.

Colour

One important parallel lies in the quality and intensity of colour of a tea and a wine. More often than not, we can already guess, from the colour of a beverage, whether it is light and refreshing or bold and zesty. The lighter the Colour, the more cooling and refreshing we expect it to be, and the darker the colour the warmer it may seem, regardless of the actual temperature of the beverage (Roque et al., 2018; Kosuke et al., 2020; Zellner & Durlach, 2002; Li-Chen Ou et al., 2012).

Thus, the sight of both green teas and white wines will engender expectations of coolness and lightness, while the sight of a black tea and, say, a Cabernet Sauvignon will evoke a hotter sensation (as shown in Figure C.1.1).

These photos show the colour parallels among green, oolong, and black teas, and Pinot Grigio, Pinot Noir, and Cabernet Sauvignon wines. Teas are from The Great Mississippi Tea Company and wine photos are by Chelsea Pridham on Unsplash.

Figure C.1.1: Wine meets tea: similarities of colours.
Source: Author

Furthermore, with respect to food, we speak of "green" flavours and "brown" flavours. "Green" flavours are associated with freshness, particularly in vegetables, while "brown" flavours are associated with foods that have been cooked, and therefore become brown. As we will see next, colours and flavours and perceived temperatures are based on the major chemicals present in foods and beverages.

Why do we have these associations between colour, temperature, and "fresh" or "cooked"?

In order to answer this question, we first need to understand how temperature is experienced in the mouth, nose, and throat, and how the chemicals in wines, teas, and foods cause "temperature" experiences.

Temperature is experienced in the mouth, nose, and throat through activation of receptors on the trigeminal nerve. This nerve has three branches, one to the eye, one to the nose and upper palate, and one to the tongue and the lower mouth, hence its name. In the nose the olfactory patch is rich in trigeminal nerve endings, as are the taste buds on the tongue and palate.

Receptors on the trigeminal nerve respond to a number of qualities, not just temperature, but also texture (= mouthfeel) and wetness – in other words, chemesthetic sensations. The nerve then transmits its messages to the brainstem, and then the brain, where they merge with sensations of smell and taste to inform of us of the qualities of what we are smelling and ingesting.

The receptors on the trigeminal nerve that respond to temperature are each termed Transient Receptor Potential (TRP). There are at least six of these that can be activated by food chemicals as well as actual temperature. Here are some of the characteristics of these receptors.

TRPV1 can be activated by temperatures greater than 40°C, strong acid, high amounts of salt, pepper, and peppers (capsaicin), by some compounds in cinnamon, and by roasty/toasty compounds produced by Maillard browning, caramelisation, and burning. Its excessive activation can lead to pain – for example the burn felt with high concentrations of alcohol is due to activation of TRPV1. This receptor is inhibited by fat and its activity attenuated by sweetness.

TRPV3 is activated by temperatures in the range of 30–40°C. Compounds in herbs and spices such as oregano, basil, and vanilla activate this receptor.

TRPV4/5 are heat sensors with a similar temperature sensitivity, in the range of 25–38°C. They are also activated in the presence of bitter, sweet, and umami compounds.

TRPM8 is activated by temperatures in the range of 17–25 °C and modulates the function of TRPA1. It is activated by menthol and by compounds with a lemony quality.

Finally, TRPA1 is activated by temperatures less than 17°C. A host of pungent compounds, such as those in wasabi, mustard, garlic, onions, nutmeg, ginger, and some of those in cinnamon, all activate this receptor, and elicit sensations that range from prickling to outright pain that may have a burning quality.

Nearly all chemicals in wine, tea, and food activate these temperature receptors, and give an impression of temperature irrespective of the actual temperature of the food or beverage.

It is important to note that activation of one of these receptors may inhibit activity of another. For example, activation of receptors at the cooler end of the spectrum inhibit activation of receptors at the hotter end of the spectrum, and vice versa.

Activation of these receptors also causes what one could call an emotional response. We call chili peppers bold and zesty because activation of the hot receptor on the trigeminal nerve causes the release of dopamine in the brain. Dopamine in turn causes us to feel motivated, even adventurous, in other words, bold (Puglisi-Allegra and Ventura, 2012).

By contrast, we call the experience of activating TRPM8 and TRPA1 "refreshing." It has been argued that cold beverages may be refreshing because they appear to diminish thirst more effectively than warm beverages, and that TRPM8 activators such as menthol and TRPA1 activators such as crushed ice have been shown to improve performance (Saldaris et al., 2020).

Finally, activation of the receptors responding to intermediate temperatures leads to sensations of warmth that have been described as comforting (Lowry et al., 2009).

Why then the parallels between colour and perceived temperature?

Green flavours are characteristic of green vegetables and green tea. It turns out that flavours we call "green" are caused by chemicals in these green or greenish foods that activate the cool and cold receptors. For example, nonanal, found in white wines and green teas, gives us the characteristic flavour of cucumbers – and the sensation that we call "cool as a cucumber" in English.

Similarly, we associate "brown" flavours with foods that are visually brown, for example a black tea or the crust on a piece of bread. An example of a chemical that gives a "brown" sensation is five-methyl furfural, found in both tea and bread crust (and some wines, too). It has a "sweet, brown, caramellic, grain, maple-like" flavour, as described by perflavory.com (accessed January 11, 2022). The temperature sensations that "brown" flavour give us range from warm to hot because the chemicals involved activate the warm and hot receptors.

Parallels between wines and teas

These considerations bring us to some parallels between tea and wine that are important for pairing with foods and allow us to consider teas as accompaniments to the dishes served in a fine dining setting.

The list of chemicals shared between wines and teas is almost endless. However, there are certain patterns of chemicals that stand out, and provide us with useful parallels.

White wines and green teas

The first set of parallels lies in white wines and green teas. Both share chemicals that activate the cool/cold trigeminal receptors. These include linalool, which has a "green" citrus quality, limonene, characteristically lemony, geraniol, with its more peach-like nuance, and hexanal, which is also "green" but which confers a more apple-like quality, and a fresh lingering after-taste.

Thus, in choosing a tea to go with a dish you would otherwise serve with white wine, you might succeed with a green tea. Like white wines, of course, green teas offer a wide palette of flavours, so exactly which green tea you would choose depends on having the experience of a number of different green teas, and then exploring how they would match with, say, a food that goes with a Sauvignon Blanc or an Albariño.

There is, of course, a problem with white wines in that alcohol shifts the balance of trigeminal sensations towards the hotter end. There are two ways of overcoming the effects of alcohol: cooling the wine (which is one reason that white wines are more flavourful when chilled) and having high amounts of residual sugar. When the white wine is very dry, the sharpness of TRPV1 activation comes through and you sense fewer of the compounds that activate the cool end of the spectrum – funnily, these wines may come across as "clean," in other words less complex, because you are not able to sense the complexity provided by the "cool/cold" chemicals. An issue that you may encounter in pairing a green tea in parallel with a white wine lies in the question of oak. Oaked Chardonnays, for example, contain vanillin and guaiacol, chemicals that are not commonly present in green teas, and are more likely to occur in oolongs, and for guaiacols, black teas.

Oolongs, Riesling, Gewürztraminer, and Pinot Noirs

Which brings me to oolongs: oolongs have two characteristics that make pairing both interesting and potentially difficult. The first is that oolongs tend to have a dramatic aroma, but when sipped a much more delicate flavour. The second is that oolongs can be much more floral than most wines. For these reasons, I suggest parallels between oolongs of various degrees of oxidation and two of the more floral and herb-flavour rich white wines, Riesling and Gewürztraminer, and also Pinot Noir.

The following graph shows the relative flavours of three different types of oolongs. As you go from the least oxidised (Dong-Ding) to the most oxidised (Da Hong Pao) you also go from a predominance of chemicals that activate the cool/cold receptors to ones that activate the warm and hot receptors (as shown in Figure C.1.2).

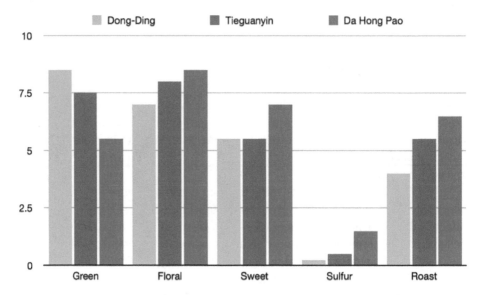

Figure C.1.2: Flavour meets Oxidation: Diversity of Oolong.
Data Source: JianCai Zhu et al. (2015). Comparison of aroma-active volatiles in oolong tea infusions using GC–Olfactometry, GC–FPD, and GC–MS. *J. Agric. Food Chem.* 63:7499–7510.

Among the floral chemicals shared by these wines and oolong teas is beta-damascenone. This chemical gets its name from the fact that it is an essential component of the aroma of damask roses. It is derived from carotenoids, chemicals in both grapes and tea leaves. In the grape beta-damascenone is formed during berry maturation, while in the tea leaf it is the result of processing (Jiaquiang et al., 2019).

Beta-damascenone, like vanillin, activates the pleasantly hot receptor, TRPA3, so will go with foods such as tomatoes and strawberries that also primarily activate this receptor.

Another flavour-forward compound that these teas and wines share is benzaldehyde with its stone fruit quality – cherry and peach. Therefore, foods that go well with these fruits can be expected to go well with these wines and teas. Wuyi Rock teas gain their name through their flinty mineral flavour, associated with the present of quercetin and kampferol. If the "coolness" of a white wine is accompanied by a mineral quality, consider using a Wuyi Rock tea as your non-alcoholic offering. It is worth noting here that Darjeelings resemble oolongs in their flavour profile more closely than they resemble black teas, even though they are frequently classified as black teas.

Black teas and red wines

Black teas offer parallels with less floral red wines, for example Merlots and Cabernet Sauvignons. These wines have a number of chemicals that they share with black teas, primarily pyrazines and thiol compounds. These compounds and other shared compounds primarily activate the hot receptor TRPV1, so both teas and wines will go well with "browner" foods with more roasty flavours. Note that black teas are generally the most astringent teas, while green teas can be the most bitter, depending on how the teas are brewed, so for successful parallel pairing it is worthwhile to consider the astringency and bitterness of the wines you have chosen.

A note about white, yellow, and puer teas

While the generalisations above are useful for considering parallel pairings of wine and tea with foods, it is more difficult to create generalisations concerning white, yellow, and puer teas. Yellow and puer teas are green teas that have been allowed to ferment, with highly variable types of microorganisms, for highly variable lengths of time. The result is flavour profiles that vary from batch to batch of processed leaf.

White tea is made from leaves that are simply allowed to wither, with relatively little manipulation at the end of the wither, the chemicals formed will tend to be more characteristic of the leaf cultivar as well as the characters of the withering environment.

As a consequence, it is difficult to even predict in general terms what wine would parallel these teas.

Parallels and challenges for presenting tea in a fine dining setting

Wine comes ready-made in a bottle, while tea must be brewed – another obvious point but one that needs to be explored for a tea service to be successful.

Brewing teas

A major reason why tea service can be problematic in a fine dining situation is that each type of tea (white, green, yellow, black, oolong, and puer), and even each individual tea, requires its own water temperature and brewing time to develop the desired taste. As you vary these parameters you will sometimes experience wildly different flavour profiles even with a single tea batch. The point behind the *gong fu* method of serving tea, where leaves are steeped multiple times for very short times, is that the drinker will experience a succession of flavours. You can match this experience when you brew the tea table-side, as is done, for example, at Heinz Reitbauer's Steirereck, but this process interrupts the flow of a fine meal when the goal is to pair teas in parallel with wines throughout the meal.

It makes better sense, then, to prepare the tea elsewhere, but again each tea served will need individualised care in brewing. In theory this can be accomplished by having specialised brewing systems.

The highly controlled brewing systems currently available for hot tea are designed for single cup service and are therefore inefficient. By contrast, a bottle of wine will serve a whole table. So, in order to serve more people an appropriate tea for each dish, a restaurant will need to have several good water heaters, at appropriate temperatures for the chosen teas. This requires room either in the kitchen or the service area.

Another approach is to serve teas at cooler temperatures – they can be brewed ahead of time and kept cool until needed. This approach works well with green teas, where the physical temperature of the beverage matches the temperature profile of the chemicals in the tea. A lightly or moderately oxidised oolong is particularly delicious when served cool, while black teas served cool may need sugar to cut the bitterness and astringency that becomes more prominent when cooled.

When you want to be serious about serving teas in parallel with wines there is a need for training. A well-trained sommelier will have abundant knowledge of all the wines in a wine list. To serve tea meaningfully, the sommelier will need an equally abundant knowledge of the teas in a tea list. importantly, I believe that the sommelier will need to understand the parallels between these teas and the wines in the list in order to make recommendations about pairing for a table where both wines and teas will be served. All training comes at a cost, another reason to have a limited tea list, at least to start.

Ultimately, I believe that the best compromise is to have a limited menu of exquisite teas that your sommelier knows well and that you can brew and serve successfully. This approach is in direct contrast to the approach with wine, where the best restaurants often have extensive cellars.

Serving teas

Finally, it should be considered that the appearance of the tea at the table plays an important role, too. You can serve the tea from a teapot placed in the service area, or perhaps have a stand for teapots next to the table, or you could choose to brew the tea in a clear glass teapot over a tea light at the table, as done by Kristin van Eetvelt, Culinaire Theesommelier in Lier, Belgium.[1]

I took the following photo at L'Espalier, a fine dining restaurant in Boston sadly no longer with us, at a tea and food pairing event hosted by tea sommelier Cynthia Gold and Nepali tea expert Jeni Dodd. As you can see, tea can be served in wine glasses, even as hot tea, provided the glasses are on the sturdy side – these were standard restaurant glasses.

Wine glasses in fact have the added advantage, particularly obvious with oolongs but appreciable with other teas as well, that the aroma chemicals emanating from the tea are concentrated below the lip of the glass so that a tea can be appreciated just as one appreciates a wine.

That said, we should recognise the extremely complex cross-modal associations among colour, flavour, and the receptacle in which a beverage is served. These associations vary among populations, even within Europe (Wana, Woods, Jacquot et al., 2016).

Conclusion

As Broecker noted, "The potential offered by tea and tea culture is increasingly being seen, understood and used." Believing that, with this (admittedly rough) guide to finding parallels between wines and teas presented here, and a modicum of exploration on the part of chefs and sommeliers, it can be stated that the use of teas during a meal in the fine dining context by exploiting what is known about wines and how to pair them with food is a comfortable, favourable and advanced pairing idea.

References

Allen, A.L., McGeary, J.E., & Hayes, J.E. (2014). Polymorphisms in TRPV1 and TAS2Rs associated with sensations from sampled ethanol. *Alcoholism: Clinical and Experimental Research, 38*(10), 2550–560. https://doi.org/10.1111/acer.12527.

Lowry, C., Lightman, S., & Nutt, D. (2008). That warm fuzzy feeling: Brain serotonergic neurons and the regulation of emotion. *Journal of Psychopharmacology, 23*(4), 392–400. https://doi.org/10.1177/0269881108099956.

---

1 https://kristinvaneetvelt.be (accessed January 12, 2022).

Luo, J., Brotchie, J., Pang, M., Marriott, P.J., Howell, K., & Zhang, P. (2019). Free terpene evolution during the berry maturation of five Vitis vinifera L. cultivars. *Food Chemistry, 299*, 125101. https://doi.org/10.1016/j.foodchem.2019.125101.

Motoki, K., Saito, T., Nouchi, R., & Sugiura, M. (2020). Cross-modal correspondences between temperature and taste attributes. *Frontiers in Psychology, 11.* https://doi.org/10.3389/fpsyg.2020.571852.

Ou, L., Ronnier Luo, M., Sun, P., Hu, N., Chen, H., Guan, S., Woodcock, A., Caivano, J. L., Huertas, R., Treméau, A., Billger, M., Izadan, H., & Richter, K. (2010). A cross-cultural comparison of colour emotion for two-colour combinations. *Color Research & Application, 37*(1), 23–43. https://doi.org/10.1002/col.20648.

Puglisi-Allegra, S., & Ventura, R. (2012). Prefrontal/accumbal catecholamine system processes high motivational salience. *Frontiers in Behavioral Neuroscience, 6.* https://doi.org/10.3389/fnbeh.2012.00031.

Roque, J., Lafraire, J., Spence, C., & Auvray, M. (2018). The influence of audiovisual stimuli cuing temperature, carbonation, and color on the categorization of freshness in beverages. *Journal of Sensory Studies, 33*(6), e12469. https://doi.org/10.1111/joss.12469.

Saldaris, J.M., Landers, G.J., & Lay, B.S. (2020). Physical and perceptual cooling: Improving cognitive function, mood disturbance and time to fatigue in the heat. *Scandinavian Journal of Medicine & Science in Sports, 30*(4), 801–11. https://doi.org/10.1111/sms.13623.

Wan, X., Woods, A.T., Jacquot, M., Knoeferle, K., Kikutani, M., & Spence, C. (2016). The effects of receptacle on the expected flavor of a colored beverage: Cross-cultural comparison among French, Japanese, and Norwegian consumers. *Journal of Sensory Studies, 31*(3), 233–44. https://doi.org/10.1111/joss.1220.

Zellner, D., & Durlach, P. (2002). What is refreshing? An investigation of the color and other sensory attributes of refreshing foods and beverages. *Appetite, 39*(2), 185–86. https://doi.org/10.1006/appe.2002.0502.

Nicole Klauß and Henrik Scander
C.2 Tea as a sophisticated food companion

After water, tea is the most consumed beverage in the world. In many nations, especially in Asia, tea is the everyday drink. And yet it is wine that has dominated the
drinks menus in gastronomy for decades. Tea is, still, rarely found on restaurant
menus; it is primarily found on hotel breakfast menus or on café and hotel drinks
menus at Afternoon Tea. In many European countries, individual tea trading companies have specialised in catering and offer hotels and restaurants the whole range of
tea, teapots, tea strainers as well as training courses on tea.

Large and international hotel chains in particular often buy centrally and so tea
from the same producer can be found on menus in Singapore, Berlin, Bangkok, and
Washington. Tea in tea bags still dominates and the selection of teas is limited and
unimpressive. It seems as if the (tea) world only consists of Earl Grey, English Breakfast, and flavoured green tea. Matcha's triumphant march into the world's coffee
shops in the form of Matcha Latte and Military Latte (in combination with espresso)
seems unstoppable.

In upscale gastronomy, sommeliers are only slowly discovering tea as a dining
companion. There are many reasons for this development, and it needs dedicated
sommeliers or dedicated staff behind the in-house bar who recognise the quality of
tea as a food accompaniment and educate and train themselves to offer an adult food
accompaniment even to guests who do not drink alcohol, because this subject is not
taught in sommelier schools (Klauß, 2017).

To understand the singular role of wine as a food accompaniment, it is worth taking a look at the history books. Wine has been firmly anchored in Central European
drinking culture in particular for centuries and has been the gold standard for food
accompaniment in gastronomy for decades. The great culture of restaurant and hotel
establishments that characterised the nineteenth century gradually laid the foundations for the classic serving of wine at table. French restaurant and hotel owners undoubtedly have the merit of having made the profession of sommelier known to a
wide public. The career of the sommelier is in fact a very astonishing one, since in the
fourteenth century a sommelier was only the so-called mule driver, a guide of draught
animals (bêtes de somme), and since he often also passed vineyards he later took over
the transport of wine at the same time! He was then promoted to cupbearer and in
the nineteenth century to wine waiter, responsible for selecting the wines and recommending the right bottle at the table.

It was then that the first sommeliers appeared in Paris, working at the city's most
famous restaurants. This was triggered by the "grand Cuisine," which became the cuisine of hotel restaurants, which led to the wait staff being given French designations
and the term "sommelier" becoming known worldwide from 1812, with the new professional figure associated with it. Tea had a small supporting role in the morning

https://doi.org/10.1515/9783110758573-008

and afternoon, while wine was given to the big stage (Sommelierverband Deutsch-Schweiz, 2023).

In no European country does tea have a similar significance to this time as it does in today's United Kingdom and, by extension, Australia. It was the English who brought tea to America, and in the New World tea quickly became the third most imported commodity. However, one will search in vain for a pronounced tea culture there, where coffee still dominated. As early as the middle of the seventeenth century, black tea arrived in East Frisia from India and China via the East India Company in Amsterdam (Standage, 2008). There, in the north of Germany (and only there), a special tea culture developed that is still cultivated today. "Teetied" (east Frisian for tea-time) is an important part of everyday life, and the strong aromatic East Frisian tea, a blend of Assam and Ceylon teas, has become a real brand. The East Frisian tea ceremony has been listed as UNESCO Intangible World Heritage Site since 2016 (UNESCO, 2016). Despite the fact that tea is also an everyday drink there, you will look for it in vain as a dining companion in the upscale gastronomy of northern Germany (Rene-barg & Kaufmann, 2018).

Tea was introduced to Australia by the British fleet, which landed in Australia in 1788 with prison inmates. Tea is an important part of modern Australian drinking culture, partly because of its British origins. Australians drink their morning and afternoon teas the way the British do. Because of the climate, tea can be grown and produced in northern Australia, sometimes to an excellent quality (Griggs, 2020).

Thus, Vitis vinifera in Central Europe has not only a historical but also a clear locational advantage over Camelia sinensis: the climatic conditions for growing grapes in Central Europe are optimal, while tea growing in Central Europe is still in its infancy. Although the Tea Grown in Europe Association lists members in the Azores, Belgium, France, Georgia, Germany, Ireland, Italy, Jersey, Portugal, Scotland, Switzerland, the Netherlands, Ukraine, and the United Kingdom, the plantations are not really visible. In the sommelier schools wine dominates, non-alcoholic accompaniment is still not taught, and so the non-drinking guest is mainly not given tea with the food, but juices, lemonades, or water.

In short, wine simply had a head start of several centuries and has secured its prominent place as a food accompaniment. So, it is not surprising that the New World is clearly ahead of the game when it comes to non-alcoholic food accompaniments: the wine and beer history is short, and so people view beverage accompaniments with much less bias. The countries in Europe that do not grow wine because of the climatic conditions, such as Scandinavia or the U.K., are pioneers in Europe for non-alcoholic food accompaniments. Upscale gastronomy in Central Europe only discovered non-alcoholic food accompaniment a few years ago, restaurants with non-alcoholic accompaniments at the fine dining level are still rare to find, and tea is rarely found here. An increasing number of guests who drink no or little alcohol and a social downshift in alcohol consumption in general and a new generation of young consumers in particular, for whom alcohol is not of great importance, ensure that more and more restaurateurs and sommeliers (have to) deal with the topic of accompaniment without alcohol. There are many good reasons to work with tea as a food accompaniment, but from a restaurateur's point of view there may also be one or two reasons not to do so.

There is a lot to be said for tea as an alternative to wine. Wine drinkers appreciate the wine talk: information about the vineyard, the terroir, the climate, the harvesting technique, and the cellar work. Cellar master is the equivalent of tea master; if the sommelier speaks of mash fermentation or must fermentation, ageing in steel barrels or wooden casks, the tea sommelier speaks of withering, steaming, oxidation, kill-the green, or roasting methods. So there is plenty of material to address the discerning guest.

A positive point for tea is that it is flexible, much more flexible than wine. The same type of tea can be made into completely different drinks by using different methods of preparation: iced brew (tea leaves steep in melting ice cubes) and cold brew (tea leaves steep for a few hours in cold water) bring fruity notes to the fore, which is a remarkable effect, especially with green teas and oolongs. Since tea can be drunk ice-cold, cold, lukewarm warm or hot, this makes it a very flexible companion. There is also the possibility to elaborate with steeping time and the amount of tea in relation to water, to increase or decrease certain flavours or textures such as tannins to perfect the food pairing (Beckett, 2020).

Whereas with wine the sommelier has at most a small amount of control through the choice of grape variety, bottle size, and perhaps the temperature, he is otherwise dependent on the quality that the winemaker has delivered to him. Wine is basically a convenience drink, whereas with tea it is the type of tea, dosage, choice of water, infusion time, drinking temperature, and, last but not least, the number of infusions. With a little practice, the drink can be adapted to the food, like a tailor-made suit.

A lack of knowledge in the preparation of tea is a relatively predictable reason for a dulled tea experience. It is not uncommon for tea in restaurants to be brewed with the boiling water from the hot water nozzle of the filter machine. In hotels, you will find a vending machine for hot water on the buffets, but it only dispenses 100 degrees. Black tea and some oolongs and Pu-Erh can be prepared well with it, but very few green or white teas will benefit from it. Professionals only order black tea in cafés to be on the safe side. Untrained staff can really ruin a good tea with the wrong temperature.

It is always astonishing to see how much money is invested in lavish machinery for coffee preparation, while savings are made on the simplest appliances, such as a kettle with adjustable temperature. Incidentally, this also applies to the private sector. The same applies to the quality of tea in cafés, hotels, and restaurants; one could write books about this, with these rarely having a happy ending. Often, the people in charge of purchasing work together with large tea trading houses. These offer everything from teas, tea caddies, displays, teapots, strainers, and other accessories, in principle everything for tea preparation. Thus, even in five-star hotels, guests sometimes find the same quality of tea as in the café around the corner: tea in tea bags, rather fannings than loose leaf and flavoured white, green, or black teas, with training courses sometimes offered for the staff, but due to the short time employees spend in the gastronomy, the knowledge then quickly meanders away. In gastronomy schools, the topic of tea is only briefly addressed, and in sommelier schools it is searched for in vain (Klauß, 2017).

While many sommeliers work with winemakers, even keeping an eye on the development of the wines themselves on site, and then curate the wine list accordingly in an elaborate way, and of course do not have the wholesaler who supplies them with the drinks, this happens relatively reliably when it comes to tea.

The selection of teas for pairings should be made together with tea experts; a knowledge of tea pairing is often available here, but detailed information about origin, production, and cultivar can help with a selection. It is important to clarify what job the tea should do. Should it be a subtle accompaniment, support the dish or provide a counterpoint?

Another point to consider is the quality of the water used for tea. Not everyone lives in the Black Forest, the north of the UK or the Vosges mountains with a hardness level of 8 °dH (in Germany), which is optimal for tea, which corresponds to 14.2 °f in France and °e 9.96 in the UK. In the UK, Taylors of Harrogate, a company from the north of the UK, adapts its blend to the hard water in the southern areas of the country (D' Offay, 2017). Anyone can find out the hardness levels of regional drinking water from the water supplier. In places with calciferous water, a water filter prevents disappointment in the cup: if chlorine is added to the drinking water, as for example in many regions of the United States, in Italy, Spain, and some regions of France, no water filter will help, but a low-calcium mineral water.

One small rule: if you ignore the issues of water quality and temperature during preparation, as well as brewing time, you can save on the quality of the tea with a clear conscience. The above reasons speak against choosing tea as an accompaniment to food, and tea also ensures respect for the material. In addition, classically prepared tea can be a time challenge for the service: if the food is ready, the tea must also be ready.

Good coordination between the kitchen and the bar is essential here. If there are several dishes accompanied by tea, different teas may have to be prepared for different tables and brought to the guests, as well as the wine or other drinks for other guests.

This means that, for example, a green tea from Taiwan with a temperature of 80 degrees would have to be brewed and brought to the guest at the moment the food is about to be served, so a short brewing time of only a few seconds can quickly increase the potential for stress, which is already present in sufficient quantities in restaurants anyway. With oolongs, for example, the fourth infusion can suit the dish better than the second – here the preparation needs a little more attention.

By the way, the principle of the double brew is exciting: this is not tea hipster chichi but was already used in the Ming Dynasty: a pot was filled with (hot) water, and the tea leaves were added. The tea was steeped in the teapot for three breaths, then the infusion was distributed to the teacups. The tea from the cups was put back into the pot and allowed to steep for another three breaths and only then was finally poured into the cups and drunk. The method has the advantage of having the results of two different temperatures in one cup. The result is a stronger tea than if you ever do a simple infusion. You need less tea than with the classic method and – a small advantage when drinking – the tea has a lower drinking temperature. But here, too, timing is crucial (D' Offay, 2017). A good solution here, by the way, is cold brew tea, which only needs to be taken out of the fridge and served, much like wine. The only challenge here is the quantity to be prepared in the morning or the day before. If you don't plan generously enough, you can't make more at short notice, because a cold brew tea needs a few hours' preparation time. Iced brew teas are therefore more suitable as aperitifs than as accompaniments to food because the serving time can be planned reasonably well.

One argument against tea as a food accompaniment is often the caffeine content. While wine tends to make many people more tired, the caffeine in tea makes for more alert evenings or nights and is therefore often used as an argument, also on the part of guests, against a tea accompaniment. A second argument against tea as a food accompaniment is that polyphenol-rich tea decreases iron absorption. The still decreasing effect of the iron absorption after drinking tea lasts only for about one hour. On the other hand there is a growing body of evidence that suggests that a moderate consumption of tea could actually protect against several forms of cancer, cardiovascular diseases, the formation of kidney stones, bacterial infections, and dental cavities, so as long as you do not suffer from iron deficiency there is no need to worry, but if you do you should also reduce your consumption of coffee and wine as well.

A look at the biology book helps here: the tea plant produces caffeine to protect itself from insects. There is often talk of theine, but it is exactly the same substance; it is just a different name, so tea also contains caffeine. The difference lies in the way it works in the body: tea leaves contain less caffeine than coffee beans and the active ingredient is bound to tannins so that the organism cannot fully absorb the caffeine in tea. One reason for this is L-theanine, an amino acid found only in tea leaves, a rather powerful psychoactive substance that crosses the blood/brain barrier and, in combination with caffeine, ensures that the stimulating effect that tea undoubtedly has rises more slowly but also falls off more slowly. In addition, ECGC (epigallocatechin gallate), a substance that belongs to the catechins, and the secondary plant substances contained in tea leaves, the polyphenols, can strengthen the positive aspects of caffeine, i.e., ensure a clear head and clearer thinking, but reduce the negative effects of caffeine, nervousness, and anxiety. Both substances are said to slow down the absorption of caffeine in the body, but also the breakdown. In comparison to caffeine absorbed with coffee, a "quick on/quick off" effect is observed and a second or third cup of coffee is needed to prolong the wakefulness effect. A well-considered selection of teas and their individual preparation makes tea accompaniment possible even for caffeine-sensitive people (Rabia et al., 2013).

Here are a few pieces of information that can serve you well when choosing teas:

1. The buds and young leaves therefore have a greater proportion of caffeine than the older and larger leaves further down the tea bush. The higher the proportion of buds and young leaves in the tea, the higher the caffeine content.
2. In summer there are more insects around, and the caffeine content in the leaves is then higher. Teas from spring or autumn harvests have a lower caffeine content and the larger and therefore older leaves contain even less caffeine.
3. Shaded teas, such as Gyokuro, produce more caffeine than, for example, unshaded Sencha.
4. A longer oxidised tea has a lower caffeine content than a shorter oxidised tea.
5. There is less caffeine in the stems and panicles than in the leaves.
6. The more leaves are used for the infusion, the higher the caffeine content in the tea.
7. The longer the tea is steeped, the higher the caffeine content. The Gong Fu Cha method with short infusion times is more suitable than the Western style with longer infusion times.
8. The number of infusions in the Gong Fu Cha method is crucial: the more infusions, the more caffeine is released from the tea leaves.
9. Hot water extracts more caffeine than cold water. A cold brew is a solution here.
10. Karigane or kukicha, i.e., stem tea, consists of leaf panicles and stems rather than leaf parts and contains less caffeine.
11. The longer the tea has been oxidised, the less caffeine it contains. Roasted or smoked tea contains less caffeine than less heated tea – caffeine is only stable up to 175 degrees. Here a Houjicha or a Lapsang Souchong would be a solution (Klauß, 2023).

Some words about decaffeinated tea: this is a highly industrialised process involving dichloromethane or ethyl acetate. In Europe, dichloromethane is more commonly used; this is a halogenated hydrocarbon and is classified as harmful to health. The residual amount of 5/mg per kilogram must therefore not be exceeded. In the USA, the use of dichloromethane for decaffeination is prohibited. Incidentally, the selection of decaffeinated teas is small and the aroma very often unconvincing.

Instead of an espresso with a caffeine content of 212 mg per 100 gr, caffeine-sensitive guests can also be offered a Houjichaespresso. For this, Houjicha is brewed in a portafilter machine like an espresso. In the cup, there are more tart notes than with the classic preparation technique and only a little caffeine. For a 0.0% tart shot after the meal, a rooibosh espresso is recommended: for this, the highest-quality rooibosh possible is made with the portafilter machine, and it goes without saying that the portafilter has been cleaned of possible coffee aroma beforehand.

Accompanying a multi-course meal in the evening with tea does not necessarily mean a short night for the guest, whereas a lunch menu can be accompanied with caffeinated teas, leaving the guest stimulated for the second half of the day.

A basic knowledge of tea, its harvest, and processing are therefore always a good idea, and that is precisely the challenge for sommeliers, who have spent their long and intensive training almost exclusively on wine and spirits. Guests who order a tea accompaniment can be practised tea connoisseurs, but also curious teen novices. This is where the sommelier schools are in demand, which as training centres usually lay the foundation for the knowledge of later sommeliers. A broader-based drinks training would be a first approach.

As with pairings with juice, water or other drinks, the sequence of dishes should first be clarified and then the appropriate drink selected. It is advisable to involve the kitchen team because a dish is usually designed to work on its own. Every drink (including water) influences the taste, so the accompaniment should be decided by the team.

Tea is a versatile companion and can accompany a complete menu. Many white and green teas, oolongs, but also black teas are ideal. More aromatic teas, such as Lapsang Souchong (smoked tea) or Pu-Erh, are a little more challenging. For example, a dish that would be accompanied by a lightly toasted barrel-aged American oak Chardonnay can also be well accompanied by a 60% oxidised Oolong, as Oolongs also contain vanilla notes.

The most important basic rule in pairing also applies to tea:

The beverage should match the basic taste of the food, and blend in, and more importantly the food should be in front, and the beverage should accompany.

This is an important, if not the most important, proposition. Applied to tea accompaniment, this means that the tea must not outshine the food.

There are several approaches to accompanying food with tea. Here follows more detailed pairing recommendations.

Tea pairings – in general and into the specific:

Let us focus on the theoretical foundations for combining food and drink in general and tea parings more specifically. We begin with a historical overview of the research situation around food and beverage combinations. Then we go deeper into what cause and effect mean. This helps you understand what happens purely physiologically in a combination, whereupon it is important to understand the importance of flavour of your pairing items and focus less on the food items themselves, i.e., a chicken can taste neutral, spicy, hot, or sweet depending on the flavouring and can also have different texture depending on cooking preparation. We will here explain how basic taste work, but also what texture is and how it effects, as well as the importance of aromas for a combination. We will show you how to create different objectives, such as a refreshing effect, a neutrality, and how to highlight different flavours so that a synergy effect arises, based on what is usually called Harrington's taste pyramid (Harrington, 2006).

To increase your understanding of how we lay the foundation of tea pairing, we will start from the pairing research in combination with our years of practical experience of preparing tea matched with food. As you understand, tea has many properties that make the drink an exciting partner for food. Basic tastes are what you feel in your mouth, that is, sweet, sour, salt, bitterness, and umami. For tea, the basic tastes are generally lower than if we compare with wine and tea (Scander, 2019). With that in mind tea can still have sweetness, acidity, and bitterness, although salinity usually shines with its absence for most beverages (Rune et al., 2021).

Some things that you will read repeatedly here are that it is not about the food items but that it is how it tastes that is most important. If you, as we suggest, start thinking about taste, textures, and aromas you will soon realise that it is easier to combine "flavours with flavours" instead of "tea and food." This will also make it easier for you to transfer this knowledge and apply it to any other beverage such as wine or tea or any other beverage option of yours. As said, this chapter is about tea and we are tea lovers, and therefore tea in combination with food, but you can of course turn it in the other direction, combining food with tea. Because even though we can change tea, it is more difficult to change the taste and character of a specific tea than to change how a dish tastes, the dish we can actually spice up, salt or simply add or change accessories or cooking methods. Still here is also one of the strengths, working with tea, as it is a craft to brew it; with tea we have the advantage to change brewing time, temperature, amount of tea leaves, to make the final impact of the paring perfect.

Another important thing is to think about what it is we want to achieve with a combination. So, what is the objective? What kind of experience do we want to focus on? Here we can assume that the idea is usually that we want the combination to taste good, but it is of course not necessary; maybe you want a heat sensation in your mouth, so that you wake up after a long sitting, so that your objective might be an awakening effect.

Moreover, it is also important to remember that there may be several dishes to be combined and then you want to create some variations. The kind of variation we are talking about is three basic concepts common to when it comes to objectives that can be achieved with a combination: refreshing, neutral, and synergy effect (Harrington, 2006). The refreshing or cleansing effect, which is common if we use cold or high acidity to freshen up an experience. The second is that it should be "neutral" and more just be a little in harmony with each other without something taking over, something that is practical when we have several different types of food like on a smorgasbord for example, then we do not want the tea to add too much but rather behave a little friendly in the background, as someone floating around mingling with everyone and letting everyone else participate. The last effect is about one plus one becoming three which is called a "synergistic effect." The synergy effect means that the combined effect is greater than the sum of the individual parts, or in short when one plus one becomes three, sometimes mentioned as the "third flavour."

Then there are other theories that can be interesting, such as using traditions as a way to match tea and food; for example you take tea and food from the same geographical area that has "grown" side by side and therefore with a long tradition create a good combination. We can call these traditional combinations such as combining sushi with Gen mai cha, which is a green tea mixed with roasted rice. Because it is mixed with roasted rice, it gets a special taste that many who are new to Japanese green tea or who do not like Japanese tea often like. Gen mai cha also has the effect on the food that it reduces the taste of fish and instead enhances other aromas. These types of combinations can be said to have been traditionally grown together.

What we are looking at is first and foremost about seeing how tastes either balance or contrast with each other (Harrington, 2006). An example of a contrast is when we have something salty and pair it with something sweet, for example like the saltiness of parmesan cheese with a sweet green tea such as Jasmin Tai Nu Long Zhu, where the sweetness of the jasmin flavour will contrast the salinity of the cheese. At the same time, the fat and hard structure of the cheese contrasts with the smoothness of the tea. Here we have both contrast in basic taste and in texture. But we can also have similarities that balance, as in a broth where we have a creamy silk texture similar to a beverage. Or when we have matcha tea powder in a batter to be able to pick up the notes of the tea; when it meets the tea we drink together with the baked cookie.

Now we have talked about the goal of the combination of food and tea and how we can work with either balance or build on contrasts. There is also a "hierarchy" when it comes to taste combinations (Harrington, 2006; Harrington & Hammond, 2005, 2009). This helps to easily create a structure or order in how you combine food and drink. This is based on the fact that we have basic components or in simple words basic taste; then we have different forms of textures, i.e., that which connects to feeling and finally aromas, that is, the characters we perceive in the form of flavour aromas. This can be seen as hierarchically arranged where basic tastes lay the foundation for the combination by working to balance or contrast basic tastes with each other. Furthermore, you build on this staircase with textures, that is, the things we know as astringency, tannins or just the body of tea. Similarly, food also has a body, but also fattiness, and other textures that come from cooking techniques such as fried, crunchy, moist, and creamy or hard or soft. Then we top this staircase with the aromas, which are then also contrasted or balanced based on what intensity and how long-lasting these aromas are and how they smell. The aromas are also the scents we feel in our fragrance centre, and they have different molecular structures that are similar (Spence, 2020; Spence et al., 2017; Spencer & Dalton, 2020; Spence, 2020a, 2020b; Spence et al., 2017), such as that nettles and currant leaves both have a green aromatic scent or that raspberries and licorice harmonise by contrasting each other, which gets really interesting in relation to tea more specifically.

Tea is in general consumed during breakfast or as cold refreshing tea, and pairing tea with particular types of food, is still an evolving art far away from being a consolidated habit of consumers (Donadini & Fumi, 2014). Still, different chocolate producers, restaurateurs, and gourmets are beginning to explore pairing tea with food. Even if this is done in a more systematic way to offer consumers guidelines in how to pair tea only a hand full of research articles have been published, which is aimed at just tea pairing (Donadini & Fumi, 2014; Donadini et al., 2012; Sato & Kinugasa, 2019).

Principle of similarities

One way to accompany food with a beverage would be the principle of similarities: if flavours that are present in the food and in the beverage, the probability that it is a match is relatively high. Ton-sur-Ton, so to speak. Black tea leaves are fully oxidised, resulting in a slightly more astringent flavour, as well as malty, woody, and toasty aromas reminiscent of bread. Black teas have a natural, complex aroma profile that includes fermented, fruity scents of bananas, apples, and pears, as well as herbaceous aromas of cooked potatoes, courgettes, and aubergines. This makes black teas good accompaniments to vegetables, as well as fruitcake or banana bread, but dishes with strawberries, raspberries, pears, courgettes, cooked aubergine, sweet potatoes, and pumpkin are also good pairings.

An Earl Grey, with its bergamot notes, is always a good match for toast with orange marmalade. Roasted green teas generally go well with dishes that have roasted notes, Genmaicha is an all-rounder for Asian cuisine (where originally dishes were not accompanied by drinks, even the most obvious one: tea).

Green teas usually have pronounced floral apple and rose notes as well as certain green, fatty, cucumber-like aromas. The fresh flavours of green tea go particularly well with dishes containing other vibrant ingredients such as lemongrass, ginger, saffron, pineapple, apricot, tomato, artichoke, bacon, and rum but also nuts and anchovies.

Principle of enrichment

Drinks can also enrich a dish, elevating the dish to a new level. A kagabucha, for example, is a good accompaniment to tuna. Kaga¬bōcha (in direct Japanese translation "stem tea") is a kind of houjicha, with the difference that with houjicha the entire leaf is roasted and with Kaga¬bōcha only the stems are roasted. With its roasted notes, the kaga¬bōcha balances the strength of the fatty tuna and provides a good balance.

Principle of contrasts

The supreme art of pairing is contrasting – the drink takes on a clear role and provides a contrast with certain flavours, for example Karigane with raw salmon, where the Karigane brings an extra boost of green freshness and balances the sweetness from the salmon. With a sweet dessert, a tea with bitter notes is a good partner, with a classic example a matcha with sweet Japanese desserts or an Assam with chocolate mousse (Man, R., & Essrich, R., 2019).

The versatility of tea – brewing and flavour

A real plus point of tea (compared to wine) is its flexibility with temperature. With foie gras, one would classically offer a well-chilled Sauternes or a Monbazillac. And this is undoubtedly a great combination, but in the mouth a cold wine (10–12 degrees Celsius) and a fat foie gras meet first. A warm oolong, oxidised to 60%, melts the foie gras already in the mouth and ensures a harmonious combination. It is similar with a goose rillette: an oolong with a degree of oxidation of 40% catches the spicy notes of the rillette well, and the warmth of the tea provides the necessary melting, so that the rillette literally melts in the mouth. And pairings with cheese and tea are also such a winner because the warm tea really melts the cheese in the mouth, a clear advantage over wine.

If you send different types of tea through the gas chromatograph, as Belgian engineer Bernard Lahousse did, you can see, for example, that a Sencha has similar aromas to a pear, but also overlaps with dry-aged beef, black garlic, or vanilla. Lahousse and his team have analyzed countless foods for their aroma components using a gas chromatograph. The result should help chefs in food pairing, but the result of these analyses can also be very helpful in beverage pairing.

Some teas are all-rounders when it comes to pairing, while others are more specialists and not always simple accompaniments. As an aperitif, white tea is a good choice. A cold-steeped Pu-Erh Ba Ya, made only from the buds of old tea trees, has floral and slightly woody, sometimes sweet notes; it is also an excellent palate cleanser and can prepare the taste buds for the next course between two courses. With sushi, diners have many different small dishes to choose from, so a cold brew of a white Pu-Erh Ba Ya can serve well as a palate cleanser.

The leaves and buds of white tea are virtually only dried, not oxidised, its colour is very light, more yellow than green, its aroma is flowery, its taste rather delicate. As a food companion, it is only suitable in the rarest of cases, for example with raw vegetables or fruit (without citrus fruits). A light poached fish with a little dill and rice goes well with a delicate white tea. If you choose a special fish, such as monkfish or

Arctic char, you can also accompany it with a special tea: for example, a white tea from Kenya.

Or a cold brew of an Oolong Dancong from the Phoenix Mountains in Guangdong Province in China; flowery and sweet, it does its job as an aperitif with flying colours.

Green tea often has notes of hay and grass and goes well with rice, poultry, fish, or melons. Green teas that are only steamed and not roasted, usually Japanese green teas, go well with seafood and steamed vegetables.

Japanese green teas are dominated by vegetal (grassy) and mostly umami notes. These teas go well with seafood, sushi, dishes flavoured with soy sauce, Gouda and Manchego cheeses, and white chocolate. Japanese green teas contain a greater amount of catechins, which are antioxidants and a real health booster (Coucquyt et al., 2020).

Fruity green teas, such as a Sencha, are good partners with chicken, fruity salads, and sandwiches. They are usually also suitable in the iced tea or cold brew variety. Sencha also goes well with white chocolate.

Roasted green teas usually come from China, but some also from Japan (Kamairi-cha). Here, the leaves are roasted after wilting, and go well with briefly fried dishes, roasted vegetables, and rather light meat. Indian green teas (e.g., green Assam) have rather fruity notes and harmonise with salads and desserts that are not too heavy. Green teas from India and Ceylon very often have slightly sweet notes and also go well with wholemeal bread and meat dishes.

Oolong teas vary greatly in terms of aroma and flavour. They tend to have a more complex aroma and their pairing possibilities are exceptionally wide. Oolongs are the jokers among teas when it comes to food accompaniment: depending on the degree of oxidation, this varies from slightly oxidised to very oxidised. The first are similar to green teas and go better with shellfish and light salads, while the more oxidised varieties are good accompaniments to grilled meats and vegetables, smoked fish and indeed French fries or desserts with chocolate, waffles or cakes with nuts and lemon cake.

Black teas are teas that are almost completely oxidised, and can be roughly divided into three categories: fruity, malty, or smoky. Fruity black teas, for example a Darjeeling second flush, are good with foie gras (there are now also unstuffed foie gras available, for example from Gioachino Palestro from Mortara in northern Italy), not too spicy curries, and with fruity-sweet desserts.

Malty black teas, such as Assam, go well with dishes with sheep's cheese, chocolate cake and desserts with chocolate, and smoky black teas, such as Lapsang Souchong from China or a Kyobancha from Japan, harmonise wonderfully with all dishes with roasted aromas, grilled food, and strongly spiced dishes.

Pu-Erh teas are distinguished between Sheng Pu-Erh (raw) and Shu Pu-Erh (ripe). This is a black tea, often ripened over many years by microorganisms such as yeasts, noble moulds, and bacteria, which ferment the tea leaves. The enzymes are not completely deactivated by the heating in the wok, so Pu-Erh tea is already slightly oxidised by the slow drying. The time for which the Pu-Erh tea leaves are heated in the wok determines how many enzymes are still active and thus has a very great influence on the later taste.

These microorganisms occur naturally on the leaves of the tea plant. During fermentation, the microorganisms convert polyphenol, sugar, and amino acids from the tea leaves into aromatic substances. This also explains why Pu-Erh tea is less bitter (less polyphenols) and also less sweet. The mineral content of the tea is not changed by fermentation. The minerals are decisive for the body and aftertaste of the tea. Fermentation makes the tea softer and rounder and changes its flavour profile. A Pu-Erh has earthy-woody notes and can rival a Roquefort as well as fatty and strongly spiced food, but also dark chocolate with 70–80% cocoa content.

Tea is a very flexible accompaniment to food: the different parameters of harvest time, type of tea, quality, processing, and preparation technique offer countless variations for a successful accompaniment to food. (Tea) sommeliers can thus flexibly respond to the needs of guests and the food and thus offer the optimal beverage accompaniment.

A certain basic knowledge is absolutely recommendable here, as with wine, in order to be able to act flexibly. Last but not least, a tea accompaniment, even with high-quality teas, is an economically highly attractive alternative to wine, because tea is a real winner in terms of the ratio between material input and sales price per cup. And also, from a PR point of view, this is always a good idea: very few food journalists report on new wines on the menu, but they report relatively reliably on new approaches to non-alcoholic food accompaniments.

Looking into the specifics on tea pairings, using Pu-Erh pairing as an example in practice

When describing basic tastes, mouthfeel, and flavours, we can show that one combination between food and tea cannot be built on the same foundations as a combination with food and wine. This is because the properties of the drinks differ significantly and therefore cannot be treated in the same way in a combination. According to Harrington and Hammond (2005), the texture and mouthfeel of food depends on the protein source, amount of fat, and which cooking method has been used. The other accessory on the plate is also of great importance for the experience of the texture and the mouthfeel. Therefore, a powerful and intense dish, containing many fatty components, usually requires a strong and full-bodied wine in order to be balanced. Among the organic acids found in the teas are tannic acid, and theaflavins, which in connection with tannic acid are believed to be the reason for the roughness and bitterness which is often found in tea (Alasalvar et al., 2012). The concept of roughness is explained by Lee and Chambers (2007), as part of the mouthfeel. The roughness is caused by a combination of various amino acids and polyphenols (Lee & Chambers, 2007). Analysis of green tea also showed that caffeine has an effect on the roughness and the perceived bitterness in the tea.

Taste of Pu-Erh

Pu-Erh tea is a hugely popular tea in China, both as a beverage and as a medicine. In the West, tea is often known as a Chinese slimming or banting tea. A variety of myths surround this tea, and its history goes back thousands of years. Yunnan, the area where Pu-Erh tea originates, is believed by many scholars and historians to be the cradle of the entire first cultivation of tea.

The tea leaves used for Pu-Erh come from the old and broad-leaved tea bushes that grow in Yunnan, so-called daye (large leaves). The leaves are allowed to oxidise for a while and then are either dried or compressed into cakes. Pu-Erh was originally compressed into different forms for more efficient transit, and acquired its dark colour and flavour due to natural fermentation in transit to its final destinations. The aging process results in a slow fermentation, and it can take about 15 years for a "raw" (unfermented) Pu-Erh to get the dark colour and its taste. Therefore, good quality Pu-Erh tea has a deep, rich taste that many consider earthy or even a bit spongy. Pu-Erh also has a very fresh, clean taste and aroma of autumn leaves and sometimes with hints of plums, dates, and chocolate. Moreover, long storage makes the tea softer and at the same time more complex. The tea is usually said to be optimally aged after between 15–20 years, but you also do not want an overcooked tea that instead dulls the taste.

So, how do we combine these flavours? To start, Pu-Erh tea is often to be served with Dim Sum, with its strong and special taste known for its beneficial effect on digestion. One might say that Pu-Erh also goes well with meat dishes, chicken, and fried food but it is still dependent on matching flavours. Applying the recommendations for a good pairing, we start matching the components of sweetness and acidity, in this case, where both the tea and the food do not exhibit these properties, which means that they are in balance. Furthermore, the saltiness of the food will reduce the experience of bitterness in the tea. while the umami intensifies the flavours. Both the food and the drink are still relatively light and elegant, although we can say Pu-Erh is the stronger tea. But it is rather in the concentration of taste whereupon we also want to meet with the same resistance. At the same time, perhaps the most important thing is to access the complexity, whereupon we would like complex dishes for this complex tea. This is where the aromas become important to understand. As Pu-Erh is dominated by very earthy, slightly spongy tones, at the same time some slightly dried fruity aromas and leather tones can develop, which is often easy to find in dishes that have been left to simmer for a long time. You then might want to take the opportunity to try dishes that you would traditionally combine with very mature and elegant red wines, such as old wines from Burgundy. And if you also have a slightly stronger dish such as meat stews, you have the advantage of tea that that you can brew slightly stronger, extracting a little more tannins to increase the resistance to the food.

Tea as a food accompaniment means a very flexible beverage that can be tailored to the food.

The countless production techniques, starting with cultivation, through harvesting and harvesting time, to the different preparation possibilities, allow for a wide range of possible food accompaniments. With a little more tea knowledge, attention to quality, and care in storage and preparation, tea can be a reliable yet maximally flexible accompaniment to any dish.

References

Alasalvar, C., Topal, B., Serpen, A., Bahar, B., Pelvan, E., & Gokmen, V. (2012). Flavor characteristics of seven grades of black tea produced in Türkiye. *Journal of Agricultural and Food Chemistry, 60*(25), 6323–332. https://doi.org/10.1021/jf301498p.

Beckett, F. (2020). *How to drink without drinking*. Kyle Books/ Octopus Publishing Group.

Coucquyt, P. et al. (2020). The art & science of foodpairing. Mitchell Beazley Publishers.

D'Offay, T. (2017). *Easy leaf tea*. Ryland Peters & Small and CICO Books.

Donadini, G., & Fumi, M.D. (2014). An investigation on the appropriateness of chocolate to match tea and coffee. *Food Research International*, 63 (Part C, 2nd Conference on Coffee Cocoa and Tea Science (CoCoTea2013)), 464–76.

Donadini, G., Fumi, M.D., & Lambri, M. (2012). The hedonic response to chocolate and beverage pairing: A preliminary study. *Food Research International, 48*(2), 703–11. https://doi.org/10.1016/j.foodres.2012.06.009.

Freeman, M., & D'Offey, T. (2018). *The life of tea*. Mitchell Beazley.

Griggs, P. (2020). *Tea in Australia: A history, 1788–2000*. Cambridge Scholars Publishing.

Gmür-Stadler, J., & Wagner-Lange, T. (2019). *GONG FU CHA- Die Chinesische Teezeremonie. Tee als Handwerkskunst und das bewusste Geniessen*, AT Verlag.

Harrington, R.J. (2006). The wine and food pairing process. *Journal of Culinary Science & Technology, 4*(1), 101–12. https://doi.org/10.1300/J385v04n01_11.

Harrington, R.J., & Hammond, R. (2005). The direct effects of wine and cheese characteristics on perceived match. *Journal of Foodservice Business Research, 8*(4), 37–54. https://doi.org/10.1300/J369v08n04_04.

Harrington, R.J., & Hammond, R. (2009). The impact of wine effervescence levels on perceived palatability with salty and bitter foods. *Journal of Foodservice Business Research, 12*(3), 234–46. https://doi.org/10.1080/15378020903158509.

Klauß, N. (2017). *Die neue Trinkkultur. Speisen perfekt begleiten ohne Alkohol*. Westend.

Klauß, N. (2023). Alkoholfrei. at Verlag.

Koch, H.-J. (1972). *Weinrecht. Richard Boorberg* Verlag.

Lee, J., & Chambers, D.H. (2007). A lexicon for flavor descriptive analysis of green tea. *Journal of Sensory Studies, 22*(3), 256–72. https://doi.org/https://doi.org/10.1111/j.1745-459X.2007.00105.x.

Man, R., & Essrich, R. (2019). *Geniale drinks alkoholfrei*. Riva.

Masui, C., et al. (2013). *Thés japonais*. Grund.

Mein, D. (2017). Caffeine in tea. Retrieved October 10, 2023, from https://meileaf.com/article/caffeine-in-tea-facts-and-myths/.

Rune, C.J.B., Münchow, M., & Perez-Cueto, F.J.A. (2021). Systematic review of methods used for food pairing with coffee, tea, wine, and beer. *Beverages*, *7*(2), 40. https://www.mdpi.com/2306-5710/7/2/40.

Parker Bowles, T. (2021). *Time for tea*. Fourth Estate.

Renebarg, T. (2018). *Teetied*. Grabener Verlag.

Sato, K., & Kinugasa, H. (2019). Influence of Japanese green tea on the Koku attributes of bonito stock: Proposed basic rules of pairing Japanese green tea with Washoku. *Journal of Sensory Studies*, *34*(6), Article e12539. https://doi.org/10.1111/joss.12539.

Scander, H. (2019). Food and beverage combinations: Sommeliers' perspectives and consumer patterns in Sweden (Publication Number 14) [Doctoral thesis, comprehensive summary, Örebro University]. DiVA. Örebro. http://urn.kb.se/resolve?urn=urn:nbn:se:oru:diva-74611.

Rabia, S., Syed Waquas, A., Hirra, A., Naveed, R., & Shahid, R. (2013). Effect of infusion time and temperature on decaffeination of tea using liquid–liquid extraction technique. *Journal of Food Process Engineering* 37.

Sösen, T. (2019). *The story of Japanese tea*. Independently published.

Spence, C. (2020). Multisensory flavour perception: Blending, mixing, fusion, and pairing within and between the Senses. *Foods*, *9*(4), 407.

Spence, C., Wang, Q.J., & Youssef, J. (2017). Pairing flavours and the temporal order of tasting. *Flavour*, *6*(1), 4.

Spencer, M., & Dalton, P. (2020). The third dimension of flavor: A chemesthetic approach to healthier eating (a review). *Journal of Sensory Studies*, *35*(2), Article e12551. https://doi.org/10.1111/joss.12551.

Standage, T. (2008). *A history of the world in six glasses*. Walker.

Sommerlierverband Deutsch-Schweiz. Retrieved March 5, 2023, https://svs-sommeliers.ch/index.php/der-sommelier/geschichte-entstehung-des-berufs.

Topic, S., & Wells, A. (2012). Warenketten in einer globalen Wirtschaft. In E.S. Rosenberg (Hrsg.), *Geschichte der Welt 1870–1945*. Weltmärkte und Weltkriege, Verlag C. H. Beck.

UNESCO. (2016). East Frisian Tea Culture. Retrieved February 20, 2023, from https://www.unesco.de/en/east-frisian-tea-culture.

Utermohlen Lovelace, V. (2020). *Tea. A Nerd's Eye View*. VU Books.

Von Paczensky, G., & Dünnbier, A. (1994). *Kulturgeschichte des Essens und Trinkens*. Btb.

Woolrich, D. (2022). *The Oxford companion of spirits and cocktails*. Oxford University Press.

Carina Pardek and Hartwig Bohne

C.3 Hospitality in harmony: Mergers of tea and chocolate

Introduction

Both, tea and chocolate are remarkably distinctive yet so compatible. The perception, understanding, and way of consuming these two has considerably changed with time. Starting as a delicatesse, being accessible only to representative people, chocolate was consumed in a liquid way, while tea was discovered by mistake. Today, every citizen can easily purchase it, with a large variety of flavours and brands to choose from. As the understanding of tea and chocolate grew, so did the ways of producing, consuming, and presenting it. From two distinctive products, which were separately consumed, by deeply studying their compatibility, we are today witnessing it as one. Even though both are known to be consumed in a liquid way, such as tea with chocolate flavour, this chapter of the book will focus on the solid presentation: chocolate bars and pralines infused with tea. Starting with a short history of both, a following sub-chapter elaborates the resulting and final product, with examples of companies that produce and reinvent both tea and chocolate.

The short history of chocolate

Beginning with what was once known to be liquid, chocolate has won the hearts of many, having both a delicious taste and several benefits when consumed correctly. Requiring a complex process, what is today known to be chocolate has a completely different appearance in its real form. The cacao tree, which is located in the tropical part of the world, also known as the "cocoa belt," is the one that produces the fruit called pod or cabosside, the colours of the pod ranging from brown to yellow and purple (Verna, 2013). As a result of an intense process, the fruit is transformed into what we know today to be chocolate.

However, the history of using cocoa started a long time ago, when in 3500 BC the cocoa plant was discovered and cultivated in a region which today is known as Ecuador (Zarillo, 2018). Being an extremely important drink in the region, and also in Central America, cacao is presented by Coe (2006) as the real name of the chocolate, while the tree was known as "Theobroma cacao," translated from Greek as the "food of the gods". Furthermore, Poelmans and Swinnen (2019) claimm that despite of existing for millennia, cacao started to be known outside the Central America only in the early sixteenth century, when the Spanish population arrived. Representing such an old plant, as the years passed, the cacao evolved and was transformed. Verna (2013) ar-

https://doi.org/10.1515/9783110758573-009

gues that the result we know today was made possible due to crossings and selections that started 35,000 years ago. Coming back to the roots of it, Maya empire not only discovered but also took advantage of the ingredients. Being perceived as food, today's chocolate has lost many of its roles. However, Rosenblum (2005, cited in Poelmans and Swinnen, 2019, p. 3) emphasises what was once one of the important functions of cocoa beans, being seen as an exchange in trade during the Maya empire. Additionally, it was not only perceived as a basic ingredient, but as an essential part of the religious rituals, being offered to the gods (Poelmans & Swinnen, 2019).

Since 1815, people transformed the cacao bean, making much use of it. Verna (2013) presents the evolution, specifying that the first solid bar of chocolate was produced in 1847, followed by the first mint flavour in 1875. From 1879, famous brands consumed by many today such as Lindt, Dairy Milk, Kiss, and Mon Cheri opened their doors. As a result of the increasing production, chocolate became famous around the world. Desired by a large number of people, the prices slightly increased. Poelmans and Swinnen (2019) illustrated this increase, arguing that compared to 1900s, by 1940 the production became ten times higher.

Not only is chocolate one of the most desired deserts, but also a product that brings many properties beneficial for one's health. Verna (2013) cites "anti-inflammatory, anti-diabetic and anti-obesity" benefits, mentioning improvements in liver functions, intestinal flora, stress and glaucoma symptoms reduction as well. Having a specific taste, chocolate is known to be consumed in stressful or sad situations, offering the human body a needed boost. Dopamine, serotonin, anandamide, and phenylethylamine are psychoactive substances found in the beloved product. While dopamine produces pleasure, serotonin controls the mood, anandamide brings happiness, and phenylethylamine is responsible for the state of mood and pleasure (, 2013). For this reason, when pricing chocolate, four essential steps are to be considered: fermentation, drying, winnowing, and griding (Coe, 2006).

The short history of tea

While being the second most drunk beverage in the world, tea has become the number one choice of many. The history of the beloved drink started many years ago, tea being discovered by mistake. Such a fortunate accident is the reason behind the possibility of enjoying the nourishing drink today. The legend started with Shen Nung, the Emperor of China who, believing that boiled water was promoting health, was outside preparing his hot drink (DeWitt, 2000). Finding himself under a bush of Camellia sinensis, some leaves accidently fell into his boiling water, with tea being produced for the first time (DeWitt, 2000). Used in the beginning as a medicine, over time people came to realised that there is much more to be discovered and enjoyed about tea. Okakura (1989) argued that news about a pleasant drink made from leaves of a certain bush was brought to Hollanders at the end of the sixteenth century. The pleasant taste of it conquered countless populations, with consumption rising considerably. Its charm made it irresistible and suitable for idealisation (Okakura, 1989).

While tea includes a large variety of flavours, the majority are not considered to be tea. The real tea comes from one plant and has six different types: white, yellow, green, Oolong, black and Pu Erh. Apart from these, beverages such as hot water with herbs, peppermint, ginger, lemon, or forest fruits "tea" are considered to be infusions. However, the possibility of plucking leaves from the same plant and transforming them into six different types of tea is explained by DeWitt (2000) as a result of varying the fermentation process and the time allocated for this. With the possibility of purchasing it from many shops today, tea has become an unexpensive product. However, at the time of its discovery, the beverage was seen as a luxury (DeWitt, 2000). Therefore, hundreds of years ago, laws that ensured the safety of the final drink were implemented. In 1724, while George I was reigning, mixing tea with other substances was forbidden through law (DeWitt, 2000, p. 8).

The everyday drink which originated from China was slowly spread across the world. With time, the way the plant was presented changed considerably. For example, DeWitt (2000) explained the invention of the tea bags, claiming that a retailer from Boston provided some samples of tea to a customer, using small silk pouches. From that moment on, a visible evolution in regards to the presentation of tea was comprehended.

Tea incorporated in chocolate

Once the understanding of tea and chocolate became clearer, and a small percentage of the history was brought to light, the only missing information is the purpose, aim, and desire behind the mix. Even though both are enjoyable and have specific tastes, combining them might have resulted in an unfavorable product. Fortunately, this was not the case. Green and yellow tea found within chocolate is an often researched topic.

Weerasingha, Wijayaratne and de Silva (2012) announced that the development of white chocolate and green tea is of great interest for both industries (tea and chocolate). When it comes to analyzing their harmony, certain elements enhance their benefits and aromas mixed together. For instance, the low pH value of tea makes it compatible with many products (Chatterjee, Das & Das, 2018). However, until the final and perfect result was possible, many attempts were made, ensuring that what is offered to customers is actually satisfying their needs. Aroyeun (2016) emphasises that in order to incorporate the green tea, different combinations were made (Gramza-Michalowska et al. 2021). Nevertheless, green tea is often found as an ingredient of a chocolate bar. Not having much of a taste, the chocolate needs additional elements. Apart from tea, honey is as well added, the final taste being enhanced (Chatterjee, Das & Das 2018).

While the perfect pairing requires background knowledge of both tea and chocolate, similarities and differences can be identified. Table C.3.1 highlights these characteristics, illustrating some of the general information.

Recently, people are moving towards a healthier life, carefully choosing the food they are purchasing. In order to keep up with the consumer's expectations and the surrounding competition, many companies and businesses started producing chocolate bars with different tea flavours or infusions. The already existing brands have also promoted their new and healthier products. While both tea and chocolate consist of several nourishing elements, concluding with a combination of these two will lead to one single product their combination implies double the benefits. Aroyeun (2016) claims that the prevention of cancer and cardiovascular diseases are linked to antioxidant properties found in chocolate and green tea (see Table C.3.1).

Table C.3.1: Characteristics of tea and chocolate.

Tea	Chocolate
Origin: Asia	Origin: South America
Discovery: 2737 BC in China **First arrival to Europe: 1610** imported by Dutch traders to Amsterdam	Discovery: 3500 BC in Ecuador **First arrival to Europe: 1544** as a gift for Prince Philippe of Spain
Plant's name: Camellia sinensis	Plant's name: Theobroma cacao
3–5 steps of production	9 steps of production
Six main types: Green, yellow, white, Oolong, black, Pu-Erh	Three main types: Dark, Milk and White
Best growing conditions in the "Tea belt"	Best growing conditions in the "Chocolate belt"
Improves brain function	
Reduces heart disease risks	
Antioxidant properties	

Source: Author, based on Zarillo (2018) and Rohrsen (2022).

Tea and chocolate pairing

Being individually two beloved small luxuries, once combined, the experience of the taste palate will enter a world of new flavours. In order for the final product to be a success, different knowledge and steps are required. The first element is quality.

While any type of chocolate can be paired with tea, quality will enhance the conclusive product. Altitude, climate, and soil are three relevant factors understood as key roles for a good and qualitative production. Craftmanship and the passion of maker are representing the next step. When the cocoa beans are handled by an experienced artisan, the final output is enjoyable. Flavoured teas have to be avoided and a successful pairing will allow the taster to feel both tea and chocolate at the same time.

In order for the best result to be achievable, it is essential to match the most suitable sort of tea with a good choice of chocolate. Starting with the milk chocolate, which is the most popular in the world, rich and creamy types of black teas, having natural sweetness and perfectly blending with spices are needed. Some examples are Chai Tea, Earl Grey, English Breakfast and Darjeeling Black Tea. Next analyzed chocolate is the dark one, with a high percentage of cocoa and a strong taste, matching smokey teas with citrus, mint or ginger notes. Red Robe Oolong, Ceylon Black Tea and Pu-Erh are some of the mentioned examples. Last but not least, white chocolate which can be very sweet and never bitter, pairs with astringency, malty and hay notes teas that are rich in flowery notes. Masala Chai, Jasmine Green, Pai mu tan and Hojicha are the illustrated combinations (Ahmad, 2022).

For a clear view, Table C.3.2 highlights the perfect matches.

Table C.3.2: Matching tea and chocolate types.

Chocolate type	Tea type
Dark chocolate	Red Robe Oolong Pu-Erh Ceylon Black Tea Earl Grey Mint Green
Milk chocolate	Chai Tea Earl Grey English Breakfast Sencha Green Tea Black Tea (Assam, Darjeeling) Matcha
White chocolate	Masala Chai Green tea (Jasmine, Hojicha) Assam Black tea Pai mu tan white tea Lightly-medium roasted Oolong Tea Matcha Earl Grey

Source: Author, based on Ahmad (2022)

Ahmad Tea in London, one of the largest tea traders worldwide, is celebrating the idea of tea pairing during the "chocolate week" every year underlining the advantageous options of matching the melting sweetness of chocolate with the hot and clear beverage: "Tea and chocolate is a winning combination" (Ahmad, 2022).

Combining these two elements requires a procedure of preparation that needs time, devotion and precision. The final product might be delicious or, when the chosen tea does not match the chosen chocolate, the result might be less enjoyable. Nevertheless, a huge interest is visible, as more and more companies are moving towards this combination, introducing chocolate bars and pralines with different teas as ingredients.

European companies that introduced chocolate bars or pralines with tea flavours

Once companies realised that having chocolate as diverse as possible, including bars with tea flavours or infusions, will bring a substantial advantage to the business, increasingly more started producing it. In the following, more than 30 European companies will be presented in order to show the variety of tastes, and options. These companies are representative of the chocolate industry, using tea as an essential benefit for their portfolio.

Being located in St. Petersburg, the first company is Amazing Cacao. Existing since 2016, the brand uses bean-to-bar technology, importing all their organic coffee beans, organic flavour beans, the cacao butter, and cane sugar in order to ensure the high quality. Having the aim of letting the true taste of chocolate come to light, Amazing Cacao allows their customers to discover the origins of their products. No artificial flavours are added; experts regularly visiting the farms and places of the cacao origins, ensuring that the processes are smooth. Regarding their offers concerning chocolate tea, some of the existing products are: "White Chocolate with Black Tea and Lemon," 'White Chocolate and Green Tea," and "White Chocolate with Rooibos Tea and Chocolate-nutty Filling."

The next company is Ara Chocolate, located in Paris, France. Founded by a Venezuelan couple, the company is one of the few chocolate roasters within France. They choose their cocoa beans from small producers from Latin America, using only natural and organic ingredients, having vegan and gluten free products. The high quality of the used ingredients enhance the aromas of the cocoa. The only product they offer is "Black Tea Ganache."

In the north of Sweden, the small "Åre Chokladfabrik" is producing truffles, chocolate cream and chocolate nips. Among their truffles, one sort is based on regional fruity ingredients and black tea as a flavour (Åre Chokladfabrik, 2024). In Amsterdam, Arte & Zayne offers a nice variety of different tea-chocolate pairings. Based on the passion for organic tea blends and organic chocolate, recipes for tea pairings with food have also been developed. In addition, different chocolate tablets and bars using organic teas offered in the shop have been created in order to underline the holistic approach of tea and suitable companions.

The British Bird & Blend tea company is offering two sorts of Easter eggs: white chocolate flavoured with matcha and cocos as well as creamy vegan oat milk chocolate infused with Earl Grey Creme tea (Bird & Blend, 2024).

ChocoCard, a company from Hungary, was founded in 2011 by a small family that had a big passion for chocolate and was looking for a job that offered both a good living and challenged them. In 2015, they decided to make their own chocolate, seeing it as an advantage. They have subsequently participated in many competitions, winning almost 50 international awards. The chocolate with tea flavours offered by the company are "Ginger and Matcha" and "White and Dark Chocolate with Matcha Powder."

The next company is Chocolat Café Tasse, founded in 1989. They import high-quality beans from Africa and South America, seeing chocolate as a constant source of inspiration. Their desire is to make every bite of their chocolate an unforgettable experience, working with the best chocolatiers masters. Being the ambassador for Belgian chocolate, customers can purchase their products from more than 40 countries. The two offered products are "White Chocolate Family Bar with Japanese Matcha Tea" and "Dark Chocolate Family Bar with Earl Grey Tea."

Dallmayr is another example. Being a typical Bavarian delicatessen shop, the brand has existed for more than 300 years. With its roots in Munich, the company grew over the years, developing considerably. Mostly famous for coffee, Dallmayr started producing its own branded products including tea and chocolates. As for the tea and chocolate combination, Dallmayr offers their customers a "Praline Truffle Chocolate," having 12 different varieties, two having tea as an ingredient, being named "Earl-Grey-Truffle".

The Polish company Datovita is one of the companies with the most offers in regards of chocolate with tea. The brand uses top quality and 100% natural ingredients. Using a traditional recipe, the chocolate makes their consumers healthier and full of energy, while the produced sweets remind people of their childhood times. Some of their offers regarding tea are: "White Chocolate with Caramelised Black Milk Tea Essence," "Dark Chocolate with Caramelised Green Tea Essence and Mint Leaves," "White Chocolate with Japanese Matcha Tea and Candied Ginger," and "Honey Chocolate with Caramelised Black Tea Essence and Spices."

Since 1992, The Hague, Rotterdam, and Schiedam based chocolate company "de bonte koe" has been one of the few companies producing chocolate bonbons/pralines with the flavour of Assam. This praline is includes milk chocolate and a strongly brewed Assam tea.

Another Polish chocolate company is Desco, primarily offering white chocolate with the taste of matcha tea. Based on a small, handcrafted business, this company also underlines the advantages of pairing white chocolate (60%) with the green colour of matcha and its typical flavour.

A well-known Belgian company is Dolfin, founded in 1989 by two brothers. Their goal of having chocolate respected worldwide slowly became a reality. The product line represents a mix of both unique and natural ingredients, using the highest quality of chocolate. "Sencha Green Tea Milk Chocolate" and "Dark Chocolate with Earl Grey Tea" are some of the existing products when it comes to tea infusions and flavours.

Being a German company, the mission of GEPA is developing and selling fair trade products. Contrary to other brands and businesses, profit maximisation and distribution is not one of GEPA's principles. Existing for more than 40 years, an important role in formatting the public awareness towards product condition was presented by the passioned company. Not only do they offer quality and fair prices, but also partnerships within forty-five countries. Regarding the chocolate offers, "Earl Grey Blanc" and "Matcha Blanc" are the two available varieties.

The chocolate expert Georgia Ramon developed special chocolate bars for the German tea company TeeGschwendner, e.g., white chocolate with Earl Grey (TeeGschwendner, 2024).

Harrer Chocolat is the next company to be presented. Being both a confectionary and chocolate factory, the owner opened the first shop in 1995, located in his hometown in Hungary. The dream of the family was to open a workshop, a dream that became reality in 2009. Regarding tea, "Milk Chocolate with Toasted Rice and Green Tea" and "Matcha Tea with White Chocolate" are two of the offered products.

A British chocolate brand is Kacao, situated in North Yorkshire, United Kingdom. The first location was in Sedbury Hall, surrounded by lavenders and roses. The fascination towards cacao beans was enhanced while the owner was traveling and working in Central and South America. Putting an accent on the quality of products, the company uses raw materials from sustainable sources. "The Yorkshire Rose Bar," a delicate infusion of black tea, and "Aztec Chai Bar" are the two existing products from the brand.

LABYs represents the next company that makes chocolate bars, pralines, cakes, and other chocolate products. Being located in Sweden, most of the final production is made from local ingredients and lots of love. When it comes to tea and chocolate, "Mailbox or Praline box chocolate" is the only offer, having different mixes of pralines, some including Earl Grey.

Lady Lavender is another European brand, being located in Budapest, Hungary. The owner understood with time that quality is an essential factor in order to have a successful business. Expertise, patience, love, and tradition are the essence of a prosperous company. In order to offer the best for her customers, together with her family, the owner tasted the sweets until the final result was pleasing. Two products are found to contain tea: "Bonbon Selection" with masala chai and smoky tea and "Chocolate Bar" with the same infusion of tea.

As a fourth German company presented here, Lauenstein has an impressive variety of chocolate with tea, e.g., tea leaves made from chocolate, but also different types of black (e.g., Earl Grey) or green (e.g., Matcha + Yuzu) tea combined with different types of dark, milk or white chocolate. In addition, Lauensteiner Tea Truffles are a unique product of this company. Lauensteiner Tea Chocolate can be found as Chai Latte, Mate Tea Curied Mint, Rooibos Orange, Earl Grey or Green Tea Matcha Lime, to name only some of their variations (Lauensteiner, 2024).

Existing since 2009, the Dutch brand "Lovechock" produces a chocolate that nurtures the well-being of both the planet and its people. Their real and pure chocolate enhances the vitamins and minerals found in the raw cacao, having a delicious and distinctive taste. Due to its a strong relation with nature, the only ingredients used are organic. Regarding tea chocolate, the only existing product is "Hazelnut Matcha Bar."

The following brand known as Love Cocoa, located in Great Britain, has existed since 2016 and started from a kitchen table. The founder, known as James Cadbury, was inspired by his great-great-great grandfather, wishing to create an amazing and great tasting chocolate bar in Great Britain. Making use of the world's finest cacao, the company is environmentally responsible, planting a tree for each chocolate bar, nibbles or truffles. They offer one chocolate bar with tea, named "Earl Grey," consisting of 41% milk chocolate from Colombia.

Located in Nottingham, United Kingdom, the company called Luisa's is named after the owner, who being a teacher was constantly carrying chocolate in her bag. Having a strong passion for chocolate, the brand only offers their consumers quality, making sure that the farmers from where the chocolate is brought live in good conditions. "Casholate Infusions Tasting Bundle" with matcha white casholate and "Superboost Casholate Collection" consisting of 12 pralines are the two products with tea flavour.

The famous french tea company Mariage Frères is also offering delicious tea chocolates (mostly pralinés) flavoured with some of their teas, e.g., Darjeeling-based Earl Grey in dark chocolate or milk chocolate with green tea and Japanese cherry blossom. Both sorts belong to the tea-chocolate brand "Chocolat des Mandarins", developed by Henri Mariage and presented first in 1860 (Mariage Frères, 2024).

A special collection of tea flavoured almond based pralines is offered by the Spanish company Mi & Cu Gourmet in Barcelona. It is a courageous blend of pralines, e.g. dark chocolate with Pu Erh tea and berries, milk and white chocolate with Assam tea, white and dark chocolate with Matcha tea, white chocolate with Matcha tea and bergamotte flavour. A very special edition is mixed of Pai Mu Tan white tea and white chocolate, ginger, coconuts, and the additional flavour of bergamotte, while the blend of white chocolate, green tea, mint, and lemon flavours shows a creative approach of tea pralines.

Paola Francesca Bertani is another well-known brand, being located in the Island of Elba. Always experimenting with new decorative techniques, in 2020, the company started an amazing collaboration with Chiara Pieraccioni. After the owner participated at a tea course, and finally entered the world of tea, the plant was also introduced within the company. They offer three chocolates with tea: "Fruits and Flowers," "Alcohol," and "Winners and Wishes," representing boxes of pralines with Earl Grey Tea, Lincang sheng tea, and Darjeeling tea.

The Paper and Tea company was founded in 2011, starting its journey in Berlin. Having a passion towards the enjoyment and uses of tea, the company focused on the tradition and knowledge of tea origins. Perceiving tea as a healthy, fulfilling, and creative lifestyle, the company values the tradition behind tea, seeing it as a way of human communication. Offering only high-quality products, P&T has developed an impressive range of tea-flavoured chocolate bars, such as white chocolate coloured with matcha, milk chocolate fused with a chai tea blend, fruity dark chocolate with sencha tea and nutty milk chocolate blended with Japanese green tea (Paper & Tea, 2024).

Being a multi-award-winning company, Piccola Pasticceria is an Italian company focussing on unique recipes of chocolate. Among its specialties, "Tea alla rosa con litchi" chocolate is offered.

The Amsterdam chocolate company "Pucchini bomboni" offers dark chocolate pralines with the flavour of strong black tea and lemon, covered with chocolate chips (Pucchini Bomboni, 2024).

The next one is Rococo Chocolates, another brand from United Kingdom, existing for 36 years and selling exceptional chocolate. Established in 1983, an international reputation was built over the years, as a result of their great attention to detail. "Earl Grey Tea Dark Chocolate Thins" and "Artisan Bar Dark Earl Grey Tea" are the two existing tea products.

Wagner Pralinen, located in Brunsbüttel/Germany, melts Matcha tea powder with milk chocolate to form a square praline ("Matcha Happen"), often used as a supplement for tea or coffee.

Winchester Cocoa Company has won many awards for designing special pairings of chocolate for the customers. This brand was inspired by classic and contemporary flavours. They offer two box selections which include Chai vanilla, Earl Grey, and Assam tea.

Another Hungarian chocolate producer, Zangio, started as a workshop in 2010, named after a combination of family names. The company was created from a desire to raise awareness for high quality chocolate and particular flavours such as Jasmine Pearl Tea.

Country	Corresponding Chocolate or Tea Brand	
Belgium	Café Tasse	Dolfin
Finland	Northquist	
France	Ara Chocolate	Mariage Frères
Italy	Paola Francesca Bertani	Piccola Pasticceria
Germany	Dallmayr	Paper & Tea
	GEPA	Tee Gschwendner
	Lauenstein	Wagner
Hungary	Amazing Cacao	Lady Lavender
	Harrer	Zangio
Netherlands	Arte & Zayne	Lovechock
	De bonte koe	Pucchini
Poland	Datovita	Desco
Russia	Amazing Cacao	
Spain	Mi & Cu Gourmet	
Sweden	Åre Chokladfabrik	Labys
United Kingdom	Bird and Blend	Luisa's
	Kacao	Willie's
	Love Coçoa	Winchesters

Figure C.3.1: European countries with tea chocolate bar and pralines production.
Source: Author

Figure C.3.1 provides an overview of the locations of the chocolate and/or tea companies presented above.

Conclusion

More than 30 chocolate and/or tea companies in Europe are developing and offering chocolates and/or pralinés with tea flavours, many of them being awarded for special tastes and high quality. Taking this into consideration, tea pairings with chocolate are a profitable opportunity symbolising hospitality, warmth and relaxation. To enjoy a good chocolate you also need a bit of time – the same you need to enjoy a good cup of tea. These simple similarities understandably underline that tea and chocolate, either as a joint product or as two parts of a light snack, are a perfect combination for a moment of hospitality. Consequently, chocolate is a perfect companion for tea and offers a large variety of options for courageous chocolatiers and hoteliers in Europe.

References

Ahmad Tea London. (2022, October 17). Chocolate and tea pairings. retrieved 20 March 2023 from https://www.ahmadtea.com/chocolate-tea-pairings/.

Amazing Cacao. (2016). Cacao beans and coffee for taste and quality connoisseurs. Retrieved September 29, 2021, from http://www.amazingcacao.com/.

Ara Chocolat. (2021). Les Accord Avec Le Chocolat. Retrieved September 29, 2021, from https://www.arachocolat.com/.

Åre Chokladfabrik (2024). Alla produkter, Retreived March 12th, 2024 from https://arechokladfabrik.se/alla-produkter/.

Aroyeun, S.O. (2016). Effects of green tea extracts on the caffeine, tannin, total polyphenolic contents and organoleptic properties of milk chocolate. *Journal of Food Processing & Technology, 7*, 1–5.

Bird and Blend (2024). Chocolate. Retrieved March 12th, 2024 from https://www.birdandblendtea.eu/products/tea-infused-chocolate-easter-egg?_pos=3&_sid=5af0972b4&_ss=r

Cafe-Tasse. (2021). Chocolat Café-Tasse Bruxelles-Brussels. Retrieved September 29, 2021, from https://cafe-tasse.com/en/

Chatterjee, G., Das, S., & Das, R. (2018). Development of green tea infused chocolate yoghurt and evaluation of its nutritive value and storage stability. *Progress in Nutrition, 20*, pp. 237–45.

Chococard. (2021). Craft Csokoládék. Retrieved September 29, 2021, from https://chococard.hu/.

Coe, M. (1996). The True History of Chocolate. Dallas Museum of Art Horchow Auditorium, pp. 1–18. Retrieved September 19, 2021, from http://dma.org/TermsConditions/index.htm.

Datovita. (2017). Datovita Original Polish Food. Retrieved September 29, 2021, from http://datovita.eu/

Debontekoe. (2023). Retrieved June 12, 2023, from www.debontekoe.nl.

DeWitt, P. (2000). A brief history of tea: The rise and fall of the tea importation act. Harvard University's DASH, pp. 1–46. Retrieved September 22, 2021, from https://dash.harvard.edu/.

Dolfin. (2021). The art of blending. Retrieved September 29, 2021, from https://www.dolfin.be/fr/.

Gramza-Michalowska, A., Kulczynski, B., Skopiec, Kobus-Cisowska, J., & Brzozowska, A. (2021). The effect of yellow tea leaves Camellia sinensis on the quality of stored chocolate confectionery. Retrieved September 21, 2021, from https://www.mdpi.com/journal/applsci.

Harrerchocolat. (2021). Legújabb Büszkeségeink. Retrieved September 29, 2021, from https://harrerchocolat.com/.

Kacao. (2021). Fresh Cream Truffles. Retrieved September 29, 2021, from https://www.kacao.co.uk/.

Labys. (2021). Välkommen till den lilla chokladbutiken i Hedemora, med sin egna chokladfabrik. Retrieved September 29, 2021, from https://labys.se/.

Lady Lavender. (2021). We are professional in chocolate. What can we help you with? Retrieved September 29, 2021, from https://en.ladylavender.hu/.

Lauensteiner. (2024). Lauenstein Confiserie. Retrieved March 12th, 2024 from https://www.lauensteiner.de/de/search/?input_search=tee.

Lovechock. (2021). Lovechock. Pure Goodness. Retrieved September 29, 2021, from https://www.lovechock.com/.

Luisa's Vegan Chocolates. (2021). Food of the Gods. Retrieved September 29, 2021, from https://luisasveganchocolates.co.uk/.

Mariage Frères (2024). Tea chocolate. Retreived March 12th, 2024 from https://www.mariagefreres.com/en/tea-delights/tea-chocolate.html.

Mi and Cu. (2023). Tea chocolates. Retrieved May 12, 2023 from https://miandcu.com/delicias.

Okakura, K. (1989). *The book of tea*. Tuttle publishing.

Paper & Tea (2024). Teeschokolade. Retrieved March 12th, 2024 from https://www.paperandtea.de/collections/tee-schokolade.

Poelmans, E., & Swinnen, J. (2019). A brief economic history of chocolate. LICOS Discussion Paper, No. 412, pp. 1–44. Retrieved September 19, 2021, from http://hdl.handle.net/10419/200496.

Pucchini Bomboni (2024). Bonbon collection. Retreived March 12th, 2024 from https://puccinibomboni.com/en/bonbons.

Rococo Chocolates. (2021). Discover expertly-crafted luxury British chocolates, decadent flavours and classic style. Retrieved September 29, 2021, from https://www.rococochocolates.com/.

Rohrsen, P. (2022). *Das Buch zum Tee*. C.H. Beck.

TeeGschwendner (2024). Teeschokolade. Retrieved March 12th, 2024 from https://www.teegschwendner.de/Teeschokolade-Georgia-Ramon-Matcha-BIO/3056?gad_source=1&gclid=Cj0KCQjwncWvBhD_ARIsAEb2HW8xzPI4HBFFrJDfY70MG3Ldg2f-Cp6vQnfcxpmNet8cmWUw38gEqHoaAlT_EALw_wcB.

Verna R. (2013) The history and science of chocolate. *Malaysian Journal of Pathology*. Vol. 35(2):111–21. PMID: 24362474.

Weerasingha, W.N.D., Wijayaratne, L.K.W., de Silva, W.A.N.T., & Wanniarachchi, M. (2012). Development of a green-tea-incorporated white chocolate. Proceedings of the Research Symposium of Uva Wellassa University, pp. 199–201. Retrieved September 19, 2021, from https://www.erepo.lib.uwu.ac.lk/.

Winchester Cocoa. (2021). Award-Winning fine chocolates, handmade in Winchester. Retrieved September 29, 2021, from https://www.winchestercocoa.co.uk/

Zangio. (2021). Tisztelt vásárlóink! Retrieved September 29, 2021, from https://zangio.hu/index.php?language=de.

Zarillo. S., et al. (2018). *The use and domestication of Theobroma cacao during the mid-Holocene in the upper Amazon*. Springer Nature.

Felix Bröcker

C.4 The importance of tea for European fine dining

A culinary approach to tea

Tea is a product that combines complex production methods, cultural history, and special taste experiences and is thus in no way inferior to wine, which is so important for European fine dining. But while wine is a central aspect of French-influenced fine dining, tea plays a comparatively minor role. Yet, fine dining in Europe has a long-standing connection to tea. Grand hotels traditionally serve "Afternoon Tea" as a luxurious treat, offering high quality teas together with a selection of sweet and savoury snacks like scones and sandwiches (Bohne & Jolliffe, 2021). This classic English light meal already is an example of a staged culinary experience, for which tea plays the leading part. Afternoon tea lives on as a reminiscence of the heyday of grand hotels. But even beyond this classic institution, tea plays a special role in the context of high cuisine. Tea is of fundamental importance in European high cuisine in various ways. This importance manifests itself on different levels:

–   The philosophy of the "tea ceremony" has influenced modern European high cuisine.
–   Tea is present in high cuisine as an ingredient, technique, and form of presentation.
–   Tea, like espresso, is traditionally served after a meal but increasingly plays an important role as a non-alcoholic accompaniment to food.

With this article, it will be presented that these areas give suitable examples of how European cuisine integrates the culture of tea.

How the tea ceremony has influenced modern European high cuisine

European restaurants emerged around the time of the French Revolution. At that time, the aim was to eat healthy food in a beautiful ambience. For this purpose, fine bouillons were served, which combined exquisite taste with a strengthening, health-promoting effect. So-called "restaurants" restorative broths were consumed, that gave their name to an institution that today is predominantly associated with pleasure and less with health (Spang, 2000, p. 42). These broths are not unlike teas. Both are extracts of solid ingredients in a hot liquid, to release flavour, and both are expected to have a positive effect on the body. Broths are associated with principles of the Asian

https://doi.org/10.1515/9783110758573-010

drink in recipes such as for beef tea and, similar to the "restaurants," they were used for healthy nutrition, in the case of beef tea also explicitly as a tonic for the sick.

The history of Japanese high cuisine also begins with a healthy, hot liquid - tea. In Japan, the local high cuisine, kaiseki, developed in the context of the tea ceremony in the late sixteenth century (Rath, 2013, p. 68). The tea ceremony developed in relation to Zen Buddhism and the vegan monastic cuisine – Shojin Ryori – was also inspired by values that are relevant to the tea ceremony (Härtig, 2016, p. 148).

In the sixteenth century, through the tea master Rikyū, the idea of wabi, the aesthetics of the imperfect, became central to the tea way and the food served (Rath, 2013; Härtig, 2016, p. 124). A light, simple meal, the cha kaiseki, was served with the tea. The food should be prepared for the tea and be subordinate to it (Härtig, 2016, p. 125). The tea way is determined by an interplay of simplicity and complexity of the "offensively beautiful and a discreet aesthetic" (Härtig, 2016, p. 127).

All these elements are related to today's restaurant kaiseki. It is still about simplicity and reduction. Seasonal and regional ingredients are central, served within a traditional menu structure. It is a light, seemingly simple meal that deals with the regional ingredients available at the time. The Kaiseki chef Yoshihiro Murata answers the question of what kaseki is: "It is eating the seasons" (Murata, 2006, p. 17). Only lightly seasoned, the food should not distract from its own taste (Tsuchiya, 1985, p. 54).

The flavour of the ingredients is important, but taste alone is not the focus (Tsuchiya, 1985, p. 38; Härtig, 2016, p. 162). The presentation should appeal to all the senses (Tsuchiya, 1985), with the sense of sight taking on a special position (Rath, 2013, p. 69). However, the presentation is not aimed at effects; it is about emphasising the naturalness, simplicity, and freshness of the food (Tsuchiya, 1985, p. 54). The empty spaces, the free areas on the plate, take on a significance of their own (Tsuchiya, 1985, p. 37). Nature, the season, i.e., the here and now, is depicted. This is not only achieved through the food: the vessels are also carefully selected, certain materials create references to the seasons (Tsuchiya, 1985, p. 12). For kaiseki menus, different materials like wood, ceramic, earthenware or lacquered are used. For the kaiseki as well as the tea way, the three ki are elementary: the season (kisetsu), the vessel (ki), and the occasion (kikai) (Tsuchiya, 1985, p. 37). The timing, the rhythm of the meal sequence, is also an important element to consider. It becomes clear that a kaiseki meal cannot be reduced to taste. It is an event in which different elements interact and constitute an experience in the sense of a performance, exactly what a tea ceremony is (Kirshenblatt-Gimblett, 2007). There is also a European tradition in which the communal meal becomes a total work of art, such as in medieval banquets (Normore, 2015). The entire staging conveys an attitude through many details. "I try to send a message," says Murata, "It's not just a dish but an atmosphere, a mood. Look for the message. The taste is important, but it's not the most important thing" (Brenner & Busico, 2007). The food served thus becomes a medium to express something. But how has this development affected Western high cuisine? In the course of Nouvelle Cuisine around 1970, French chefs for the first time intensively studied Japanese cuisine, exchanged ideas with Japanese colleagues, drew inspiration from it, and adopted elements of this cuisine.

Nouvelle Cuisine and tea

Some aspects that were important for Nouvelle Cuisine can also be found in traditional European high cuisine and direct forerunners such as Fernand Point also shaped this style. However, Japanese cuisine appears as a clear influence that can hardly be overestimated and continues to inspire and shape Western high cuisine to this day. Nouvelle Cuisine chefs discovered many of the principles of Japanese kaiseki for themselves and transferred these into their own system of cooking.

The first two of the ten commandments of Nouvelle Cuisine written by Henri Gault and Christian Millau in 1973 illustrate this:

1. Thou shalt not overcook.
2. Thou shalt use fresh, quality products.

The lightness of Japanese high cuisine is expressed in two further commandments:

7. Thou shalt eliminate rich sauces.
8. Thou shalt not ignore dietetics.

And the special way of plating food is also discussed:

9. Thou shalt not doctor up thy presentations.

For the chefs of Nouvelle Cuisine, seasonal and regional products prepared à la minute have gained in importance. The product and its characteristics should be brought out in the best possible way by the chef and served fresh. The product should not be overcooked and stand on its own. It is particularly noticeable that the way of presentation has changed. It was no longer served from lavishly filled platters; now the dishes were arranged individually on the plate for each guest by the chef. This has led to chefs thinking more about colours, shapes, and the arrangement of individual components. Food should not only taste good, but also look appetising. This led to smaller portions, which are common in kaiseki. In Western high cuisine, where large quantities were historically important, such delicate and reduced cooking irritated and provoked previous habits. Wholesomeness and health were taken into account and vegetables gained in importance over meat. The new basic orientation of Nouvelle Cuisine, which turned itself against traditional French cuisine, stands for the turn towards Japanese high cuisine. A new image emerged that is reflected in the numerous cookery books of the time. This is particularly evident in some of the pioneers who are mentioned here as examples:

The Troisgros brothers committed themselves to the new lightness and were presumably the first to prepare a dish directly on the plate for the guest. Salmon with sorrel from 1963 stands for this simple product cuisine (Labro 2014). As a self-taught chef, Michel Bras has practiced a cuisine that is close to nature and characterised by bringing the environment onto the plate. Asian cuisine and philosophies have influenced his vegetable-focused style (Heller, 2002). Influential and iconic is his "gargouillou," which uses a variety of herbs and vegetables to represent the region. Lightness, colours, shapes, and textures define the dish. His way to prepare and plate the food was pioneering a new style of cuisine in Europe (Muhlke, 2009). Other chefs such as Paul Bocuse, Pierre Gagnaire or Michel Guérard have taken up influences from Japanese cuisine and integrated them into French cuisine.

More tea today

Nouvelle Cuisine has thus already transferred important features of Japanese cuisine into European culture and made it a new standard. Building on this, further aspects were adopted, and the examination of Japanese cuisine intensified. It is noticeable that today influential restaurants in European high cuisine all over the world orient themselves on the values and appearance of kaiseki and thus on values of the tea ceremony.

Ferran Adrià has studied Japanese high cuisine and adopted aspects of it: "There's an element of kaiseki in the cooking at El Bulli," says Adrià (Brenner & Busico, 2007). His former student René Redzepi, who has been a trend-setter with Nordic cuisine at Noma for a good ten years, sounds similar: "In a sense there is a part of Japan in the Noma kitchen, floating in every single serving – although a Japanese person would not see them as a Japanese ingredient, but the DNA and inspiration comes from our journeys in Japan" (Swinnerton, 2016). Looking at the already mentioned peculiarities of kaiseki, it becomes clear what these parallels are: at elBulli, menus with up to 30–40 small courses were served. Each dish was carefully arranged and served on a wide variety of materials. Adrià did not reduce his dishes to taste. For him, all the senses were important, and he also wanted to communicate something with his food: for him, cooking is a language. Food is understood as a staged experience, for which the location, the journey or the interaction with the guests are just as important as the food itself. This approach is also expressed in the rules describing this cuisine (elBulli, 2021a):

1. Cooking is a language through which all the following properties can be expressed: harmony, creativity, happiness, beauty, poetry, complexity, magic, humour, provocation, culture.
9. The information given by a dish is enjoyed through the senses: it can also be enjoyed and rationalised through reflection.
10. Taste is not the only sense that can be stimulated: touch can also be played with (contrasts of temperatures and textures), as well as smell, sight (colours, shapes,

trompe d'oeil, etc.), whereby the five senses become one of the main points of reference in the creative cooking process.

16. Local cooking tradition as a style is a sense of bonding with the local geographical and cultural context, as well as with its culinary tradition. The link with nature complements and enriches this relationship with the environment.
20. Recipes are conceptualised that give harmony to small servings.
21. Decontextualisation, irony, spectacle and performance are completely legitimate, providing they are not superficial but closely bound up with a process of gastronomic reflection.

Nordic cuisine, in turn, adopts the corresponding rules of previous cuisines such as those of Nouvelle Cuisine and elBulli and introduces further elements from Japan.

With Nordic Cuisine, these become even more visible. Not white porcelain but earthenware from local craftsmen and also wood, stones or textiles are used to serve the food. The ingredients are meant to represent the Nordic region: Noma is about perceiving time and place through the food served. Food processing techniques, above all fermentation, also become an important foundation of this Nordic cuisine, which is obviously very Japanese at the same time and feels connected to the philosophy of the tea ceremony. This is made clear by some of the rules of the New Nordic Manifesto from 2004 (Nordic Council, 2021):

1. To express the purity, freshness, simplicity, and ethics we wish to associate with our region.
2. To reflect the changes of the seasons in the meal we make.
3. To base our cooking on ingredients and produce characteristics which are particularly in our climates, landscapes and waters.

A signature dish of Noma "vegetable Field" reveals Redzepi's closeness to Bras but also to the ideas of kaiseki. This extreme regional cuisine, which combines unusual ingredients from the region to create new dishes, shares a clearly Japanese-inspired philosophy, which is already evident in the presentation of the dishes. Like Nouvelle Cuisine or elBulli, New Nordic cuisine has established a style that is now being implemented and varied worldwide. Something of Japan and thus something from the tea ceremony can now be observed around the globe in restaurants of Western high cuisine. The dishes show visual similarities to kaiseki dishes. They are small, carefully arranged seasonal and regional dishes served in various small bowls. Whether it's Ernst in Berlin, Septime in Paris, Attica in Melbourne or Central in Lima, you can already see the similar philosophy in these dishes. Even the supposedly classic French chef Alain Ducasse had been relying on the plant-based shojin cuisine to offer contemporary high cuisine with few animal products (Etcheverria, 2020, p. 107). The Basque restaurant Mugaritz serves over 20 courses and aims to appeal to all the senses and the intellect in order to trigger emotions. It is more connected to elBulli than to the New Nordic Cuisine, but the Japanese influence is also obvious (Mugaritz, 2021).

Eleven Madison Park in New York is consistently moving towards shojin cuisine. Chef Daniel Humm, known for his modern cuisine based on classic French luxury products such as foie gras, poultry or lobster, has been serving purely vegan cuisine since 2021 and has sought the advice of Toshio Tanahashi, a shojin chef (Begay, 2021). Tanahashi has already accompanied Ducasse in the transformation of his restaurant in 2014 (Etcheverria, 2020, p. 107).[1]

For most modern restaurants, the focus is not on the food alone, but on individual dishes and their presentation:

> The excellence of the cooking is almost beside the point at Osteria Francescana – and Eleven Madison Park, and Can Roca, and Noma. You expect it to be perfect, the way you expect an opera orchestra to be impeccably rehearsed, but its most important task is to propel the narrative dream. (Gold, 2018)

Thereby food is used as a medium to express something, just as food is used in kaiseki menus.

The philosophy of kaiseki also serves the longings of today's society: the contemplative nature of the tea ceremony and kaiseki form an antithesis to modern's faster, higher and further. At the same time, the traditional vegan cuisine of the shojin is a way to deal with resources in a more sustainable and conscious way. Responsibility, mindfulness – traditional values are becoming more important in a world that is in the process of becoming more sustainable. Restaurants see themselves as multipliers or simply as places that enable their guests to find peace: a meal as a contemplative act, comparable to a tea ceremony.

Tea as an ingredient, a technique, and a form of presentation

In addition to the fundamental philosophical influence of tea on European cuisine, tea also plays a role as an ingredient in Western cuisine. Nouvelle Cuisine has looked at various ingredients from around the world and combined them with regional products. The variety of teas can add aromatic accents to sweet or savoury dishes. The way of serving and the technique of steeping aromatic leaves in hot water has inspired dishes and enriched Western high cuisine.

This is seen with tea sorbet by Jean-Jacques Lacombe or Michel Guérard (see Besser, 1977, p. 239; Guérard, 1977, p. 300), as mousse with black tea by Eckart Witzig-

---

1 The Buddhist French chef Eric Ripert of New Yorks Le Bernadin invited Jeong Kwan, a cook who prepares temple cuisine at a Korean buddhist monastery to New York; her work was also covered by the Netflix series *Chef's Table* (Gordinier, 2015).

mann (Witzigmann, 1991/2004, pp. 108/109 and 176) or as egg cream with jasmine aroma by Ducasse (Ducasse, 2007, p. 212). Tea was also used in savoury dishes like by André Jaeger for a tea-smoked monkfish with Chinese cabbage salad (Willsberger, 2013, p. 123). Michel Bras used the regional "tea" Calamintha grandiflora for his iconic dish "Le Biscuit de Chocolat coulant aux arômes de cacao, sirop chocolaté au thé d'aubrac" to flavour the dessert by means of an infusion (see Bras, 1991, p. 162). In 2008 Ferran Adrià served a European "Matcha" tableside. Instead of using original green tea, the "tea" was prepared with a powder based on chervil (elbulli, 2021). Heston Blumenthal drew inspiration from tea for several dishes. "Nitro Poached Green Tea and Lime Mousse" is used as an appetising and refreshing intermediate course, using liquid nitrogen and matcha powder. "Hot and iced Tea" (Blumenthal, 2009, pp. 132 and 283) simultaneously serves cold and hot Earl Grey in one cup. Blumenthal, the Mad Hatter, invites us to a tea party where he challenges taste habits and at the same time brings British tea culture to the table. At Noma, Earl Grey already appears in the first cookbook. The tea is used to cook parsley root in it (Redzepi & Meyer, 2006, p. 97). In the 2010 cookbook, a recipe for "Spinach steamed in Tea" is presented, for which black tea is used (Redzepi, 2010, p. 119). Tea is not a regional ingredient in Denmark, but it is part of everyday culinary life. This is also evident in the dessert "Cloudberries from Pitea, burnt meringue and herbal tea", for which Earl Grey is used in addition to regional leaves and herbs (Redzepi, 2010, p. 263).

But tea is not only used as an ingredient in dishes. Some dishes have less to do with tea as an ingredient than with the way tea is served, like the recipes of Bras and Adrià already demonstrated. At Noma, a hot drink is served as a separate course as a welcome drink in winter or as an intermediate course as a tongue cleanser to prepare for further courses. A cup with a bag containing regional herbs and spices is served (Redzepi, 2013, p. 32). The presentation is reminiscent of the ordinary cup of tea at home but the unusual tableware, the tea bag on a sprig of lemon pine and the ingredients make it a unique Nordic tea experience. Daniel Humm serves his Clam Bake with a velouté in a teapot (Goldberg, 2017) and a light tomato essence is also presented in a teapot and poured at the table as "Tomato Tea with Parmesan Lavash and Lemon Thyme" (Mc Leod, 2013). Christian Jürgens uses a Cona coffee machine for his "Hong Kong Crayfish Tea" and brews a "tea" with flavours of Asia tableside (Sinzinger, 2015).

Tea for teetotallers

These are just a few examples of how tea is used in European high cuisine as an ingredient, a technique or as a form of presentation. Of course, tea is also used as a beverage, and not only for the aforementioned classic afternoon tea. If one does not want the classic espresso to round off the meal, not just any tea is served nowadays. Many restaurants offer a rich selection and a special service, making tea a highlight at the end of the meal. Alain Ducasse's Plaza Athenée (Miseviciute, 2015) or Heinz Reitba-uer's Steirereck have their own tea trolley (Hardin, 2017). In addition to special teas from all over the world, it is stocked with fresh herbs that are cut and brewed table-side. Sometimes in-house tea sommeliers, such as Christopher Day at Eleven Madison Park in New York, provide a selection of high-quality teas that are prepared and ex-plained at the table – as is common for wine (Chan, 2014).

This elaborated tea service is not limited to the end of the menu. Still rather new is the idea of serving tea as a beverage with food in Western high cuisine. Tea is an ideal beverage for a non-alcoholic menu accompaniment. For some restaurants, a pure tea accompaniment is a matter of course alongside wine, as is the case at Adeline Grattard's Yam' Tcha in Paris. At Tim Raue in Berlin, green tea was already used as a menu accompaniment for his Asian-inspired cuisine in 2009 (Seiser, 2009).

When tea is integrated into the non-alcoholic menu accompaniment, it is not nec-essarily served hot for this purpose, but possibly cold or at room temperature. Cups are then not the appropriate drinking vessel; instead wine glasses are used (Lockhart, 2019). Teas are used pure or as part of mixed drinks. Tea-based drinks such as kombu-cha also play an important role for varied enjoyment without alcohol. Especially for aperitifs with no or little alcohol, some producers such as "Copenhagen Sparkling Tea", "Ama Brewery" or "Viez und Töchter" rely on the complexity of fermented tea drinks for exciting alternatives to sparkling wines. The trend of accompanying food with non-alcoholic beverages is just gaining broader acceptance (Klauß, 2019) and tea seems to occupy an important position in this development.

Conclusion

This short overview shows that tea is more than a simple hot beverage in European culinary art. The potential offered by tea and tea culture is increasingly being seen, understood and used. For some chefs, this goes beyond an ingredient, an exciting bev-erage or certain rules for a menu. They are addressing the cultural significance of tea. These chefs are taking essential aspects of the tea ceremony and kaiseki and combin-ing this philosophy with their own culinary roots, resulting in a cuisine that unites global and regional aspects. Perhaps it will soon be self-evident to enjoy a plant-based cuisine with alcohol-free tea-based drinks? Thereby we return to the roots of Asian and European culinary culture, where a healthy way of life was combined with good taste, and enjoyment and well-being were understood as everyday needs – exactly what is true for a good cup of tea.

References

Begay, T. (2021). The Shojin Master On That Eleven Madison Park Menu, The Controversy Of Plant-Based & Why We Must Respect Plants. Restaurantrecs. Retrieved December 30, 2021, from https://restaurantrecs.com/the-shojin-master-on-that-eleven-madison-park-menu-the-controversy-of -plant-based-why-we-must-respect-plants.html.

Besser, K. (1977). *Die hundert besten Rezepte der großen Köche Europas*. Ullstein.

Blumenthal, H. (2009). *The fat duck cookbook*. Bloomsbury.

Bohne, H., & Jolliffe, L. (2021). Embracing tea culture in hotel experiences. *Journal of Gastronomy and Tourism*, 6(1–2), 13–24 (12).

Bras, M. (1991). *Le Livre de Michel Bras*. Rodez. Editions du Rouergue.

Brenner, L., & Busico, M. (2007, May 16). Eating the seasons. *Los Angeles Times*. https://www.latimes.com/ archives/la-xpm-2007-may-16-fo-kaiseki16-story.html.

Chan, K. (2014, December 3). How Eleven Madison Park, Brushstroke, and Atera Are Taking Tea to the Next Level. Eater New York. https://ny.eater.com/2014/12/3/7326909/eleven-madison-park-brushstroke-atera-tea-

Ducasse, A. (2007). *Der Ducasse: Die besten Rezepte vom Meisterkoch der französischen Küche*. Bassermann Verlag.

Elbulli. (2021a). Synthesis of elBulli cuisine. Retrieved December 30, 2021, from https://elbullifoundation. com/en/synthesis-of-elbulli-cuisine/.

Elbulli. (2021b). Chervil tea. Retrieved December 30, 2021, from http://elbulli.com/catalogo/catalogo/anyo. php?lang=en&anyo=2008&id=1487.

Etcheverria, O. (2020). *The restaurant, a geographical approach: From invention to gourmet tourist destinations*. ISTE / Wiley.

Gold, J. (2018, June 10). Jonathan Gold looks over the 2018 World's 50 Best Restaurants list and names some notable omissions. LA Times.

Goldberg, A. (2017, April 30). Eleven Madison Park. Retrieved December 30, 2021, from http://www.alife wortheating.com/posts/2017/eleven-madison-park.

Gordinier, J. (2015, October 16). Jeong Kwan, the philosopher chef. *New York Times*. https://www.nytimes. com/2015/10/16/t-magazine/jeong-kwan-the-philosopher-chef.html.

Guérard, M. (1977). *Die leichte große Küche*. Ullstein.

Hardin, J. (2017, April 13). Tea at 10 of the World's Best Restaurants. Retrieved December 30, 2021, from https://www.killgreen.io/main/tea-at-the-worlds-best-restaurants.

Härtig, M. (2016). *Einfachheit: Eine kulturphilosophische Untersuchung der japanischen Kaiseki-Küche*. Königshausen & Neumann.

Heller, A. (2002, December 1). *Zen oder die Kunst ein Ei zu kochen*. Neue Zürcher Zeitung. Retrieved December 30, 2021, from https://www.nzz.ch/folio/zen-oder-die-kunst-ein-ei-zu-kochen-ld.1618229.

Kirshenblatt-Gimblett, B. (2007). Making sense of food in performance: The table and the stage. In S. Banes & A. Lepecki (Eds.), *The Senses in Performance*. Routledge.

Klauß, N. (2019). *Die neue Trinkkultur: Speisen perfekt begleiten ohne Alkohol*. Piper.

Labro, C. (2014, October 23). L'escalope de saumon à l'oseille de la maison Troisgros. Retrieved December 30, 2021, from Le Monde. https://www.lemonde.fr/m-styles/article/2014/10/23/l-escalope-de-saumon-a-l-oseille-de-la-maison-troisgros_4510760_4497319.html.

Lockhart, K. (2019, September 9). The restaurants making tea pairing the new wine pairing. Robb Report. Retrieved December 30, 2021, from https://robbreport.com/food-drink/dining/tea-pairing-replacing-wine-pairing-fine-dining-2867969/.

Mc Leod, M. (2013, September 15). Eleven Madison Park. Mel Mc Leod Lifestyle and Travel Blogger. Retrieved December 30, 2021 from https://melmcleod.com/2013/09/15/eleven-madison-park/.

Mugaritz. (2021). Food? We love to feed our minds . . . Retrieved December 30, 2021, from https://www.mugaritz.com/en/food/co-9/.

Muhlke, C. (2009, February 10). Gargouillou: A new meaning to 'garden variety'. *New York Times*. https://www.nytimes.com/2009/02/11/dining/11gard.html.

Miseviciute, A. (2015, August 29). Alain Ducasse at Plaza Athénée. Luxeat https://www.luxeat.com/blog/alain-ducasse-plaza-athenee/.

Murata, Y. (2006). *Kaiseki: The exquisite cuisine of Kyoto's Kikunoi restaurant*. Kodansha.

Nordic Council. (2021). Retrieved December 30, 2021, from https://www.norden.org/en/information/new-nordic-food-manifesto.

Normore, C. (2015). *A feast for the eyes*. The University of Chicago Press.

Rath, E. C. (2013): Reevaluating Rikyū: Kaiseki and the origins of Japanese. *The Journal of Japanese Studies*, *39*(1), 67–96.

Redzepi, R. (2010). Noma. Time and Place in Nordic Cuisine. Phaidon.

Redzepi, R. (2013). *A work in progress*. Phaidon.

Redzepi, R., & Meyer, C. (2006). *Noma Nordisk Mad*. Politiken.

Seiser, K. (2009, March 27). Raue kocht Raue. Esskultur. https://www.esskultur.at/raue-kocht-raue-33/.

Tsuji, S. (1980/2012) *Japanese cooking: A simple art*. Kodansha.

Sinzinger, S. (2015, March 31). Signature dish: Christian Jürgens "Hongkong Crayfish Tea." https://steffen sinzinger.de/blog/2015/03/31/signature-dish-christian-juergens-hongkong-crayfish-tea/.

Spang, R. (2000). *The invention of the restaurant: Paris and modern gastronomic culture*. Harvard University Press.

Swinnerton, R. (2016, December, 13). When Rene Redzepi brought Noma to Japan. *The Japan Times*. https://www.japantimes.co.jp/life/2016/12/13/food/rene-redzepi-noma-japan/#.XJ3sVmaX-Rs.

Tsuchiya, Y. (1985). *A feast for the eyes*. Kondansha.

Willsberger, J. (2013). *Best of gourmet: Die große Zeit der neuen Kochkunst*. Umschau.

Witzigmann, E. (1991/2004). *Highlights*. Nikol.

Nicole Klauß

C.5 Tea in a bag – The history of the tea bag

A small bag of dried tea leaves that is soaked in hot water to make tea.
(Encyclopedia Brittanica, 2023)

Introduction

Teabags are the result of an obviously very widespread need: to be able to prepare tea in a convenient way, without scales, sieves or pots. Today, teabags can be found on almost every supermarket shelf: single-chamber tea bags, double-chamber tea bags, round tea bags or even tea bags in the shape of a pyramid. These are made of tasteless paper, but plastic fibres are also used.

Who actually invented the tea bag?

This question is answered almost unanimously in tea literature, on the websites of tea merchants and also in many scientific studies with the name of the New York tea merchant Thomas Sullivan, who sent his customers tea samples in small silk bags in 1908 in order to save shipping costs – the customers dipped the silk bags directly into the teapot without having to handle a teaspoon and strainer. The circumstances under which the tea bag was invented is a classic example of serendipity: Thomas Sullivan, tea merchant from New York is, nolens volens, the inventor of the tea bag. And because the story is so beautiful, one encounters Thomas Sullivan in most articles about tea. One reason for this is that the story fits in with other romanticised tea legends, such as the one about the discovery of tea. In China, the story goes that Emperor Shen Nong, who was born in 2700 BC, was walking through his garden, holding a cup of hot water. Then leaves of a tea tree fell into his cup and he enjoyed the vitalising and tasty infusion (Protheroe, 2016).

The legend of how tea became a drink is a similarly unplanned serendipitous discovery like how tea leaves found their way into the bag, with typical examples of serendipity. This describes the phenomenon of finding something that one was so explicitly not looking for. For example, the discovery of America by Christopher Columbus, who was actually looking for the sea route to India, or the attempt to develop a strong adhesive, when the adhesive did not stick properly and the removable adhesive of the Post-it was the result. The name for this phenomenon is derived from Serendip, the ancient Sanskrit name for Ceylon, now Sri Lanka, and it is there that the ancient saga of "The Three Princes of Serendip" is set. It tells of the three sons of King Jafer. They set out on

https://doi.org/10.1515/9783110758573-011

foreign journeys, often drawing curious conclusions from their experiences. After many adventures they return and all three become wise rulers (Meichsner, 2002).

The term serendipity was coined by the English writer Horace Walpole, the fourth Earl of Oxford, who wrote in a letter to the politician Horace Mann on January 28, 1754 that he possessed a special ability, namely to always find exactly the right thing when needed, and compared this with the events in the story "The Three Princes of Serendip." It was to be another 80 years before the word made a career for itself (Merton, 2004).

Thomas Sullivan went down in history as the inventor of the tea bag. In fact, however, it was Roberta C. Lawson and Mary Molaren of Milwaukee who, in 1901, well before Thomas Sullivan discovered the tea bag, developed a tea leaf holder which was patented on March 24, 1903 under patent number 723287 (Begley, 2015; see Figure C.5.1).

The advantages of the tea bag are obvious, as only enough of the tea leaves are used to make one cup and the bag holds the tea leaves together so that they do not get into the tea drinker's cup, while also being large enough for the leaves to unfold and extract the flavour of the tea. Their patent application stated, "To obviate this, our object in the present invention is to provide means whereby a small quantity of tea, so much only as is required for a single cup of tea, can be placed in a cup and have water poured thereon to produce only a cup of tea fresh for immediate use."

Regardless of the two discoveries of the tea bag, this invention was primarily for the purpose of preparing tea in a convenient way, without the need for other aids such as a pot, strainer, spoon or scales. Timothy D'Offay sums it up in his book *Easy Leaf Tea*: "The Tea Bag is a terrible invention for brewing tea but a brilliant piece of portion control" (D'Offey, 2017).

The company Ilola Tea from Vancouver meets the demand for easy portioning of whole leaf teas with their Tea Discs©: the tea leaves are pressed into small discs, and resemble Pur Erh tea, pressed into round bricks. However, the infusion must then be filtered. For this purpose, a so-called Tea Disc Infuser is offered. Oprah Winfrey's recommendation (Oprah's favourite things, 2022) has certainly benefited the distribution.

In the 1930s, several manufacturers were already experimenting with different shapes and materials. The materials used were cheesecloth, perforated paper or gauze. Paper fibre bags finally prevailed.

Various manufacturers quickly started working on different materials for tea bags. Some of the materials they worked with were similar to the gauze Sullivan then used, while others included cheesecloth and perforated paper. However, it was the paper fibre bags that became the most popular and well-known. Originally, these tea bags were sewn by hand. In the 1930s, machine production was added.

William Hermanson, a founding member of the Technical Papers Corporation in Boston, invented the heat-sealed paper fibre bag in 1930. This invention revolutionised the manufacture of tea bags, which had previously been sewn by hand. Hermanson, however, sold his patent to the Salada Tea Company in 1930, and by the end of the decade tea bags were being mass-produced in large numbers (Katevas, 2023).

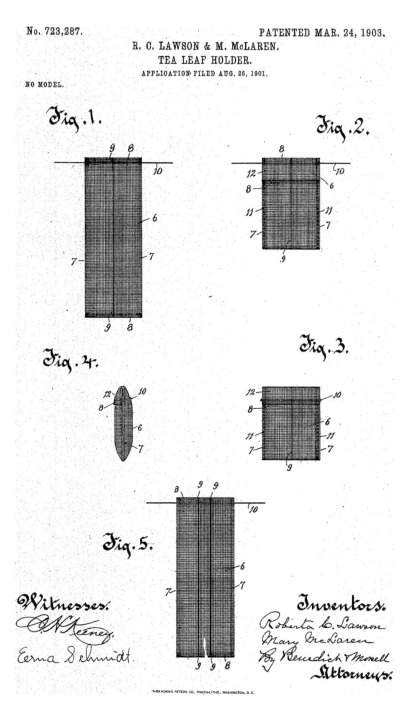

Figure C.5.1: Patent "Tea leaf holder" (1903).
Source: United States Patent Office (1903)

In 1931, William McKercher invented the CTC (Crush Tear Curl) process, which enabled tea leaves to be crushed into tiny particles. Tea bags could thus be filled more easily by tea companies and this processing technique revolutionised the production of black tea. The advantage of the granulate was that the brewing time could be significantly reduced. To this day, around 95% of black teas are processed in this way. Tea in most tea bags is Fannings or Dust, i.e. tea in its lowest quality grade, for which consumers pay around 30 EUR per kilo at the discounter, is purchased for a maximum of 5 EUR in India, according to Peter Rohrsen (Rohrsen, 2022; see Figure C.5.2).

Figure C.5.2: Timeline of Lipton Tea bags.
Source: Ekaterra (2024)
Note: Ekaterra was Unilever's tea business company, sold in 2022 to CVC Capital Partners, and rebranded to *Lipton Teas and Infusions* in 2023.

Adolf Rambold, an employee of the German company Teekanne, developed tea packing machines, and in 1949 applied for a patent for the "Constata – Teepackmaschine," which could produce 160 double-chamber bags per minute (Deutsches Patent- und Markenamt, 2021; see Figure C.5.3).

The idea of the double-chamber bag was to divide the tea portion into two equal halves, thus the water can flow through the tea faster, meaning the brewing time is shortened and the filter paper used is neutral in taste. The Constata was a machine that, driven by a motor, could fill, count,and pack the tea bags into boxes in a very small space. Rambold then founded Teepack Spezialmaschinen GmbH & Co KG, a subsidiary of the Teekanne company, in 1948. The Perfekta is the successor to the Constata and processes 420 bags per minute. The path of the tea granulate is as follows: the granulate falls through a funnel, is dosed, falls onto the filter paper, this paper is then cut, the double-chamber tea bag is then formed, the tea bag is folded in the middle, and finally is closed with an aluminium clamp (Rohrsen, 2022).

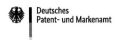 **Deutsches
Patent- und Markenamt**

Teebeutel

Adolf Rambold, Viersen 1944

Patentschrift Nr. 914 425

„Faltbeutel, insbesondere Aufgußbeutel"

Der Doppelkammer-Teebeutel, den sich Adolf Rambold 1944 patentieren ließ,
löste genähte Mullsäckchen und geklebte Papiertütchen ab, deren Aufguss kaum
Teearoma, aber viel Beigeschmack hatte. Dank einer speziellen Falttechnik wurde
aus einem rechteckigen Filterblatt ohne Kleber oder Klammern ein praktischer
und geschmacksneutraler Faltbeutel. Der Schlauchfalz (4) dient zugleich als
Verstärkung für die Halteklammer. Der Erfinder Rambold, der als Techniker
bei der Firma Teekanne beschäftigt war, entwickelte auch Hochleistungs-
maschinen, die hunderte Doppelkammer-Teebeutel pro Minute
produzieren und noch heute weltweit im Einsatz sind.

© Deutsches Patent- und Markenamt, München 2021

Figure C.5.3: Patent files Tea bag.
Source: Deutsches Patent – und Markenamt (2021)

The company cwTec GmbH from East Frisia in northern Germany developed an alternative to the metal closure of the tea bag for Teekanne: the knot aggregate, which was integrated into the tea packing machine, met customers' demands for more natural packaging and complete compostability (Maeck, 2014).

While Sullivan first used silk, then gauze, the producers later experimented with cotton and mixed materials. John Horniman, founder of Horniman's Tea Company, wanted to counteract the poor reputation of tea quality in tea bags in the first decade of the twentieth century by vouching with his name for the good quality of tea in his company's tea bags. He now used paper for the tea bags which were, however, sealed with glue which affected the taste of the tea. The bad reputation of tea in tea bags cannot be discarded even today; most people only know the often only moderate quality of tea in tea bags, which they put into hot water from the tap, boiled up several times (Le Compte & Bramah, 2005).

To this day, Teekanne processes tea bags from the abacá, which is a plant from the banana family. Its hard fibres, which can be up to two meters long, are dissolved in water and processed into a pulp. Besides tea bags, the albacá is also used to make cigarette paper, filters, and banknotes (Japan). Papers made from abacá fibre are fine-pored, tear-resistant, and neutral in taste.

In 1992, the English company Tetley brought round tea bags onto the market; these were suitable for large cups and also were without strings and paper tags. Tetley was instrumental in making round tea bags popular in the UK. This was a great success and over the years the British have embraced these bags very well. A survey conducted in 2020 found that Britons use 61 billion tea bags every year. As more people become concerned about our global plastic waste problem, tea bags that contain plastic are being used less and less. However, many of the mass-produced bags contain a thin layer of plastic to increase their strength when wet (Le Compte & Bramah, 2005).

Brooke Bond, the then parent company of PG Tips from England (PG Tips is now part of Ekaterra, which was renamed Lipton teas and infusions in 2023 (Bolton, 2023), launched the pyramid tea bag in 1997. These allow the tea leaves to unfold better and are particularly suitable for whole leaf teas and were also suitable for large cups and pots. Tea may expand three or four times its original volume so bigger space is needed for a good release of aromes (Erkens, 2022). While the pyramid tea bags were initially made of polypropylene, the development department worked on reducing the amount of plastic in the tea bags, which, with nine billion tea bags produced per year, is roughly equivalent to 60 million plastic bags or an area of 31,000 football fields (Jing Tea, 2021).

The poll by the London-based, single-origin tea brand found that the lockdowns from March 2020 have not only led to an increase in tea drinking in the UK, but that Brits are making more mindful decisions about their teas, with people choosing to drink more loose-leaf tea, which benefits both tea drinkers and the environment.

Plastic tea bags not only create more plastic waste, but also microplastics in tea. Tea leaves come into contact with plastics in two ways: firstly, tea leaves need to be protected from heat, moisture, light, and odours for transport; and secondly they are transported in polypropylene bags. The tea associations recommend either plywood boxes lined with aluminium foil or multilayer paper bags.

A study by Wuhan Polytechnic University from September 2022 analyzed the amount of microplastic from three commercial types of plastic tea bags. Microplastics were found in the brewed tea from 94% of the filter bags used, and in some cases the strings had plastic in them. The scientists concluded that pre-washing the teas is an effective way to reduce the uptake of microplastics. In comparison, using woven nylon filter bags to pack tea and coffee has a lower risk of releasing microplastics during steeping, and using plastic-free strings can largely avoid the release of microplastics.

An experiment with three different plastic tea filters showed no more microplastics in a solution of distilled water after washing five times, and that no microplastics could be detected on the surfaces of the tea bags even after the first wash (Wang, 2022).

They then heated the emptied teabags in water to simulate brewing tea. Using electron microscopy, the team found that a single plastic teabag at brewing temperature released about 11.6 billion microplastic and 3.1 billion nanoplastic particles into the water. These levels were thousands of times higher than those previously reported in other foods (Tufenkij, 2019).

The industry responded to customers' demands and worked on more sustainable plastic-reduced pyramid bags, first the pyramid bag, which consists of 80% compostable paper fibre and only 20% polypropylene, and since 2018 there are bags made of 100% compostable corn starch.

The Kräuterrebellen, tea producers from South Tyrol, go one step further and process the starch of genetically-free cultivated maize for their tea bags. Their tea pyramids are almost transparent and show the quality of the herbal infusions (Kräuterrebellen, 2023).

Länggasstee from Bern in Switzerland not only offer high quality teas, but also source most of their teas themselves and have been supplying the catering industry for a long time. They have tackled two problems at once: the predominantly poor quality of tea in tea bags and the difficulties that staff in the catering trade have with preparing loose leaf tea: brewing times, the amount of tea, and temperature – the right timing for tea is usually often a challenge in the daily routine of restaurants and cafés; training courses are usually provided by the large tea suppliers, but the turnover in the gastronomic businesses is high and the knowledge then leaves the company with the employees. In training, the topic of tea is covered, but rarely in depth, and more than the basic knowledge that there is black, green, and herbal infusion is rarely taught. For example, the often unfiltered water for green tea is often poured onto the tea (bag) at 100 degrees through the hot water nozzle of the portafilter machines and brewing times of five minutes or longer, because the teas are left at the dispenser even longer, are not uncommon. Most green teas then usually taste mediocre. Professionals only order black teas in cafés; they forgive longer brewing times and the teas are then still enjoyable with milk and sugar.

Katrin Lange (Länggasstee) states: *"At Länggasstee, we have therefore worked intensively on tea varieties that could be suitable for use in the catering industry and forgive any handling errors. We developed a tea bag without an exactly specified brewing time and brewing temperature. The idea behind this is that the choice of tea is the key to success; only high-quality tea that has been carefully processed can withstand less than optimal handling. Aiming to support the gastronomy and to serve the guest a good tea with the simplest handling, we focused on our idea to develop a tea bag without infusion time. The selection of the tea from hundreds of tea varieties is the decisive factor. If the tea is of high quality and carefully processed, it will tolerate improper treatment (too short or too long infusion time, too cold or too hot water) better. In addition, there are teas that are more suitable simply because of the way they develop their flavour (over time)."*

The tea selection process took almost two years, with hundreds of teas tasted and in the end 18 varieties remaining. It is a basic assortment of teas that are preferred in the hospitality industry, with all processing techniques and the main herbs represented.

The Sélection Grand Hotel assortment currently includes 11 teas, White Needle, Sencha, Long Jing, Tie Guan Yin, Earl Grey, Jasmine, Oolong, Qimen Haoya, Assam, Chai, and Pu Erh and seven herbal infusions, Edelweiss, Mint, Verveine, Rooibosh, Fruit infusion with Rose, Fruit with Mint and Hibiscus, and Ginger-Lemon (Länggass, 2023).

The tea bags of Länggass tea are made of fibres from sugar cane, the so-called bagasse, and are compostable. Bagasse is the fibrous residue that is mainly produced during the processing of sugar cane. In this process, the sugar cane is pressed out in mills after harvesting. The dry fibres that remain after the juice has been squeezed out are mixed with water and fine-meshed materials can then be made from this pulp.

There are no ribbons or labels either, and the tea bags are delivered in cardboard boxes made of pressed cardboard without any outer packaging. The herbal infusions all passed the critical practical test with tea experts with flying colours. Among the teas, only three of the teas are not so forgiving of grossly improper treatment with infusion times of over six minutes. It seems that the classic preparation of tea leaves is too complicated even for tea bags in these fast times: alternatives to tea bags are tea balls (Teaballs, 2023) or tea as cubes (Waterdrop, 2023). Tea leaves are ground into powder, pressed into shape, and dissolved in hot water like an effervescent tablet.

Even matcha is not spared the desire for quick and easy tea enjoyment without equipment. Instead of being whipped with a chasen in a bowl, freeze-dried matcha is now pressed into cubes and can thus, convenience at its best, be added to hot milk.

Tea connoisseurs use tea cigars from Kaley Tea in Sri Lanka. Here, the tea bag 2.0 is made by hand: the Tea Cigars. Leaves of green or black tea are tied into a bundle with a thread on one side and put into the glass as a natural tea bag (Kaley, 2022).

In any case, the invention of the tea bag has one good thing for research in the field of soil quality: with the tea bag index, scientists detect the activity of microorganisms in the soil, so it can be found out how quickly organisms living in the soil break down plant residues. To do this, plant material, for example tea, the contents of which are precisely weighed, is put into a tea bag, and this bag is sealed and buried in the soil for three months. The tea leaves decompose and after three months the contents of the bags are weighed again. The difference in weight between the starting weight and the final weight is calculated by the TBI: the tea bag index. The lower the TBI, the higher the biological activity in the soil (Keuskamp, 2013).

Conclusion

Tea bag producers act flexibly to the needs and wishes of the customers for quality in the tea bag: the abandonment of adhesives and aluminium clips, the enlargement of the tea bags with the double chamber bag, the pyramid bag or the change to compostable tea bags. The development of tea bags has come a long way over the years. Today, they continue to serve their purpose of providing a convenient way to drink tea. In addition to drinking, people also use tea bags to treat dark circles under their eyes, to absorb odours, and to soothe sunburns. In addition, it is a convenient and easy option for the hospitality industry to offer a large variety of teas and infusions without a big stock of loose teas. The guests meanwhile got used to this type of presentation and the question for loose tea is becoming a symbol of exclusivity or a wider expertise of tea.

References

Bolton, D. (2023, January 13). Ekaterra Rebrands as LIPTON Teas and Infusions. Retrieved March 5, 2023, from https://tea-biz.com/2023/01/13/ekaterra-rebrands-as-lipton-teas-and-infusions/.

Deutsches Patent- und Markenamt. (2021). Postergalerie: Teebeutel, Adolf Rambold, Viersen 1944, Patentschrift Nr. 914 425 "Faltbeutel, insbesondere Aufgußbeutel". Retrieved July 19, 2023, from https://www.dpma.de/docs/postergalerieneu/25_teebeutel.pdf.

D'Offey, T. (2017). *Easy leaf tea*. Ryland Peters.

Ekaterra (2024). *Lipton's tea bags – a historical overview*. Ekaterra Group.

Encyclopedia Brittanica. (2023). Tea-bag. Retrieved February 20, 2023, from https://www.britannica.com/dictionary/tea-bag.

Erkens, M. (2022). *Tea wine's sober sibling*. Terra.

Harisson, B. (2018, December 8). Design moment: Tea bag, 1901. https://www.irishtimes.com/life-and-style/homes-and-property/fine-art-antiques/design-moment-tea-bag-1901-1.3720851.

Jing Tea. (2021). Thirst for better tasting & sustainable tea drives change in tea habits. Retrieved February 20, 2023, from https://jingtea.com/journal/taste-and-sustainability-driving-change-in-uk-tea-habits.

Kaley Tea. (2022). Tea cigars. Retrieved February 15, 2023, from https://kaleytea.com/product/black-tea-cigar/.

Katevas, C. (2023, March 20). Tea bags: their history. Retrieved March 5, 2023, from https://tea.gr/en/tea-bags-their-history/63.

Keuskamp, J., et al. (2013). Tea Bag Index: a novel approach to collect uniform decomposition data across ecosystems. Retrieved February 23, 2023, from https://besjournals.onlinelibrary.wiley.com/doi/full/10.1111/2041-210X.12097.

Kräuterrebellen. (2023). Retrieved February 20, 2023, from https://rebellen.it/de/gastro.

Länggass. (n.d.). Sélection Grand Hotel – Premium tea line combining tea culture and comfort ieved February 20, 2023, from https://www.laenggasstee.ch/index.php?menuid=48&getlang=en.

Le Compte, C., and E. Bramah. (2005). *The bramah tea and coffee walk around London: A guided tour of 400 years of tea and coffee history around the city and Southwark*. Christian le Comte.

Maeck, S. (2014). *Meßmer- Vom Zauber einer Weltmarke*. Wachholtz Publishers.

Meichsner, B. (2002). Drei Prinzen aus Serendip. Retrieved February 27, 2023, from https://www.forschung-frankfurt.uni-frankfurt.de/36050189/serendip_93.pdf.

Merton, R., & Barber, E. (2004). *The travels and adventures of serendipity: A study in sociological semantics and the sociology of science*. Princeton University Press.

Nagy, K. (2017). The history of the tea bag. Retrieved February 25, 2023, from https://tea-shirt.co.uk/blogs/news/history-of-the-teabag.

Okafor, J. (2022). The history of tea bags from invention through popularity. Retrieved February 23, 2023, from https://www.trvst.world/sustainable-living/eco-friendly/history-of-tea-bags.

Protheroe, S. (2016). Just your cup of tea: the history (and health claims) of the nation's favourite brew. Retrieved February 23, 2023, from https://www.cam.ac.uk/research/discussion/just-your-cup-of-tea-the-history-and-health-claims-of-the-nations-favourite-brew.

Rohrsen, P. (2022). *Das Buch zum Tee. Sorten – Kulturen – Handel*. C.H. Beck Verlag.

Tea and coffee.net. (2021). New survey reveals increase in loose-leaf tea consumption in UK during lockdowns. Retrieved February 20, 2023, from https://www.teaandcoffee.net/blog/26250/new-survey-reveals-increase-in-loose-leaf-tea-consumption-in-uk-during-lockdowns/.

Teaballs. (2023). The tea without bags. Retrieved from February 20, 2023, from https://en.teaballs.eu/.

Tufenkij, N. (2019). Some plastic with your tea? Retrieved February 23, 2023, from https://www.mcgill.ca/newsroom/channels/news/some-plastic-your-tea-300919.

United States Patent Office. (1903). *Patent tea-leaf holder*. Specification forming part of Letters Patent No. 723, 287, dated March 24, 1903. Retrieved July 20, 2023, from https://patents.google.com/patent/US723287A/en#citedBy.

Wagner-Langer, T., et al. (2019). *Gong Fu Cha: Tee als Handwerkskunst und das bewusste Genießen*. AT Verlag.

Wang, J., et al. (2022): Identification and evaluation of microplastics from tea filter bags based on raman imaging. Retrieved February 20, 2023, https://www.ncbi.nlm.nih.gov/pmc/articles/PMC9497986/.

Waterdrop. (2023). Hot hydration. Made Simple. Retrieved February 20, 2023, from https://en.waterdrop.com/collections/microtea.

D Presenting tea in style

Honouring tea means to use also proper teaware, porcelain or glass, cups, mugs and tea-pots or vessels, but also spirit kettles and samovars – all this is showing pride and wealth underlining the valuable function of tea in a private, social or business context.

Petra Werner
D.1 The historic development of tea pots

Introduction

After the discovery of sea routes, tea was brought to Europe by the Portuguese, Dutch and English. The decisive role was played by the Dutch East India Trading Company, founded in 1602. It delivered tea in large quantities from Asia to Holland. Closely related to the tea trade was the business with Chinese porcelain (Sandgruber & Kühnel, 1994).

Europe enthusiastically embraced everything that had an exotic origin. The first teahouses were built in the big cities around 1680, and Chinese fashion conquered almost all the princely courts. Initially valued as a curiosity, Asian porcelain became a prized luxury item from the middle of the seventeenth century. Collecting it was part of the lifestyle of the European nobility and the monarchs created precious collections. The porcelain treasures were set up and presented on consoles in specially equipped rooms, the porcelain cabinets. The most famous and important porcelain collection in the West was established in Dresden by Augustus the Strong (1670–1733), King of Poland and Elector of Saxony.

With the decline of courtly culture and the slow rise of bourgeois society in the second half of the eighteenth century, porcelain fever also took hold of the small landed gentry and the wealthy middle classes. From now on, porcelain collecting and tea drinking were an integral part of the wealthy bourgeois circles. From the twentieth century onwards, porcelain finally became the ideal commodity for everyone. Likewise, tea consumption rose steadily.

Vessels for tea culture

Various utensils were necessary for the storage, preparation, and enjoyment of tea. In China and Japan, certain types of vessels had developed, such as the pot, cup, and tin, which were then imported from the Far East. In the long run, however, the vessel forms were no longer sufficient for the Europeans. Porcelain products were ordered and made in China specifically for European tastes.

In Europe in the seventeenth century, the individual parts of a tea set were still different in shape, material, and decoration.

It was not until after the founding of the first porcelain manufactory in Europe, in Meissen in 1710, that drinking utensils for coffee and tea were produced in porcelain on a significant scale. From the middle of the eighteenth century, almost all German sovereigns established porcelain manufactories and produced service pieces for

https://doi.org/10.1515/9783110758573-012

the preparation and drinking of the exotic hot beverages. The private company foundations in Thuringia followed this trend.

No other material is more suitable for the vessels than porcelain. It is as exotic as it is precious. And although it is very thin and fragile, porcelain can withstand hot liquids. In addition, it does not conduct heat as much as metal and is tasteless. Vessels for hot beverages eventually accounted for a considerable portion of the companies' total porcelain products.

As a sample, the manufacturers used both the Chinese porcelains and the goldsmith's work. The teapots were initially mostly small, low, and bulbous with a low-set spout. This design prevented the sinking aromatic substances from being lost.

For larger tea parties, which became more and more common in the second half of the eighteenth century, larger teapots were required.

The oldest form of cup, the handle-less tea Koppchen in a hemispherical design, also has its origins in Chinese porcelain. The East Asians sip hot tea from these small bowls, which still exist today and are common in Germany under the Dutch name Koppchen.

Until about 1730, teacups had the same shape as coffee cups. Only then did the teacup evolve into a wider bowl and the coffee cup acquire a steeper wall.

The handle on the cup and the saucer are an addition or ingredient that European customs required. The handle (Schiedlausky, 1988) was to protect the drinker from the heat of the drink. To cool down the hot drink, the tea was tipped into the saucer and then drunk from it. Therefore, the saucers were often quite deep in their design. This widespread custom was by no means against good manners in Germany until the end of the eighteenth century. In some areas, this custom even persisted into the early twentieth century (Mielke, 1988). Gradually, however, the original meanings fell into oblivion. The cup with handle and saucer were part of the coffee or tea ritual. The saucers now served as a tray for the spoon and protected the tablecloth from coffee and tea stains.

The tea was prepared either in the pots or in the cups.

So-called Kummen speak of a tea preparation at the beginning of the eighteenth century in the Koppchen. The loose tea leaves were placed in the koppchen and hot water was poured over them. Before the next infusion, they were rinsed in a bowl, the kumm, to remove any tea leaves left behind. This rinsing bowl had a deep shape and was essential for a complete service. During the nineteenth century, cumbers increasingly disappeared from the porcelain manufacturers' assortments. At the latest, after the invention of infusion bags at the beginning of the twentieth century by the New York tea merchant Thomas Sullivan, they were finally superfluous (Sandgruber & Kühnerl, 1994).

The loose tea leaves were stored in tea caddies, which in Germany were also modeled after Chinese caddies. They usually have an angular shape and a narrow, short opening at the top.

After tea, originally a medicine and luxury food for the upper classes, became steadily cheaper in Europe in the nineteenth century, it advanced in Germany, England, and many other countries to become the popular drink for every time of day. As a result, not only the teapots but also the teacups became larger (Vollers, 1985).

At the same time, the inexpensive production of porcelain by the factories created the possibility of using the industrially produced mass product in gastronomy.

Over time, the stylistic design of the individual service parts changed, but the types of vessels have partly survived to the present day.

Components of tea set

The composition of the service also remained. From the eighteenth century, the manufactories developed suitable arrangements for every occasion. The déjeuner or tête-à-tête was designed for two people with a coffee or tea pot, cream pourer, sugar bowl, and two cups and saucers. The solitaire, the breakfast service, served for drinking in private seclusion, consisted of an appropriately scaled-down pitcher and a cup and saucer. In both sets, the individual service pieces were placed on a platter.

A larger party required a complete set of teapots, cream pourer, sugar bowl, at least six tea bowls with saucers, and a kumm. The teapot was larger, as the previous forms were much too small in volume for these tea parties. Since cakes and pies were served, plates were also part of the service. A special feature is the lidded cup, which can be found today in the assortment of various porcelain companies. It is used especially for drinking green tea or Oolong. Since both types of tea are infused with hot water rather than boiling water, the lid prevents the tea from cooling quickly.

The tea set – shapes and decorations

As already mentioned, the basic shapes of tea vessels have not changed much over the centuries, but the details, handles, lids, lid knobs and spouts, and especially the proportions and decoration, have.

The design of porcelain was influenced by the fashion of the time. Already in the second half of the eighteenth century, the range of shapes and decorations in the manufactories was extremely rich. The individual tea service pieces in baroque design and playful rococo manner were decorated with flowers, birds, landscapes, gallant scenes, and other subjects.

A wide variety of influences in the design and decoration can be seen in the service from the nineteenth century. There were no limits to the imagination and the results were not only squat-bellied vessels with lids, handles and spouts, and bowl-shaped cups; there were also service creations, which were completely based on na-

Figure D.1.1: Teapot and cup in tomato shape.
Note: Teapot and cup in tomato shape, manufacturer Sontag & Söhne, Tettau, around 1880,
Porzellanikon, permanent loan Seltmann, Weiden
© Porzellanikon – State Museum of Porcelain Selb /Hohenberg a.d. Eger
Source: Thomas Meyerhöfer

ture. Presumably, these pieces, e.g., service pieces in the shape of tomatoes, were hardly ever used, but were rather displayed as collector's items in the showcase (see Figure D.1.1).

Towards the end of the nineteenth century, it was vogue to converse and drink tea in the course halls of seaside resorts and on the terraces of grand hotels. Following the taste of the time at the end of the century, the porcelains had body shapes in the style of the Third Rococo, which came back to full bloom from about 1870. The tea service pieces captivated with their varied knob and handle shapes, and round, angular-broken or richly intertwined variants. They were a reflection of the social conventions of the time.

In private households, blue decorations such as the onion pattern, which was developed in the Meissen manufactory as early as 1730 and subsequently imitated by many porcelain manufacturers, also enjoyed particular popularity (see Figure D.1.2).

The conservative, bourgeois social class usually preferred historicising forms and decorations. They liked to take possession of aristocratic lifestyle goods and thus expressed their desire for representation. In order to satisfy the wishes of this clientele, the companies continued to offer traditional services. However, they also reacted to new fashions and produced tableware for a clientele that was open to new things.

Around the turn of the century, porcelain companies consciously turned away from the models and patterns they had previously imitated. Art Nouveau, which reached its peak at the World's Fair in Paris in 1900, made its way into service design. New vessel silhouettes and modern decorations determined the appearance from now on. The initially organic-vegetable shapes and floral patterns were increasingly replaced by geometric designs. The artists of the Darmstadt Artists' Colony and the studio of the Vereinte Kunstgewerbler Darmstadt (United Arts and Craftsmen Darm-

Figure D.1.2: Tea service pieces form 29.
Note: Tea service pieces form 29, manufacturer Lorenz Hutschenreuther, Selb, around 1870/75,
Porzellanikon, stock Hutschenreuther archive, permanent loan of the Upper Franconia Foundation,
Bayreuth
© Porzellanikon – State Museum of Porcelain Selb /Hohenberg a.d. Eger,
Source: Thomas Meyerhöfer

stadt), which was founded in 1902, played a significant role in the development of this style. Among them was Hans Günther Reinstein, who created the Botticelli service form for the Rosenthal company in Selb. This is characterised by a taut design, with the decoration of the standing hearts, a rarely achieved unity of form and decoration. The tea service was used in private households as well as in the catering trade (see Figure D.1.3).

Figure D.1.3: Botticelli tea service pieces.
Note: Botticelli tea service pieces, design by Hans Günther Reinstein, 1903, manufacturer Philipp
Rosenthal & Co. AG, Selb, Porzellanikon, Rosenthal Archive collection, on permanent loan from the Upper
Franconia Foundation, Bayreuth
© Porzellanikon – State Museum of Porcelain Selb /Hohenberg a.d. Eger
Source: Thomas Meyerhöfer

For the catering industry, porcelain also plays a not insignificant role as an advertising medium. Vignettes and advertising imprints on the dishes keep the name of the café or restaurant permanently in front of the guest's eyes. The service thus becomes the business card of the establishment (Träger, 1996).

The Bauscher brothers in Weiden had already recognised this need at the end of the nineteenth century and specialised in the production of hotel and restaurant porcelain in their porcelain factory. A teapot and a milk jug, for example, display emblems of the Gibson Hotel in Cincinnati and of a hotel in Davenport, respectively. The design also features outstanding functional properties. The handles on this teapot and milk jug were placed on the side and not opposite the spout as is usually the case. This design has the advantage that the thumb can be placed on the lid when pouring the tea. At the same time, this holds the lid in place. This type of design reveals the influence of Japan, where side handle teapots, called yokode kyusu, are used for making tea (see Figure D.1.4).

Figure D.1.4: Tea service parts for hotel, Gebr. Bauscher AG.
Note: Tea service parts for hotel, Gebr. Bauscher AG, Weiden, molding 1914, Porzellanikon, inv. no. 23855/12
© Porzellanikon – State Museum of Porcelain Selb /Hohenberg a.d. Eger
Source: Thomas Meyerhöfer

From 1914 onwards, the development of new service forms had to be cut back or completely stopped by porcelain producers, as the outbreak of the First World War brought shortages of personnel, raw materials, and coal.

Even after the end of the war in 1918, there was initially little that was new in tableware production. Well-tried service in historicising style was produced and sold (Werner, 1992). These were still in demand among customers. It was only in the course of the 1920s that new tableware shapes and decorations emerged in keeping with the spirit of the Golden Twenties. Everything that looked exotic was extremely popular. Imitations of Japanese motifs and depictions associated with Asia adorned countless porcelain items, especially tea sets (Werner, as cited in Eger and Selb, 2014). It was not uncommon for porcelain companies to use foreign scenes in their advertisements (see Figure D.1.5).

Figure D.1.5: Advertisement of porcelain factory Heinrich & Co. (1927).
Source: Die Schaulade (1927)

In the 1920s, the Rosenthal porcelain factory included a teapot with an unusual shape in its production programme in Kronach. The so-called Sparteekanne, made of fireproof porcelain, could be placed on the table in the supine position with the spout facing upwards. A small compartment was provided for the tea leaves. Boiling water was then poured over them and then the lid was put on. After the tea had steeped sufficiently, the pot was placed. This method of preparation had special advantages. The tea could be brewed several times and, since it did not come into contact with any metal, it retained its natural flavour (Neiseke, 2005; see Figure D.1.6).

Figure D.1.6: Advertising leaflet Sparteekanne, Porzellanfabrik Rosenthal & Co. AG.
Note: Advertising leaflet Sparteekanne, Porzellanfabrik Rosenthal & Co. AG, Kronach, around 1930

Other designers had already been trying since the mid-1920s to help a contemporary, functional design achieve a breakthrough. The focus was clearly on function. Utility porcelains were developed that had an absolutely clear form. Superfluous, ornamental accessories were omitted. The tableware was suitable for machine production and at the same time inexpensive to manufacture. The Arzberg porcelain company made a clear commitment to this industrial design at the beginning of the 1930s. It presented the 1382 service form at the 1931 Leipzig Autumn Fair. The Stuttgart architect and later Werkbund director Hermann Gretsch had designed the shape. This mass-produced dinnerware, whose no-frills vessels were based on the spherical shape, could be purchased inexpensively and individually as needed, which made it easier to buy in times of economic crisis. Until 1947, there was only a bulbous half-height cup size to be used for coffee and tea. Only then was the service expanded to include a tall cup shape. Since then, the former universal cup has served as a teacup. To this day, 1382 is considered the German series dinnerware of good form par excellence and the tea service is still very popular (see Figure D.1.7).

Until the end of the Second World War and even in the first post-war years, the services hardly differed from those of the 1930s. Plain, unadorned, simple forms were offered in the porcelain manufacturers' assortments, just as much as those that showed a recourse to baroque and rococo forms.

With the economic upswing in the Federal Republic of Germany, purchasing power increased and prosperity moved into households. As a result, porcelain was no longer just a commodity, but once again became a cultural asset.

The services were mostly available as complete table settings, i.e., coffee, tea, and dinner services. The tea and coffee services had the same design. Only the sizes of the individual service pieces varied. The palette of decorations ranged from gold rims and simple surface decorations to flowers and grasses.

Figure D.1.7: Jug wall with the shape 1382.
Note: Jug wall with the shape 1382 from Arzberg in the permanent exhibition at Porzellanikon –
Staatliches Museum für Porzellan, Hohenberg a.d. Eger
© Porzellanikon – State Museum of Porcelain Selb /Hohenberg a.d. Eger
Source: Andreas Gießler

Since the 1960s, there has also been a noticeable trend towards pure tea service. Companies are increasingly including services in their programme that were explicitly designed by the designers only for the hot beverage tea.

Examples can be found in countless manufacturers. A special role may be attributed to the Rosenthal company, which has collaborated with a large number of international artists and designers and has launched extraordinary models alongside its traditional line. Tea service designs such as "Tea for Two" from 1964, "Assam" (1968), "TAC I" (1969), "Drop" (1971) (Fritz, 1989), "Hommage à Darmstadt" (1989) or "Cha" (2015) reveal the most diverse influences. In their design, they could hardly be more different. For commercial reasons, such contrasts are nothing unusual. The Arzberg company also had a lot to offer, as evidenced by excellent services such as "Teaworld" (1984) or "Tea for one" (1987) (Siemen, 1987; Fritz, 1998).

The growing interest in modern tea culture led producers to offer more and more new commodities.

The classic tea set, consisting of a teapot, milk jug, sugar bowl, cups, and saucers, can still be found in the sales offers of manufacturers. However, there are also sets reduced to a few pieces. Königliche Porzellan-Manufaktur Berlin, for example, offers products with a glossy glazed top and matte underside made of bisque porcelain, combining functional laboratory aesthetics and Far Eastern tea culture. The LAB series tea set for the minimalist tea ceremony consists of the LAB teapot with a side handle, an integrated, particularly fine-mesh stainless steel strainer, an oak wood board and mug, and an Oolong tea (KPM, 2023).

Summary

Tea, once a luxury good, is now the most consumed beverage on earth alongside water. In Germany, too, tea consumption is growing steadily. Tea is drunk on all occasions, whether outside the home or in private. There is no special "teatime." Restaurants offer an extensive tea menu and in cafés the guest gets a lot of quality teas. In tea stores and even in supermarkets, the customer can find, in addition to the classic tea bag, various loose teas and pyramid-shaped tea bags for the high-quality leaf teas. Tea culture from around the world and tea ceremonies interest many consumers.

This development has not escaped the attention of porcelain producers. They are responding with modern tea service designs and combinations, whether for the catering trade, private drinking pleasure or for the office.

References

Advertising booklet Hommage à Gropius. Rosenthal.
Advertising booklet Über die Kunst (1983). *Tee und Mokka zu trinken*. Rosenthal.
Becher, U. (1990). *Geschichte des modernen Lebensstils. Eating, Living, Leisure, Travel*. C.H. Beck.
Bedford, J. (1964). *Talking about teapots; and thus about porcelain, pottery, silver, Sheffield plate, etc.*
Dexel, T. Equipment for tea and coffee. Work reports from the Städtisches Museum Braunschweig.
Die Schaulade, 3 (1927), Heft 10, Verlagshaus Meisenbach & Co., p. 506.
Fritz, B. (1979). *The porcelain dishes of the Rosenthal Group 1891–1979*. Union-Verlag.
Fritz, B. (1995). *Utility porcelain of the 20th century*. Klinkhardt und Biermann.
Fritz, B. (1998). *The tea service tac 1 by Walter Gropius*. Verlag form.
Funke, N. (2010). Kaffee- und Teegeschirre der Manufaktur Wallendorf im 18. Jahrhundert. In
    Porzellanland Thüringen. 250 years of porcelain from Thuringia, Museumsverband Thüringen e.V.
Garth, C. (1989). *The crazy teapot*. Heyne.
Gaylard, L. (2015). *The tea book*. DK Publishers.
Goss, S. (2005). *British tea and coffee cups 1745–1940*. Reprint, Shire Library.
KPM Königlich Preussische Porzellanmanufaktur. (2023). The LAB tea-set white. Retrieved July 20, 2023,
    from https://en.kpm-berlin.com/products/lab-tea-set?variant=42310324813982.
Krueger, T., and Urban, A. (2010). The hot 3. 300 years of coffee, tea and chocolate in Northern Germany,
    Schriften des Historischen Museums Hannover, Vol. 37.
Mergenthaler, M. (2013). *Teewege. History, culture, enjoyment*. J. H. Röll Verlag.
Mielke, H.P. (1988). *Coffee, tea, cocoa*. Verlag Müsers.
Morel, A. (2001). *The laid table*. Verlag Hier und Jetzt.

Neiseke, A. (2005). Coffee maker and division pot made of fireproof porcelain, Rosenthal porcelain.

Renovanz, P. (1957). *Tee, Seide, Porzellan*. Brockhaus Verlag.

S.K. (1991). A fragile treasure for the 5 o'clock tea. In: *Essen und Trinken in alter Zeit, Mainfränkisches Museum Würzburg*, pp. 95–97.

Sandgruber, R., & Kühnel, H. (1994). Genuss & kunst. Coffee, tea, chocolate, tobacco, cola. Innsbruck (Catalog of the NÖ Landesmuseum, New Series No. 341).

Schiedlausky, G. (1961). *Tea, coffee, chocolate*. Prestel Verlag.

Siemen, W. (1987). 100 Years of the Arzberg Porcelain Factory 1887–1987. *Publications and Catalogs of the Museum of the German Porcelain Industry, 9*. Hohenberg/Eger.

Stahlbusch, T.A. (2009). *Weißes Gold aus Meißen. Service and tableware*. Battenberg-Gietl-Verlag.

Teekanne GmbH. (2007). *Teekanne has been making tea for 125 years*. Teekanne.

Träger, S. (1996). Around the world in 80 cups. Gastlichkeit und Porzellan – ein Beitrag zur Geschichte des Porzellans für die Gastronomie vom Ende des 19. *Jahrhunderts bis in die Gegenwart, Schriften und Kataloge des Deutschen Porzellanmuseums, 46*. Hohenberg/Eger.

Viehoff-Heithorn, T. (2012). Tea – from luxury drink to mass product – and back again. In *Zum Wohl! Getränke zwischen Kultur und Konsum*, catalog for the exhibition of the LWL-Industriemuseum. Essen.

Vollers, A. (1985). *Tea and porcelain. Two treasures from the Middle Kingdom*. Bremen.

Werner, P. (1992). The twenties. German Porcelain between Inflation and Depression –The Time of Art Deco?! *Publications and Catalogs of the Museum of the German Porcelain Industry, 30*. Hohenberg/Eger.

Werner, P. (2014). "Golden Times"? Between Inflation and World Economic Crisis 1918–1933. In *Exhibition Catalog Porcelain for the World*. 200 Jahre Porzellan der bayerischen Fabriken, Volume I, Schriften und Kataloge des Porzellanikons, Vol. 113. Hohenberg a.d. Eger / Selb.

Zischka, U., Ottomeyer, H., & Bäumler, S. (1994). *Die anständige Lust*. Edition Spangenberg bei Droemer.

Lyudmila Britenkova* and Hartwig Bohne

D.2 Tea on stand: Samovars and spirit kettles

Introduction

Mostly in the nineteenth century, teapots made from different types of metal symbolised the pride and wealth of households. Teapots from copper or messing as well as from silver were used to be placed on tea tables in order to heat the freshly brewed tea or only the hot water. In addition, producers of metal represented this trend at the tea occasions and in the tea gardens and at home, where most of the people were drinking their tea in nicely decorated rooms. The atmosphere and the style of tea sets signalised the meaning of tea for the daily routine but also as a symbol of hospitality (Belge, 2023; Carver Wees, 1997).

Technically, the teapots were heated by an oil-based heater (spirit kettle on stand) and placed on a tray. In addition, the specially designed teapot warmer was created to make the tea experience more comfortable. Therefore, it was not necessary to take the teapot from the warmer, but only to push the teapot slightly to pour the tea into the tea cup placed under the hanging teapot. For some of the tea pots, the milk and sugar pots were produced from the same material in order to have a basic set of tea utensils (Rothermund, 2004; Pettigrew, 2003; Scarce, 2003).

Samovars and the origins of the craft at XVIII century Urals

The Russian samovar is a unique phenomenon deeply rooted in the development of the Russian history, life and the culture of tea drinking. In a fairly short time, the samovar became integral to any Russian life that not a single-family event or reception took place without. Whether in the capital or in the provinces, practically every family had "miracle water heaters." (Takako, 2018)

The first samovars in Russia appeared in the Urals, the largest metallurgical cluster where they also made huge quantities of copper dishes starting from the 1830s. The manufacture of copper dishes became the origins of the samovar. However, the earliest documented evidence of the Russian samovar remained at the Verkhne-Irginsky plant of the Osokins. The report from Yekaterinburg city customs of February 7, 1740 listed the goods seized from people traveling from the Verkhne-Irginsky plant. Among others,

*Lyudmila Britenkova (curator) and the entire team of the Museum of Samovars and Bouillottes, Private Collection of Mikhail Borshchev/Grumant, developed this chapter in order to show the variety of samovars and spirit kettles as well as the heritage and innovative engery of handicraft in this field.

https://doi.org/10.1515/9783110758573-013

there was "a copper samovar with an instrument, tin-plated, 16 pounds of weight of own manufacture." The Irginsky plant was founded by two cousins, Peter and Gavrila Osokin, from the town of Balakhna, in the Nizhny Novgorod province. In September 1738, the Irginsky plant began making tableware for sale at the markets, upon obtaining the applicable permits from the regional administration. They began with the most popular items, cauldrons and pipes, and then the craftsmen came up with the idea to connect a boiler to a pipe and thus make a portable boiler that would heat up by itself, without a stove or a boiler. The first Russian samovar thus appeared between September 1738 and February 1740. In 1741, one of the Osokins merchants' clerks was hired by Akinfiy Demidov's plant, to work for Osokin's main competitor, and could have possibly passed on the production technology for this new product: from that very moment samovar-making immediately began at Demidov's factory in Suksun (Korepanov, 1700–1950); (Belge, 2023; Schütz, 1986; Yoder, 2009).

Figure D.2.1: Travel-Size Samovar Sunduchok, or the Chest by the Demidov's Factory.
Source: Urals, mid- century, Museum of Samovars and Bouillottes, Private collection of Mikhail Borshchev/Grumant

By the middle of the eighteenth century samovar- and coffee pot-making took an important place in the metalwork industry of the country. Samovars were made in the Urals (Suksunskiy and Nizhne-Tagilskiy Demidovskiy factories), in Moscow (Alexander Shmakov's factory), Perm province (Troitskiy Zavod by Turchaninov), while Yaroslavl, Arkhangelsk and Tula joined a bit later. By 1812 the largest samovar-making enterprise was the plant of Peter Silin (in Moscow province) with an output of 3,000 items a year, but then Tula took over as the true samovar capital, with its status confirmed even in the saying that "One does not come to Tula with own samovar" (see Figure D.2.1) (Schütz, 1986; Yoder, 2009).

Development of manufacturing in Tula, Moscow and other cities of the Russian Empire

In 1778 Tula gunsmiths (or weapon-makers) Ivan and Nazar Lisitsyn applied to the administration of the Armory Plant for a permit to open a samovar factory. At that time samovar-making was still a new and profitable business due to their being few competitors: samovar factories operated only in Suksun and Nizhny Tagil, and also in Moscow. Their factory located in a residential building, in a small room, and there was a smithy with only two forges, to solder samovars and for casting, which remained separately in the same house's courtyard.

The Lisitsyn brothers worked together until the early 1810s until their split up, when each one had opened their own production and had their own brand. In 1823 the factory of Nazar Lisitsyn produced 450 items, and 10 years later already 625 samovars a year. Half of the products were sold in Tula, while the rest went to the other cities of Russia. In Nizhny Novgorod, the Lisitsyns kept their own shop in Gostiny Dvor (trade house). Furthermore, the Lisitsyn samovars became known in Central Asia, like Khiva or Bukhara.

The Lisitsyns' example was soon followed by many other gunsmiths: by 1808 there was already eight samovar factories in Tula, by 1850 the number became 28, and by 1900–1905 it got to as high as 85 (see figure D.2.2).

Products of the samovar factories were widely exhibited domestically and internationally. The first All-Russian exhibition took place in 1829 in St. Petersburg, where the Tula samovar-maker Nikolai Malikov was awarded a silver medal.

In 1836, at the Moscow Manufacturing Exhibition, samovars of the Tula merchant Vasily Lomov were awarded with silver medals, and after a while they received an appreciation from Iran (Persia): the Order of the Lion and the Sun. In 1837, on the occasion of the arrival of the heir to the throne, the future Alexander II, Tula organised an "Exhibition of Fabrications." The heir with his retinue, together with his tutor Vasiliy Zhukovsky (born in Tula), traveled "to view the state." On June 9, he visited Tula. At the exhibition, in addition to army weapons by Tula factories, there were hunting rifles and pistols, daggers and cones, steel products, door devices, clocks, compasses and other products of Tula makers. There were also works of the best samovar factories: hereditary honorary citizens by that time, the Lomovs and the Chernikovs, and the merchants Lisitsyn and Khruslov. Some, like samovars and coffee pots by gunsmith Malikov, attracted attention because of their intricate shapes, fine metal and impeccable décor compared to others (see Figure D.2.3).

By the end of the nineteenth century, several large samovars-making clusters also making other so-called copper utensils had emerged in Russia, and Tula was the first of them, catering to "regular" consumers, and therefore mass production was focused on not the most expensive samovars, but of different styles and sizes. Moscow and St. Petersburg (factories of Ksimantovsky, Pets, Sevryugin, Kondratyev and Dubinin)

Figure D.2.2: Vase-like Samovar Ampère, presumably by the Lisitsyn Brothers, made in Tula in the first quarter of nineteenth century.
Source: Museum of Samovars and Bouillottes, Private collection of Mikhail Borshchev/Grumant

made products often plated with silver and widely used white metal and cupronickel in décor, while Warsaw (Fraget, Plevkevich, the Henneberg brothers or the Buch brothers) mainly made elegant vase-like samovar with rich decor, and a variety of bouillottes. Samovars were also made in the Urals and in the provinces of Yaroslavl and Vladimir (Belge, 2023; Schütz, 1986; Yoder, 2009).

Samovars ran by the factories of Konstantin Pets, Pyotr Sevryugin and Alexander Matissen in Moscow in the second half of the nineteenth century turned out to be exceptionally beautiful. In the late nineteenth and early twentieth centuries the market was filled with products by Moscow factories of Alenchikov and Zimin, successfully competing with the makers from Tula.

Especially noteworthy are the products by Konstantin Pets: it was his products which represented Russian samovars (there were no Tula makers at all) at the Global Exhibition in London in 1851. The Moscow silver-plating factory of Konstantin Pets exhibited two expensive samovars of red copper lined with silver from the outside and from the inside: these pieces were intended to decorate the festive tabling (rather than samovars, those reminded more of luxurious 50-cup vases) and a travel-size 30-cup samovar with detachable legs and a crane (according to the reviews back from

Figure D.2.3: Vase-like Samovar Facets by Malikov factory. The Russian Empire, Tula, mid-nineteenth century.
Source: Museum of Samovars and Bouillottes, Private collection of Mikhail Borshchev/Grumant

International London Exhibit of Main Industries by L. Samoilov and A. Sherer from External Trade Dept written in St. Petersburg in 1852 (see Figure D.2.4)).

Products by another Moscow manufacturer, Matissen, appeared remarkable for their full correspondence to the "Russian style" that was in fashion in the second half of the nineteenth century, including romantic national tendencies in art. The motifs of Russian embroidery and carving, images of birds, roosters or mythological creatures were all over the decor of Matissen samovars (see Figure D.2.5).

In addition to samovars, the manufacturers exhibited all kinds of accessories like trays, rinse bowls and service sets. Some of the manufacturers were quite widely engaged in the making of various hardware, or copper and metal utensils.

Samovars always came with trays, to protect the table from overheating and make tea drinking more convenient and elegant. Trays were made at the same samovar factories from the same materials and offered to customers in sets with samovars: they came in brass, copper, or nickel-plated brass. The shapes of these trays differed from round to oval or rectangular, while the most preferred one was

Figure D.2.4: Vase-like Samovar Lions by Pets factory. The Russian Empire, Moscow, middle of the nineteenth century.
Source: Museum of Samovars and Bouillottes, Private collection of Mikhail Borshchev/Grumant

so-called "oblong" or "semicircular", looking like the extended rectangular one but with one of the short sides rounded (Schütz, 1986; Yoder, 2009).

Another popular design was "Peterburg", called so in some price lists: complicated in shape and made of two parts. There was a narrow rectangle connected to a circle: while the rectangle usually accommodated the samovar, the round one was for rinse bowls, cups and other tea-drinking accessories.

All old trays had wide rims bent outward, often with raised ornaments or engravings, while the central part of the tray could also be decorated with engraving, usually something to do with florals.

Another part of the samovar set was rinse cups or simply rinses, quite specific items designed for samovars only. This kind of a cup would go under the samovar tap, to collect the rest of the water from the lower part of the samovar, or the rest of the tea from used cups after drinking was over. Rinsing bowls looked like low and wide vessels and had a supporting leg with a wide flat base.

Figure D.2.5: Egg-like Samovar by Mattisen factory. The Russian Empire, Moscow, the 2nd half of the nineteenth century.
Source: Museum of Samovars and Bouillottes, Private collection of Mikhail Borshchev/Grumant

Its body was shaped as a round bowl ("ordinary" style) or a wide and short cylinder, slightly narrowed upwards, with the upper edge bent outward ("Raphael" style).

Samovars of exquisite shapes made of expensive materials were usually ordered with a service set: in addition to a tray and a rinse, it also included a teapot, a creamer or milk jug, a sugar bowl, and sometimes a tea strainer. In these cases, the only tray shape available was rectangular, almost square, and wide enough for a special service set, so that all items on the service set fit along with the samovar.

Samovar design. Shapes, fashions and functions

So how is a samovar differ from a teapot? How is a samovar designed? The most prominent part, often beautifully shaped, is the body or the wall, as the samovar-makers call it. First, the water to be boiled is poured inside. The second detail, no less important, is a special cavity for fuel inside, in the middle of the body, called a brazier or a jug as it often resembles its shape. There is a grate at the bottom of the jug or the brazier to place the fuel on.

The body is connected to the lower part, the pallet, or the tray, i.e., the base of the samovar where the legs attach. This transition from the body to the tray is called the neck, being narrower than the body itself. Up the neck there are the blowers, i.e., the holes usually decorated, where the air needed to maintain the combustion process in the brazier goes. On the side of the body there are handles to carry the samovar, and in the front there is the faucet including a stem, a key (locking mechanism) and a branch, soft of a curved plate connected to the key to make it easier to turn. The faucet is connected to the body via a burr, a special thickening around the faucet to reinforce this part and make it more reliable. The lid with a hole in the middle closes the samovar body, and the diameter of the hole is equal to that of the brazier pipe, so that it is strung onto the brazier in a way. The lid itself often has small round holes, each with a hinged lid of its own: these are so-called steamers: when the samovar boils, steam is released through them. The lid is usually covered with a hotplate, a beautifully designed stand for a teapot often placed on top of samovars. The same hotplate also disguises the part of the brazier rising above the lid. At the very top there is a small cap or a plug to close the upper hole in the brazier and stop the combustion inside by preventing the constant air flow through the brazier pipe, while for the samovar to work the cap must be removed. Both caps and lids have round wooden handles (see Figure D.2.6) (Belge, 2023; Schütz, 1986).

Fire-stove samovars are fueled by wood like wood chips, chunks, even pinecones, but charcoal is the best: even a small amount provides strong and even heat.

The main thing is that the chocks and chips are dried really well, otherwise the ignition will be poor. In this case, a folk remedy well-known from films and literature came to aid: put an old boot on top of the brazier and squeeze the leg rhythmically, pumping air to the fuel, until the first signs of fire appear. Coals could also be inflated with the help of special devices, "blowers", looking like small triangular bellows with narrow noses and a pair of handles, the same as is done with the old charcoal irons.

Draught is a must for good combustion: air flow through the brazier pipe should remain constant. To increase the draught and bring out the smoke in case the samovar is heated indoors, one needed an additional pipe, most often L-shaped, with a handle attached to the vertical part. The horizontal part was attached to the vent hole in the stove (the samovar was always placed next to the stove) so that smoke could escape through the chimney on the roof.

Putting the samovar on, meaning to prepare it for work and heating up, was something common for a nineteenth century commoner. Now it may seem like a kind of mysterious ritual, despite its simplicity, however it may cause considerable difficulties for people of today. So, here's how to "put up" the samovar:

- first you shake out the remains of old ash,
- then pour water inside,
- close the lid,

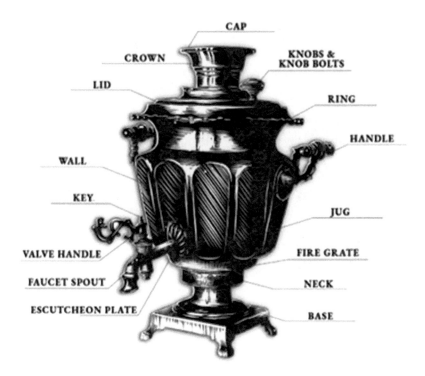

CAP

CROWN

LID

KNOBS &
KNOB BOLTS

RING

HANDLE

WALL

KEY

JUG

VALVE HANDLE

FIRE GRATE

FAUCET SPOUT

NECK

ESCUTCHEON PLATE

BASE

Figure D.2.6: Fire-Stove Samovar Design Layout.
Source: Museum of Samovars and Bouillottes, Private collection of Mikhail Borshchev/Grumant

- put fuel in the brazier pipe,
- set it on fire with a long splinter
- put it on the chimney by connecting it to the oven vent and finally,
- once your water has boiled, remove the pipe, and put the plug on the brazier.

The air flow inside stops, and all coals are immediately extinguished – as simple as that.

Now you can put a teapot on top of the hotplate for better extraction (or infusion). Tea is brewed with boiling water from a samovar at the earlier stage of boiling, when small bubbles appear on the surface of the water.

The design of a fire-type samovar working on wood fuel shaped at the very origins of its manufacture has survived to this day: only the décor or art details changed.

Numerous samovars made in Tula met the various needs in Russian life. Perhaps the earliest type of samovar could be *sbitennik*, a mix of a samovar and a teapot. These round teapot-like vessels with a heating pipe-brazier inside and blow-out holes in the lower part of the body were used to boil water, and also well to prepare an ancient Russian drink, sbiten that became popular in Russia much earlier than tea itself.

Figure D.2.7: Sbiten Samovar. The Russian Empire, the first half of the nineteenth century.
Source: Museum of Samovars and Bouillottes, Private collection of Mikhail Borshchev/Grumant

Sbitens were prepared by brewing various fragrant herbs in boiling water (sage, St. John's wort, valerian, mint or oregano) with honey and various spices added to the liquid. Sbiten was meant to be only drank hot, so to sell it at fairs or bazaars or in the streets sellers placed a heating pipe inside the device. Such *sbitenniks* were common at the end of the eighteenth and early nineteenth centuries but later were replaced with special street trade samovars with swing-over handles, like one of a bucket.

Such samovars were named *shop samovars*. In addition to sbitennik, street vendors selling sbitnen usually wore a wide belt with pockets for glasses or mugs, and several bundles of bagels or bagels thrown over the shoulder. One of the old sbiten recipes lived up to our time, so maybe the following quote was just the thing once traded at fairs, when the customers were loudly invited to have some instead of "chugging beer": "So, the sbiten recipe calls for six liters of water, 500 grams of honey, 700 grams of molasses, five to ten grams of spices (cinnamon, cloves, hops, and mint)/ Boil the water, add all the ingredients and boil for 30 more minutes."

At the end of the nineteenth century, old sbitenniks were replaced with store-bought samovars, much more convenient ones, with the faucet keys securely locking the liquid inside and not allowing it flow out in case the body was accidentally tilted: when walking, it was swayed regardless of holding the rocker handle. Even when filled to the brim, store-bought items would not cause trouble to its owner, which could not be said about the sbiten ones.

Travel samovars were in great demand in the first half of the nineteenth century as well. Those days, when journeys were long and tiring, not only the famous Russian roads and robbers, but also bad food and often lack of any at post stations were a real disaster for travelers. Post stations were only available about 18 to 25 kilometers away. Inns and taverns were only available at the first and second "category" stations in provincial and district towns, while the rest offered none (see Figure D.2.7).

Train stations in smaller settlements could not offer travelers anything but rumpled and poorly cleaned samovar, so those who did not stock up on provisions and their own travel samovar would be in deep trouble. The bulky road carriages had a wide variety of devices to carry provisions and kitchen utensils and a whole cellar for tea and cutlery. There was everything needed to eat or have some tea, and in addition to those cellars there were dedicated crates for travel samovars. Such samovars always had detachable legs, on screws or inserted into grooves, with hinged handles tightly fitting to the body. The shape of travel samovars was always been simple and convenient for packaging: a cylinder or rectangle (see Figure D.2.8).

Samovars-kitchens were also used on the go: when on the road, you could cook several dishes at once. The samovar body had partitions on the inside dividing it into several compartments, and a faucet attachable to the boiling compartment. Each compartment had its own lid, and one more, common one, covered the entire samovar, so it could also be used as a whole bowl. Such samovars came with bailers, too. Travel food, very simple like porridge or stew, would not cool down for a long time, thanks to the hot coals inside the brazier pipe keeping them hot.

Samovars were not only made to boil water for tea: they could also be used to make coffee. Coffee samovars were always cylindrical, with the lower part of the body decorated with an intricately shaped grate (air flow holes), faucets with similarly shaped burrs, and their brazier pipes having removable frames on the inside: this is where a canvas bag for ground coffee beans went to hang. Later, at the end of the nineteenth century, coffee samovars became similar to the rest, so that even from the outside they would not look any different from regular ones, the only distinguishing feature being the bag frame inside.

With the spread of tea and tea drinking in Russia, another type of samovar appeared, a tavern type. Generally, those were huge and voluminous and had the simplest shape possible, cylinder. These stood near the stove so that the smoke would come out through its vent and could immediately boil large amounts of water. The volume reached 15, 27, 45 and even 70 liters. Boiled water from such samovars was then poured into glasses or cups for customers, or into small teapots with side handles with long spouts allowing to top up boiling water from behind for those sitting at the table. The same huge samovars were taken out during festivities outside the city, and

Figure D.2.8: Travel-sized Samovar with GP monogram, by Pushkov factory The Russian Empire, mid-nineteenth century.
Source: Museum of Samovars and Bouillottes, Private collection of Mikhail Borshchev/Grumant

neat innkeepers earned a lot of money this way: who would refuse a cup of tea outside, in the fresh air, enjoying both a delicious drink and excellent weather at the same time?

Samovars in crafts and arts. Ways to décor, designs and styles

In its early days in Russian life, the samovar served as a dish used by the nobles, due to the fact that tea drinking came to the country in the mid-seventeenth century, and until the first half of the nineteenth century it used to be mainly for nobles. Accordingly, like all other nobles' tableware, samovar had to meet very high standards; it must have looked elegant and natural in the house environment (Takako, 2018).

At the end of the eighteenth century both architecture and interior design were all about the "classic" style, and its main principle was a nod to ancient arts, strictness and clarity, and structured shapes, as well as compliance between the image of an object to its function. During this period samovars reminded of vases or antique urns, i.e., were egg-shaped with a deep wide belt in the middle and a spoon-like bottom. The wall was embossed with a spoon-like or rocaille ornament and flower garlands, overlays of leaves (acanthus, palmettes) and mascarons, floral or geometric.

At the same time, forms associated with established patterns of everyday things come into use, like samovars shaped like a four, six or eight sided box, or a barrel.

Since the 1830s Russian art generally came to a new stage, almost like searching for new styles. Along with the works of classicism, others appeared, mainly referring to historical styles. This phenomenon was named eclecticism or historicism. The favourite form of neo-Greek style samovar was an antique vessel called a crater.

This shape, apparently borrowed from porcelain vases, became a mass market thing at that time, made in large quantities by the Imperial Porcelain Factory. The feeling of the solidity of such crater-shaped samovars was enhanced by a low, usually deaf neck without a grate. Such samovars had quite little décor: only the burr and the place where the handles were attached had a pattern resembling acanthus. As a rule, the handles were shaped to echo the curve of the upper part of the body.

The neo-Greek style also manifested itself in samovars shaped like other antique vessels, kiliks, tending to be even more horizontal. The original shape was emphasised by the tray line, handles, a flat lid and a crane with horizontal branch-bracket. One of the ways to enhance the samovar décor and avoid the use of purely decorative parts was faceting the wall.

From the mid-nineteenth century shapes of Tula samovars began to develop in their own, special way, losing the influence of the styles observed at the late eighteenth and early nineteenth centuries. This phenomenon was mostly associated with changes in the social status of its users. By the end of the 1840s tea drinking in Russia spread wider and wider in the life of common people.

The nobles, with their refined cultural requirements, stopped being the only consumers of samovars, and by the second half of the nineteenth century so many new, never-seen samovar shapes had appeared that the device became traditional. The craftsmen themselves called most of these shapes "a vase", and they only varied in the complexity of structure and the soft transition from one volume to another.

The vase shape has rooted and, being popular with the consumer, has existed until the present, changing and growing new solutions. As a rule, vases became more complicated by faceting, adding "spoons", "drops", "columns" and "twisted columns", as well as other décor and images. Often custom-made samovars were made from famous artists' sketches and casts in special anvils. Such samovars were expensive and rare (See figures D.2.9 and D.2.10).

Due to manual manufacturing process, the craftsman had the opportunity to vary the shape using various types of parts during the assembly. Along with the complex

Figure D.2.9: Vase-like Samovar Facets by Lukyanov factory. The Russian Empire, Tula, 1850s.
Source: Museum of Samovars and Bouillottes, Private collection of Mikhail Borshchev/Grumant

"vase" shape, simpler ones were created, also not devoid of beauty and expressiveness of their own, with the most common ones "glass", "egg", "ball", "dula" (or pear; see Figure D.2.11).

At the turn of the nineteenth and twentieth centuries, samovar production manifested a connection with stylistic changes in the "greater art", technical progress and a changing concept of beauty more than before. In the 1890–1900s *moderne* made its appearance in Russian art, with the trend of the new aesthetic and the concept that the line is an expression of volume.

Samovar products however, rarely included samples embodying the character of Art Nouveau as fully as porcelain, glass or ceramics could. Traditionally the nature of the samovar as a functional object and slow reaction of production to the new trends have ended up so that, in relation to samovar shapes or styles, you could only talk about echoing the modern style.

The spirit of the times found its way in a new approach to the factory products. Industrial products became part of everyday life, and simple shapes like a can (cylin-

Figure D.2.10: Vase-like Samovar Arrowed by Vanykin factory. The Russian Empire, Tula, the second half of the nineteenth century.
Source: Museum of Samovars and Bouillottes, Private collection of Mikhail Borshchev/Grumant

der) have became widespread. This has also been facilitated by technical innovations introduced at some large factories.

F.i., the factory of the Trading House of B.G. Teile and Sons began forging the wall of the can samovar. Stamps were also used to make trays and lids, however these innovations were not been applied everywhere, and a huge number of craftsmen working at home continued making samovars parts literally by hand (see Figure D.2.12).

The samovar today. Modern craftsmen and manufacturing techniques

The traditional brazier samovar design shaped by the second half of the eighteenth century existed in a single version for just over half a century. Already by the first half of the nineteenth century, new original solutions for the device began to appear,

Figure D.2.11: Pear-shaped Samovar on ornately shaped tray, presumably by Pekin factory.
The Russian Empire Moscow, second half of the nineteenth century.
Source: Museum of Samovars and Bouillottes, Private collection of Mikhail Borshchev/Grumant

and, although these did not gain wide recognition for the most part, their appearance marked the development of technical thought in samovar making.

1864 was the year when the production of samovars by engineer-colonel Voloshinov began: the model named after the maker in the newspapers took off in Moscow, where a small series got made at the factory of Pyotr Sevryugin and in Tula, where the Chernikov brothers had their eyes on the new original design. The inventor himself, having received a 10-year privilege on his product, offered drawings and descriptions to all interested manufacturers and craftsmen for a small fee. The main feature of such samovar was a brazier pipe: not straight like in all others, but curved at the top at a 45-degree angle. The top holes of such pipes were placed on the side of the lid and covered with flat extinguisher lids. The samovar's own lid was flat, and had no protrusions or décor like overlays. The handle of Voloshinov samovar resembled the teapot's: shaped as a flat curved bracket and placed on the side of the body. Advertisements for the new samovar especially emphasised the fact that the draught was more intense, and the speed of boiling was higher.

Figure D.2.12: Wineglass-like Samovar with intricate raised circle and double tap by the Batashevs factory. The Russian Empire, Tula, early twentieth century.
Source: Museum of Samovars and Bouillottes, Private collection of Mikhail Borshchev/Grumant

In the late nineteenth to early twentieth century new original designs fell like from a cornucopia. In the early twentieth century B.G. Teile and Sons in Tula started making patented kerosene samovars. Reinhold Teile himself invented the kerosene burner for these and filed a patent for it (privilege No. 3303/1866). The factory advertisements for these products stated that they "[. . .] by no means smoke, produce no coal gas and boil quite fast, so you can put one indoors [. . .]" (Kalinichev, S.P. & Britenkova, L.V., 2010, p. 136).

The bottom of the kerosene samovars looked very similar to the base and burner of a kerosene lamp, with the only difference being that, instead of a glass lampshade, a samovar body was put on and secured with special clamps. Usually, such samovars were made in can or glass shape, with a capacity of ten to 30 glasses (a glass being a common measure of volume in samovar-making, 200 milliliters). A detachable body made it easy and quick to fill the tank with kerosene, while the side screw made it possible to control the flame of the burner, and the wick could be ignited through a slide window in the samovar neck (see figure D.2.13).

Figure D.2.13: Can-shaped Kerosene Samovar by Teile and Sons factory. The Russian Empire, Tula, early twentieth century.
Source: Museum of Samovars and Bouillottes, Private collection of Mikhail Borshchev/Grumant

The Shemarin brothers bought a patent for the production of alcohol or *spirit* samovars. Inside such a samovar there was no longer a brazier pipe: it was replaced with two hollow tubes placed crosswise and connected to each other in the centre. One of the tubes went outside and connected to external reservoir for alcohol via an adapter. Said reservoir, or a tank, was usually conical and had a small ignition hole. Such samovar could also be put in indoors since no soot, smoke or smell came out during the combustion of alcohol. Alcohol samovars were manufactured in small batches as they were not particularly in demand, possibly due to the higher cost of fuel.

A similar design of alcohol samovars was used by *Norblin and Co.* working in Warsaw. Samovars by this company were sonorously named after Edison (patent No. 22900). Over time, the design of the alcohol burner in these somewhat changed, but the principle itself remained the same (see Figure D.2.14).

A small firm, *Shakhdat Brothers and Co.* in Tula, directed all its small output to the making of new design samovars, developed by engineer Juriy Parichko, who filed an application for his invention on January 20, 1897 and obtained a patent for it num-

Figure D.2.14: Spirit Samovar Edison. The Russian Empire, the Polish County, Warsaw, early twentieth century.
Source: Museum of Samovars and Bouillottes, Private collection of Mikhail Borshchev/Grumant

bered 1604 on January 20, 1899. The Parichko design samovars had no grate at the bottom of the brazier, and the brazier itself was easily removable from the body and could be fixed on the samovar circle with a wide ring.

It had as many as three compartments: the central one, as usual, and the side ones connected to the central compartment at the bottom. The samovar's neck was deaf and had no blower holes: the air to combust the fuel came through wide openings on the burner support. An original device like this made it possible to use not only wood for fuel, but also liquids like alcohol or kerosene. In an effort to interest buyers in their product, the Shakhdat brothers advertised in Tula newspapers and spread numerous advertisements and leaflets. Despite active advertising, the number of orders remained small, so the samovar would not live up to expectations, and the company soon went bankrupt. No one else dared to buy out the patent for this type of samovar after this.

In 1912, the bourgeois from Kharkov city with the last name Epelbein patented a boiling device for household needs, as well as for baths looking like a cylinder mounted on a plate, with two compartments equipped with outlet pipes and taps inside. A chimney went inside the cylinder with the upper compartment rested on top of it, to heat water for bathing.

Below it, around the chimney, there was another compartment that was intended for household needs, also heated from the stove and with water supplied from the home water supply system (or a pipe). The Moscow factory of two merchants, Alenchikov and Zimin, took advantage of this invention and received the "privilege" for making samovars that would heat water when installed on a stove. These samovars had covered containers inside, connected to the tap to allow water to be added during the heating process without spoiling the quality of already boiling water. The device, in fact, very original, also suffered the same fate: these designs did not become massively popular or recognised. The ordinary wood-burning (heating) samovar remained the "master" of them all because of its convenience and ease of use, availability and cheap and common wood as a fuel (see Figure D.2.15).

Figure D.2.15: Cooker/Slab-heated Samovar by Alenchikov and Zimin factory. The Russian Empire, Moscow, early twentieth century.
Source: Museum of Samovars and Bouillottes, Private collection of Mikhail Borshchev/Grumant

Fundamental changes in the samovar design and its production technology came much later, after the Second World War. Now almost all samovar parts became mechanically made: be it the body, neck, lid, tap branch or jug, all of those were made using premade stamps. Dedicated machines "ironed" the walls and the lid; handles were made solid, under single press, taps were injection-molded, and tinning of the entire samovar altogether became galvanic. The samovar turned into a product of continuous production and, unfortunately, lost the last remnants of individuality; even the souvenir products were developed with regard to the batch manufacture. In 1964, miniature 125-gram souvenir samovars appeared in stores: those were in fact an exact copy of the one that belonged to the family of Leo Tolstoy and in the Yasnaya Polyana Estate Museum, so the model received the same name. It took 24 stamps and fixtures to make those and a dedicated small machine to give a finishing touch to a 5mm handle. This souvenir was a huge success at both domestic and foreign markets, and huge numbers of these were made.

By the mid-1950s, in the premise of changes in the living conditions of Russians there was a remarkable novelty, the electric samovar. During the second half of the twentieth century the Soviet Union began civil engineering and massive construction of residential buildings, albeit not very comfortable, but good enough for millions of people to be able to move to new homes with centralised steam heating. In such apartments, with no stove or a chimney system and air vents, you no longer could put up a regular heating samovar – these thus became impractical for use.

In 1957 Tula plant *Shtamp* developed a samovar with an electric heater instead of a tube connected to chimney. At that time, it looked like a ceramic insulator with an electric spiral wound around. Such three-liter samovars would boil water in 30 minutes, without troubles like ash or smoke, but unfortunately its heater's service was only 800 hours, so these had to be changed quite often. A few years later inconvenient ceramic heaters were replaced by tubular heaters having a service life of already 3,000 hours, and the heating time for the same three liters was reduced to 18 minutes.

Electric samovars remain the most popular products in the industry. Tula makes 14 types of them, e.g., pear-, ball-, vase-, acorn-, can-, cone or oval-shaped, with a capacity of 1.5 to ten liters (so-called "family" ones; see Figure D.2.16).

Despite the emergence of electric samovars, the love for the old "heating" version has not gone away. In the 1970s Stamp plant made nine types of fire samovars, five and seven-liter ones, and in addition a combined type developed in the 1960s, with a fire tube and a tubular electric heater around the body, as a kind of fusion between fire and electric types.

Modern and high-tech methods found their use in samovar décor: reliefs got applied to the body using hydraulic forging (extrusion of ornaments using liquid under 400-bar pressure), surfaces got primed and were polished using galvanising machines to prepare for nickel coating and then cleaned with ultrasound in addition. Instead of painstaking and expensive engraving on individual samovars, the photographic method was now used. With it, a photosensitive emulsion is applied to the surface, and then

Figure D.2.16: Electric Samovar with service set Metelitsa by Vannikov Works Stamp. USSR, Tula, 1980s.
Source: Museum of Samovars and Bouillottes, Private collection of Mikhail Borshchev/Grumant

there is a negative of an image. The resulting print is covered with a thin layer of protective mastic, and unprotected areas are etched in hydrochloric acid solution.

Another samovar metamorphosis came at the very end of the twentieth century: they began to get covered with artistic painting on various subjects. Smooth-surface glass type samovars were prepared for painting, then the artists covered their bodies and lids with multi-colour painting using special heat-resistant paints, with the samovars then dried in dedicated ovens and, to finish, the surface got covered with double layer of varnish.

Samovars have always been used also to rely to the life of people and day-to-day situations. In the design of the samovars shown as figures D.2.17 and D.2.18 a rooster is connected to the samovar as well as a witch ans a wooden house, symbolising natur and heritage.

Figure D.2.17: Rooster Samovar made following the design by Ippolito Monighetti. The Russian Empire, 1869.
Source: Museum of Samovars and Bouillottes, Private collection of Mikhail Borshchev/Grumant

Figure D.2.18: The Teremok/ Attic Story Samovar by Panferov and Co. The Russian Federation, Tula, 2018.
Source: Museum of Samovars and Bouillottes, Private collection of Mikhail Borshchev/Grumant

Spirit kettles

Following the structure of a stand with three or four legs and a burner at mid, a spirit kettle is a silver teapot that sits upon this stand heated by the burner usually filled with spirits to fuel a flame, which can be seen by the host and the guests. Often, the spirit kettles are combined with a tray to prevent drips and heat reaching the table. There are diverse varieties of spirit kettles, e.g., being attached to the stand with a chain, and secured by a removable locking pin, or in different shapes, e.g., pear shaped, bulbous, bullet-shaped, oval, spherical, or melon-shaped. The shape and the volume of the kettle also indicate the wealth and pride of the family and the appreciation for drinking tea as a social event (AC Silver B, 2023; Pettigrew, 2001; Pettigrew, 2003; Carver Wees, 1997).

The raising attractiveness of spirit kettles started in the late 1680s, during the reign of the British Queen Anne, but also in the Victorian era when spirit kettles were reintroduced and this resurgence was possibly due to the discovery of odourless spirits for the burner. Spirit kettles became an extravagant accessory to any elaborate formal tea party: not just the aesthetic appearance of these tea vessels, usually highly ornate and decorative, but the simple reason to avoid several replenishments of normal teapots when brewing tea made the bigger kettles more requested than usual teapots as they were usually rather small at this time (AC Silver, 2023; Pettigrew, 2001; Pettigrew, 2003).

A variety of spirit kettles from the Kingdom of Poland, Austria, Germany, France, Great Britain and the United States show European preferences and tastes: those were also used to make tea, coffee or mulled wine, to boil eggs or serve hot dishes.

Figure D.2.19: Spirit kettle, with service set owned by Prince Golitsyn (Norblin and Co). The Russian Empire, the Polish County, Warsaw, early twentieth century.
Source: Museum of Samovars and Bouillottes, Private collection of Mikhail Borshchev/Grumant

Figure D.2.20: Spirit kettle set.
Note: Spirit kettle set with milk jug and
sugar bowl, material: brass.
Origin: Germany
Photo: Kaleef Oladele Lawal
Source: Collection Bohne/Berlin

Spirit kettles, made from brass, copper, tin, and especially silver, symbolise a wealthy
handling of tea and the consumption of this beverage. Sets of a swinging tea kettle
with a milk jug and sugar bowl as well as elaborated decorations were used to make
these vessels attractive, although they are "only" used for keeping the water for tea
on the tea table warm (see Figures D.2.19+D.2.20).

Brass has been used as a solid material for (spirit) kettles since ancient times. As an
alloy of copper, zine, and other materials, brass needs to be polished regularly – similar
to copper. During the reign of Queen Victoria of England, kettles made of brass with a
big volume (up to 2 liters) and a stand were very popular. Spirit kettles on a pivoting
stand, made from brass or copper, were also developed due to the different colours in
comparison to silver, and had a faster impact on the heat of the boiled water, and were
also simply made for decorative reasons (Carter, 1994) (see Figures D.2.21+D.2.22).

Also, famous producers like WMF recognised the trend of spirit kettles and developed different designs, decorations, and technical constructions to present the hanging kettle the best way possible. In addition, the impact of the "Art Nouveau" and the
high price of silver lead designers and producers to also differentiate the materials of
kettles. Consequently, more people got access to these tea related vessels (Street-
Porter, 1981; see Figure D.2.23).

Figure D.2.21: Spirit kettle on a pivoting stand.
Note: Spirit kettle on a pivoting stand, material: brass. Origin: Germany
Photo: Kaleef Oladele Lawal
Source: Collection Bohne/Berlin

Figure D.2.22: Tin spirit kettle on a pivoting stand.
Note; Spirit kettle on a pivoting stand, material: tin.
Origin: Great Britain
Photo: Kaleef Oladele Lawal
Source: Collection Bohne/Berlin

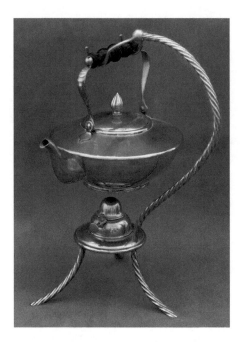

Figure D.2.23: "Swinging" Spirit kettle.
Note; Swinging Spirit kettle, material: tin.
Origin: Germany
Photo: Kaleef Oladele Lawal
Source: Collection Bohne/Berlin

This special silver tea kettle was made in London in 1737/38 by the silversmith Charles Frederick Kandler. It has the preferred spherical shape, the playful decoration with blossoms, acanthus leaves, and cartouches decorated with roncailles, and underlines the decorative language of the late baroque, also the reign of King George II, from 1727 to 1760. Until the beginning of the nineteenth century, the handles of English teapots were made of various materials, usually wood, ivory or silver, and only later wrapped with leather or with two-tone bast. In addition, a representative storage box was often provided (Fahrenson-Baaten, 2023).

Conclusion

Samovars or tea (spirit) kettles are symbols of a noble and representative handling of preparing tea – and presenting tea. Obviously, the Russian approach to developing Samovars heated by coal, wood, kerosine or later electricity (with the first mention of Samovars in Russia in 1730), and the more British approach to have kettles on stands with candles or spirit lamps, were both ways of keeping boiled water hot and/or offering a big vessel of prepared tea, and were attractive in their times, for normal households but also for the royals and their entourage. Still, in contemporary settings, samovars and spirit kettles give a warm and pleasant feeling, initiate storytelling around tea, and make the moment of tea a special occasion of enjoyment and relaxation.

Figure D.2.24: Silver spirit Kettle by Charles Frederick Kandler.
Note; Silver spirit Kettle by Charles Frederick Kandler, material: Silver 925.
Origin: Great Britain
Photo: Kerstin Fahrenson-Baaten
Source: Silbersuite – Antiquitäten & Altes Tafelsilber, Schweitenkirchen/Germany

Figure D.2.25: Spirit Kettle and storage box.
Note; Silver spirit kettle by Charles Frederick Kandler,
material: Silver 925.
Origin: Great Britain,
storage and travel box made from wood
Photo: Kerstin Fahrenson-Baaten
Source: Silbersuite – Antiquitäten & Altes Tafelsilber, Schweitenkirchen/Germany

References

AC Silver. (2023 A). What is a spirit kettle? Retrieved from July 28, 2023, from https://www.acsilver.co.uk/shop/pc/Samovars-Spirit-Kettles-c131.htm.

AC Silver. (2023 B). History of spirit kettles. Retrieved from July 28, 2023, from https://www.acsilver.co.uk/shop/pc/Samovars-Spirit-Kettles-c131.htm.

Altoner Museum in Hamburg. (1977). *Tee-Zur Kulturgeschichte eines Getränke*s. Trebe.

Belge, B. (2023). *Der Samowar*, retreived 12 November 2023 from: https://www.dekoder.org/de/gnose/samowar-alltagskultur-teekultur-geschichte.

Carter, T. (1996). *Teapots*. Apple Press.

Carver Wees, B. (1997). *English, Irish, and Scottish Silver at the Sterling and Francine Clark Art Institute*. Hudson Hills Press.

Clark. G. (1989). *Die verrückte Teekanne*. Heyne.

Clark, G. (2001). *The artful teapot*. Watson-Guptill Publications.

Emmerson, R. (1992). *British teapots and tea drinking*. HMSO.

Fahrenson-Baaten, K. (2023). Expertise für eine Teekessel auf Rechaud. Silbersuite – Antiquitäten & Altes Tafelsilber, Schweitenkirchen/Germany.

Gaylard, L. (2021). *Das Teebuch*. DK Penguin Random House.

Hahn, B. (2022). *Eine Reise in die Welt des Tees*. Brunnen Verlag.

Kalinichev, S.P. & Britenkova, L.V. (2010). *Samovars of Russia*. Hobby Press.

Masset, C. (2010). *Tea and tea drinking*. Shire Publications.

Museum of Samovars and Bouillottes, private collection of Mikhail Borshchev/Grumant. (n.d.).

Pettigrew, J. (2001). *A social history of tea*. The National Trust.

Pettigrew, J. (2003). *Design for tea*. Sutton Publishing.

Rohrsen, P. (2022). *Das Buch zum Tee*. C.H. Beck.

Rothermund, D. (2004). *Der Siegeszug des Tees um die Welt*. Deutsches Tee-Institut.

Scarce, J. (2003). Russia, Iran and Turkey. In R. Faulkner (2003). *Tea – East and West*. V&A Publications.

Schäfer, D. (2003). *Samowar*. Verlag für die Frau.

Schütz, J. (1986). *Russlands Samowar und russischer Tee: Kulturgeschichtlicher Aufriss*, Verlag Lassleben.

Spouer, K. (2022). *Tea Cyclopedia*. Skyhorse Publishing.

Street-Porter, J., & Street-Porter, T. (1981). *British teapots*. Angus Robertson Publishers.

Takako, M. (2018). Tea drinking culture in Russia, in: Journal of International Economic Studies, Vol. 32/2018, pp. 57–74.

Yoder, A. J. (2009). Myth and Memory in Russian Tea Culture, in: *Studies in Slavic Cultures* (8), 08/2009, pp. 65–89.

E Scouting tea culture and hospitality

Celebrating tea and hospitality is the essential combination of spaces, occasions, and artful atmosphere. It means to enjoy the feeling of hospitality, to see the socially binding elements of tea, and to sustainably use the time needed to relax.

Hartwig Bohne
E.1 Tea venues in Europe

Introduction

Hospitality is embracing tea – not only in teahouses and at home, but also in specific tea venues. Tea rooms and tea gardens reflect social developments, but also different approaches for woman and men using tea as an element of communication or (strategic) gathering by serving refreshments, pastries, coffee and mostly tea. In Great Britain, the tea gardens were a symbol of welfare, also underlined by elaborated gardening concepts. This approach was also adapted in The Netherlands, Georgia, and Türkiye. Another approach of making tea more visible and accessible can be seen in different types of "moving tea," e.g., on boats, in buses or even in carriages or on "tea bikes". Apart from the characteristic teahouses, these venues underline the diversity of places dedicated to tea and the creativity in offering tea to different customers.

Tea room/salon de thé

Tearooms are an integral part of the local tea culture in many European countries.

In France, tearooms are called *"salon de thé"*. The oldest existing tearoom is Maison de Théo by Mariage Frères. It was founded on 1 June 1854, so it can already look back on almost 170 years of existence. The founders, the two brothers Edouard and Henri Mariage, took the family heritage in a new direction with their manufactory. As traders in tea, spices, and oriental goods, the family had been importing tea to France since 1660. Nicolas Mariage had already been personally commissioned by King Louis XIV to import teas from Persia for the royal court, among other things (Mariage Frères, 2023).

The British perspective on tearooms is also remarkable. A female manager of London's Aerated Bread Company is credited with creating the bakery's first public tearoom in 1864. In the UK today, a tearoom is a small room or restaurant where beverages and light meals are served, often having a sedate or subdued atmosphere. The food served can range from a cream tea (also known as Devonshire tea), i.e., a scone with jam and clotted cream, to an elaborate afternoon tea featuring tea sandwiches and small cakes, to a high tea, a savoury meal.

The Royal Family's favourite food hall, Fortnum & Mason, is one of the oldest and most famous stores in Piccadilly. Fortnum & Mason's success began with lights. The insistence of Queen Anne's household on fresh candles every night spelled a legitimate perk for an enterprising footman: spare palace wax to sell on. By 1707, William Fortnum's enlightened sideline had declined enough to leave royal service and start a

https://doi.org/10.1515/9783110758573-014

business with his landlord. Hugh Mason Tea is pivotal to the storied past of Fortnum & Mason. In 1902, the brews came to boast a royal pedigree thanks to a bespoke blend specially created for King Edward VII. From contemporary infusions to home-grown blends, tea is still reigning and pouring today (Fortnum & Mason, 2023).

Tea gardens

Besides Great Britain, Türkiye and Azerbaijan are also famous for their ancient and traditional tea culture. In both countries, tea is part of everyday life and is drunk at every opportunity around the clock. Tea gardens (Cay Bahcesi) are a widespread sight in the Turkish city and village landscape, meeting places for sharing news, celebrate family gatherings, or just relaxing and enjoying a glass of tea (typically tulip-shaped). In Türkiye tea gardens popping up in the 1950s aren't always a garden in the traditional sense. In fact, unlike the serenity and reflection of Japanese tea gardens, Turkish tea gardens are loud and lively with music, conversation, and sometimes even hookah (typical water pipes). Today, there are many tea gardens in the tourist metropolis of Istanbul and in the tea-growing region around the city of Rize. While tea gardens vary little in terms of tea, service, or outdoor furniture, they are distinguished by their location (Wohl, 2017).

Figure E.1.1: Wannock House Tea garden (1920).
Source: Garden Museum, London

In England, tea gardens established themselves in British society between the sixteenth and nineteenth centuries. Over 200 tea and pleasure gardens were established in London during this period. A tea garden was a place to drink tea, walk around lawns and ponds, and look at statues. Examples were Cuper's Gardens and the area that became the Caledonian Cattle Market in London. Mainly frequented by the working class, these tea gardens quickly became a hit all over Great Britain. One of the reasons why gardens in the suburbs began to be more frequented than the centrally located but wholly masculine coffeehouses was that they offered their attractions to women as well as to men. All sorts of beverages were served, including tea, coffee, and chocolate, but tea soon acquired an outstanding vogue (Aysha, 2019; Pettigrew, 2001; Masset, 2010). Similar to this development, taking a cup of tea in a tea garden became more and more popular in Georgia too (Pettigrew, 2003). And, also in the Netherlands, tea gardens became an interesting model of gardening culture in the eighteenth century (Way, 2017; see Figures E.1.1–E.1.4).

Figure E.1.2: Grand Walk Vauxhall Gardens (1760).
Source: Garden Museum, London (Photo: J. Muller)

As shown in Figure E.1.5, hotels in Great Britain adapted their gastronomic offers to the requests of guests offering tea and snacks in their facilities, but also on roof top gardens or similar spaces. The idea combining classic food and beverage with a specific view or perspective is still a favourable element of hospitality, as the contemporary offers of afternoon tea in destinations like London, Dublin or other European metropoles illustrate.

Figure E.1.3: Embankment Gardens Tea Lawn (1890).
Source: Garden Museum, London

Figure E.1.4: Mrs West's Tea garden (1909).
Source: Garden Museum, London

Figure E.1.5: The Roof garden at Mayfair Hotel.
Source: Garden Museum, London

Tea on the move

Other ways to have afternoon tea in the UK are to enjoy it on board a ship, in a carriage or on the roof of the famous British double-decker buses. In London, Dublin, Cheshire, and Brighton these are popular tourist attractions but locals also enjoy their tea on the move. City cruises, for example, offer a several-hour cruise on the Thames where you can enjoy afternoon tea while taking in London's most famous sights like the London Eye or the Big Ben. On the other hand, the tours on the Lady Diana or the Mark Twain through Old Cheshire are somewhat smaller, while afternoon tea cakes and sandwiches are served.

Afternoon tea cruises can be found in Cheshire operated by the award-winning Davenports Tea Room. Belinda Davenport, the owner, set up the concept with her husband, Ian, so that they could use their own boat and their love of canals and justify it in the name of afternoon tea! Belinda's family has a long history of involvement in canals after her great-grandfather started a coal carrying company in 1840, servicing the tanneries in Runcorn, Cheshire. The Horsefield family business continued until the last tannery closed in 1963, over 120 years of canal boating history. In 1972 Belinda's parents bought a holiday hire boating business, next to where her husband Ian was born, and soon after that a 50-seater trip boat where they started their love for each other. Premier Narrow Boats and Lapwing Cruises survived until the late 1980s. Davenports Cruises was set up soon after the tearoom opened in 2006 as a way of utilising the boat they owned, albeit that they realised it had to be changed to a more suitable boat ultimately to pass on their love of the English canals and afternoon teas (Davenport, 2023; see Figure E.1.6, and E.1.7).

Figure E.1.6: The Tea Boat of Davenport's of Cheshire.
Source: Belinda Davenport

Figure E.1.7: Swimming afternoon tea space.
Source: Belinda Davenport

On the street, the typical afternoon tea is also served in buses. In Brighton, London, and Dublin, these tea tours are common. In Brighton, for example, you can have afternoon tea on the iconic Routemaster bus RML 2333 while enjoying Brighton's city centre sights: Royal Pavilion, Palace Pier or Hove's Grand Avenue. Popular carriages to book in London are the Cinderella carriages, where you can have tea and cake in a fairytale carriage while being driven around London.

Conclusion

Tea places can be developed and created in relation to different customers, different venues, and different types of mobility. It is impressive to see the social function of tea related gatherings, which have been playing an important role since the sixteenth century. Still today, for example in Türkiye or Azerbaijan, tea consumption is an instrument for communicative meetings or for positively melting cultures. The documented tea places mostly connect people by using a freshly brewed tea and some snacks, offering a space for a quiet meeting or for a typical cocktail atmosphere. It shows again the vast potential of and opportunities for tea to bring people together and bridge social and also political differences.

References

Aysha, T. (2019). The pleasure of tea gardens of the 18th century. Retrieved March 27, 2023, from https://www.thehillcarttales.com/tea-tales/tag/tea-garden/.

Fortnum Mason. (2023) Our history. Retrieved March 22, 2023, from https://www.fortnumandmason.com/our-history.

Mariage Frères. (2023). La cuisines au thé – French cuisine with tea. Retrieved March 22, 2023, from https://www.mariagefreres.com/UK/french_tea_salon_and_restaurant.html.

Masset, C. (2010). *Tea and tea drinking*. Shire Library.

Pettigrew, J. (2001). *A social history of tea*. National Trust.

Pettigrew, J. (2003). *Design for tea*. Sutton Publishing.

Rappaport, E. (2017). *The thirst for empire*. Princeton University Press.

Way, T. (2017). *Tea gardens*. Amberley Publishing.

Wohl, S. (2017). The Turkish tea garden: Exploring a 'third space' with cultural resonances. *Space and Culture, 20*(1), 56–67.

Carina Pardek and Hartwig Bohne

E.2 Contemporary European teahouse concepts

Introduction

While tea can easily be enjoyed in many places, special locations are dedicating all their focus to the beloved drink. Teahouses are representing the perfect example of such sites, illuminating a place of harmony. Representing firstly a place that serves tea, a deeper emotion gathers people to both socialise and enjoy a much beloved drink. As for the history of teahouses, it is believed to have firstly appeared in China, during the Tang dynasty's Kaiyuan era, followed by times of entertainment. Primarily introduced with actors, opera, singers, and storytellers, teahouses embodied artistical elements. Looking around the world, countries have interpreted in a certain way how such a place should be presented and its meaning towards local people. While in China teahouses are associated with gatherings and social actvities, in Japan the term was once understood as the place where geisha would entertain her clients, seeking privacy or a private tea ceremony. As for Europe, tea rooms or houses are often encountered, with minimalistic designs that allow the main actor (tea) to be the centre of attention. Evolving with the rest of the world, teahouses have changed their appearance, keeping up with futuristic designs and out of the ordinary architectural plans. A clean and peaceful atmosphere is experienced as a common characteristic.

To offer a better overview of the architectural evolution of the teahouses, several examples located across Europe are to be presented within the following.

Teahouses examples around Europe

Black Teahouse represents the first example of teahouse concepts that already exist. This project was designed by Czech Studio A1 Architects and is situated next to a peaceful lake near the city known as Česká Lípa. The place illustrates and encourages visitors to admire the beauty of nature. As for the interior, certain design items have been introduced in order to create a unique and attractive experience. Focusing on tea culture, the room has as a central attraction point a teapot carried by a woven rope suspended from the ceiling (Frearson, 2011) (as shown in figures E.2.1 and E.2.2).

The round walls that form the building are coated in clay plaster, with flower vases as a distinguishable design elements. The large doors emphasise the surroundings, reaching the sheltered deck. As previously mentioned, the outside area is bordered by nature, the Teahouse representing a part of a carefully designed scenario.

https://doi.org/10.1515/9783110758573-015

Figure E.2.1: Black Teahouse interior.
Source: Frearson (2011). Black Teahouse by A1 Architects (n.d.).

Figure E.2.2: The exterior and surroundings of the Black Teahouse.
Source: Frearson (2011). Black Teahouse by A1 Architects (n.d.).

The following example is represented by Three-winged wooden teahouse in Leiden. Designed by a Dutch architecture studio known as GAAGA, the Netherlands has to offer a beautiful teahouse with an incredible panoramic view. The project began as a community desire, characterised by a remarkable story. Wishing for an ideal place, sizable enough to welcome the neighbourhood, the "green heart" was built. With a long waiting time of ten years, the idea of the teahouse started from a need of a place where different social activities could be possible. After a considerable planning of the financial spectrum, the community's dream became slowly a reality. Regarding With regards to its design, the house has wooden walls and a cantilevered roof, as well a beautiful decked terrace. Emphasising a continuity between the interior and exterior, the place has an all-round shape, without any traditional front or back side (Morby, 2015) (as shown in Figure E.2.3).

Figure E.2.3: Three-winged wooden teahouse in Leiden-Noord by GAAGA.
Source: Morby (2015a)

In addition, the interior is spacious enough for a kitchen, toilet, game room, and small museum exhibition. The most attractive place is represented by the sitting area, allowing the community to easily communicate with each other, located at the intersection of the three legs of the house (as shown in Figure E.2.4). Having the aim of strengthening social cohesion, the focus is attributed to the largest space within the house (Morby, 2015). The designer's inspiration came from a nearby similar teahouse, a building that was well constructed with several legs.

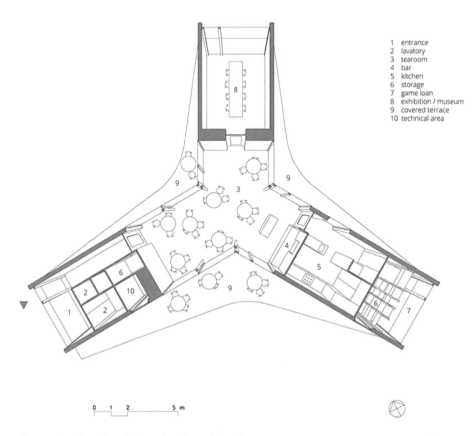

1 entrance
2 lavatory
3 tearoom
4 bar
5 kitchen
6 storage
7 game loan
8 exhibition / museum
9 covered terrace
10 technical area

0 1 2   5 m

Figure E.2.4: Floor plan of three-winged wooden teahouse.
Source: Morby (2015b) / Photo: Marcel van der Burg

Nevertheless, sustainability embodies a significant perspective, the house being designed accordingly. The glazed windows and tall walls with a beautiful panoramic warm the interior, while the green vegetation from the roof improves the water management and supports biodiversity. This teahouse was initiated as a social concept by the community offering a transparent architecture for everybody, using tea as an invitation to meet and spend time together (Morby, 2015).

The third teahouse concept example is represented by Floating Teahouse Ø in Copenhagen. Located in Copenhagen's canals, the building was designed by PAN-Projects, a London architecture studio. Helene Christina Pedersen, the teahouse designer, explained the connection between the water and the teahouse design, emphasising that the water surface reflects both the seasons and the environment on the construction.

Made of wood structure clad in fiber-reinforced and plastic-covered Styrofoam, the roof holds the acrylic tubes (Carlson, 2021) (as shown in Figure E.2.5).

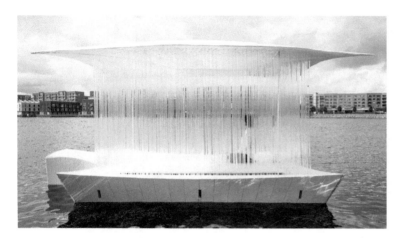

Figure E.2.5: Floating teahouse: acrylic tubes and roof design.
Source: Cabo (2021)

The role of these tubes is to create a running water effect, contributing to a remarkable and fascinating result. Primarily used as a teahouse, the place offers the possibility of holding variable events, designed for the Danish citizens to use it in their favour. The project, exclusively planned for the capital's citizens, has been already used as a DJ stage, floating concert, or yoga venue. This place enables activities that were not possible before, bringing joy and efficiency to the local people. Having the aim of enriching a positive and sustainable culture, the project enhanced the beauty of a natural phenomenon, created by the surface of water. By embracing the natural phenomena, the Floating Pavilion Ø highlights a positive and sustainable culture. The construction was planned in such a way that within the inside a feeling of being surrounded by water is created (Carlson, 2021).

Pursuing further, Teahouse by David Maŝtálka represents another project created by A1 Architects, this time in collaboration with the sculptor Vojtech Bilisic. The house is situated in Prague, Czech Republic, and illustrates a minimal place for gatherings, following the Japanese tradition. Situated in a wild garden with several spring apple and cherry blossom trees, the outside is ready to surprise the visitors, while the inside offers a different perspective of the surroundings. Focusing on an intimate and small sacred building, the house was built on a circular platform, with a translucent dome that enables light to enter the place. The shape directs the guests' attention to the heart of the building, where tea is carefully prepared (Etherington, 2009) (as shown in Figure E.2.6).

Figure E.2.6: The interior perspective of the teahouse by David Maštálka.
Source: Havlova (2009)/https://www.a1architects.cz/en/works/teahouse-in-the-garden/

The house depicts a place where both the guest and the host can enjoy a cup of tea in quiet contemplation. Constructed from oak that stands on stones brought from a nearby pond, the project was finished within 35 days, creating a mimicing colouring effect, emphasised by the surrounding garden (Etherington, 2009).

Example number five is the *Ein Stein Tea House*, which reflects the exact history and principles of tea ceremony, with a personal interpretation from the architect Terunobu Fujimori. While at the age of 45, the architect developed his first design, his work being distinguishable through the use of natural materials and stubborn ideas. For the *Ein Stein Tea House*, materials such as untreated robinia trunks and wooden boardings were used. Being characterised by the relation to the surrounding landscape, the house was designed together with a Japanese architect. Surrounded by nature, the teahouse is situated above the ground (Boehm and Panzenböck, 2021) (as shown in Figure E.2.7).

The following teahouse is situated within two bunkers (as shown in Figure E.2.8). The bunkers were implemented back in 1936, as part of the widespread defensive works. While firstly a national centre for polo sport was supposed to be developed, the UNStudio won the tender for a teahouse project. The first bunker provides a place designated for business partners, in a stainless-steel cover. Due to a huge window, the interior can be visualised. Regarding the teahouse, this is located above the ground level, consisting of a spacious room. The staircase is leading to a strong light coming from a panoramic window (UNStudio, n.d.).

Figure E.2.7: The *Ein Stein Teahouse* illustration.
Source: Santorini (2021)

Figure E.2.8: The bunkers illustration.
Source: Richters (2007)/https://archello.com/project/tea-house-on-bunker

The subsequent example is known as Fata Morgana Teahouse and is located in north-west Cambridge, United Kingdom. The inspiration behind the project lies in an Anglo-Saxon poem "The Wanderer," poem that illustrates a movement without any destination of purpose, triggering a process of reflection and contemplation. The same reflection is highlighted through the architecture of the teahouse (as shown in Figure E.2.9). Inviting guests to a different perspective of the area, the house inspires people towards art, representing the perfect place for self-reflection (Buildner, n.d.).

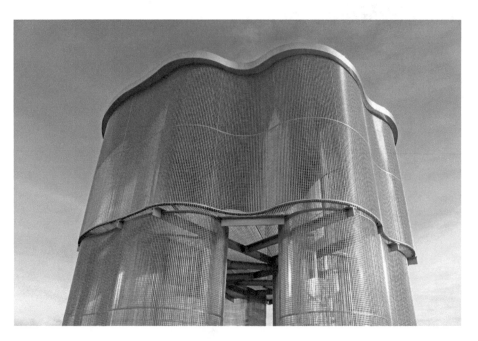

Figure E.2.9: The outside perspective of the Fata Morgana Teahouse.
Source: Winter (2018)/https://winter-hoerbelt.de/fatamorgana-teahouse/

The rebuilt Berliner Stadtschloss (Humboldt Forum) houses a Japanese teahouse, which is part of the Museum of Asian Art. Apart from its role as an art object in the exhibition, the teahouse is a place for practicing tea ceremonies, being presented to the guests as an act of art. As for the design, the emptiness in Japanese aesthetics was highlighted, with elements that define the interior as a classical tearoom (as shown in Figure E.2.10). At the same time, the space metaphorically presents the cultural connection between Japan and Berlin. The name of the teahouse is "Bôki-an" and is represented by two distinctive rooms which highlight a space of cultural understandings. Illustrating a contrast between both old and modern concepts, the space was made using traditional materials such as Japanese paper (Humboldt Foum, n.d.).

The following teahouse, known as The Flying Teahouse, represents a portable space in a traditional Japanese style. Salzburg based architect and scenic designer Gerhard Feld-

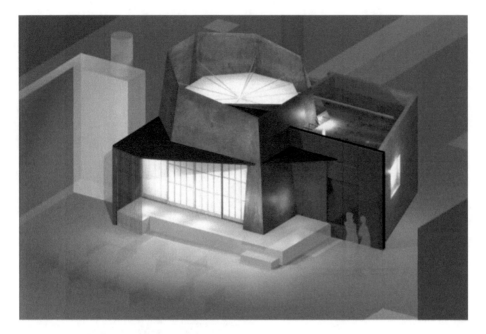

Figure E.2.10: Teehaus "Bôki-an" at Humboldtforum Berlin.
Source: URA Architects & Engineers (n.d.)

bacher built the house in such a way that it can be easily transported on a car trailer. The house has the size of 4 tatami mats and weights less than 300 kg or about 900 kilograms including the trailer (see Figure E.2.11).

The presented project has been carefully described by Gerhard Feldbacher as the following: *"The Flying Teahouse is a Japanese-style mobile tearoom. It can be towed by car and set up in almost any location with relative ease. In its original form, the Japanese teahouse was supposed to embody a kind of primitive mountain hut that transfers so-called wild nature into the owners' domestic garden. In contrast to this, The Flying Teahouse brings the visitors back to nature."*

The initial aim of Feldbacher was to make the archaic elements of architecture tangible. The focus of the teahouse is represented by the sound of boiling water, an open fire, and the shadows of the outside world leaving traces on the translucent walls. Above the fire, a teapot is hung from a jizaikagi, specially bought from an antique shop in Tokyo. No directions are given, the user experience only depends on the way the individuals would interact with the architecture and the question of how deep into the space they wanted to go. *"This type of architecture enables us to experience nature and our surrounding in a much more intensive way than ever possible in a modern house or apartment"* Feldbacher says.

Further, the actual function of the space was originally not clearly defined. Even tough it is called a tearoom it can serve many purposes. Here, the architecture only provides certain conditions. In the past years, The Flying Teahouse was used as an informal

Figure E.2.11: The Flying Teahouse.
Source: Gerhard Feldbacher @theflyingteahouse

meeting room for congress participants of the Salzburg Global Seminar held at Schloss Leopoldskron (2018). It was several times seen at the Schmiede festival in Hallein (2017, 2018, 2019) as an extension of the festival into public space or at the OFFCITY Pardubice in the Czech Republic to draw attention to an abandoned part of the town (2019). The content was herby always different, depending on the actual situation. Often, the classical tea ceremony was mixed with modern elements as video-projections using the translucent walls or sound installations, usually in cooperation with other artists.

After years of experimenting the main interest shifted to a one-on-one theatric intervention, where the creator of the teahouse is occupying his shelter for several days non-stop to draw attention to a specific area, as in Pardubice 2019. Curious by passer as well as designated visitors could stop by for a cup of tea or use the teahouse to rest or meditate. Usually on the first day people are just watching from the distance. But after the second or third day people usually get curious and they decide to have a closer look. That's why the teahouse is usually set up for at least for 3 days at one location to draw the audience into the space and atmosphere.

However, after seven years of experiences it became transparent, that more attention had to be paid to the aspect of the tea ceremony in its conventional setting. Therefore, the ceremony will be used in future as a framework story for a new type of space intervention. To be presented as of 2024 somewhere at a remote sport in the mountains surrounding Salzburg (The Flying Teahouse, 2024).

Due to the contribution of Jörg Schilling from Hamburg, the *"Teehaus in den Großen Wallanlagen"* in the city of Hamburg can also be analyzed and interpreted. When "Little Teahouse Hamburg" is entered into the search engine, the first thing that appears is the Chinese teahouse in Feldbrunnenstraße, built in 2008 as a symbol of the twinning of Shanghai and Hamburg. This sheds a significant light on the situation of the *"Teehaus in den Großen Wallanlagen"*, which – once a proud landmark of the International Horticultural Exhibition of 1963 – long enjoyed an unnoticed existence. After the recent restoration in accordance with the regulations for monument preservation, it once again increasingly breathes the atmosphere of a teahouse, which the architect Werner Blaser (1924–2019), author of the 1955 book *Temple and Teahouse in Japan,* described as follows: "Emptiness is the imperishable." The reference to this architecture, which is characterised by the spirit of the Japanese tea ceremony, because of its free division of space as well as clear and sober construction, should, combined with the modern-technology structure of the pavilion, convey to the visitors of the IGA the new cosmopolitanism and the striving for the progress of Hamburg (Schilling et al., 2021).

The teahouse must be seen in the context of the Japanese garden, which was laid out at the same time and to the north of it, which goes back to the ideas competition for the IGA announced in 1958 and the design of the garden architect Günther Schulze (1927–94). As a structural architect, Heinz Graaf (1910–80) was part of the award-winning consortium. He designed the square and glass pavilion, which was built together with three asymmetrically laid-out wooden platforms of different sizes over a watercourse. The widely cantilevered building appears to float above the water, supported by a narrow access core and held in place by a then state-of-the-art tension cable structure stretched across the roof and four piers. A flat lantern and the horizontal profiles of the development area and roof support the East Asian association (Schilling et al., 2021).

The intended use was catering. The Gesellschaft für Teewerbung mbH leased "Das Teehaus," as the location was called for simplicity's sake (as shown in Figure E.2.12). It developed into a popular meeting place, which was due to the inviting outdoor areas as well as the exotic impression. However, the teas on offer were from India and Ceylon. The range also included a "lemon iced tea" and a "Hawaiian tea cup" with Darjeeling, pineapple, and rum.

In fact, the teahouse had been planned as a temporary exhibition building. Various offers of use supported considerations for its preservation. Thus, it was converted into the headquarters of the "Special Service Office IGA 73" in preparation for the next horticultural exhibition. At the beginning of 1967, the senator responsible inaugurated it and did not spare those present a stereotype inherent in the building's name: "With the romantic word teahouse, each of us probably associates the terms Japan, geisha, cherry blossom." He wanted to emphasise the "compared to tea drinking certainly sober, in part much more tangible" activity to prepare an international horticultural exhibition. After this was completed, the building was primarily used as a day care centre for the elderly.

Figure E.2.12: Teehaus in den Großen Wallanlagen.
Source: Ries (2022)

It was not until 2015 that the teahouse, now a listed building but increasingly leaning because of the moving subsoil (the old Hamburg moat), received a commitment of funds for its renovation. This was completed at the end of 2021 and honored in a publication, the hamburger bauheft 37 "Das Teehaus in den Wallanlagen" (Schilling et al., 2021).

The Cottage English Tea Room, located in the "Gärten der Welt," highlights a special example of a teahouse in an English garden project in Berlin. The Cottage is divided into three main areas: the fireplace room, the public toilets, and circulation area or the space reserved for the management. Within the fireplace, which connects the terrace and garden, 32 people can be accommodated, while small dishes and tea being served (as shown in Figure E.2.13). Within the small teahouse, the British tea culture is the entire focus, tea time being celebrated in a British way with cucumber sandwiches and homemade scones with clotted cream. Having a considerable variety of teas, Darjeeling, Earl Grey and Ceylon are only some of the possible offers. Situated far from the hustle of the city, the teahouse is located next to a lake, with beautiful flowerbeds and small fountains (Haas Architekten, 2018).

Teehaus Timmendorf illustrates another beautiful example, being located at the Baltic Sea. First, the special design of the new pier (length 135 meters, developed by PPL Hamburg) symbolises a Japanese tea ceremony influenced by Zen Buddhism. The guests are comfortably guided to the teahouse at the pier's end (Developed by Schuberth Architects, Hamburg). The pier and the teahouse standing on a platform at the end form a unit and appear as an architectural ensemble (see Figure E.2.14). Built in 2013 and having 525 square meters space, the inspiration regarding the design and architecture style was embodied by the sea, spectacular views and strong winds. This teahouse offers a peaceful atmosphere where art is worshiped and tea is enjoyed.

Reaching the end of the examples and much information being reflected, for a precise view of all of the presented teahouses, Tables E.2.1–E.2.3 will gather the specifics, representing a comparison between the teahouses that have been analyzed and described above.

Figure E.2.13: Cottage – Englisches Teehaus.
Source: Haas Architekten/Atelier Dirk Altenkirch (2018)/https://www.thecottageberlin.de/

Figure E.2.14: Teehaus Timmendorf Strand.
Source: PPL Architektur und Stadtplanung (2012)

Table E.2.1: Contemporary teahouse concepts in the Netherlands, the UK, and Denmark.

Information	Teahouse name			
	TeaHouse in a bunker	Three-winged wooden teahouse	Floating Teahouse Ø	Fata Morgana Teahouse
location	Netherlands	Netherlands	Denmark	UK
year of construction	2004–2006	2011	2019	2018
architect + its location	UNStudio (Netherlands)	GAAGA (Netherlands)	PAN-Projects (London, UK)	Wolfgang Winter and Berthold + AECOM master planners
specific location (on the water, at a lake)	Dutch polder landscape	Located in a local park	On water (Canals)	Next to a small lake
size	80 m²	–	11 m²	700x700x660 cm
materials	Concrete and metallic	Reusable, demountable and massive wood	Acrylic tubes	Modified stainless steel grid, stainless steel sheets and bars
surrounding area	Stables and polo fields	"green heart" of the district	Water	Water
symbols	Historic structure	strengthen social cohesion and mutual respect amongst local residents	A place that can be used by locals for many purposes	Offering the idea of Fata Morgana
specifics	–	Possibility of serving tea	Possibility of hosting tea ceremonies	–

Source: Author.

Table E.2.2: Contemporary teahouse concepts in the Czech Republic and Austria.

	Teahouse's name		
Information	Flying teahouse	TeaHouse by David Maštálka	Black Teahouse
location	Austria	Czech Republic	Czech Republic
year of construction	2017	2009	2011
architect + its location	Gerhard Feldbacher (Austria)	A1 Architects (Prague)	A1 Architects (Prague)
specific location (on the water, at a lake)	The location is constantly changing	Around gardens	Next to a lake
size	–	2.13 m²	10 m²
materials	White paper walls	Oak and clad in burnt larch wood	Natural and sustainable
surrounding area	–	Cherry trees blossom	Garden, lake, trees
symbols	A communication place	Minimal place to gather	A minimal place for gathering
specifics	Teapot, Jizaikagi	Teapot hanging from the ceiling	Teapot hanging from the ceiling

Source: Author

Table E.2.3: Contemporary teahouse concepts in Germany.

Information			Teahouse's name		
	Bōki-an teahouse (Humboldt Forum Berlin)	The Ein Stein Tea House (Neuss)	Teehaus in den Großen Wallanlagen (Hamburg)	The Cottage English Tea Room (Berlin)	Teehaus Timmendorf
location	Germany	Germany	Germany	Germany	Germany
year of construction	2019	2020	1963 reopened 2022	2017	2013
architect + its location	Jun Ura (Japane)	Terunobu Fujimori (Japan)	Heinz Graaf	-	Andreas Schuberth (Hamburg)
specific location (on the water, at a lake)	Inside the Museum for Asian Art of the Berlin State Museum	Within a outdoor area of a musem	Wallanlagen (public park)	English Garden as part of the "Gärten der Welt" (public park)	at the Baltic Sea
materials	Corten steel echo	Natural materials	-	-	wood
symbols	The relationship between Germany and Japan	A relationship to culture and the museum's area	Place for social gathering, meeting point for elderly people	English gardening concept	Typical bridge facing the Baltic Sea
specifics	Design	Possibility of serving tea	Possibility of enjoying tea	British tea culture	Tea drinking

Source: Author

Conclusion

Teahouses are unqiue places of enriching experiences that extend beyond enjoying a simple cup of tea. As the previous examples have shown, these places serve as cultural centres, cultivating a sense of community and spirituality. With offers of selected and carefully picked tea blends, teahouses represent a place of reconnection with nature and oneself. Due to their strong relation towards history and traditions, it is clear that such establishments play a pivotal role in preserving and sharing the art of tea. In this fast moving word, teahouse remain a space for peacefulness, inviting visitor to not only drink a cup of tea, but also find solace and reflect.

References

Archello (2024). https://archello.com/project/tea-house-on-bunker. Retreived Jan 26th, 2024.

Boehm, F., & Panzenböck, L. (2021, 5 April). *Ein Stein Tea House and Other Architectures. Stiftung Insel Hombroich*. Retrieved December 29, 2021, from https://www.inselhombroich.de/de/veranstaltungen/terunobu-fujimori.

Buildner (n.d.). The acrrchitecture of iconic teahouses. *Bee breeders architecture competition organiser*. Retrieved January 14, 2022, from https://architecturecompetitions.com/the-architecture-of-iconic-teahouses.

Cabo, D.H. (2021). Floating Pavilion Teahouse. Retrieved January 25, 2022, from https://static.dezeen.com/uploads/2021/03/floating-pavilion-teahouse-o-by-pan-projects_dezeen_2364_col_2-191x191.jpg.

Carlson, C. (2021, 9 March). *Pan projects creates floating teahouse on Copenhagen canal. Dezeen.* Retrieved December 29, 2021, from https://www.dezeen.com/2021/03/09/teahouse-o-floating-pavilion-copenhagen-canals-pan-projects/.

Etherington, R. (2009, 19 March). *Tea house by David Maŝtálka. Dezeen.* Retrieved December 29, 2021, from https://www.dezeen.com/2009/03/19/tea-house-by-david-mastalka/.

Frearson, A. (2011). *Black Teahouse by A1 Architects*. Retrieved January 30, 2022, from https://static.dezeen.com/uploads/2011/09/dezeen_Black-Teahouse-by-A1Architects_11.jpg.

Frearson, A. (2011, 8 September). *Black Teahouse By A1 Architects. Dezeen.* Retrieved December 29, 2021, from https://www.dezeen.com/2011/09/08/black-teahouse-by-a1architects/.

Haas Architekten/Atelier Altenkirch, D. (2018). Retrieved July 20, 2023, from *The Cottage in den Gärten der Welt Berlin*. https://www.haas-architekten.de/projekte/oeffentliche/the-cottage-englisches-teehaus/.

Havlova, E. (2009). Tea house by David Maŝtálka. Retrieved January 25, 2022, from http://static.dezeen.com/uploads/2009/03/teahouse_david_a1_02.jpg.

https://static.dezeen.com/uploads/2011/09/dezeen_Black-Teahouse-by-A1Architects_11.jpg. (accessed January 30, 2022)

https://static.dezeen.com/uploads/2015/09/Teahouse-Leiden-Noord-by-GAAGA_dezeen_468_12.jpg. (accessed January 30, 2022)

https://static.dezeen.com/uploads/2015/09/Teahouse-Leiden-Noord-by-GAAGA_dezeen_1_1.gif. (accessed January 28, 2022)

https://static.dezeen.com/uploads/2021/03/floating-pavilion-teahouse-o-by-pan-projects_dezeen_2364_col_2-191x191.jpg. (accessed January 25, 2022)

https://winter-hoerbelt.de/wp-content/gallery/fata-m-teahouse/thumbs/thumbs_IMG_3189.jpg. (accessed January 25, 2022).

https://www.haas-architekten.de/projekte/oeffentliche/the-cottage-englisches-teehaus/. (accessed July 20, 2023).

https://www.humboldtforum.org/wp-content/uploads/2019/12/HF_eb00093213-Teehaus-Rendering -768x508.jpg. (accessed January 10, 2022).

https://www.metalocus.es/sites/default/files/styles/mopis_news_carousel_item_desktop/public/metalo cus_teronobu_fujimori_2020_ein_stein_teehaus_01.jpg?itok=MsKd_Cho. (accessed January 30, 2022).

https://www.ppl-hh.de/timmendorfer-strand-seeschloesschenbruecke/. (accessed July 20, 2023).

Morby, A. (2015a). Retrieved January 30, 2022, https://static.dezeen.com/uploads/2015/09/Teahouse-Leiden-Noord-by-GAAGA_dezeen_468_12.jpg.

Morby, A. (2015b). Floor plan. Retrieved January 28, 2022, from https://static.dezeen.com/uploads/2015/ 09/Teahouse-Leiden-Noord-by-GAAGA_dezeen_1_1.gif.

Morby, A. (2015, 2 September). *GAAGA uses prefabricated wooden walls to build "three-legged" tea house in a Dutch park. Dezeen*. Retrieved December 29, 2021, from https://www.dezeen.com/2015/09/02/gaaga-prefabricated-wooden-walls-three-legged-tea-house-dutch-park-leiden-netherlands/.

PPL Architektur und Stadtplanung. (2012). Timmendorfer Strand Seeschlößchenbrücke.

Neubau einer Seebrücke. Retrieved from July 20, 2023, from https://www.ppl-hh.de/timmendorfer-strand-seeschloesschenbruecke/.

Richters, C. (2007). *UNSTUDIO*. (n.d.). Retrieved January 30, 2022, from https://divisare-res.cloudinary.com/ images/f_auto,q_auto,w_600/v1/project_images/510657/2004924487/unstudio-christian-richters-tea-house-on-bunker.jpg.

Ries, A. (2022). *Planten un Blomen*. Retrieved July 20, 2023, from https://plantenunblomen.hamburg.de/frei zeit-und-erholung/teehaus-grosse-wallanlagen-565142.

Rosen, D. (2020, 27 August). The History of Chinese Teahouses. Teamuse. Retrieved January 2, 2022, from https://www.teamuse.com/article_200828.html.

Santorini, L. (2021). Retrieved January 30, 2022, from https://www.metalocus.es/sites/default/files/styles/ mopis_news_carousel_item_desktop/public/metalocus_teronobu_fujimori_2020_ein_stein_teehaus_ 01.jpg?itok=MsKd_Cho.

Schilling, J., et al. (2021). *hamburger bauheft 37: Das Teehaus in den Wallanlagen*. Schaff-Verlag.

Tea House. *Archello*. Retrieved December 29, 2021, from https://archello.com/it/project/tea-house.

The Cottage Berlin (2024). www.thecottageberlin.de. Retreived Jan 26th, 2024.

The Flying Teahouse. (2024). Fliegendes Teehaus (@theflyingteahouse).

UNSTUDIO. (n.d.). Tea house on bunker. Retrieved January 30, 2022, from https://divisare-res.cloudinary. com/images/f_auto,q_auto,w_600/v1/project_images/510657/2004924487/unstudio-christian-richters -tea-house-on-bunker.jpg.

URA Architects & Engineers. (n.d.). Retrieved January 10, 2022, from https://www.humboldtforum.org/wp-content/uploads/2019/12/HF_eb00093213-Teehaus-Rendering-768x508.jpg.

Winter, W. (2018). Fata Morgana Teahouse. University of Cambridge, U.K. Retrieved January 10, 2022, from https://winter-hoerbelt.de/wp-content/gallery/fata-m-teahouse/thumbs/thumbs_IMG_3189.jpg.

Irena Weber

E.3 Tea with art: Dialogical imagination and hospitality

Prologue: Tea is exactly like Fellini

At the 2019 Ljubljana International Film Festival (LIFFE), the Japanese film *Every Day a Good Day* won an audience award. The film is based on a book by Noriko Morishita, who also collaborated on the screenplay. The original title of Morishita's book, first published in English in Japan in 2019, was *Every Day a Good Day: Fifteen Lessons I learned about happiness from Japanese tea culture*. When it was published a year later by Allen & Unwin in the UK, the title was changed to *The Wisdom of Tea: Life Lessons from the Japanese Tea Ceremony*. Some nuances were lost in this "cultural translation" and the change of title. Every Day (is) a Good Day is a proverb in the Japanese Zen tradition and is often used on scrolls in teahouses, in what we usually refer to as a "tea ceremony." In Japan, however, as an English translator of the book notes, the term "tea ceremony" is avoided by the practitioners of Cha No Yu (The Way of Tea), and instead simply "Tea" is used. When the Zen saying is dropped from the title, so is the complexity as well as one of the central points of the book, which cannot be reduced to "wisdom" alone. Moreover, "Life Lessons" hardly correspond to the original "Happiness."

While it can be argued that the expression "tea ceremony" is more readily understood in a Western cultural context than "The Way of Tea," and therefore the translation (and transliteration) is reasonably accurate, the absence of the Zen proverb nonetheless makes unclear the multi-layered gradation of learning with and about tea over time. Without the proverb, we do not ask ourselves, as the Japanese characters in the film do, "What does this mean?" but rather assume that the book is about using tea to gain knowledge or "wisdom" about life. Fortunately, the film has retained the original title.

The film's opening scene shows a family of four coming home from the cinema, which we learn from the off-screen voice of a narrator: "When I was ten years old, my parents took me to see a movie called 'La Strada' by a director named Fellini. It was about poor street performers, it was depressing and in black and white. I could not make sense of it." The little girl's voice announces itself on the screen in a tiny plaintive voice: "We should have seen Disney!" The family enters the house, the parents apologise good-humoredly and laugh, and the door closes. In the next scene, the girl who complained about Fellini comes through the same door, ten years older, and the story of learning about tea and, indeed, Fellini unfolds. In the book, the connection is made clear in the preface, while in the film the references to Fellini are scattered in selected sections where the "metamorphosis," as Morishita describes it, is

https://doi.org/10.1515/9783110758573-016

more visual and theatrical. To understand the referenced scenes, one must be familiar with Fellini's film, as the main character takes on the role of Gensomina and reenacts her role in traveling to the sea with her cousin. The gradual appreciation of the tea is likened to the way one comes to appreciate Fellini based on life experiences and accumulated knowledge of art or, as Morishita explains it, in a time frame:

> there are things we understand immediately and things that take time to grasp. For the first kind of experience, a single experience is enough. But things in the second category, like Fellini's La Strada, open up to us only gradually, undergoing a slow metamorphosis over several encounters. And each time we understand a little more, we realise we have only seen a tiny slice of the whole. Tea is exactly like that. (Morishita, 2020, pp. xii–xii)

When one picks up a book about Japanese tea or watches a film about it, one does not expect it to start with a reference to a cult Italian director. Constructions of travel imaginaries supported by contemporary tourism marketing tend to reproduce notions of cultures as clearly rounded and separate entities, putting gauze over the gaze, as it were, of the view of the history of cultural borrowing and, in certain cases, cultural appropriation (Young, 2010). On the other hand, academic interest in cultural influence and exchange between Japanese and Western art continues to offer new insights beyond the well-known influence of Japanese art on Monet and Impressionism (see Morena, 2022). Contemporary cultural borrowings include examples of Japanese-inspired teahouses in Prague designed by a1architects (https://www.a1architects.cz/en/works/tea house-in-the-garden/), while European-inspired design can be found in Hiro Ajiki's homage to Cubism in chawan (https://www.katiejonesjapan.com/artists/hiro-ajiki/cubism-cha wan-tea-bowl/) or Yoko Zeltserman Miyaji's application of one of the British idioms with a cherry on top to the design of a teapot (https://kammteapotfoundation.org/prod uct/yoko-zeltserman-miyajiteapot/).

Complex cultural borrowing and cultural appropriation in the art are both historical and contemporary. The present chapter, while focusing on European tea culture as represented in art, also acknowledges a dialogical character of tea culture not only in the geographical East-West and Transatlantic sense but in cosmopolitan outlook and sensibility, which Beck (2008, p. 89) understands as a prerequisite to opening a space for dialogical imagination.

The chronotope of tea in literature and film

In the Cha Jing, the first book on tea, art was already an integral part of the work. Ostensibly designed as a handbook on the origins of tea, as well as the cultivation, production, tools, material culture, tea drinking habits, historical encounters, and dialogues, it was written on the silk scroll by Lu Yu in the eighth century during the Tang dynasty, in which calligraphy – itself an art form – was combined with illustrations and poetry. In one of the poems by the revered Wang Wei, a poet, painter, and musician, we encounter a motif that centuries later can be found in British literature, namely the soothing and restoring power of tea, the tea as a panacea.

Starting with "tea exaltation poems" such as Panacea: A Poem upon Tea: in Two Cantos written in 1701, literature played a significant role in "domesticating" tea outside the narrow circle of the court elites (Ellis et al. 2015, p.83). By the time Jane Austen set her pen to paper tea was such an everyday occurrence in Britain that it fell into the background of decor as it were. It was already part of the familiar setting in the Victorian novel (Farrell 2002, p. 162) in which tea scenes were somewhat surprisingly described and emphasised more by male than female writers, although tea preparation was a female domain.

In an attempt to analyze the significance and the role of tea in a selection of literary works and films, we turn to Bakhtin's concept of the chronotope and introduce the novel chronotope of Tea. Bakhtin introduced his concept of chronotopes in four essays, especially in Forms of Time and of the Chronotope in the Novel, translated from Russian and published under the title *The Dialogic Imagination* (2001). He acknowledged borrowing from Einstein's theory of relativity to apply to literary criticism, more or less as a metaphor, but expressing the key notion of the inseparability or fusion of time and space. He used the chronotope in various contexts, and the closest definition that can be found is as follows: "We will give the name chronotope (literally, "time-space") to the intrinsic connectedness of temporal and spatial relationships that are artistically expressed in literature" (Bakhtin, 2001, p. 84). Chronotopes are understood as "organising centres" for narrative (Bakhtin, 2001, p. 250) in which events and characters represent social relations and cultural practices. Polysemic in nature and applied in various forms in literary studies, the concept of the chronotope also links to Kant's *Critique of Pure Reason*, in which space and time are defined as indispensable forms of cognition. Unlike Kant, Bakhtin understood them as forms of the most immediate reality. His goal was to show what role these forms play in the process of concrete artistic cognition or artistic visualisation (Bakhtin, 2001, p. 85). Before applying this concept to the realm of the literary novel, Bakhtin invoked the image of the chronotope of real life, i.e., the agora, the public square where a citizen's life was shaped, completed, and publicly approved. Bakhtin's chronotope is a timespace in which narratives are intertwined and unraveled. His case studies were examples from classical literature from antiquity to Dostoevsky.

Bakhtin scholars understand and use the concept in very different ways, pointing out that Bakhtin himself did not give a precise definition, but there seems to be agreement that the concept is plural, that is, there is not just one chronotope but a multiplicity of them, and one large chronotope may contain several smaller ones.

In the case of the chronotope of encounter or meeting, its most salient feature seems to be the saturation of the experience with excitement and pronounced emotional familiar features of the travel experience. The derivative chronotope of the road expresses the same combination of saturation and acceleration; it is the literary symbol par excellence for the "flow of time," and the road is formed by the fusion of time and space (Bakhtin, 2001, p. 244). For Bakhtin, the road was often a familiar path to follow, representing the measure of saturated time, but the road itself could also stand for exploration and adventure.

The chronotope of tea that we are introducing in this chapter is at once understood as a motif in a novel or a film and as a set of larger and smaller chronotopes that are intertwined. The chronotope of tea, a liquid chronotope as it were, should not be confused with the so-called "edible chronotope" that Kirshenblatt-Gimblett (2004) introduced briefly without acknowledging Bakhtin, and with no explanation as to how exactly the tourist experience forms a chronotope when experience is formed within the chronotope or else it would somehow exist outside timespace.

Aside from tea forming part of the background, general environment, stage setting, and even soundscape, several chronotopes of tea were identified in selected novels and films (see Figure E.3.1).

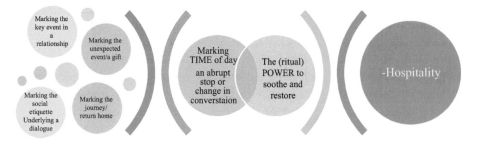

Figure E.3.1: The chronotopes of tea.
Source: Author

The major chronotope from which other smaller chronotopes of tea can be connected or derived from is the chronotope of tea hospitality. In the contemporary hospitality industry, the notion is reduced or limited to commercial hospitality, while in the anthropological sense of traditional hospitality the scope is broader, including the obligation and cultural exchange, and like with Mauss's gift it needs to be reciprocated. As Selwyn (2013, p. 172) points out in his analysis, hosts offer guests hospitality by giving them a combination of space, food, warmth, respect, and an opportunity to initiate or consolidate relationships.

In one of his famous lectures entitled Hostipitality Derrida (2000) enters into a creative dialogue with Kant's famous third article of A Perpetual Peace in which Kant makes an argument for universal hospitality in connection with the Cosmopolitan Right and Derrida embarks on the question of language which shows hospitality and hostility in close proximity as they share the same Latin root. Hospitality can be understood as an opportunity or indeed necessity to keep hostility at bay.

In literary works and films based on them, the rules of hospitality when serving tea are rather pronounced both in homes and at social gatherings like balls and outings and in the context of travel. As already indicated, the power of tea to restore balance, soothe, and transform both body and mind is known from the first writings on tea and is in Europe particularly associated with British literature and cinematic tradition. Tea is offered in times of turmoil, anxiety, unexpected events, and celebrations. It marks the abrupt change in conversation or underlines the end of the journey. It supports dialogue and marks the time in a sense of a particular time of day – something happens at tea time or before/after tea.

At this point, it is also worth noting the impact tea culture had on everyday expressions. Tea penetrated the English language with numerous idioms that non-native speakers need to learn even when they are not tea drinkers. When Auden (2019) writes the refrain "You are my cup of tea" the meaning of the expression needs to be understood or the poem does not make sense. The expression that something is a "tea party" may be wrongly understood as a literal tea party instead of something that is easily achieved or done. Not for all the tea in China means one is not prepared to do something and indeed tea cup itself may be fine "china." In idioms, as with the chronotopes, a dialogical imagination is key. When the often cited expression about tea and hope is encountered we tend to perceive it as an emic English feature when in fact in the literary work in which the phrase first appears it is uttered by an American character. Horace Bream (a young American) in Pinero's play *Sweet Lavender* is an example of an outside etic view on English culture when he comments upon being offered tea in a slightly awkward situation: "In English society, while there is tea there is hope" (Pinero, 1893, p. 77). Admittedly the etic point of view is envisioned by the English author who puts words into the mouth of the American character.

Cups of sense and sensibility: Tea with Jane Austen

Although tea is not a central topic in Austin's novels, as both Ellis (2015) and Farrell (2002) would agree, tea nevertheless "speaks to her" as Markman Ellis put it in his lecture on Austin in a sense of particular temporality, materiality, and representation (Ellis 2022, p. 11, 16). It is perhaps indicative that Ellis does not mention Austen in his co-authored book *Empire of Tea* (2015) although the importance of literary works has been discussed in the book in some detail, particularly in a way literature pertains to shaping the rituals and reflect social structure. It was only in a debate on the Regency period in the time when we all took to Zoom lectures that the focus has been turned to Austen and her tea as well.

Wilson (2011), in her book *Tea with Jane Austin,* based her analysis on Austen's personal correspondence while literary examples in the book come from various authors and are combined with recipes and anecdotes. It is clear from the structure of the book that the author tried to extend rather thin historical evidence into more embellished, imagined importance that tea played in Austen's life which as we shall see later is also pronounced in films and TV series that are based on Austen's books. The daily tea routines of the Austen family can be glimpsed at the Hampshire Cottage, Austen's house turned museum. From the display, we know that the family predominantly used porcelain teapots, but silver ones were also part of the family teaware, perhaps resembling Paul Storr's one (Figure E.3.2).

Figure E.3.2: Paul Storr Teapot.
Note; Paul Storr/ Storr & Mortimer, "Teapot" 1838–1839. Sterling silver.
Photo: Kamm Teapot Foundation
Source: Kamm Teapot Foundation

As was already noted, tea was such an integral part of everyday life that Austen never really elaborates on it in her novels. In terms of narrative structure and details, she is much more focused on dinner scenes. As Farrell (2002, p. 163) points out, an invitation to tea was a minor one compared to a dinner invitation, although this pertained more to the situation in the city than in the countryside because travel was still more arduous in the country and visitors were expected to be treated to tea as well as dinner.

Comparing the writing in *Emma* with two films (1996 and 2020), it is noticeable that both films open with tea scenes while the introduction in the novel has none. The 2020 film adds an intriguing sound element to it, namely the conversation is punctuated by the rhythmic placement of a teacup on the saucer. Director Autumn de Wilde is well-known for directing music videos and has added a layer to the interpretation of Austen by creating a soundscape chronotope of tea. The often cited passage from *Emma* marking the stop in conversation or changing the direction of a conversation by serving tea when a particular visitor is rather rambling comes from Mrs. Bates's monologue at the ball: "No coffee, I thank you, for me – never take coffee. – A little tea if you please, sir, by and bye, – no hurry – Oh! here it comes. Every thing so good!" (Austen, 2014, p. 2876)

In terms of the presence of tea chronotopes and dialogical imagination, the 1995 film *Sense and Sensibility* is a prime example. The script was written by Emma Thompson and together with director Ang Lee, who had poor command of English at the time, created an interpretation, and formed a dialogue with Austin that is at once very English yet with Chinese sensibility regarding a sense of duty, tea hospitality, ethics, and the importance of family obligations. Ang Lee, when approached to direct the film, initially thought that a mistake must have been made. After reading Austen he agreed to direct the film as he recognised the Confucian ethics in Austen's social relations and rules of obligation as well as in the attitude toward the landscape, insisting the film had to be shot where Austen lived. Thompson, in her diaries that accompanied the script, commented on Ang Lee's directorial approach as "sensibility without sentimentality" (1995, p. 222) and that Austen would be astonished as it corresponded to her own, or at least that is how Thompson herself interprets and imagines Austen.

In the 1995 version of *Sense and Sensibility*, alongside domestic scenes of breakfast and afternoon tea meal with family or visiting neighbours and relatives there are several prominent chronotopes of tea shaping the narrative. In a scene where Fanny Dashwood, a greedy and insensitive new mistress of the Dashwood house, is displeased with the tone and content with the conversation she changes the course with a sharp exclamation, "Tea!," effectively ending the scene and demonstrating her power in cutting the discussion short. When Marianne Dashwood is unexpectedly presented with the musical instrument as a gift from Colonel Brandon, the immediate response from Elinor is to turn to a servant to fetch some tea as the joyous occasion clearly had to be marked by a cup. In an emotional scene in which Marianne in great anguish locks herself in the room, the teacup is passed from the youngest to the oldest sister in front of the locked door in the hope it could be handed over to the middle sister to soothe the pain. When the door remains closed Elinor eventually sits on the stairs and drinks the cup herself. Since the scene is shot from above tea is clearly seen in a teacup, meaning that the teacup was not a mere prop. In another prolonged scene of anguish when Marianne goes missing from her walk Elinor is offered one cup after another in quick succession that would be quite improbable to handle in real life. The end of the journey and homecoming is marked in several scenes, the most pronounced one when Mrs. Palmer, halfway out of the carriage, exclaims loudly, "Oh, Mrs. Bunting: We are in desperate need of tea! What a journey we've had. My bones are rattling still."

After re-watching the arguably more popular *Pride and Prejudice* TV series and two films, no tea chronotopes of note could be identified, which perhaps attests to the particular dialogical sensibility of Thompson and Lee. In 2000 Lee directed the film *Crouching Tiger, Hidden Dragon* which he described as "Sense and Sensibility with martial arts" (Köhler and Palmer, 2013).

"Just the ticket": Tea at Downton Abbey

Downton Abbey's globally successful TV series (2010–2015) and two films (2019, 2022) are not based on literary work but on an original script of a period drama genre. The TV series starts with a historic event, the sinking of the Titanic in 1912, and follows the Crowley family and their servants for six seasons to 1926. The subsequent film *Downton Abbey* (2019) and its sequel *Downton Abbey: A New* Era (2022) take place in 1927 and 1928. Though several actual historical events are depicted it is entirely a work of fiction reinforcing both an emic view of English society and an etic response from the audiences in Europe, the USA, and Asia to what is considered quintessential British-ness, interior design and tea culture included. Some direct references to Jane Austen are found both in TV series dialogues and in characters and behaviours. When Dowager, Countess of Grantham (played by Dame Maggie Smith), hosts one of her acquaintances, Lady Shackleton, to run interference with a single peer, Lady Shackleton remarks: "Of course, a single peer with a good estate won't be lonely long if he doesn't want too be," to which Dowager countess replies "You sound like Mrs. Bennett" (Season 5, episode 1), referring to the famous opening statement in Pride and Prejudice: "It is a truth universally acknowledged, that a single man in possession of a good fortune, must be in want of a wife" (Austin 2014, p. 984). *Pride and Prejudice* is again referenced when Downton Abbey, a stately home, is to be opened to the public with charged entrance fees and skepticism was raised whether anyone would be interested in a visit. At an afternoon tea scene, Dowager Countess of Grantham raises the question of why would people be interested in a perfectly ordinary house with chairs and tables, to which her guest Mrs. Crowley responds that not everyone lives in such a house and that people are curious, sealing this with a statement: "Even Elizabeth Bennett wanted to see what Pemberley was like inside" (Season 6, episode 6). These direct references serve to support and reinforce the accepted culturally constructed imagery of Austin's world and its enduring popularity.

In most TV episodes, and the first of two films, tea is a part of the family's daily routine. In the last film tea nearly disappears from view and no tea chronotopes could be identified. The reason for that absence is hard to pronounce without further research. The chronotopes of tea in the series and the first film are in part similar to the ones found in Austen: determining the time of day, and changing the course of conversation (are we going to have tea or not?). Others are specifical to mark the social status, as is the case of the invitation to tea by a member of the Royal family and on the opposite side the Crowley family going to tea at the cottage of their cook to help her build a positive image in a cottage rental.

Dowager Countess regularly summons individual members of the family to tea when she needs to discuss matters of importance to her. In all those cases the servants only bring in the teaware but the tea itself is prepared by the Dowager herself. In close-up scenes it is visible that tea is being elaborately prepared, cups are not empty, and several pots and tea urns are used – there is great focus on detail although it is fiction. In one of the scenes where tension among the family is about to boil over the door opens and tea is brought in, with Dowager Countess exclaiming "Just the ticket." The phrase "just the ticket" is a shortened expression of "that's the etiquette," which conveys that something is just the proper thing to do. The word is of French origin and refers to specific instructions for proper behaviour at court ceremonies (https://www.etymonline.com/word/etiquette).

In a published Downton Abbey tea cookbook, in essence a tourist souvenir, several photographs featuring tea are prominent (see Figures E.3.3 and E.3.4) and have been made into a collage by the author, due to demands of the copyright. Collages are made with an inclusion of a teaware.

Figure E.3.3: Collage, "Downton Abbey afternoon tea".
Source: Author

Downton Abbey afternoon tea cookbook with the image of the dowager having tea outside with a view of the estate and the vintage Davenport teacup owned by the author.

Downton Abbey afternoon tea cookbook with the image of Mary Crawley holding a cup of tea in the library and the porcelain teacup that was designed for the author by the renowned Slovenia artist Katja Bricman.

Figure E.3.4: Collage, "Downton Abbey cookbook".
Source: Author

In re-reading and particularly re-watching familiar works of art entirely through the lens of tea which used to be undistinguishable from the surrounding, just part of the background suddenly emerges into focus as a versatile prop, a chronotope, and an element of dialogical imagination that shapes and supports the narrative like Bakhtin's organising centre. It opens an intriguing new layer and insight not much different from Morishita's sentiment on Fellini.

From Samovar to Suprematism: Tea with Kazimir Malevich

Samovar is perceived as an indistinguishable part of Russian tradition and culture. Its status was well established by the corpus of nineteenth-century Russian literature of Puschkin, Tolstoy, Chekhov, and Dostoevsky. It is represented as a part of the Russian identity in films such as *An Unfinished Piece for Mechanical Piano* based on Chekhov's play or *The Last Station*, a biographical film of the last days of Tolstoy who was known for his passion for tea drinking and could not imagine writing without it. When Malevich painted his *Samovar* in 2013 in a cubist style it marked his path toward the new artistical style and the movement of Suprematism (see Figure E.3.5).

Figure E.3.5: Samovar by Kazimir Malevich.
Source: https://commons.wikimedia.org/wiki/File:
Samovar_(Malevich,_1913).jpg

In 2019 two distinct exhibitions marked the two hundred and seventy-fifth anniversary of the Imperial Porcelain Factory in St Petersburg Russia. One opened in May at the St. Petersburg City Museum, the other in December at the Winter Palace.

The prominent place was given to tea sets designed for the Russian Imperial family through Soviet revolutionary transformation for the masses from the early 1920s till contemporary Russian porcelain engaging diverse artists.

Kazimir Malevich and his students used porcelain as the medium in which they expressed a new art of Suprematism in which the utilitarian perfection as they called it may be expressed in a teapot that is not necessarily designed as a utilitarian object (Karpova, 2019, p. 198). They were not expressing contempt for utilitarian application but rather emphasising the effort of preparing and pouring tea in such an object which reminds us of the Chinese expression of the gong fu cha, which carries a meaning of preparing tea with effort (as well as skill and practice).

Several teapots that are part of the Hermitage Museum collection were designed not as useful everyday objects but as transcending objects of the new art movement. Malevich contributed designs for the porcelain work but has not worked in the factory himself; this task was left to his students (Figure E.3.6).

In the famous white teapot from 1923, the geometrical shapes that were already seen in the cubist painting are here in three dimensions that underline the effort of tea pouring as a very conscious performance (Figure E.3.7).

Figure E.3.6: Malevich's teapots design at St Petersburg exhibition.
Source: Author

Figure E.3.7: Malevich's Suprematist Teapot (designed 1923).
Note; Kazimir Malevich (Russian, 1878–1935) / State Porcelain Factory (USSR), Suprematist Teapot
designed 1923, manufactured circa 1930. Porcelain
Photo: Kevin O'Dwyer
Source: Kamm Teapot Foundation

Tea with contemporary artists: Museum performances

In our everyday life, we may refer to tea as a "ritual" or may practice the tea ceremony in its prescribed ritualistic element. While our tea can be performed for us alone in the context of an art performance, an audience is required.

Every type of performance is, in Turner's sense, an explanation and explication of life. Ancient Greek dramas, which developed out of certain religious rituals, were the social meta-commentaries of the society of the time, the stories that a group told itself about itself, or the plays it performed about itself. Each society has its metacommentaries, active mirrors that it sets up to analyze the social structure. Ritual as the transmission of a collective message is a classical assumption that derives from Durkheim's axiom that a ritual is an internal act through which a group celebrates or glorifies itself and binds itself together in the affirmation of shared values, creating and affirming a world of meanings or symbols that the group shares. The performance of ritual is not only an internal matter for the group; it can be oriented towards cultural change or in public rituals can be directed at non-participants, even when they are present only as categorical referents, i.e. only symbolically.

Four contemporary art performances on the theme of tea are compared as rituals and metacommentaries and not from the point of view of art criticism. Tea for Five: Opium Clippers was attended in person. Let me get you a nice cup of tea was seen as an exhibition at the Tate Modern while the other two, The tea set and Tea On The Table, were analyzed based on the published videos, and the latter was also discussed in personal correspondence with the artist (see Table E.3.1).

Tea for Five: Opium Clippers by Slovenian artist Neja Tomšič has been running since 2017 and has been performed in museums and diverse other settings well over one hundred times. When living in Baltimore the artist became acutely aware of the opioid crisis and learned that one of the first opium clippers was built right in Baltimore. She became interested in that particular history which brought her to the tea and opium trade and the conflicts that resulted in the opium wars. The performance she envisioned was from the very beginning focused on the clippers. She has commissioned a ceramic tea set and hand-painted it using historical events and elements (see Figure E.3.8).

In April 2022 the author participated in the performance at Cukrarna Gallery, the contemporary art space in Ljubljana. In the dimly lit setting with a black cloth on the table the artist was preparing Dahongpao wulong in a gong fu cha style while explaining the design of the individual teacups and narrating selected aspects of the opium and tea history. Although she was performing a tea ceremony with skilled smooth gestures and appeared to be rather knowledgeable of gong fu cha she was for some reason using tea tongs, cha jia instead of a tea digger spoon cha shi, or even tea pin cha zhen. It was a choice that simply didn't make sense. The group of participants was too diverse to become connected by participating in the tea ritual so the performance in

Table E.3.1: Tea in art performances in museums.

Performance	Artist	Museum/Year	Content focus	Audience participation	Additional material
Tea for five: Opium clippers	Neja Tomšič	Tate Modern, London, 2019/ Cukrarna, Ljubljana, 2022	History of tea; critical social and cultural reflection; tea ceremony	Group drinking tea & limited conversation	An artist book
Let me get you a nice cup of tea	Yasmin Jahan Nupur	*Tate Modern*, London, 2022 (exhibition till the end of 2023)	History of tea; British colonialism; exchange of ideas	One-on-one drinking tea & conversation	A book of tea recipies
Tea On The Table	Oksana Yushko	Tarusa Branch of the Pushkin State Museum of Fine Arts, 2021	Collective work on the unfinished sketch by Russian artist Eduard Steinberg & tea ceremony; memories	Group drinking tea & co-creating a tea design; collective action; tea ceremony; immersed participation, collective action	Co-created tea design as part of the museum collection
The tea set	Rain Wu	Design Museum, London, 2016/ Tate Modern, London, 2017	History of tea; cultural exchange and borrowing; design; tea ceremony	Group tea tasting & individuals measuring the tea for the teapot	

Source: Author.

that regard did not achieve its goal of a shared, bonded experience that would in any sense be transformative. This, however, does not diminish the scope and depth of the performance that is based on well-researched tea history and critical reflection of the contemporary inequalities in global neoliberal capitalism. In these aspects, it is much broader in scope and content than the other three performances.

Also impressive was the nice cup of tea which was performed in Tate Modern by Yasmin Jahan Nupur, a Bangladeshi artist as part of the colonial histories. The room setting with various elements that testify to colonial heritage as well as the video is still on display. Participants that had to reserve the spot to sit down with the artist were given a cup of herbal infusion while the narrative was about tea which is to a certain extent perplexing. A nice cup of tea actually included herbs from the artist's garden (see Figure E.3.9).

Tea on the table was a site-specific performance by contemporary Russian artist Oksana Yushko who happened upon an unfinished graphic sketch with two circles and the word "service" when researching Eduard Steinberg's work. As the artist herself explained in a personal communication Steinberg was from the second wave of

Figure E.3.8: Tea for five.
Source: Author

Figure E.3.9: Tate modern display.
Source: Author

the Russian avant-garde, and is famous for his metaphysical still lives. The unfinished work gave an idea to design a performance in which the local community as well as guest visitors and even passers-by would become engaged in a conversation and participate in collective action.

In the artist's words, the tea cups used in the performance were "from different tea sets and times, which we collected from various people, composing an 'impossible tea set'. People drank tea, talking and changing places and imprinting tea rings on a paper roll, which was shifted every time after new people came in. Steinberg has compiled the whole alphabet of his own signs in painting. 'Tea marks' left by people refer to their own memories and imagination. The tea ceremony is a ritualised social situation in which each piece has its symbolic meaning. Drinking tea in the artist's studio shows hospitality and openness of the place." The performance was site-specific and commissioned by The Pushkin State Museum of Fine Arts. The artist communicated that she intends to repeat the performance in a new setting but retain the core idea of collective action and exploration of memories.

The tea set by the Taiwanese artist Rain Wu currently living in Europe combines tea history narrated or rather read from the notes with an originally designed tea set that appears difficult to use – perhaps not in the same sense as Malevich's teapot but more in that the shapes are not readily practical. She served English breakfast tea and invited some participants to measure tea into the teapot. From the video, it is difficult to hear what exactly she is narrating from the tea history. The tea set is referred to as a narrative sculpture.

All four performances are to some degree focused on tea history. All include audience participation, although to various degrees, and three of them have produced additional artistic material.

Epilogue: Back to the future of tea design and culture

As the EU adopted the Communication on the New European Bauhaus in September 2021 (https://new-european-bauhaus.europa.eu/about/about-initiative_en) it seems fit to conclude the chapter by looking back at the original Bauhaus and its influence in the teaware design. Arguably the most famous piece was designed by the founder of Bauhaus. Gropius's teapot designed for Rosenthal remains in circulation today (Fritz, 1998) (see Figure E.3.10).

In his manifesto, Gropius called for a new unity among diverse stakeholders in the art and craft: "Let us then create a new guild of craftsmen without the class distinctions that raise an arrogant barrier between craftsman and artist!" (Bauhaus Manifesto, 1919). If the personal story of Grete Marks (Margarete Heymann-Loebenstein) is anything to go by then the noble sentiment of unity and abandoning the "arrogant

Figure E.3.10: Walter Gropius, TAC Teapot 1969 Porcelain.
Note: Walter Gropius (German, 1883–1969) / Rosenthal (Germany est. 1879)
Photo: David H. Ramsey
Source: Kamm Teapot Foundation

barriers" in Bauhaus did not stretch to gender equality. Grete Marks joined the Weimar Bauhaus and studied under famous artists including Paul Klee but was repeatedly denied enrolment in ceramics. Instead, she was kept in the bookbinding workshop and eventually gave up and left. After her marriage, she founded a ceramics business together with her husband and brother-in-law. She applied the knowledge gained at Bauhaus and followed the Bauhaus motto of designing and producing "modern, useful, and beautiful household items for [the] individual" (Otto & Rössler, 2019, p. 36; see Figure E.3.11).

Figure E.3.11: Grete Marks "Teapot" (1928).
Note: Margarete Marcks (German, 1899–1990), Teapot circa 1928. Silverplated alpacca, ebony
Photo: David H. Ramsey
Source: Kamm Teapot Foundation

The modern design of her silver teapot readily reminds one of teaware designed for Alessi several decades later which would attest to her talent that was not entirely recognised in her lifetime. The New European Bauhaus as envisioned by the EU calls for imagination, creativity, sustainability inclusivity, and cooperation. Tea culture in its potential – hospitality, dialogical imagination, and co-creation – should well be part of it. Designing a different future that is sustainable, creative, and inclusive should in effect be our cup of tea.

Acknowledgements: The author would like to thank the artist Oksana Yushko for providing the vital information about her performance Tea on the table.

References

Auden, W.H., & Isherwood, C. (2019). *The complete works of W.H. Auden: Plays and other dramatic writings, 1928–1938*. Princeton Legacy Library.

Austen, J. (2014). *The complete works of Jane Austen*. Delphi Classics. E-book.

Bakhtin, M.M. (2001). *The dialogic imagination*. University of Texas Press.

Bauhaus Manifesto. (1919). https://gropius.house/location/bauhaus-manifesto/#:~:text=Together%20let%20us%20desire%2C%20conceive,WALTER%20GROPIUS%201919.

Beck, U. (2008). *The cosmopolitan vision*. Polity.

Derrida, J. (2000). Hostipitality. Angelaki. *Journal of Theoretical Humanities, 5*(3), 3–18.

Ellis, M., Coulton, R., & Mauger, M. (2015). *Empire of tea*. Reaktion Books.

Ellis, M. (2022). Jane Austen and the British way of tea. Online lecture. Retrieved October 11, 2023, from https://www.janeaustenandco.org/asia-and-the-regency.

Farrell, M. (2002). *From cha to tea. A study of the influence of tea drinking on British Culture – a mini-anthology of British Literature from 1660*. Universitat Jaume.

Fritz, B. (1998). The Tea Service TAC1 by Walter Gropius. Verlag Forum.

Karpova, Y. (2019). 'A thing of quality defies being produced in quantity': Suprematist porcelain and its afterlife in Leningrad design. In C. Loder (Ed.), *Celebrating suprematism. New Approaches to the Art of Kazimir Malevich* (pp. 198–218). Brill.

Kirshenblatt-Gimblett, B. (2004). Foreword. In L. Long (2004), *Culinary tourism*. The University Press of Kentucky.

Morena, F. (2022). *Gli impressionisti e il Giappone. Arte tra Oriente e Occidente Storia di un'infatuazione*. Giunti.

Morishita, N. (2020). *The wisdom of tea: Life Lessons from the Japanese tea ceremony*. Allen & Unwin.

Köhler R., & Palmer, S. (2013) "What do you know of my heart?" The role of sense and sensibility in Ang Lee's Sense and Sensibility and Crouching Tiger. *Hidden Dragon Philosophy Book* Chapter 9. https://researchonline.nd.edu.au/phil_chapters/9.

Neame, G. (2020). *The official Downton Abbey afternoon tea cookbook*. Frances Lincoln Publishers.

Otto, E., & Rössler, P. (2019). *Bauhaus women: A global perspective*. Herbert Press.

Pinero, A. (1893). Sweet Lavender. A comedy in three acts. Digitalized by Google Books. https://www.google.si/books/edition/Sweet_Lavender/-Wo-AAAAYAAJ?hl=en&gbpv=1&dq=sweet+lavender&pg=PA165&printsec=frontcover.

Prezelj, P. (2021). Koordinate spomina. O knjigi Opium Clippers Neje Tomšič. Membrana 95/96. https://www.membrana.si/recenzija/koordinate-spomina-o-knjigi-opium-clippers-rostfrei-publishing-2018-neje-tomsic/.

Selwyn, T. (2013). Hospitality. In M. Smith and G. Richards (Eds.), *The Routledge handbook of cultural tourism* (pp. 172–77). Routledge.

Thompson, E. (1995). *The sense and sensibility. Screenplay & diaries. Bringing Jane Austen's novel to film*. Newmarket Press.

Wilson, K. (2011). *Tea with Jane Austen*. Frances Lincoln.

Wu, J. (2017). *An illustrated modern reader of the classic of tea*. Shanghai Press and Publishing Development Company.

Young, J. (2010). *Cultural appropriation and the arts*. Wiley-Blackwell.

Yu, L. (2011). *Cha Jing. El clásico del té*. Ediciones Librería Argentina.

Filmography

An Unfinished Piece for Mechanical Piano. 1977. 2020 digitally remastered. [film] Directed by Nikita Mikhalkov.

Alexander, J. (Director). (1995). *Sense and Sensibility* [Tv series].

Curtis, S. (Director). (2022). *Downton Abbey* [Film].

de Wilde, A. (Director). (2020). *Emma* [Film].

Engler, M. (Director). (2019). *Downton Abbey* [Film].

Hoffman, M. (Director). (2009). *The Last Station* [Film].

Lee A. (Director). (2000). *Crouching Tiger, Hidden Dragon* [Film].

Lee, A. (Director). (1995). *Sense and Sensibility* [Film].

McGrath D. (Director). (1996). *Emma* [Film].

Omori T. (Director). (2018). *Every Day a Good Day* [Film].

Percival, B., et al. (Directors). (2010–2015). *Downton Abbey* [Tv series].

Video

Tea on the table. Performance Oksana Yushko. (2021). https://www.youtube.com/watch?v=ASXjZ3kabkI.

Sit down for tea with artist Yasmin Jahan Nupur | Tate. (2023). https://www.youtube.com/watch?v=T_3cU1udmH8.

Neja Tomšič – The opium clippers – performance. (2022). https://www.youtube.com/watch?v=ouymRPC5lrM.

The tea set. Film by Agnes Yu-Hsin Su. Project by Rain Wu. (2017). https://vimeo.com/204457116.

Neja Tomšič – The opium clippers – performance. (2022). https://www.youtube.com/watch?v=ouymRPC5lrM.

The tea set. Film by Agnes Yu-Hsin Su. Project by Rain Wu. (2017). https://vimeo.com/204457116.

Katrina Wild and Gundega Silniece

E.4 TEA TEA ME: Digital tools towards more accessibility

Introduction

This chapter investigates the role of digital innovations in relation to tea tourism, education, and hospitality. It describes and explores the potential implications of the TEA TEA ME mobile app, which is a booking platform for tea tours, events, and education, serving as a global community space for both tea industry professionals and tea enthusiasts. Relevant literature is reviewed about tea tourism, European tea plantations, tea education, tea apps, and the establishment of online communities via technological innovations. Empirical methods have been employed, such as focus groups and interviews with tea industry specialists and tea producers, adding up to a total of 13 personal correspondences. This chapter was written at the beta testing stages of the development of the TEA TEA ME app, and, as such, statistical data to underpin the model are yet to be produced in volume. In summary, the chapter examines the current state of tea-related experiences in Europe and what role platforms like TEA TEA ME play in this context.

Tea tourism

Tea tourism has emerged as a new paradigm in the tourism industry, offering unique and authentic experiences to contemporary tourists. This niche segment has the potential to enhance the brand image and marketing of tea-producing destinations while fostering relationships with potential customers. Moreover, it provides an additional source of income to farmers and producers, while showcasing tea planting areas, beautiful natural environments, as well as the historical and cultural heritage of the land. As a result, some travel agencies in the tea-producing areas have incorporated various tea-related activities such as tea trails, exhibits, festivals, homestays in plantations, teahouse and shop visits, pottery kilns, and museums in their tour packages (Fernando et al., 2017). Tea tourists have expectations concerning relaxation, homely environments, and tea plantations when visiting a tea destination (Jolliffe & Aslam, 2009) and incorporating leisure activities such as tea leaf plucking, plantation visits, tea tasting, and knowledge sharing with workers who do the tea plucking holds great potential (Fernando et al., 2017). Developing sustainable tourism in tea regions could help develop market retention and stability of the tea industry, which has gradually fallen in the face of competition. The industry recognises the need for more investments in value addition rather than focusing on bulk exports. By providing an

https://doi.org/10.1515/9783110758573-017

experiential value proposition, tea tourism adds value to the generic business model of the tourism industry and enhances the potential for the tea sector to extend its value margin beyond the traditional tourism business model and increase the net gain (Sultana & Sultana Khan, 2018). Recently emerging innovations in the tea tourism field have showcased promising value proposition strategies, for instance, the development of a further niche: gastronomical tea tourism. It was demonstrated by two village tea communities in Japan (Umegashima, Shizuoka) and Thailand (Phaya Phrai, Chiang Rai) during a two-year project (2020–2022) funded by The Toyota Foundation, where the two groups developed tea cuisine, tea cocktails, and a package of tea trails with unique small-scale activities benefiting the community members by exhibiting their unique tea heritage as well as recognising its value (Goswami, 2023). Another example is that both Taiwan and North America have introduced English-style teahouses that attract tourists; these trends demonstrate the transference of tea cultures and traditions across borders and continents (Jolliffe, 2007).

Tea tourism has the potential to foster collaboration with local communities and small tea estate holders through the promotion of homestay units and unique cultural immersions. Such collaboration is particularly relevant for individuals and families facing socio-economic challenges, such as poor housing, insufficient land, or income, who are often excluded from ecotourism development. In order to maximise the benefits of tea tourism to the local community. Despite the growing interest in tea tourism, there is a lack of consideration regarding its impact on the local communities and how to ensure a positive community impact, therefore, present-day tea-related tourism has the potential to be an instrument of social change in terms of sustainable development projects (Jolliffe, 2007). However, the adverse effects of tourism must also be taken into consideration. Whilst infrastructure development, such as roads, railways, airports, etc., can have a positive impact on rural areas, mass commercial tourism can be detrimental to local communities, leading to an inadequate generation of income and employment opportunities. It has been argued that ethnic minority regions can benefit from tourism by reviving cultural traditions, which inbound tourists desire to experience. However, it can also result in the distortion and commercialisation of local traditions to suit the consumptive desires and gaze of the inbound tourist. This is compounded by large-scale tourism, which at times harms the natural environment and causes exploitation of local cultures and communities. Regrettably, local communities where mass tourism is developed do not always receive direct benefits, as governments and tourism authorities often work with tourism developers without adequate consultation or involvement of the local communities. To address the challenges of mass commercial tourism, cultural sensitivity and community-based sustainable tourism must be prioritised. This requires targeting the key stakeholders involved in the production and consumption of tourism, namely the government, tourism operators and developers, local communities, and the incoming tourists themselves. Achieving this objective will necessitate a significant shift in the mindset and practices of the tourism industry (Sigley, 2010).

Tea production and tourism in Europe

Tea tourism aligns with cultural tourism and shares similarities with other beverage and food-related forms of tourism such as wine tourism in European countries like France in terms of its history and connections with travel; thus it is motivated by an interest in the history, traditions, and consumption of the beverage tea (Jolliffe, 2007). This type of tourism has gained attention from researchers studying concept-based tourism and has been found to share attributes with eco-tourism, agro-tourism, and sustainable tourism as defined by various authors. The scale of European tea gardens is not meant for mass production at the moment, hence it is not significantly exploiting of either the natural or cultural resources. Thus, the cultural heritage preservation of tea traditions in Europe relates more to tea consumption practices (British Afternoon tea and East Frisian Tea, for instance). Engagement in tea and cultural appreciation of tea traditions of foreign lands can also be witnessed, such as Chinese Gong Fu Cha, which is a peculiar phenomenon occurring in many European teahouses, for instance in Czech Republic's teahouses (čajovny). In the pursuit of attracting tourists, not only tea-producing countries but also tea-consuming countries are starting to incorporate tea tourism as a means for visitors to engage in tea-related activities and experiences.

The emergence of tea tourism in Europe in the form of tea garden visits is a rather modern phenomenon attributable to the recent inception of tea plantations on the continent. The cultivation and production of tea in Europe have primarily occurred in the regions surrounding the continent, including the Azorean Islands (Portugal), Georgia, Azerbaijan, Russia, and Türkiye, since the end of the nineteenth century. Notably, most of these plantations are still operational. Tea cultivation in the Azores was initiated in 1874, and at the beginning of the twentieth century, 14 tea gardens were in operation in the north of the Island of São Miguel, two of which, Cha Gorreana and Porto Formoso, remain operational and represent important local tourist attractions. These two gardens comprise a combined total of approximately 40 hectares. According to Ukers (1935), tea production in Georgia began in 1893, on the eastern coast of the Black Sea near Batumi, with the cultivation of 150 hectares of tea using seeds sourced from China, India, and Ceylon. The plantation employed 15 Chinese labourers to manage its operations. The Russian Ministry of Agriculture set up an experimental station in Chakvi in 1900, which offered local landowners seedlings free of charge, leading to a rapid increase in tea production. By 1913, the tea plantations had expanded to cover 960 hectares and were established in other regions such as Guria and Martvili. After the First World War and the Russian Revolution, tea production in the region experienced a sharp decline. However, the Soviet Union government sought to attain self-sufficiency in tea production and increased the land dedicated to tea cultivation to 34,000 hectares in 1933. The tea plantations in Sochi (Russia) and Rize (Türkiye) were primarily developed using the material and expertise from Georgia. Tea plantations in Lankaran, Azerbaijan were initiated at the start of the twentieth century and developed under Soviet rule. Geographically, the Lankaran-Astara region is proximal to the Iranian region of Lahijan, where Iranian tea is predominantly grown (Mazerolle, 2016).

Based on the data provided by the United Nations World Tourism Organization (UNWTO), more than 900 million international tourists travelled in 2022, representing a twofold increase compared to 2021, albeit accounting for only 63% of the pre-pandemic levels. This surge in tourism was evident in all global regions, with the Middle East experiencing the most substantial relative increase as arrivals reached 83% of pre-pandemic levels. Similarly, Europe recorded nearly 80% of pre-pandemic levels, hosting 585 million arrivals in 2022. In light of the challenging economic climate, tourists are expected to seek value for money and opt for domestic travel (UNTWO, 2023). Amidst the COVID-19 pandemic, tea tourism has also encountered significant challenges, particularly concerning travelling to tea-producing regions in Asia and Africa from the West. Such travel has become increasingly daunting, given the stringent travel restrictions imposed globally. Nonetheless, the impediments to European tea lovers' travels to tea-producing areas in Asia and Africa have always existed, primarily regarding distance and accessibility. This challenge is not limited to Europe alone but also extends to other regions, such as the North and South American continents. As a result, travel to European tea-producing areas holds potential, thereby opening new opportunities for innovation, education, and growth in the domestic tea tourism industry.

The Tea Grown in Europe Association, established in 2016, handles a number of tasks, from routine (joint purchase of equipment, exchange of information, joint events) to ending with the backbone issues for emerging European tea farming. For instance, the association is engaged in giving tea the status of a subsidised agricultural crop because currently it does not formally belong to such crops in Europe. This, among other things, prevents tea farmers from receiving farm subsidies. Another area of the association's work is the development of tea-growing technologies in Europe and the creation of a set of models for building tea businesses, including ones that work at the intersection of industries, for example, tea business models with tourism components (Malyhin et al., 2021). The association currently has tea-growing members from 14 European countries, including three national associations: the Georgian Organic Tea Producers Association, the Tea Scotland Association, and the National Association for the Promotion of French Tea Producers (Tea Grown in Europe, 2023).

Most of these gardens offer guided tours, scheduled visits, tastings, and other activities. Over the last 150 years, there have been several experiments in Europe growing the Camellia sinensis plant and making tea from it. Some of the earliest experiments can be found in Portugal and France. Tea plants across the world grow under diverse geographic and climatic conditions, and, at least, parts of Europe are potentially suitable for tea growing. As an association, they intend to promote the growth of tea as an economic activity in Europe. Since 2016, the association continues to grow rapidly and includes a large number of projects and members (Tea Grown in Europe, 2023).

It is noteworthy to acknowledge the existence of numerous emerging tea cultivators in Europe who are currently not affiliated with the "Tea Grown in Europe" Association (Hardin, 2020).

Tea education

If education within the coffee and wine sommelier industry is compared to tea education, then we can conclude that a globally recognised and unified certification system is still lacking. Wine has the International Sommelier Guild (ISG), Court of Masters Sommeliers (CMS), Institute of Masters of Wine (IMW), and Wine and Spirit Education Trust (WSET), while the leading professional barista certification is offered by Speciality Coffee Association (SCA). It is worth pointing out that long-established tea-producing countries are entirely different; for instance, in Japan, there is the Nihoncha Instructor Association's certification and in China one can complete majors in tea science and culture at the university level, however the focus is primarily focused on the tea produced in the respective country and is not easily accessible to tea professionals from abroad who do not speak the local language. And yet again, there is a phenomenon in tea-producing countries with courses tailored for both foreign and local tea specialists, for example, Asian School of Tea India/Thailand (Tea Sommelier, Tea Connoisseur, Tea Tasting & Blending Masterclass), Ceylon Tea Academy (Tea Tasting & Technology Diploma and International Tea Mastery designed together with Australian Tea Masters), Global Japanese Tea Association (Japanese Tea Foundation, Intermediate & Advanced Courses, Japanese Tea Master Course), amongst others. Meanwhile, the hospitality segment focusing on tea in the West still is falling short on education as there are no hospitality degrees at universities and HoReCa (hotel/restaurant/catering) institutions include tea as part of their curriculum.

When taking a closer look at tea education in Europe, currently there are several key players in this field. For instance, the European Speciality Tea Association (ESTA) was established in 2018. It is a non-profit membership organisation, which focuses on the speciality tea segment and contributes to the tea community through innovation, research, education, and communication. The International Development Committee is responsible for ethical and environmental issues, organised trips to areas of origin, collaborations, and partnerships supporting the tea value chain and its issues and problems, and the role of tea culture, traditional and modern, in the tourism and hospitality sectors. ESTA has developed a system specifically for educators in the tea industry, aimed at establishing a reliable certification process with accompanying exams. The professional teaching license obtained after completing a module or the full course is valid for two years, after which authorised tea certifiers must pass repeated exams to ensure that the information provided in their lessons is reliable and of high standards. All subjects, except the introductory module "Introduction to Tea," are taught and certified at three levels: foundation, intermediate, and advanced.

These subjects cover a range of topics such as botanicals, Camellia sinensis, sensory skills, barista skills, hospitality, cultivation, and processing (European Speciality Tea Association, 2023). Silniece (2023) emphasised that tea is a lifelong education venture and it is incomprehensible that in the West some try to condense the education material to one week or so. The majority of educators offer simple and short courses of tea 101 or a few online lessons, while only a few offer long immersive courses that go deep into the topic of tea covering origins, culture, brewing skills, production, etc. Nevertheless, there are a few certified educational institutions in Europe worth mentioning: International Tea Education Institute (UK), UK Tea Academy, Tea Academy Italy, Tea Academy Spain, Palais des Thés Tea School and L'École du Thé (France), Eastern Tea Academy (Eastern Leaves, Yunnan: available online), Chadō Urasenke Tankōkai Berlin Association, Ronnefeldt Tea Academy (Germany), Tea Masters Sweden (through ITA), Urasenke Finland, and Dilmah School of Tea EU, amongst others.

Analysis

Innovative tools to revitalise tea tourism

The World Tourism Organization (UNWTO), a United Nations Specialized Agency, has partnered with MUST Travel & Tech, a travel mobile app, to provide digital tools for promoting sustainable tourism development. The visibility provided through technological tools offers an opportunity for tourism service providers to restart their activity sustainably, from new rural destinations to destinations with high infrastructure development. The digital transformation of tourism service providers and the promotion of programs related to innovation, education, and investment for tourism destinations are encouraged. The agreement aims to create global and regional innovation ecosystems that accelerate the recovery of tourism in the post-pandemic years. The implementation of digital solutions aligned with new trends in the tourism sector enables the development of a differentiated, personalised, and safe tourism product focused on behaviour patterns and space management, contributing to the recovery of the economy (UNWTO, 2021). Relevantly, another case study states that Bangladesh's tea tourism industry has identified a challenging marketing environment as consumers become more technologically savvy, distracted, and demanding (Sultana & Sultana Khan, 2018). This can be applied to other countries also as it is the reality of the twenty-first century. Fernando, Kumari, and Rajapaksha (2017) advocated for a range of promotional strategies for tea tourism destinations, including social media marketing, e-word of mouth, blogs, and printed media when proposing methods for promoting tea tourism in Sri Lanka in the context of the development of the Ceylon tea brand:

Many tourists use travel apps to find out useful information about destinations, transportation, accommodations, places to eat, and experiences. Most apps offer simple general information that does not focus on special interests. But the TEA TEA ME app is different from others. It's a tailor-made app for tea travellers and tea lovers which helps them decide to select tea tourism destinations and events easier and faster. It's a very powerful tool towards the travel decision and useful device for gathering the information for tea events, tea business, and tea tourism. (Assoc. Prof. Dr. Amnaj Khaokhrueamuang, The University of Shizuoka, Japan)

As much as tea tourism is defined as a niche, a key opposing view to this was presented by tea expert Denis Shumakov, curator at TeaTips.Ru, as he argues that, fundamentally, tea tourism is no different from any other type of tourism. As soon as roads, beaches, and hotels appear near the objects of tea tourism and sightseeing and food-tourism-like activities are involved, it fits into the framework of the traditional vacation tourism industry without any distinctive features. Therefore, when it comes to information technology, tea tourism does not require specific solutions for its technological support. Therefore, ordinary booking systems, customary websites, common geographical information systems (GIS), and standard package services of travel agencies can cover the information needs of tea tourism. It is also more profitable for tea tourism projects to cooperate with large universal information services, rather than with specialised ones. At the same time, of course, there will always be independent phenomena at the intersection of information technology and tea tourism. For example, a high-profile occurrence like the "Afternoon Tea UK" platform provides convenient bookings and features over 500 venues for afternoon tea experiences in the UK and Ireland (Shumakov, 2023). Essentially, the argument is true, and vacation-type large-scale tourism gains reasonable benefits by employing standard tourism promotion strategies and is not in dire need of specialised solutions. However, it is believed that a niche platform tailored for niche tea-drinking audiences will be useful for all parties involved, especially smaller-scale authentic experiences. Therefore, modern tools like tea apps, online platforms, and communities are potential tools to revitalise the interest in tea, especially in younger generations who have been showing an increased interest in value propositions like speciality tea, and healthier and more sustainable choices. In many countries, we can witness decreased interest in "traditional tea" as new more "convenient" and trendy concepts like bottled tea, bubble tea, tea bags, and tea lattes have been taking over. For example, Japan faces an issue of an ageing population with more than half (or about 56%) of tea farmers being 65 years or older (Suzuki, 2021). Young people move out of rural areas and have no interest in pursuing agriculture. Making tea-related activities more appealing and easily accessible, interactive education is the key. It holds the potential to both preserve culture, as well as create jobs and prospective careers in the field. Anil Cooke, MD Asia Siyaka Commodities PLC and Chairman of Ceylon Tea Road Map 2030, commented that TEA TEA ME can be positioned as a timely value-added service that brings the world of tea to a whole new generation of enthusiasts and an opportunity for tea lovers to discover all that is special about the infinite elements surrounding tea (Cooke, 2023).

TEA TEA ME app

The TEA TEA ME mobile application, developed by Gundega Silniece, Vadim Chirkov, and Katrina Wild, endeavours to provide an all-inclusive and comprehensive database of tea-related events, tours, and educational programs worldwide, accessible via Google Play and the App Store, as well as a web version. In 2017, Gundega Silniece, founder of the TEA TEA ME app and board member of the European Specialty Tea Association (International Development of Tourism, Hospitality, and Sustainability), participated in the seventh International Tea Forum held in Enshi, Hubei province, China, which devoted a considerable portion of the event to the advancement of tea tourism. During the conference, the speakers emphasised the importance of developing tea tourism as a cohesive driving force for the tea industry, rather than a fragmented phenomenon. Silniece expressed initial skepticism, as similar ideas had been proposed at prior industry meetings of this nature, but little had been accomplished in terms of promoting the entire tea industry through tourism and education. While she recognised the logic behind promoting personal business interests above all else, she believed that it was short-sighted when considering the industry as a whole. Silniece put forward that the solution to the problem of segmentation could be a common platform that unites all market players, making tea events, education, tours, garden visits, and tasting sessions (herein referred to as events) easily accessible in one place. Her vision for the industry is seen as a panacea that caters in a mutually beneficial manner to businesses, producers, farmers, and tea enthusiasts alike (Silniece, 2022). Since then, several industry specialists have expressed their support for the establishment of an app of this nature. Nishchal Banshota, CEO of Nepal Tea Collective, commented that the TEA TEA ME app is a potential solution to a perceived void in the market, which has not previously provided a single platform exclusively tailored to the interests and needs of tea enthusiasts. TEA TEA ME is an opportunity to bring tea professionals and enthusiasts together in the form of a cohesive community around tea (Banskota, 2023). The primary objective of this app is to facilitate a globally inclusive community, which serves as a unifying tool for the tea industry to resolve issues related to segmentation, while contributing to the general awareness of an informed consumer. By consolidating information on tea-related experiences, the mobile app seeks to offer the convenience of accessing and booking all the events in a single place. This platform lists an abundance of tea education opportunities, ranging from novice-level education to professional certification. Moreover, TEA TEA ME intends to aid travellers in identifying and visiting tea gardens and producers while staying informed about the available tea-related experiences in the area. Addressing the challenges presented by the demands of modern customers, TEA TEA ME thus promotes niche tourism and adds publicity to the host while addressing the technical challenges.

> The TEA TEA ME app is an innovative resource for those who love to travel for tea and represents a further stage of development of tea tourism. The app fills a need in the tea tourism community for the sharing of information, making tea tourism experiences more accessible to all. (Lee Jolliffe, tea tourism consultant and retired hospitality and tourism professor; lead editor for the *Routledge handbook of tea tourism*)

For registered members, the TEA TEA ME application offers the ability to create or book events directly with organisers. Events can be filtered by geographical location, event type (such as tea ceremonies, tastings, workshops, garden visits, tours, certified courses, etc.), online or offline accessibility, price, and dates, among other criteria. This allows users to quickly and easily find relevant events that match their needs. Furthermore, the platform offers a convenient system of communication with event organisers, as well as a rating and review function to help users make informed decisions. As discussed priorly, the issue within the industry is that education is quite segmented and hard to find; therefore, the app's goal is to promote trustworthy education in the field. Filters like "Tea Blending," "Tea Tasting," "Sommelier," "Tea Farming and Production," "Botanicals," "Japanese Tea Ceremony," "Gong Fu Cha," certified professional education, internships, etc., would make it easier to find a specific field of interest and appropriate certification. The TEA TEA ME also provides the option for individuals and organisations to create a professional profile that highlights their specific offerings and specialties such as education, retail, tourism, events, and more. This feature allows them to showcase their unique skill sets and expertise, ultimately enhancing their networking capabilities and career prospects within the tea industry, potentially opening new doors for easier direct sourcing with other tea businesses. The platform aims to attract a wide range of growers and producers, providing them with the opportunity to showcase their products and services, resulting in greater accessibility and discoverability for all parties involved, and benefitting all stakeholders in the tea industry (see Figure E.4.1).

The TEA TEA ME team commented that spearheading the establishment of a strong community of both enthusiasts and industry specialists will take time as it is a gradual process, yet they are ambitious about forming collaborations with tea associations, official tea boards, tour operators, and tea representatives from various countries. Ratings and reviews will take some time to lay the foundation as it depends on the users to put into service the offerings of the app and give back feedback. Additional features like blogs, live streams, improved networking tools, and other innovative functions will continue to be developed as the TEA TEA ME team comes up with further ideas and solutions for the benefit of the tea industry.

Mobile tea apps, technology, and community building

In recent years, several tea-related apps have emerged, mainly tea timers, journals, and online tea shops of respective brands. Denis Shumakov commented on various aspects of tea apps in the context of the World Tea Awards 2023, for which apps like Harney &

Figure E.4.1: TEA TEA ME mobile app.
Source: Author

Sons, Snackpass, Mighty Timer, Adagio Teas, and Peet's Coffee were nominated as mobile app innovations. The list contained applications that were primarily focused on selling tea and brewing timers, which, in his opinion, did not meet the criteria of an innovative tea application. He believed that this was due to reasonable inertia in the industry, where companies tended to replicate their online store as a mobile app (Shumakov, 2023). When referring to tea and smartphone technologies, for instance, Chinese scientists have developed a compact near-infrared spectrometer (NIR spectrometer) that connects to a smartphone app and can assess the moisture content of green tea during the fixation process (Lan et al., 2022). Another curious invention by Vietnamese researchers has developed a low-cost and portable method for rapid assessment of phenolic content (chemical compounds of polyphenols like catechins, theaflavins, tannins, and flavonoids that affect flavour and mouthfeel) in tea infusions using the smartphone camera and a homemade photo box. The results obtained using this method were comparable to those obtained with expensive laboratory equipment, and the device was successfully tested on various types of tea (Minh-Huy et al., 2023). Overall, Shumakov suggests that there is still much room for innovation and development in the tea app industry and acknowledged that progressive solutions would likely emerge on the market in the future (Shumakov, 2022). When speaking of tea journals, it is worth mentioning MyTeaPal, Steeped, and Teahead Timer amongst many others. Apart from the tea timer tools, MyTeaPal and Steeped have established strong tea communities and features like a global tea club, educational guidelines for brewing, as well as vendor features. Vincent Liu, the founder of the MyTeaPal app, created an all-in-one mobile app for tea enthusiasts to record their tea journey and connect with other tea drinkers worldwide. The app includes a global tea club with members from 40+ countries, where users can share tasting notes and attend weekly virtual events to taste tea together. Liu emphasises community building in MyTeaPal, demonstrated by the Discord server and Facebook group, MyTeaPal Community, which gained 2,000 members in two years (Liu, 2023). Tristan Otto, the Marketing & Sales Manager of Steeped App, similarly suggested social platforms Facebook and Discord played a crucial role in establishing a community, building brand identity, and engaging with a wide spectrum of audiences. Satisfied users have also provided invaluable word-of-mouth promotion that pivoted the success of the application (Otto, 2023).

There's a growing realisation that digital technologies are actually a seamless, indivisible combination of artefacts, people, organisations, policies, economics, histories, cultures, and knowledge: that they are socio-technical products. The UX/UI designer and developer of the TEA TEA ME app Vadim Chirkov (2023) commented that digital innovations hold the capacity as a socio-technical product and that a lack of ethics within the digital product industry can be witnessed, leading to negative influences in society, for instance, unhealthy consumption of social media. Each stakeholder, from the everyday user/co-creator to the government and corporate official, brings their unique history, intersectionality, and expertise, amplifying the influencing social and technical structures of the digital technologies around us. These personal and social factors influence the development of code, software, information, and physical electronics. Simultaneously, the aforementioned elements shape the individuals and social structures that utilise them. To ensure vibrant, engaged, and diverse participation, it is crucial to incorporate social justice-oriented progressive community interaction and critical social and technical skills (Wolske, 2020).

Discussion

Tea experiences and technological implications

The offering of a cup of tea is a universal sign of hospitality, in either a home or commercial hospitality setting. Practitioners recognise that tea offered in the lodging setting is an "experience" and that the current evolution of tea into a "trendy" product is not a surprise. For hospitality, tea consequently serves as both a symbol and a resource with considerable potential for the provision of commercial hospitality as the tea culture revolves around creating a comfortable and positive experience for guests (Fernando et al., 2017). The value proposition of TEA TEA ME, as described by Hassan Afshari, organiser of the Iran Tea Masters Cup and National Coordinator and Judge of TMC, is that the platform provides a means for tea enthusiasts and professionals from around the world to connect and share their knowledge and passion for tea. Through the exchange of information on tea culture, brewing methods, and pairings, TEA TEA ME has the potential to facilitate the discovery of new perspectives and ideas. Additionally, Afshari emphasises the importance of TEA TEA ME as a tool for connecting tea specialists from different countries and promoting their unique tea cultures to a global audience (Afshari, 2023). The TEA TEA ME platform is an internationally inclusive app for all regions, not exclusive only to Europe. This is its strong point since it can be a great tool for both domestic European tourists, as well as international ones visiting Europe to explore what is available regarding experimental tea plantations and local tea culture. TEA TEA ME's mission is to secure a regular flow of customers attending events and tours with the convenience of a comprehensive database of available tea experiences with the opportunity to book it directly with the organisers in a single place, thus making the experiences more accessible.

Gaëlle Rousseau, founder and main farmer of Jardins de Thé in France, highlighted the importance of tea knowledge, especially in terms of farming and processing. She expressed her concern about the shared misconception among guests, who visit her farm, that tea is just a flavoured drink in Europe since aromatised teas and blends in France are fairly popular at the moment, not appreciating the natural flavours of the tea plant itself. Jardins de Thé's mission is to educate consumers about the hard work involved in growing and processing tea and to develop a better understanding of the world of plants, as well as awareness of what they eat or drink. The establishment of the tea garden in 2022 attracted more than 200 visitors, and 90% of them were tea drinkers with no prior knowledge of tea. Rousseau hopes that with the TEA TEA ME app, Jardins de thé will attract more international tea enthusiasts, who can explore not only the famous Deauville seaside in Normandy but also unique French tea cultivation and enjoy Japanese-style tea ceremonies, tea lunches, herbal plants, and organic vegetables as part of the tea tour (Rosseau, 2023). Similarly, Hannes Saarpuu, the founder and main tea maker of the Renegade Tea Estate in Georgia, has noted the potential benefits of tea garden visits as a value proposition for the tea industry. By providing visitors with an insight into the otherwise opaque and concealed processes of tea growing and production, such tours facilitate interaction between tea farmers and consumers, promoting the development of trust and long-term partnerships. This personal approach is particularly beneficial for small-scale producers seeking to distinguish themselves from larger, more established tea brands and foster a strong sense of community around their products. According to Saarpuu, Renegade Tea Farmers view tea growing and production as a beautiful process, and welcome opportunities to share their passion with others (Saarpuu, 2023). The educational value of tea tourism in Europe may have an indirect, yet positive impact on the global tea industry. As tea consumers become better informed, their appreciation of the product may increase, potentially benefiting not only the European tea industry but also other tea-producing regions around the world (see Figure E.4.2).

Figure E.4.2: Renegade Tea Estate in Georgia.
Source: Renegade Tea Estate (2022)

Conclusion

A limitation of the chapter is that there is currently no literature or statistical data on digital tools that offer comprehensive databases of tea-related experiences on a global scale apart from TEA TEA ME, in its early stages. This is briefly reflected in the chapter by the identification of other tea apps. The role of digital tools in support of the tea industry, tourism, hospitality, and education is however worthy of further investigation. Finally, limited resources that have thoroughly investigated the field of tea education are available. In conclusion, tea tourism presents unique opportunities for the tea industry and the TEA TEA ME app holds the potential to be a valuable tool for providing convenient access and facilitating the growth of tea-related experiences on an international scale. While the industry lacks a globally recognised unified certification system and accessible education, digital innovations like TEA TEA ME can be an invaluable tool to aid in making information about education opportunities easily discoverable. Socio-technical tools of this nature present an opportunity to bring tea professionals and enthusiasts together in the form of an impactful community around tea. Interactions between tea market participants are verified by hundreds of years of cross-cultural tea selling and consumption practices; therefore, tea traditions expressed and linked digitally could potentially make a positive impact on the future of the tea industry.

References

Afshari, H. (2023, March 10). TEA TEA ME App and Networks of Tea Culture (K. Wild, Interviewer).

Banskota, N. (2023, March 8). Potential of TEA TEA ME App for the Benefit of the Tea Industry (K. Wild, Interviewer).

Chirkov, V. (2023, March 21). TEA TEA ME App Developer Perspectives: Digital Products as Sociotechnical Tools (K. Wild, Interviewer).

Cooke, A., (2023, March 21). TEA TEA ME App within the Context of the Tea Industry (G. Silniece, Interviewer).

European Speciality Tea Association. (2023). European Speciality Tea Association. Retrieved October 10, 2023, from https://specialityteaeurope.com.

Fernando, I., Kumari, K.W.S.N., & Rajapaksha, R.M.P.D.K. (2017). Destination marketing to promote tea tourism socio-economic approach on community development. *SSRN Electronic Journal*.

Goswami, R. (2023, March 22). Communities in Thailand and Japan show the way when it comes to tea & local cuisine. world tea news. Retrieved October 10, 2023, from https://www.worldteanews.com/ori gins/communities-thailand-and-japan-show-way-when-it-comes-tea-local-cuisine.

Jolliffe, L. (2007). *Tea and tourism: tourists, traditions and transformations*. Channel View Publications.

Jolliffe, L., & Aslam, M.S.M. (2009). Tea heritage tourism: evidence from Sri Lanka. *Journal of Heritage Tourism*, 4(4), 331–44. https://doi.org/10.1080/17438730903186607.

Jolliffe, L., Aslam, M., Amnaj Khaokhrueamuang, & Chen, L.-H. (2023). *Routledge handbook of tea tourism*.

Jolliffe, L. (2023, March 7). TEA TEA ME App in the Context of Tea Tourism (K. Wild, Interviewer).

Hardin, J.G. (2020). Where tea grows in Europe [Review of Where tea grows in Europe]. Kill Green. Retrieved October 10, 2023, from https://www.killgreen.io/main/where-tea-grows-europe.

Khaokhrueamuang, A. (2023, March 9). TEA TEA ME App in the Context of Tea Tourism (K. Wild, Interviewer).

Koththagoda, K.C., & Dissanayake, D.M.R. (2017). Potential of tea tourism in Sri Lanka: A review on managerial implications and research directions. In *Equality and Management*, 51–68. University of Szczecin, Poland.

Lan, T., Shen, S., Yuan, H., Jiang, Y., Tong, H., & Ye, Y. (2022). A rapid prediction method of moisture content for green tea fixation based on woa-elman. *Foods*, 11(18), 2928. https://doi.org/10.3390/ foods11182928.

Liu, V. (2023, March 18). MyTeaPal app development in the context of community building (K. Wild, Interviewer).

Malyhin, M., Nikandrova, O., & Shumakov, D. (2021). Experimental tea plantation on Mount Zhornina – TeaTips. http://eng.teatips.ru/experimental-tea-plantation-on-mount-zhornina/.

Mazerolle, D., Guyomarc'h, N., Bucher, W., Kim, H.O., Gruntkowski, N., & Niepoort, D. (2016). *Tea cultivation in Europe*.

Minh-Huy, D., Anh-Dao, L.-T., Thanh-Nho, N., Nhon-Duc, L., & Cong-Hau, N. (2023). Smartphone-based digital images as a low-cost and simple colorimetric approach for the assessment of total phenolic contents in several specific Vietnamese dried tea products and their liquors. *Food Chemistry, 401*, 134147. https://doi.org/10.1016/j.foodchem.2022.134147.

Otto, T. (2023, March 10). Steeped app from a development and marketing perspective (K. Wild, Interviewer).

Rousseau, G. (2023, March 18). TEA TEA ME app and European tea tourism (K. Wild, Interviewer).

Saarpuu, H. (2023). Renegade tea estate in Georgia: Benefits of welcoming guests to tea farms (K. Wild, Interviewer).

Shumakov, D. (2023, March 17). Tea tourism and digital tools in the tea industry (K. Wild, Interviewer).

Shumakov, D. (2022). Tea paraphernalia. Retrieved October 10, 2023, from http://blog.teatips.ru/category/ paraphernalia/.

Sigley, G. (2010). Cultural heritage tourism and the ancient tea horse road of southwest China. *International Journal of China Studies, 1*(2), 531–44. University of Western Australia.

Silniece, G. (2022, September 22). TEA TEA ME app's mission & issues in the tea industry (K. Wild, Interviewer).

Silniece, G. (2023, March 9). Tea education in the context of Europe (K. Wild, Interviewer).

Sultana, S., & Sultana Khan, R. (2018). Factors determining tourism: A framework to promote tea tourism destination in Chittagong. *Global Journal of Management and Business Research: Real Estate, Event and Tourism Management, 18*(1). Southern University.

Suzuki, S. (2021, January 28). Tea reports by the Japanese government. Global Japanese Tea Association. Retrieved October 10, 2023, from https://gjtea.org/tea-reports-by-the-japanese-government/.

Tea Grown in Europe Association – Taste what European soil has to offer. (2023). Retrieved July 29, 2023, from https://tea-grown-in-europe.eu.

Wolske, M. (2020). 2A: Critical social + technical perspective. Retrieved October 10, 2023, from https://iopn.library.illinois.edu/pressbooks/demystifyingtechnology/chapter/a-critical-social-technical-perspective/.

UNTWO. (2021). Digital tools to revitalize tourism. Retrieved October 10, 2023, from https://www.unwto.org/news/digital-tools-to-revitalize-tourism.

UNTWO Barometer. (2023, January 17). Tourism is set to return to pre-pandemic levels in some regions in 2023. Retrieved October 10, 2023, from https://www.unwto.org/taxonomy/term/347.

Remark: In 2024, the UNWTO changed its name to UN Tourism, but as the references used in this chapter have been created before, the original name of the institution has been kept.

F Experiencing the islands of tea

The tea came to Europe either by sea (on ships or tea clippers) or by land (caravans). Some of the islands in Europe had and still have more favourable conditions also for tea production or were stops on the classic trade routes, so that an early and intensive tea culture developed. They have retained this tea-orientation in different forms to this day.

Vahid Ghasemi, Susana Goulart Costa, Flávio Tiago,
Duarte Nuno Chaves and Teresa Borges-Tiago

F.1 Azores tea: From industrial production to tourism experience

Introduction

Tea tourism is a tourism niche (Cheng et al., 2010) that was raised from the interconnection of other tourism concepts: nature tourism, cultural and heritage tourism, food tourism (Cheng et al., 2012), and sustainable tourism (Su, et al., 2019).

Tea, like coffee, is an agricultural product, originating as the second most popular beverage globally, perceived as a commodity product and not as part of a tourism experience. Nonetheless, in recent years, due to its particularities in wellness, culture, and lush green plantation, tea tourism is raising tourists' attention in different parts of the world.

Tea has a broad history, dating back thousands of years across various cultures. Tea originated in southwest China. During the early sixteenth century, Portuguese priests and merchants in China introduced their drinking habits to western civilisation (Weinberg & Bealer, 2004).

Although the Portuguese discovered the maritime route to India in 1497, only in 1513, with Jorge Álvares, did the Portuguese set foot on Chinese territory with a trading mission. However, tea was not among the products the Portuguese initially sought to bring to Europe. According to several authors, the Portuguese started importing tea to Lisbon around 1580 (Hobhouse, 1985; Hobhouse, 1985; Martin, 2018). However, the accepted document date for the tea entrance in Europe dates to 1610 Dutch shipments. In the early years, the trade of green tea in Europe was carried out by Dutch merchants for medicinal purposes. With the increased tea consumption in England, in 1670, Charles II of England encouraged the British East India Company to trade this product (Martin, 2018; Silva, 2014).

Until the eighteenth century, Europe was only a tea consumer. Then, in October 1763, the first living specimens arrived in Europe by Captain Eckburg, who brought the developing plants from China to Uppsala, Sweden (Silva, 2014). In mainland Portugal, the first experimental tea production project occurred in early 1800 (Moura, 2019). Some plantations were also introduced on the island of Madeira, and the crop was discontinued. In

Acknowledgements: We gratefully acknowledge financial support from FCT – Fundação para a Ciencia e Tecnologia (Portugal) through research grants UIDB/04521/2020 of the Advance/CSG and ISEG; and UIDB/00685/2020 of the Centre of Applied Economics Studies of the Atlantic. This study is a contribution to the research project "TASTE" (Ref. ACORES-01-0145-FEDER-000106) funded through FEDER (85%) and regional funds (15%) via "Programa Operacional Açores 2020."

https://doi.org/10.1515/9783110758573-018

the Azores, the tea plantation introduction occurred during the nineteenth century, and the industrial tea cultivation began in S. Miguel around 1820 (Moura, 2019; Silva, 2014) and remains active today. The present study adopted a triangulation method involving a first phase analysis of historical evolution and retrieval of culture and traditions manifestation related to tea, followed by interviews conducted with different stakeholders regarding the relevance of tea for the tourism experience and development in the Azores. This study presents the importance of tea tourism and sustainable tourism experiences for tourists and locals to enable new potentials for different stakeholders in the Azores. It also contributes to the literature on European tea culture.

Literature review

Tea cultures and drinking habits vary around the globe, giving space to an emerging trend: tea tourism. Although the relationship between tourism and tea can be found many centuries ago, one of the earliest studies linking tea and tourism was written in 2003 by Jolliffe. The author explored the tea trilogy – history, heritage, and industry – considering tea as an element of the tourism destination offer and a motto to traveling. As Chen, Huang, and Tham (2021) noted, tea tourism research follows this growth of interest, but the concept is still relatively underexplored, especially outside Asia, where significant productions are placed.

Publications are very suitable data sources to understand the relevance and interest of a specific topic. Therefore, a well-known database – Web of Science – was chosen, and current data up to the publication year 2022 was retrieved and analyzed across all disciplines. Using the search keyword "tea tourism," 274 papers were retrieved, being dispersed worldwide, although with a clear focus on China and Twain (62%).

Tea tourism has been a topic addressed in different research fields: hospitality, leisure, and sports tourism are in the central area. And even within the field of tourism and hospitality, tea tourism has received some attention from different perspectives (Cheng et al., 2012).

Over the decades, tourism has experienced continued growth boosted by several factors (Akadiri, Akadiri, & Alola, 2019). This growth goes hand in hand with increasing offers of diversification and competition among destinations, which enhances the search for unique forms of differentiation and communication of the local uniqueness that enriches experiences and appeals to tourists (Veríssimo et al. 2017).

Tea tourism as a tourist's experience has related to the natural environment of tea garden, tea leaves plucking, tea production, tea packaging, and tea labour-culture (Datta, 2018). However, few studies have looked into the specificities of tea growers (Huang & Qian, 2005) and, more specifically, how these tea growers' resilience led them to reinvent their industrial business model and become a player in the tourism industry.

The case study of the Azores

By nature and geographical conditions, islands are quite different from the rest of the territories (Hampton & Hampton, 2009; Lai, 2002). Tiago and Borges-Tiago (2022) highlighted that most small islands have economies dependent upon a limited base of industries and constrained by external elements. Due to their natural beauties and landscapes and the natural resource constraints and dependency, as Roudi, Arasli, and Akadiri (2019) mentioned, tourism is an economic activity suitable in small island contexts. With nine small islands, the Azores archipelago is no exception, having recently elected tourism as a strategic industry.

These nine volcanic islands are located in the middle northern hemisphere of the Atlantic Ocean, approximately 1,000 miles (1,600 km) west of mainland Portugal and about 600 kilometers (373 miles) wide (see Figure F.1.1).

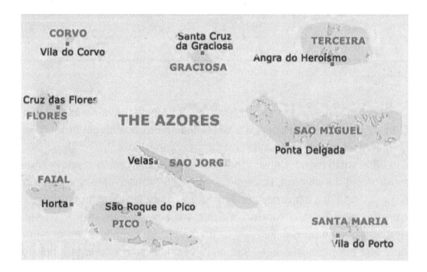

Figure F.1.1: Azores' Map.
Source: Whats on in Azores (2023)

The islands were recognised by Portuguese navigators back in 1427. These islands were considered difficult places to live for many centuries due to their remoteness and natural conditions and hazards. The newcomers were first established in the two most east islands, and agriculture was their primary activity. Regardless of the rudeness of its volcanic soils, the newcomers were able to develop different cultures and industries that evolved over the centuries to respond to locals' and importers' demands. For instance, during the sixteenth and seventeenth centuries, attention was given to perishable products sold to galleons crossing between Europe, America, and India. In the eighteenth and nineteenth centuries, agriculture focuses on orange production and exportation to

England (Dias, 1995). The fluctuation and existence of cycles in regional agricultural output appear to allow farmers to respond to changes in demand and their natural production constraints. One natural condition that makes the islands unique is their tepid, oceanic, subtropical climate. However, temperatures ranging from ten to 30 degrees Celsius and an average annual mean relative humidity of 76% are unsuitable for all cultures. Adding to natural climate constraints, it cannot be forgotten that the islands' geography and the soils' volcanic nature limit the cultivated areas. For instance, as observed in the map, the tea production in the Azores is around 50 tons, while in China it is more than three million tons and in India over 1.3 million tons (see Table F.1.1).

Table F.1.1: Tea Production worldwide 2021.

TOP 4 tea producing countries worldwide				
China	India	Kenya	Sri Lanka	others
3,120,000 t	1,329,040 t	533,000 t	299,339 t	1,188,152 t
48,23%	20,54%	8,24%	4,63%	18,36%

Source: (Deutscher Tee- und Kräuerteeverband 2022)

Compared to global producers, the tea growers in the Azores have no expression. Nonetheless, the organoleptic characteristics of the tea and its traditional production, history, and role in the tourism industry highlight their importance.

As noted in other small island contexts, the natural conditions and the cycle cultures profoundly transformed the physical, economic, social, and cultural landscape (Silveira, 2012). Nowadays, the primary industries are agriculture, dairy farming (for cheese and butter products primarily), livestock ranching, fishing, and recently tourism.

Several initiatives have been developed in the region over the last two decades, aiming to value and maintain heritage from a cultural and environmental perspective. Thus, tourists visiting the Azores look to its volcanic landscapes and the surrounding sea for contemplation and pleasure during various activities in the natural environment (Lima et al., 2013). But they will also experience local heritage through visiting museums, monuments, and factories, tasting local food and enjoying locals' experience sharing (Faria et al., 2014).

The background of tea production in the Azores

Tea results from drying the leaves of the Camellia sinensis tree of the Teaceas family, which has around 300 varieties. Three types of tea originate from the Camellia sinensis: green tea, which does not undergo fermentation during processing and thus maintains the original colour of the leaves; oolong tea, with oxidation between green and black; and black tea, which, because it is more fermented than the other two, acquires a darker shade (Campos, 2014).

The production and consumption of this beverage have their origins in various legends and traditions. One of them identifies the Chinese Emperor Shen Nung (2737–2697 BC) as the first promoter of tea (Saberi, 2010), while another narrative associates this beverage with Bodhidarma, the founder of Zen Buddhism (Silva, 2014). Regardless of these uncertain origins, the tea plant was first cultivated and consumed in Asia in the area between the province of Yunnan in China and the state of Assam in northern India (Silva, 2014).

With its initial consumption limited to the Chinese elite (Wu, 2020), tea attracted increasingly different social circuits from the thirteenth century, benefitting from its dissemination by Taoist monks, who were particularly attentive to tea's healing properties (Silva, 2014). Thus, the growing appreciation of tea in China consolidated it as an instrument of harmony between human beings and nature in a philosophical and religious context, which was mainly influenced by Confucianism, Taoism, and Buddhism (Wu, 2020). It generated a deepening of its cultivation, processing, and storage techniques, along with the improvement of the protocol associated with its consumption (Han, 2007).

Europeans would only learn about the existence of tea in the sixteenth century through maritime expansion to the East. It is rumored that Portuguese missionaries in Japan and China had made this drink known in Portugal; however, as Portuguese commercial interests were more focused on spices, drugs, precious goods, and manufacturers, tea was not an appealing product for them. Therefore, the first European record of the existence of this plant was made in Italy in the mid-sixteenth century, then called Chiai Catai, namely, "tea from China" (Silva, 2014).

A reliable record of the first shipment of tea to Europe was only made in 1610 by the Dutch East India Company. The Dutch became the first traders of this product, which gained popularity in the various European monarchies. In England, for example, it is recognised that the habit of drinking tea at the British Court was introduced by the Portuguese Queen Catherine of Braganza when she married the English King Charles II in 1662 (Wu, 2020). However, throughout the seventeenth century, the beverage was still considered exotic and valued mainly for its medicinal characteristics, with its consumption limited to higher social groups. Its importation from the East made it more expensive in European markets (Van Driem, 2019).

In the eighteenth century, with the development of the Chinese production of black teas and the strengthening of the British East India Company, it was possible to reduce the price of tea, making it more accessible to different social groups (Wu, 2020). This factor fostered the dissemination of this beverage, which was also adapted to Western tastes by adding milk and sugar, transforming tea from a mere tonic into a social drink (Wu, 2020). With the worldliness of tea, all the protocols associated with its consumption were also imported into Europe, with the attraction of oriental exoticism exemplified by the porcelain utensils, such as teapots, saucers, cups, spoons, sugar bowls, and so forth, which was in line with eighteenth-century artistic chinoiserie.

However, until the beginning of the nineteenth century, the tea consumed in Europe was only produced in Asia. The methods for its cultivation and production outside this geographical area were unknown. The massification of this beverage justified the experimentation of tea growers in various places, including those that were part of the Portuguese Empire. In the 1810s, the first experiments with Macau tea were conducted in Brazil in an attempt to ensure that Brazilian production would satisfy the growing demand from Western countries. From there, production was encouraged in mainland Portugal and the archipelagos of Madeira and the Azores, especially after 1822, when Brazil gained independence (Silva, 2014).

While the experiments in Portugal and on the island of Madeira were not very fruitful, the climate, relief, and quality of the soil in the Azores proved propitious to growing tea from the very beginning. On this archipelago, the first news about tea dates back to 1801, when D. Lourenço José Boaventura de Almada, Captain-General of the Azores, sent two crates with Chinese tea plants to the King of Portugal through the circuits of Macau and Goa (Moura, 2019). However, at this stage, the Azores would only function as a revolving stage for tea passage between the East and West. In 1820, the first seeds for cultivation from Brazil arrived on São Miguel. On the island, the crop location chosen was in São António in the municipality of Ponta Delgada, whose success would have allowed its cultivation to expand to the area of Capelas. During this experimental phase, the tea plantation on the island of São Miguel was only for ornamental purposes (Melo, 2008), following in the footsteps of the botanical experiments that, since the eighteenth century, have marked the landscape of São Miguel, adorning it with several British-inspired picturesque gardens that can still be visited today.

With the decline of orange cultivation in the Azores, from 1830 onwards, tea, among other agro-industrial innovations, was seen as a promising investment. The new crops in the primary sector decisively altered the island landscape, which was increasingly dotted with tea, tobacco, sweet potatoes, and pineapples (João, 1991). In the 1870s, the Sociedade Promotora de Agricultura Micaelense (Promoting Society of Agriculture of São Miguel), founded in the 1840s (Enes, 2008), began to encourage tea cultivation and production, with the first experiments conducted by the leading landowners of Micael. In these first trials, although the environmental context of São Miguel, particularly in the northern part of the island, proved very suitable for the planting of tea trees, it failed in terms of their handling (Silva, 2014). For this reason, the Sociedade Promotora decided to hire two Chinese men from Macao to teach them oriental processing techniques. In March 1877, master Lau a Pan and his assistant Lau a Teng arrived in São Miguel (Moura, 2019). Despite only staying until 1879, the latter was instrumental in promoting tea on the island, generating increasingly positive reviews. In 1878, the Micaelense tea was praised by members of the Clube Micaelense and Clube Lisbonense for its quality (Machado, 2016).

The success of the tea from São Miguel led to an increased strengthening of its production, for which greater scientific and technical rigor was required. Thus, in 1892, the "Manual do cultivador e manipulador do chá" (The Tea Grower and Handler

Handbook) was published in Ponta Delgada. This publication also included a chapter dedicated to accounting, reflecting the commercial demands of the beverage. Consequently, the increase in production allowed greater outlets for tea; in 1898, the quantity exported reached five tons (Silva, 2014), and in 1904 that number reached close to 40 tons, exceeding 60 tons in 1911. In this way, in the 1910s, almost 5% of the arable area of São Miguel was occupied by tea plantations, 80% of which were located in the municipality of Ribeira Grande (Cabido, 1913), with around 10 large processing units spread around Ribeira Grande, Rabo de Peixe, Fenais da Ajuda, Sete Cidades, Arrifes, Lagoa, and Ponta Delgada (Silva, 2014), accompanied by around 30 other smaller structures, mainly located in São Miguel (Machado, 2016). The island of Faial also had a tea factory (Moura, 2019).

In addition to the increase in cultivable area, the growth in production on the island greatly benefited from the technical modernisation that occurred at the end of the nineteenth century and the beginning of the following century, particularly with the introduction of steam engines in the industrial sector. The first steam engine arrived in São Miguel in 1848, brought from England by Simplício Gago da Câmara to serve his mill located in Calheta, Ponta Delgada. From then on, increasing use of these machines was observed in the milling, wood, nails, candles, typography, and tea industries.

José Maria Raposo do Amaral, owner of a factory in Ribeira Seca da Ribeira Grande called "Casa do Chá," José do Canto in Caldeira Velha da Ribeira Grande, and José Bensaúde in Ponta Delgada were the first to include steam engines in their factory structures between the end of the nineteenth century and the beginning of the twentieth century, soon to be followed by other producers. For example, in 1907, the Mafoma Tea Factory installed its first English steam engine built by Marshall, Sons and Company Ltd. This factory operated until the last quarter of the twenty century (see Figure F.1.2).

Figure F.1.2: Mafoma Tea Factory wrapping paper, 1953–1974.
Source: Regional Government of the Azores/ Regional Secretariat for Culture and Digital Transition, Carlos Machado Museum

The proliferation of production expanded the competitive market, forcing local producers to invest in product diversification and marketing. In 1910, José Maria Raposo do Amaral reported that, faced with the dominance of black tea production, he experimented with the handling of green tea, although still without great success. The intense competition between producers, particularly between José Maria Raposo do Amaral (Raposo d'Amaral Tea), José do Canto (Canto Tea), and José Bensaúde (Bensaúde Tea) in the markets of Lisbon and Porto, to where most of the island's tea was exported, required concrete innovations to lower costs and attract customers, as José Maria Raposo do Amaral stated in 1911:

> This tea business is going from bad to worse, and I see that it is necessary to change the sale system, making the purchase more accessible to the small consumer. To this end, I think my intentions would be achieved by dividing it into tins of 1, 2, 5, and 10 kg and small paper packets of 125 gr. The cans, even the smallest ones, should be parallelepiped-shaped because the round boxes make you lose a lot of space. (Pimentel, 2018)

The outbreak of the First World War in 1914 led to a decline in island tea due to the constraints on its export. These difficulties were aggravated by the crisis of 1929, which was particularly damaging for another of Micael's agricultural exports, the pineapple, which represented 90% of the island's sales abroad during this period (Dias, 1995). Nevertheless, in the 1930s, the island had 16 small tea factories, whose production reached the highest figures since the beginning of its cultivation, with around 70,000 tons per year (Machado, 2001).

In the 1940s, due to the world conflict and the political consolidation of Estado Novo, Azorean tea suffered a new setback in the face of competition from Mozambican tea, particularly protected by the Portuguese state. Mozambique, a Portuguese colony at the time, first experimented with growing tea at the end of the nineteenth century, mimicking what had occurred in the Azores. Since then, the success of this crop was notorious in the Mozambican climatic context, particularly in the area of Upper Zambezia, assuming particular economic importance since 1940, given the support granted by Estado Novo. In the Azores, however, little investment in tea production, the stagnation of techniques, the rivalry between producers on the islands, small cultivation areas, and the taxes imposed by the government on tea from the island of Micael contributed to the decline of this agro-industrial production. Additionally, the growing number of Azorean families emigrating to the United States and Canada in the 1950s and 1960s also depleted the labour force in this sector, in which female labour was vital, accounting for almost half the workforce. The label of the packages reflected the traditional method adopted and the relevance of female work (see Figure F.1.3). Thus, in 1966, only five tea factories remained on the island of São Miguel, most of which closed down over the next 20 years. This decline was accompanied by a new change in the landscape, with an increase in pastures due to investment in agriculture and cattle breeding, which is still a key sector in the Azorean economy today.

In the 1980s, the only surviving tea factory in the Azores and operating in Europe was Gorreana, founded a century earlier. Located in Maia, a municipality of Ribeira Grande, it was the only factory in the Azores that never interrupted its activity, remaining in operation even today, with tourism potential that stems from its history and adaptation to the demands of consumers and the guidelines of the European Community. Gorreana tea, produced using the Hysson method of steam, is considered a traditional tea with an organic production profile. The plantation area covers around 32 hectares and is fertilised exclusively with plant manure.

Figure F.1.3: Gorreana Tea Factory packaging label, second half of the twentieth century. Source: Regional Government of the Azores/ Regional Secretariat for Culture and Digital Transition, Carlos Machado Museum

The Gorreana factory currently produces around 33 tons of tea per year, distributed between black tea (Moinha, Broken Leaf, Pekoe, Orange Pekoe, Orange Peko, Ponta Branca, and Oolong varieties) and green tea (Hysson, Encosta de Bruma, and Pérola varieties). In addition to regional and national consumption, Gorreana's teas are also exported to Germany, the United States, Canada, Austria, France, Italy, Brazil, Angola, and Japan, among others.

Currently, Porto Formoso is the other factory producing teas in São Miguel, located in the parish of the same name in Ribeira Grande. After its closure in the 1980s, it reopened to the public in 2001, producing the following varieties of black tea: Orange Pekoe, Pekoe, Broken Leaf, and Azores Home Blend (see Figure F.1.4).

Looking from an industrial point of view, Gorreana presented a higher resilience since it never closed and was able to open the doors of the factory and later on of the tea plantation to tourists since the early 1980s.

The Gorreana and Porto Formoso factories are top-rated tourist facilities on the island of São Miguel due to their cultural and natural attraction to visitors. They can simultaneously offer the contemplation and experience of a gastronomic heritage that assumed global relevance in the 21st century.

Figure F.1.4: Porto Formoso Tea Factory Label, 1920–1980.
Source: Regional Government of the Azores/Regional Secretariat for Culture and Digital Transition,
Carlos Machado Museum

In addition, there is a third, more experimental, tea plantation to be found on the main island of the Azores: Agrarian Development Services of São Miguel. There, the authorities of the Azores plant and harvest different types of tea, but mainly white tea. The Agrarian Development Services of São Miguel (S.D.A.S.M.) initiated at the beginning of the 1980s the study of the adaptation of the Camellia sinensis var. assamica on the climate of the Azores on two small plantations (0.4 ha). The plantation is maintained without the use of synthetic or pesticides and the idea is to analyze the chances for sustainable growth of white tea and other sorts on the islands. This plantation is also open for guided tours, offering a very rural and authentic type of tea tourism, directly in the fields and among the tea plants (Tea grown in Europe, 2023).

From production to tourism orientation

The preliminary findings pointed to a non-linear path of evolution of the tea production since only one was operating from the 18 small factories for a period. This drawback was primarily due to improper planning and marketing efforts and limited collaboration among stakeholders, combined with competition from other agro-industrial products such as sweet potatoes or tobacco. For Gorreana, tourism became a natural path since, in the earliest years, the plant factory was open to visitors without changing the business model.

The tourism growth seeds the reignition of old factories plants in the island, not only linked to tea. For instance, the former Tobacco Factory – Museu de Tabaco da Maia, located near the two tea factories, was converted into a museum. It is dedicated to the investigation, documentation, conservation, interpretation, and dissemination of the tobacco industry from the perspective of social and local development of rural communities. One of the most important objectives of this museum is to create synergies and become a nucleus of attractiveness linked to tourist and cultural activities. Therefore, the factories' recovery and reorientation towards tourism arise not only as a way to increase the experience of tourists but also as a way of valuing the cultural and industrial heritage under a sustainable paradigm. This perspective is quite visible in the interviews collected with the owners of the two active factories.

Presently tea tourism potential is acknowledged by local people, tourists, DMO, and tea factories, under the tea trilogy: history, heritage, and industry. Therefore, to assess the overall strategy underlying tea factories, an adaptation of the model presented by Khaokhrueamuang, Chueamchaitrakun, Kachendecha, Tamari, and Nakakoji (2021) was adopted.

These authors considered that to understand the tourism interpretation, the analysis should focus on five properties: 1) motivating visitors to visit the destination; 2) communicating the place's meaning; 3) targeting potential tourists; 4) differentiating the destination from other sites; and 5) activating value co-creation (Khaokhrueamuang et al., 2021). In the present study, the focus will be on the three last elements combined: how tourists co-created the image of the tea factories, how owners project their factory brand image, and how that differentiates it from other experiences.

The initial work was based on the interviews made with the two CEOs of the two factories. In the testimonial of Porto Formoso Tea factory owner and CEO José António Pacheco, the tourism purpose walks hand-by-hand with the reopening of the factory:

> We started the project of reopening the plant in 1998 by increasing the plantation area. And, in 2001, we reopened the factory to be a functional factory to efficient production and pleasant for those who visit us.

> The experience was designed for tourists visiting the island of São Miguel and looking for an exotic reality, which does not exist in their countries of origin. Most of these tourists do not know the tea plant, and here they get to know the process from the plant to the cup. (José António Pacheco)

The commitment to environmental and cultural sustainability is evident in the activities developed in this plant. Not only do they seek to maintain a process of orthodox production, in which one works the whole leaf tea and without aroma, one does not pack the tea in wallets, but in packets. In addition to minimising the ecological footprint, it maintains the main rituals of tea consumption and its aroma and traditional taste. Additionality, tea production has a biological production accreditation, issued annually by an international entity.

In the testimonial of Maria Madalena Mota, CEO of Gorreana Tea Factory, it was possible to understand that they also use a conventional method to produce the tea and differentiate from other international competitors. Furthermore, this plant's great quantity of tea is exported to Germany, being sold as a premium biological product. Although she acknowledges the relevance of exportation and tourism, she stressed that:

> Those who visit us always, regardless of the crises that may be occurring worldwide, are the locals. Our Micaelenses are our Sunday customers. They come here and have a cup of tea that we

offer for free and then buy tea at the supermarket [. . .] This is the way we thank them, for always being with us, even in the most troubled moments. (Maria Madalena Mota)

Both interviews showed that the traditional production processes are valued and enrich the tourism experience offered. Therefore, tourism and production are considered almost as one since tourists are welcome to walk in different plant sessions and over the plantations. Gorreana Tea Factory also recently started to explore the tourism potential of the plantation more, creating the tea walking trails, where tourists and locals are invited to walk and explore the tea plantation.

In the case of Porto Formoso Tea Factory, the first of May is dedicated to recreating the picking of tea leaves. Locals and tourists alike are invited to dress up as in the old days and manually collect the tea leaves into a vine basket while singing traditional songs.

In recent decades, tourists have used social media networks, primarily those thematic, to share their experiences with peers (Amaral et al., 2014). Moreover, their ratings and comments are helpful for those planning a trip to a destination (Xu et al., 2021), becoming influencers of their destination image formation. Moreover, tourists become active cocreators of destination brand images.

As referred by Yeap, Ooi, Ara, and Said (2021), some of the elements communicated, such as sustainable practices, might influence the tourists' global image and preference formation. To assess this component, the reviews available at TripAdvisor for these two-tea plantations were retrieved, and a content analysis was conducted.

The data extracted examined 318 reviews made to the Porto Formoso Tea Factory and 1,123 reviews made to Gorreana Tea Factory, with an average rating of 4.5 and 4. The initial word cloud for both factories shows that tea plantation and factory are regularly present in the comments made by tourists (see Figure F.1.5). The vast majority of the tourists have a pleasant experience at the tea factories (Porto Formoso – 85.25; and Gorreana – 82%).

Gorreana Tea Factory

Porto Formoso
Tea Factory

Figure F.1.5: Tea Tourism interpretation.
Source: Author

Comparing the outcome of both factories reveals how the Gorreana tea factory is considered oriented to tea production, with a less explicit focus on tourists, while the Porto Formoso factory is considered more like a tourist spot than a working factory. Moreover, tourists visiting Porto Formoso tea factory made some comparable comments in their experience in Gorreana, considering Porto Formoso as less crowded, even having a smaller factory and plantation area, and therefore being more suitable for tourism experiences.

Tourists tend to classify themselves as tea-drinkers or not, showing their knowledge and taste related to this specific drink. However, regardless of being tea-drinkers or not, a common point was found in both factories related to tea quality: 96.8% of all comments asserted that the tea had a great flavour and quality. On the other hand, some tourists mention that the tea freely offered had less quality but advise peers to spend a "little" amount of money to have a "tea-rrific" experience.

In the general comments, particular attention was given to references related to tourist guides, displaying objects, and on-site signs (El-Menshawy, 2016), since these components are considered differentiating variables. For example, there is a projection room in both factories, where tourists get acquainted with the factory's history and tea history in the region. On the other hand, there were no particular references to the tour guides' information. However, in global comments, it was possible to see that tourists complained about not having very informative materials available, indicating that the tour booklet and projected movie did not have enough information. In an opposite sense, tourists complement the tours around the factory and plantations and positively evaluated the displayed objects. However, in the Gorreana factory, some comments made to the display objects led to inferring that they might need additional information and background to fulfill their function.

The landscapes and views from both factories were also found in the reviews. However, although acquainted with the different lushes of green and other natural appointments, tourists did not make specific references to both factories' sustainable efforts. This absence might lead us to question if the factories do not fully communicate their efforts or if it happens because tourists aren't expecting any less from a destination with a sustainable tourism destination accreditation, as is the case of the Azores.

Final considerations

Despite the increasing recognition of tea tourism, there is limited research on how tea owners move from a tea factory into a tourism experience. Moreover, most evidence is related to tea plantations in eastern regions, such as China, Taiwan, or Japan. In Europe, there is a small island (S.Miguel – Azores – Portugal) where tea plantations are part of the local heritage.

In this chapter, we have unveiled the history of the tea in the Azores and showed how, after the decline of the tea industry, one factory – Gorreana Tea Factory – was able to prevail, opening to tourism and exportation. This work also illustrates that old and abandoned factories can overcome their past when combining tea production with tourism. The clear tourism orientation and success case of the Porto Formoso Factory proves it.

The reviews made by tourists show that tea tourism is a growing niche, with potential, especially when integrating tea degustation with beautiful landscapes and welcoming people. However, they also unveil the need for a more consistent communication model that provides information, such as on enhancing the experience. These conclusions are similar to the ones found in the work of Tiago, Fonseca, Chaves, and Borges-Tiago (2021) that analyzes the role of food in tourism experiences in the Azores.

Findings also highlighted that tea tourism is a suitable format of sustainable tourism: (1) not only because it promotes the economic growth and sustainability of traditional factories; (2) but also as it prompts social and cultural sustainability by valuing heritage and local traditions; (3) and environmental sustainability through conscious and biological production. Perhaps not all these dimensions are indeed acknowledged by tourists since they were not highlighted in their comments. But some of the elements well-rated in their experiences mirror these dimensions. Future research is therefore needed to better understand how to transfer heritage value to tourism experience based on tea. Future works should consider questioning tourists and locals and compare the results with other destinations and other industry-driven tourism experiences.

References

Akadiri, S.S., Akadiri, A.C., & Alola, U.V. (2019). Is there growth impact of tourism? Evidence from selected small island states. *Current Issues in Tourism, 22*(12).

Amaral, F., Tiago, T., & Tiago, F. (2014). User-generated content: tourists' profiles on Tripadvisor. *International Journal of Strategic Innovative Marketing, 1*(3).

Cabido, A.G.F. (1913). A indústria do chá nos Açores. Boletim do trabalho industrial, 88.

Campos, M.A.M.M. (2014). Caracterização de propriedades nutricionais e antioxidantes de chás do Arquipélago dos Açores e valorização dos seus resíduos.

Chen, S.-H., Huang, J., & Tham, A. (2021). A systematic literature review of coffee and tea tourism. *International Journal of Culture, Tourism and Hospitality Research.*

Cheng, S., Hu, J., Fox, D., & Zhang, Y. (2012). Tea tourism development in Xinyang, China: Stakeholders' view. *Tourism Management Perspectives, 2.*

Cheng, S.W., Xu, F.F., Zhang, J., & Zhang, Y.T. (2010). Tourists' attitudes toward tea tourism: A case study in Xinyang, China. *Journal of Travel & Tourism Marketing, 27*(2), 211–20. Retrieved October 10, 2023. doi:10.1080/10548401003590526.

Datta, C. (2018). Future prospective of tea-tourism along with existing forest-tourism in Duars, West Bengal, India. *Asian Review of Social Sciences, 7*(2).

Deutscher Tee- und Kräuerteeverband. (2022). Teereport 2022. Retrieved April 20, 2023, from https://www.teeverband.de/files/bilder/Presse/Marktzahlen/Tee%20Report%202022__DS.pdf.

Dias, F.S. (1995). A importância da "economia da laranja" no Arquipélago dos Açores durante o século XIX. ARQUIPÉLAGO-Revista da Universidade dos Açores.

El-Menshawy, S. (2016). Effective rapport in tourist guiding (interpretation of themes). http://dx.doi.org/10.4172/2167-0358.1000172.

Enes, C. (2008). Sociedade Promotora da Agricultura Micaelense. In *Enciclopédia açoriana*. Ponta Delgada.

Faria, S.D., Tiago, M.T B., Tiago, F.G.B., & Couto, J.P. (2014). Tourism on the Azores and Madeira islands: issues of peripheral and development Regions. Paper presented at the second Annual International Interdisciplinary Conference, AIIC 2014.

Hampton, M., & Hampton, J. (2009). Is the beach party over? Tourism and the environment in small islands: A case study of Gili Trawangan, Lombok, Indonesia. *Tourism in Southeast Asia: Challenges and new directions*, 286.

Han, K. (2007). Tracing the history of tea culture. *Tea and tourism: Tourists, traditions and transformations*, 23–37.

Hayes, D., & MacLeod, N. (2007). Packaging places: Designing heritage trails using an experience economy perspective to maximize visitor engagement. *Journal of Vacation Marketing, 13*(1), 45–58.

Hobhouse, H. (1985). Seeds of change. Five plants that transformed mankind. *Fünf Pflanzen verändern die Welt*, 128–86.

Huang, Z.-H., & Qian, F.-Y. (2005). Tea growers behavior's impact on tea safety [J]. *Journal of Nanjing Agricultural University, 1*.

João, M.I. (1991). Os Açores no século XIX: economia, sociedade e movimentos autonomistas: Edições Cosmos.

Jolliffe, L. (2003). Chapter 6: The lure of tea: history, traditions and attractions. In *Food Tourism Around the World*.

Jolliffe, L. (2006). Tea and hospitality: More than a cuppa. *International Journal of Contemporary Hospitality Management*.

Khaokhrueamuang, A., Chueamchaitrakun, P., Kachendecha, W., Tamari, Y., & Nakakoji, K. (2021). Functioning tourism interpretation on consumer products at the tourist generating region through tea tourism. *International Journal of Culture, Tourism and Hospitality Research, 15*(3). Retrieved October 10, 2023. https://doi.org/10.1108/IJCTHR-08-2020-0187.

Lai, T.-W. (2002). Promoting sustainable tourism in Sri Lanka. Linking Green Productivity to Ecotourism-Experiences in the Asia Pacific Region.

Lima, E.A., Machado, M., & Nunes, J.C. (2013). Geotourism development in the Azores archipelago (Portugal) as an environmental awareness tool. *Czech Journal of Tourism, 2*(2). doi:10.2478/cjot-2013-0007.

Machado, M.V.D.R. (2016). O chá Raposo d' Amaral: contributo para o estudo do chá em S. Miguel. In *Percursos da História. Estudos In Memoriam de Fátima Sequeira Dias*. Ponta Delgada: Universidade dos Açores.

Martin, L.C. (2018). *A history of tea: The life and times of the world's favorite beverage*. Tuttle Publishing.

Melo, P.P.D. (2008). A locomóvel da antiga fábrica de chá da Mafoma: Uma máquina a vapor na indústria micaelense do dealbar do século XX. Insulana, 64.

Moura, M.F.D.O. (2019). Introdução da cultura do chá na ilha de São Miguel no século XIX (subsídios históricos).

Owen, C. (1992). Changing trends in business tourism. *Tourism Management, 13*(2). 224–26.

Pimentel, A.A.P. (2018). José Maria Raposo Amaral Um Progressista Convicto? Universidade dos Acores (Portugal).

Roudi, S., Arasli, H., & Akadiri, S.S. (2019). New insights into an old issue–examining the influence of tourism on economic growth: evidence from selected small island developing states. *Current Issues in Tourism*, *22*(11).

Saberi, H. (2010). *Tea: A global history*. Reaktion Books.

Seyitoğlu, F., & Alphan, E. (2021). Gastronomy tourism through tea and coffee: Travellers' museum experience. *International Journal of Culture, Tourism and Hospitality Research*.

Silva, R.M.E.D. (2014). O chá em Portugal: História e Hábitos de Consumo.

Silveira, P. (2012). A produção e a exportação de laranja nos Açores. Um olhar a partir da periferia: o caso da ilha de São Jorge. *Povos e Culturas* (16).

Su, M.M., Wall, G., & Wang, Y.N. (2019). Integrating tea and tourism: a sustainable livelihoods approach. *Journal of Sustainable Tourism*, *27*(10). Retrieved October 10, 2023. doi:10.1080/09669582.2019.1648482.

Tea grown in Europe. (2023). Tea grown in Europe 2023 – in focus. Retrieved July 20, 2023, from https://tea-grown-in-europe.eu/wp-content/uploads/2023/06/EuT-2023-Leaflet-digital-version.pdf.

Tiago, F., & Borges-Tiago, T. (2022). Small island destination. In *Encyclopedia of Tourism Management and Marketing* (n.p.). Edward Elgar Publishing.

Tiago, F., Fonseca, J., Chaves, D., & Borges-Tiago, T. (2021). A look into the trilogy: food, tourism, and cultural entrepreneurship. Turismo sénior: Abordagens, sustentabilidade e boas práticas, 10.

Van Driem, G.L. (2019). *The tale of tea: A comprehensive history of tea from prehistoric times to the present day*. Brill.

Veríssimo, J.M.C., Tiago, M.T.B., Tiago, F.G., & Jardim, J.S. (2017). Tourism destination brand dimensions: An exploratory approach. *Tourism & Management Studies*, *13*(4).

Weinberg, B.A., & Bealer, B.K. (2004). *The world of caffeine: the science and culture of the world's most popular drug*. Routledge.

Whats on in Azores. (2023). Map of Azores photograph. Retrieved March 24, 2023, from https://www.whatsoninazores.com/map/.

Wu, J. (2020). What makes bubble tea popular? Interaction between Chinese and British tea culture. *The Frontiers of Society, Science and Technology*, *2*(16).

Xu, H., Lovett, J., Cheung, L.T., Duan, X., Pei, Q., & Liang, D. (2021). Adapting to social media: the influence of online reviews on tourist behaviour at a world heritage site in China. *Asia Pacific Journal of Tourism Research*, *26*(10).

Yeap, J.A., Ooi, S.K., Ara, H., & Said, M.F. (2021). Have coffee/tea, will travel: Assessing the inclination towards sustainable coffee and tea tourism among the green generations. *International Journal of Culture, Tourism and Hospitality Research*.

Belinda Davenport and Hartwig Bohne

F.2 Trading and traditions – The British and tea

Introduction

The British and tea seems to be an emotional and economic partnership forever. Based on colonial experiences and the import of tea plants from China to the former British colony India and visionary people like Earl Grey, Thomas Twining or Josiah Wedgewood, tea culture became a synonym for British culture and vice versa (Pettigrew, 2003; Twinings, n.d.).

The "wedding for tea" and entrepreneurial impacts

After the first direct import of tea to Great Britain in 1644, the promotion of tea consumption was empowered by the marriage of Catherine de Braganza (origin Portuguese) and King Charles II in 1662 as the new queen transferred her tea related preferences from Portugal to Great Britain (Krieger, 2021). In addition, in 1670 the first silver teapot in Great Britain was presented by Lord Berkley to the East Indian Tea Company in order to underline the importance and value of tea as well as the pride of silver tableware (Pettigrew, 2001). Also, other silversmiths and craftsmen followed the trend of tea and illustrated their abilities by developing teapots, e.g. Paul Storr (1771–1844; Figure F.2.1).

Consequently, entrepreneurs like Thomas Twining followed this trend, opening the first tearoom in London in 1706. Elsewhere, the potter Josiah Wedgwood saw the opportunities of tea porcelain and started producing tea pots and teacups in Stoke-on-trend in 1759 (Pettigrew, 2003).

The land of afternoon tea

The custom of having afternoon tea is symbolic for British hospitality and is embedded in its traditional culture, dating back to the 1800s. Traditionally taken between 4–5 p.m., the times taking it have shifted as modern evening meals aren't as late, meaning afternoon tea may now be taken anytime in the afternoon. The concept of afternoon tea was believed to have been invented by Anna Russell, Duchess of Bedford in 1840, as she was Queen Victoria's friend and lady of the bed chamber (inner circle of the Queen's ladies in waiting), however this is likely to be a corruption of the

https://doi.org/10.1515/9783110758573-019

Figure F.2.1: Paul Storr Teapot.
Note: Paul Storr (British, 1771–1844), Teapot 1838–1839. Sterling silver
Photo: Kamm Teapot Foundation
Source: Kamm Teapot Foundation

truth. With the invention of the gas lamp, work and mealtimes were stretched later so that evening meals were taken at 8 p.m., suggesting there were social changes in Britain at that time. The date the Duchess was believed to have first had her afternoon tea though was most likely 1843 during a visit to Belvoir Castle, Leicestershire, when she was eating alone in her room, due to her hostess being unavailable and her husband out shooting. As the Duchess of Bedford travelled to Prussia before, it can not be excluded that the initial impuls for combining snacks and tea was taken from Prussia (today: Germany) to Great Britain. It was actually Queen Victoria who visited Germany in August 1845 and experienced 'tea, quite in the German way' and where 'excellent cakes of all kinds were served, while the Queen's ladies made the tea' referring to the German Queen. http://www.queenvictoriasjournals.org/ 15 Aug 1845)

From the 1880's afternoon tea in Britain was mostly found in larger hotels particularly in London, until it's resurgence in popularity after the popular Downton Abbey TV series in 2010, and is still very popular today with both British people and visitors alike (Emmerson, 1992; Pettigrew, 2001; Rohrsen, 2022; Ellis, 2022).

Until today, the combination of tea and snacks is connected to the British tea culture and heritage, showing the close relation of tea and the pride of a big nation. Also, the "rule" of "Milk in or tea first" is an interesting development of culinary habits, based on the warming effects of tea in a cup and the proper handling of thin porcelain cups, which would be easier with the cooling effect of milk. In Great Britain, 85% of tea drinkers prefer to have milk with their tea – a singularity in Europe (Smith, 2020).

Centre of tea trade

In addition to the cultural importance, Great Britain was also important for the international tea trade. For this, the London Tea Auction, established in 1679, was a symbol of tea trading efforts as well as the branded tea companies, e.g., Lipton, which were influencing the development of tea visibility and awareness for hundreds of years globally. Until the 1950s, one third of the European tea trade was still administered there, but due to more independency of producing countries and less of a need for an international auction hall, this institution closed in 1998 (Rohrsen, 2022; Lipton Teas, n.d.).

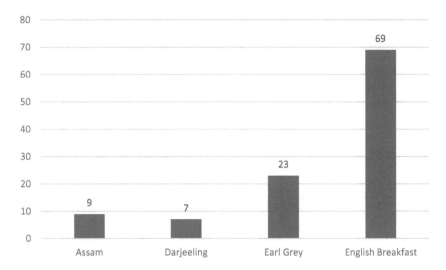

Figure F.2.2: British preferences for black teas.
Source: Smith (2020)

The tea consumption in Great Britain has shown a black preference till today. Earl Grey is still elegant and famous (23% of consumers prefer this sort), but more than half of the British tea drinkers regularly prefer English Breakfast (69%). Interestingly, more female than male tea drinkers prefer the strong sort of English breakfast (57% versus 51%) and the consolidated preference for this type of tea starts around the age of 25 and remains stable. Until the age of 25, the preferences are wider and one third of the people do not drink tea. Obviously, in their mid-twenties, they change views and perspectives (Smith, 2020; Figure F.2.2).

British tea pot design – The CUBE

Following the pride and tradition of Great Britain as a well-known tea drinking country, British teapots were usually spherically shaped and lavishly decorated. But, for the operations in guest-oriented operations, the British entrepreneur and designer Robert Crawford (1882–1937) focused a specific approach, and developed the most efficient, non-drip, non-chip, and easily stacked teapot, the "CUBE" (pot and cover made from ceramics), patented in Leicester in 1917. The design is influenced by "Art Deco" and can be seen as the British interpretation of the aesthetic principles of the German Bauhaus (although it was initiated later). And, mostly, the purpose to be used in hotels and gastronomic establishments influenced the industrial design – perfectly pourable and storable. Initially scheduled as a product made of ceramics only, it also got a version based on silver plated metal in the 1920s. Consequently, it was also intensively used on transatlantic ocean liners (e.g., Cunard Line) and railways. As the world's largest selling patented teapot, it is the symbol of British tea related perfectionism as well as the impact of tea culture for industrial design and the passion of British ceramic designers (Victoria and Albert Museum, 2009; Anderson, 2000; Figure F.2.3).

Figure F.2.3: The CUBE teaset (1950s, Cunard Line Gastronomy Equipment).
Note: CUBE shaped three piece set. Teapot with lid, creamer, and open sugar in cream colour with yellow, gray, and black stripes. Designed by Robert Crawford (British, 1882–1937), Foley Bone China/glazed ceramics.
Photo: Kamm Teapot Foundation
Source: Kamm Teapot Foundation

Conclusion

The British culture is embodying tea culture at its best. The blend of royal background, entrepreneurial and cultural impacts as well as dominating global trade and creating tableware shows the variety of British understanding of tea. Consequently, the British tea culture is often mentioned as a synonym for tea consumption if consumers are asked for any European tea tradition. And, also in other European countries, the reference for afternoon tea, sorts of tea or typical tea tableware very often is the British role-models. There is no doubt that the "English Breakfast Tea" is one of the strongest brands of tea known and respected globally.

References

Anderson, A. (2000). *The cube teapot: The story of the patent teapot*. Richard Dennis Publisher.

Ellis, M. (2022). *Jane Austen and the British way of tea*. Retrieved March 30, 2023, from https://www.janeaustenandco.org/asia-and-the-regency.

Emmerson, R. (1992). *British teapots and tea drinking*. HMSO.

Krieger, M. (2021). Geschichte des Tees. Böhlau Verlag.

Lipton Teas. (n.d.). *History in the beginning*. Retrieved March 30, 2023, from https://www.lipton.com/ca/en/our-purpose/lipton-tea-history.html.

Pettigrew, J. (2001). *A social history of tea*. National Trust.

Pettigrew, J. (2003). *Design for tea*. Sutton Publishing.

Rohrsen, P. (2022). *Das Buch zum Tee*. C.H. Beck.

Smith, F. (2020). How do British tea drinking habits compare with other Europeans? Retrieved March 30, 2023, from https://yougov.co.uk/topics/consumer/articles-reports/2020/11/24/how-do-british-tea-drinking-habits-compare.

Twinings History. (n.d.). *About us*. Retrieved July 6, 2022, from https://twinings.co.uk/blogs/news/history-of-twinings.

Victoria and Albert Museum. (2009). The Cube. Retrieved July 30, 2023, from https://collections.vam.ac.uk/item/O186718/the-cube-teapot-and-cover-cube-teapots-ltd/.

Carol Bailleul

F.2.1 Afternoon tea or high tea – Tea traditions in England, Scotland, and Wales

What comes from faraway, is good – Tea as an exotic luxury in the seventeenth century

Although many people associate tea with Great Britain, it was a Dutch trading company bringing tea from Japan (Green) and China (Black) to Amsterdam in 1610. Thanks to the English East India Company, Chinese gold made its first sea voyage to England in the seventeenth century. In the beginning, this was only a very small quantity: 65 kilograms per year. That is less than three bags of cement! This made this product very scarce and expensive. It is quite logical that only the richer class could afford this exotic luxury! They liked boasting with this new beverage. Tea was a status symbol, a sign of wealth. Whoever served this infusion was apparently at the top of the social ladder.

Tea was discovered in China some 5,000 years ago. According to a Chinese legend, Emperor Shen Nong invented tea by accident. For reasons of hygiene, he ordered his subjects to always boil water before drinking it. When he was travelling with his entourage, they paused in a remote part of the empire. Emperor Shen Nong had his subjects boil water while he took a nap. Nearby stood a tea plant, whose leaves were blowing into the kettle. The Emperor woke up and perceived a pleasant smell. He drank the water with the tea leaves and was very impressed by the delicious taste and the uplifting effect of the drink.

In Europe, people could have tea for the first time in the so-called coffee houses. They were meeting places exclusively for men. In particular, businessmen, politicians, poets, and the clergy know how to find their way there. Because of high taxes, people only brewed the infusion once: in the morning. For the rest of the day, they heated the drink every time a customer asked for tea. Fortunately, this situation changed at the end of the century, as the tax was suddenly levied on the leaves instead of on the infusion. This made the sale of tea possible, and men took this product home. That way, their wives could also get acquainted with the Chinese gold. As women were not allowed in the coffee houses, they organised parties at home and consequently friends met regularly and had tea. The hosting lady even bought furniture and crockery especially for the occasion, and the first British tea ceremony was born (Bailleul, 2018).

https://doi.org/10.1515/9783110758573-020

From smuggler to pleasure garden – Tea as a status symbol in the eighteenth century

What turbulent times! The Kingdom of Great Britain was regularly entangled in wars. In the field of tea, too, this period was not without controversy. The precious leaves had been the exclusive preserve of the wealthier classes. When the ships entered the City of London, a guard came on board with them until they reached the warehouse. That is how precious tea was! The demand for this exotic article grew by the day. To meet the enormous demand, a trade in fake tea was created: used tea leaves were mixed with ash and the leaves of the well-known herb, hawthorn. Tasting the difference, the typical British answer was: "Better an infusion that doesn't taste so good than no tea at all."

It was much more important to fix where and how the tea was drunken. This infusion was preferably served with milk, bread, and butter. Having tea was not only done in the living room, but also in the so-called pleasure gardens. These were theme parks *avant la lettre* and guaranteed an intense experience. You could go for a quiet walk, enjoy a boat ride, take part in fun folk games, enjoy a quiet concert or a magical firework display. Ladies flaunted the most expensive outfits.

Tea was originally only drunk with sugar. Milk only appeared around 1720. In addition, the British started discussing the controversy about pouring tea into the cup first

Figure F.2.1.1: British silver teapot (1670).
Source: Bailleul (2018)

or milk first. This nationally important question was solved by using scientific support: the Royal Society of Chemistry decided that milk should be poured into the cup first.

For the many accessories, it was booming business. There was a huge range of teapots, storage boxes, cups and saucers, water kettles, sugar bowls, milk jugs, trays, teaspoons, spoon holders, etc. There were even holders for the wet, used spoons! And teaspoons were often numbered. So, when refilling, the hostess knew exactly which spoon belonged to which person (see figure F.2.1.1).

The reputation of tea

Firstly, tea offered a solution for the success of cheap gin of the moment. The combination of low gin prices and higher wages led more and more people to turn to this drink. However, the excessive use of gin led to a lot of misery. Health problems, arguments at home, accidents at work, aggressive behaviour and even death were the sad consequences. Tea was seen as a better beverage to get enthusiastic without alcohol.

Figure F.2.1.2: British tea caddy.
Source: Bailleul (2018)

Another reason for the success of this new beverage was the prestige it gave people. Tea was a status symbol because tea was a precious possession. It was therefore kept in very expensive and decorative holders. The first ones were made of Chinese porcelain, then there were beautiful boxes in various types of wood, subtly inlaid with ivory or silver knobs. The proud hostess was the only one in the household who kept the key to this box. This gave her more power and independence in relation to her husband and the staff, and was the woman's first steps towards taking her place in society (see figure F.2.1.2 and F.2.1.3).

Birth of afternoon tea – Tea as the national drink in the nineteenth century

Based on previous events in British SPA towns and also in France, the raising attraction of tea and pastries (mostly for women) in the afternoon in England, altered to, the Duchess of Bedford is primarily credited for having increasing the popularity of high/afternoon tea, although she was not the inventor but a passionate follower of this tradition. Since good food tasted better in company, the Duchess invited friends over for tea. Here "tea" meant not only the infusion, but also a light meal with a selection of small dishes, and a second form of a delicious afternoon tea was created (Moore, 2023, Coffey, 2010).

Figure F.2.1.3: British China tea set.
Source: Bailleul (2018)

The custom of drinking tea in the late afternoon became so popular that the wealthy classes organised genuine tea receptions. We are talking about an event where up to 200 guests were invited! Ladies even had a tea dress specially designed for the occasion. This so-called tea gown was made of a light fabric, worn loose, which was nice and comfortable for at home.

Workers were also discovering tea. Because they returned late from work, they developed their own ritual in the evening: high tea. The term "high tea" referred to the high table at which workers sat to eat this meal. This was in comparison to the low tables of afternoon tea. Today, the terms "afternoon tea" and "high tea" were often used interchangeably to refer to the afternoon tea ritual.

Black or Green – why the British preferred Assam tea

Suddenly, there was a significant event. Something that transformed tea into the British national drink. From the very beginning of tea importation until now, the British have imported their tea from China. How did they do this? Well, they illegally exported opium from India to China and in return they got tea. This opium trade led to many addicts in China: around three million opium addicts by 1830! However, the Chinese government eventually no longer put up with this and burned the annual volume of opium. The British were furious and declared war on China, and the Chinese in turn reacted by imposing an embargo on tea exports. The British had to find an alternative source of tea.

They found this alternative in India, in Assam, a state in the Northeast of this "Jewel in the Crown." The British had tea produced there in large quantities, which lowered the price of tea. Plantations producing British tea also appeared elsewhere in Asia, for instance in Darjeeling, India, and in Ceylon. The tea landscape in Britain suddenly looked completely different. Tea was no longer an exotic product. It had become a British drink because it came from British colonies.

Tea entrepreneurs

With the growing consumption of tea, tea shops sprang up like mushrooms. In 1717, Thomas Twining opened the first tea shop in London, the Twinings Golden Lyon Shop on the Strand. Above the entrance there are two Asian figures and a golden lion. To this day, guests and customers can taste tea in this place and get a piece of British tea history through the numerous memorabilia in the small museum at the back of the shop.

The greatest influence on the price of tea came from Thomas Lipton. He bought some tea plantations himself and thus eliminated the many intermediaries in the tea trade. In addition, halfway through the nineteenth century Lipton developed its famous "yellow label" which became one of the most famous tea brands all over Europe.

Healthy enjoyment – Tea as a trendy treat in the twenty-first century

One cup of tea is not like another. The popularity of tea remains high. Despite growing competition from coffee with the advent of slow coffee and latte art, there is a growing interest in loose leaf tea, preferably organic and sustainably grown. A new generation of trained tea sommeliers is ready to let you discover the thousand and one aromas of tea.

Hotels are experiencing glory days in serving afternoon teas. In addition to the traditional formula, you can usually opt for a festive variant with champagne or cava, or, if you want to stand out from the competition, put a gentleman's tea or a kid's tea on the menu. People are looking for a unique experience together with friends or family.

Elsewhere, cream tea is in a class of its own. Cream tea is typical of Devon and Cornwall. It consists solely of scones with clotted cream and strawberry jam. So, what do you put on your scone first? Clotted cream or jam? That depends on where you order this delicacy. In Devon, the clotted cream is spread on the scone first, followed by the jam. In Cornwall, it is the other way around. Here, they use the jam first and add the clotted cream last.

This makes it clear that in the seventeenth century tea was seen as a means of socialisation. Tea was indeed the best way to spoil your guests with culinary delight, also by using and respecting certain rules, illustrated in table F.2.1.1.

Afternoon tea or high tea in Ireland, Scotland, Wales versus England

If you take the very posh afternoon teas like in hotels in London, there is very little difference in what's being done, except in the price. If you go to a 4-star hotel in the London area, it is really expensive, up to as much as 65–70 pounds for an afternoon tea, particularly if you have a glass of champagne or something similar. In other parts of Britain prices can range from 15 to 60 pounds with quite a lot of places selling an afternoon tea for 30–35 pounds, so for much more reasonable prices.

The other difference that people may see is the ingredients that they use. You may find things like locally caught smoked salmon and local specialties, both savoury and sweet.

Scotland is very famous for shortbread: Scottish shortbread. That might easily be a component dependent on who's running the show. And oats. Flapjacks and things like that. Maybe even gingerbread. The really fine leaved oatmeal is often used in gingerbread. And also things using whiskey, like whiskey cake. And of course there is a lot of fishing, so obviously salmon. You might have beef as well. The ingredients may well be locally sourced.

British tea etiquette

Table F.2.1.1: The do's and don'ts of afternoon tea.

Do's	Don'ts
The greeting between hostess and guest is done with a firm handshake.	The right order to eat an authentic afternoon tea is to start with the sandwiches and savouries. Then eat the scones. Finish with the other sweet pastries.
Don't put your handbag on the floor when you sit down at the table. Place it on your lap or behind your back against the back of the chair!	As a hostess, never ask for an extra piece of cake or an extra cup of tea. You ask your guests this question and expect them to reply, 'No, thank you. Would you like something else?
Wait for the hostess to signal that you can start eating.	Don't dip your biscuits in the tea.
Once the afternoon tea begins, take the napkin, unfold it and place it on your lap. When you must leave the table during the afternoon tea, fold the napkin nicely and put it on your chair. You should hold a piece of cake with your left hand.	Don't stick out your little finger. Never put the napkin back on the table when you leave it during the afternoon tea. Afternoon tea is finger food. You do not eat with knife and fork.
Knife and fork lie together on the right-hand side of the plate or on the napkin on top of the plate.	Scones are not cut with a knife. Scones are torn or broken in two.
Cups and saucers are picked up simultaneously if the distance between guest and table is greater than 30 cm.	No elbows on the table.
The cup is taken separately if the distance between guest and table is less than 30 cm.	No putting tea and something to eat in your mouth at the same time.
Scones are eaten in small bites. Spread some clotted cream and jam on each one.	Do not put too manypieces on the plate at once.
If the clotted cream and jam are served in only one pot on the table, each guest takes a piece of it with his/her knife and puts it to the side of the plate.	Never leave your spoon in the cup after stirring.
For individual jars of clotted cream and jam, spread directly from the jar onto the scone.	
When adding milk to your tea, stir so that your spoon does not touch the rim of the cup. When finished, place the spoon on the saucer behind the cup.	

Source: Bailleul (2018)

And there are also traditional specialty cakes. For instance, if you go to Wales, you would be given really local cakes. There, you will get something called the bara brith. That is, again, a fruit loaf, with the fruit steeped in something, perhaps tea. They also have Welsh cakes, which are flat and look like a pancake, but they are made with a fairly short mixture of flour, sugar, and butter, which is quite dry. You roll it out and you cut rounds, and they are cooked on the top of the stove. They go on a griddle and then you flip them like a pancake, which is still very common in Wales. If you go to Wales, they will be a tourist gift usually packed in 6-ies or 8-ies.

The jam may also differ. There may be local fruits. Scottish marmalade is very fruity and intense. And Dundee cake, which is a fruit cake with almonds laying on top of the cake, which is a very popular cake in Scotland. In hotels things are usually not British let alone Irish or Scottish. They have a more international feel to what they are serving. Another difference may be between the big hotels and the smaller tea-rooms Here the people owning the tearooms are much more likely to go for local and organic. This could be anything: beef, eggs, cheese, almost anything depending on the style of cakes they make.

If you have fish and chips in Scotland as your supper, it is sometimes called a fish supper or a fish tea. That's probably also prevalent in the North of England, from Manchester upwards. If they say, "I am going to have tea now," they might not be talking about afternoon tea, but might well be talking about supper. In some soap operas on television, you might hear someone having a conversation like the following. The man might be outside repairing the car and round about 5.30–6 p.m. the wife might come out into the garden and say, "Are you coming in for your tea?" This doesn't mean afternoon tea, this means supper. There's always been some confusion about what the term actually means.

As soon as afternoon tea became more mainstream towards the 1870s, it was almost certainly copied in Ireland. There used to be a lot of very wealthy people, aristocrats in Scotland. Not so much in Wales. Wales had always been a bit more down in terms of wealth and aristocracy. There were more farmers. Ireland certainly had a lot of quite posh aristocrats and Scotland a lot of big landowners who are still there today. And they would probably be serving afternoon tea in their homes, in their castles.

The type of tea was partially standardised. The English breakfast blend united Assam and Java, while an Irish breakfast was a blend of Assam and Ceylon while Scottish breakfast blend was rare and dominate by Assam, Ceylon, and Oolong.

As the four nations England, Wales, Scotland, and Ireland have been together for a very long time since the beginning of the eighteenth century, it is difficult to identify a purely British trend separating it from the other regions. But there is one big difference indeed: the Irish drink much more tea than the British (and Welsh and Scottish). The Irish drink between four and six cups a day, the British more like three cups a day. And they drink it strong, really strong.

References

Bailleul, C. (2018). *Afternoon tea or high tea?* Houtekiet.

Bohne, H., & Jolliffe, L. (2021). Embracing tea culture in hotel experiences. *Journal of Gastronomy and Tourism*, 6(1–2), December 2021, pp. 13–24.

Bohne, H. (2022a). Tea ceremonies. In D. Buhalis (Ed.), *Encyclopedia of tourism management and marketing* (pp. 331–35). Edward Elgar Publishing Ltd.

Bohne, H. (2022b). Tea consumption heritage. In D. Buhalis (Ed.), *Encyclopedia of tourism management and marketing* (pp. 335–37). Edward Elgar Publishing Ltd.

Coffey, M. (2010). Is the Duchess of Bedford a fraud? (Aug 31st, 2010), retreived Jan 28th, 2014 from https://teageek.net/blog/2010/08/is-the-duchess-of-bedford-a-fraud/.

Krieger, M. (2021). *Geschichte des Tees*. Böhlau Verlag.

Moore, S. (2023). Why The Duchess of Bedford did not invent afternoon tea (Aug 08th, 2023), retreived Jan 28th, 2024 from https://theenglishmanner.com/insights/wwwwhy-the-duchess-of-bedford-did-not-invent-afternoon-tea/.

Pettigrew, J. (2001). *A social history of tea*. National Trust.

Rohrsen, P. (2022). *Das Buch zum Tee*. C.H. Beck.

Robin Emmerson
F.2.2 The British tea ceremony

"[. . .] When the clock strikes four, everything stops for tea."

These are the words of a song from the 1930s, and each of its verses ends like this. "Everything Stops for Tea" celebrates afternoon tea as a British institution, and the repetition suggests that it is unchanging. By the 1930s afternoon tea at four o'clock had ruled polite British drawing-rooms for almost a century, as a light meal with bread, butter, and cake.

The most striking thing about the British and tea, however, is that they drank it at almost any time (see figure F.2.2.1). The man-about-town Captain Gronow recalled in his memoirs:

Figure F.2.2.1: Chelsea porcelain tea set at Temple Newsam House, Leeds.
Source: Author

When our army returned to England in 1814, my young friend, Augustus Stanhope, took me one afternoon to Harrington House, in Stableyard, St James's, where I was introduced to Lord and Lady Harrington, and all the Stanhopes. On entering a long gallery, I found the whole family engaged in their sempiternal occupation of tea-drinking. Neither in Nankin, Pekin, nor Canton was the teapot more assiduously and constantly replenished than at this hospitable mansion . . . As an example of the undeviating habits of the house of Harrington, General Lincoln Stanhope once told me, that after an absence of several years in India, he made his reappearance at Harrington House, and found the family, as he had left them on his departure, drinking tea in the long gallery. On his presenting himself, his father's only observation and speech of welcome to him was "Hallo Linky, my dear boy! delighted to see you. Have a cup of tea?"

https://doi.org/10.1515/9783110758573-021

In the early nineteenth century Lady Harrington, like other hostesses, would make the tea herself in front of her guests. She would open the tea caddy and spoon the tea leaves into the teapot. Then she would take the lid off the teapot, place the teapot in front of an urn of simmering hot water, and turn the tap to fill the pot. Once the tea had brewed, either she or one of her daughters would pour it out into the cups and hand them round. Almost everyone seems to have taken both milk and sugar. As part of the campaign against the slave trade in the 1790s there were attempts to persuade people not to take sugar in tea. A cartoon shows King George III and Queen Charlotte trying to persuade their reluctant daughters (Emmerson, 1992; Pettigrew, 2001; see Figure F.2.2.2).

Figure F.2.2.2: King George III and Queen Charlotte trying to persuade their reluctant daughters from taking sugar.
Source: Author

Once your teacup was empty, the hostess would take that as a sign to refill it without asking you. To show that you had had enough, you had to leave your teaspoon in the cup. This was a trap for foreign visitors who did not know the code. The Prince de Broglie reported in 1782:

> I partook of most excellent tea and I should even now be still drinking it, I believe, if the Ambassador had not charitably notified me at the twelfth cup, that I must put my spoon across it when I wished to finish with this sort of warm water. He said to me: it is almost as impolite to refuse a cup of tea when it is offered to you, as it would be indiscreet for the mistress of the house to propose a fresh one, when the ceremony of the spoon has notified her that we no longer wish to partake of it.

François de la Rochefoucauld, visiting England in 1784, noted that drinking tea "[. . .] gives the rich an opportunity to show off their fine possessions: cups, teapots, etc., all made to the most elegant designs, all copies of the Etruscan and the antique." Fashionable design and good workmanship demonstrated taste and wealth, just as management of the tea ritual showed off your good manners. Jane Austen used the tea service to suggest the vanity of her villain General Tilney in *Northanger Abbey*:

> The elegance of the breakfast set forced itself on Catherine's notice when they were seated at table; and luckily, it had been the General's choice. He was enchanted by her approbation of his taste, confessed it to be neat and simple, thought it right to encourage the manufacture of his country; and for his part, to his uncritical palate, the tea was as well flavoured from the clay of Staffordshire, as from that of Dresden or Sevres. But this was quite an old set, purchased two years ago. The manufacture was much improved since that time; he had seen some beautiful specimens when last in town, and had he not been perfectly without vanity of that kind, might have been tempted to order a new set.

Tea held a special position compared to the other hot drinks, coffee, and chocolate. Inventories of grand houses in the eighteenth century show that the pots and equipment for making coffee and chocolate were kept in the room of the lady's maid, not that of her mistress. When her mistress wanted coffee or chocolate, the servant made it for her. A tea service, however, was generally kept in the mistress's boudoir or study. When she wanted tea, she called for her maid to bring a kettle of boiling water with a spirit lamp beneath it to keep it bubbling. Then the mistress would dismiss the servant and make the tea herself. In this way the service of tea became associated with a special kind of privacy which the rich did not have for much of their time. Some of the most luxurious ceramics were made for this private use: Georgiana Duchess of Devonshire, ancestress of Diana Princess of Wales and the subject of the film *The Duchess*, bought a tea set for one, made of Wedgwood's jasper ware, from the firm's London shop in 1786 for three guineas (Elllis, 2022; Pettigrew, 2001; Emmerson, 1992; see Figure F.2.2.3).

The two most important times of the day for the social drinking of tea in the eighteenth century were in the morning and after dinner. Morning calls were the brief visits which polite people made to each other's houses when they were staying in London or other social centres such as Bath or York. Once you had sent a message to say you were in town, it was normal to visit without further announcement, and you did not know who else might be visiting when you arrived. Tea was the normal accompaniment to one of these visits, which should not last more than half an hour.

You had to make sure you did not visit too close to the family's dinner time. The fashionable time for dinner gradually became later and later, so there was a risk that those used to fashionable late dinners – especially in London – would overstay their welcome when making calls on people who still dined at two o'clock. As the time of dinner slipped later and later, so did the morning calls. By Victorian times, with dinner at half past seven or eight, the calls had also moved later, to the afternoon, but with typical British stubbornness they were still known as "morning calls" (Pettigrew, 2001; Emmerson, 1992).

Figure F.2.2.3: Wedgwood's Jasper Ware teapot.
Source: Author

Once dinner had moved later, to about eight, a hungry gap opened between lunch and dinner, and a "little something" was needed in-between the two. This is how "afternoon tea" as a light meal with bread, butter, and cake began, in the houses of society hostesses like the Duchess of Bedford and the Duchess of Rutland. Before "afternoon tea" became an institution, the most formal occasion for drinking tea was after dinner. In the 1720s foreign visitors to England were already noting with horror that after dinner the women all left the dining room, while the men remained at table and became drunk and disgusting. The excuse was that the women went to make tea in the drawing-room and that the men, after a short interval, would join them to drink it. In practice the men extended this interval and altered its purpose to suit themselves (Pettigrew, 2001; Emmerson, 1992).

Eventually the inebriated men would stagger into the drawing-room, where the women had been drinking tea by themselves for some time. When Georgian books of instructions to servants talk about serving tea, they always talk about serving it in the drawing-room after dinner. The first stage was that servants would bring in the container of boiling water with a device for keeping it hot. Until the 1760s this was a kettle, which for the rich would be of solid silver, mounted on legs with a spirit burner underneath. The whole thing would often be placed on a specially designed stand like a tripod table, and occasionally this would also be of solid silver rather than wood. In the 1760s people began to find that the kettle needed refilling too frequently and replaced it with a much larger hot-water urn. Something more powerful than a spirit lamp, however, was needed to keep the water really hot. A heavy iron bar was heated in the kitchen fire until it was red-hot. A servant carefully lifted it by passing a metal rod through a hole in the top of the bar. Then the urn was filled with boiling water and the hot iron bar was dropped into a metal sleeve in the centre of the urn, and a cover quickly placed on top. The full urn was carried very carefully into the drawing-room (Pettigrew, 2003; Roth, 1961).

The poet Thomas Cowper described it as "the bubbling and loud hissing urn throwing up a steaming column." This is the ritual which Jane Austen and her readers would have known. Her novels, like other literature of the period, do not trouble to describe it because it was so familiar. Cartoonists, however, sometimes showed a tea-table being accidentally overturned and the contents of the urn being spilled on the company (see figure F.2.2.4) (Austen, 1975).

Advantages of wearing Muslin Dresses! —— dedicated to the serious attention of the Fashionable Ladies of Great Britain

Figure F.2.2.4: The hot water urn upset.
Source: Author

Once the servants had brought in the teakettle or hot-water urn, the mistress would unlock the small chest or trunk in which she kept the tea and sugar. Eighteenth-century tea trunks usually had three compartments inside: one for black tea, one for green tea, and a central one for sugar. The three containers might be of silver, enamelled metal, or occasionally ceramic. The containers themselves were likely to be precious, but a greater risk was that servants would help themselves to some of their contents. Both tea and white refined sugar were expensive, and in some households it became the custom to provide servants with tea and sugar as part of their allowance in order to persuade them not to steal them (Pettigrew, 2003; Pickering, 2013)

Directions to Servants, by Jonathan Swift, was written in 1745 in the form of the real books of instruction intended to explain to servants how to perform their duties. It is really a satire, however, which exposed how servants could trick their employers and help themselves. His "Advice to the Waiting Maid" describes the 'execrable Custom got among Ladies [. . .] the Invention of small Chests and Trunks, with Lock and Key, wherein they keep the Tea and Sugar, without which it is impossible for a Waiting-maid to live. For, by this means you are forced to buy brown Sugar, and pour Water upon the Leaves, when they have lost all their spirit and taste." As he says, used tea leaves were re-used by servants, and in some houses they were sold by servants from the back door. Swift's "Advice to the Butler" is a good deal worse: "When you are to get Water on for Tea after Dinner (which in many Families is part of your Office) to save Firing, and to make more Haste, pour it into the Tea-Pot, from the Pot where Cabbage or Fish have been boyling, which will make it much wholesomer, by curing the acid and corroding Quality of the Tea." One hopes that few servants were so shameless (Pettigrew, 2003; Scarfe, 1988).

At this time tea was trickling down through the British social system. The poor desired it because they associated it with the leisurely life of the gentry, including the rituals and equipment which accompanied it (see figure F.2.2.5). Hogarth in *The Harlot's Progress* shows his prostitute determinedly drinking tea while living in great poverty.

Charles Dering was shocked in 1751 by the behaviour of a poor stocking-weaver in Nottingham:

> Being the other day at a grocer's, I could not forbear looking earnestly and with some degree of indignation at a ragged and greasy creature, who came into the shop with two children following her in as dismal a plight as the mother, asking for a pennyworth of tea and a halfpennyworth of sugar, which, when she was served with, she told the shopkeeper [. . .] I do not know how it is with me, but I can assure you I would not desire to live, if I was debarred from drinking every day a little tea.

The upper class thought tea was too good for the poor. Samuel Johnson, himself a tea addict, declared "Tea is a liquor not proper for the lower classes of the people, as it supplies no strength to labour, or relief to disease, but gratifies the taste without nourishing the body." The poor, however, were determined to have their tea anyway. Tea's rise in popularity in Britain dates from the years between 1700 and 1720. In 1700 the British East India Company imported about 20,000 pounds' weight of tea. By 1721 they were importing over a million pounds' weight. From 1700 they also began importing huge amounts of Chinese porcelain and red stoneware for drinking tea, which ensured that the prices would be modest. The fashion for tea-drinking spread very

Figure F.2.2.5: A poor prostitute drinks her tea.
Source: Author

quickly through the whole country. In 1717 John Sutcliffe, a pious apothecary in Cli-
theroe, Lancashire, wrote a poem in which the Devil tempts a young girl by presenting her with a tea service (Street-Porter, 1981; Pettigrew, 2001; Emmerson, 1992).

He describes her sitting with her friends showing off the fancy tea things and
their fancy manners in holding the teacup:

> Upward the little fingers distant stand [. . .]
> They praise the making of the tea/ then where it was bought and what it cost and how
> More of that savour may be bought as low/And ever one must her own story tell
> As if she only knew to buy as well/from teas they pass to coffee by degrees
> And chocolate and talk as much of these/as nauseating as profuse and vain
> And then perhaps return to tea again/unless they straggle to the China dishes
> And thus, you'll hear them simper out their wishes/ that they a set such like knew where to buy
> When perhaps every word they speak's a lie [. . .]

From its beginning the British tea ceremony involved the hostess making the tea herself.
It began in 1662 when Charles II married a Portuguese princess, Catherine of Braganza.
Portugal had been the first European country to directly trade with China by sea, and
tea was a long-established drink there. Catherine brought the taste to the court in London. The place where traces of this courtly tea-drinking survive is Ham House near London. Elizabeth, Duchess of Lauderdale, kept an exotic tea table of Javanese lacquer in

her private "closet" or sitting room, and next door an "Indian furnace for tea garnished with silver." This was presumably for heating the water. She had chairs made in England in an exotic style to go with her tea-table. The ensemble shows how tea-drinking created a taste for exotic objects and decoration in exotic styles, which were part of its attraction. The duchess also had a copy of one of the first European books to explain how to make and drink tea, *Les Voyages d'Alexandre de Rhodes*, published in 1666.

The first detailed account of tea-drinking in English was a translation from another French book, by Jacques Spon alias Dufour. The English translation was by John Chamberlayn in 1685, entitled *The Manner of Making of Coffee, Tea, and Chocolate, as it is used in most part of Europe, Asia, Africa, and America, with their Vertues*. It describes how Chinese aristocrats prepared tea for their friends with their own hands, using precious and delicate vessels which they kept in special private rooms in the middle of their palaces. When European aristocrats read this, they had before their eyes some of the delicate and unfamiliar Chinese objects which the East India Companies had brought with them from the other side of the world. This text remained the only description of Chinese tea-drinking in English for more than a generation and had a great influence on how the British tea ceremony developed. British aristocrats wanted to copy what they thought was the polite behaviour of Chinese aristocrats, even though they really knew very little about it.

The other hot drinks, coffee and chocolate, could not compete with the advantages of tea. It was not only that they were more messy to prepare and serve; they did not have the right cultural associations. Coffee came from the Turkish empire, and when seventeenth-century European ladies thought of Turkish ladies drinking coffee, they thought of the harem. That would not do. Chocolate came from the tribes of Central America, whom Europeans then regarded as savages. Tea was associated with polite Chinese aristocrats, and you could actually imitate them by preparing it yourself. It was a winner.

The delicate and decorated objects which came with the tea from China helped to sell tea-drinking as a habit, and to sell the idea of China itself. The courtly figures painted on porcelain and lacquer screens fired the imagination of Europeans to create an imaginary China and its embodiment, the chinoiserie style. But the delicate Chinese porcelain, thin, white, and translucent, was surprisingly strong. For a century British potters tried in vain to match it. They had difficulty in making porcelain which would not break when boiling water was poured in. The shop of Robinson and Rhodes in Leeds advertised in 1760 "a good assortment of Foreign China and a great variety of useful English China of the newest improvement, which they engage will wear as well as foreign, and will change gratis if broke with hot water." As late as the 1780s the Derby porcelain factory was regularly receiving complaints from the manager of its London showroom that he "wished something could be done respecting the teapots to prevent them from flying [*i.e., flying to pieces*] for the disgrace is worse than anything, and it loses the sale of many sets." All the factory could suggest was that customers warm up the teapots gradually. The teapots of the Worcester factory gained a reputation for resisting boiling water. Their porcelain contained soapstone which resisted thermal shock, and other factories copied the recipe. The potters of Staffordshire developed white salt-glazed stoneware and then cream-coloured earthenware which were also reliable and very much cheaper. Their pottery quickly captured European markets, and, long before Josiah Wedgwood, in 1749 the French government set up at the Pont-aux-Choux in Paris the *Manufacture Royale des Faiences a l'imitation de celles d'Angleterre* in order to try and compete (Street-Porter, 1981; Pettigrew, 2001; Emmerson, 1992).

The Staffordshire wares were popular at every level of British society, and because they were affordable even the poor could drink tea. Some teapots were so small that it is not always clear whether they were for adults or toys for children. Many were "one-dish" teapots made for adults, designed to hold just one cup of tea for those who perhaps could not afford to drink very much, because tea was still expensive. Despite their small size and low price, they were often beautifully finished (see Figure F.2.2.6).

Figure F.2.2.6: A small teapot in Staffordshire creamware, about 1770.
Source: Author

This was the beginning of a fiercely competitive industry of the modern type, with over a hundred factories aiming to sell in Europe and beyond. It was the need to compete with imported Chinese tea wares which kick-started the industrial development of the Staffordshire potteries (Ellis, 2022; Pettigrew, 2001; Emmerson, 1992).

The importance of tea for the development of the British economy was extraordinary. This was the first time that the daily diet of ordinary British people depended on two commodities, tea and sugar, brought from the two opposite ends of the world and finally united in the teacup. In 1782 the eruption of the volcano Laki in Iceland filled the atmosphere with dust and ruined the harvest in northern Europe for several years. In Britain the high price of grain made it impossible for the poor to afford beer. Since water was usually not safe to drink unless it was fermented or boiled, the government recognised this was a national health emergency, and that tea was the answer. In 1784 they removed most of the high tax on tea to enable the poor to afford it as their principal drink. Francois de la Rochefoucauld, visiting in the same year, noted:

> The drinking of tea is general throughout England. It is drunk twice a day, and although it is still very expensive, even the humblest peasant will take his tea twice a day, like the proudest: it is a huge consumption. Sugar, even unrefined sugar, which is necessary in large quantities and is very dear, does nothing to prevent this custom from being universal, without any exception.

From this point onwards, tea was Britain's national drink.

References

Austen, J. (1975). *Northanger abbey*. Folio Society edition.

Ellis, M. (2022). Jane Austen and the British way of tea. Retrieved October 10, 2023, from https://www.ja neaustenandco.org/asia-and-the-regency.

Emmerson, R. (1992). *British teapots and tea drinking*. HMSO.

Pettigrew, J. (2001). A *social history of tea*. The National Trust.

Pettigrew, J. (2003). *Design for tea*. Sutton Publishing.

Pickering, O. (2013). The Quaker's tea table overturned: An 18th century moral satire. *Quaker Studies, 17*(2), 244–64.

Roth, R. (1961). Tea drinking in 18th century America: Its equipage and etiquette. *Bulletin of the Smithsonian Institution*, 225: *Contributions from the Museum of History and Technology*, 72.

Scarfe, N. (1988). *A Frenchman's year in Suffolk*, Suffolk Record Society, vol. 30.

Street-Porter, J., & Street-Porter, T. (1981). *British teapots*. Angus Robertson Publishers.

Belinda Davenport
F.2.3 The true story of Earl Grey

Earl Grey tea is well-known throughout the world and a popular tea in the UK. Known for its slightly smoky blend, floral aroma, infused with the essence of bergamot orange rind, it can however have a love/hate relationship with consumers, certainly in the UK. Few consumers are aware that in fact there are many different variations to the flavour depending on the company blending it. Despite the general belief that Earl Grey only gets its flavour from bergamot, this is not true since some companies use neroli, an essential oil produced from the blossom of the bitter orange tree (citrus aurantium), and there is a reason for this difference. That reason is embedded in history, intrigue, and is steeped in mystery. Importantly, some of those companies claim to be the first commercial business to offer the recipe, possibly to gain competitive advantage or the prestige of being the first. This article considers the evidence to try and establish the truth.

The story

The story of how Earl Grey came about suggests that the blend was given to Charles Grey, second Earl Grey (1764–1845), British Prime Minister in the 1830s, to counteract the hardness of the water found at his home Horwick Hall in Northumbria, England. In a 1994 interview for *The Daily Telegraph* the sixth Earl Grey is reported to have said that:

> The story I tell is this: during his period as Prime Minister, Earl Grey sent an envoy to China, who supposedly saved the life of a mandarin's son. In gratitude, the mandarin shipped a special blend of tea, plus the recipe to make it. Earl Grey must have taken the tea and purported recipe to his tea merchant and asked him to copy it [. . .] Unfortunately, he added, we don't know who Earl Grey's tea merchant was and we don't know what the original blend tasted like.

Twinings claim that after Lady Grey introduced it to London's society they were asked to produce it, since London water was similarly hard. Jacksons of Piccadilly also lay claim to being the first company to produce it, while East India Company claim they had the recipe before Earl Grey was given it.

Fact or fiction

So much distortion to this story has taken place as internet blogs and articles are published, many with slight deviations from the aforementioned that are then passed on.

https://doi.org/10.1515/9783110758573-022

An example is that Earl Grey himself travelled to China, however Charles, second Earl Grey, is not known to have travelled to China, especially since during that period Britain was on the brink of war with China.

According to Oxford English Dictionary contributor Stephen Goranson,

> there was a flurry of advertisements for 'Earl Grey's Mixture' dating from 1884. With his earliest documentary evidence yet found of a connection between 'Earl Grey' and a particular blend of tea, sold by Charlton and Co. Goranson, the date suggests that Henry, the 3rd Earl Grey (1802–1894), who served as Victoria's Secretary of State for War and the Colonies in the 1840–50s, might have been the Earl Grey associated with the tea, rather than his more famous predecessor. Oxford English Dictionary (2013)

But is the story plausible? Apart from a confusion between the first and second Earls Grey, China was completely diplomatically isolated in the 1830s and bergamot as an added flavouring is unknown there. So where did Earl Grey tea originate?

According to Austin of Sevencups, the truth is likely to be slightly more mundane, yet still historically interesting. The second Earl of Grey, Charles Grey, spent a short though politically important four years as Prime Minister of the United Kingdom, from 1830 to 1834. His administration is responsible for significant reform, including the abolition of slavery throughout the British Empire in 1833. His link to the world of tea came in 1834, when shortly before retiring from public life, he removed the trade monopoly with China held by the East India Company. The newly opened trade routes allowed tea clippers, a fast-traveling trade ship, to be entirely packed with this single product, drastically reducing the import cost and causing a surge in the popularity and consumption of tea in the United Kingdom. With this in mind, it seems likely that a Chinese ambassador presented Charles Grey with a gift of high-grade Chinese tea out of gratitude for the sudden profitability of the tea business. Using bergamot oil to scent and flavour tea was a technique unknown in China at this time, which reinforces the probability that this came later, when British tea manufacturers were attempting to recreate the taste of Earl Grey's special tea (Food of England, 2022).

Austin spoke with Zhuping about which variety of tea Charles Grey might have been given, as their sources both online and in textbooks were disparate on this note; popular guesses were Qimen or Lapsang. Zhuping quickly ruled out the former. Production of Qimen tea did not begin until 1875, when Yu Gancheng, founder of Qimen tea and once a Wu Yi Shan officer, brought the technology to produce this variety back to his hometown. Their guess is that Charles Grey was given Lapsang Bohea, a fine black tea scented with pine smoke. According to research by Foods of England, one of the most highly prized Chinese teas is the Fo Shou, a green tea from Yongchun in Fujian Province. It is said to have a taste reminiscent of the bergamot orange used in perfumery, and is sometimes called "bergamot tea," though it does not contain any sort of added flavouring. Other teas, such as the black Keemun (or Qimen), present a similar natural flavour.

It appears to have been the case that some English tea dealers took to adding bergamot flavouring to fairly ordinary tea in order to increase its value:

> To render Tea at 5s. a Pound equal to Tea at 12s. – The cheapest and most expensive teas are all the leaves of the same tree, at least they should be so. The high flavour, therefore, of some of the sorts of tea and the want of flavour in others, must arise from the manner of preparing them, and must, consequently, be in some measure artificial. It follows if we can discover any fine flavoured substance and add it to the tea in a proper manner, we shall be able to improve low-priced and flavourless tea into a high-priced article of fine flavour. The flavouring substance found to agree best with the original flavour of tea is the oil of bergamot, by the proper management of which you may produce from the cheapest teas the finest flavoured Bloom, Hyson, Gunpowder and Cowslip. [. . .] When it is thus improved, it is often sold at 18s and a guinea a pound. Cowslip tea has been as high as 32s. ('Lancaster Gazette', Saturday May 22, 1824, p. 3)

This was fine, if you were open about what you were doing. Otherwise, you could get caught out, such as when Brocksop and Co. found themselves in court in May 1837 accused of supplying what was said to be "Howqua" black tea which had been "artificially scented and appeared to have been drugged with bergamot in this country." It can be claimed that this was the first tea company to produce Earl Grey commercially.

Claimant one: Jacksons of Piccadilly

Jacksons of Piccadilly claimed to be the original blenders of the original recipe, and there is evidence of adverts dated from 1928 which states that the tea was "introduced in 1836 to meet the wishes of the former Earl Grey" (see Figure F.2.3.1).

According to "A Social History of Tea" by Jane Pettigrew and Bruce Richardson (Benjamin Press), there was no proof to substantiate the claims either way. Compounding the issue is that Twinings bought Jacksons of Piccadilly in January 1990, after it was sold to Fitch and Lovell Ltd., a food distribution company, in 1986.

Jacksons of Piccadilly, founded by Robert Jackson in 1700, was a London based teahouse, which earned the reputation for selling pre-blended teas direct to customers. This was uncommon during that period as people tended to blend teas themselves at home. They claim to have been given the recipe by Earl Grey to George Charlton, a partner of Robert Jackson and Co in 1830. In the 1800s tea was a new beverage in UK; Robert Jackson used to blend tea at home and by 1815 he was an established blender of tea. By 1890, the Jackson blends were a favourite of the Royalty, and they gained the right to use the royal warrant (Pettigrew, 2001).

Oxford English Dictionary researchers, however, found no advertisements for Earl Grey tea until the 1880s and state that the first reference to Earl Grey tea dates only as far back as the 1920s (see Figure F.2.3.2).

Figure F.2.3.1: Earl Grey's Mixture advertisement.
Source: Jacksons of Piccadilly (1928)

Claimant two: Twinings

R. Twining and Company Ltd. also claim to be the original blenders of Earl Grey tea, in order to counter the hardness of London water, whilst Earl and Lady Grey visited London. According to Oxford English Dictionary researchers, it is only from the early twentieth Century, and not before, that the London tea merchants Twinings in The Strand advertised Earl Grey. Twinings, however, had more recently obtained the endorsement of Richard, the sixth Earl Grey (b.1939), whose signature appeared on their packages. However, the Oxford English Dictionary conducted research to substantiate the claim and have never found any evidence that either Jacksons of Piccadilly or R. Twinings and Company Ltd. were connected with the origin of the Earl Grey brand.

Despite this, the current Earl Grey's home Horwick Hall promotes on their website and in their tearoom that it is Twinings. Richard, the sixth Earl Grey, contradicts this claim when he was interviewed by Bernadine Tay, Director or European Speciality Tea Association and Quintessential Teas. The video, re-posted on YouTube 2020, states that the tea was created due to complaints about the lime in the water to a mandarin, and that the recipe was given to counteract the taste. He then went on to say that it was Lady Grey's visit to London that introduced the recipe to society; on the

By Appointment to HIS MAJESTY THE KING.

CHINA TEAS

The Celebrated

"EARL GREY'S" MIXTURE.
The Perfection of Choicest China Teas **4/6 per lb.**

BROOKS' CLUB BLEND. A choice selection of fine China Teas. ‥ ‥ **3/6 per lb.**

INVALID CHINA TEA. Carefully selected Blend of Pure China, containing less tannin than any other Tea. Easily digested and strongly recommended for Invalids and Dyspeptics **4/- per lb.**

DR. MILTON'S BLEND. A combination of the Choicest Growth of Pure China Tea. Recommended by the late Sir Andrew Clark and J. H. Milton, Esq., of St. John's Hospital.. **4/- per lb.**

KUMQUATA TEA. An exquisite Afternoon Tea. A Pure China Blend ‥ **3/- per lb.**

HOUSEHOLD TEA. ‥ ‥ **2/4 per lb.**

ROBERT JACKSON & CO.,
Tea and Coffee Merchants,
171-172, PICCADILLY, LONDON, W.1.

Figure F.2.3.2: China Teas advertisement – Early Grey.
Source: *The Times*, March 28, 1919, p. 4 (Foods of England, 2022)

video, he names Jacksons of Piccadilly as the company who was asked to blend it commercially (Quinteassential Fine Tea, 2017).

Claimant three: East India Company

East India Company's records date back to the Boston Tea Party, which took place on December 16, 1773. It was their tea that was thrown into the harbor in response to Britain's taxes on tea. East India claims that "their archives revealed that the use of the neroli orange blossom flavouring with tea was first observed in China in 1793 by Sir George Staunton, an East India Company botanist" (East India Company, 2021). East India Company uses a blend of neroli and bergamot to flavour their Earl Grey, claiming it to be more like the original flavour of the Earl Grey blend (East India Company, 2021).

Bergamot, more commonly used in most Earl Grey tea today, is a subspecies of Citrus Aurentium or Neroli, the original flower used in China. Sir Joseph Banks, to whom Staunton reported his findings, experimented with various flavourings, and according to the East India Company this recipe was devised long before Earl Grey heard of it from Sir Banks, his friend.

Other possibilities

It may be that the name originates from a tea dealer called Grey, such as William Grey and Co, situated at Morpeth, only a few miles from the home of Earl Grey's family seat at Horwick. According to Foods of England researchers,

> Grey's Tea was very widely advertised from at least 1852, sometimes with the rhyme (see Figure F.2.3.3):
>
> If your pockets and palates you both want to please,
> Buy William Grey's finest of Teas,
> His, at Four Shillings, is unequale'd they say,
> Then come with your money, and purchase of Grey (Foods of England, 2022).

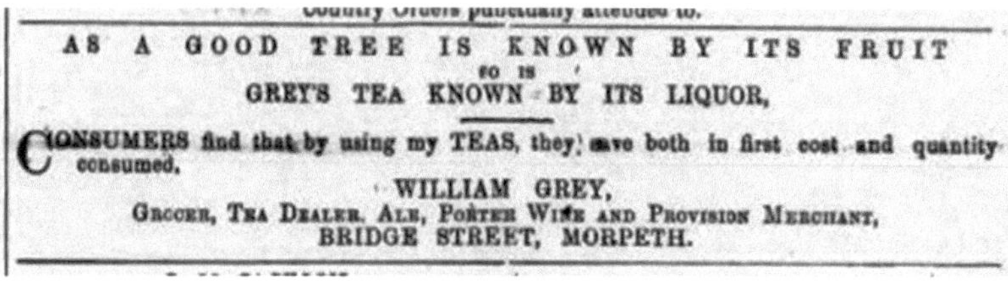

AS A GOOD TREE IS KNOWN BY ITS FRUIT
SO IS
GREY'S TEA KNOWN BY ITS LIQUOR.

CONSUMERS find that by using my TEAS, they save both in first cost and quantity consumed.

WILLIAM GREY,
GROCER, TEA DEALER, ALE, PORTER WINE AND PROVISION MERCHANT,
BRIDGE STREET, MORPETH.

Figure F.2.3.3: Morpeth Herald, Saturday April 16, 1864.
Source: Foods of England (2022)

According to Foods of England researchers, "shortly after this, Grey's of Morpeth seem to disappear from the record, and 'The Celebrated Grey Mixture' Tea then turns up in advertisements for the London blenders Charlton & Co" (Foods of England, 2022; see Figures F.2.3.4 and F.2.3.5).

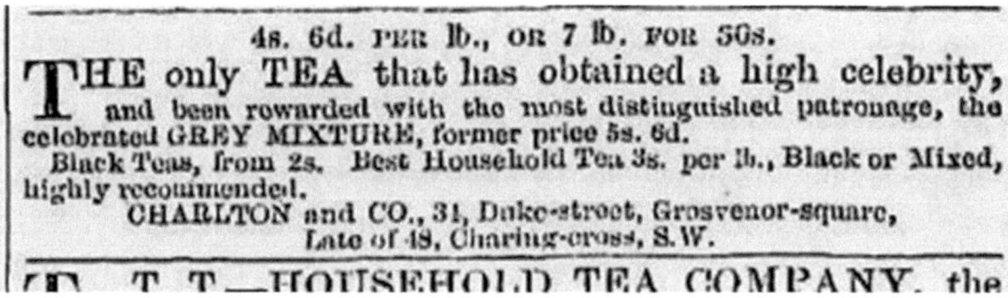

4s. 6d. PER lb., OR 7 lb. FOR 30s.

THE only TEA that has obtained a high celebrity, and been rewarded with the most distinguished patronage, the celebrated GREY MIXTURE, former price 5s. 6d.

Black Teas, from 2s. Best Household Tea 3s. per lb., Black or Mixed, highly recommended.

CHARLTON and CO., 31, Duke-street, Grosvenor-square,
Late of 48, Charing-cross, S.W.

Figure F.2.3.4: John Bull, Saturday, September 7, 1867.
Source: Foods of England (2022)

Earl Grey, rather than Grey's mixture, was mentioned in the book *Revelation of High Life Within Royal Palaces*, published in the USA around 1891 (Foods of England, 2021) which seemed to gain it its link to royalty (see Figure F.2.3.6).

Established 1847.

THE Celebrated TEA, EARL GREY'S MIXTURE.
This choice Tea can only be obtained of the Introducers and Sole Proprietors,
CHARLTON and CO.,
20, Jermyn-street, near Regent-street, late of 198, Piccadilly.
Importers of the Genuine Nepaul Pepper, Madras Currie Powder, and other Indian Condiments.

F. STEWART and CO., BREAD and BISCUIT

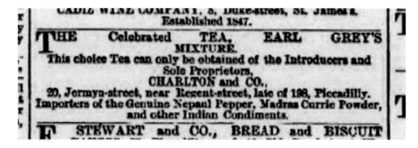

Figure F.2.3.5: "Morning Post," Thursday, June 19, 1884.
Source: Foods of England (2022)

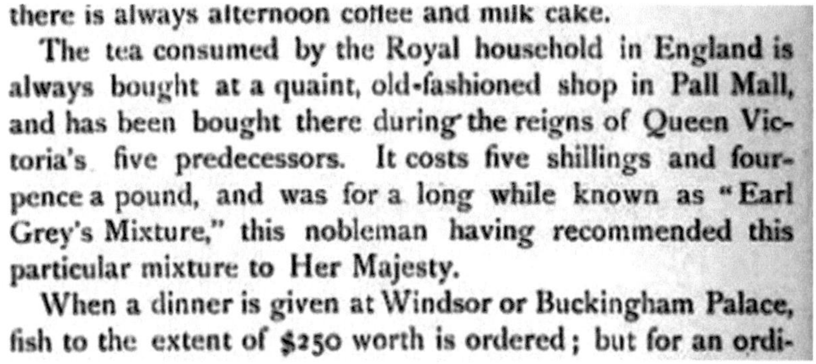

there is always afternoon coffee and milk cake.

The tea consumed by the Royal household in England is always bought at a quaint, old-fashioned shop in Pall Mall, and has been bought there during the reigns of Queen Victoria's five predecessors. It costs five shillings and fourpence a pound, and was for a long while known as "Earl Grey's Mixture," this nobleman having recommended this particular mixture to Her Majesty.

When a dinner is given at Windsor or Buckingham Palace, fish to the extent of $250 worth is ordered; but for an ordi-

Figure F.2.3.6: Revelation of High Life Within Royal Palaces, 1891.
Source: Foods of England (2022)

Earl Grey culinary uses

Modern day Earl Grey tea would be considered any grade of black tea flavoured with bergamot or the lesser-known versions with neroli, with variations including Lady Grey (a sweeter version flavoured with bergamot and vanilla or lavender) and Russian Earl Grey (flavoured with bergamot and lemongrass).

Its distinctive flavour makes it the most popular tea for culinary uses. Whole leaves or bags of Earl Grey are used to infuse cakes, scones, creams, sauces, jams, and even dark chocolate. While the flavours of other teas can be difficult to strongly infuse, the essential oils in Earl Grey help it to stand out strongly against other ingredients (Table F.2.3.1).

Table F.2.3.1: Types and pairing of Earl Grey Teas.

	Lady Grey	Earl Grey	Russian Earl Grey
Flavours	bergamot and vanilla or lavender	bergamot or neroli	bergamot and lemongrass
Teas	Mostly a blend of Ceylon, Darjeeling and Assam . . . or pure black tea . . . but rarely green tea		
Pairing	Sweet: Milk and dark chocolate Salty: creamy cheese, grilled salmon, steamed shrimps, (very) spicy food, e.g., curries or Mexican food		

Source: Author

Conclusion

Considering the evidence presented, it is most likely that it was the high grade of Chinese tea, such as Lapsang Bohea or Fo Shou with their naturally orange flavour was presented to Earl Grey and due to it counteracting the hard water in both Horwick and London, proved popular to demand a UK viable commercial alternative. It is likely that East India Company's George Staunton was aware of the original flavours of tea being in the right place at the right time. Jacksons of Piccadilly was known for their blends, unusual at the time, so could have been one of the first major players, particularly as Richard, 6th Earl Grey named them as being the first company. The link to Earl Grey is believed to be important to Twinings since it is understood from a former employee of Twinings, that an oil painting of Earl Grey hangs in their board room. Since the family did not earn royalties from the commercial production of the tea bearing their name, it is likely that they now earn something from Twinings now being promoted in their tearoom and who can blame them. One thing is for sure, there is a mystery surround the origins of Earl Grey Tea and we may never know for sure.

References

East India Company. (2021). Earl Grey Teas. Retrieved July 20, 2023, from https://lifestyle.theeastindiacompany.com/collections/earl-grey-tea.

Foods of England. (2022). Earl Grey Tea. Retrieved February 20, 2023, from http://www.foodsofengland.co.uk/earlgreytea.htm.

Oxford English Dictionary. (2013). Earl Grey – The results of the OED Appeal on Earl Grey tea. Retrieved July 22, 2023, https://www.oed.com/discover/earl-grey/?tl=true.

Pettigrew, J. (2001). *A social history of tea*. National Trust.

Quinteassential Fine Tea (2017). An interview with Earl Grey. Retreived July 21st, 2023, from https://www.youtube.com/watch?app=desktop&v=f4gzxQurNY4+Quinteassential+22+Dec+2017.

Lee Jolliffe
F.2.4 British tea heritage and branding

Introduction

This chapter investigates the role of British tea heritage and culture in the branding of tea products and experiences. Relevant literature is reviewed, on British tea heritage and its culture, British tea brands and tea and hospitality. Then the major branded teas currently trading in the U.K., many with a long history and heritage but now owned by multinational entities, are identified. Though the comparison of two case study examples the use of tea heritage and hospitality in the branding of tea commodity products and experiences is examined, profiling how heritage and culture has been employed in the commodification of these products. In summary, the chapter explores the current state of the use of tea heritage and related culture for the branding of tea products in the U.K. while examining the link of these brands to tea culture and hospitality.

Britain's tea heritage and culture

Tea heritage and its culture here is briefly identified here as a context for discussing the role of branding tea as a beverage in British society. Some studies identify tea as a source of identity for the English (Fromer, 2008) and as a national drink (Boniface, 2017). Dating back to Victorian times tea united the various classes in England to a certain extent while also reflecting middle class values, as the demand for tea led to it being cultivated in British controlled colonies such as India and Sri Lanka as part of the building of the Empire (Skinner, 2019).

The need for and interest in tea being affordable, safe, and sanitary led early on to branding and packaging. The issue of affordability also led to the blending and direct sourcing of teas so that a consistent product could be offered at a lower price. For example, Thomas Lipton created and marketed an affordable tea product, cutting out the middleman by operating his own plantations, then blending and marketing the tea under the slogan of "Direct from the tea gardens to the teapot" (Lipton, n.d.). The marketing of tea brands thus dates back to these early tea times, when companies created slogans to promote their tea. British tea traditions such as afternoon tea and high tea also encouraged the consumption of tea. Skinner (2019) noted that with tea drinking and afternoon tea established across various socio-economic classes there were different forms of informal versus formal consumption.

History and its heritage elements have played a large part in creating the tea brands that are dominant in the U.K. tea market today. While tea companies have changed hands in terms of ownership, for the most part their corporate heritage has

https://doi.org/10.1515/9783110758573-023

been maintained within their brands, demonstrated by the examples of Twinings and Taylors of Harrogate (Yorkshire Tea), thus contributing to their marketing.

Tea packaging is known to convey brand essence through graphics and design and is also a part of promotion. Colour can also be used strategically in brand packaging as it can attract the attention of consumers and affect perceptions at the point of sale (Kauppinen-Räisänen, 2014). An example is the bold red packaging of Typhoo with a design that was updated and relaunched in 2018 in an effort to engage with shoppers while enhancing the history and heritage of the brand (FOODBEV Media, 2018). This redesign also incorporated a new slogan relating to the tea experience, "Coming together over tea."

Corporate heritage branding

Heritage can be employed in the branding of products, and for some historic firms this can occur at the corporate level. Balmer (2011) discusses the concept of corporate heritage branding, especially in the case of companies with a long history. Also, in the U.K. the system of the royal warrant plays a role in branding. Some of the major tea brands have a royal warrant, a certification of providing goods to the royal family for at least five years. For example, Twinings has a certificate issued by the both the former HM The Queen and HRM Prince of Wales (as tea and coffee merchants) and Taylors of Harrogate has one issued by the Prince of Wales (as supplier of beverages), and now King Charles III. The appropriate royal crest is on the tea packaging of these firms.

Today's tea consumers are also interested in sustainability and the origins of their tea (Saberi, 2010) and this is another element that now affects branding. Ethical trading and sustainability are thus now taken into account by the major tea brands and their controlling companies, such as Unilever (Henderson & Nellemann, 2011).

Tea is a branded commodity. In the case of corporate tea branding this brief literature review indicates that this history and heritage of the brand can play a role. Consumers may exhibit attachment or committed purchase intentions to certain brands, and it is possible that the heritage elements of the brand are a contributing factor.

Tea brands and hospitality

Tea is linked to hospitality, and this enters into the use of and connections to hospitality by the various tea brands. The major tea brands are likely to use hospitality to promote their products, for example by linking up with well-known hotels featuring their brands and blends for their afternoon tea services. Skinner (2019) reflected on the popularity of afternoon tea services in hotels as an added service and luxury product and added revenue stream. Likewise, Jolliffe (2006) highlighted the potential for hotels to develop afternoon tea services to make use of dining facilities in the time between lunch and dinner. Bohne and Jolliffe (2021), in their review of how hotels embraced tea culture, found that many establishments offer various forms of afternoon tea services, some linked with specific brands of tea.

In London the historic afternoon tea venue (circa 1927) at the Palm Court in the Sheraton London Grand Park Lane Hotel at one time featured a Twinings Afternoon Tea (Twinings Blog, n.d.) and is now partnered with The Exotic Tea Company. In addition, numerous global hotels feature a Twinings Afternoon Tea, playing on the recognition and heritage of the brand. For example, in Hong Kong, the restaurant Three on Canton at the Gateway Hotel in winter 2020 collaborated with the British Twinings tea brand to offer a Twinings Romance in London Afternoon Tea (Dimusum Daily Hong Kong, n.d.).

Likewise, a number of afternoon tea hotel venues feature Taylors of Harrogate, for example Yorkshire's Crawthorne Hall Hotel and Middlethorpe Hall where the promotional information states that Afternoon Tea at Middlethorpe is enhanced by a local luxury connection with the old established family tea merchants "Taylors of Harrogate" (Yorkshire Good Food Guide, n.d.).

Methods

The research purpose of this chapter is to investigate the branding of major British tea brands, especially with regards to corporate heritage brands in relation to hospitality. This chapter is based on secondary sources. The major tea brands in the U.K. were identified based on web sources (see Table F.2.4.1) profiling their establish-

Table F.2.4.1: Establishment, History and Heritage of Major U.K. tea brands.

Brand	Establishment	History/Heritage	Ownership
PG Tips	Brand launched by Brooke Bond (est. 1845) in the 1930's.	Links to Lipton (est. 1871) through Unilever.	Unilever
Tetley	Founded 1837 in Yorkshire, England by grocer brothers Joseph and Edward Tetley.	First to sell tea bags in U.K. (1953) and to introduce round bags.	Tata Tea Limited
Typoho	Launched in 1903 in Birmingham by grocer John Sumner.	First to sell pre-packaged tea rather than loose over the counter.	Zetland Capital (2021)
Twinings	Established in London in 1706 by Thomas Twinning.	Oldest tea brand in the world. Family still involved with brand.	Associated British Foods
Yorkshire Tea	Established 1977, Taylors of Harrogate dates to 1886 and Betty's Tea Rooms to 1919.	Incorporates history, heritage and traditions of Taylors and Bettys.	Bettys and Taylors of Harrogate

Source: Author

ment, heritage, and history as well as current ownership. Information on brand ownership is correct as of the time of writing the chapter in the middle of 2022.

Several of these brands with a strong heritage component were selected for case studies in order to allow for the comparison of heritage branding approaches. Case studies are known to be a useful research method, in particular when dealing with bounded phenomena, and are recognised as a stand-alone qualitative method (Denzin & Lincoln, 2011). In addition, word clouds are also employed as a method of analyzing the heritage branding elements of the websites for the case study brands. In both of the cases the text from the "About Us" pages profiling the history of the brands was analyzed.

Due to their long and historic corporate histories, both Twinings and Yorkshire Tea were selected for case studies, the first, Twinings (established in 1706), being the oldest tea brand in the world, and the second, Yorkshire Tea, combining the history of two companies, Taylors of Harrogate (established in 1886) and Betty's Tea Rooms (established in 1919). The comparison of the cases offers the opportunity to gain insights into the corporate heritage branding of these British tea brands.

Major British tea brands

The five tea brands profiled also ranked highest in a 2019 survey of tea brand awareness within the general population in the U.K.: PG Tips at 94%, Tetley at 90%, Yorkshire at 87%, Twinings at 79%, and Typhoo at 79% (Harker, 2019). Other brands in the U.K. market, such as Pukka Herbs, Teapigs, Brew Tea, Jacksons, and Ahmed Tea, had drastically lower brand awareness out of the 1,000 consumers surveyed. Pukka Herbs, established in 2001, was acquired by Unilever in 2017. Teapigs, established in 2006, is now owned by Tata Tea. Jacksons of Piccadilly is a historic brand now owned by Twinings. Ahmad Tea, established in 1986, is an independent company. The ownership of four out of these five brands by the major tea conglomerates demonstrates a deep penetration of the historic tea companies into the marketplace. Overall, the survey concluded that longstanding brands do better in the marketplace (Harker, 2019).

PG Tips

While the heritage of PG Tips brand only dates to the 1930s, the current parent company Ekaterra also owns and markets Lipton which has a much longer history dating back to the 1800s, with Thomas Lipton credited with bringing low-cost tea to the masses in England (Lipton Teas, n.d.). The "Tips" in the PG Tips name is a reference to only the tips of the tea leaf being picked, the bud and the first two leaves under it (PG Tips, n.d.). Produced by the company Ekaterra, now owned by CVC, a private equity company, since 2022 and formerly by Unilever, the brand was originally under Brooke Bond (Unilever, 2022). Marketing taglines have included "We all need a PG moment." Like the other British tea brands PG Tips is also paying attention to the sustainability of their tea (Henderson & Nellemann, 2011). The brand is a member of the Ethical Tea Partnership and certified by the Rainforest Alliance (PG Tips, n.d.). Ekaterra, founded by Unilever in 2021, also markets the tea brands of Lipton, Lyons, PG Tips, Pukka, T2, Tazo, and Red Rose.

Tetley

This brand dates back to the mid 1800s and in the 1950s was reportedly one of the first to introduce tea bags (1953) and also round ones. An early marketing promotion was through Petula Clark's single "Anytime Is Teatime Now" that was used on Radio Luxembourg to advertise the tea (Tetley History, n.d.). Since 2000 the brand has been owned by Tata Consumer Products, headquartered in Kolkata, India. This change in ownership consolidated the supply sources of the tea from Tata's plantations in India and Ceylon (Sri Lanka). Tetley is now reported to be the largest tea brand sold in the U.K., by volume of tea sales.

Typhoo

This brand was launched in 1903 in Birmingham by grocer John Sumner. It was reportedly the first branded tea to be sold packaged over the counter versus loose tea. The tea was marketed as medicinal with the tagline of "The tea the doctor recommended." In 1906 the founder started selling Typhoo branded teapots and including circulars on the benefits of the tea along with picture cards in the packages (Typhoo, n.d.). In 1910 he travelled to Ceylon (now Sri Lanka) to begin directly sourcing from the tea gardens there (Typhoo Tea, n.d.). Today the teas are sourced from different continents and countries including Africa (Kenya), South America (Argentina), Ceylon (Sri Lanka), India, and Indonesia. Once in the U.K. the teas are blended to achieve a consistent taste and packaged in tea bags which are then sealed into several foil bags before being boxed. The major shareholder of the company is now Zetland Capital (2021).

As discussed earlier, a relaunch of the branding in 2018 still incorporated strong elements of the heritage of this tea. Current marketing themes include "From Garden to Cup" and the tagline "Create your #Typhoo Moments" for use on Facebook, Instagram, and Twitter.

Twinings

Twinings is the oldest established tea brand, dating their history back to the 1706 when Thomas Twining opened his tearoom on The Strand in London, a location that still operates today. The commercial logo of the company dates back to 1796. While the brand is now owned by a multinational food processing and retail company, Associated British Foods, a representative of the Twining family still has a role in the company. Twinings is marketed globally and is a featured tea in many hotel afternoon teas. It also has several Royal Warrants as discussed earlier in the chapter. The tagline for the tea invites the customer to experience the world of this tea company, to "Take a moment to pause, and immerse yourself into the world of Twinings tea."

Yorkshire tea by Taylors of Harrogate

The Yorkshire Tea brand was launched in 1977 based on the heritage of the family company Taylors of Harrogate that dates back to 1886. The core of the brand is the blending of the finest teas and the proper preparation of the tea. Branding taglines for the brand reflect this philosophy: "Where everything's done proper," "Let's have a proper brew," and "Try It, You'll See." The signature packaging features a country scene from Yorkshire.

Summary

It should be noted that all of these brands are marketed internationally and thus have a European and international presence. In general, these brands have seen an increase in home consumption during the COVID-19 pandemic. A survey of 2,000 British tea drinkers in December of 2020 during the pandemic related lockdowns reported an average daily consumption of four tea bags per participant, while also highlighting an increased interest in loose leaf teas, sustainability, and the origin of the tea (Facenda, 2021).

Case study examples

The following section considers two of the popular brands in more detail, as a basis in a later section for comparing both their histories and how they use both heritage and hospitality in their branding. Due to their long and historic corporate histories, both Twinings and Yorkshire Tea (Taylors of Harrogate) were selected for case studies, the first Twinings (established in 1706) being the oldest tea brand in the world and the second combining the history of two well established companies, Taylors of Harrogate (established in 1886) and Betty's Tea Rooms (established in 1919).

Case 1 – Twinings

Twinings was established in 1706 when Thomas Twining opened his tearoom in London on the Strand, at a location that is still operational today. The brand reportedly uses the oldest commercial logo in use dating back to 1796. Although now owned by Associated British Foods, a multinational food processing and retail company with headquarters in London, a representative of the Twining family, Stephen Twining, still has a role in the brand.

In terms of hospitality the company supplies what they call luxury teas to hotels and bed and breakfast operations across the UK, and globally through licencing arrangements. Many of the afternoon tea services at hotels feature Twinings. For example, the company lists five afternoon tea destinations featuring their loose-leaf teas in London, some with custom blends such as the Waldorf Tribute Blend at the Waldorf. At their flagship store in London (216 Strand), billed as the oldest tea shop in London, they offer retail teas, a premium loose leaf tea sampling bar, tea experiences, and tea master classes as well as exhibits on the history of the brand, thus creating a tea attraction. Tag lines used by Twinings include the promotion of the flagship store at 216 Strand in London with "Take a moment to pause and immerse yourself into the world of Twinings tea" (Twinings History, n.d.; see Figure F.2.4.1).

Figure F.2.4.1: Word Cloud of Twinings About Us Page.
Source: Author

Case 2 – Yorkshire Tea by Taylors of Harrogate

Taylors of Harrogate represents the amalgamation of two historic companies, Taylors (est. 1886) and Bettys (est. 1909), resulting in the unique partnership of a tea merchant company with a tearoom operator. Charles Edward Taylor and his brother created their company, CE Taylor and Co., in 1886. Bettys Tea Rooms was established by Frederik Belmont in 1919 in Harrogate England (Visit Harrogate, 2020). The two companies joined together in 1962 when Bettys acquired Taylors. The family-based company known as Bettys and Taylors of Harrogate now has three main brands, Bettys, Taylors of Harrogate, and Yorkshire Tea, launched in 1977. Bettys Café Tea Rooms are traditional tea rooms serving traditional tea and meals and also featuring Bettys Tea Room Blend. The new company therefore has a strong link to both the tea and hospitality trades. This allows for cross promotions and the branding of products, for example the Bettys special tea blends. Both Bettys and Taylors of Harrogate have online shops. Bettys has its own line of tea blends, marketed as a souvenir in tin caddies, a chain of six cafés, and also operates Bettys Cookery School offering both master classes and practical classes (Visit Harrogate, 2020).

The taglines for the marketing of the now popular Yorkshire Tea introduced in 1977 include: "Where everything's done proper," "Let's have a proper brew," and "Try It, You'll See." This draws upon the history and heritage of the company in terms of the "proper" serving of tea, but also a "proper" brew, with both references to hospitality in terms of the preparation and serving of tea. There is also an emphasis on heritage in Yorkshire Tea, of being a third-generation family business (Yorkshire Tea, n.d.; see Figure F.2.4.2).

Figure F.2.4.2: Word Cloud of Yorkshire Tea About Us Page.
Source: Author

Analysis

The following is a comparison and then a discussion of the two companies in terms of establishment, heritage, corporate branding, royal warrants, hospitality and retail operations, and marketing (see Table F.2.4.2).

Table F.2.4.2: Case study comparison.

Factors	Case 1 – Twinings	Case 2 – Yorkshire Tea by Taylors of Harrogate
Establishment	1706	1886 and 1909
Heritage	Oldest tea shop and logo	Combines two old established firms (1962), Yorkshire Tea introduced in 1977
Corporate Brand(s)	Twinings	Taylors of Harrogate, Yorkshire Tea, Bettys
Royal Warrants	Former HM the Queen and HRM Prince of Wales (tea and coffee merchants) now King Charles III	Former Prince of Wales (supplier of beverages) for Taylors of Harrogate now King Charles III
Hospitality Operations	Tea Tasting Room at Flagship Store in London	Chain of Bettys Cafés in Yorkshire
Retail Operations	Tea Shop at Flagship Store in London (In Person) and online site for purchase of teas and related gifts	Bettys Tea Rooms sell tea and related goods. Both Bettys and Taylors of Harrogate have online shops
Word Clouds Dominant Themes	Name of tea company, name of founder, tea types (blends), royal warrant holder, aspects of history (East India Company)	Name of tea, name of founder, name of company, aspects of tea, occupations (tea buyer), locations (store, café)
Marketing Tag Lines	"Take a moment to pause, and immerse yourself into the world of Twinings tea."	"Where everything's done proper", "Let's have a proper brew" and "Try It, You'll See"

Source: Author

Both tea brands of Twinings and Yorkshire Tea by Taylors of Harrogate have the foundation of a long history and deep heritage. The history of Twinings is much longer whereas the history of the Yorkshire tea brand is short but founded on the long history of the amalgamated Taylors of Harrogate that dates back to the late 1880s. The two brands have in common the involvement of the descendants of the original founding families. However, Twinings has only one unified brand whereas Taylors of Harrogate has Taylors of Harrogate, Yorkshire Tea, and Bettys.

It is of note that the current branding of Twinings is focused on the broad-based world of tea, whereas the Taylors of Harrogate Yorkshire tea has a focus on the proper preparation of the brew. However, both brands connect with the customer experience, Twinings by inviting tea drinkers to immense themselves in a world of tea, and Yorkshire by encouraging customers to try the proper brew themselves. For both brands their retail locations (The Strand for Twinings and Betty's Tea Rooms for Yorkshire) provide in-person tea experiences that also contribute to the reinforcement of the brand and the experience of customers. Links with hotel chains and their afternoon tea services also provide the in-person experience, creating memories and encouraging brand loyalty.

Comparing the word clouds generated from the text on the "About Us" pages of the websites of Twinings and Yorkshire Tea, it is evident that history and heritage plays a dominant role in the information conveyed. Especially featured in both cases are the names of the founders and the companies. Types of tea are also mentioned (such as green tea for both and black tea for Yorkshire Tea). Aspects of tea (blending, brewing, infusing) are to some extent mentioned by both brands. Of course, the term most mentioned on both sites is tea.

In terms of hospitality both brands are directly involved in retail and hospitality operations, Twinings through their flagship store and Yorkshire tea through the companies' chain of Bettys Tea Rooms. The use of both brands by higher end hotels in their afternoon tea services further reinforces the brand positions, for Twinings globally and for Yorkshire tea primarily in the U.K.

In marketing these brands use packaging (reflecting their royal warrants) and taglines to invite customers to experience their tea. The distinctive designs of the tea packages are notable, as they contribute to the marketing of the product. Elements of the heritage of both brands are used in the advertising taglines. The websites of Twinings and Yorkshire Tea also convey the histories of the company to consumers, inviting them to share in that heritage by purchasing and brewing their respective teas.

Discussion

This chapter has investigated the role of British tea heritage and culture in the branding of tea products and experiences, using the cases of two of the leading heritage tea brands in the U.K., Twinings and Yorkshire Tea from Taylors of Harrogate. It is apparent that the long histories and rich heritage legacies of both cases examined are used in their branding, and conveyed to the customers through package design, royal warrants, marketing tag lines, and website histories. The brands invite customers to experience their tea, both through the retail marketing and their use in exclusive afternoon tea experiences in luxury or higher end hotels. The family connections to the founders of both brands are also emphasised in the marketing of the teas. However, a limitation of this chapter is the primary focus on the five major tea brands in the U.K.

The case studies of Twinings and Taylors of Harrogate demonstrate that these heritage brands also use hospitality to reinforce their brand positions with consumers, through their association with the afternoon tea services offered by higher end hotels. In this way, hoteliers are also offered an opportunity to build their afternoon tea products and services on the heritages of these iconic tea companies. This use of hospitality also plays on the rich history and heritage associated with both of these brands.

However, beyond the case study tea brands and the top five in the U.K. market, many other British tea brands (e.g., Northern Tea Merchants, Birchall Tea Darvilles of Windsor), including the others in the top ten mentioned earlier, also use their history and heritage in promoting their tea. They all do this with references back to their origins, founders, and development over time. Some brands use timelines on their websites to benchmark major events and developments of their companies.

Conclusion

A limitation of the chapter is the main focus on Britain, while all of these British tea brands have international markets and profiles and thus strong links in Europe. This is briefly reflected in the chapter by the identification of dominant tea brands with afternoon tea services in international hotels. The global role of British tea brands is however worthy of further investigation.

It is evident that the deep history and rich heritage of the British tea brands makes a definite contribution to the branding of these products. The cases of the well-established and historic brands such as Twinings and Yorkshire Tea (Taylors of Harrogate) could provide marketing and development lessons for other emerging tea brands, for example in the specialty tea market in the U.K., Europe, and beyond. Hotel operators can also find insights and best practices in the way that these brands have enhanced and added value to hotel afternoon tea services and customers' tea experiences.

References

Addy, R. (2021). Typhoo Tea acquired by Zetland Capital. Retrieved April 5, 2022, from https://www.foodma nufacture.co.uk/Article/2021/07/19/Typhoo-Tea-acquired-by-Zetland-Capital.

Bohne, H., & Jolliffe, L. (2021). Embracing tea culture in hotel experiences. *Journal of Gastronomy and Tourism, 6*(1–2), 13–24.

Boniface, P. (2017). *Tasting tourism: Travelling for food and drink*. Routledge.

Balmer, J.M. (2011). Corporate heritage brands and the precepts of corporate heritage brand management: Insights from the British monarchy on the eve of the royal wedding of Prince William (April 2011) and Queen Elizabeth II's Diamond Jubilee (1952–2012). *Journal of Brand Management, 18*(8), 517–544.

Dimsum Daily Hong Kong. (n.d.). Retrieved July 6, 2022, from https://www.dimsumdaily.hk/twinings-love-is-in-the-mail-afternoon-tea-at-at-three-on-canton/.

Denzin, N.K., & Lincoln, Y.S. (Eds.). (2011). *The Sage handbook of qualitative research*. Sage.

Ekaterra. (2023). Timeline of Ekaterra. Retrieved March 17, 2023, from https://ekaterratea.com/uk/en/pur pose-and-sustainability/story/.

Facenda, V.L. (2021). New survey reveals increase in loose leaf tea consumption in U.K. during lockdowns. Online in Tea and Coffee Trade Journal. Retrieved July 6, 2022, from https://www.teaandcoffee.net/ blog/26250/new-survey-reveals-increase-in-loose-leaf-tea-consumption-in-uk-during-lockdowns/.

FOODBEV Media. (2018). Typhoo launches new positioning with package design. Retrieved June 24, 2022, from https://www.foodbev.com/news/typhoo-launches-new-positioning-with-updated-packaging-de sign/.

Fromer, J. E. (2008). *A necessary luxury: tea in Victorian England*. Ohio University Press.

Harker, L. (2019). English tea brand rankings uncovered. Retrieved July 26, 2022, from https://latana.com/ post/english-tea-brand-ranking.

Henderson, R.M., & Nellemann, F. (2011). Sustainable tea at Unilever. *Harvard Business School Case* (712–438).

Jolliffe, L. (2006). Tea and hospitality: More than a cuppa. *International Journal of Contemporary Hospitality Management, 18*(2), 164–68.

Jolliffe, L. (Ed.). (2007). *Tea and tourism: Tourists, traditions and transformations*. Channel View Publications.

Kauppinen-Räisänen, H. (2014). Strategic use of colour in brand packaging. *Packaging Technology and Science, 27*(8), 663–76.

Lipton Teas. (n.d.). *History in the beginning*. Retrieved April 5, 2022, from https://www.lipton.com/ca/en/ our-purpose/lipton-tea-history.html.

PG Tips. (n.d.). Our brand heritage. Retrieved April 6, 2022, from https://www.pgtips.co.uk/about-us/our-brand-heritage.html.

Saberi, H. (2010). *Tea: A global history*. Reaktion Books Limited.

Skinner, J. (2019). *Afternoon tea: A history*. Rowman & Littlefield.

Tetley. (n.d.). *Tetley Tea heritage.* Retrieved July 8, 2022, from https://www.tetley.com/history-tetley.

Twinings History (n.d.). *About us.* Retrieved July 6, 2022, from https://twinings.co.uk/blogs/news/history-of-twinings.

Twinings Blogs. (n.d.). Twinings Afternoon Tea – The Palm Court. Retrieved July 15, 2022, from https://twin ings.co.uk/blogs/news/our-communi-tea-about-twinings-partnerships-twinings-afternoon-tea-the-palm-court.

Typhoo Tea. (n.d.). Our heritage. Retrieved April 6, 2022, from https://typhoo.co.uk/about-us/great-british-tea-since-1903/.

Unilever. (2022). Unilever announces completion of the sale of its Tea business, ekaterra, to CVC Capital Partners Fund VIII. Retrieved March 17, 2023, from https://www.unilever.com/news/press-and-media/press-releases/2022/unilever-announces-completion-of-the-sale-of-its-tea-business-ekaterra/.

Visit Harrogate. (2020). The history of Bettys. Retrieved July 6, 2022, from https://www.visitharrogate.co. uk/blog/the-history-of-bettys.

Yorkshire Food Guide (n.d.). Retrieved May 27, 2022, from https://yorkshirefoodguide.co.uk/blog/after noon-tea-in-york/.

Ann T. Conway and Detta Melia

F.3 Tea and Irish Hospitality

Introduction

History of tea and Irish hospitality: From elite beginnings to everyday hospitality

Tea first entered Irish society in the eighteenth century when Ireland was still part of the British Empire. At the beginning it was a tradition and part of the elite culture, as importing the commodity was not only time consuming due to the long shipping time from the East but also, as you can imagine, quite costly.

The elite in Britain retained the best quality imported tea and the lower quality was released to Ireland. The trouble with the lower quality import was that it required extra milk and meant that brews had to be stronger, a custom that continues and allow enough space in the pot for a second "cuppa." In fact, there is always a pot of tea brewing when you call to someone's house, or the kettle will be put on as quick as you cross the threshold and say, "God bless all here [and who used to dwell within (extn.)]", or "Dia an daoine sa teach."

A mug of tea in Irish households to "dainty" China cups?

When most people think of tea, they think of English breakfast or afternoon tea with dainty China cups and a hotel's tiered trays with delicate finger sandwiches and tiny tea biscuits. In Ireland taking Irish tea is sometimes referred to as "high tea," and it is more widely known as the workman's tea. High tea was practical as it was filling, and it was a reward for a hard day's work. The hot tea comforted and warmed while the food fed hard-working men and women. It may not have been fancy, but it became a solid tradition.

When Anglo-Irish aristocracy first introduced tea to Ireland via colonialism and the East India Company in the eighteenth century, the aristocratic English created a tradition of taking tea in the afternoon, at 2–4 p.m.: Paul Kelly from The Merrion Hotel in Dublin states that "afternoon tea (or Low tea) is a light meal typically eaten at 4 o'clock" (Kelly, interview) with those tiered serving plates and "dainty china cups." When the English shipped the remaining stronger blended black teas to Ireland, the Irish, a lower "working class" people, acclimatised themselves to the stronger blend with lots of milk.

https://doi.org/10.1515/9783110758573-024

As they would have would have been "labouring" in the fields at that time, "high tea" became a tradition of taking this strong tea with their dinner, taken in, sometimes, large mugs, and accompanied by cold meats and potatoes, typically occurring after the work was finished at around 6 or 7 o'clock in the evening.

The best tea and the best "china" were kept for the "best" visitors, usually the clergy, the teacher, doctor, or family home from abroad, and kept safe in a cabinet. This tea was served in the "best" room in the house, the parlor. This was separate to the "high tea" and became a tradition in its own right with visitors coming to the house being offered a cup of tea.

Are we tops when it comes to tea or is it Türkiye?

Up until recently the Irish were the top consumers of tea per capita, surpassing the Chinese themselves – the consumers of the most tea per country, obviously due to a higher population – but more remarkable is the fact that they have more of it daily than neighbouring Britain, who introduced them to tea in the first place. The consumption rate in Ireland is approximately 2.19 kg or 4.83 lb, loose black tea leaf being their preference – like Türkiye who are now the top consumers of tea (Blue Hare, 2022; Ferdman, 2014).

Irish breakfast tea: Barry's, Bewley's, Lyons or Robert Roberts?

Not that dissimilar to English Breakfast Tea, Irish Breakfast tea is generally a blend of Assam and/ or Ceylon black tea, usually no more than two blends and of a stronger nature, but sometimes only with Assam. The importer of Assam tea came via the British East Indian Company, who for years had a monopoly of Assam production and exporting teas from India from the former British Empire (Blue Hare, 2022)

Bewley's: First importer of tea directly to Dublin from China

Samuel Bewley and his son Charles broke the monopoly in 1835 by bypassing India and importing 2,099 chests of tea from Canton in China. Bewley's hence established a brand and name for themselves from around 1840 after Joshua Bewley established the China Tea Company, a precursor to Bewley's, and set up "tea rooms" in Dublin, first in South

Great Georges Street (1894) and Westmoreland Street (1896) [where one of the authors worked during college], and then the iconic Grafton Street café with its famous Harry Clarke-stained window which was established in 1927 (Bewley's, 2022 (online), www. bewleys.com/ie). Bewley's was taken over by Patrick Campbell in the 1980s, establishing the Campbell Bewley group, but the Bewley's name remains on the front of the cafes as it is synonymous in tea and coffee society in Ireland, but in particular in Dublin. For years Bewley's had a monopoly of tea (and coffee) in the Irish market – again in middle to upper class circles – until the Lyons company was established (see Figure F.3.1).

Figure F.3.1: Bewley's Café Grafton Street.
Source: Bewleys (2022)

Lyons: The tea of the Liffey

Lyons was a family-run business founded in 1902. They began operations in High Street, Dublin, close to Christchurch Cathedral. Their original tea was known as Lyons Green Label (which is now the Original Blend). They moved to Marlborough Street, behind the Gresham Hotel in 1932, which then became part of the College of Catering, Cathal Brugha Street, when the company moved to a state-of-the-art facility in Golden-bridge in 1963 (F. White, 2014) [The College of Catering then became part of the Dublin Institute of Technology, then the Technological University of Dublin, City Campus where both authors are based].

In the 1970s, the introduction of the round tea bag saw Lyons increase their share of that market to 65%. Then in 2004 they brought in the pyramid tea bag which, they say, allows better circulation to extract the full flavour of the brew. Lyons was sold to Unilever in 1996 and their blend is now used worldwide under a "sustainabli-ti" culture (Lyons Tea & Unilever, 2021). In 2022 this part of Unilever was transferred into Ekaterra and sold to investors. In 2023 Ekaterra was rebranded "Lipton Teas and Infusions."

Lyons Tea is one of the more popular tea brands used in Ireland as it was a huge sponsor of Irish TV programs and can also be seen in other popular culture settings such as in the iconic movie *The Quiet Man* – starring Maureen O'Hara and John Wayne and directed by John Ford – where a Lyons Tea brand sign is visible in the background in Castletown (The Quiet Man, 1952).

Elsewhere, in the current BBC/RTE production of Mrs. Brown's Boys (2011 series) there is a box of Lyons Tea sitting on top of the bread bin in Mrs. Brown's kitchen, alongside other well-known Irish branded goods. In fact, when Mrs. Brown's friend calls for a "daily" visit, they sit and gossip over a "cuppa".

Barry's tea: "a real broth of a brew"

Barry's tea is the other big player on the Irish tea market and would hold second place to Lyons as regards market share, but would be the bigger exporter of Irish-blended teas. And depending on who you talk to and sometimes where they live, Barry's is the number one tea blend: this is also seen according to Newstalk's Biggest Selling Brands (2016), where Barry's came in ahead of Lyons (29th) at twenty-fourth overall, behind the likes of Tayto and Brennan's bread – but that is another day's story, over a cup of Barry's tea, which according to Bowe (2005) is a "real broth of a brew".

The company was founded by James J. Barry in 1901 and operated from a shop in Prince's Street, Cork. It has remained in the family since then, with his grandson Peter, a former Fine Gael TD and Tánaiste, now the company chair (Barry's Tea, 2022).

You will find Barry's in many countries. Their tea has a unique flavour and is blended from leaves supplied from Assam, Kenya, and Rwanda. Due to demand in the 1960s, Barry's went national and then followed up by exporting their products to Britain, the United States, Canada, Australia, Spain, France, Germany, South Korea, New Zealand, and the Middle East.

Anthony Barry, the current chair's father, won the Empire medal in 1934 for his blending, and this family trait of getting it right is still top of their list to the present day (Barry's Tea, 2022).

Robert Roberts: Another roaring success in tea trade on Dublin's Southside

An in the *Irish Independent* from 2011 detailed that Robert Roberts (RRs) is one of Ireland's oldest businesses founded in 1905 and was selling 190 million teabags and 350 tons of coffee a year in Ireland. Today it employs more than 200 people in Tallaght, Dublin.

"Irish people are still predominantly tea drinkers," Ken Maguire, Company Director with RRs said: "we sell higher volumes of tea than coffee. And, as a nation, we are bigger consumers of cappuccino-style coffees compared to other countries where espresso is the most popular."

In its early years, Robert Roberts was known for its coffee houses in Suffolk Street and later in Grafton Street. It was here in Roberts Café in Grafton Street in 1921 that Lady Augusta Gregory established and convened her Irish PEN literary society (Brady, 2017) [a branch of the worldwide writers' association] and Maud Gonne McBride, amongst other literary giants of the time, were regular customers.

The company's founders, the Goodbody family, who were Quakers from Tullamore, Co. Offaly, were involved until recent years, when the business was taken over by the DCC group. By then, Robert Roberts coffee had merged with the tea company Baker Wardell, a business that goes back to the 1700s and was also founded by a Quaker, John Wardell, in Dublin's Liberties area.

Today, Robert Roberts' teas and coffees account for about 25% of this market in Ireland and, like every other business, is constantly dreaming up new ways to win new customers and keep its loyal tea and coffee drinkers happy. Its teas come from India, Kenya, and China, while the coffee beans are imported mostly from Indonesia, Costa Rica, and Columbia. Sacks containing the different varieties are piled high with the name of the farms they come from stamped on each one. Robert Roberts was among the first companies to introduce herbal infusions in Ireland in the 1970s and 1980s. Mr. Maguire said the firm was a bit before its time then, as it began offering Darjeeling and Assam teas here (Anon, 2011).

Are these the only tea brands in Ireland?

There are other Irish tea blenders, but the above dominate the market. Lesser-known brands such as Punjana, blended in Belfast, Northern Ireland, and Nambarrie; elsewhere, McGrath brothers from Dublin, set up in 1969, are the main tea suppliers to Aldi.

The Ceremony of Tea and Irish Hospitality

As was suggested earlier, if you are ever invited into an Irish household, you can be sure that as soon as you cross the front door (or the back door in the country), you will be offered tea as an icebreaker. And by any chance you decline the first offer, you will most certainly get a second and a third, and more, until you accept – just like with Mrs. Doyle and Fr Ted in the famous Irish television show named after the latter. This continuous offering actually dates back to poorer times in centuries past where it was polite to offer and refuse in case the host didn't have a lot to provide for the guest. But if the host offered again, it was an indication to the guest that there was enough to go around for everyone.

Offering the visitor a cup of tea is the backbone of Irish hospitality, and one of which everyone is immensely proud. Once you have finished that first cup, you will be offered more tea, and so on, until you have had your fill, or the gossip has been exhausted. The tea is never presented alone and an offer of a homemade cake or bread or biscuit is produced with the "cupán tae."

A great example of this can be seen when a visit of dignitaries to Ireland are pictured in the Aras taking tea with the President of Ireland, or of course pictured with a pint of the (other) black stuff [at Guinness's]. But maybe most famously of all, John Fitzgerald Kennedy (JFK) when visiting Ireland in the 1960s went to visit his family homestead in County Wexford and was welcomed "home" by the Bean an Ti with the traditional tea and home bakes (Murphy & O'Beachain, 2021).

More recently, former President Barak Obama, while visiting his ancestral homeplace of Moneygall in County Offaly, stopped off at a craft shop in the town to purchase a "tea set" for his mother-in-law back in the USA (Andrews, 2011).

How to make tea the "Irish" way – "you'll have a cuppa tay!"

The making of tea can be a ritual, but you are always shown from an early age in an Irish house how to make the "right" cup of tea. This may differ from person to person and from household to household but might not vary too far from the following:

If you use tea leaves or tea bags (some say using a tea bag in a mug is sacrilege!), Irish tea is at its best if you "scald" the tea pot first with boiling water, swirling the water around the pot to warm it up before rinsing it out, then adding the tea (loose leaf or tea bags – a spoon of tea per person/ cup and then one for the pot) and then keeping the tea warm once the boiling water is added, but never, ever letting it re-boil. Once this happens, the tea is destroyed or, as the saying goes, "boiled tea is spoiled tea."

A tea pot is kept warm on the "range," by the fire, or on a hob, but one must be incredibly careful not to allow the pot to become "stewed" which then renders the tea undrinkable. Keep it hot, but do not stew it. To make tea properly, again, be it a pot or a cup, it is recommended to pour an adequate amount of boiling water over the tea and let it soak for three to five minutes.

Some say you add the milk to your tea, but in earlier times when the tea that was first imported was so strong, many would have a third of their cup full of milk before the tea was added, with the amount of tea judged by the "colour" of the tea in the mug. Others nowadays would shirk away from tea with your milk and say milk should only be added to "colour" the tea. Others like it completely black, but then again this might stem from "Lent" days when you were never allowed "colour" your tea during the Lenten fast in Catholic Ireland, or affect the pure taste.

The brand of tea becomes an emotional loyalty after time and respective to households and locations in Ireland. You could not have multiple brands sitting side by side on the shelf – that is a complete no, it is one or the other! From the two authors' perspectives, Ann prefers tea being able to stand her spoon on the strength of the tea, Barry's, made in the kitchen of her family home in the west, drank from her favourite mug, held with two hands, none of the pinkie finger style, mind you with the "dainty china cup," with a drop of milk, just to colour it, and a slice of her Mam's homemade brown bread spread with butter and Dad's homemade jam; whereas, where Detta is from in the east of the country, the preference is for Lyon's tea but made the same way, and no matter the occasion as soon as she has reached the back door of the house the kettle is put on, with whatever tart has been made, apple, or rhubarb, put on the table with the tea.

Some superstitions still exist from reading tea leaves (the traditional way to make tea is using tea leaves and not using a tea bag): floating tea leaves and rising bubbles predict the arrival of strangers, and bubbles that rise to the top mean money is coming. Some also say you need to be able to lift these bubbles with a teaspoon or else this financial windfall will be lost.

From hospitality in the big (and little) house to hotels

Tea is usually served multiple times throughout the day: upon waking, mid-morning, afternoon tea, evening tea, and a late-night tea. Traditional tea times provided throughout the industry are: elevenses, which are unsurprisingly from 11:00 a.m. served with scones. Then there is afternoon tea, which is usually between 3:00–5:00 p.m. with some sweets, to follow the English tradition, and, finally, high tea at 6:00 p.m. with more substantial foods, which is typically more Irish. But there is no stopping you to have a cuppa before bed, and there will always be the self-service kettle and selection of teas and coffees in your room just in case you did not have enough.

What is "afternoon tea"?

According to McElwain (2019) food historians generally credit Anna Maria Russell, the Duchess of Bedford for popularising afternoon tea in the 1830s as she needed to fulfil her "peckishness" [sic], as the gap between luncheon and dinner after the Industrial Revolution had flipped the main meal from noon to evening, by asking her butler to bring tea, bread, and butter to her chambers around five o'clock. Soon these teas in the afternoon contained both sweet and savoury snacks brought to her and her husband's, Sir Francis Russell, rooms at Woburn. Soon she invited her close friends to partake of afternoon tea with her in her inner drawing room close to her boudoir, soon to become known as her "tea room."

As the house has been open to the public since 1955 visitors can visit the Duchess' Tea Rooms. However, the custom of taking a small snack in the middle of the afternoon pre-dates Anna but she may be noted as being the first "influencer" of afternoon tea customs as she soon started to invite friends along to this tea in the afternoon. As she was a lady in waiting and lifelong friend to the Queen, Victorian Britain soon took up the custom of having tea and light snacks in the afternoon.

Victorian-era teas assumed many forms, according to purpose. Ranging from informal feminine gatherings to elaborate ornate events attended by hundreds, this versatile meal played a unique role in British life, enjoyed throughout the Empire, except for the USA, until the last quarter of the nineteenth century. Americans embraced coffee as a way to forge a national beverage identity separate from England.

Due to high taxation it was expensive and only affordable for the very wealthy. Despite the cost, tea drinking became widely popular, and English tea sellers such as Twining's [still in operation today – Irish branded teas are listed above] started selling dry tea, so that ladies who could not frequent the coffee houses could enjoy it. Tea was very valuable and was kept by the lady of the house rather than in the care of the housekeeper. It was the lady of the house also who would serve the tea, in imitation of the Japanese tea ceremony.

When the Duchess of Bedford had her friends join her in her tea room for this new social event "the table was laid [. . .] there were the best things with a fat pink rose on the side of each cup; hearts of lettuce, thin bread and butter, and the crisp little cakes that had been baked in readiness that morning" (Pettigrew, 2001).

Eventually, the tea beverage became generally affordable, and the growing upper middle class imitated the rich and found that the meal with tea was a very economical way of entertaining several friends without having to spend too much money, and afternoon tea quickly became the norm. By the end of the century, afternoon tea had crossed all class barriers.

According to Pettigrew (1999), during the first half of the twentieth century, tea, along with sandwiches, scones, and cakes, was served in smart hotels. And on market days in the main towns, wealthy market goers would spend the day shopping and then treat themselves to the luxury of afternoon tea before travelling home in time for dinner.

The early development of the afternoon tea menu

Much of what is known about the earliest tea menus were not recorded in cookbooks, but literature. Jane Austen and her contemporaries chronicled the rise of this meal with great care and detail. Kim Wilson's (2004) *Tea with Jane Austen* offers tea notes, menu suggestions, and modernised recipes gleaned from Mrs Beeton's books, such as Milk Dough for Children's Cakes, Tea Cakes, Bread for Tea, Seville Orange Biscuits, Ginger Cake, Gingerbread, Buttered Eggs, Soda Cake, Macaroons, Sponge Cake and Cheap Bread (Wilson, 2004, 2011; Beeton, 1892).

In 1879, Mrs Beeton's Book of Household Management explained the organisation of a nineteenth century "little tea" where "a pretty little afternoon tea service is placed upon a small table and there are plates of rolled bread and butter, as well as biscuits and cake" (Pettigrew, 2001, pp. 107–108). These writings of Mrs Isabelle Beeton would have originally come from her 24 newspaper columns which she wrote between 1859 and 1861, and which could have reached the "upper middle classes."

However, the following is a more detailed excerpt from Mrs Beeton's *Everyday Cookery and Housekeeping book* (1892) which describes the importance of tea and afternoon tea to the Victorian households:

> In Victorian country houses, preparing recipes for tea was carried out not in the kitchens, but in the stillroom, where the maid was under direct supervision of the housekeeper. The stillroom in previous centuries had been the province of the mistress of the house, where she prepared sweetmeats, confectionery and cordials for the banqueting or dessert course – providing yet another link between luxury food items and tea. Afternoon teas, as Marie Bayard wrote in 1884 in Hints on Etiquette, was 'not supposed to be a substantial meal, merely light refreshment'. The food and drink were then (and still are today) less important than the event itself. 'Cakes [. . .] thin bread and butter, and hot buttered scones, muffins, or toast is [sic] all the accompaniments strictly necessary.' [. . .] Neat, crustless sandwiches were a particularly useful tea-time food, allowing hostesses the possibility of introducing more exciting flavours. More important, perhaps, they could be eaten without risk of soiling gloves and other articles of clothing. Sandwiches intended for afternoon tea are dainty trifles, pleasing to the eye and palate, but too flimsy to allay hunger where it exists. (Mrs. Beeton, 1892, in Pettigrew, 2001 p. 117)

This then transferred into the "common middle class" households with Craig (1936) suggesting home tea menus for a week to include (for Afternoon Tea) brown bread and butter, potted salmon sandwiches, picklets, rock cakes, scotch jam sandwiches, and other delicacies long since gone from modern day palates.

Pettigrew (1999) continues that the tradition of afternoon tea in hotels remains today, and the same irresistible selections of savouries, warm scones, and artistic displays of little pastries attract as much excited attention as elsewhere around the globe. Most hotels and tearooms focus on the time-honoured classic menu, often using local Irish ingredients, but a few have tweaked the tradition by theming the food or by adding a little extra treat such as a tea cocktail or a mini feast of special desserts – just enough to intrigue and tempt.

This has become a separate meal as part of the hotel offering of breakfast, lunch, and dinner. Now afternoon tea is part of an all-in package. It is also a growth sector for apa centres and spa treatments with an afternoon tea package included for after your treatment – with a bottle of bubbly as an optional extra. Some foods that are typically served with an Irish afternoon tea include:

- Sandwiches of salmon, dill, cream cheese, and cucumber
- Roast Irish beef with horseradish and tomato
- Buttermilk fruit scones with clotted cream and homemade strawberry jam
- Victoria sponge cake or sticky date and walnut cake

Afternoon tea at The Merrion Hotel Dublin

Based on an interview with Paul Kelly, Executive Pastry Chef at The Merrion Hotel and judge at the the Great Irish Bake-off, Dublin, it is possible to gain an insight into the afternoon tea service at The Merrion.

In recent times afternoon tea has had a resurgence in popularity in Ireland, with the range in price and quality of afternoon teas around the country highlighting this consumer trend. While an afternoon tea break was a normal occurrence for ladies in Victorian England as stated earlier, it has now become a very viable and lucrative option for hotels and restaurants in Ireland. This chapter will shed light on how the development of this once British tradition has become one of the nation's favourite experiences.

Afternoon Tea is always an elegant affair, creating a feeling of grandeur that comes with dining like a Duchess. The gracious surroundings of The Merrion's Drawing Rooms (see Figure F.3.2 below) are the perfect place to relax and enjoy Art Afternoon Tea. The Merrion Art tea is a witty interpretation of the hotel's extensive collection of art, featuring portraits of primarily the eighteenth and nineteenth century inspired by the works of J.B Yeats, William Scott, Louis Le Brocquy, and others.

Figure F.3.2: Drawing Room at The Merrion Hotel, Dublin.
Source: Hartwig Bohne

The Drawing Room

The "Art Tea" is served over two courses: first, the tiered plates you'd usually associate with afternoon tea holding small bite sized dinky sandwiches, a selection of cakes inspired by the paintings to be found in the hotel and, of course, mini scones with clotted cream, lemon curd, and raspberry jam on the side (Figure F.3.3).

The second course comes in the form of three pastries inspired by pieces of art on display in the hotel, chosen weekly by Chef Paul Kelly; three paintings (Figure F.3.4) are reimagined as culinary delights. Flavours range from salted caramel and apple to white chocolate and orange blossom. It's an overall lovely experience but the service really makes it that extra bit special.

There are 19 different tea choices on the menu. While the guests enjoy dining, the Art experience is completed with a complimentary The Merrion Art Catalog for guests to browse the artworks which surround them. The experience and art connections can be further extended as guests can choose to enjoy a self-guided art audio tour.

Figure F.3.3: First Course: Cakes like paintings at The Merrion.
Source: Hartwig Bohne

Chef Paul Kelly explains:

> We really love our Art Afternoon Tea and the feeling it has created for our guests; it is a very creative product that is constantly evolving, the Vegan Afternoon Tea is our newest offering from The Merrion, guests can enjoy a wide range of delicious Vegan delights from sandwiches, scones, cakes, and pastries.

In 2015, The Merrion's Art Experience was awarded the Leading Hotels of The World Remarkably Uncommon Award [see also: https://www.merrionhotel.com/all-about-the-merrion/awards-acolades/, accessed July 20, 2022).

Figure F.3.4: Second course: Pastries inspired by art at The Merrion.
Source: Hartwig Bohne

From afternoon tea and coffee houses to tea rooms and back?

An interview with Blathnaid Bergin, management consultant in the hospitality industry and owner of The Business of Food, provided a detailed insight into the trends and developments in the hospitality industry in Ireland.

From anecdotal evidence, the tea business is a slow boil. The last two decades has seen the exponential growth of coffee shops, roasteries, cafes, and coffee culture. Across the globe, more than two billion cups of coffee are drunk every day (Robson, 2019 (online), www.bbc.com/). Dublin is the second most "coffee crazy" capital city in the world, with 180 coffee shops per 100,000 people, and imports of 94.94 EUR per person per year (Mellett, 2021).

Popularised by such coffee haunts as "Central Perk" in the hit series *Friends*, cafes have become the go-to social venue for friends, family, and workmates, a resurgence of a pre-Victorian era. The universal phrase "meet you for a coffee" may well be repeated thousands of times a day in Irish life. But where does this leave our national brew? As illustrated earlier, we apparently consume more tea per capita than any other country, apart from Türkiye. A decade ago, excitement over specialist teas gave a renaissance rise to Tea Rooms and specialist Tea companies, the likes of which had not been seen since the 1800's.

Are you having tea or coffee?

Cafes and coffee shops alike will confirm that their coffee sales outstrip tea sales by some margin, whereas tea/ coffee supply companies still say their teas are their biggest sellers.

A recent advertising campaign featured several builders stopping for a break. One of them came back to the truck with the coffee order. One poor chap had ordered tea and bore the brunt of his mates' derision. The distinct message in this advert was that drinking tea was no longer cool! The term "builders tea" is widely used when referring to a properly strong cup of black tea. It seems that our builders have now embraced coffee culture and the tea break on sites has morphed into the coffee break.

Black tea lends itself to being paired with any number of foods, both sweet and savoury, and we Irish are known for pairing it with foodstuffs from bread and jam to a full Irish. However, to enjoy a tea of delicate flavour, an education in tea pairings is necessary. Trying to enjoy a "high tea" with a cup of White Tea with a strongly flavoured fry up is unlikely to reveal the subtleties of said tea; likewise, matching a cup of Early Grey with lashings of milk and a lamb chop will not do this delicate tea experience justice.

Speciality teas

Can it be that we are now in need of the same education regarding the myriad range of teas as coffee? Although there are specialist teashops across the country and the tea conversation had a significant moment around about a decade ago, they are nowhere near as abundant as cafes and coffee shops. Every village and town have at least one and usually multiple cafes where competition to sell the best coffee (and thus gain the most customers) can be fierce. The same conversations are not usual regarding tea. It is a rare café indeed where tea leaves are served. In fact, younger staff are often not even familiar with black tea leaves. Most cafes will stock the obligatory herbal and fruit infusions such as Camomile, Mint, Green, and Berry served in bags of varying degrees of questionable quality. But tea leaves are a thing of the past, or are they?

One such company The Rare Tea Company, based in London [see also www.ther areteacompany.com] has been working directly with loose leaf tea farmers since 2004 and prides itself on its sustainability, a reflection of society and also one which Lyons Tea also prides itself in doing more recently. The Joy of Cha [see also https://thejoyof cha.com] was established in Dublin in 2006 and sells both tea and coffee, as do most of the specialist tea shops. Word on the ground is that a quiet revolution is stirring in the world of tea. It is rumored that tea will take on the same significance as coffee and specialist tea companies are scouring the world for superior quality.

Will there be a time when during the office "coffee break" the chat in the queue at the neighbourhood café will be around Oolong, Earl Grey, Yerba Mate, Pu-Erh, rather than the merits of the americano or the signature blend? The traditional strong black tea that we all know and love so much that we consume it in vast quantities still accounts for 85% of the total tea consumption in the western world (Research Drive Global Tea Market Report, 2021). As with any revolution, it begins slowly and then becomes an unstoppable force. Watch out, it seems that tea is in the nascent stages of revolution. Only time will tell.

Finally, a fun fact: Irish pubs are legally required to serve tea!!

Tea, amongst other things of course, defines our Irish culture, and whether you can believe this or not, all Irish pubs across the country are, today, legally required to offer tea on their menu (Section 81 of the 1872 Licensing Act). It is officially against the law in Ireland to own a bar and not serve a "cupán tae." That is how important tea really is for the Irish, or is it because those who do not part take in an alcoholic beverage are referred to as "tea totallers"?

And: The Irish merger of tea, tradition and technology

In 2021, the city of Dublin build a special artwork: "Smithfield Utah" by Alan Butler, an Irish artist from Dublin. At the recently developed Smithfield marketplace, a large bronze teapot with an obvious connection to Irish culture across generations symbolises warmth and connection. This extraordinary teapot sculpture is designed to be seen from near and far as well as an invitation to stop and to relax. It is also a reference to the rich history of congregation and trade at the Smithfield marketplace, but also with a technological background (Dublin Sculpture, 2021; Figure F.3.5).

The special tea vessel on Smithfield marketplace is a "Utah Teapot," referring to a virtual teapot form created by mathematician Martin Newell in 1975. His idea of a special design was a page of computer code describing, numerically, this most common 3D object. Till today, this technology, the code, has been used to create and test 3D computer graphics and builds an essential element for the application of 3D software used by designers, architects, artists, and engineers across the world (Dublin Sculpture, 2021).

This combination of tea culture and technological innovation is unique. And Irish.

Figure F.3.5: Teapot artwork "Smithfield Utah" by Alan Butler.
Photo: Hartwig Bohne

References

Andrews, A. (May 26, 2011). Obama will use hurley stick to put manners on congress. *Irish Central* (online). https://www.irishcentral.com/opinion/amyandrews/obama-will-use-hurley-stick-to-put-manners-on-congress-122655054-238085951.

Anon. (2011). Brewing up a recipe for success over 100 years. *The Irish Independent* (online). https://www.independent.ie/business/brewing-up-a-recipe-for-success-over-100-years-26804522.html.

Barry's Tea. (2022). Our story (online). Retrieved October 10, 2023, from https://www.barrystea.ie/our-story/.

Beeton, I.M. (1879). Book of household management. good form. In J. Pettigrew (2001), *A social history of tea*. The National Trust.

Beeton, I.M. (1892). Mrs. Beeton's cookery book and household management. in J. Pettigrew (2001), *A social history of tea*. The National Trust.

Bewley's. (2022). Our heritage (online). Retrieved October 10, 2023, from https://www.bewleys.com/ie/about-us/our-heritage/.

Blue Hare. (2022, March 4). Won't you have a cuppa? The Irish way with tea (online). Retrieved October 10, 2023, from https://blueharemagazine.com/have-a-cuppa-the-irish-way-with-tea/.

Bohne, H., & Jolliffe, L. (2021). Embracing tea culture in hotel experiences. *Journal of Gastronomy and Tourism*, *6*(1–2), 13–24.

Bohne, H. (2022a). Tea ceremonies. In D. Buhalis (Hrsg.), *Encyclopedia of tourism management and marketing* (pp. 331–35), Edward Elgar Publishing Ltd.

Bohne, H. (2022b). Tea consumption heritage. In D. Buhalis (Hrsg.), *Encyclopedia of tourism management and marketing* (pp. 335–37). Edward Elgar Publishing Ltd.

Bowes, T. (2005, March 5). A real broth of a brew. *The Telegraph*.

Brady, D. (2017). Writers and the international spirit: Irish PEN in the post-war years. New *Hibernia Review*, *21*(3), 116–30. Retrieved October 11, 2023, from https://www.jstor.org/stable/44807310#metadata_info_tab_contents.

Craig, E. (1936). Cookery illustrated and household management. In L. Olver (2010), *Afternoon Teatime*. Retrieved October 11, 2023, from https://www.foodtimeline.org/teatime.html.

Ferdman, R. (2014; updated 2022). Where the world's biggest tea drinkers are. QUARTZ (online). Retrieved July 21, 2022, from https://qz.com/168690/where-the-worlds-biggest-tea-drinkers-are.

Father Ted. (1995–1998). *Channel 4 Comedy Series*. https://www.channel4.com/programmes/father-ted.

Irish PEN Papers 1935–2022 (online). Retrieved October 11, 2023, from https://catalogue.nli.ie/Collection/vtls000508010.

Licencing Act 1982 (Section 81). Government of Ireland (online). Retrieved October 11, 2023, from https://www.irishstatutebook.ie/eli/1872/act/94/enacted/en/print.html.

Lyons Tea (Unilever). (2021). sustainabili-tea (online). Retrieved October 11, 2023, from https://www.lyonstea.ie/.

McElwain, A. (2019). Who invented afternoon tea? *The Irish Times* (online). https://www.irishtimes.com/life-and-style/food-and-drink/who-invented-afternoon-tea-1.3809973.

Mellett, L. (2021, December 4). Deja brew: The growth of Ireland's coffee industry. *Trinity News*. https://trinitynews.ie/2021/12/deja-brew-the-growth-of-irelands-coffee-industry/.

Mrs Browns Boys (2011) comedy. Retrieved October 10, 2023: https://www.comedy.co.uk/tv/mrs_browns_boys/.

Murphy, B., & O'Beachain, D. (2021). *From whence i came*. Irish Academic Press. Retrieved October 11, 2023, from https://irishacademicpress.ie/product/from-whence-i-came/.

Newstalk. (2016). Ireland has a new favourite tea according to the biggest selling brands (online). https://www.newstalk.com/news/ireland-has-a-new-favourite-tea-according-to-the-biggest-selling-brands-576436.

Olver, L. (2010). Afternoon Teatime (online). Retrieved October 11, 2023, from https://www.foodtimeline.org/teatime.html.

Pettegrew, J. (1999, October 21). Teatime in Ireland. *Teatime magazine*. Retrieved October 11, 2023, from https://www.teatimemagazine.com/teatime-in-ireland/https://www.teatimemagazine.com/tag/jane-pettigrew/.

Pettigrew, J. (2001). *A social history of tea*. The National Trust.

Research Drive. (2021). Global tea market report (online). Retrieved October 10, 2023, from https://www.researchdive.com/4659/tea-market.

Robson, D. (2019). How the world came to run on coffee. Retrieved October 10, 2023, from https://www.bbc.com/future/bespoke/made-on-earth/how-the-world-came-to-run-on-coffee/.

Sculpture Dublin. (2021). Smithfield Utah. Retrieved July 28, 2023, from https://www.sculpturedublin.ie/new-commissions-smithfield-square/.

The Merrion Hotel. (2022). Awards and accolades. Retrieved June 2023, from https://www.merrionhotel.com/all-about-the-merrion/awards-acolades/.

The Merrion Hotel Art Afternoon Tea. (2019). Drawing rooms and afternoon tea. Retrieved June 22, 2023, https://www.merrionhotel.com/dine/drawing-rooms-afternoon-tea/.

The Quiet Man (1952) movie. Retrieved October 10, 2023: https://www.imdb.com/title/tt0045061/.

White, F. (2014, September 5). History of the cup of tea: Part 2. *Carlow Nationalist*. https://carlow-nationalist.ie/2014/09/05/look-history-cup-tea-part-2/.

Wilson, K. (2011). *Tea with Jane Austen*. Francis Lincoln.

Wilson, K. (2004). *At home with Jane Austen*. Abbeyville Press Publishers.

G Exploring tea by the sea

Tea arrived in Europe either by the sea, initially via Dutch ports, or by land with caravans from China via Russia. This chapter focuses on the tea culture in countries
where tea was mainly imported across the Atlantic using tea clippers (1843–1869), and
later bigger ships through the Suez Canal.

Christian Hincheldey and Allan Lindgaard Winther

G.1 The Danish tea heritage

Introduction

Danish pharmacists are thought to have been the first to bring tea to Denmark, according to historian Annette Hoff of Denmark. Small quantities of tea were rumored to have been brought from Amsterdam, suggesting that teas were utilised as a form of medicine – likely recommended by Chinese healers. One of the first official references to tea in Denmark is made in 1668. There is evidence that tea was consumed at the time of the bishop of Aalborg. Studies show that tea was initially introduced as a medicinal herb in China, where it has long been believed to be a useful herb for medicine purposes.

In the seventeenth and eighteenth centuries, Denmark experienced a huge trade boom with China. Early in his reign, King Christian IV (who ruled from 1577 to 1648) dispatched his ships to Southeast Asia, aiming to unravel the mysteries of the East and secure a share of its captivating goods and wealth. The East India Company, established in Denmark in 1616, initially held a trade monopoly. However, in 1732, the first Danish ship, the Crown Prince Christian, completed the return journey to China, marking the foundation of The Asian Company (Asiatisk Kompagni) in the same year. Before 1732, the East India Company exclusively managed the trade with China, which gradually became more organised and significant. Subsequent years witnessed a substantial influx of tea, spices, silk, and porcelain to Denmark. When ships set sail for China, they first docked in colonies like Macao (then part of Portugal) or Java in Indonesia (then part of the Netherlands). Denmark's own colony, Tranquebar, located on the eastern coast of India, briefly played a role in the tea trade with China, with the first ship departing in 1674. During the eighteenth century, tea emerged as a pivotal commodity in trade. A considerable portion of the ship's cargo comprised tea, reflecting the growing popularity of this beverage. Trade transactions with the East flourished, bringing prosperity to Copenhagen's historic districts.

Tea trading anchoring tea in Denmark

The foundation of A.C. Perchs Thehandel in 1835 by Niels Broch Perch in Copenhagen marked a significant development. Niels, the son of the renowned seventeenth-century merchant Jens Bay Perch, had developed a passion for tea during his travels to Asia in 1807. In his pursuit of quality tea, he opened a small retail shop at No. 5 Kronprinsens Street in Copenhagen in 1835, where the teashop still operates today. Niels Perch personally oversaw tea imports for many years before naming the shop after

https://doi.org/10.1515/9783110758573-025

his third-oldest son, Axel Christian, before passing on the teashop. Today A.C. Perch operate 6 tea shops and tearooms in Denmark. The shops and tearooms can be found in the heart of the historic Scandinavian cities of Copenhagen, Aarhus, Odense, Oslo in Norway and Stockholm in Sweden and Copenhagen Airport (Hincheldey, 2009; see Figure G.1.1).

Figure G.1.1: A.C. Perch's teashop.
Source: Christian Hincheldey https://perchs.dk/en/copenhagen/

Tea embracing hospitality

In 2006, 172 years after the opening of the tea shop, another part of tea related hospitality became a reality. Perch's Tea Room opened above the old shop in Kronprinsens Street. It had long been a wish to find a suitable location in the street for tea lovers to enjoy the lovely leaves. The goal with the opening of Perch's Tea Room was to create an oasis for tea in Copenhagen, a place where tea drinkers could enjoy everything from afternoon tea, Japanese teas and iced teas to modern tea smoothies. The menu in Perch's Tea Room includes classic English scones with lemon curd, clotted cream, and a variety of marmalades, alongside plates with cucumber sandwiches, extravagant cakes, and petit-fours as well as delicious lunch platters and cheese. The Tea Room is inspired by both Chinese teahouses and English tea salons offering more than 150 different teas from around the world (Hincheldey, 2009).

Hospitality as a family business

One of the success factors of A.C. Perch's has been to preserve the knowledge and expertise about tea that have been accumulated over many generations. This enthusiasm for the product has been a key element. The capacity to provide the customer with a unique experience and to tell a story has been another key. For a specialty store and tearoom like Perch's, the idea of storytelling has long been significant to the brand and is a timeless value. The unique company's history and reputation, ongoing aspects of modernisation as well as a deep understanding of Danish hospitality, are essential to authentically provide the longtime experience. Consumers and guests are increasingly looking for added-value experiences. High ratings are given to goods and services that are connected to quality, feelings, aesthetics, identity, and individualism. These are ideals that specialty stores can frequently encourage. Consequently, A.C. Perch's tea shop is the oldest tea shop in Scandinavia still in business. The shop's success is a result of the work of many generations and it has been honored by the loyalty of customers and guests. The authentic spirit of the shop must be retained, which necessitates a commitment to hospitality and an outstanding quality of products sold (Hincheldey, 2009).

Danish tea preferences

Denmark is not only famous for plastic bricks, beaches, and the liberal city of Copenhagen, but, also for the varieties of liquorice. In the context of hot beverages, the tea culture in Denmark is dominated by a selection of black tea preferences. If they drink tea, then Danes particularly favour black tea (50% Earl Grey, 30% English Breakfast, 13% Darjeeling, 5% Assam), and 40% of the Danes also like green tea (multiple answers allowed, 1.018 Danes participated in the survey in 2020). Black teas are therefore not exclusive, but have a clear advantage. Within the black tea consumers – if they choose Earl Grey or English Breakfast – 73% drink their tea without milk, and only 21% with milk, while 36% sweeten their beverage (11% with one sugar per cup, 12% with two, and only 4% with three sugars per cup). The Danish show a preference for strong teas, but not as much as their Swedish neighbours. Meanwhile, the Danish people are less milky, but sweeter than the tea drinkers in Sweden (Smith, 2020; see Figure G.1.2).

Tea, experience economy and hosting

As a traditional Danish tea business, Perch's shows how to create memorable events or experiences in order to impress their customers. The memory becomes the product: the experience. Also, two other institutions are providing tea related hospitality in Copenhagen, the Nimb Hotel and Dronning Louises Tehus (Queen Louise's Tea-

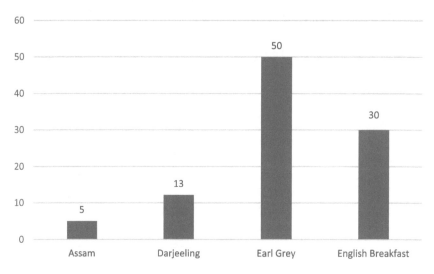

Figure G.1.2: Black tea consumption in Denmark.
Source: Smith (2020)

house) serve their afternoon tea by using experience economy concepts to create memorable experiences. The price for this (on average 30–120 EUR/pers.) is a lot of money for some tea, biscuits, sandwiches, and scones, but what you also get is the storytelling and staging of the experiences. This stage, the decoration, the interior design, the utensils, the porcelain, and also the teapots and teaspoons – this all is part of the stage underlining a unique experience, just as the theatre does for every show (Dronning Louises Tehus, 2023b; Nimb Hotel Copenhagen, 2023; see Figure G.1.3).

In addition, the set up surroundings, the right temperature, maybe some nice music, excellent service by the waiters, the story of tradition and family business, and a tea related success story including explanations about the products you get during the session – these details make the tea drinking experience a special one. Often the story is focused on the tea: where it's from, how it has been farmed by this special farmer, harvested under special conditions, dried under the sun, and gently sent to the consumer. The story could also be about the authentic Scandinavian set-up with the salmon sandwiches, scones, and jam from local fruits making the tea ready for drinking. The customers could buy all the ingredients themelves and make this at home, but then they wouldn't get the staging and this wouldn't create a memorable experience. So, the tea ceremony also depends on the surroundings, as well as the storytelling. This is what A.C. Perch, Nimb Hotel, and Dronning Louises Tehus (Queen Louise's Teahouse) do so well, by offering the tea ceremony in perfect and authentic surroundings which contributes to the full experience (Nimb Hotel Copenhagen, 2023; Dronning Louises Tehus, 2023a).

This is also part of the hospitality that is offered by hotels and restaurants. They need to have a standard level of hospitality that every customer always experiences.

Figure G.1.3: Danish teatime.
Source: Christian Hincheldey https://perchstearoom.dk/

One could also call this "hosting" or "hostmanship," where we find the concept of the host and the guest. The waiter and the company become the host and the customer becomes the guest. When this happens you can, as a company, lift the experience to a new level of memorable experiences. The interaction between the host and the guest is crucial in creating memorable experiences that the guest will seek out again and again. Maybe the guest will bring friends and family to experience a good afternoon tea and often the guest will post the experience on social media, which will be the best and free marketing the company can get. When we are talking hosting in general, this demands that the host is prepared, authentic, attentive, proactive and helpful, knowledgeable, has the desire to give service, and is motivated and passionate about the experience. If these items are fulfilled, there will be a very good chance to succeed with creating a memorable experience for the guest and making them feeling expected, welcome, and that they belong, which is what hosting is all about (Winther & Simonsen, 2021).

Conclusion

Tea and food itself will not create a memorable experience by themselves. Only if they ae wrapped in hosting and authentic surroundings will there be a very high chance of creating the perfect memorable experience that will bring the guest back for more and make a good business. These guests will feel the hospitality and the link to tea.

References

Dronning Louises Tehus. (2023a). Queen Louise's Tea House. Retrieved March 27, 2023, from https://www.dronninglouisestehus.dk/en/.

Dronning Louises Tehus. (2023b). Teatime. Retrieved March 27, 2023, from https://www.dronninglouisestehus.dk/wp-content/uploads/2022/03/Menukort_-_Dronning_Louises_Tehus_-_Marts_2022.pdf.

Hincheldey, C. (2009). *Tea from leaf to elixir*. N.T. Production & Divine Tea. www.acperch.com.

Li, Y.R. (2022). A study on tea drinking, behavior, and attitudes in the Nordic countries. Master Thesis at Halmstad University.

Nimb Hotel Copenhagen. (2023). Nimb Bar. Retrieved November 12, 2023, from https://www.nimb.dk/~/link.aspx?_id=AA324B44E1B449F5869598E3D2D5810F&_z=z#lamerenda_afternoontea.

Smith, F. (2020). How do British tea drinking habits compare with other Europeans?. Retrieved March 30, 2023, from https://yougov.co.uk/topics/consumer/articles-reports/2020/11/24/how-do-british-tea-drinking-habits-compare.

Winther, A., & Simonsen, D. (2021). Informal & relaxed: Exercising the role of host in the hospitality industry. EuroCHRIE conference paper, Aalborg 2021.

Arnaud Bachelin and Hartwig Bohne

G.2 La perspective Française –
The French and tea

Introduction

Tea in France is a beverage of quality and precision. Famous brands, royal links, impressive porcelain, and innovative entrepreneurs as well as creative tea farmers illustrate the diverse French approach to tea, its cultural roots, and varieties.

Arrival of tea in France with a little fanfare

After a gentle period of acclimatisation in France, tea has been given its letters of nobility. With its demanding standards and refinement, tea has had to be patient. It was hard to imagine the destiny tea was designed for when it first appeared in France alongside chocolate and coffee. It was at the dawn of the seventeenth century, probably around 1630, that tea made its mid entry into France. It would take around 20 years for tea to find its place on French tables and in French homes. Its high price was the main reason why it was so difficult to develop. There were many detractors of the "impertinence of the new century," as Guy Patin amusingly called it almost a century after its appearance. It timidly took the place of sage, which until then had been widely consumed in France, starting with its sovereign, King Louis XIV. However, the medicinal aspect of the plant led to a number of adepts and found ambassadors in the upper echelons of the state. Among the most prestigious was Cardinal Mazarin, who took it daily to treat his gout. It wasn't long before he set the trend and saw tea consumption spread around him and throughout the court. The Marquise de Sévigné was also a great lover of the little herb, as were many of the literati of the time. At the time of the French Revolution, tea was considered a luxury product and its consumption was very limited. It wasn't until the middle of the nineteenth century that tea gained a whole new following (Bachelin, 2023; McCulloch, 2022).

Development of consumption and consumption patterns

If there was one factor that led to a considerable increase in tea consumption at the dawn of the nineteenth century, it was the cholera epidemics that were ravaging Europe. For health reasons, people were advised to boil the water before using it. From then on,

https://doi.org/10.1515/9783110758573-026

tea had a clear path to spread through the different classes of the population, even the most modest. On one hand, the quality of the tea was mediocre and the varieties few and far between. On the other hand, coffee, a product from the French colonies, was a major competitor. Tea retained a special aura that was appropriated by the bourgeoisie and women of good society. Fortunately, at the end of the nineteenth century, with the development of the Japanese movement and the great Parisian exhibitions promoting exoticism, tea was given a new lease of life. Indian teas, freshly produced by the British, and the first teas from Ceylon were discovered at the Universal Exhibition in 1900.

During the second half of the nineteenth century, under the Second Empire, tea consumption in France benefited from a new fashion, Anglomania, which spread throughout France. It was then that the British model of drinking tea spread to France, using large, generous teapots generally produced by French factories such as those in Limoges or Sèvres for the most prestigious. This new fashion meant that English factories were even able to set up shop on the capital's main thoroughfares, such as under the arcades of the rue de Rivoli or in the heart of the Louvre department store near the museum and hotel of the same name. This fashion was encouraged by the private tearoom that the Empress Eugénie de Montijo had built to welcome, in the style of the literary salons of the eighteenth century, the men of letters and intellectuals of the time, such as Alexandre Dumas, Gustave Flaubert, Louis Pasteur, and Eugène Delacroix, whose work also evoked the taste for exoticism at the end of the century (Bachelin, 2017; Bush, 2023).

The development of tea rooms also meant that women of good society could go out without compromising their reputation. The primary target clientele for these tea rooms were women and intellectuals. In other European countries, tea was even used to promote the emancipation of women and their access to the right to vote. The tea most commonly consumed at the time was black tea, which was more accessible and which Europeans tended to understand better. Green teas on the market at the time were rare and their consumption was not encouraged. The consumption of black tea and the use of porcelain gave rise to the habit of putting milk in one's cup. While some saw this as a way of avoiding temperature shocks on the fine porcelain, others saw it as a way of having a drink that was higher in calories and tastier, given the quality of the tea leaves available from the merchants of the time (Pettigrew, 2003).

In France, black tea was in the majority until the 1970s, before a trend towards flavoured teas developed and, finally, green tea, in the mania for seeking benefits in everything eaten or drunk, began to be consumed at the dawn of the twenty-first century. Since the beginning of the twentieth century, tea consumption in France rose steadily, tripling between 1995 and 2015, nowadays at an average of 250g tea per person per year. Today, two out of three French people drink tea, mainly natural and pure (77% avoid milk, only 17% add milk), and the market is worth some €500 million, 20% of which is generated by independent teahouses. But, there is a clear preference for Earl Grey (35%) teas as well as for English Breakfast (18%) and Darjeeling (17%) (see Figure G.2.1). And, also in France tea has become an attractive companion of food, deserts, and sweets (Smith, 2020; Bush, 2023).

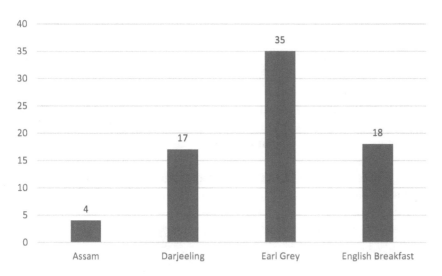

Figure G.2.1: Black tea preferences in France.
Source: Smith (2020)

France and tea objects – porcelain and famous ceramists

It's always the same story: new products are generated by the appropriation of new fashions: new clothing customs, new food products requiring new and precise utensils. This was a recurring theme in eighteenth century France, with the discovery of numerous exotic products. Among the most common were chocolate, coffee, and tea, which we are interested in here. It was against this backdrop that teapots, chocolate and coffee makers, as well as sugar bowls began to appear in French homes. At first, the necessary utensils were imported directly from the countries producing these exotic foods. Teapots, bowls, cups, and trays were imported on a massive scale throughout the eighteenth century.

But the discovery of porcelain gave a new impetus to French and European craftsmen. It was then that a royal factory was created in France, the one in Vincennes, which a few years after its foundation became the famous Sèvres factory, still in operation today. It produced a large number of teapots, at first imitating Chinese models, then completely emancipating itself and reinventing the object. The dimensions and designs would differ. The most surprising thing would be to see these same models copied later by Chinese and Japanese craftsmen. What would French craftmanship be without porcelain and ceramics in general? To imagine France without the porcelain workshops of Limoges, the stoneware of Puisaye or the soft porcelain of Chantilly would be like cutting out tea, coffee, or chocolate (Bachelin, 2017).

Even if all these manufacturers continue to bring prestige to France through their products, there are an increasing number of independent ceramists and veritable goldsmiths who create tea-drinking utensils in Europe today. One example is the work of Jean Girel, who focuses much of his work and research on the creation of Tenmoku bowls, the same bowls that were produced in China during the Song dynasty and used for the ritual of brewing tea. Jérôme le Potier and Pierre Auriol also stamp small porcelain bowls with precious enamels that are used for Gong Fu Cha tasting, a Chinese tasting method that has become increasingly popular in France over the last 10 years.

Apart from porcelain, French silversmiths and designers were also interested in presenting their craftsmanship, using tea as a theme (Figure G.2.2).

Figure G.2.2: Silver Teapot (1937).
Note: Silver Teapot, 1937 (Jean-Emile Puiforcat (French, 1897–1945)
Photo: Tony Cunha
Source: Kamm Teapot Foundation

Exploring tea and tea brands in France

While tea used to be sold by apothecaries, particularly when it first arrived in France, it is undoubtedly thanks to the traders and specialist shops that tea has found its way into French homes. These merchants have been the standard-bearers for the cause and the product. They gave tea its letters of nobility and, above all, a high profile in the capital.

It's important to distinguish between two types of tea sellers in France: teahouses and tea merchants. The former offer on-the-spot tasting of teas and often pastries and dishes, whether cooked with tea or not. The latter simply sell tea in bulk or already packaged. Historically, their best representative was the *A la Porte* Chinoise shop in the Galerie Vivienne. It sold Chinese and Japanese teas, as well as furniture and exotic objects imported from China. It was a shop frequented by many celebrities, including Emile Zola, Edgar Degas, Charles Baudelaire, and Claude Monet. Unfortunately, the shop no longer exists. However, there are several famous French tea brands currently operating:

1. Angélina
Opened for the first time in 2005, Angélina shares a strong passion towards tea, helping customers to experience "the finest things life has given us." While in the beginning the consumers could choose from among 300 teas, with time the shop extended the number of varieties. As tea represents the main focus, white, green, Oolong, black, China black, Pu-Erh, Matcha, chai and English blends teas are available. Flavoured, herbal, fruity, organic, and decaf teas and infusions are also within the company's product selection (Angelinas tea, 2023).

2. Betjeman and Barton
The Betjeman & Barton tea company not only emphasises a century-old brand, but also a company defined by excellence and originality. Relying on men with experience and entrepreneurial spirit, the business celebrated the tea masters and tea from the best tea gardens and plantations across the world. However, ladies took over the management of the company, bringing inventiveness, elegance, and determination. Furthermore, a new look was brought to the company, inspired by the slogan "Paris tea merchants since 1919." For example, Katherine Gregory was responsible for the artistic side for more than 20 years, while Agnés Defontine developed the heritage of the company through luxury and refinement. In addition, Laurence Miletti took over the tearoom, whereas Mariane Pinto gave impetus to the amazing company. Concerning the tea variation, classics such as black, green, oolong, smoked, white, and metal are offered. Within the flavoured section, spicy, gourmet, flowery, sweety, and Earl Grey tea are some of the options, while Assam, Ceylon, Darjeeling, China, and Japan are also present. An interesting factor concerning the company is reflected by the tasting pack amateur, tasting pack connoisseur, or tasting pack luxe options for the passioned tea guests. Betjeman and Barton has also opened the first tea bar in Paris, where a whole tea tasting experience can be enjoyed by customers. Both hot and iced tea can be tasted, in a unique, alternative place where traditions are preserved (Betjeman & Barton, 2023).

3. Compagnie & Co.

Founded in Paris in 1848, Compagnie & Co. (formerly Compagnie Coloniale) is the oldest French tea brand, although its business model started with the production and selling of chocolate. But as of 1860, tea became more and more important and was growing to the second pillar of success. France-based tea leaf processing and packaging process has led to the company being awarded the title of "Quality Artisan Producer" by the Collège Culinaire de France, representing and transmitting essential values of excellence in French cuisine (Compagnie, 2023).

4. Dammann Frères

The history of the Dammann Frères tea company started many years ago, more exactly in 1692, when Louis XIV allowed Sir Damame to exclusively sell tea in France. Over the years that followed, several factories were opened across the world, in Batavia in 1825 and later on in Tamatave in 1925. Even though the company continued to expand, opening another factory in New York in 1926, only in 1949 did tea become the company's sole trade. More recently, in 2005, the company started to supply the finest restaurants, creating their own products, designs, and recipes. The online sale website of the company was launched in 2007, while one year later the first store opened in Paris. The success of the company was visible, operating in 2012 within 62 different countries across the world. Keeping and respecting the traditions gathered from great blenders, the company transferred all collected experiences within the value chain, focusing their attention on each step, from the harvesting and drying to the transporting of the product. Emphasising their entrepreneurial spirit, Dammann Frères changed the way people perceived the individual tea bag in the 1980s, turning tea into a drink that can be served at each hour of the day. Furthermore, the quality and ethical policy as well as sustainable development are relevant and crucial factors for the company (Dammann, 2023).

Having a wide selection of products, some of the offered teas are black, green, white, Oolong, dark, yellow, mate, and matcha tea, flavoured teas such as citrus fruits, flowery, red fruits, gourmet, minty, orchard, and exotic, as well as many others that are found within the company product selection.

5. Kusmi

Kusmi Tea represents another company with a long and fascinating history, dating from 1867 and founded in St. Petersburg by Pavel Kousmichoff. Following the Russian revolution, the company relocated to Paris. The company flourished, with new offices opened in New York, Hamburg, Constantinople, and Berlin during the year of 1927. When the owner of the company, Viatcheslav Kousmichoff, passed away, his son took over the business. Unfortunately, due to a bigger focus on artistry and tea than business, the company declined during this time. However, in 2003 the owner of the company changed, with Kusmi bought by Sylvain and Claude Orebi. Furthermore, in 2017, after exactly 150 years of existence, the business had already opened 85 stores in 35 different countries, offering their guests 100 various tea blends. Recently, in 2020, Kusmi tea company became organic. The company has also focused on charitable cases, such as fighting against the threat of extinction to wild tigers, launching their own blog where several distinctive topics are discussed (Kusmi, 2023).

Regarding the offered products, black, green, and white tea, as well as organic blends, yerba mate, herbal, fruit, and rooibos tea and infusions, are the existing options. Apart from the ordinary tea types, the product can be bought in tea-filled tins, tea bags, loose leaf pouches or tea samplers. Concerning the flavour of the above-mentioned tea types, spicy, unflavoured, citrus, fruity, sweet, floral or vegetal are offered.

6. Mariage Frères

The Mariage Frères French company was opened in 1854, being the oldest French importer of tea. The company come from an active family in regards of colonial trade, founded by two brothers, Henri and Edouard Mariage. Trading with China and Ceylon, the company provided exclusive retailers, hotels, and tearooms with their products. The last owner who was part of the Mariage family found two enthusiastic young people who started working for the tea company and spread the tea culture of the company worldwide. The Mariage Frères teahouse made a major contribution to the development of tea drinking in France. From the 1980s onwards, they cleverly developed a luxurious image for tea, playing on the charm of luxury à la Française, which enabled the brand to be widely exported around the world and to become synonymous with French tea. The tea menu is extremely extensive, offering both natural and flavoured teas (Bush, 2023).

Tea represents the main focus of the company, an aspect also seen in the tea related spaces the company offers. In Paris, a typical *salon de thé* has been successfully established, in order to underline the quality of tea with a specific environment, where tradition and refinement is suggested. The place allows guests to appreciate amazing tea blends as well as food baked with tea. In addition, a unique tea museum is part of this tea experience, and Mariage Frères illustrates a poetic adventure, with some of the rarest tea objects in history presented here. Luxury and refinement, as well as silver, porcelain, and clay are some of the materials found in the museum (Bachelin, 2023; Cosmopolis, 2004;, Stella, 2003).

7. Palais des Thés

The company emphasises the tea experience, traveling across the world in order to offer their customers the best teas. The important partnership and relationship the company has with their providers gives the business the opportunity to sell various flavours and emotions. In addition, Palais des Thés is designing their own flavoured tea in Paris, emphasising innovation. François-Xavier Delmas is the founder of the company, and has spent at least 30 years visiting gardens and plantations, in order to find the best for his clients. Due to these travels, the founder has gained much experience and knowledge about tea; therefore, within the store, limited-edition and rare teas are available. Mathias Minet is also an important person within the company; joining the business in 1990s, he and François-Xavier Delmas have built the success of the company that is seen today. In 1999 both partners set up the Tea School, sharing their experience in tea tasting. Aiming to offer only the best for their customers, the company has in-store sommeliers who guide and advise the consumer concerning various tea types, flavours, and aroma (Palais des thés, 2023; Bachelin, 2023).

Independent tea merchants are now more numerous. They mainly offer flavoured teas, although the trend has been towards natural teas since 2015, and even natural teas sourced directly from producers. The Parisian tea trade is also made up of specialised tea merchants, such as Jugetsudo, which offers prestigious Japanese teas and accessories, Thés de Chine, which until 2022 offered precious, fair-trade Chinese teas in its shop on Boulevard Saint Germain, and Terre de Chine, which only offers natural Chinese vintages. Recently, the prestigious Taiwanese teahouse Wisteria opened its doors in Paris, offering the chance to discover the great vintages of Chinese and Taiwanese teas in the traditional way, encouraging the consumption of tea using the gong fu cha method, all with high-quality and often antique accessories.

The sale of loose teas is also increasingly present in the various French provinces, notably through the Palais des thés outlets, but also thanks to the distribution of Dammann teas in many fine grocery shops in France. Elsewhere, Thé-ritoires is a natural teahouse founded in 2016 that aims to offer a different tea experience. Halfway between an English tea room and a Chinese teahouse, it is possible to discover hundreds of teas here, directly sourced from the producers. This world of tea is also documented by entrepreneurial spirit and individual teashops, e.g., Thé Cha Yuan, La Fabrikathé or Human and Tea and Les thés sur terre – all Lyon based.

France is also one of the countries that has elevated tea to the highest ranks of gastronomy. As a result, tea is increasingly making its way to chefs' tables. These include the work of chef Anne-Sophie Pic, a great lover of green teas, and the Yam Cha restaurant in Paris, which offers tea and food pairings.

Tea production in France

From the early days of the nineteenth century, the French government has been looking into tea production, with the aim of finding new ways of producing tea that would enable France to develop economically. With this in mind, the Ministry of Agriculture sent Jean Baptiste Guillemin, a botanist from Burgundy, to Brazil with the mission of understanding all the principles of tea growing and returning with the information needed to develop it in France. On his return, a number of trials were carried out, some in Brittany, others in Corsica and even in the Tuileries gardens, as described by the Parisian tea merchant Houssaye in his colossal work on tea in 1839. These attempts were not very successful. Tea and porcelain production went ahead in the French colonies, particularly in Indochina (between 1887 and 1954), where numerous plantations were developed and production was encouraged by French colonists. It wasn't until the early 1960s that tea-growing was developed on modern French territory, on Réunion island on more than 300 hectares. In 2017, the plantation covered 587 hectares and produced 53 tonnes of tea. Projects were also launched in French Guiana, with less satisfactory results (Bachelin, 2017)

Today, there are many tea-growing projects in France, from Brittany to the Pyrenees, via the Basque Country, the Cévennes, and the Morvan with the Terres Eduennes project. But there is still a long way to go before French production plays a major role in the global and national tea trade. The products that come out of these gardens are true luxury products, whose quality is uneven and only needs to improve. Among the projects that catch my eye are those of Denis Mazerolles in Languidic, Brittany, with his Filleule des Fées tea garden, and Lucas Ben-Moura in the Pyrenees on the terraces of Arrieulat. The variety of cultivars and the quasi-scientific approach make their projects important models for anyone interested in growing tea in France today (Tea grown in Europe, 2023).

Conclusion

After a timid start in France, tea is on the way to becoming one of the most widely consumed drinks in France after water, gaining a little more of the market share every year. The teas on offer to French consumers are of increasingly high quality, allowing producers of natural teas to express themselves to the full. The future certainly holds some wonderful surprises for the world of tea, however tea in France will have to be able to adapt to its audience and show patience.

References

Angelinas Tea. (2023). About. Retrieved January 30, 2023, from https://www.angelinasteas.com/.
Bachelin, A. (2023). *L'heure de véri-thé*. Epure publishers.
Bachelin, A. (2017). *L'heure de véri-thé*. Baker Street publishers.
Betjeman and Barton (2023). Retrieved January 30, 2023, from https://www.betjemanandbarton.com/en/.
Bush, C.W. (2023, February 17). Tea in France – Ooh, la la! Teatime Magazine. Retrieved July 20, 2023, from https://teatimemagazine.com/tea-france-ooh-la-la/3/.
Compagnie & Co. (2023). Retrieved July 5, 2023, from www.compagnie-co.com/en/.
Cosmopolis. (2004). The French tea company in Paris. History and teas. Retrieved January 30, 2023, from https://cosmopolis.ch/mariage-freres-en/.

Dammann. (2023). History.Retrieved January 30, 2023, from https://www.dammann.fr/en/cms/history.htmll.

Kusmi Tea. (2023). Our brand. Retrieved January 30, 2023, from https://www.kusmitea.com/us/our-brand.html.

McCulloch, B. (2022, May 25). Did you know? France has a longer history of tea drinking than the UK (May 25, 2022). Retrieved July 20, 2023 from https://www.connexionfrance.com/article/Mag/French-Facts/Did-you-know-France-has-a-longer-history-of-tea-drinking-than-the-UK.

Palais des thes. (2023). About us Retrieved January 30, 2023, from https://www.palaisdesthes.com/en/.

Pettigrew, J. (2001). *A social history of tea*. National Trust.

Pettigrew, J. (2003). *Design for tea*. Sutton Publishing.

Smith, F. (2020). How do British tea drinking habits compare with other Europeans? Retrieved March 30, 2023, from https://yougov.co.uk/topics/consumer/articles-reports/2020/11/24/how-do-british-tea-drinking-habits-compare.

Stella, A. (2003). *French Tea: Mariage Frères – Three Centuries of Savoir-Faire*. Flammarion.

Tea grown in Europe. (2023). Tea grown in Europe 2023 – in focus. Retrieved July 20, 2023, from https://tea-grown-in-europe.eu/wp-content/uploads/2023/06/EuT-2023-Leaflet-digital-version.pdf.

Teatimemagazin (2023, Feb 17). Dammann Frères: France's Oldest Tea Company. Retrieved 12 November 2023 from: https://teatimemagazine.com/dammann-freres-frances-oldest-tea-company/.

Hartwig Bohne

G.3 Tea culture and cultivation in Germany

Introduction

Tea in Germany? The country of beer and coffee is one of the most important tea trading places worldwide – mainly due to Hamburg port, but also Bremen and Emden (Krieger, 2021). As Germany did not have any colonies with tea plantations – in differentiation to Great Britain – the main business activities have been importing, then nobeling, and afterwards exporting tea (Rohrsen, 2022). Three major companies are dominating the German tea business: OTG (e.g., Meßmer and OnnO Behrends brands), Ronnefeldt, and Teekanne, with a big variety of products (Maeck, 2014). But there are also innovative entrepreneurs who have started planting, harvesting, and producing tea on a small scale: tea cultivation in Germany is also possible.

Sweet taste and increasing consumption

Regarding their taste, German tea drinkers are sweet ones. In particular, for black teas (English Breakfast or Earl Grey), 26% of the German tea drinkers prefer one piece of sugar, 16% take two, and 3% need three. In addition, 28% of the tea drinkers like to add milk, but the majority of 63% prefers pure tea (Smith, 2020).

In terms of consumption, people in Germany consume 20,000 tons of black and green tea per year (with increasing tendency), of which approximately 18% is organic tea. Calculating the prepared beverage, people in Germany drink 28 litres of brewed black and green tea per person per year on average, with one sizable exception: East Frisians drink 300 litres brewed black tea (East Frisian blend) per person per year. It can be noted that German customers developed a preference for higher qualities and more loose tea than tea bags (55:45) and that infusions (fruit, herbal) are highly demanded. Figure G.3.1. shows in total 61,954 tons of consumed teas and infusions, of which green tea accounts for about 8% and black teas about 24%, while approximately 68% is related to herbal or fruit infusions (Deutscher Tee- und Kräuterteeverband, 2022; Rohrsen, 2022)

https://doi.org/10.1515/9783110758573-027

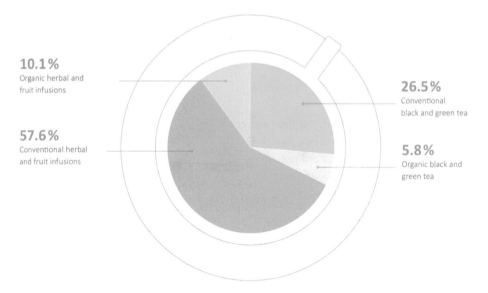

10.1%
Organic herbal and
fruit infusions

26.5%
Conventional
black and green tea

57.6%
Conventional herbal
and fruit infusions

5.8%
Organic black and
green tea

Figure G.3.1: Organics on the rise.
Source: Deutscher Tee- und Kräuterteeverband (2022)

Black is black

Also, the preferences within the black teas differ compared to other European countries. The German tea drinkers like Earl Grey very much (33%), then Darjeeling (28%), and afterwards English Breakfast (17%) and Assam (16%). These results, to be seen in figure G.3.2., are based on a survey with 2,048 tea drinkers and multiple answers were possible (Smith, 2020). Either "Earl Grey" or "Darjeeling" is mostly offered in restaurants and hotels, if only one black tea is available. Obviously, there are two reasons for this: first, Darjeeling is not as strong as Assam, so that more (non-experienced or occasional) tea drinkers can easily accept it and get an access to tea and, second, the marketing of "Earl Grey" and the light lemon flavour make this sort also easily accessible, so that both are widely accepted as a "black tea" in the gastronomy. This also underlines a certain undifferentiated handling of sorts of tea and unspecific knowledge of many consumers and the hesitantly gastronomic response to this consumer's behaviour. While on a coffee vending machine or on coffee menu cards the consumers can easily find six to ten different coffee specialties, you have to go to luxury hotels or specialised cafés in order to find a good tea menu.

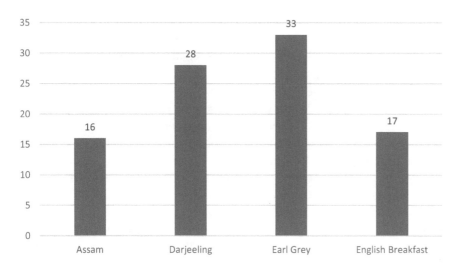

Figure G.3.2: Black tea preferences in Germany.
Source: Smith (2020)

Tea trade

Trading tea is very European. Hamburg port is one of the most important ports in terms of tea import and export. And, although Germany is not relevant regarding producing tea, it is one of the biggest marketplaces for tea worldwide. In 2021, Germany imported about 47,500 tons from 80 countries, but also exported 22,300 tons to 108 countries (Deutscher Tee- und Kräuterteeverband, 2022). In addition, Germany had a unique tax on tea between 1953 and 1993, but this tax did not apply as long as the tea did not leave the Hamburg free trade zone. Therefore, Hamburg port was one of the most frequented tea trading ports and more than 50% of the tea consumed in Europe is still handled in Hanburg port. The London tea auction was a symbol for international tea trading and operated between 1679 and 1998, also underlining the role of London and Great Britain for the international reputation of tea. And, while the auction was closed in 1998, the function of Hamburg port for European and international tea trade was stabilised and is still one of the anchors of global tea trade (Pompetzki, 2017).

Tea made in Germany

India, Sri Lanka, Japan, China, Türkiye, and Kenya – they all are famous for their tea plantations. But Germany? Yes, there are innovative entrepreneurs, passionate and creative, who started planting and harvesting tea in different places in Germany. In the western part, the Tschanara Tea garden is operating on 4,000qm in a village called Odenthal-Scheuren, harvesting tea plants mostly from South Korea, but also from China, Japan, India, and Türkiye. They grow successfully in these climate conditions and the harvest is about 9 kilograms per year of white, yellow, green (majority), Oolong, and black tea (Tschanara Teagarden, 2023).

A second tea planation is Wudang Daoist Tea Garden by Wenzhuo Liu, in operation since 2017 near Hanover. Following the name of the garden, the tea plants are originally from the Wudang Mountains in Hubei Province, China. The idea is to extend the tea fields and to develop a mountain tea garden, also adding a Daoist temple beside the garden. It should become a centre of Chinese tea culture and a representative of Wudang Daoist tea, art, and culture in Europe. The focus is on white, green, black (red), and dark tea (Wudang teagarden, 2023).

Going to the northern part of Germany, in the village of Hardebek, 200 seedlings were planted in 2022, which are to yield tea from 2025. This project is the most northern in Germany and is based on tea plants coming from Brittany/France (NDR, 2022).

These entrepreneurial activities show the passion for tea, but also for tea culture and the use of opportunities, also due to climate change and unusual ideas for agriculture. Tschanara and Wudang tea gardens are open for guided tours and tea tastings and are part of regional tourism. As the produced quantity of tea is not yet sufficient for being constantly sold to restaurants or hotels, it is still a unique opportunity to be directly hosted in the tea plantations' drinking tea made in Germany as a special moment of hospitality.

Tea enjoyed in Germany

Enjoying tea in Germany is a diverse challenge. There are trends like bubble tea and ice tea to make tea easily accessible – although these two beverages do not really have much in common with a good tea. And there are the exclusive developments like tea pairing instead of wine pairings in exclusive restaurants or non-alcohol gastronomy. A qualitative approach is certainly the hotel's offers like afternoon tea or cream tea. In big cities many five star hotels offer afternoon tea mostly on Fridays and weekends, between 14:00 and 18:00, and they are focused on a copy of typical British afternoon tea service. It would be an exception to get a Japanese or Chinese tea ceremony offered in a hotel in Germany (Grundmann, 2023).

Apart from the social and cultural links, the art scene also used tea for demonstrating their abilities. As one of the most famous porcelain companies worldwide, Meissen porcelain developed creative and innovative teapots and cups, tea sets and colourful arrangements in order to underline the sensitivity of China being a perfect material to enjoy tea (Figure G.3.3).

Figure G.3.3: Meissen Porcelain Grotesque teapot, 1726–1730.
Note: Meissen Porcelain Factory (Germany, est. 1710), Hausmaler
Photo: Kamm Teapot Foundation
Source: Kamm Teapot Foundation

Figure G.3.4: Tea service (1929).
Note: Tea Service 1929 (Copper, brass, ebony wood) from Karl Heubler (German, 1884–1961)
Photo: © Quittenbaum Kunstauktionen GmbH, München
Source: Kamm Teapot Foundation

Figure G.3.5: Silver teapot (1935).
Note: Silver teapot (1935) from Hayno Focken (German, 1905–1968)
Photo: David H. Ramsey
Source: Kamm Teapot Foundation

Not only was porcelain highly recommended and requested by customers to drink tea and to show the pride of a household or the service level of a hotel. Other materials, e.g., silver or sheet metal or cupper, were also used for impressive and useful tea sets (Figures G.3.4 and G.3.5).

Conclusion

Tea culture in Germany is mainly based on the extraordinary consumption of black tea in East Frisia. But the development of Meissen porcelain also had an important impact on the tea tableware, as well as the Dresmer blue and red porcelain, used in East Frisia. In Bavaria, the first teapots for hotels were developed by Bauscher porcelain and in the middle of the eighteenth century travelers in Thuringia and Saxony preferred a special "tea table" for travelling in order to take their own teapots, tea cups, and a small tablet to prepare loose tea with them, including water from their home.

It can be stated that there always was a strong entrepreneurial spirit and a close link between the sort of tea and the style of consumption in Germany (Krieger, 2021). Products which followed the habits or needs of consumption as well as the initial function of tea for health issues or later as a royal beverage show the development and meaning of tea for regional cultures and societies. The global power and market share of German tea producing companies as well as the use of exclusive German porcelain for tea ceremonies underline the high quality of entrepreneurial decisions and tea related products as well as the power of consumers. East Frisia, meanwhile, clearly illustrates the pride and power of traditions and social anchoring of tea as well as the regional connectivity. In sum, Germany is much more than coffee and beer; Germany's tea culture is sweet, black, and entrepreneurial.

References

Deutscher Tee- und Kräuterteeverband. (2022). Teereport 2022. Retrieved March 30, 2023, from https://www.teeverband.de/files/bilder/Presse/Marktzahlen/Tee%20Report%202022__ES.pdf.

Grundmann, C. (2023). Cultural and social functions of tea ceremonies and their implementation into the hotel industry. Bachelor Thesis at the SRH Dresden School of Management.

Krieger, M. (2021). *Geschichte des Tees*. Böhlau Verlag.

Maeck, S. (2014). *Meßmer- Vom Zauber einer Weltmarke*. Wachholtz Verlag-Murmann Publishers.

Norddeuscher Rundfunk NDR. (2022). Kreis Segeberg statt Tropen: Tee made in Schleswig-Holstein. Retrieved April 23, 2023, from https://www.ndr.de/nachrichten/schleswig-holstein/Kreis-Segeberg-statt-Tropen-Tee-made-in-Schleswig-Holstein,tee402.html.

Pompetzki, Carola V. (2017, April 26). Teemetropole Hamburg – ganz schön aufgebrüht!. Retrieved April 22, 2023, from https://www.welt.de/sonderthemen/tee/article164033666/Teemetropole-Hamburg-ganz-schoen-aufgebrueht.html.

Rohrsen, P. (2022). *Das Buch zum Tee*. C.H. Beck.

Smith, F. (2020). How do British tea drinking habits compare with other Europeans?. Retrieved March 30, 2022, from https://yougov.co.uk/topics/consumer/articles-reports/2020/11/24/how-do-british-tea-drinking-habits-compare.

Tschanara Teagarden. (2023). Der Teegarten. Retrieved April 23, 2023, from https://tschanara-teagarden.de/der-teegarten/.

Wudang Teagarden. (2023). Wudang Tea Garden & Tea House. Retrieved April 23, 2023, from https://wudang-pai.de/wudangteahouse/.

Hanne Klöver

G.3.1 German delight: East Frisian tea culture

Introduction

Tea has been drunk in East Frisia for more than 300 years. Today, the East Frisian tea ceremony significantly contributes to the cultural identity of the region. East Frisians call themselves a nation of tea drinkers. This is also underlined by three special museums in the towns of Leer and Norden with permanent and special exhibitions all about this pleasurable drink.[1] In 2016, the German UNESCO Commission also listed East Frisian tea culture as an Intangible Cultural Heritage in Germany – as the first tea-related UNESCO cultural heritage worldwide (UNESCO, 2016). Five years later, it was included in the Book of Records (formerly the Guinness Book of Records). The Record Institute for Germany had calculated that East Frisians drink an average of 300 litres of tea per capita annually, while the national average is just 28 litres (Rekord-Institut, 2021). Accordingly, the East Frisians even surpass the annual tea consumption of the inhabitants of Libya (287 liters) and Türkiye (277 liters).

In 1610, tea landed in Amsterdam for the first time. But how did it get to East Frisia and how did tea drinking become an integral part of East Frisian life? Was it initially only a luxury for the wealthy or did tea also reach poorer sections of the population? Why did tea prevail in this part of the country against coffee, which was introduced in Europe at about the same time and gained the upper hand in the surrounding area?

For the perfect East Frisian teatime, the "ingredients" are fixed; it is not only the preparation, the way of serving, and how the tea is drunk that matters: just as important are tea spoons and a special cream spoon (designed with the so called "Ostfriesenmuster" (a specific pattern),[2] the tableware, and the teapot. All this together forms the East Frisian tea ceremony and makes it unique. It is possible to understand how and under what conditions this habit became an identity-forming custom over the centuries thanks to a distinctive awareness of regional values ("Heimatbewegung") and is still perceived as such by the population today.

This is a tradition that finally received the accolade of being included in the UNESCO-list of "Intangible Cultural Heritage in Germany 2016 (UNESCO, 2016)." The presentation ends with an outlook: what benefits does a region derive from such a title? What approaches are there to valorise and market it for tourism?

---

1 Ostfriesisches Teemuseum, Norden; TeeMuseum - Sammlung Oswald-von Diepholz zur internationalen Kulturgeschichte des Tees, Norden; Bünting Teemuseum, Leer.
2 Cream spoons are specially shaped: a circular flat spoon cavity attaches to a small, curved handle.

https://doi.org/10.1515/9783110758573-028

"East Frisian coziness always has a cup of tea ready"

The saying goes, "In East Frisia, the teapot never gets cold, because East Frisian Gemütlichkeit always has a cup of tea ready."

The reason for this is the social anchoring of the East Frisian tea culture - it is practiced by young and old. Moreover, the preference for certain tea blends is often passed down from generation to generation. Because the tea itself is also an East Frisian speciality, the "Genuine East Frisian blend" may only be called this if it was produced in East Frisia. The strong black tea should contain at least 50% Assam teas, and Java, Ceylon, Sumatra, and Darjeeling varieties can also be added. There are three traditional tea trading houses in East Frisia. In Leer, Johann Bünting started selling tea in 1806 (today Bünting Teehandelshaus as part of J. Bünting Beteiligungs AG). Other large tea trading houses still in existence today were founded in 1873 (Thiele & Freese in Emden) and 1887 (OnnO Behrends in Norden, today under the umbrella of Ostfriesische Tee Gesellschaft GmbH & Co. KG).

East Frisian tea is prepared in different ways. As a rule of thumb, eight to 10 grams of tea – about three heaped teaspoons – are poured over with fresh, boiling water in a preheated pot until the loose leaves are covered. The teapot should have a bulbous shape so that the tea can "float" and the aroma can fully develop. Then after three minutes it is poured over with the remaining but reheated water and then the tea is served. It then has a stimulating effect. For a calming effect it brews for two to three minutes longer. Before the tea is served, it is poured through a sieve into another preheated serving pot. The teapots are intended only for the East Frisian tea ceremony and are never used, for example for the preparation of flavoured or herbal infusions. Regarding the dosage: Some families also use the tea measure "Döpsels", low German for "tea can lid". Depending on the size, one to two "Döpsel" of tea are enough to prepare one litre of tea.

East Frisians drink tea with rock candy and cream. The pieces of rock candy are placed in thin-walled cups and the cups are filled three-quarters full with the hot tea. The tea ceremony is characterised by a soft crackling sound (a British visitor therefore called East Frisian tea "tinkletea" for the tinkling sound it makes). The first cup is poured by the host or hostess. This is because the cream spoon is moistened in it so that the absorbed cream runs off better. It is placed on top of the tea counterclockwise. This is how time is stopped, they say in East Frisia, because teatime is a period of rest and pause. The cold cream first glides down in the hot tea and then rises as a little cloud (Klöver, 2008; Klöver, 2016).

The tea is not stirred before drinking. As a result, a different taste develops with each sip: first the mildness of the cream, then the astringency of the hot tea, and finally the sweetness of the rock candy. Regular tea times together characterise the daily routine and the family and professional togetherness in East Frisia, with at least three cups of tea served: "Three cups of tea are East Frisian law." Anyone who has not put a spoon in the cup afterwards will continue to be served tea. Many East Frisians use the traditional Red Dresmer or Blue Dresmer tableware for the tea ceremony on Sundays and holidays. But there is a wide range of shapes and patterns.

East Frisian Tea – a pleasurable drink for all social classes

Due to maritime connections and geographical proximity, it is considered certain that tea came to East Frisia via the Netherlands. Starting in 1610, Dutch merchant ships brought the first small shipments to the European continent. A few decades later, Great Britain began to dominate the European tea trade with the East India Company. Representatives of orthodox medicine were "pioneers and companions of the stimulants on their triumphal march in Europe" who, among other things, presented tea as a "miracle drug" (Menninger, 2004, p. 273).

Through Bremen merchants, who were also active in the seaport city of Emden, the work of Jano Abrahamo á Gehema may have become known in East Frisia. It was published in Bremen in 1686 with the title "Edler Thee-Tranck." The physician praised tea as "a proven means to a healthy long life" and as a wonderful "water drink" and "useful and even necessary for all social classes" (á Gehema, 1686).

Towards the end of the seventeenth century, tea was not only widespread in the Netherlands, France, and England. In the seaport city of Emden, "Thee und Coffe ausgezapfft" (Emder Stadtarchiv, 1691, quotation from Kaufmann, 1989, p. 72) had been served in four privileged houses from 1691 at the latest.

Emden thus drew level with the port and trading metropolises of Italy, England, and the Republic of the United Netherlands, where coffee houses that also served tea had been set up on the model of the Orient. In the seventeenth century, moreover, an enthusiasm for the Orient had formed in courtly circles, and with it a preference for tea and coffee (Menninger, 2004, p. 321).

The East Frisian dynasty of princes was not unaffected. The diary of the margraves of Brandenburg-Bayreuth, who also visited the Aurich court during their cavalier tour in 1728, bears witness to this. An unknown scribe meticulously noted down, day by day, what was on the young princes' "educational programme." Tea and coffee times were obviously important, because he mentions them again and again in the reports. For example, on the "7th of January," a Wednesday: "All of the most illustrious lords and ladies were in the allhiesigen Reith-Hauße and had most of the school horses (of which there were quite a few true ones) ridden by the stable master, and also drank Thée and Caffée there" (Jhering, 2005, p. 115). On the "27th of April," a Tuesday, it says: "at 8 o'clock, however, the two most illustrious lords of the Margraves drank Thée once again at the Reigning Princess [. . .]" (Jehring, 2005, p. 129).

At the time, tea was not reserved for the dynasty of princes in East Frisia. In 1718, it is reported that among the marsh farmers on the coast, "it was becoming fashionable to drink tea." Around that time, there were already three tea merchants in the town of Norden. Also, in the neighbouring town of Aurich, a Dutch distiller dealing with tea asked for a settlement permit (Haddinga, 2015, p. 55). In 1725, the Drost of the provincial towns of Greetsiel and Pewsum offered a silver tea box to the person who would sell the most expensive horse at the newly established Pewsum market (Drees, n.d.).

Information about the spread of tea in East Frisia is also provided by events in the last third of the eighteenth century. The then sovereign Frederick II, King of Prussia, also ruled over East Frisia. At first, the Prussian state itself earned money from the imports of coffee and tea. In 1751, the "Royal Prussian Asian Company from Emden to Canton and China" was founded. Two years later, the company ship "König von Preußen" landed half a million pounds of tea in Emden after its first voyage. However, the Prussian merchant fleet was only granted six voyages. It was disbanded in 1764 (Suebsmann, 2015, p. 35).

The Prussian state could now no longer earn money from the Asian trade and from the import of tea and coffee. The royal advisors made it clear to King Frederick II that if consumption continued, large sums of the money earned in his East Frisian province would flow abroad. Finally, in 1778, tea and also coffee drinking were to be banned. The East Frisian authorities defended themselves massively because all classes of the population were used to drinking tea. Even the servants could not be deprived of tea without running the risk that they would migrate to the Netherlands:

> The use of tea and coffee is so general and so deeply rooted in this country that the nature of man would have to be reversed by a creative force if they were suddenly to say good night to these beverages [. . .]. If the state has to save money, it must not be at the expense of the man in the street [. . .] Tea and coffee, however, belong to the true comforts of life according to traditional custom. (Acta, 1779)

Useful tea delight: covering your thirst

The climate and drinking water conditions in East Frisia certainly contributed to the spread of tea drinking. The harsh coastal climate with high rainfall and high humidity almost demanded a hot drink. Buttermilk and beer were the first two options prior to the introduction of tea. Drinking water, on the other hand, was scarce and often not very digestible. In the coastal marshlands, only brackish water – a mixture of salt and fresh water – could be obtained. The groundwater in the wells was quickly contaminated with insects and plants, and foul odors developed in hot weather. The same was true for the so called "Backen" (cisterns).

Tea and also coffee offered the possibility of obtaining a wholesome and hot beverage despite the poor quality of the water. The poor population in the newly founded moor colonies from the eighteenth century onward preferred tea to coffee, because coffee beans had to be elaborately roasted and ground before processing (Kaiser, 1995, pp. 11 ff.). Tea, on the other hand, could be infused several times and thus stretched. This practice can be seen in an article published in the Emder Zeitung in 1820. Many thousands of people would have drunk tea "only as warm water," "by simply puring the tea leaves over and over again with brewed water" (Emder Zeitung, May 18th, 1820, quotation after Kaufmann, 1989, p. 144).

One of the poorest moor colonies in East Frisia at that time was Moordorf. Today, the open-air museum "Museum of Poverty" presents the extremely difficult living situation of the first inhabitants who began to settle there at the end of the eighteenth century. Around 1820, the moor colonists mainly subsisted on potatoes with salt, bread, and buckwheat pancakes. There was no clean drinking water (Arends, 1818, pp. 429 ff.). The schoolmaster of the village criticised in a letter to the authorities in Aurich that children used to drink from a waterhole to quench their thirst. The waterhole, however, was a cattle watering place (Viehtränke, 1846).

Despite this obvious poverty, the inhabitants afforded tea and also the accessories necessary for its preparation. The parish of Victorbur received the estate of those who had received poor relief in Moordorf. After the colonist Folkerts died, the church received, among other things, a teapot and a tea caddy. After the death of the colonist Casjens, it received from her estate a teapot, a "Teesackje," a tea caddy and small utensils for the preparation of tea (Protocollum, 1782).

Black tea on the rise

Torsten Kaufmann, in his very detailed analysis of tea drinking in East Frisia, concludes

> that [also] in the cities – especially in Emden – a solution to the drinking water problem took place through an accelerated change from beer to coffee and tea since the first half of the 18th century [. . .]. There, the servants belonging to the lower class and the labourers employed on the farms also received these beverages as part of their everyday diet (Kaufmann, 1989, p. 114).

He notes the same for the coastal marshlands: "Even the servants and hired day labourers there received thin tea infusions daily, which were also cheaper than other beverages or the traditional porridge diet" (Kaufmann, 1989, p. 143).

Kaufmann concludes that around 1820 almost one third of the then approximately 134,000 inhabitants of East Frisia, and thus all social groups in East Frisia, drank tea daily. At that time, however, tea was mostly consumed as a thin infusion because it was expensive. At most, "visitor tea," i.e., tea for guests, had a stronger consistency. Also, around that time, the same amount of black tea (varieties such as "Pecco," "Souchong," "Congo," and "Bohe," estimated by Kaufmann as mediocre) and green tea was sold (Emder Zeitung, May 18, 1820, p. 330, quotation after Kaufmann, 1989, p. 130).

In the years 1815 to 1866, East Frisia belonged to Hanover and at times also to Great Britain, because King George IV was King of the United Kingdom of Great Britain and Ireland and of Hanover in personal union from 1820 to 1830. The so called "England fashion" led to the urban and rural upper classes (rich marsh farmers) increasingly drinking tea: "As a result, tea – especially green tea – received a social revaluation" (Kaufmann, 1989, p. 143). On special occasions, marsh farmers served their guests green tea – "Uxim" and "Haisan" – as a contemporary account states (Arends, 1820, p. 428). Around the middle of the nineteenth century, black tea already accounted for two-thirds of the amount of tea consumed (Kaufmann, 1989, p. 154).

Cheers tea!

There could be another reason why tea drinking spread quickly and to all social classes. As early as 1530, the East Frisian scholar Henricus Ubbius had criticised the excessive consumption of alcohol in East Frisia. He wrote about his compatriots that through the excessive consumption of Hamburg beer they "squandered a good part of their fortune in it and in the process killed each other in intoxication" (Ubben, 1930, pp. 9 ff.)

Around 1700, Calvinists and then also Pietists took massive action against excessive alcohol consumption. Karl Wassenberg evaluated a large number of the pious writings that appeared after tea became known in East Frisia in the seventeenth century. He writes of a changing perception of drinking: "[. . .] the strict Calvinist social ethic made 'boozing,' like all revelry, a problem" (Wassenberg, 1992, p. 239).

Tea and coffee seemed to be sent by God. Thus, at the beginning of the eighteenth century, the reformed preacher and pietist Wilhelmus Schortinghuis, who was active for a time in the East Frisian town of Weener, praised tea and coffee beyond all measure in one of his songs of edification. In "De Sondaar ontdeckt, Coffy of Thee drinkende," the third stanza reads (loosely translated): "While drinking tea or coffee, the sinner discovers: the East brings us coffee beans,/ With the pleasant tea,/ Abundant for refreshment,/ And the water of your throne in the/ Clouds, makes that escape us:/ You have done all well" (Schortinghuis, 1727, quoted in Wassenberg, 1991, p. 64).

Karl Wassenberg stated that religiously motivated opponents of the drug alcohol made tea, in particular, popular in East Frisia as an alternative to coffee. The drug tea[3] "became a "God's drug" and "with increasing tendency, the East Frisians seem to define themselves by their drug tea. It has become so far removed from its reference that it has become one itself. One is no longer a tea-drinking Calvinist, one is a tea-drinker" (Wassenberg, 1991, p. 129).

---

3 Black tea contains caffeine (formerly known as "tein") and is one of the legal stimulant drugs.

Small peculiarities on the fringe of the East Frisian tea ceremony may remind us of this time. During the dignified tea ceremony, East Frisians often jokingly bring the first cup to their mouths with a "Cheers Tea!"[4] They toast each other as one would do when drinking beer. Bourgeois households stored their precious tea sets in the "Buddelei," a small single door hanging cupboard with sloping side walls. Actually, the "Buddel" brandy and some drinking glasses stood there. In East Frisia, however, it housed everything needed for the tea ceremony: "blue- and red-flowered Dresden porcelain teaware, a teapot (low german 'Trekpot') and cups [. . .] as well as saucers (low german 'Schöddelkes' – for pouring over quite deep) [. . .] cream spoons and sugar tongs" (Lüpkes, 1925, p. 44).

Fine tea parties

In the East Frisian towns, "Theegesellschaften" came into fashion. As elsewhere, the East Frisian middle classes adopted certain forms of aristocratic culture. In doing so, it oriented itself on supraregional models. In 1809, for example, the Weimar court chef François le Goullon described in his work *The Elegant Theetable* how tea should be served when having company. The book also contains recipes for pies, cakes, and pastries (le Goullon, 1829). At the beginning of the nineteenth century, the historian Hofrath Tileman Dothias Wiarda reported on evening gatherings in his hometown of Aurich that lasted up to four hours: "Ladies have now also begun to hold *theegesell-schaften* among themselves, as they then often gather 20, 30 and more ladies together [. . .]. Now the finest pastries are ordered from confectioners, who were previously unknown, and served up" (Wiarda, 1832, p. 114).

There was no shortage of fine porcelain. On its first voyage to China alone, the afore-mentioned merchant ship "König von Preußen" brought around 140,000 pieces of porcelain back to Emden in 1751. More than two thirds of these were tea and coffee cups. In addition, 255 tea sets and 239 teapots had been taken on board. The goods were sold at public auction. Not only German, but also Dutch, Brabant, and Scandinavian traders participated in these auctions in the duty-free Emden free port (Suebsmann 2015, pp. 35 ff.)

The teaware also found buyers in East Frisia. Emden merchants advertised in 1756 with "allerhande Soorten van het nieuws aangekoomen Porcellain en Thee, in 't kleine en in 't groote to een civile Prys te bekoomen" ("Porcelain and tea, newly arrived and available in small and large quantities at a civil price") (Weekly Ostfriesische Anzeigen und Nachrichten, Sep 20th, 1756, citation after Suebsmann, 2015, pp. 44–45)

---

4 A brochure published on the occasion of the newly designed experience exhibition in the East Frisian Tea Museum Norden was entitled "Cheers Tea" (Cf. brochure "Cheers Tea").

Towards the end of the eighteenth century, porcelain from Thuringian manufactories also entered the East Frisian market. The Wallendorf "Rood Dresmer" and "Blau Dresmer" became fashionable. In addition, East Frisian porcelain painters had unpainted teaware brought to them to design and sell themselves. "Dresmer" is the Low German expression for "Dresdener." The porcelain got its name from the old "Dresdener Hofform." The typical hemispherical ribbed cups and accessories were exported from Thuringia to East Frisia until shortly before the Second World War and then again after the fall of the Berlin Wall. Even today, both shapes are considered typical for the East Frisian tea table. Red Dresmer is sold under the name "East Frisian Rose" (botanical model: "Centifolia, the hundred-leave") (see figure G.3.1.1.), while the Blue Dresmer with blue intertwined lines and flowers is offered under the name "Strawflower".

Figure G.3.1.1: East Frisian Tea China, designed with the typical pattern "East Frisian Rose".
Source: Ostfriesisches Teemuseum, Norden (www.teemuseum.de)

The tea ceremony also boosted the arts and crafts. The eighteenth and nineteenth centuries were the heyday of goldsmithing and silversmithing in East Frisia. Elaborately decorated teapots, tea caddies, kluntje tongs (for crushing candy pieces), cream spoons, tea scoops, tea strainers, and teaspoons were created. Even today, artisans make brass teapots. A silverware factory near Hanover – founded in 1821 – still produces teaspoons with the "original Burgdorf East Frisian pattern."[5] They are an important part of the traditionally set tea table (Klöver, 2008, pp. 18 ff.)

The paintings of the painter and silhouette artist Caspar Dilly show that all these things were in use. He traveled around East Frisia around 1825 and portrayed peasant families on the Geest and in the Marsch. About 30 of his works are still in family pos-

---

5 The "Frisia" model was designed by company founder Otto Kropp, https://burgdorfer-silberwaren fabrik.de/, accessed February 8th, 2024. The silverware factory was founded in Burgdorf near Hanover in 1821.

session or are kept in museums and collections. Often women, men, and children are sitting at the set table: sugar pots, milk jugs, large and small pots, porcelain for tea or coffee, plus water containers made of pewter and brass with a crane as a serving device, étagères, and cake trays (Ottenjann, 2003, p. 35; Krueger & Urban, 2010, p. 23). Dilly also depicts the custom at that time of drinking tea from a saucer. Even around the year 2000, there were occasional East Frisians who let the hot tea cool with rock candy in the saucer and then sipped it with relish.[6]

Drinking tea creates East Frisian identity

After the British began to export Assam and Darjeeling teas produced in India, among others, around 1860, more and more black tea was drunk in East Frisia. The organisation of British planters and manufacturers in India joined together to form a "Calcutta Tea Syndicate." They also operated a branch in Emden since 1884 and thus not only gained influence on the East Frisian tea market, but also pushed back coffee. "From a pound of coffee you can make 50 to 60 cups of drink, from a pound of tea, on the other hand, 250 to 260 cups (with double infusion even 500 cups)," it was said in a newspaper article in 1887. Calculated per cup, tea cost only half as much as coffee (Leerer Anzeigenblatt June 16h, 1887, quotation after Kaufmann, 1989, p. 150).

Towards the end of the nineteenth century, East Frisia felt itself to be a "tea nation," as the following report suggests:

> How significant the consumption of thee is in East Frisia, especially in the western part of it [. . .] can be seen from the fact that in 1878, 7876 'Kwart' crates weighing 37,5 kg each were exported from Amsterdam to East Frisia alone, 5686 to Russia, 1415 to Hamburg and Bremen, and only 115 crates to the rest of Germany. The whole of Germany imported 31358 centners of tea in 1868 [. . .] so at least 8000 hundredweight (of it), thus over the fourth part of the whole German consumption, is consumed in East Frisia (de Vries; Focken (1881), pp. 276 ff.)

Consequently, the people of East Frisia increasingly focused on regional values and cultural heritage ("Heimatbewegung") and developed identity-forming characteristics. The recollection of local customs was booming. Local history societies were also founded in East Frisia, such as the Norderland Local History Society in 1922.[7]

An explicit East Frisian tea ceremony did not yet exist at that time, states Torsten Kaufmann. It was only "crowned" as such at that time. Social differences between the wealthy farmers of the marsh, the less well-off people on the Geest, and the poor moor colonists were ignored. In the households of wealthy marshland farmers, valuable teaware became a benchmark for cultural heritage. "Magnificent silver utensils for tea"

---

6 Note Matthias Bergmann, Aurich, in January 27, 2022.
7 Today the sponsor of the East Frisian Tea Museum Norden.

were regarded as an example of local pride, documenting the East Frisian custom of drinking tea. *"What could be more obvious than to assume that tea drinking was also a 'Frisian custom', even to regard tea as 'the East Frisian national drink of the house, especially of the women', which had been prepared 'in the trekpot – be it a silver one or one made of Dresden porcelain with red or blue flowers on a ribbed base'?"* (Kaufmann, 1989, p. 162, quotation after Lüpkes, 1925, p. 61).

The East Frisian middle class, who remained loyal to the "Heimatbewegung" in order to preserve local values and customs, would have subordinated their way of enjoying tea to the broad masses of the people. This included drinking tea as a strong infusion with cream and rock candy. This way of consuming tea, which was declared to be the norm, was eventually adopted as a pattern of action by all strata of the population. It was this that made it the East Frisian tea ceremony. And it led to coffee being drunk – if at all – in many families only on Sundays and holidays.

"Wenn wi kien Tee hebben, dann mutten wi starven"

The identification with the East Frisian tea culture was shown again and again over the course of the twentieth century by reactions to actual or feared shortages of tea. After the beginning of the Second World War, tea was classified as an expendable luxury food. From the age of 35, each adult was entitled to only 20 grams of tea per month. Apparently, the discontent about this became so great among the population that the National Socialists proclaimed the officially defined "East Frisian Tea Drinking District" and introduced a "tea card" for extra tea rations according to an "Oldenburg Tea Distribution Key." The common saying that is still widespread in East Frisia today probably dates from that time: "Wenn wi kien Tee hebben, dann mutten wi starven!" ("If we don't have tea, then we have to die!"). Even after the war ended, tea was still scarce. Some women sewed bags in their petticoats and smuggled tea from the neighbouring Netherlands across the border in them. In 1952, a few overweight ("overloaded") women were caught. They had hidden almost 1.5 hundredweight of tea in their dresses and had appeared a bit too bulky to the customs officials.[8]

The times of the "tea deficiency" were obviously burned deep into the collective memory of the East Frisians. Employees of tea companies reported that older people in particular still tend to stock up. This became clear in 2003 in the run-up to the Iraq war. At that time, boxes of up to 25 kilograms of tea were reportedly sold to private individuals (Klöver, 2008, p. 81). Families also stockpiled tea at the beginning of the Covid pandemic.

---

8 Exhibition Bünting Tea Museum Leer.

Summary and outlook

Tea has been drunk in East Frisia for more than three centuries. The hot beverage was able to establish itself very quickly and in all strata of the population for two main reasons. There was a lack of good drinking water. Only tea made it drinkable. At the same time, Calvinist and pietist circles used it as a non-intoxicating substitute for alcohol. The drug "tea" became the "God's drug" and finally the "everyday drug." By 1820, more than a third of the population drank green and black tea. Toward the end of the century, there was a marked shift toward black tea. Today, the "Echte Ostfriesische Mischung" (Original East Frisian blend – trademarked, if blended in East Frisia) is produced in East Frisia from mainly Assam teas and various other varieties. Due to porcelain imports and products of the local silversmiths, fashions of tea drinking developed in upscale circles in the eighteenth and nineteenth centuries, following the English model. This was recognised and declared universally valid by those who were committed to preserving cultural heritage and customs ("Heimatbewegung"). The "East Frisian tea ceremony" developed into an identity-forming "national" cultural asset that is still practised today. The German UNESCO Commission listed the East Frisian tea culture in 2016 as an Intangible Cultural Heritage in Germany. This is another reason why the East Frisian tea ceremony is becoming increasingly significant for tourism marketing. The of East Frisia (Ostfriesische Landschaft) put tea drinking on its agenda from October 2020 to March 2022, in particular to once again highlight the value of this intangible cultural heritage for tourism. The central question is how to achieve a valorisation of the intangible cultural heritage in an entire region with bundling cultural, tourist, and gastronomic competencies (Ostfriesische Landschaft, 2021).

In addition, two other tea related awards have been recognised: In 2021, the inclusion of the East Frisian tea consumption as world record in the Book of Records (formerly the Guinness Book of Records), and also the award to be one of the best local history museums in Germany for the Ostfriesisches Teemuseum Norden (East Frisian Tea Museum, Norden) as an acknowledgement of presenting the East Frisian, but also national and international tea cultures impressively, being an extra curricular and digital place of learning to address also children, young people, and new citizens.

However, local officials see a need for action in the development of standards for the hotel and restaurant industry, which often has foreign owners and employees. Bagged tea served in glasses and mugs is not uncommon in East Frisia, even in these areas. The East Frisian tea ceremony should be brought back into focus there and also be made accessible to tourists and visitors. At the cultural agency of the regional association of East Friisa (Ostfriesische Landschaft) an expert advisory board, "Tea culture East Frisia," develops among other things a quality seal, which vouches for the quality of the East Frisian tea ceremony practiced in the respective gastronomic mechanisms. Multilingual flyers with information about the East Frisian Tea Ceremony will be available in hotels, vacation apartments, restaurants, and tea rooms. Training courses for tour guides and gastronomic staff are being planned (Ostfriesische Landschaft,

2022, p. 15). The Ostfriesland Tourismus GmbH is marketing the theme of "tea" as a special culinary feature (Ostfriesland Kulinarik, 2024).

References

Acta (1779). Die Abstellung des übermäßigen Thee und Caffe trinken. Dep I Nr. 3129/ 1778–79, Niedersächsisches Landesarchiv, Abteilung Aurich. Bericht vom 11.5.1779.

Arends, F. (1818). Ostfriesland und Jever in geographischer, statistischer und besonders landwirtschaftlicher Hinsicht. Emden 1818 Bd. 1. Unveränd. Nachdruck Verlag Schuster 1974.

Arends, F. (1820). Ostfriesland und Jever in geographischer, statistischer und besonders landwirthschaftlicher Hinsicht. Emden 1820 Bd. 3. Unveränd. Nachdruck Verlag Schuster 1974.

De Vries, J.F. & Focken, T. (1881). *Ostfriesland. Land und Volk in Wort und Bild*. Unveränd. Neudruck d. Ausg. Sändig Wiesbaden.

Drees, H. (n.d.). Gehörten Tee, Kaffee, Zucker, Sirup und Tabak in Ostfriesland schon vor 1665 zum Bedürfnis des täglichen Lebens? Unveröff. Manuskript 413 (284 A * B) Landschaftsbibliothek Aurich.

à Gehema, J.A. (1686). *Edler Thee-Tranck*. Bremen.

Haddinga, J. (2015). Die ostfriesische Teekultur und ihre Geschichte. In A. Kanzenbach & D. Suebsmann, pp. 55–63.

Jhering, M. (2005). *Hofleben in Ostfriesland*. Hannover.

Kaiser, H. (1995). Der große Durst: Von Biernot und Branntweinfeinden – rotem Bordeaux und schwarzem Kaffee. 2. Auflage, Stiftung Museumsdorf Cloppenburg.

Kanzenbach, A. & Suebsmann, D. (2015). Made in China. Porzellan und Teekultur im Nordwesten im 18. Jahrhundert. Ein Kapitel Handelsgeschichte. Isensee Verlag.

Kaufmann, T. (1989). Un drink ʼn Koppke Tee . . . Zur Sozialgeschichte des Teetrinkens in Ostfriesland. Museumsfachstelle der ostfriesischen Landschaft.

Kloever, H. (2008). *Tee in Ostfriesland*, Sambucus Verlag.

Klöver, H. (2016). Tee in Ostfriesland – Ostfriesische Teezeremonie. Retrieved February 7, 2024, from https://www.youtube.com/watch?v=d78fZJX3lmE.

Krueger, T., Urban, A., Linnemann, H., & Ziegan, U. (2010). Die heißen 3: 300 Jahre Kaffee, Tee und Schokolade in Norddeutschland. Historisches Museum Hannover.

le Goullon, F. (1829). Der elegante Theetisch, oder die Kunst, einen glänzenden Zirkel auf eine geschmackvolle und anständige Art ohne großen Aufwand zu bewirthen. Verlag Wilhelm Hoffmann. Reprint der 2. Aufl. Weimar 1829. Leipzig 1985.

Lüpkes, W. (1991). Ostfriesische Volkskunde, 2. durchges. und erw. Auflage Emden 1925. Reprint Verlag Schuster.

Menninger, A. (2004). Genuss im kulturellen Wandel. Tabak, Kaffee, Tee und Schokolade in Europa (16. –19. Jahrhundert). Franz Steiner Verlag.

Meyer, T. (2019). Das regionalgeschichtliche Phänomen 'Moordorf'. Ostfrieslands berüchtigster Ort im 18. und 19. Jahrhundert. Diplomica.

Ostfriesische Landschaft. (2022). Praxisleitfaden nachhaltiger Kulturtourismus: Inwertsetzung von Immateriellem Kulturerbe in Niedersachsen am Beispiel der Ostfriesischen Teekultur. Kulturagentur der Ostfriesischen Landschaft.

Ostfriesland Kulinarik. (2024). Tee. Retrieved February 7, 2024, from https://www.ostfriesland.travel/urlaubsthemen/kulinarik/tee.

Ottenjann, H. (2003). Wandel der Stuben- und Kleidungskultur ländlicher Oberschichten im Weser-Ems-Gebiet in der 1. Hälfte des 19. Jahrhunderts, dokumentiert durch die Silhouetteure Trümpelmann und Dilly (1804–1841). In K.-H. Ziessow &. K. Thomas (Eds.). *Die gute Stube*. Museum im Schloss, Porzellanmanufaktur Fürstenberg.

Protocollum. (1782). Protocollum oder öffentliches Verzeichnis derjenigen so seit 1782 in der Victorburer Gemeinde, zur beständigen Armenpflege aufgenommen worden und vermöge Königlichen Befehls von da an, hierin als solche verzeichnet stehen, deren Güter der gedruckten Armenordnung gemäß nach ihrem Tode der Armencasse hierselbst zufallen sollen). Quoted in T. Meyer (2019). Das regionalgeschichtliche Phänomen 'Moordorf'. Ostfrieslands berüchtigster Ort im 18. und 19. Jahrhundert. Diplomica, p. 46.

Rekord-Institut. (2021). "Und was ist mit Tee?" Retrieved February 1, 2022, from https://rekord-institut.org/und-was-ist-mit-tee/.

Schortinghuis, W. (1727). *Geestelike Gesangen tot Ontdekkinge, Overtuiginge, Bestieringe, en opwekkinge van Allerley Soorten van Menschen*. Jurjen Spandaw Publisher.

Suebsmann, D. (2015). Das chinesische Porzellan der "Königlich-Preußischen Asiatischen Compagnie von Emden" 1753–1756. In A. Kanzenbach & D. Suebsmann, *Made in China. Porzellan und Teekultur im Nordwesten im 18. Jahrhundert. Ein Kapitel Handelsgeschichte*. Isensee Verlag, pp. 33–47.

Teetied. (2016). "Teetied – die Teezeremonie in Ostfriesland." Retrieved Feb 7th, 2024 from https://www.youtube.com/watch?v=WnjzFSE_zDM.

Ubben, H. (1930). Die Beschreibung Ostfrieslands von Henricus Ubbius vom Jahre 1530. Ohling.

Ubbius, H., & Ritter, F. (1913). Die Beschreibung von Ostfriesland vom Jahre 1530. Gesellschaft für bildende Kunst und vaterländ. Altertümer zu Emden.

UNESCO. (2016). "Ostfriesische Teekultur." Retrieved February 7, 2022, from https://www.unesco.de/kultur-und-natur/immaterielles-kulturerbe/immaterielles-kulturerbe-deutschland/ostfriesischer-tee.

Viehtränke (1846). Schreiben an das Amt Aurich v. 8.8.1846. Niedersächsisches Landesarchiv, Abteilung Aurich, Rep. 26 b, Nr. 365. Zitat in Meyer, T. (2019). Das regionalgeschichtliche Phänomen 'Moordorf'. Ostfrieslands berüchtigster Ort im 18. und 19. Jahrhundert. Diplomica, p. 178.

Wassenberg, K. (1991). *Tee in Ostfriesland: Vom religiösen Wundertrank zum profanen Volksgetränk*. Verlag Schuster.

Wassenberg, K. (1992). Tee im Prozeß ostfriesischer Zivilisation. In *Rondom Eems en Dollard*, pp. 237–243. Van Dijk & Foorthuis REGIO-Projekt Groningen.

Wiarda, T.D. (1832). Auricher alte und neue Zeit. In *Bruchstücke zur Geschichte und Topographie der Stadt Aurich, bis zum Jahre 1813*. Reprint d. Ausg. 1832 Verlag Schuster Leer.

Marion Roehmer

G.3.2 Special elegance: East Frisian tea China

Origins and establishment of tea drinking in East Frisia

East Frisia and the Netherlands have always had a close cultural and economic relationship.[1] Since the late Middle Ages, coastal traffic in these neighbouring areas provided for lively trade with all kinds of merchandise. After the creation of the Vereenigde Oostindische Compagnie, a long-distance trade company with official privilege, Dutch ships took up sailing to China and Indonesia on a regular basis in 1602 and far eastern goods started to arrive in Dutch and East Frisian ports. Large scale importation of spices was soon followed by green tea from China, before the mid sixteen hundreds.

Initially, tea used to be a noble beverage for princely courts, but it soon became popular among the bourgeois classes in the first half of the eighteenth century. In East Frisia, however, even among the peasant population, tea replaced the consumption of beer, which had been the everyday beverage up to then, by 1760. This everyday beverage of the rural population, which had to be highly nutritious and full of calories, was not only meant to nourish and fortify, but also had to replace full meals. Water by itself was no use in this respect.

Thus, with the introduction of cane sugar from the British and Spanish colonies, tea became the ideal energy drink for East Frisia. Different methods and customs of eking out sugar candy, which was very expensive, stem from that time. Tea became part of everyday life. At every break in working hours, working men and women had some, even among the lower classes, for it was cheaper than coffee, another stimulant which the rich upper classes were fond of.

By the beginning of the eighteenth century, the British East India Company had managed to take over the larger share of the tea trade to Europe, and consequently Great Britain had become a tea drinking country, too. The British upper classes elevated tea-drinking to a social event. At the beginning of the nineteenth century, the British way of life became fashionable all over the continent and in East Frisia, too.

Britishness was celebrated in the way people designed their gardens and parks, how they dressed, how they ate and drank, including the distinguished evening tea parties. Evidently, this kind of influence also affected the East Frisian upper class, and so having teatime became the hallmark of the upper class and of East Frisian society as a whole. Since the early eighteen hundreds, tea had become the "national" beverage of the East Frisians.

---

1 I am much obliged to Gerd Thieltges for translating.

https://doi.org/10.1515/9783110758573-029

Even when, during the nineteenth century, coffee became the favourite drink of all strata of German society, the East Frisians held on to their tea, even if it was merely for economic reasons, which was served nevertheless in thin white porcelain cups.

Chinese porcelain for Chinese tea

Before the middle of the seventeenth century, the Dutch traders were importing, along with Chinese tea, Chinese porcelain, which was used as a drinking vessel for the new hot drink, combined with such accessories as kettles etc. So, Chinese porcelain was largely used in East Frisia, when, at the same time, in the eastern parts of Germany it could only be found in the porcelain cabinets of princes. The shape of the vessels that were sold corresponded strictly to their function, namely tea drinking (Roehmer, 2010). Only small bulbous cups with a circular foothold were to be used. At the same time in China, these were used for the drinking of tea, but also for rice wine – sake – and for religious offerings. Upon their arrival in the ports, these new drinking vessels, called "Koppchen" in modern German, "Kopje" in Dutch, and "Koppke" in low German, were immediately auctioned off to intermediaries.

These drinking cups, however, following the well-known example of cacao, were not to be put on the table such as they were, without any support, although this was customary in China and Japan. What the traders imported and sold, was a combined offer of kopjes and small flat dishes with an ascending rim, which was to be used as "sauce dish" or "saucer." In China they were not manufactured as a set, since the Chinese used them as small plates to offer food. Consequently, at the beginning, there were no same patterned cups and saucers. It can be mentioned here that the saucers were always intended to serve as a kind of tray or platter for putting the cups, which were without a handle and possibly steaming hot, on the table or lifting them up to the mouth. Drinking from the saucers was a habit which was frowned upon by all and sundry, and the contemporaries often made ample fun of such behaviour (Roehmer, 2019).

A major element of tea drinking sets was the kettle, with a strongly accented bulbous contour, and a steep spout situated at the upper third of the vessel. This original form, which was transformed in Europe later, also stems from contemporary Chinese moulds and was imported together with the rest. The preparation of the tea served in these kettles followed the example of Chinese tea preparation in the seventeenth and mostly eighteenth centuries: the basis was green tea, from which, following the Far Eastern example, an extract was concocted that was diluted with water according to everybody's taste. Therefore, the extremely small tea kettles from this period can be regarded as special mini kettles meant to provide for a highly concentrated solution. From these kettles, a small amount of tea was poured into the kopje and replenished with water. It was only over the course of the eighteenth century that people started serving pastry and biscuits for teatime. These were proffered on a porcelain tray (see Figure G.3.2.1) and one took them with their fingers to eat them, one at the time, when they were offered the tray. This is a custom that continues to exist in East Frisia today.

Figure G.3.2.1: Wallendorf rose décor tray.
Source: Ostfriesisches Teemuseum Norden

Chinese porcelain for Europe

Nowadays porcelain, to us, appears to be very ordinary, but it is a man-made, artificial material, which could not but fascinate people when it first made its appearance in Europe. The main reason for this is the snow-white look of the substance whose lustrous splendour is heightened by its brilliant glaze. Up to the end of the Middle Ages, Europeans, in their material world, were acquainted with only one single substance that, with its glossy white surface, came close to this wondrous new stuff. There was, since Antiquity, a kind of shell from the Pacific Ocean, which was known all over the Mediterranean due to long distance trade: the Kauri- or Venus-snail. The Italians, because of its form, called it *porcella* (= piglet), and this term was instrumental in the naming of "porcelain" (see Figure G.3.2.2).

Figure G.3.2.2: Kauri shell.
Source: private

There was no real "invention" of porcelain in China; you might rather speak of an evolution. From the seventh century argillaceous earth was mined at Kaoling Mountain near the town of Jingdezhen in Eastern China, which gave its name to Kaolin, or China clay, the main ingredient of porcelain. This earthen clay was not homogeneous, but over several centuries the mines advanced to layers that were richer and richer in Kaolin. So, the original grey stoneware that resulted from the firing of the clay from Kaoling Mountain became brighter and brighter, until white vessels could be produced from it. Natural traces of feldspar and quartz sand made the vessels ever denser and more homogeneous so that they became close to modern day China. In the middle of the fourteenth century, the emperor of China turned the Jingdezhen production sites into imperial manufactories. Some of this white porcelain was traded to Persia and the Arabic empires, from where the merchants returned with cobalt and vessels painted with cobalt blue designs. Soon, the Chinese recognised the positive qualities of cobalt, which, after firing in the kiln, turns into an immutable and brilliant blue colour. They started cobalt painting under the glaze, a kind of decoration technique that was strongly fostered by the imperial household and which, up to the present, has remained the most popular porcelain design (see Figure G.3.2.3).

The re-invention of porcelain in Germany

During all of the sixteenth and seventeenth centuries, foremost in France and Italy, learned alchemists strove to uncover the secret of how to make porcelain. The results of all these attempts have been summarised under the telltale name of "Pseudoporzellan." It was either very clear stoneware or earthenware with a white glaze, or the so-

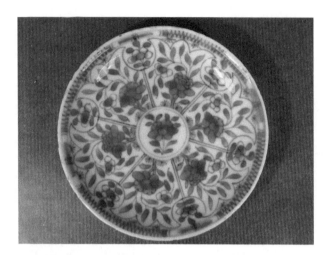

Figure G.3.2.3: Chinese underglaze blue painting plate.
Source: Ostfriesisches Teemuseum Norden

called "Frittenporzellan" which does not contain any kaolin or clay in their mass, but consist mainly of feldspar, quartz, and alabaster. Any small bruise made the substitute apparent, despite the shiny and perfect surface.

Finally, the reinvention of China was successfully performed by Johann Friedrich Böttger (1682–1719). At his side, at the Saxon court in Dresden, there were outstanding experts like Count Ehrenfried Walter von Tschirnhaus, who had been studying, for quite some time, the melting process in clay and glass, especially at temperatures higher than usual. He introduced Böttger to the physical side of the preparation of the material and of the firing process. Of equal importance for Böttger was the Saxon "Bergrat" and chemist Carl Eugen Pabst von Ohain, who knew all about minerals in the kingdom of Saxony and the quality of the materials contained therein. These two learned men, in turn, benefitted from Böttger's assiduous zeal and stubbornness in experimenting. So, the second invention of porcelain was performed in Saxony at the beginning of the eighteenth century. In the year of 1708, the first porcelain manufactory of Europe was founded at Dresden, soon to be transferred the Albrechtsburg at Meißen. In 1717, there was the successful creation of the highly appreciated and much coveted "Blaumalerei," a cobalt-blue transparent glazing décor.

It was in vain that they tried, in Meißen, to keep the chemical and technological mysteries of porcelain production secret. Already in 1718, another manufactory was founded at Vienna, which in 1720 was followed by Venice. Up until 1755 further manufactories were established at Höchst, Fürstenberg, Wegely at Berlin, Frankenthal, Ludwigsburg, and Ansbach. Outside of Germany, you can name Naples, Mennecy-Villeroy, Sèvres-Vincennes and Saint Petersburg. The arcane knowledge of porcelain production had begun to spill over much of Europe.

The founding of porcelain manufactories in Thuringia

It is well known that, for a long time, the Meißen manufactory set the standards and styles of porcelain production in Germany. But its clear commercial success made it also a prime example in the economic thinking of the period. Many a prince pondered the economic advantages of granting the privilege of founding a porcelain manufactory. Essential for the success of such an enterprise was the possibility of attracting trained specialists, and disposing of the respective raw materials. In Thuringia, both requirements were united in its proximity to Saxony and the similarity of geological conditions, including the abundant forests.

This made for a rapid sequence of new porcelain manufactories from 1760 onwards. These early foundations were provided with exclusive privileges in order to ascertain financial viability for the entrepreneurs; at the same time the extreme division of the dukedom of Thuringia, a consequence of the "Ernestine Separations," made possible the existence of eleven manufactories in a relatively restricted area. Consequently, by the beginning of the nineteenth century, the reputation of Thuringia as a porcelain country was obvious.

Concerning exportation to East Frisia, the most important Thuringian manufactories are Wallendorf (privilege of 1763), Limbach (privilege of 1772) and Rauenstein (privilege of 1783), while smaller quantities of porcelain were imported from Volkstedt (start of production in 1762), Ilmenau (privilege of 1777), and the more recent manufactories of Eisenberg (privilege of 1796) and Elgersburg (start of production in 1806). These new manufactories took their forms and decors from the Meißen example. However, after the founding period, they had to open up new markets in order to continue to exist in the face of the great manufactories like Meißen, Vienna or Fürstenberg. This was achieved, firstly, by the production, from porcelain, of household items and consumer goods, which previously had been fabricated from other materials, and secondly by expanding into rural areas. It was no coincidence for the rural north-west to fit this description: the Thuringian carriers, who were paramount in the distribution of all kinds of wares and finished goods from the Thuringian Forest region, were quite familiar with this area because they were wont to collect their young horses from the Oldenburg country (Roehmer). Bremen and Hamburg quickly became the centres of porcelain trade to the north, and also served as distribution hubs for the more distant rural areas. The volume of the trade increased rapidly: one Hamburg merchant receiving goods worth 495 Reichtaler (currency at that time) in 1789 from Wallendorf, and received delivery of 2,233 Reichstaler worth of porcelain in 1799 (Jena, 1902). Strangely for this porcelain, it lost its place of origin in the process. The intermediaries thought that they could ask for a higher price if they called their wares "Dresmer Teegood," i.e., Dresden tea table ware, which was to suggest that it stemmed from the Meißen manufactory. As a consequence of this, the East Frisian tea drinkers never knew that their tea porcelain had been produced in Thuringia (Roehmer, 2010).

The East Frisian market

The Thuringian manufactories exporting to East Frisia had to consider the preferences and the limited financial means of their customers, which led to the fact that the porcelain destined to these regions took a special place in the range of their products. While, at the beginning, they marketed traditional vessels according to the Chinese canon, the cups, kettles, and dishes soon took on a more contemporary look. The surface of kettles and saucers, following the Meißen example, was structured by oblong vertical flutings, and later the broken fluted design for cups was also introduced. From approximately 1790, cups with handles were introduced, which initially cost double the price of those without handles, because their manufacture was more complicated. Since these cups represented the new fashion, they prevailed. Around 1810, cylindrical cups, some of them with square handles, were marketed, but this did not win the day with conservative East Frisian buyers (see Figure G.3.2.4).

Figure G.3.2.4: Wallendorf cups with different handles.
Source: Ostfriesisches Teemuseum Norden

Basically, décor was limited to four plainly executed simple patterns. Colourful décors, or even gold-rimmed ones, for obvious financial reasons, rarely or never found their way to the East Frisian customers. These simple patterns, however, from the 1870s at the very latest, were removed from the regular range of products of the manufactories and were commissioned to homeworkers.

Traditional decors and their development

A) Red Indian Flowers decor

Since the start of porcelain importation to East Frisia in the late eighteenth century, Red Indian Flowers, i.e., simple flower designs in a woodcarving manner, was the most popular décor in East Frisian households. In traditional East Frisian families, it is well-remembered even today that the red pattern was the first one to reach their homes, and then the blue décor followed.

In fact, Red Indian Flowers was the first floral design created by Meißen, after the Eastern models, to be quickly copied in Thuringia. It progressively went through different stages of simplification that developed even further with the tea services destined for the north-west. It ended up as a schematic design there that was barely reminiscent of its floral origins (see Figures G.3.2.5 and G.3.2.6). Because of the limited timespan of exports lasting up to the 1820s, as it seems, the Red Indian Flowers decor today figures among the rarer decors in households and museums in the North-West.

Figure G.3.2.5: Wallendorf Indian flowers cup.
Source: Ostfriesisches Teemuseum Norden

B) A Distinct Form of Indian Flowers: Straw Flower-Décor (Strohblumendekor)

The Straw Flowers pattern, a blue underglaze décor, is the most fabricated décor of the eighteenth century by far, and it has lost none of its popularity up to now. It originated early, after 1730, in Meißen and was soon copied in Thuringia. Strawflowers, long lasting and universally appreciated, became a most successful décor in East Frisia, too. On the surface of the small rotund vessels of the tea table, its intricacy made for an impression of extraordinary dynamism that was highly decorative (see Figures G.3.2.7 and G.3.2.8). Without any simplifications, it was produced in Thuringia and ex-

Figure G.3.2.6: Rauenstein Indian flowers plate.
Source: Ostfriesisches Teemuseum Norden

ported up to the twentieth century, when commercial relations between Thuringian manufactories and their East Frisian customers came to an end.

Figure G.3.2.7: Wallendorf straw flowers pattern teapot.
Source: Ostfriesisches Teemuseum Norden

C) Monochrome Architectures and other Classicist Patterns

Another early pattern for exportation to East Frisia was a very simple execution of "Monochrome Architectures." Coloured or monochrome, the popular architectural drawings were a common décor of late baroque that continued to belong to the more elaborate and therefore more expensive décors in the classicist period. The Thuringian

Figure G.3.2.8: Wallendorf straw flowers pattern cup.
Source: Museum "Otto Ludwig" Eisfeld

manufactories produced tea porcelain with different architectural illustrations, only the simplest of which were exported to the north-west (see Figures G.3.2.9 and G.3.2.10).

Figure G.3.2.9: Monochrome architectures Wallendorf teapot.
Source: Ostfriesisches Teemuseum Norden

A frugal kind of drawing with heavy contours and planes composed by parallel traits, it exhibits a style of depiction common in Dutch fayence painting of the period. Large ornamental Fayence plates and tiles were popular and widespread in East Frisia at the time; they belonged to the common inventory of a well-to-do-household (see Figures G.3.2.11). There may have been a kind of reverse influence: the long-distance traders, always on the lookout for new motifs to appeal to their clients, possibly related back to the Thuringian manufactories the drawing style and the pictorial cosmos

Figure G.3.2.10: Monochrome architectures Wallendorf cup.
Source: Ostfriesisches Teemuseum Norden

of fayence painting, as a booster for new porcelain motifs (Roehmer, 2010). This familiar décor was produced for East Frisia up to the second half of the nineteenth century,
at a time when elsewhere, and for quite some time, there had been no more buyers
for this design.

Figure G.3.2.11: Harlingen Fayence plate.
Source: Schlossmuseum Jever

Even more than the Monochrome Architectures, purely classicist motifs were subject to fashion, which meant, for the East Frisian market, that they consisted exclusively of cornucopiae, friendship altars, and initials in flower garlands, in a plain form (see Figure G.3.2.12). Porcelain sets with these motifs that were first imported in limited numbers became ever more popular at the beginning of the nineteenth century, when tea gatherings became more fashionable in bourgeois circles. Elsewhere, China bedecked with friendship motifs, even if it was more expensive, was a much appreciated and prestigious gift in a region that held porcelain in high esteem.

Figure G.3.2.12: Wallendorf friendship Altar Décor.
Source: Ostfriesisches Teemuseum Norden

D) The East Frisian Rose
Next to the blue Strawflowers pattern, the East Frisian Rose was the most successful and typical décor in East Frisia. It is a variety of "German Flowers" that were, among others, produced in Thuringia under the name of "Colourful Flowers" or "Bunte Blumen."

The German Flowers design had been developed in Meißen shortly before 1740; it evidently consisted of flowers painted in a naturalist style. Among these, a certain type of rose was supreme: It was a large centifolia in delicate violet or vividly pink tones, a flower that had been cultivated in Holland in the late sixteenth century (See figure G.3.2.13). You can find it at the centre of many Flemish still lifes, and was considered the queen of roses in the eighteenth century. It comes as no surprise that this décor was among the earliest to be taken up in Thuringia, with the rose as the main element, but associated with other flowers hemmed in by a floral bouquet. The further Meißen evolution into a rose décor with a solitary flower was not taken up in Thuringia as such. It was, however, introduced in East Frisia in a simplified and less expensive form, probably at the beginning of the nineteenth century. It was so successful and appreciated from the start that not only did its name change to "East Frisian Rose," but it was in constant demand throughout the nineteenth and up to the second half of the twentieth century.

Figure G.3.2.13: Rosa Centifolia.
Source: private drawing

As the simplified rose décor was part of those executed by homeworkers, who had been introduced to their trade on the spot but had not been trained systematically, the decors turned out in different ways, according to the hand that had made them. These differences appear not only with respect to their painting styles, but also in the distribution of the motifs on the surface, as shown in this example of three kettles from Wallendorf (see Figures G.3.2.14–G.3.2.16).

Figure G.3.2.14: Wallendorf Rose décor teapot.
Source: Private collection Leer

Figure G.3.2.15: Wallendorf Rose décor teapot.
Source: Ostfriesisches Teemuseum Norden

Accordingly, the motifs on the decors were different, so that there was basically no way of assembling matched sets, although people tried to do so. This becomes apparent when you look at the tea ensembles that can still be found in traditional households that do consist of very similar specimens (see Figures G.3.2.17 and G.3.2.18).

Figure G.3.2.16: Wallendorf Rose décor teapot.
Source: Private collection Leer

Figure G.3.2.17: Wallendorf Rose décor cup.
Source: Private collection Leer

Figure G.3.2.18: Wallendorf Rose décor plate.
Source: Private collection Leer

Over the course of the nineteenth century, there was an increase in more simplified types of rose décor. It can be surmised that this happened especially in the second half of the nineteenth century when the traditional rose décor had gone completely out of fashion and was only manufactured for the conservative clientele in the north-west. This schematic rose décor was called "geschlossene Rose," "Closed Rose" (see Figure G.3.2.19). Its simple design did not impair its popularity in East Frisia. Nowadays, this variety is often called the "East Frisian Rose of the old time" or "True Frisian Rose" (echte Ostfrie-senrose), as only this type of closed rose porcelain can still be found in private hands (Roehmer, 2015).

Figure G.3.2.19: Wallendorf Rose décor teapot.
Source: Ostfriesisches Teemuseum Norden

The history of East Frisian China in the twentieth century

Thuringian porcelain exports to the North-West were temporarily interrupted by the First World War. It seems that, subsequently, only the exportation of the Straw-Flowers décor was resumed, since this was a pattern belonging to the general range of products manufactured by the Thuringian companies. The production of Rose-patterned tableware, however, was not immediately renewed in Thuringia, as it seems. Instead, the highly efficient Silesian manufactories, that experienced a strong upturn after World War I, took over this business (Schmidt, 1996). The Rose décor, by then more naturalistically styled and with a slightly clearer colouring, was put on the teacups with their assorted saucers (see Figures G.3.2.20 and G.3.2.21).

Figure G.3.2.20: Waldenburg in Schlesien, Krister Porzellan-Manufaktur AG Rose décor cup. Source: Ostfriesisches Landesmuseum Emden

It did not belong to the standard repertoire of Silesian manufactories. In the thirties again, so far as it is known up to now, two Thuringian firms, at the very least, delivered a considerable stock of small cups and dishes with the East Frisian Rose décor to the North Sea coast: Elgersburg and, to a lesser degree, Wallendorf, A typical feature of Elgersburg is the fluted surface with a smooth rim around the dishes (See figure G.3.2.22). A sample sheet that has been conserved shows this décor as "Wartburg"; it also presents, in great details, a classical tea table with all its accessories (Figure G.3.2.23).

Figure G.3.2.21: Waldenburg in Schlesien, Krister Porzellan-Manufaktur AG Rose décor plate.
Source: Ostfriesisches Landesmuseum Emden

Figure G.3.2.22: Elgersburg rose décor teapot.
Source: Private collection Norden

Figure G.3.2.23: Sample sheet Elgersburg Porzellanmanufaktur.
Source: Arbeitsgemeinschaft Massemühle Elgersburg e.V.

After the Second World War, porcelain deliveries from Thuringia came to a décors halt, due to the fact that Thuringia was situated on the other side of the Iron Curtain. At Wallendorf, as old porcelain painters can tell you, no more Frisian Roses were painted after the resumption of production in 1949.[2] The same was true for Elgersburg, where the last porcelain painter of Elgersburg manufactory died in 1956.[3]

Notwithstanding, this did not mean the end of the East Frisian Rose décor. Its unabated popularity led to the Hamburg trading company of August Warnecke, that had been importing porcelain from China since 1925, reintroducing the East Frisian Rose décor in the 1950s. The porcelain was manufactured in Japan and hand-painted in lively colours with the so-called "Closed Rose" (see Figure G.3.2.24). There were considerable quantities of China involved in this import business, which included not only tea porcelain but also crockery featuring the same design. Subsequently, these motifs were printed; the production of Rose décor was ended in 1993. A few other companies also tried to partake in this abiding interest in traditional tea porcelain, like Robert Oskar Meyer in Bremen, but none of these firms could ever reach the Warnecke market share.

---

2 For this oral information, I am grateful to Heiko Heine, Museum "Otto Ludwig" Eisfeld.
3 For this oral information, I am grateful to Wilfried Rath, Arbeitsgemeinschaft Massemühle Elgersburg e.V.

Figure G.3.2.24: August Warnecke trading company Rose décor teapot.
Source: Private collection Norden

After German Reunification in 1989, Wallendorf tried to revive the traditional décors by handicraft, but, evidently, the use of manual skills led necessarily to a price tag that foreclosed distribution on a large scale (see Figure G.3.2.25). Although it had held its rank constantly for close two hundred years, the motif itself, additionally, did not find any buyers anymore, except with the small number of connoisseurs and traditionalists who kept on appreciating it for its marked historical and aesthetic appeal. Contrary to the Straw Flowers pattern that continues to thrive, the Rose décor appears to have come to the end of its long way from Meißen German Flowers to the printed Closed Rose design from Japan.

Figure G.3.2.25: Wallendorf Rose décor teapot.
Source: Ostfriesisches Teemuseum Norden

References

All pictures have been made by the author herself. Figures, not related to private collections, are related to the permanent exhibitions at
- Museum "Otto Ludwig" Eisfeld, Marktplatz 2, 98673 Eisfeld, Germany,
  www.museum-eisfeld.info
- Schlossmuseum Jever, Schlossplatz 1, 26441 Jever, Germany,
  www.schlossmuseum.de
- Ostfriesisches Landesmuseum Emden, Brückstraße 1, 26725 Emden, Germany,
  www.landesmuseum-emden.de
- Ostfriesisches Teemuseum Norden, Am Markt 36, 26506 Norden, Germany,
  www.teemuseum.de

Roehmer, M. (2010). *Ostfriesisches Teeporzellan. Vom Thüringer Wald an die Nordseeküste*. Soltau-Kurier-Norden.

Roehmer, M. (2015). Der Weg der Rose. Thüringer Porzellan für die Nordseeküste. S. Gläser, Keramik im Spannungsfeld zwischen Handwerk und Kunst. Germanisches Nationalmuseum Nürnberg.

Roehmer, M. (2019). Tee- und Kaffeegeschirr auf dem Falkenhof. In G. Hülsmann, *Keramik*. Schnell & Steiner.

Schmidt-Stein, G. (1996). *Schlesisches Porzellan vor 1945 – Ein Beitrag zur Geschichte der deutschen Porzellanindustrie und zur schlesischen Landeskunde sowie ein Handbuch für Sammler*. Bergstadtverlag Wilhelm Gottlieb Korn.

Stieda, W. (1902). Die Anfänge der Porzellanfabrikation auf dem Thüringerwalde. G. Fischer.

Gabriella Lombardi

G.4 The Italian tea culture

Introduction

In Italy, the tea culture still needs to be discovered. Most Italians identify tea with the "normal" tea in teabags, and baristas serve it with a slice of lemon. This lack of knowledge about tea is not to blame: Italy is a relatively young country and does not have centuries of history like Great Britain. For this reason, it is justifiable. But before exploring the emerging trends in the Italian tea market, let's take a few steps back to understand its spread.

The origins

Going back through the centuries, the *Book of the Marvels of the World* created much curiosity towards Asia and its rituals. The *Book of the Marvels of the World* (Italian: Il Milione, lit. "The Million," deriving from Polo's nickname "Emilione"), in English commonly called *The Travels of Marco Polo*, is a thirteenth-century travelogue written down by Rustichello da Pisa from stories told by Italian explorer Marco Polo. It describes Polo's travels through Asia between 1271 and 1295 with his father Niccolò Polo and his paternal uncle Matteo Polo, Venetian merchants and travellers, and his experiences at the court of Kublai Khan (Polo, 1982).

The manuscripts of this book found all over the libraries and archives of Italy and Europe amount, with the latest discoveries, to one hundred and fifty. The fact that they are written in various languages (French, Latin, Italian, and Veneto dialect) and, in many ways, in a simplified and abbreviated form proves that the book had, from its first appearance, the greater diffusion allowed in those times by the lack of printing. They were the first manuscripts that satiated curiosity about distant worlds (Polo, 1982).

Compared to other travel reports written during the thirteenth century, the *Book of the Marvels of the World* was exceptional because Marco Polo testified to the existence of a very sophisticated Mongolian civilisation, absolutely comparable to European cultures: the Mongols, in short, were not just the "savage" nomads who lived on horseback and moved around in tents, but they inhabited walled cities, knew how to read, and had very elegant customs and traditions. Marco Polo is said to have been the first to describe a drink that could, most likely, be tea (Ricci, 2001).

Besides this epic book, the first European tea accounts were written in Italy during the late Renaissance, in the sixteenth century. The cultural and artistic revival was evident in Rome, Venice, and Naples, three cities of great wealth, power, and so-

https://doi.org/10.1515/9783110758573-030

phistication. The Italian peninsula accumulated increasing knowledge about Asia through its influential political, religious, and economic institutions (the Vatican, merchants, and bankers). The earliest Church reports and correspondence from Asia were compiled and published in Rome; tea descriptions are found mainly in the lively Neapolitan histories of the Orient and the colourful oriental travelogues of Venice (Teasenz Tea-Blog, 2016; Clark, 2001).

Ramusio and Venice

In particular, being strategically located on the Adriatic Sea, Venice was once the most powerful city in Europe, dominating trade by land and sea between the West and the Eastern empires of Byzantium and the Islamic world. Venice competed with Rome and other European cities in almost every field. Knowledge in Venice was like a spiral, concentrated in the city and then spread in the form of books to all parts of the continent. Venetian merchants, scholars, and printers excelled in translating, collecting, and publishing information. The city's publishing houses played a crucial role in the propagation of data and opinions: "before 1501, Venice had printed more books than any other European city, and was equalled in Italy only by Rome" (Teasenz Tea-Blog, 2016).

In Venice, a statesman, historian, and linguist, Ramusio, translated into Italian various accounts of travels to Asia by Europeans. His monumental three-volume work, *Delle Navigationi et Viaggi* (1550–1559), spread many revelations about the Orient throughout the continent. A great storyteller, Ramusio entertained his readers with tales of personal encounters with foreigners from the East. In one of these tales, he mentioned a meeting with a Persian merchant from Yazd (now in Iran) on his way to Italy, who had just returned from China with a rhubarb root. Since ancient times, the West regarded the root of the Chinese Rheum palmatum as a purgative. As a medicine against numerous ailments, the European trade in Chinese rhubarb was highly profitable like no other plant. But instead of praising rhubarb, the Persian merchant said that the Chinese held this root in low esteem and used it as incense or fodder for horses, and then he began to describe the healing powers of tea (Teasenz Tea-Blog, 2016; Clark, 2001).

Valignano and Rome

As the capital of the Catholic faith, the Vatican has demanded faithful obedience from almost all Western kings and queens. Moreover, the language of the Holy See has been an essential vehicle of communication and control and, thus, a power source for Rome. Latin remained, as in previous centuries, the lingua franca of cultured Europe, while nascent Italian was the most comprehensible language. Through intrigue and diplomacy, the city of Rome was the focal point for relations with foreign intelligence and the spread of knowledge. The apostolic nuncio in Goa, the Vatican's ambassador to the Indies, wrote official letters to Italy, sending annual reports via East India Company ships back to Lisbon. Travelling across the Mediterranean and later to Rome via the Tiber River, letters from the diplomatic missions began to circulate; before long, they were published by the Vatican in Italian and Latin to announce to the faithful the success of the Church in Asia and to disseminate information about the extraordinary discoveries of the East (Teasenz Tea-Blog, 2016).

In Rome, the Vatican authorised the publication of Jesuit reports from Japan to promote Catholic interests in Europe. The books, in particular, helped demonstrate the activities of a vigorous and prosperous Church to Catholics and Protestants. In particular, the Jesuit accounts of tea satisfied the curiosity of European readers about exotic plants, medicine, and oriental customs to a great extent. Chanoyu, the Japanese ceremonial service of tea, was the topic that particularly interested readers. In 1591, the Jesuit Alessandro Valignano, a powerful ambassador on a mission to Asia, encouraged the use of tea further to increase the religious and commercial interests in that territory, instructing Jesuits in Japan in the observation of chanoyu to welcome better visiting Japanese lords and officials (Teasenz Tea-Blog, 2016).

Three Chinese in Naples

In 1545 Naples was the most populous city in Europe and an important port on the Mediterranean. As the capital of the Kingdom of Naples, the city was a destination for a long time for European and Asian emissaries, travellers, and maritime correspondence in Italy. During the sixteenth century, extensive construction and renovation of buildings, shipyards, and fortifications were undertaken by the Spanish-appointed viceroys of the Habsburgs. The city's wealthy patrons began to create art collections, museums, libraries, and botanical gardens, making Naples one of Europe's outstanding artistic and cultural capitals. In 1576 the Neapolitan academic Giovanni Lorenzo d'Ananias wrote a treatise on world history that dealt with contemporary knowledge of Asia. It also recorded the surprising arrival of three Chinese merchants in Naples on their way to Spain. In the treatise, the historian described tea as a Japanese substitute for alcohol: "[. . .] all those who do not drink wine, take water mixed with a very soft powder [. . .]" (Teasenz Tea-Blog, 2016).

From Waldensian culture to imported tea sachets

From the Renaissance until the nineteenth century, tea was a privilege for high officials, diplomats, scholars, bishops, and popes, being a sporadic reference only in rare books. These limited editions graced the collections of a cultured élite, and the rest of the population was excluded entirely. Also, the teapot was present in the excellent table services of Italian royal families, but it was just a fad. This ornamental object was displayed in the company of foreign guests. Thanks to the Waldensian community and two wars, tea in Italy acquired a popular dimension (Vola, 2017; Grivetti, 2023).

To seek an authentic tea culture in Italy, we have to leap into the history of the Waldensian community. Today, the Waldensians are spread mainly in Piedmont, where they have their centre in Torre Pellice, in the province of Turin. The Waldensian Evangelical Church is a reformed Christian Church inspired by the Protestant reforms of the sixteenth century. The Waldensian Church takes its name from a merchant from Lyon, Valdo (1140–1206), who decided to live the Christian experience following the example of the community of the apostles: selling his goods, he lived on alms without abandoning his loyalty to the Pope. His movement was excommunicated and expelled from the city at the end of 1184 as part of the fight against heretical movements. Following the persecutions of 1208 in the south of France under Innocent III, the Waldensians retreated to northern Italy, mainly to the western valleys of Piedmont, such as Val Pellice, Val Chisone, and Valle Germanasca (Vola, 2017; Grivetti, 2023).

In the seventeenth century, the Duchy of Savoy gradually suppressed the Waldensian community's freedoms. Throughout the eighteenth century, the Waldensians were discriminated against as second-class citizens in these valleys, called the Alpine ghetto. It was not until 1848 that King Carlo Alberto granted the Waldensians civil rights and political freedom. Nevertheless, what does this have to do with tea and its spread?

Already in the seventeenth century, young daughters of Waldensian pastors or professors went to serve English families as governesses. Their work was particularly appreciated in England, Odesa (Ukraine), and Poland because of their knowledge of French (the "noble" language of the time) and their high education. These girls also became governesses and "nursemaids" for Russian aristocratic families (Vola, 2017; Grivetti, 2023).

Living in this aristocratic environment, they learnt the custom of drinking tea. When they returned to their homeland in the valleys, they maintained and spread this habit of having an afternoon snack with a cup of black tea. Thanks to them, tea and its culture arrived in the Waldensian Valleys. In this mountain area of the Piedmont region, tea immediately spread to every social level, unlike in other European countries and the rest of Italy, where it was initially drunk only by the aristocracy and upper class. Furthermore, they used loose leaves, not bagged tea. They knew how to brew them in the teapot and then use a strainer while pouring the liquor to prevent leaves or particles from falling into the cup. The tea was prepared very strongly, in the English tradition, and served in bowls or Chinese porcelain services if the family was particularly wealthy. The tea was sweetened by adding sugar and a cloud of fresh milk (Vola, 2017; Grivetti, 2023).

Sweet tarts with butter and jam (elderberry or blueberry) or savoury tarts of bread, butter, and anchovy paste were the ideal pairings with tea. On special occasions or when there were guests, the canapés were replaced by apple pies and sultana biscuits (Vola, 2017; Grivetti, 2023).

Returning to the contribution of the wars to spread tea culture, Italians made their first real acquaintance with tea during the Crimean War. However, this war did not interest us, tea lovers, but it was fundamental in our Risorgimento for two reasons: the constitution of the Kingdom of Italy and a better knowledge of this drink. The tremendous strategic head, Camillo Benso Conte (Earl) of Cavour, following his desire to annex Lombardo-Veneto, at the time under Habsburg Austria, to the Kingdom of Sardinia, sought essential alliances. The Crimean War broke out in 1853, pitting Russia against France (Lombardi, 2013; Lo Blundo, 2017).

At this diplomatic juncture, Cavour saw an opportunity to make France an ally by intervening on its side. The Kingdom of Sardinia entered the war in 1855. During meetings between high-ranking army officers and diplomats, our Italians began to drink tea (the French had been drinking it for at least a century, the Russians for much longer). Tea reached as far as Turin. One of the fathers of the unification of Italy, Massimo d'Azeglio, owned a complete tea set, which today belongs to the Museum of Palazzo Madama in Turin.

However, it took a few decades and another tragic event, the Second World War, for tea to be cleared to all social classes. The Allied soldiers who landed in Sicily and crossed the peninsula, liberating city after city from south to north, brought chocolate, chewing gum, and tea in sachets. In the 1950s, some people who emigrated abroad, to America or England, and returned brought tea with them. Italian families began to drink it, it became a habit, and it entered the Italian breakfast alongside caffè latte, coffee, and milk. In Italy comes Lipton, so reassuring (mainly since the 1980s, thanks to a commercial in which Dan Peterson exclaims, 'For me, number one!'), while Twinings, Infrè and Té Ati are absolute market leaders (Lombardi, 2013; Lo Blundo, 2017).

Contemporary Italian tea trends: What's new on the Italian market

How has tea culture evolved since the 1950s? Does tea continue to be a traditional drink, or is the fresh air of novelty also blowing on the Italian scene? But above all: are Italians becoming tea lovers? The answer is yes: the land of the espresso is slowly falling in love with tea! Let's take a look at the tea trends that have established themselves around the world and that have just begun arriving or consolidating in Italy as well.

Better less but good

Italy is known worldwide as the motherland of espresso, and Italians remain undisputed strong coffee drinkers. However, tea consumption constantly grows, and consumer demand increasingly focuses on high-quality or "trendy" teas. Market data suggest that tea is a significantly less popular drink in out-of-home consumption than coffee. Adults are the most frequent drinkers of traditional black tea, while young people between the ages of 25 and 40 are more likely to drink flavoured black teas, green teas, scented or flavoured teas, whether floral or fruity and relaxing herbal infusions (G. Lombardi, 2022b).

Despite the still uncertain economic situation, the demand for tea remains stable in volume and there has only been a slight decline in value due to the shift of demand towards cheaper products. In particular, newcomers who have approached the world of tea since 2020 have had the opportunity to learn how to prepare it properly during the long lockdown months or while still working from home. For this reason, the tea consumer has become more demanding and been constantly searching for loose and bagged value-for-money products. Those who opt for loose products prefer teas of origin, pure or naturally perfumed by contact. They know how to prepare them correctly, they know the secrets of the most suitable water to enhance the quality of the leaves, and they have the accessories to transform the tea ritual into an experience to be enjoyed at home. On the other hand, those in search of practicality prefer pyramid-shaped tea bags that can hold whole tea leaves or larger tea leaves rather than traditional bags, which are quick, easy to prepare and carry, as well as being of sound quality.

For a niche of experienced consumers with high purchasing power, on the other hand it does not matter if the value of premium teas has increased: tea offers pampering, and it is better to have just a tiny quantity of a premium one because the taste must satisfy the palate (Lombardi, 2023).

Tea to-go

Single servings of soluble tea are excellent alternatives to pyramid bags for those who live in a hurry but want to keep their taste. The tea leaves selected to produce these soluble mono doses from usually organic cultivation undergo a crystallisation process. Pour the contents into a small bottle of cold water or a cup of hot water, and the tea is ready! Also, more brands offer travel mugs and thermos flasks to drink one's favourite tea anywhere. There are many proposals: attractive colours and patterns, different materials (aluminium, ceramic, glass, double-walled glass), ergonomic shapes, and internal filters to infuse the tea (Lombardi, 2023).

Matcha, the undisputed king

Matcha is everywhere and takes the podium as the absolute protagonist in the world tea scene. Whether in the ceremonial premium version, the cooking variant, or the houjicha (roasted) type, it is the most versatile tea that can be "declined" into products that have nothing to do with tea. Some examples? Sweets (tiramisu and cheesecake revisited with matcha), ice cream, Easter eggs and Christmas Panettone, chocolates and candies, cocktails and matcha lattes, but especially supplements and cosmetic products. Matcha, never again without it! (Lombardi, 2022a).

Nitro tea

One of the latest international tea trends is also gaining ground in Italy. What is it? A real revolution! Thanks to nitrogen, nitro tea offers a unique tactile experience: a velvety and creamy cold tea, sweet and free of astringency, with a crown of foam similar to draught beers. This delightful texture makes it the most fabulous cold drink of the moment. In the United States and Australia, the nitro tea version in cans is already becoming popular, and we tea lovers are waiting for it with open arms here in Italy, too (Lombardi, 2022b).

Turning tea into an experience

Conscious and sophisticated consumers want to turn the tea ritual into an experience at home. But that is not all! Going to a tea shop is about more than just choosing a good product. Consumers are constantly looking for specialised shops, tea rooms, or, more simply, bakeries and bars that also know how to brew teas competently and create an entire experience around the infusions on the menu. A recommendation to all Horeca professionals: attracting and retaining new customers depends to a large extent on the ability to make the customer experience more than just what they are drinking. It is essential to find ways to transport them into a parallel world and educate them about quality. Let's impress them by showing professionalism and creating the right atmosphere with a mise en place appropriate to the context (Lombardi, 2022b).

The awareness, especially among young people, of the desire to adopt a healthy lifestyle continues to shape habits and increase consumer demand for hot drinks. Better information and social media have been the keys to spreading and pushing this trend, driving this post-Covid-19 and post-lockdown return to normality. There is an increasing demand for valuable allies of our health and well-being that can stimulate relaxation and improve sleep. This need will increasingly drive herbal infusions and rooibos. In particular, rooibos, improperly called red tea, pure or mixed with other health stimulants such as goji berries, acai, and ginseng, is a must-have for consumers who do not want caffeine (Lombardi, 2023).

Tea mixology

Still talking about bubbles, when poured into a glass and rising to the top, sparkling tea increasingly wants to establish itself as a terrific alternative to the classic champagne glass. For the curious sober drinker, the aperitif can be non-alcoholic or low in alcohol but still satisfying and trendy. On the other hand, for those in search of unconventional alcoholic blends, tea is an excellent ingredient for creating tea cocktails that combine taste and originality. Mixology, conversely, continuously experiments with bitters and other homemade preparations to break free from commercial products and differentiate itself in an increasingly competitive and demanding market. This research naturally opens the door to countless uses for a drink as age-old, "aesthetic," and refined as tea (Lombardi, 2023).

Sustainability and respect for the environment

This trend goes beyond the world of tea and concerns marketing across the board. Choosing the sustainable option was not always possible during the pandemic. However, with the lifting of restrictions, the focus on environmental friendliness is back: 75% of Gen Z say that sustainability is more important than branding. This figure should be considered because it is a good indicator of the factors influencing the purchasing choices of the next generation of tea drinkers (Ghosh, 2022).

To achieve commercial success, all producing countries and big brands in the tea world will increasingly have to meet these requirements: ethical tea, food factory, chemical free tea, ethical management, zero child employment, sustainable agriculture (soil and water conservation), small holders, environmental management, product traceability to source, and carbon neutrality, to name just a few (Lombardi, 2022b).

Increasing demand for professional tea education

The need for tea-specific training has significantly increased over the past three years. Many schools and academies specialising in coffee, wine, or sensory analysis, in general, have included tea-specific modules to supplement their training offerings.

Among the various academies and after the proven success of the TAC TEA SOMME-LIER® programme (in an exclusive partnership for Italy with the Tea and Herbal Association of Canada), the Protea Academy Association has recently widened its training proposals by launching two innovative professional courses on tea and herbal infusions aimed at tea enthusiasts and specialists: Herbal Tea Expert and Tea Barista PRO.

The culture and promotion of quality tea in Italy can and must also pass through the bar, the place par excellence of friendliness, hospitality, and the fusion of tradition and innovation. With this targeted training, Protea Academy has been awarded the role of reference point for tea enthusiasts and professionals. This association is a critical player in promoting tea across Italy (Protea Academy, 2023).

What a challenge! – Tea is growing in Italy!

Today, two tea plantations are operated: one in Tuscany and the second in Piedmont. The first one in Sant'Andrea di Compito, in the province of Lucca, can be considered the earliest pioneering attempt to adapt tea plants, which, as we all know, love tropical and subtropical climates, to the harsher temperatures of the Tuscan mountains. The experiment began in '87 after an initial selection to find the tea plants most resistant to the harsh winters. Today in the Antica Chiusa Borrini – the name of the property – there are 2,500 tea plants in the open ground distributed over five tea gardens (terraces).

Small-scale, non-commercial production now sees four families of tea produced: white tea, green tea, oolong tea, and black tea (De Francesco, 2020; Moroni, 2021; Prete, 2017).

Apart from Tuscany, there is another magical tea place near Lake Maggiore: the unique territory of the Ossola Valley, rich in parks and natural oases of rare beauty, dotted with historic villages and a treasure trove of culture, ancient traditions, and folklore. In the Ossola Valley, the Premosello plantation, the first commercial production came to life: an exclusive all-Italian tea cultivated and produced in small quantities (La Via del Tè, 2023).

Everything was born from the encounter between La Via del Tè and La Compagnia del Lago Maggiore, from the union of the experiences of the Carrai family (tea importers since 1961) and the Zacchera family, expert growers of flowering camellias who several years ago also began successfully breeding camellias for tea.

The Premosello plantation currently has around 20,000 Camellia Sinensis plants, many of which have been reproduced from seeds of plants from Rize, Türkiye, in various stages of growth, with plans to expand it in the coming years. It is, by extension, the second-largest plantation in Europe and the first in Italy to guarantee appreciable and constant tea production, a special place with a unique microclimate, watered by the Toce River and surrounded by the unspoilt majesty of the Alpine peaks (Compagnia del Lago, 2023).

Conclusions

Tea in Italy was probably the best-kept secret until the last decade.

What is Italy in the big ocean of the European tea market?

It is a small fish wandering in the vast waters and searching for potential opportunities.

Italy is the motherland of caffè espresso (espresso coffee), and Italians are heavy coffee drinkers. Still, tea consumption is constantly growing, and consumer awareness is more focused on high-quality and trendy teas. Italy is a fresh and virgin market that until now is waiting to be explored. The current situation is just the tip of the iceberg; you can only see a small portion of endless possibilities merging from the unexplored ocean (see Figure G.4.1).

Figure G.4.1: Tea Business Outlook in Italy.
Source: Protea Academy, 1st International Green Tea Conference, International Green Tea Trade Meeting, March 2019, Shengzhou.

Under the surface, which are the business potentials to unlock for those pioneers who believe in the future Italian tea market?
–   Fast-growing demand
–   Higher prices
–   Speciality business
–   Direct import (instead of local European sourcing)
–   Improved range

- Lifestyle
- Experience
- Traceability

In this day and age, innovation, convenience, storytelling, transparency, and a new generation of trained tea professionals are the keys to achieving a new dynamic market such as Italy (AITC, World Tea Industry Review, May 2022).

References

AITC. (2022). *World Tea Industry Review*.

Clark, G. (2001). *The artful teapot*. Watson-Guptill Publications.

Compagnia del Lago. (2023). Piantagione del tè. Retrieved March 28, 2023, from http://www.compagnia dellago.com/fiori-e-piante/pianta-del-the/.

De Francesco, A. (2020). Ma che storia fantastica è quella dell'unica piantagione di tè in Italia. 25 Nov 2020. Retrieved March 29, 2023, from https://www.identitagolose.it/sito/it/44/27241/dallitalia/ ma-che-storia-fantastica-e-quella-dellunica-piantagione-di-te-in-italia.html.

Ghosh, S. (2022, July 22). Gen Z generates demand for sustainable supply chain practice. Retrieved March 31, 2023, from https://sustainabilitymag.com/supply-chain-sustainability/gen-z-generates-demand-for-sustainable-supply-chain-practice.

Grivetti, M. (2023). Studi Valdesi. Retrieved March 29, 2023, from https://studivaldesi.org/video.php#.

Il Mondo del Tè, (2016, May 20). Il tè e il Rinascimento italiano: La Storia del Tè in italia. Retrieved March 29, 2023, from https://mondodelte.wordpress.com/2016/05/20/il-te-e-il-rinascimento-italiano-la-storia-del-te-in-italia/.

La Via del Tè. (2023). La piantagione. Retrieved March 28, 2023, from https://www.laviadelte.it/la-piantagione.

Lo Blundo, M. (2017, February 14) Breve storia del té in Italia. Retrieved March 28, 2023 from: https://ilmiote.wordpress.com/2017/02/14/breve-storia-del-te-in-italia/ (accessed March 28, 2023).

Lombardi, G. (2022a). L'oro verde: il matcha. Retrieved March 31, 2023, from https://www.vinhood.com/ magazine/recensioni-prodotti/loro-verde-il-matcha/.

Lombardi, G. (2022b). *The handbook for professional training*. Milano.

Lombardi, G. Tea trend: le novità del mercato. Retrieved March 31, 2023, from https://www.vinhood.com/ magazine/curiosita-ed-educazione/tea-trend-le-novita-del-mercato/.

Lombardi, G. (2013). *Tee Sommelier*. White Star Publisher.

Moroni, S. (2021, December 23). Le mirabolanti avventure del signore del tè italiano. Retrieved March 27, 2023, from https://www.lifegate.it/original/le-mirabolanti-avventure-del-signore-del-te-italiano.

Polo, M. (1982 reprint). Il libro di Marco Polo detto millione. Einaudi publishers. Retrieved March 31, 2023, from https://docenti.unimc.it/giulia.corsalini/teaching/2022/26828/files/il-libro-di-marco-polo-detto-milione-edizione-einaudi-torino-1954).

Pretre, M.L. (2017, October 16). Guido Cattolica, e la folle idea (realizzata) di coltivare il tè in Italia. Retrieved March 27, 2023, from https://www.repubblica.it/sapori/2017/05/24/news/lucca_antica_chiusa_borrini_unico_produttore_te_italiano-165579035/.

Protea Academy. (2023). Retrieved March 27, 2023, from https://www.proteaacademy.org.

Protea Academy. (March 2019). 1st International Green Tea Conference Review, International Green Tea Trade Meeting, Shengzhou.

Ricci, M. (2001, October 24,). Il primo té nel deserto del catai. Il Corriere della Sera. Retrieved March 28, 2023, from https://www.quodlibet.it/recensione/400.

Teasenz Tea-Blog. (2016, May 20). Il tè e il Rinascimento italiano: La Storia del Tè in italia. 20 May 2016. Retrieved March 28, 2023, https://mondodelte.wordpress.com/2016/05/20/il-te-e-il-rinascimento-italiano-la-storia-del-te-in-italia/.

Vola, B. (2017). Viaggio intorno al tè blog. Retrieved March 29, 2023, from https://viaggiointornoalte.net/2017/02/17/il-te-valdese-la-storia-e-la-cultura-del-te-in-italia/.

Lysbeth Vink and Annette Kappert-White

G.5 It is a man's world: The "Business of Tea" in the Netherlands and beyond

Introduction

The main purpose of the chapter is to explore the historical role women played in promoting, distributing, and establishing tea consumption in The Netherlands. Despite being the first nation to introduce tea to the Western world, and the abundance of literature and images documenting women as sapless tea drinkers, languishing their afternoons away, entertaining and sipping the amber brew in their teahouses, the latter is far from reality. Preliminary research indicates Dutch women were also instrumental in establishing the tea industry in The Netherlands and beyond.

As such, this chapter aims to rectify such misrepresentation by using two aspects of critical theory, namely a feminist approach to critique literature surrounding the role, position, and influence of women in establishing the tea industry in The Netherlands and the new historicist approach to illustrate how literary and visual texts by their own reflection of ideas and attitudes of the time in which they were written have caused a stereotype and created a perverse narrative.

The authors aptly utilise desk research and explore visual and narrative data dating from 1610 to present to find evidence of women's role in tea production, tea importation and its distribution to the rest of Europe and beyond, to include but not limited to royal patronage, the establishment and management of large teahouses, and the implementation of tea museums and tourist attractions across the Netherlands.

Findings confirm that majority of the visual and narrative data surrounding tea depicts women as hostesses and are family or household based. This further implies that in terms of the "tea business" women have indeed been left out of the narrative. By utilising the new historicist approach, we can further rationalise those mass-market writings and visual narratives about tea culture were written for women and not by women. However, whilst this may be applicable for early material, by analyzing current material we also see that despite the time in which they were produced, this has had very little impact on more recent texts which still fail to illustrate women as businesswomen but more as a nostalgic representation of former years (see Figure G.5.1).

Despite playing such a pioneering role, the Dutch have not been forward in acknowledging the role of women in the establishment of their tea industry. As such this chapter aims to set the record straight by initially setting tea in its political and social context and detailing the journey of tea to and throughout The Netherlands. To understand the role of women, the chapter further subdivides the Dutch tea historical landscape into three periods: Elitism, Popularisation, and Massification. It concludes

https://doi.org/10.1515/9783110758573-031

with a critique of more recent visual and narrative tea literature to identify the way women have been and are to a large extent still being portrayed in the modern day.

Figure G.5.1: "Teascapes": an historical elucidation of the Dutch "tea business".
Source: De Theefabriek (2022)

The earliest mention of tea in literature dates to 1559 and refers mainly to it being consumed for medicinal purposes (Martin and Cooper, 2015): "one per two cups of this decoction taken on an empty stomach removes fever, headache, stomachache, pain in the side or in the joints, and it should be taken as much as you can bear it [. . .]" (Tannahill, 1988, p. 267). The first mention of a tea trade between India and the West was documented by a Dutch author in 1598 (Weisburger & Comer in Kiple & Ornelas, 2000). Following this we see extensive data in the form of ship logs taken from the Dutch East India Company (V.O.C) which has also been credited as the first to bring tea from Japan to Europe in 1610 (Hohenegger, 2006) and later from China in 1637.

The first V.O.C. shipment of tea to arrive in Amsterdam originated from the former Dutch colony, Batavia (Saberi, 2010; Molen, ter, 1978; Voskuil, 1988). However, not only did it transport tea, but also social, cultural, economic, and political transformations, and a rich cultural heritage with fine examples of tea memorabilia (Trumpie & Bosmans, 2007). The latter tended to be auctioned in the V.O.C. "chambers" in Amsterdam, Hoorn, Enkhuizen, Rotterdam, Delft, and Middelburg (Molen, 1978) and today offer a unique source of information about the seventeenth and eighteenth century history of many countries and cultures. However, during its early period of operation, the V.O.C. forbade women from travelling out to the East Indies (Sen, 2015). Similarly, although literature suggests that there were quite a lot of traders involved in the tea business, in 1766 there were over 40 tea exporters in The Netherlands (Molen, 1978); from the said archives we can glean that this only means men (see Figure G.5.2).

Figure G.5.2: Tea Auction House, Amsterdam.
Source: Nationaal Archief (1950)

Elitism

Eventually, tea spread from Amsterdam to the rest of the Netherlands, but rather than travelling logistical routes, tea travelled with the elite Dutch society. By example, on account of tea being the beverage of choice for Countess Maria Louise, van Hessen-Kassei, the mother of Willem IV, the then Governor of the United Provinces of The Netherlands (Vink et al., 2022), it travelled from the west of The Netherlands to the provinces in the east and eventually to the north. It is believed that the said Countess introduced tea to Fryslân, and according to Kooijmans (1997) the countess would always ask her friends in Utrecht and Amsterdam to send her some tea.

In 1643, the importation of tea itself began to gain momentum and there is an invoice showing tea from the "Chineese Coopmandschappen to The Netherlands for 1400 pounds of tea and 7675 teacups" (Molen, ter, 1978, p. 20) and unsurprisingly, by the 1700s, tea became a status symbol and a means for women to climb the social ladder. Some of this status can also be attributed to the said expensive vessels required to steep, serve, and drink it. By example, at the courtship of Amalia van Solms, Princess consort of Orange by marriage to Frederick Henry, Prince of Orange, there was the first known porcelain vessels used for drinking tea in the Netherlands, dating to 1654 (Voskuil, 1988). It is also rumored that when an envoy of Friedrich Casimir of Hanau, the ruling count of Hanau-Lichtenberg, came to Amsterdam for dealings with the Dutch West India Company (W.I.C.), tea was served during each of the courses of their 12-hour dinner (Brugmans, 1920).

By 1660 the affluent Dutch had begun to accept tea as a household commodity and we see the appearance of tea caddies fitted with special locks to avoid pilfering, handmade tea boxes made from silver and from paper, and tea became a symbol of wealth and status, with affluent families setting aside special rooms where tea was prepared, served, and drunk: "The furniture consisted of tea-tables and chairs with cabinets for the cups and sugar boxes as well as for silver spoons and saffron pots [. . .] The tea and saffron were served together. The mixture being hot, sweetened and covered in a cup to persevere its aroma" (Voskuil, 1988, p. 73).

These rooms were soon to progress into actual teahouses (theekoepels) with said families erecting them in their backyards. Many were influenced by Chinese and Turkish designs and situated next to small streams, canals, or rivers, and used as status symbols (Molen, 1978; Meulenkamp, 1995). Some of these structures have been restored and are visible monuments throughout The Netherlands today, for example at the Kröller-Müller Museum, Kasteel Rosendael, and extensively throughout Fryslân.

Tea was also a luxury good for much of its early European history. Indeed, the first English tea was a gift to the king from Dutch merchants in 1664 (Hohenegger, 2006). It became especially fashionable, among high society in The Hague. Charles II, after having grown up in exile in The Hague, took his penchant for tea to England and his newly acquired Portuguese wife, Catherine of Braganza, followed suit. Similarly, Lord Arlington and Lord Ossory, courtiers of Charles and Catherine, purchased a large quantity of tea for themselves during a mission to The Hague and as such Catherine was soon known as a tea-drinking queen. With a pound of Dutch imported tea costing 60 shillings in London in 1660 and with the average daily wage for a labourer less than a shilling a day, tea was well out of the average price range (Martin, 1832; see Figure G.5.3).

Popularisation

Whilst tea was initially determined for the social elite, by the seventeenth century tea visits were also used to educate the "lower placed" women; however, tea was always purchased by the lady of the house due to the specialist knowledge and expertise required to select the right tea (Molen, ter 1987). As per routine, tea merchants would

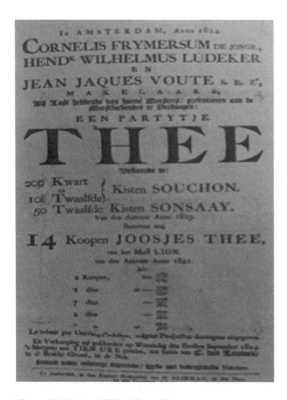

Figure G.5.3: Aanplakbiljet Theeveiling.
Source: Gemeente Amsterdam Stadsarchief (1824)

first present the dry tea leaves for the lady to smell the aroma and then chew on a small sample; once a selection was made the tea merchant would prepare a couple of small pots with the selected teas, pouring it into customised small teacups, "vinkepotjes," for the lady to taste, and should the tea be to her liking it would be purchased (Molen, ter 1978).

Despite this, the Dutch domestic market remained relatively limited throughout the seventeenth century. This pattern is comparative to the Dutch neighbours; the French nobility initially gave "English-style" tea parties, but once the novelty had worn off they returned to their national wines and dark-roasted coffee. Similarly, the Germans, after the first flurry of excitement, came to ignore the new drink, preferring their old and true favourite, beer. However, tea went on to become something very British with professor of the Royal Medico-Botanical Society Samuel Phillips Day claiming:

> What was first regarded as a luxury, has now become, if not an absolute necessity, at least one of our accustomed daily wants, the loss of which would cause more suffering and excite more regret than would the deprivation of many things which once were counted as necessities of life. (Fromer, 2008, p. 70)

Similar sentiments came from other learned scholars, "We are now almost justified in calling tea the English national drink; the more so as we take of it as much as all the rest of Europe put together" (Denyer, 1893), and from George Gissing: "Nowhere is the English genius of domesticity more notably evident than in the festival of afternoon tea. The mere chink of cups and saucers turns the mid to happy repose."

Returning to The Netherlands, we see that tea as medicine became a daily necessity in Dutch life as quickly as people could learn how to enjoy it. The Dutch writer, Cornelius Bontekoe, claimed that tea could demolish ill-health and "200 cups daily would not be too much" (Sigmond 1839, p. 94), and it could cure any fever (Hohenegger, 2006). This contributed to its popularisation amongst the lower classes. Initially sold to consumers in pharmacies (Molen, ter, 1978), by the seventeenth century tea was sold in grocery stores to rich and poor alike and was in general use throughout Holland, with a pertinent example being the city of Leiden which had a population of 36,000 in 1749 and 50 stores where coffee and tea were sold, five tea specialty stores, and 23 tea street sellers (Molen, 1978).

The latter would sell "milk tea" to the passer-by, as illustrated in the print of a tea seller by Cornelius Dusart (see Figure G.5.4). Female street sellers also sold tea at carnivals in Amsterdam and The Hague (Molen, ter 1978) and pamphlets were often printed with the slogan "Kees die drinkt by mooye Kee, een lekker kommetje melkthee" (Molen 1978).

Figure G.5.4: The tea seller by Cornelius Dusart.
Source: Rijksmuseum Amsterdam (1695b)

Massification

By the eighteenth century, coffee shops had become popular destinations for conversation, political discussions, and exchange of local news items, however no respectful Dutch woman would be seen in such establishments and so they tended to serve tea at home and, whenever possible, in their gardens. Tea visits often encompassed rituals, with memorabilia being made of precious materials, like gold or silver, which enabled the owner to show her wealth and status (Molen, ter, 1978).However, as the price of tea dropped and it became more widely available many of these traditions began to change, involving cultural and social transformations and material revolutions in The Netherlands. A befitting quote for this era comes from Muurling (2011): "The poorer the household, the greater the proportion of Delft porcelain." The transition from a luxury to a mass- consumed staple good also meant that tea began to lose its novelty and potential for social and cultural distinction and came to belong to the realm of daily routine.

To meet the then modern consumer's needs, we see in the eighteenth century Dutch "Theekransjes," which were initially simple tea tasting ceremonies with tables laden with a variety of tea cannisters and a "brouillaire" with hot water. Each participant was given their own small porcelain teapot to make a pot of tea, to be judged by the other participants based on the following: "astringent," "rising," "hearth strengthening," or "a little dull." The group members merely enjoyed showing off their degrees of knowledge of tea making and tasting.

By the nineteenth century this ceremony evolved into brewing a large pot of tea, from which small cups were filled. Rock sugar was used as a sweetener and the tea was served with marzipan and biscuits. The tendency was to slurp the tea and chase it down with a glass of brandy or two. The playing of cards and gossiping became befitting attributes. Many of these latter customs were frowned upon and people who participated were seen as disdainful and, more so, women who 'wasted' their time with tea visits who also they squandered their money on precious tea items (Voskuil, 1988). Such squander is easily illustrated by the *Theegezelschap* by Pieter van den Berge, 1694–1737 (see Figure G.5.5).

The Dutch widows

Historically, both visual and narrative literature have not been relatively kind to Dutch businesswomen, and only a little information and basic details about the widows Johanna Borski, Sara Bols, Susanna van Eeghen, Cornelia van Eeghen, Lysbeth Mintjes, and Hendrica van Nelle are available. Theytook over the companies after the death of their husbands and left successful businesses for their offspring, many still in existence today. Pertinently, both Lysbeth Mintjes and Hendrica van Nelle became successful proprietors in the "Tea Business."

Figure G.5.5: Theegezelschap, Pieter van den Berge, 1694–1737.
Source: Rijksmuseum Amsterdam (1695a)

Lysbeth Mintjes

In 1753, the Dutch businessman Egberts Douwe and his wife Akke Thijsses opened their first store called *de Witte Os* in Joure, Fryslân. They sold "colonial goods": tea, tobacco, coffee, and spices. In 1780 their son Douwe Egberts and his wife vrouw Ymke Jacobs Visser took over the business and in 1806 after his death the company was taken over by his second wife Elisabeth Pot (Lysbeth Mintjes) and one of his sons. They renamed the company the *Weduwe Douwe Egberts* and this name was used until 1925, when her sons eventually took over and renamed the company *De Compagnie – Firma Weduwe Douwe Egberts '1806–1833'* (Groeneweg, 2021). In 1937, Douwe Egberts introduced their own tea brand, Pickwick, after Charles Dickens' *Pickwick Papers* and in 2015 they merged with Jacobs, to become JDE (Groeneweg, 2021). Today, what was once a small Frisian village shop has now become part of the large beverage conglomerate known as JDE Peet's.

Lysbeth Mintjes was married to Douwe Egberts for 16 years and had nine children. She died in 1835 at the age of 66. Unfortunately, due to a fire in 1881 any material that might have existed about the *Weduwe Douwe Egberts* was lost, and we are also unable to confirm if any of the images in Douwe Egberts logos on the tea or coffee packaging of either 1983 or 2012 are in the likeness of Lysbeth.

Hendrica van Nelle – Brand

Similarly, Johannes Van Nelle started his small shop selling coffee, tea, and tobacco in 1806 (Bantje & Kind, 1981) in Rotterdam. After his death in 1811, the company was taken over by his widow, Hendrika Brand, who renamed the company the *Weduwe J. van Nelle*; upon her death in 1813, the name was changed to *De Erven de Wed. J. van Nelle* and remained so until 1982 (Bantje & Kind, 1981, p. 16). Despite taking over for a relatively short time, Hendrika's legacy lies in the company's ability to market and promote their products through slogans such as those used in the seventeenth century, for example "Tasting is buying" (Bantje, 1981). That is not the only influence the early tea business had on the company as they also promoted their wares through tea tastings at special fairs, such as the Industrial Fair for Women. Initially, they sold samples of tea for ten cents, but after a while they became complimentary as, according to Bantje (1981), they soon realised the tea would sell itself in this way. Van Nelle also courted the local press, by attending fairs and by ensuring their stands were designed and decorated by young promising artists, and of course these activities delivered quite a lot of free press moments (1981). The Van Nelle company, as per Douwe Egbert, later went on to introduce tokens on their packets of tea. These tokens could be saved up and exchanged for gifts such as children's books. But marketing prowess is not the only thing Hendrika and Lysbeth had in common; unlike the other successful widows previously mentioned, only these two women who worked in the "tea business" identified themselves as widows and rebranded their companies accordingly.

In comparison, we see a plethora of literature documenting the success of British widows, for example Maria Tewkes of York and Mary Little Twining, the widow of Daniel Twining. To ensure her legacy was well documented, the latter wrote a diary and noted that it was her proudest achievement to have stuck to her commitment to only sell the finest quality teas. This said, today there are fewer Dutch women who are breaking from tradition; they are not widows, and as such breaking the mold as tea proprietors in their own right. With their inclusion in this chapter we begin to write a new narrative, with Mikkel Lévelt and Linda Rampen, who have documented their own journeys and bring us up to the current state of the "Tea Business" in The Netherlands.

Mikkel Lévelt

Simon Levelt was also a Dutch proprietor who opened up a coffee, tea and other "colonial goods" store in 1826 in Amsterdam. He sold an assortment of national and international brands of tea. Although there is no documentation in regards to his wife, the company has been passed down through six generations and to date there are 37 stores in The Netherlands and Belgium. In, 2003, Simon Levelt's great granddaughter, Mikkel Lévelt, became the first female director of the company. However, whilst there are numerous articles about Mikkel in the popular press, in academic literature we see more of her penchant for sustainability (Cramer, 2005) than about the actual tea itself (see Figure G.5.6).

Figure G.5.6: Mikkel Lévelt.
Source: De Volkskrant (2015)

Figure G.5.7: Portrait of Linda Rampen.
Source: ITC Academy (2022)

Linda Rampen

Linda Rampen started Het Zuyderblad, Theeplantage Soerenonk, North-Brabant in 2011. Not too dissimilar to the other female proprietors mentioned in this chapter, she inherited the family small holding, with cows, pigs, strawberries, asparagus, and of course several domestic animals, but instead of continuing with this line of heritage Linda decided to set up the first tea Dutch tea plantation. Today, the plantation annually produces 70 kilograms of high-grade tea and Linda is responsible for her own literary and visual contributions. How times have changed (see Figure G.5.7)!

Unfortunately, despite change the Dutch tea industry and tea in itself have not been able to regain their former glory. The original Pickwick brand was sold to the American conglomerate Sara Lee, which controls 65% of the Dutch tea market, and teabags are preferred by its consumers (Wal van der, 2008). This said, the legacy of Dutch women in the "tea business" lives on, and half of the 10 main tea companies based in The Netherlands today have female members on their board of directors.

Research design

As indicated, this chapter is based on secondary data, by which visual and narrative literature was critically analyzed to identify the role women played in establishing the tea industry in The Netherlands and to some extent to wider Europe. To add depth to the study the main literature search was taken from 1610 to the present day and focused mainly on Dutch women. The literature provided recurrent themes that served as codes for the visual data. The codes were used to aid a visual search from which a total of 62 images including paintings, advertisements, photographs, and television commercials were found to depict Dutch women in relation to varying aspects of tea. The majority of other images relating to tea found in the search tended to be of the tea itself or tea memorabilia. Unfortunately, due to editorial limitations only eight of the actual images featuring women were displayed in this chapter, however the authors feel that they are a representative sample, since it was never about how many images but more about what the images depict.

Further, the chapter utilises two aspects of critical theory, a feminist approach (Clark, 2007) to analyze literature surrounding the role, position, and influence of women in establishing the tea industry in The Netherlands and the new historicist approach to illustrate how literary and visual texts by their own reflection of ideas and attitudes of the time in which they were written have caused stereotypes and created a perverse narrative.

Critical theory for this chapter embraces the work of Alvesson and Deetz (1999) who define the term as the skewing of historical discourse through reification, the universalisation of sectional interests, the domination of instrumental reasoning, and the critique of hegemony. By combining this with a feminist approach, the authors are able to reveal obvious and subtle gender inequalities in the Dutch Tea business, in order to call for change in reducing such inequalities (Martin, 2002). Further, by embracing the new historicist approach the authors have been able to illustrate "how the interests of men have been assumed or asserted to be universal, silencing the voices and ignoring the concerns of women" (p. 5). As per example, much of the early tea literature was disseminated through private networks or in manuscript form. This resulted in male oriented audiences, since so few women could read or write or had access to the networks. Furthermore, the use of visual data used to advertise tea tells us very little about women of the time and even less about the time in which they were produced. As such, in keeping with the feminist approach, in the concluding section we present our observations rather than findings.

Observations

In paintings women tended to be dressed for the occasion, adorned with capes and feathers or with pearls with long dresses. In most cases they are having tea with others, including men, other women, and, in rare cases, with children. The teapot tends to be either on the table and women are served rather than them serving it themselves. In contrast, in many of the adverts we see women take on a more domestic role and dressed accordingly. They are either serving the tea or sitting down with a cup of tea with the teapot on a table next to them.

The found photographs from the current era show in both cases the women as depicted as being at work i.e., either tasting or promoting tea, in some way reminiscent of the former tea sellers. However, in all of the Dutch television commercials, we identified extensive nostalgia, particularly so in the promotion of black tea. In most cases women were placed in domestic roles, serving tea to their families and in others only to their sons. However, in both the adverts and television commercials we also found evidence of the health benefits of green tea and other herbal infusions being demonstrated, with the use of young women, women at the spa or women relaxing.

Tea "would be nothing, nothing . . . without a woman"

Despite the paltry amount, the authors were able to locate evidence of women promoting, distributing, and establishing tea consumption in The Netherlands. However, many of these women tended to be widowed, be diversified from tea, and add coffee, tobacco, and a wide selection of porcelain to the business (Trumpie & Bosmans, 2007). That said, some managed to hold on to the business until it was eventually sold, merged with large conglomerates, or passed down to a male heir. We can also conclude that men were the main promoters, distributers, and establishers of tea consumption in The Netherlands.

It is also difficult to say with any certainty what the actual role of early women tea practitioners would have been. Even if we widen our search to include a more global perspective, what we can glean from tea literature is scarcely more than their name and family background. For example, the Portuguese Catherine of Braganza, wife of Charles II, is claimed to have brought tea with her to the court of St. James (Hill, 2000), some credit has been given to Anna, Duchess of Bedford, as the inventor of the afternoon teatime (Hill, 2000), while there is paltry mention of the British female tea merchants Maria Tewkes of York and Thomas Twining's widow Mary Little Twining who kept the business going and indeed flourishing for almost two decades (Hill, 2000).

As such, more extensive research needs to be conducted in order to determine if this is just Dutch phenomena. Hence, the authors intend to use this research as a prelude to a much larger comparative piece of research in which the narrative is further explored as it relates to the rest of Europe and a consecutive piece relating to coffee. In sum, we will continue to analyze visual and narrative data, for although we cannot change it we can at least contribute to writing a new narrative.

References

Alvesson, M., & Deetz, S. (1999). An introduction to critical research. In *Doing Critical Management Research*, 1–22. SAGE Publications.

Bantje, H., & Kind, W. (1981). Twee eeuwen met de weduwe: geschiedenis van De Erven de Wed. J. van Nelle NV: 1782–1982. Van Nelle. P 15–16, 185–187.

Bedford, J. (1964). *Talking about teapots; and thus about porcelain, pottery, silver, Sheffield plate, etc.* London.

Brugmans, H. (1920). Een Duitsch geleerde te Amsterdam. *Amselodamum*, 7, 25–27.

Clark, D.S. (2007). Critical feminist theory. In *Encyclopedia of law & society: American and global perspectives* (Vol. 1, pp. 349–350). Sage Publications.

Cramer, J. (2005). *Duurzaam ondernemen uit en thuis*. Uitgeverij Van Gorcum.

Denyer, C.H. (1893). The consumption of tea and other staple drinks. *The Economic Journal*, 3(9), 33–51. https://doi.org/10.2307/2956036.

De Theefabriek. (2023). De Theefabriek . . . een paradijs voor de theeliefhebber!. Retrieved January 15, 2022, from https://www.theefabriek.nl/theelezingen/.

De Volkskrant. (2015, October 5) De vloek van goede koffie en. Retrieved January 15, 2022, from https://www.volkskrant.nl/economie/de-vloek-van-goede-koffie-en-thee~b5c7e076/ 5 Oct 2015.

Fromer, J. (2008). "Deeply indebted to the tea-plant": Representations of English national identity in Victorian histories of tea. *Victorian Literature and Culture*, 36(2), 70, 531–47.

Gissing, G. *The private papers of Henry Ryecroft*.

Groenewege, L. (2021). Thuis sinds 1753 Unpublished Manuscript, Reinwardt Academie & JDE Heritage Center, 27, 30, 51 .

Hill, E. (2000, August 4). Women's place in tea history. Retrieved January 20, 2022,from m https://www. teamuse.com/article_000804.html.

Hohenegger, B. (2006). *Liquid jade: the story of tea from east to west*. Macmillan.

ITC Academy (2022). Over ITC Academy. Retrieved January 15, 2022, from https://itcacademy.nl/about/.

Kiple, K.F., & Ornelas, K. (2000). *The Cambridge world history of food*. Cambridge University Press.

Kooijmans, L. (1997). Friese adel en het huis van Nassau. *Virtus| Journal of Nobility Studies*, 4(2), 57–59.

Martin, L., & Cooper, R. (2015). A world history of tea – from legend to healthy obsession. *Alternative and Complementary Therapies*, 17(3), 162–68.

Martin, J. (2002). *Feminist theory and critical theory: Unexplored synergies. Research paper series*. Stanford Graduate School of Business. Sage Publications.

Martin, R.M. (1832). *The past and present state of the tea trade of England, and of the continents of Europe and America: And a comparison between the consumption, price of, and revenue derived from, tea, coffee, sugar, wine, tobacco, spirits, & parbury*. Allen, & Company.

Meulenkamp, W. (1995) Theekoepels en tuinhuizen in de Vechtstreek, uitgeverij Heureka, Weesp.

Molen, ter, J.R. (1978). Thema thee: de geschiedenis van de thee en het theegebruik in Nederland. P 20–21, 26–36, 38, 45–46.

Muurling, S.T.D. (2011). Een schatkamer in Europa: Koffie, thee en porselein in de Hollandse materiële cultuur. *Historisch tijdschrift*, 43(3), 218.

Nationaal Archief. (1950). Retrieved January 15, 2022, from https://www.nationaalarchief.nl/.

Rijksmuseum Amsterdam. (1695a). Retrieved January 15, 2022, from https://www.rijksmuseum.nl/nl/collec tie/RP-P-1908-4729.

Rijksmuseum Amsterdam. (1695b). Retrieved January 15, 2022, from https://www.rijksmuseum.nl/nl/collec tie/RP-P-BI-7291.

Saberi, H. (2010). *Tea: A global history*. Reaktion Books.

Sen, Amrita. (2015). Traveling Companions: Women, Trade, and the early East India Company. *Special Issue on "Transcultural Networks in the Indian Ocean, Sixteenth–Eighteenth Centuries: Europeans and Indian Ocean Societies in Interaction,"* edited by Su Fang Ng. *Genre: Forms of Discourse and Culture*, 48(2), 193–214.

Sigmond, G.G. (1839) *Tea; Its effects, medicinal and moral*. Orme, Brown, Green, & Longmans (facsimile by Kessinger Legacy Reprints).

Tannahill, R. (1988). *Food in history*, rev. ed. Crown.

Trumpie, A., & Bosmans, S. (Eds.). (2007). *Pretty Dutch: 18de-eeuws Hollands porselein*. 010 Publishers.

Van Der Wal, S. (2008). Sustainability issues in the tea sector: A comparative analysis of six leading producing countries. Stichting Onderzoek Multinationale Ondernemingen, June.

Vink, L., Kappert-White, A., & Bohne, H. (2022). *Cultural heritage and tourism; Friesland tea*. Routledge.

Voskuil, J.J. (1988). De verspreiding van koffie en thee in Nederland. *Volkskundig bulletin*, 14(1), 73–74.

Gihan Mauris and Henrik Scander

G.6 Tea in Sweden – Tradition and consumption

Traditions and the past

Tea arrived in Sweden early and for some time Sweden has been one of Europe's leading nations in the tea industry, exporting tea to large parts of the continent. Tea came to Sweden in 1685 via merchants from Gothenburg who imported tea via Amsterdam and Hamburg. Tea is becoming an important commodity in Sweden, not least for the Swedish East India Company, for who tea was the most important commodity and the basis for the company's finances. Because the profits were high and foreign people were happy to invest in the company's tea trade.

Gothenburg was an important European port for many years. However, tea did not become a prominent drink for Swedish culture like it grew and became in, for example, the United Kingdom, the Netherlands and Germany. However, tea drinking increased in Sweden in the eighteenth century and in cities such as Gothenburg and the Swedish capital Stockholm special teahouses were also set up and tea was more widely distributed. However, tea will never be as popular as the new eighteenth century drink – coffee. In Sweden, coffee is still gaining in popularity and today Sweden is the world's second most coffee-drinking country, second only to Finland, while Sweden is in a modest thirtieth place when it comes to tea consumption.

So from the time tea became fashionable in England in the eighteenth century it did not take long for it to spread to Sweden, even though at that time it was a distinct stimulant for the Swedish upper class and King Gustav III used tea as an exclusive gift. Furthermore, Carl Linnaeus tried during this time to plant tea bushes in Sweden. However, this never became a reality for Linnaeus despite all his attempts, especially in Uppsala, but we must not forget that it was this Swedish gentleman, Carl Linnaeus, who gave the tea its botanical name, Camellia sinensis. Carl Linnaeus named the tea bush Thea senesis in 1737 and published the name in the book *Species Plantarum* in 1753. Carl von Linné further wrote about tea in his *Herb Book* from 1725.

Carl Linnaeus criticised the importing of tea. He considered it a significant economic waste to import tea from China. He advocated domestic tea cultivation such as his attempt to grow tea in Sweden, but the climate was too harsh. Initially, tea was a medicinal plant sold by pharmacists and it was only during the eighteenth century that tea developed into a beverage among other beverages.

Even though tea was not a huge success in Sweden, there has been a large increased trend in recent years where mainly quality teas have had a renaissance in Sweden as in other countries. Clear examples of this are seen in sales but also in the

https://doi.org/10.1515/9783110758573-032

success that tea and scones or afternoon tea in various vintages have had in the hotel and restaurant industry, both in big cities but also rural hotels.

Since this versatile beverage made its way into the Swedish isles, tea was considered more of an ayurvedic beverage from the east, which is why it was sold primarily in pharmacies at that time. The Swedes, much like the rest of the western world, understood that there were medical attributes to the beverage that were advantageous to one's health. However, being rather costly at the time, and not completely perceptive to the difference between the Camellia Sinensis bush and other plants, middle-class Swedes would brew similar looking leaves and other herbs hoping to obtain similar advantages whilst enjoying a hot beverage. One example of this is "Silver Tea", a concoction of different types of leaves brewed in hot water and served with milk. Theses leaves, since not oxidised, would generate a pale liquor and would visually have a silvery to white colour when adding the milk, hence the name.

Tea as a whole in Sweden has been predominantly associated with health, relaxation and a cultured alternative to coffee. Considering the health trend that is currently sweeping Europe one would say that not very much has changed in this perception. The low caffeine in comparison to coffee and the health benefits associated with amino acids and antioxidants found in tea have resulted in a growth in overall interests and sales in Sweden. Having said that, the majority of this statistic is related to flavoured teas.

The critical change

Until the late 1970s the Swedes' relationship with tea was rather limited to what types and blends were fashionable and popular in other tea drinking nations of the west, such as Earl Grey, black current Lapsang Souchong and Ceylon breakfast tea. It was not until 1981 that a Swedish tea company, Tea Centre of Stockholm, pioneered with a unique composition of tropical fruits to create the renowned Swedish tea blend "Söderblandning", created by Mr. Vernon Mauris in his small boutique situated on the southern borough of the capital. The blend was a result of him accidently spilling several different flavoured teas on the floor, creating the blend which is today Sweden's second most consumed flavoured tea and a staple blend in many Swedish homes, so much so that there are many imitations of this blend with similar names.

Swedish trends of today

Today the focus on relaxation and mindfulness is ever increasing in Sweden and finding the small luxuries in life is imperative to be able to disconnect from one's hectic lifestyle. Tea, together with coffee, beer, wine and other foods, has been a way of supporting this behaviour and having people create genuine interests in such handcrafted items.

For the most part many Swedes are in the beginning of their travels into the world of tea and begin their journey with what they are familiar with, loose leaf flavoured black and green teas. These are still today the most common teas sold on the Swedish market and account for approximately of the overall sales of tea. These are an obvious start since they are easy to adapt to and rather forgiving when it comes to brewing techniques due to essences and oils that help mask any imperfections in the final brew. However, for the Swedish enthusiasts of tea interests vary greatly.

The tea culture in Sweden is dominated by a selection of black tea preferences. If they drink tea, then Swedes prefer (where multiple answers are allowed) black tea (65% Earl Grey, 42% English Breakfast, 15% Darjeeling, 7% Assam). Only 41% choose green tea. Predominantly, the Swedes are black tea consumers. Within the black tea consumers – if they choose Earl Grey or English Breakfast – 57% drink their tea without milk, while 32% drink it with milk. Only 23% of Swedish tea drinkers sweeten their beverage (10% with one sugar per cup, 9% with two and only 4% with three sugars per cup). Consequently, the Swedes are the top black tea drinkers in Scandinavia, showing a preference for milk (more than their neighbours), but not really for sweeteners (lowest sweetening preferences in Scandinavia – with one speciality: 13% of the Swedish black tea drinkers put lemon and honey in their cup of English Breakfast or Earl Grey.) (Smith, 2020; see Figure G.6.1).

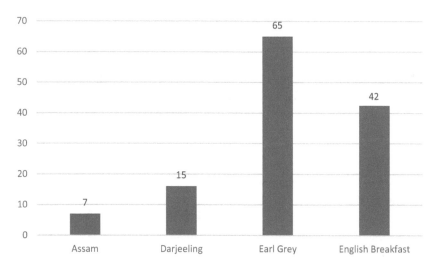

Figure G.6.1: Black tea consumption in Sweden.
Source: Smith (2020)

The general knowledge of tea in Sweden has been growing steadily for the past ten to fifteen years and one would say that the trend will continue in line with the parallel trends in health, mindfulness and craftsmanship. What differentiates the Swedish market from many others in Europe, and which can very much be assumed as a favourable trait, is the general knowledge and interests in beverages. This started with wine in the 80s and continued with single malt whiskey in the 90s. Since then, several beverage categories have trended on the Swedish market. We have seen a big trend for quality coffee and craft brewing in the last ten years. But the strongest trend for beverages in Sweden at the moment is non-alcoholic beverages, which is also in line with the health ideal that is so strong now. There is clearly a lot in it that connects to tea. First of all, we have Swedish people's general interest in knowledge surrounding beverages, the trend for non-alcoholic consumption and health, but also the interest in the craft of brewing, namely being able to brew in regards to your own taste and being able to direct the taste towards specific food combinations.

Swedish consumption patterns

Swedish imports and consumption of tea have remained relatively flat from the 1980s until today, with the exception of a certain increase between 2000 and 2010 when consumption was up to 0.4 kg per capita per year but which is now back at 0.3 kg per capita.

Looking at data from the Swedish food agency total of 1,797 (53% women) subjects who reported everything they ate and drank during four consecutive days, the average consumption of tea in Sweden is around 145 ml for women, 88 ml for men and all together 120 ml per day. In this study, 48% registered that they consumed tea. The Swedish average consumption differs between the sexes and is higher among women (56%) and lower for men (37%). Among women, the age groups 31–44 and 45–64 years have the highest intakes. Among men, the youngest age group has the lowest intake while the oldest age group the highest intake. In regard to weekdays, it is fairly evenly distributed, both for men and women. Even if tea consumption is distributed on all hours of the day, there are still two major peaks at around 8 a.m. in the morning and 9 p.m. in the evening and one lower peak around 3 p.m. in the afternoon (see Figure G.6.2 and Table G.6.1). This indicates tea as a morning and evening drink. Moreover, looking at how Swedish people have registered their consumption in regard to meals, breakfast consumption accounts for more than 40% while only a small proportion, around 15%, is consumed at lunch and dinner. This is the potential for changing consumption behaviour to an increase in tea which could be beneficial for both health and even better meal experiences, if we substitute sodas and even alcohol to some extent.

Considering consumption in regard to where we consume our tea, it is obvious that the main consumption of tea is at home and in the fika breaks at work (see Table G.6.2). It can also be seen that the consumption of tea is linear with places with a higher number of inhabitants, i.e. the big Swedish cities such as Stockholm, Gothenburg and Malmö have a significantly greater consumption of tea than in the smaller cites (see Table G.6.3). One could therefore argue that Swedish tea consumption is a metropolitan trend or phenomenon.

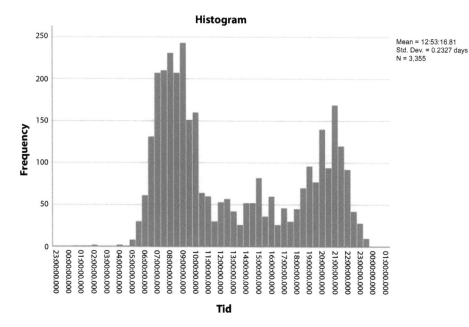

Figure G.6.2: Swedish tea consumption occasion timeline.
Source: Scander (2019)

Table G.6.1: Preferred time slot for Swedish tea consumption.

	Men %	Women %	Men and women %
Breakfast	47.1	41.2	43.5
Lunch	4.3	4.8	4.8
Dinner	10.4	11.3	10.8
Other	38.2	42.8	40.9
Total	100.0	100.0	100.0

Source: Scander (2019)

Table G.6.2: Location of Swedish tea consumption.

	Men %	Women %	Men and women %
Event e.i. sport arena theater	0.6	0.2	0.3
Lunch or "fika" room at work	10.7	13.2	12.5
At home	79.0	73.9	75.5
At friends or family	3.0	4.7	4.1
On the go	1.3	0.6	0.9
Restaurant, Bar or Café	2.1	2.7	2.5
Other	3.3	4.7	4.3
Total	100.0	100.0	100.0

Source: Scander (2019)

Table G.6.3: Swedish tea consumption region.

	Men %	Women %	Men and women %
Stockholm/Gbg/Malmoe	43.2	37.0	39.0
Lager cities	37.1	39.3	38.7
Mid-size towns	10.7	13.3	12.5
Congested	3.2	3.9	3.7
Sparsely populated	5.8	6.5	6.1
Total	100.0	100.0	100.0

Source: Scander (2019)

Table G.6.3 is based on the official classification of municipalities in H-regions (homogeneity), hence the municipalities of Sweden are classified into six such H-regions depending on population density. The three highest density categories (H1 and H2) include the three largest cities of Sweden, Stockholm, Gothenburg and Malmoe. Larger cities (H3) are municipalities with more than 90,000 inhabitants within a 30 km radius of the municipal centre (most populous parish in the municipality). Mid-size towns (H4) are municipalities with more than 27,000 and less than 90,000 inhabitants within a 30 km radius from the municipal centre and with more than 300,000 inhabitants within a 100 km radius from the same point. Congested (H5) are municipalities with more than 27,000 and less than 90,000 inhabitants within a 30 km radius from the municipal centre and with less than 300,000 inhabitants within a 100 km radius from the same point. Sparsely populated (H6) are municipalities with less than 27,000 inhabitants within a 30 km radius from the municipal centre.

Moreover, a light-meal pattern has been identified for Swedish women that is positive towards fibre-rich bread, cheese, rice, pasta and food grain dishes, while also substituting products for meat and dairy products and sweets, where tea is a common beverage (Ax et al. 2016).

Several food surveys also including beverage intake have been published in Sweden but only a few have analyzed choice of beverage at each meal and their contribution to energy intake. Certain beverage choices, such as tea, have been shown to be important for the intake of certain nutrients, in reducing obesity and controlling diabetes, in the prevention of cancer, in reducing heart and vascular disease, in protecting teeth and bones, and as antioxidant and antibacterial agents (Li, 2022; Monobe, 2018; Ng, 2018). Studies have also looked at the optimal brewing conditions for tea to obtain the best balance between sensory preferences and health effects (Perez-Burillo, 2018). With this in mind, we do promote an increase or substitution for tea especially in regard to dinner choice, where many calorie dense beverages are drunk, such as beer and wine (Scander, 2018a; Scander, 2018b). This to promote not only a healthier diet overall but also a way for people to discover the underestimated taste of tea.

Conclusion

The Swedish tea consumption habits are showing the preferences for drinking tea at home or during a break at work, but also in the morning. It can also be seen a metropolitan trend as well as the breakfast as an important meal to drink tea.

References

Ax, E., et al. (2016). Dietary patterns in Swedish adults; results from a national dietary survey. *British Journal of Nutrition, 115*(1), 95–104.

Hayat, K., et al. (2015). Tea and its consumption: Benefits and risks. *Critical Reviews in Food Science and Nutrition, 55*(7), 939–54.

Li, Y.R. (2022). A study on tea drinking, behavior, and attitudes in the Nordic countries. Master thesis at Halmstad University.

Monobe, M. (2018). Health functions of compounds extracted in cold-water brewed green tea from Camellia Sinensis L. *Jarq: Japan Agricultural Research Quarterly, 52*(1), 1–6.

Ng, K.-W., et al. (2018). Oolong tea: A critical review of processing methods, chemical composition, health effects, and risk. *Critical Reviews in Food Science and Nutrition, 58*(17), 2957–980.

Perez-Burillo, S., et al. (2018) Effect of brewing time and temperature on antioxidant capacity and phenols of white tea: Relationship with sensory properties. *Food Chemistry, 248*, 111–18.

Scander, H. (2019). Food and beverage combinations: Sommeliers' perspectives and consumer patterns in Sweden (Doctoral dissertation, Örebro University).

Scander, H., et al. (2018a). Beverage consumption patterns and energy contribution from beverages per meal type: results from a national dietary survey in Sweden. *Public Health Nutrition, 21*(18), 3318–327.

Scander, H., et al. (2018b). Food and beverage dinner combinations, patterns among Swedish adults. *International Journal of Gastronomy and Food Science, 14*, 20–26.

Smith, F. (2020). How do British tea drinking habits compare with other Europeans? Retrieved March 30, 2023, from https://yougov.co.uk/topics/consumer/articles-reports/2020/11/24/how-do-british-tea-drinking-habits-compare.

H Discovering tea by land

Tea arrived in Europe either by the sea, first via Dutch ports, or by land with caravans from China via Russia. This chapter deals with the tea culture in countries where tea was primarily imported with caravans from the Far East (China), by using different trails via Mongolia and neighbouring countries to Europe.

Stefan Nungesser, Isabell Stern and Andreas N. Ludwig

H.1 Tea in Austria – In the land of coffee houses

In his autobiography *The World of Yesterday*, the writer Stefan Zweig remembers the particular atmosphere in Vienna's coffee houses:

> It [the coffee house] represents an institution of a special kind that cannot be compared with any similar one in the world. It is actually a kind of democratic club accessible to everyone for a cheap cup of coffee, where every guest can sit for hours for this small obolus, discuss, write, play cards, receive his mail and above all consume an unlimited number of newspapers and magazines. Every day we sat for hours, and nothing escaped us.

Austrians are justifiably proud of this long-standing culture of "Kaffeehäuser", the famous coffee houses. They are one of the main reasons why coffee has always enjoyed far greater public attention in Austria than tea and why tea consumption is notoriously low (Austrian Coffee and Tea Association, n.d.). Even the history of Austria's professional representation of its coffee and tea industry reflects this fact: the current "Österreichischer Kaffee- und Tee-Verband", the country's coffee and tea business association, has existed since 1952. However, it was not until 1988 that the "Austrian Tea Institute" was founded as a part of this association, with the task of collecting and documenting knowledge about tea.

This chapter first gives an overview of the history and consumption habits of tea in Austria. Second, it briefly introduces the major contemporary Austrian tea brands, which play a non-negligeable role in the country's slowly growing affection for tea, as well as in the hotel and restaurant industry today.

History of tea in Austria

Around 1610, tea from China first reached European shores via Java through the Dutch East India Company. The monopoly passed to the British East India Company in 1669, which held it in China until 1833 (Vocelka, 2010, p. 239). It is likely that the popularity of tea had initially been rather low, as the taste was rather astringent. The good reputation of Asia's healing herbs certainly contributed to the acceptance of this novel drink, though. Less than a century later an entire continent had taken a liking to this beverage of Eastern origin. The convivial tea party developed, especially among the upper classes, as a fixed point for getting together with family and friends in a cultivated way. The various tea suppliers triggered a real price war, making tea available to the masses, as prices fell and the upper classes no longer had the exclusive privilege of enjoying it (Krieger, 2021, pp. 123–125). Tea became particularly popu-

https://doi.org/10.1515/9783110758573-033

lar in Britain where the first tea shop was opened in London in 1717 – still using the same familiar name today: Twinings. However, tea's popularity in Austria and Central Europe only began to rise late and slowly during the eighteenth century (Vocelka, 2010, pp. 239–40). Its spread in the Habsburg Empire was quite comparable to the introduction of other luxury foods in Europe at that time, and was largely due to a preference for all things Asian – Indian, Chinese and Japanese – among Europe's ruling dynasties and nobility (Bödding, 2007, p. 366). Roman Sandgruber (1994, p. 76) summarises this phenomenon as follows:

> Europe enthusiastically absorbed everything that came from across the seas, as lacquer boxes, silk fabrics and porcelain show, for example. Precious collections of Chinese porcelain were created by the absolute monarchs of Europe and concentrated at their courts. A new fashion emerged, the chinoiserie. The "herb the Chinese call tea" spread through the many international contacts of court and aristocratic society. One would not have expected anything else from the Japan and China fashions of the 18th century. It can be assumed that with the prevailing interest in all things Chinese, tea received corresponding attention everywhere in Europe. In Austria, for example, Emperor Leopold I showed considerable interest in the art and culture of China. Maria Theresia also loved the Far East. The Austrian Jesuits maintained direct contacts with the Middle Kingdom for a long time. In the first half of the 18th century, aristocracy in Lower Austria had a habit of drinking tea at breakfast.

Along with tea and especially coffee, chocolate was one of the three "warm drinks of pleasure" (Sandgruber, 1994, p. 77). It was introduced at the Viennese Court by Charles VI in 1711 at the latest. In 1752, Maria Theresia decreed that for events at court "refreshing drinks in the form of tea, coffee and chocolate were to be prepared at a cheap price, [. . .] in sufficient quantity and good quality" (Sandgruber, 1994, p. 77). Although there were regular gatherings in some Viennese salons where tea was served, tea did not become established as an everyday beverage, neither in Vienna or in Austria in general. Even for the middle classes, breakfast consisted mainly of coffee with croissants or rolls, but no tea. It was not until the age of industrialisation that coffee became an accepted part of everyday working life.

Despite this general trend, tea nevertheless became a somehow fashionable drink for a rather limited and exclusive clientele, as the "Mode à l'anglaise", the English fashion, became popular among the Austrian upper class after 1800. Although tea was much more expensive than coffee, it was easier to dilute and, with the addition of sugar, it could be made into a high-calorie drink that began to appeal to the lower classes as well. Here, alcohol was very often added to warm up during breaks at work. Additionally, this made the sometimes poor water quality less noticeable. As a result, tea was gaining popularity with broader social classes in the Habsburg Empire, along with other luxury foods such as coffee, chocolate, sugar and tobacco, but more so with the middle and upper classes, who had greater purchasing power. Even after the Second World War and until the 1950s, lower income classes very often had to make do with substitutes of similar taste and appearance (Sandgruber, 1994, p. 81).

Coffee house culture as a driver for tea consumption

While there is only little historically documented information about tea, the history of coffee in Austria is relatively well documented. Coffee was first introduced to the Austrian court in 1665 and gained wider public attention during the Ottoman siege of Vienna in 1683. Two years later, the first coffee house is said to have opened in the Habsburg capital as a result (Miedaner, 2018, p. 159). A common modern definition of coffee houses by the Austrian Economic Chamber reads as follows (Lower Austria Economic Chamber, 2022, p. 12):

> Coffee houses are catering establishments, the character of which is determined by the furnishing of the premises (arrangement of the tables, possibly lodge-like grouping, possibly separate games room) and the type of management (provision of games tables, possibly billiards, provision of several newspapers and magazines). The guest is thus invited to stay longer. The focus of the activities is the serving of coffee, tea and other hot beverages and refreshments, while the serving of food tends to take a back seat.

The importance of the Viennese coffee house culture is underlined by the fact that UNESCO has listed it as an intangible cultural heritage since 2011 (Austrian National UNESCO Commission, n.d.). Like the Stefan Zweig quote at the beginning of this chapter and other well-known novels and memories that recall the atmosphere of this institution since the nineteenth century up to the present day, Charlotte Ashby (2013, p. 9) aptly describes Austrian coffee house culture by quoting Hilde Spiel (1971) in her article "The Cafés of Vienna":

> In every large or small town throughout the Habsburg lands there is a Viennese coffeehouse. In it can be found marble tables, bentwood chairs and seating booths with leather covers and plush upholstery. In bent-cane newspaper-holders the Neue Freie Presse hangs among the local papers on the wall [. . .] Behind the counter sits the voluptuous and coiffured cashier. Near her looms the expressionless face of the head waiter, who as soon as the call 'Herr Ober, the bill!' is issued, will vanish from the guest's field of vision. The barman lurks casually, but jumps to attention readily enough, though at no time giving the impression of hurried bustle. All in good time, the junior waiter brings the quietly clinking metal tray with its full glass of water to your table.

Coffee houses have also always been important for consumption of tea in Vienna and Austria in general. There are very few surveys on how important this is, but figures on the importance of coffee houses in Austria allow at least a cautious assessment. According to the Austrian Economic Chamber, there were a total of around 5,503 coffee houses in Austria at the end of 2022. This number underlines their importance among the total of 41,227 gastronomy establishments in Austria (Austrian Economic Chamber, 2023, p. 82). In 2017, in a survey conducted by the Vienna University of Economics and Business Administration, 41% of respondents (50% men and 50% women) stated that they go to a coffee house or café in Vienna at least once a month. Some 26% go at least once a week and 8% almost daily (MindTake Research, 2017). The classic coffee house still meets the needs of the younger target groups as well. In an empirical lifestyle study of the Viennese coffee house market, Berger (2005) found that the traditional establishment type, the "old Viennese coffee house", still best meets modern consumer needs. Last but most important for our context is that another survey conducted by the opinion research institute MindTake in 2015 found that among the hot drinks consumed in a coffee house, tea ranks third with 36%, after coffee (75%) and cocoa (41%) (MindTake Research, 2015).

Following the first paragraphs of this chapter, there are two aspects to bear in mind: firstly, and perhaps contrary to common belief, tea has had a permanent place in Austria since the seventeenth century, albeit a much more marginal one compared to coffee. Secondly, and interestingly enough, this fact is largely due to the country's coffee houses and their unbroken success – as the following section will further illustrate.

Tea consumption in Austria

According to Statista, the sales volume of tea in Austria has been growing steadily over the last number of years, especially during the Covid 19 pandemic. In 2022 the sales volume was 79.7 million EUR and is estimated to reach 85.9 million EUR in 2023. More than three quarters of this turnover was spent "away from home" – in coffee houses, for example – and the smaller part, just under 23%, was spent on tea for home consumption. Accordingly, the average turnover per capita in 2023 is calculated to be 9.46 EUR (Statista, 2023). This roughly coincides with current data reporting the monthly consumption expenditure of Austrian households on tea in 2019/20 to be 2.50 EUR. This puts tea ahead of cocoa among hot beverages (0.70 EUR per month), but far behind coffee at 13.30 EUR per month (Statistik Austria, 2021). According to Nielsen Market Research and the Austrian Tea Institute, around 700 million tea bags were sold in food retail outlets in Austria in 2015/16, with tea from tea bags accounting for around 95% of the total tea market here (Austrian Coffee and Tea Association, 2016). Fruit and herbal infusions are the most popular, with Austrians being European champions in the consumption of herbal and fruit infusions, according to the Coffee and Tea Association. While the market shares in food retail in 2019 show herbal tea leading in terms of sales with 47.1% (fruit infusion 34.2%, black tea 12.9% and green tea 5.7%), a survey by Marktagent.com on behalf of Demmers Teehaus (in June/July 2019, see Figure H.1.1) saw a preference for fruit infusion (Austrian Coffee and Tea Association, 2019).

Using results from the above-mentioned market research study from 2019, the trade magazine CASH summarises other preferences for tea consumption in Austria as follows:

> More than a third of Austrians (36%) drink tea several times a week. 16.7% even drink it daily. The Tea Barometer clearly shows that Austria's women drink tea much more often than men: 42.6% even drink tea several times a week, but only 29.5% of men. One statement that can be made, laid across this result, is that the older people are (41.4%), the more tea they drink than

younger people (30.7%), and also that the higher the level of education, the more tea is drunk (43% vs. 32.6%). 'Younger' refers to the 18–24 age group.

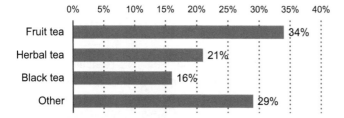

Figure H.1.1: Preferred types of tea in Austria 2019 ("Which type of tea do you prefer to drink?"). Source: Austrian Coffee and Tea Association (2019)

The Coffee and Tea Association also notes that tea consumption in Austria is very much characterised by seasonal fluctuations. A lot of tea is drunk in autumn and winter from October to January. Christmas plays a special role in tea consumption: tea and Christmas baking have a long tradition in Austria. Tea biscuits in connection with tea consumption play an important role for Austrians at this special time of year, as the Austrian Ministry of Agriculture, Forestry, Regions and Water Management (BMLRW) points out on the topic of "Culinary Heritage" (BMLRW, n.d.-a).

But there is also a trend towards year-round beverages, as bio and healthy eating becomes more and more important. This is especially true for herbal infusions and wellness teas, which are said to have both functional and emotional benefits. In addition, tea is increasingly becoming a lifestyle and trend drink, with tea not only drunk hot, but also cold, in blends or as a base for tea cocktails (Austrian Coffee and Tea Association, 2020). Unfortunately, more precise figures on these aspects of tea consumption are not yet available.

In summary, both the value and volume sales of tea are increasing in Austria, with two clear trends: firstly, Austrians seem to prefer the convenience of tea bags, and secondly, fruit and herbal infusions are becoming increasingly popular. Whether this is also true for consumption in the country's important hotel and wellness industry is difficult to assess, but the high number of leisure and wellness hotels in Austria certainly supports this assumption. This is reason enough to briefly discuss some aspects of the special importance of herbal infusions in Austria.

Selected Austrian tea brands

Numerous German and other foreign tea brands are present in the Austrian tea market through the food retail trade (Statista, 2022). Although there is only very little information available, three major Austrian brands are presented below to give a first impression of Austria's now increasingly thriving tea business, especially in the fruit and herbal infusion sector.

Demmers Teehaus

In 1981, Andrew Demmer opened the headquarters of "Demmers Teehaus" at Mölker Bastei 5 in Vienna. It was a mixture of a tea salon and a tea shop with many different types of tea on offer. Most importantly, the company also created its own tea blends. These creations led to the most famous Austrian fruit infusion blend, "Obstgarten" (fruit garden) (Demmers Teehaus, n.d.-a). As Demmer's popularity grew, so did the company. Today, it not only owns several tea shops under the name "Demmers Tee-haus" but has also won over many companies in the catering and hotel industry, and is thus represented in all gastronomic sectors.

Demmer offers practical solutions for the catering and hotel industry, with easy handling, versatile designs in the form of displays that present either open tea or the bag variant beautifully. Both sustainable and close to nature, all Demmer displays are made of wood. To complete the product range, not only is the tea itself offered, but also the necessary equipment for its preparation. Upon request, tea training is also offered to companies so that their employees can learn about different tea varieties and thus become better at active selling (Demmers Teehaus, n.d.-b).

Demmers' quality promise includes sustainability, the organic promise and fair trade (Demmers Teehaus, n.d.-c). Products are evaluated according to strict criteria and are also tasted by staff at regular intervals. Since the cultivation areas are far away and products travel far, special attention is paid to the packaging and to sustainable cultivation methods. The raw materials are therefore sourced from organic farms. Demmer's aim is to produce high quality tea using natural resources and in an environmentally friendly way.

Julius Meinl

For around 155 years, Julius Meinl has been synonymous with Viennese coffee house culture as well as coffee and tea. In 1862, Julius Meinl I opened a shop selling spices and raw materials. His son then developed his own method of roasting coffee, which for the first time removed the aftertaste from coffee beans while retaining their natural aroma. Over the years, the company grew and the product range expanded to include many different types of tea. On the occasion of its one hundred and fiftieth anniversary, Julius Meinl Tea was relaunched under the motto "East meets West". In 2018, the product range was again expanded to include cold drinks under the "Tea on the Rocks" collection (Julius Meinl, n.d.-a). This deeply Austrian company has grown into a world-renowned business with over 1,000 employees and now has branches and distributors in over 70 countries (Julius Meinl, n.d.-b).

Julius Meinl buys its teas from different regions of the world, such as Sri Lanka, the Himalayas and Assam in India, where the climate and conditions are ideal for producing high-quality products. Great care is taken in the production of the tea, which is divided into seven steps, such as correct plucking, withering under the right conditions, treatment with steam and fermentation, drying, sorting, blending and finally tasting (Julius Meinl, n.d.-c.).

Julius Meinl offers a wide range of teas for companies, restaurants and hotels, including menus or flyers. Like Demmer, Meinl also offers tea training courses so that employees can improve their knowledge of tea and thus better advise guests (Julius Meinl, n.d.-d). These training sessions include tea tastings, so that not only is theoretical information about different types of tea exchanged, but also the senses of taste and smell are stimulated.

Interview with Jeannette Meinl
Member of the owner family of Julius Meinl Industrieholding GmbH

1. Austria has a strong coffee culture. What is (was) the importance of tea for the Julius Meinl company?
For Julius Meinl, tea has always been just as important as coffee. Julius Meinl I also sold tea in his grocery shop from the very beginning (1862). In the meantime, Julius Meinl has been the largest tea and coffee importer in Central Europe and thus has 160 years of tea expertise.

2. How has the demand for Meinl tea developed and been differentiated by type (black, green, Oolong, white) and form (bagged or loose tea)?
In terms of demand, it can be seen that there is a great preference in Austria for fruit and herbal infusions, also for green and white tea, but only then for black tea. Loose tea is increasingly becoming a speciality; it is mainly packaged tea that is bought. We see the reason for this in the tendency towards convenience and an increased need for explanation of loose tea (brewing time, water temperature, amount of tea), so that in a coffee country like Austria sales tend primarily towards tea bags. Consumers' knowledge about the preparation method is not very deep and therefore tea seems more complex than coffee. People no longer take the time to prepare a beverage carefully, preferring instead to choose tea bags. In our delicatessen "Julius Meinl am Graben" we offer empty tea bags for self-filling, so that customers can decide which tea and how much they want to put into their individualised tea bags. This is our answer to the demand for bags, the "self-responsible tea bag".

3. What are the parallels/differences/national peculiarities between coffee consumption and tea consumption in Austria in terms of strength/flavouring/sweetening/use of glass or porcelain?
In Austria, a coffee country, tea is not considered to be of great importance. In this respect, the details regarding strength/flavouring/sweetening/glass or porcelain are not aspects that play a major role in tea consumption. There is no pronounced tea culture in Austria, so there is no special attention to water quality or type of tea or the like.
Interestingly, there is a parallel in the development of special varieties: Earl Grey tea was born as an "accident" because black tea was unintentionally mixed with bergamot oil. In the case of coffee, Monsoon Malabar coffee was created in a similar way by mistakenly adding too much moisture to the coffee beans, but it then developed such an interesting aroma that it is considered a speciality.

4. Which European markets are particularly exciting for you in terms of tea and what developments have taken place there in the last 5 years?
Central and Eastern Europe are very interesting for us. The demand trends there are comparable to those in Austria.

5. Is there a specific ritual or pattern in tea consumption in Austria, such as the East Frisian tea ceremony or English Afternoon Tea?
5.1 If so, what tradition has developed? Are there also special cakes or similar?
5.2 If no, why has such a tradition for tea not developed in Austria?
No. A specific tea culture has not developed in Austria. Historically, Austria has become a coffee country. The siege of the Turks in 1683 brought their drink, coffee, to Vienna and it became very popular here. This distinguishes landlocked Austria from countries such as Great Britain or France, for example, which had direct access to tea regions and traditions through sea access and their own colonies. Historically, East Frisia was also introduced to tea by the Dutch. In parallel, the Turks brought coffee to Austria.

6. The Julius Hotel has recently been built in Prague. Why there and are there further plans for similar projects?
Prague is not only the fifth largest hotel market in Europe, but had too little capacity in this segment. Moreover, we have family roots in Bohemia, so this city is close to our hearts. Further plans are open, but we can well imagine the concept in Paris or London.

7. Is the hotel industry relevant for tea consumption or is tea primarily consumed at home in Austria, so that the hotel industry is not very important as a sales market?
The hotel industry is very interesting, but tea is not particularly marketed. Therefore, a separate teahouse – analogous to the classic Viennese coffee house – would be rather unrealistic in Austria. Tea is drunk just as much at home and the strong passion for tea that has grown for coffee over centuries is missing.

8. Your assessment/comment on the tea culture in Austria.
I myself am a passionate tea drinker. But Austria is unfortunately not a tea country but a coffee country. The trends towards more health and convenience will continue and consumers expect more than just the sale of tea. It is also about good treatment of the plantations, sustainability, nature conservation and local working conditions. Transparent references to the country of production are required in order to be able to assess the quality. It is about building trust with the seller and supplier/producer. Intensive notes are recognisable as taste trends, e.g., lychee or hemp. The combination of convenience and health orientation is gaining ground. For me, however, it is always a highlight to be able to enjoy a good cup of Darjeeling 2nd flush.

Sonnentor

Johannes Gutmann, the founder of the Sonnentor company, wanted to break new ground with the term "organic" as early as the 1980s. At the time, the herbs growing in the farmers' fields were being plucked out and thrown away, a practice that Gutmann did not approve of. Little thought was given to these by-products, and the word "organic" was scoffed at. His idea was to process these neglected herbs and not only support his region, but also process food that no one wanted to eat anymore. He wanted to sell regional organic products under the roof of the laughing sun, an old symbol of the Waldviertel (Lower Austria). In 1988, he made a breakthrough with his organic herbs by attracting a number of farmers to his company, and now the Sonnentor family includes more than 300 farmers and about 500 employees (Sonnentor, n.d.-a). Sonnentor's product range includes not only organic herbs and spices, but also coffee, cocoa and snacks. The company sources its herbs from farmers in Austria and abroad. Fair trade is of course a particular concern to Sonnentor.

The focus is on sustainability and organic farming to increase added value. For Sonnentor, sustainability means not only minimising pesticides on the plate, but also independence from multinationals and the creation of regional jobs with a "hands-on" mentality. Even the packaging is made from sustainable materials. The fields are cultivated without chemicals in order to offer the best quality (Sonnentor, n.d.-b).

As well as private consumers, Sonnentor also supplies several restaurants and hotels. Twelve specially selected teas with an exclusive design are offered in a high-quality display case. The corporate range is divided into classic tea bags and loose teas. A further bonus offered to companies is a presentation specially adapted to the company (Sonnentor, n.d.-c).

Also, Austrian artists used the trend of tea consumption to underline their capabilities. Figure H.1.2 shows an impressive tea service made with brass by Josef Hoffmann during the time when only the Meinl company was trading and offering tea. The use of bass fits with the contemporary attractiveness of this material.

Figure H.1.2: Tea service (1910).
Note: Josef Hoffmann (Austrian,1870–1956), Tea Service (1910). Silverplated brass
Photo: David H. Ramsey
Source: Kamm Teapot Foundation

Conclusion

Austria – and especially its capital, Vienna – is very much characterised by its coffee house culture, which largely dominates both national and international (self-)perception. Apart from certain periods in the eighteenth and nineteenth centuries, when tea was socially cultivated in Austrian upper-class circles, tea has played and continues to play a much smaller role in public attention and popularity than coffee. However, it is clear that tea consumption has been growing steadily in recent years. In particular, fruit and herbal infusions are now the dominant types of tea in Austria, which distinguishes this market from other European countries.

Due to the country's geographical location in the Alps, various forms of herbal infusions have played an important role, sometimes regionally, and have long served not only the pleasure of drinking but also health and well-being. The trend towards sustainable and regionally produced food and drink, as well as health and fitness, is further increasing the demand for herbal infusions. Sonnentor, for example, has successfully entered the Austrian tea market and is currently among the three most popular brands in Austria (Statista, 2022).

Coffee may still be the most popular hot drink in Austria. But tea has slowly but surely secured its place in Vienna's coffee houses and beyond. Linked to particular Alpine traditions and contemporary trends, its herbal varieties seem to be its future in this country – if not the foundation of a true Austrian tea culture.

References

Ashby, C. (2013). The cafés of Vienna. In C. Ashby, T. Gronberg, & S. Shaw-Miller (Eds.), *The Viennese café and fin-de-siècle culture* (pp. 9–31). Berghahn Books.

Austrian Coffee and Tea Association (Österreichischer Kaffee- und Tee-Verband). (2016). Österreicher sind Europameister beim Konsum von Kräuter- und Früchtetees. Retrieved January 17, 2022, from https://teeverband.at/oesterreicher-sind-europameister-beim-konsum-von-kraeuter-und-fruechtetees/

Austrian Coffee and Tea Association (Österreichischer Kaffee- und Tee-Verband). (2019). Österreichischer Teemarkt 2019. Retrieved July 18, 2023, from https://teeverband.at/oesterreichischer-teemarkt-2019/

Austrian Coffee and Tea Association (Österreichischer Kaffee- und Tee-Verband). (2020). Österreichischer Teemarkt 2020. Retrieved July 18, 2023, from https://teeverband.at/mehr-tee-denn-je-krise-macht-durst-auf-tee/

Austrian Coffee and Tea Association (Österreichischer Kaffee- und Tee-Verband). (n.d.). Geschichte des Tee-Instituts. Retrieved July 18, 2023, from https://teeverband.at/geschichte-des-tee-instituts/

Austrian Economic Chamber (Wirtschaftskammer Österreich). (2023). Tourismus und Freizeitwirtschaft in Zahlen. Österreichische und internationale Tourismus-und Wirtschaftsdaten. Retrieved July 18, 2023, from https://www.wko.at/branchen/tourismus-freizeitwirtschaft/tourismus-freizeitwirtschaft-in-zahlen-2023.pdf

Austrian National UNESCO Commission (Österreichische UNESCO Kommission). (n.d.). Viennesse Coffee House Culture. Austrian List of Intangible Cultural Heritage. Retrieved July 18, 2023, from https://www.unesco.at/en/culture/intangible-cultural-heritage/national-inventory/news-1/article/vien nese-coffee-house-culture

Berger, D. (2005). Der Einfluss von Lebensstilen auf das Kaufentscheidungsverhalten von Konsumenten – Ergebnisse einer empirischen Studie. *der markt, 44*(3), 118–26. https://doi.org/10.1007/BF03032074

Bödding, M. (2007). Kaffee, Tee und Kakao. *Journal für Verbraucherschutz und Lebensmittelsicherheit, 2*(4), 365–67. https://doi.org/10.1007/s00003-007-0204-9

CASH. (2019). To tea or not to tea. Retrieved October 11, 2023, from https://www.cash.at/industrie/news/ to-tea-or-not-to-tea-19623

Demmers Teehaus. (n.d.-a). Das Unternehmen. Geschichte. Retrieved July 18, 2023, from https://www.tee. at/ueber-uns/das-unternehmen/geschichte/

Demmers Teehaus. (n.d.-b). Über uns. B2B. Retrieved July 18, 2023, from https://www.tee.at/ueber-uns/b2b/

Demmers Teehaus. (n.d.-c). Das Unternehmen. Qualitätsversprechen. Retrieved July 18, 2023, from https://www.tee.at/ueber-uns/qualitaetsversprechen/

Julius Meinl (n.d.-a). History. Julius Meinl: now and then. Retrieved July 18, 2023, from https://juliusmeinl. com/us/about-julius-meinl/our-history

Julius Meinl (n.d.-b). Who we are. Retrieved July 18, 2023, from https://juliusmeinl.com/us/about-julius-meinl/who-we-are

Julius Meinl (n.d.-c). The perfect cup. Retrieved July 18, 2023, from https://juliusmeinl.com/us/your-perfect-cup

Julius Meinl (n.d.-d). For businesses. Retrieved July 18, 2023, from https://juliusmeinl.com/us/for-businesses

Krieger, M. (2021). Geschichte des Tees. Anbau, Handel und globale Genusskulturen. Böhlau Verlag.

Lower Austria Economic Chamber (Wirtschaftskammer Niederösterreich). (2022). Infoblatt Gastgewerbe & Betriebsarten. Retrieved July 18, 2023, from https://www.wko.at/branchen/noe/tourismus-freizeitwirtschaft/gastronomie/Gastgewerbe–Betriebsarten-2022.pdf

Miedaner, T. (2018). Kaffee – der Genuss Arabiens. In T. Miedaner (Ed.), *Genusspflanzen* (pp. 155–77). Springer-Verlag.

MindTake Research. (2015). Studie zur Kaffeehaus- und Kaffeekultur in Österreich. Retrieved January 14, 2022, from https://www.marktmeinungmensch.at/studien/studie-zur-kaffeehaus-und-kaffeekultur-in-oesterrei/

MindTake Research. (2017). Infografik Kaffeehausbesuche. Retrieved July 18, 2023, from https://www.mind take.com/de/file/infografik-kaffeehausbesuche

Sandgruber, R. (1994). Genußmittel. Ihre reale und symbolische Bedeutung im neuzeitlichen Europa. *Jahrbuch für Wirtschaftsgeschichte / Economic History Yearbook, 35*(1), 73–88. https://doi.org/10.1524/ jbwg.1994.35.1.73

Sonnentor. (n.d.-a). Geschichte. Sonnentor & Johannes Gutmann. Retrieved July 18, 2023, from https://www.sonnentor.com/de-at/ueber-uns/geschichte

Sonnentor. (n.d.-b). Bio- und Nachhaltigkeit. Retrieved July 18, 2023, from https://www.sonnentor.com/de-at/ueber-uns/bio-nachhaltigkeit

Sonnentor. (n.d.-c). B2B. Angebote für die Gastronomie. Retrieved July 18, 2023, from https://www.sonnen tor.com/de-at/b2b/gastronomie

Statista. (2022). Ranking der beliebtesten Teemarken in Österreich nach regelmäßigem persönlichem Konsum im Jahr 2022. Retrieved July 18, 2023, from https://de.statista.com/statistik/daten/studie/ 630132/umfrage/beliebteste-marken-bei-tee-in-oesterreich/

Statista. (2023). Consumer Markets, Heißgetränke. Tee, Österreich. Retrieved July 18, 2023, from https://de.statista.com/outlook/cmo/heissgetraenke/tee/oesterreich

Statistik Austria. (2021). Verbrauchsausgaben – Hauptergebnisse der Konsumerhebung 2019/2020. Retrieved July 18, 2023, from https://www.statistik.at/statistiken/bevoelkerung-und-soziales/ausga ben-und-ausstattung-privater-haushalte/ausgaben

Vocelka, K. (2010). *Geschichte der Neuzeit. 1500–1918*. Böhlau Verlag.

Bernhard Bauer
H.2 Azerbaijan and Georgia: Caucasian tea habits

Introduction

"The culture of çay (tea), a symbol of identity, hospitality and social interaction" is the title of the inscription on the UNESCO representative list of the intangible cultural heritage of humanity for Azerbaijan (and Türkiye) in 2022 (UNESCO, 2022). It is regarded as a social practice that shows hospitality, creates and maintains social ties, and is an intrinsic part of celebrating important moments in the lives of communities.

Since the nineteenth century tea has been produced in Azerbaijan and Georgia and currently enjoys a culturally and economically rejuvenating moment. Both countries became the main tea producers in the former Soviet Union while still part of ex-USSR and reached a peak in production in the mid-1980s. It then represented more than 95% of Soviet tea production and around 75% of its total tea supply. Georgia led the way with production of about 150,000 tons from an area of over 65,000 ha, followed by Azerbaijan, producing 35,000 tons from an area of 13,000 ha (Prikhodko et al., 2021).

The fall of the USSR led to the loss of traditional markets and a dramatic decline in the tea industry in the Caucasus. As of 2019, only about 1,900 ha of the tea plantations were active in Georgia and 1,100 ha in Azerbaijan. About 2,000 and 900 tons of green tea leaves or about 500 and 225 tons of made tea, respectively, were obtained from these areas (Prikhodko et al., 2021).

Tea production in the Caucasus has witnessed a certain revival with the tea productive area increasing from 600 ha in 2010 to 1,100 ha in 2019 in Azerbaijan, and from 800 ha in 2014 to 1,900 ha in 2019 in Georgia. However, in the case of the tea leaf output the increase has been much slower (Prikhodko et al., 2021). This is due to the tea plants which take several years to become fully productive.

Azerbaijan and Georgia are amongst the most northern and significant tea producing areas in the world with tea plantations situated between 38°N and 43°N. Hence, tea harvesting is limited to a period of six months (May to October) as tea plants are in dormancy throughout the rest of the year due to low temperatures. However, the long dormancy period of Azerbaijani and Georgian tea plants offers potential for the production of distinctive teas, giving them individual organoleptic qualities. In comparison, major tea producers such as India, Sri Lanka or Kenya are capable of producing tea all year-round and can thus achieve higher yields.

The coastal areas, along the Black Sea in Georgia and the Caspian Sea in Azerbaijan, offer the most suitable agro-climatic conditions for tea production. This is also where most of the tea plantations are located. Lower precipitation levels along the

https://doi.org/10.1515/9783110758573-034

Caspian coast compared to that of the Black Sea, especially during the summer months, means that while Georgia is currently able to produce rain-fed tea, most tea plantations in Azerbaijan are irrigated (with the exception of rare cases of higher-altitude tea plantations).

Consumption patterns represent a key difference between the analysed countries. Azerbaijan has a strong tea drinking culture similar to that of neighbouring Türkiye and Iran. The government of Azerbaijan is supporting the development of its tea economy to substitute imports as the domestic market shows high demand. On the contrary, Georgia is working on prioritising improved market access to and the diversification of export markets.

This chapter is about the commonalities and the different features of tea between Azerbaijan and Georgia. It regards the historical background of tea production, its development during the USSR period and in the aftermath as well as today's situation dealing with the contribution of tea to the national economy and daily drinking habits. Moreover, an outlook to the future of tea culture in the Caucasus is given thanks to the many initiatives of organic farming, certification processes and integrating locally made tea into cultural and culinary tourism activities.

From 2018 to 2020 the author was living in Baku and working for the newly established Azerbaijan Tourism Board (ATB). This is when he got personally interested in the culture of tea drinking in the Caucasus. As a cultural anthropologist he used to speak with locals often about their relationship to tea as a cultural element, a food product and natural stimulant, as well as about the economic impact of the national tea economy.

Acknowledgment is made to Ms. Sakina Asgarova, industry association manager at ATB, certified international trainer at the World Federation of Tourist Guides Association and a distinguished expert of Azerbaijani culinary heritage. She has been working on upgrading Azerbaijani tea to a marketing component within the national culinary tourism strategy. Further acknowledgment goes to Mrs. Anna Vartanova[27] and Mr. Besarion Zalikiani[28] from Georgia who shared their precious knowledge about the historical and present tea culture in Georgia in two expert interviews. All of these experiences and encounters have contributed to this book chapter where the past, present and the future of tea culture in the Caucasus are combined. Much of the information was collected with informal conversations and unstructured qualitative interviews, participant observation and the author's personal notes from the field.

Historical background

The actual beginning of the habit of tea drinking in the Caucasus societies is a contested topic. It is unclear whether the popularity of tea drinking in the Caucasus goes back to the influence of the Russian or Persian empire. Yet, the beginning of tea cultivation is dated to around the mid of the nineteenth century (Battle, 2017). It is said that the Georgian Prince Miha Eristavi, who travelled to China in the 1830s, took seeds to Georgia after having been impressed by the taste of black tea. At that time though, the export of such seeds was prohibited by Chinese law. So, the prince smuggled the seeds out of the country hidden in a piece of bamboo. Eventually, the first home grown tea was harvested some years later by the prince (Georgian Recipes, 2013). Hence, it can be interpreted as the pendant to the big British tea robbery as described by Sarah Rose in her work *For all the Tea in China* (Rose, 2010). However, Georgia celebrated 170 years of tea production in 2017: governor general Vorontsov gave an order to transfer the first bushes of Chinese tea in the area of the Georgian town of Ozurgeti back in 1847 (Chanturiya, 2018). A further impact on tea production was from a Scottish officer named Jacob McNamara starting from the late 1850s onwards after the Crimean war. As his ship was wrecked along the coast of the Black Sea the British officer was captured by the local military forces. He remained in the country and married into a Georgian family. Missing the taste of black tea, he proposed to increase its production on the Eristavi estate in Orzurgeti and Chakvi. Tea from the Caucasus was later presented at an international exhibition in St. Petersburg in 1864. An article by the Russian Nouvelles quoted by the Board of Trade Journal in 1891 (Tea Cultivation in the Caucasus, 1895)[33] stated that the tea plants on the western littoral of Transcaucasia were flourishing and that the plants reached normal dimensions and full maturity. The climate of Western Caucasia was similar to that of south-east China which favoured the growing of tea plants; further, the article stated that "the quality of the tea produced is said to be good".

Towards the end of the nineteenth century, a merchant named Konstantin Popov who was in charge of the Russian imperial tea trade decided to grow tea for exporting along the Black Sea coast. He purchased vast plots of land and established tea plantations with internationally competitive exports. After a study trip to China about large-scale tea production in 1892, Popov came back with Chinese tea crop experts. They significantly helped to improve the production process and created the basis for the successful tea export economy during the Soviet era (Butrin, 2003). Lao Junzhou was the only Asian expert who wished to stay more than three years in Georgia. He became the manager of a tea plantation in Chakvi and followed his mission to create perfect conditions for quality tea in the Caucasus (Zhou, 2012). This led to the award of a gold medal for black tea at the Paris World Exposition in 1899. When he returned to China with his family in 1926, he left an impressive heritage (Liu-Kandareli, 2010). The tea business became so important that the Tea and Subtropical Cultures Research Institute in the Georgian Soviet Socialist Republic was founded in Anaseuli in Western Georgia. Its objectives were to do research on new varieties of tea that adapted to the climate of the area and experiment with different aromas.

Towards the end of the Russian Empire and the beginning of the Soviet Union, Georgia was already playing a crucial role in the tea market. An expansion programme in Georgia in the 1930s reflected Soviet determination to create a tea-growing region sufficiently large enough to satisfy the demands of the Soviet people (Bone, 1963). After coming to power, the communist leadership took over control of the tea production in Georgia with far-reaching consequences. The main focus was on increasing the volume of production, giving favour to quantity and neglecting quality. The directives for municipal authorities were to produce as much tea as possible, shifting from a manual way of collecting tea leaves to mechanical collection. As a result, not only young leaves and tips but also old leaves and other organic material from the bushes were harvested. In order to speed up the process, the fermentation stage was omitted, double drying was reduced to single drying, heat treatment was applied and any kind of quality assessment was left out. Georgian tea lost its reputation as a quality product and became one of the cheapest teas worldwide, which was often sold to the military. The lowest quality tea from Georgia was known as "brick tea", consisting of tea leaves of any grade, steamed and pressed into a two-kilogram brick form. Its trademark, the sickle-and-hammer stamp, gave it the common name of "Stalin tea" among the larger society (Butrin, 2003)

At its peak up to 133,000 tons of packed tea were produced per year from around 70 species. With the collapse of the Soviet Union tea production dropped to nearly 4,000 tons. The tea-growing cooperatives under the communist regime were simply not ready for any competition in exporting their product. Within a few years around 95% of tea factories were forced to close their doors. Parts of the equipment were sold to foreign tea production houses, disassembled, exported and reused, most often in neighbouring Türkiye where tea factories were already operating and increasing their volumes (Vorotnikov, 2017).

The first tea bushes were brought to Azerbaijan in the late 1880s. The production of tea was focused on the southern regions of Lankaran and Astara from the very beginning. Today, this area is located towards the border with Iran, with most of the plantations situated in the Talysh mountains. A land owner named Novoselov is said to be the person who industrialised tea making in Azerbaijan starting in 1912. The first governmental decree on developing the tea production in the Southern area of Azerbaijan was issued in 1931. Tea growing was heavily intensified in the 1970s and 1980s with the rapid extension of fields, agro-technical machinery as well as improvement of irrigation and water supply. With the collapse of the Soviet Union, the industry of tea production faced a similar fate as in Georgia until the late 1990s. This included the deterioration of tea quality, a steep fall in production volume and increasing imports for the country's high consumption rate (Guliyev, 2010).

The present tea culture in the Caucasus

Tea drinking among the population in the Caucasus enjoys more popularity than ever in these days. In Azerbaijan, the per capita annual consumption increased by 31% between 2008 and 2018 (Prikhodko et al., 2021). The Caucasus nation ranks among the countries with the highest tea consumption per capita per year with an average of 2–2.5 kg (Nazarli, 2016), with more tea only consumed in Türkiye. Other top tea-drinking countries are the UK and Morocco.

With domestic green leaf production below 1,000 tons (equivalent to less than 250 tons of made tea), Azerbaijan has relied on imported tea for 99% of its domestic tea supply as of 2018. Hence, protecting the origin of Azerbaijani tea is important. Domestic consumers principally believe that the tea characteristic they have become familiar with belongs to Azerbaijani tea, while in fact they are consuming mostly imported tea (Prikhodko et al, 2021). The development of a more discerning domestic tea market can be created with the enforcement of the rules of origin or geographic indications, coupled with parallel efforts to educate consumers about the unique characteristics of tea grown in Azerbaijan. Today, there are efforts to bring tea "made in Azerbaijan" closer to the quality of imported teas from South Asia – a difficult task for the producers as the local consumers have become accustomed to the Asian taste; however at the same time nationally grown tea preserves its unique organoleptic qualities.

Consumption behaviour is very different in Georgia, where per capita consumption is around 400 grams per year (five times lower than in Azerbaijan). About 100 grams of that amount are consumed within households and the rest is consumed in the restaurants and accommodation sector (National Statistics Office of Georgia, 2021). The share of locally produced tea that is consumed in Georgia is around 20%. The development of the country's tea sector will have to be strongly export-oriented, as domestic consumption patterns are unlikely to significantly shift (Kochlamazashvili & Kakulia, 2013). However, rising incomes in Georgia open up opportunities for high-end niche products, such as specialty, medicinal, health and wellness teas. The companies of Anna Vartanova and Besarion Zalikiani are working towards that direction – with a strong focus on improving tea quality while maintaining the unique characteristics of Georgian tea and protecting its identity. These are key to reaching lucrative export markets and also enhancing the consumer appeal of the tea brand "made in Georgia" internationally.

Tea holds an important place for the Azerbaijani population. It is consumed all day and at night; there is no specific tea time as it is (or was) in the UK with traditional afternoon tea. People take their time to drink tea; there is no rush neither with the preparation nor the consumption. And most importantly, it is always the right time to have a glass of tea. If someone is offered tea, he/she will not refuse it. Offering tea is a gesture of taking time to speak and listen to the person invited – and time is a precious gift for everyone. Refusing someone's tea would probably not be felt as an offense but as slightly strange or suspicious behaviour. Tea is an important element of the daily routine. Guests should never reject a glass of tea. It is not expected that every glass of tea is emptied to the last drop; therefore, an elaborated strategy for not drinking too much could be sipping slowly, stirring snugly, complimenting its mixture and taste, and not asking for a refill. On hot days a chilled glass of water in addition is a good companion.

Azerbaijanis drink tea during a visit in a hammam, on the street when having a snack, and taxi drivers usually have a large thermos flask in their trunk to enjoy a cup during their break. In Baku there are also mobile tea vendors canvassing from one shop to the other along busy shopping streets, selling tea to the sales assistants pushing re-modelled baby strollers which are used for transporting the tea pots, cups, sugar and sweets.

In addition, various tea drinking ceremonies exist throughout the country. There are certain protocols to be respected, especially during dedicated family festivities such as engagement and wedding ceremonies. The amount of sugar served and put into the armudu are important details and may give indications whether the father of the bride is in favour of the chosen one. This varies substantially throughout the regions and enjoys high cultural and traditional significance (Jafarova, 2013).

The pear-shaped glass named "armudu" is the favourite tea cup (Bayramova, 2013). The Armudu glass is associated with the figure of a hostess in Azerbaijani culture. It is believed that the classic shape of Armudu represents the ideal figure of an Eastern woman or an 18-year old Azerbaijani girl. The Armudu is made from a variety of materials, such as glass, porcelain, faience and silver (Jafarova, 2013).

At home or in a teahouse tea can also be drunk in a standard tea cup made from glass or ceramic. Street vendors serve tea in a paper or polystyrene cup. In a Chaykhana, a typical and rather modest teahouse in Azerbaijan, tea is commonly served with sugar, lemon and jams from many different fruits (Niederbrühl, 2020). Azerbaijanis like to drink their tea very sweet, especially in the morning. To have the extra sweet experience people take a piece of sugar and put it between the front teeth. The hot tea is drunk and slowly dissolves the piece of sugar. Once it has vanished, the drinker pours various teaspoons of sugar into the glass. By the second glass the fruit jams can either be mixed with the tea or eaten aside with the spoon. But actually there is no sequence to be respected; people simply follow their preference of taste. Asking the waiter for more sugar, more lemon, more fruit jam or even more tea is generally seen as a compliment.

The samovar, a traditional water boiler, is an important element for the preparation of tea. Traditional Chaykhanas, either indoor in the cities or the surrounding countryside, or outdoor somewhere in the woods along roads connecting small towns, use wood to heat up the water. Dense clouds of smoke seam such places and the smell of burning wood gives a wonderful feeling of the slowly prepared tea. Teahouses with a bigger guest capacity also use electric samovars.

Since the late 2000s tea production in Georgia has been on the rise again in terms of both quality and quantity. The industry is keen on positioning itself with high-quality products on the international market, with the emphasis on pesticide-free varieties, organic growing processes and creative marketing techniques (Seturi & Todua, 2019). One of the results is that the *Tea In Studio* of Anna Vartanova currently lists 53 locally produced tea variations with various characteristics ranging from differences in taste, intensity, being wild and planted.

Recognising the importance of the agricultural sector for the economy and the long cultural tradition of tea production and consumption, both Azerbaijan and Georgia have introduced various policies. This includes certain tea development programmes with specific support measures in order to stimulate the sector development.

In Azerbaijan, the State Programme for the Development of Tea Industry (2018–2027) aims for an increase in the tea productive area to 3,000 ha. The production target is set to expand to 8,500 tons by 2027. Current financial support measures by the state provide a financial subsidy per hectare per year for the first seven years from planting and a reduced subsidy per hectare per year thereafter. For new plantations established before 2019, a similar subsidy amount applies independently of the current age of the plantation. These newly introduced subsidies aim at stimulating investments in new tea plantations and replacing various pre-existing agricultural input-specific subsidies (Azertac, 2018).

In 2016, a Tea Rehabilitation Programme was adopted by the Government of Georgia. Unlike in the case of Azerbaijan, the Georgian approach, managed by the Ministry of Environmental Protection and Agriculture, aims to stimulate the rehabilitation of abandoned tea plantations by co-financing weeding, deep pruning, fertilisation, and other works. The objective is to reach up to 7,000 ha of rehabilitated tea plantations within the programme time frame (Ministry of Environmental Protection and Agriculture of Georgia, 2016)

The future of tea culture, production and consumption

Tea is on the rise in the Caucasus – in terms of national economic opportunities, new lifestyle habits as well as the rejuvenation in the traditional context. Chaykhanas in Azerbaijan are visited by the younger and the older generations, and urban and modern teahouses in Georgia are becoming interesting for the hipster movement. The linkage of the tea sector with tourism activities is an important economic opportunity for farmers, traders and tea experts such as Besarion Zalikiani and Anna Vartanova. In particular, the domestic tourism market is of interest to the many rural stakeholders in Georgia and Azerbaijan.

Internationally funded projects such as EU4Lankaran (UNDP, 2021) are supporting the tea-agricultural sector in the South of Azerbaijan. As a consequence, these farmers will not only benefit from the direct support to their agricultural businesses but will also be able to enter the tourism value-chain. The tourism sector is interested in integrating such tea producers into specific activities such as visits to a tea plantation, getting hands-on information about its production, having the opportunity to taste the locally made tea, and developing tea-based souvenirs. Such activities are further supported by the Azerbaijan Tourism Board and Slow Food as a strategic partner.

Tea as a cultural and culinary element packaged in a tourism activity is marketed by the Azerbaijan Tourism Board (ATB) to visitors in the form of articles (Azerbaijan Tourism Board, 2021), specific activities posted on the ATB website, and at the many international tourism fairs and exhibitions.

In Georgia, the cultural legacy of tea and Europe has been integrated into the Cultural Routes of the Council of Europe Programme. In December 2020, the Board for Strategic Development and Certification of Cultural Routes of Georgia granted five new routes, among those the route "Georgia painted by tea" (European Institute of Cultural Routes, 2020), with the Certificates of the Ministry of Education, Science, Culture and Sport of Georgia.

The members of that route are Georgian bio tea companies, tea related associations, universities, teahouses, and museums. The partners contribute to offering a variety of services to the visitors such as tasting of local types of tea, excursions with storytelling about different themes (history, literary, bio-agriculture, etc.), tea picking, and processing activities, among others. These partners must comply to certain standards of production and have a bio-certificate for all their products, adopt the "farm to table" concept, take on social responsibility projects, and offer adequate infrastructure for visitors.

Besarion Zalikiani pays attention to the demand trends of the young travellers and tea lovers, so he founded the start-up "Tea Country" in 2021. It is a tea delivery company distributing products from 15 tea growers across Georgia. With business initiatives such as "Georgian Tea in TeaHouses" and "Literary Tea" he even links national artists and literature with the tea sector. During a start-up week contest organised by Start-up Grind and USAID, Besarion was part of a winning project about a Georgian Tea Online Platform in the same year.

Moreover, his company is cooperating with regional Tourism Development Centers, airports, and other local tourism related institutions to increase the awareness of Georgian tea. In order to do so the tea industry also takes advantage of digitalisation and technology. Specific 3D virtual tours are developed at tea factories and tea plantations to create marketing material. All teabags get QR codes which are linked to websites and platforms with specific information about tea in Georgia.

Anna Vartanova is also active in the development of Georgian agro-ethnic tea tours and tourism activities linked to the production of tea. The customers visit tea farmers and are accompanied by professional tea tour guides and tea masters. They lead the groups through tea gardens, plantations, and wild tea forests at the seaside regions and conduct tea master classes with the degustation of various teas.

The tea cultural route shall act as an economic driver for rural Georgia. Its initiators count on the increasing interest in the field of tea plantation, encouraged bioproduction by new SMEs, attracting foreign investment (by diaspora Georgians), modernisation of farming, diversification of the economy, and growing visitor numbers.

Moreover, the route and modern tea farming shall have a spill-over effect to neighbouring countries and territories suffering from military confrontations and create opportunities for piece-building among the Caucasus populations.

Conclusion

Azerbaijan and Georgia are looking back to a history of more than 150 years of tea production which has undergone substantial changes during the time of the USSR and after its fall in the 1990s. For around 15 years the Caucasus countries have been celebrating a significant cultural rejuvenation of tea consumption. Their respective governments have also witnessed the economic value and incentivise the production, export, and national consumption of "home-grown" tea products. Moreover, the tea industry benefits from several farming companies which are focusing on the production of organic tea and on improving the quality of its green and black tea sorts.

However, tea produced and packaged in both Azerbaijan and Georgia by domestic producers is usually a blend of domestic and imported tea (mostly from Iran in Georgia and from Sri Lanka in Azerbaijan). Most often such information is not made visible on the product labels. The mix of tea of various origins and its packaging as a "national" product is a common practice within the industry. Sometimes the share of locally-produced tea is under 10% of the final product. The effect of such practices on the evolution of consumer preferences both domestically and in key export markets could be significant. Consumers are led to believe that the characteristics of the tea they are accustomed to drinking belong to the local tea, while in fact they are consuming mostly imported (or re-exported) tea. This could sooner or later lead to a total loss of tea identity (Prikhodko et al., 2021).

Tea companies and initiatives such as from Anna Vartanova and Besarion Zalikiani are working towards establishing a distinctive tea identity in the Caucasus. They are involved in and are leading various activities that introduce and enforce rules concerning the origin or geographic indications, or at least clear labelling guidelines allowing consumers to differentiate between locally grown and locally processed but imported tea. Their initiatives are coupled with parallel efforts to educate consumers about the unique characteristics of tea grow in Azerbaijan and Georgia. Furthermore, providing more information shall also form a basis for the creation of more discerning tea markets where Georgian and Azerbaijani teas need to popularise and protect their unique identity.

These actions are highly appreciated in the societies of both countries which are reconsidering the value of nationally grown tea products. Furthermore, the tourism sector is becoming a tool for raising awareness and the marketing of organic products, especially among the domestic tourism market. In addition, revenues from tourism activities such as tours to tea plantations, production facilities, tea master classes, seminars, tastings, etc., are an important economic opportunity for farmers, guides, and all those that are directly and indirectly connected to the local tourism industry.

May 21, the international tea day, is celebrated by tea-producing countries around the world including the Caucasus. This event seeks to draw the attention of governments and citizens to the impact that tea trade has on farmers, producers, and the larger industry. In Azerbaijan and Georgia this day is further used to raise awareness of the cultural significance of tea and the importance of its organic production.

References

Azerbaijan Tourism Board. (2021). How to spend a long weekend in Sheki, Azerbaijan. Retrieved October 22, 2021, from https://www.nationalgeographic.co.uk/travel/2021/07/how-to-spend-a-long-weekend-in-sheki-azerbaijan

Azertac. (2018). Azerbaijan to Increase tea plantations up to 3,000 hectares by 2027. Retrieved January 15, 2022, from https://azertag.az/en/xeber/Azerbaijan_to_increase_tea_plantations_up_to_3000_hectares_by_2027-1136254

Battle, W. (2017). The World Tea Encyclopaedia: The World of Tea Explored and Explained from Bush to Brew. Troubadur, London.

Bayramova, J. (2013). *God´s drink – Voyage to the land of Azerbaijan tea*. Visions of Azerbaijan. Discover the Land of Fire. Retrieved January 15, 2022, from http://www.visions.az/en/news/496/ef6bd31a/

Bone, R. M. (1963). *Soviet tea cultivation*. Annals of the Association of American Geographers, *53*(2): 161–73. Retrieved January 15, 2022, from https://www.jstor.org/stable/2561409

Butrin, D. (2003). *Georgia: Fleece, wine and mimino*. Kommersant Dengi, No. 5 (410).

Chanturiya, R. (2018). *170 years of Georgian tea*. Coffee and Tea International Business Magazine. International Tea House.

European Institute for Cultural Routes. (2020). Cultural routes of the Council of Europe programme. Activity report. Retrieved January 15, 2022, from https://rm.coe.int/cultural-routes-of-the-council-of-europe-programme-activity-report-202/1680a245ec

Georgian Recipes. (2013). How a Georgian prince smuggled tea out of China. Retrieved January 15, 2022, from https://georgianrecipes.net/2013/03/29/how-a-georgian-prince-smuggled-tea-out-of-china/

Guliyev, F. (2010). *Tea growing in Azerbaijan. The present and prospects*. Visions of Azerbaijan. Retrieved January 15, 2022, from http://www.visions.az/en/news/196/8872cf85/

Jafarova, A. (2013). Ancient traditions of tea drinking in Azerbaijan. Azernews. Retrieved January 15, 2022, from https://www.azernews.az/culture/49831.html

Kochlamazashvili, I., & Kakulia, N. (2013). The Georgian tea sector: A value chain study. Retrieved March 29, 2023, from https://iset-pi.ge/storage/media/other/2021-10-07/563ae2b0-2761-11ec-a316-b5bd50827c2a.pdf

Liu-Kandareli, M. (2010). Tea culture sources in Georgia. Chinese business in Georgia. Retrieved January 15, 2023, from https://georgiaphiles.wordpress.com/2013/01/20/georgia-tea/

Ministry of Environmental Protection and Agriculture of Georgia. (2016). Georgian tea plantation rehabilitation program. Retrieved January 15, 2022, from https://mepa.gov.ge/En/Projects/Details/18

National Statistics Office of Georgia. (2021).

Nazarli, A. (2016). Azerbaijan among leaders in tea drinking. AzerNews. Retrieved January 15, 2022, from https://www.azernews.az/lifestyle/96938.html

Niederbrühl, S. (2020, August 12). Die aserbaidschanische Teekultur. Retrieved April 15, 2023, from
https://www.auresa.de/blog/die-aserbaidschanische-teekultur/

Prikhodko, D., Sterk, B., Monzini, J., & Snell, J. (2021). Potential brewing for Azerbaijani and Georgian tea
industries. *Directions in investment, number 2*. FAO. Retrieved January 15, 2023, from https://doi.org/
10.4060/cb4736en

Rose, S. (2010). *For all the tea in China. Espionage, empire and the secret formula for the world´s favourite
drink*. Penguin Books.

Seturi, M., & Todua, T. (2019). The role of branding for success in the Georgian tea market 13. Retrieved
March 29, 2023, from https://doi.org/10.5281/zenodo.3455675

Tea Cultivation in the Caucasus. (1895). *Bulletin of Miscellaneous Information (Royal Botanic Gardens, Kew)*,
1895(99), 58–61. https://doi.org/10.2307/4118479

Vorotnikov, V. (2017). Georgia works to revitalize its tea industry. Retrieved January 15, 2022, from
https://www.teaandcoffee.net/feature/2061/georgia-works-revitalize-tea-industry/

UNESCO. (2022). Decision of the Inter-Governmental Committee 17.COM 7.B.44. Retrieved January 16,
2023, from https://ich.unesco.org/en/decisions/17.COM/7.B.44

UNDP. (2021). EU funded project for modernising fruit and vegetable sector kicks off in Azerbaijan.
Retrieved October 22, 2021, from https://www.undp.org/azerbaijan/press-releases/eu-funded-project
-modernising-fruit-and-vegetable-sector-kicks-azerbaijan

Zhou, J. (2012). Chinese in Georgia. ECMI Working Paper # 54. Retrieved March 29, 2023, from
https://www.ecmi.de/fileadmin/redakteure/publications/pdf/Working_Paper_54_en_corrected.pdf

Samuel Bartoš, Jan Hán and Kateřina Havelková

H.3 Czech tea heritage, entrepreneurship and perspective

Introduction

Tea is an important social drink, consumed by the vast majority of the Czech population. Therefore, it is necessary to pay as much attention to it as other popular beverages such as wine, beer or coffee.

The following text can be divided into three parts. The first part describes some aspects of Czech tea culture. These aspects include Czech tea consumers, purchasing preferences and consumption habits, preferred types of tea, the phenomenon of Czech teahouses and others. The second part of the text presents a selective transcription of an interview with Petr Zelik, the founder and owner of OXALIS. OXALIS is one of the most important companies in the tea and coffee business in the Czech Republic. This section focuses on the tea and coffee business in current economic, social and cultural conditions. The final part summarises the problems encountered in the development of Czech tea culture and the ways in which this tea culture can be improved.

Fragments of tea culture in the Czech Republic

Tea can be considered as an extremely popular drink in Czech society. This statement is supported by the company Nielsen Admosphere, which published the results of a survey on tea consumption in the Czech Republic in 2015. This research revealed that it is very difficult to find a single Czech who does not drink tea; the results showed that 91% of men and up to 99% of women consumed tea. In the following sections, various aspects of Czech tea culture will be characterised.

Historical references to tea in the Czech Republic

According to V. Polák (1936), today's Czech word "čaj" does not originate from Chinese language but rather from Persian and Turkish language. On the contrary, the word "thé" was implemented into colloquial Czech language from German. In its historical development, the word "čaj" first entered the written language as a Russianism, was gradually domesticated in the colloquial language and then replaced the word "thé".

Tea probably appeared in Europe around 1549, in Venice, thanks to a Persian rhubarb and tea merchant. It is not entirely clear how and when tea was brought to Bo-

https://doi.org/10.1515/9783110758573-035

hemia. But what we are sure about is the fact that tea was commonly consumed in Bohemia in the early eighteenth century. This statement is proved in a dissertation from 1720 (Černý, 2020). It can be assumed that Czech tea culture originated in the seventeenth or eighteenth century. According to some sources, at the end of the eighteenth century, Chinese tea was being sold in Prague, in a house called "U Zlatého okouna" thanks to the merchant Jan Alois Svatojánský. Other references about tea can be found in the literary works of famous Czech writers, such as Karel Havlíček Borovský or Jan Neruda (Thomová et al., 2002). Jan Neruda writes in his feuilleton in 1874:

> We drink coffee day and night, in the morning right after sleeping and at night for sleeping, in the morning for eating and at noon for digestion. Coffee is to us – at least in Bohemia, where tea is still little consumed – among drinks what potatoes and bread are among meals [. . .]. Tea is a drink somehow more modern than coffee. In the past, we used to invite for something, now we invite for Tea. It has all kinds of names – soirée, conversation, sometimes thée-dansant [. . .]. In our country, coffee still dominates, only in the cities sometimes we invite people for tea. We consider it aristocratic [. . .] (Thomová et al., 2002, p. 273)

It can be stated that tea and tea culture was being repressed until 1989. Prior to that year, it was only possible to buy high-quality loose-leaf tea in Tuzex with bons, and the majority of teas were imported from the Soviet Union and India and were packed into teabags and distributed to shops. The situation improved slightly in the 1980s when a shop called "Káva a čaj" (Coffee and Tea) was opened in Prague. This shop was the only place with a larger range of imported loose-leaf tea. The big turning point came after 1989, when a huge tea boom started in the Czech Republic. This was due to the opportunity to travel to both producing countries and the western part of the world, which was characterised by a large range of different types of tea. Another important turning point was the success of Czech teahouses, which led to their expansion. In 1993, a new teahouse was opened close to Wenceslas Square in Prague, which was the beginning of the largest teahouse network in the Czech Republic (Thomová et al., 2002).

Czech tea consumers

First of all, it is necessary to characterise specific types of consumers. According to Petr Zelik (2022), consumers can be divided into two groups – mass consumers and consumers who seek quality loose-leaf tea – "[. . .] since the invention of a tea bag and portioned teas have basically taken over the developed part of the planet, probably because of the fast-paced lifestyle [. . .]." The mass consumer can be characterised as someone who prefers the quicker and simpler preparation of tea using teabags. In Czech Republic, 70–80% belong to this category, while 20–30% are more into qualitative loose tea (Kratochvílová 2022; Zelik 2022). The preparation of loose-leaf tea cannot be regarded as difficult but certain rules must be followed to achieve the desired quality. This aspect can probably be considered as the reason for this vast difference.

A Czech tea consumer can be considered as "mostly educated [. . .]" (Zelik, 2022). It is based on the fact that there have been major changes in consumer knowledge and also acceptance of new types of tea in the last thirty years. In the 1990s, the supply of tea in the Czech Republic was very limited and therefore tea culture was developing slowly. Petr Zelik considers the existence of Czech teahouses and the greater opportunities for travel to be the main reasons for this change. It is typical for mass consumers and consumers who seek high quality loose-leaf tea that the most common place to consume tea is at home. Other places for consumption are teahouses, which play a significant role in the development of tea culture in the Czech Republic. Both groups of consumers evaluate taste and aroma when choosing and buying tea. Mass consumers also evaluate price, while for consumers seeking high quality tea, important factors are the appearance of the tea leaf, origin and the manufacturing process (Kratochvílová, 2022). According to Petr Zelik (2022), there is a large number of Czech consumers who consume tea especially when they have a cold or they feel sick. For many people tea represents "[. . .] a kick-start for the day, which is associated with the morning and maybe breakfast ritual [. . .]" (Zelik, 2022) and therefore it can be assumed that tea is largely consumed at the beginning of the day. However, if one wants to enjoy tea and combine it with some relaxation, tea is most often prepared in the afternoon: "[. . .] I think what has developed here is something like 5 o'clock tea or afternoon tea [. . .]" (Zelik, 2022).

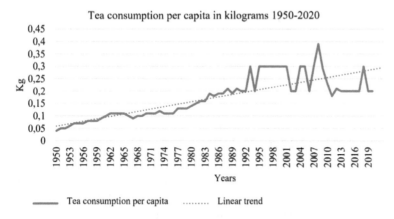

Figure H.3.1: Tea consumption per capita in kilograms, 1950–2020.
Source: Kratochvílová (2022) according to Czech Statistical Office

Figure H.3.1 shows the consumption of tea in the Czech Republic from 1950 to 2020. The data was processed with balance method based on tables from the Czech Statistical Office. The chart shows that the highest consumption of tea was in 2007, while the lowest consumption can be seen at the beginning of the chart. According to M. Kratochvílová (2022), the reasons for the growth of the curve, i.e., the growth of the amount of tea consumed, are better availability of tea and historical development.

In general, bagged tea is the more preferred form of tea, but Czech consumers also seek for loose-leaf tea – 93% of tea consumers use tea in teabags, while 46% of consumers prepare loose-leaf tea (Nielsen Admosphere, 2021). In the Czech Republic, tea is mostly purchased via e-shops, in supermarket chains but also in specialised shops focused on the sale of tea. The preferred place for purchase is shown in Figure H.3.2, based on data from a questionnaire survey conducted by M. Kratochvílová (2022). This chart compares tea lovers and ordinary consumers.

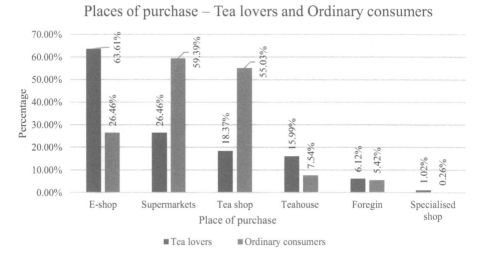

Figure H.3.2: Places of purchase.
Source: Processed according to Kratochvílová (2022)

Types of tea consumed

According to Nielsen Admosphere (2021), the most consumed type of tea in the Czech Republic is fruit infusion. In terms of consumption, it is followed by black tea and herbal infusion. In addition, it can be seen that women prefer to consume fruit infusion, while black tea is a beverage more often consumed by men (Dasaev, 2021). The top five types of tea consumed according to Nielsen Admosphere are shown in Figure H.3.3.

It is not only important which type of tea is mostly consumed but also at what times of the day specific types of tea are consumed. Figure H.3.4 shows preferred types of tea in specific times of the day. The data describe the behaviour of consumers who seek high quality loose-leaf tea (Kratochvílová, 2022).

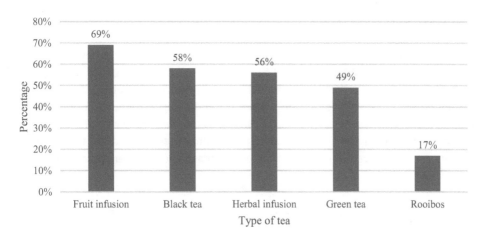

Figure H.3.3: Top five consumed teas in Czech Republic in 2021.
Source: Processed according to Nielsen Admosphere (2021)

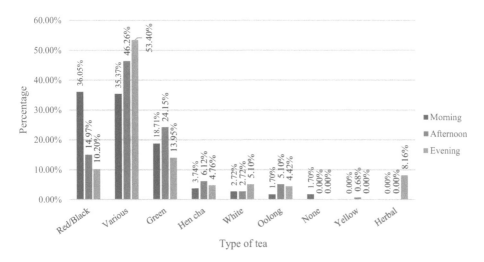

Figure H.3.4: Preferred type of tea in different times of the day.
Source: Processed according to Kratochvílová (2022)

The most consumed tea in the morning is black tea, followed by the "various" tea group. According to this master's dissertation, this group includes all types of tea. What is important for participants' preference is their mood during the day which influences their choice. This fact is also reflected in the data on tea consumption in the afternoon and evening, as the "various" category is the most frequently selected. It can be seen that most consumers do not associate a particular tea with a particular time of the day (Kratochvílová, 2022) (see Figure H.3.4).

Czech tea culture

According to Petr Zelik (2022), Czech tea culture can be characterised by certain features, including the phenomenon of Czech teahouses, the growing demand for high quality loose-leaf tea, the Čajomír association and the creation of tea rituals. When examining the transcription of the interview, another significant aspect of Czech tea culture was defined, the existence of an interest group of members of the Czech Bartenders Association called Czech Teatenders. Another aspect is also the attitude of accommodation and catering establishments towards the development of tea culture.

The phenomenon of Czech teahouses

> Teahouses are an amazing Czech phenomenon that started in the early 90s and in a way responded to the hunger for travel, which was impossible through the Iron Curtain, and I think, that teahouses also fulfilled the fast, immediate transfer of the atmosphere of the Far East or Arabic culture [. . .] (Zelik, 2022)

> I think that teahouses were a wonderful transmitter of tea culture to the Czech environment, when tea culture was slowly beginning to develop [. . .] (Zelik, 2022)

In Europe, coffee culture was and is definitely more dominant in the form of cafés, but the number of places where tea would be served and honoured was increasing. Teahouses of the Czech type are widespread like nowhere else in Europe and they have become a major phenomenon. Thus, it is not difficult to find teahouses all over the Czech Republic with a wide range of different types of tea (Korosteleva, 2021).

> There are many cultural activities and performances associated with teahouses, such as music, which is typical for tea countries and another thing is lectures and educational activity [. . .] (Zelik, 2022)

The main difference between Czech teahouses and teahouses around the world is that Czech teahouses mainly focus on quality tea and its enjoyment rather than on the combination of tea and hookah or food (Korosteleva, 2021). Thomová and co-authors (2002) state that Czech teahouses are original in their design because they mix elements of Eastern cultures and are often furnished with furniture that comes from attics or dumps. This furnishing creates a cosy, nostalgic and often meditative atmosphere.

There are more than 180 teahouses in the Czech Republic, of which over 60 can be found in Prague. According to M. Vojtěchovská from the zeměpisec.cz portal, in 2020 there were at least 199 teahouses in operation, which, in the words of expert Aleš Juřina, was the largest concentration of teahouses on the territory of one country in the world. In the Czech Republic, there are up to 1.89 teahouses per 100,000 inhabitants (Hanák and Foursquare City Guide, 2022; Teahouses in Prague, n.d.; Vojtěchovská, n.d.).

Consequently, there are also new concepts of teahouses, developed by Czech architects. Black Teahouse represents the first example of teahouse concepts, designed by Czech Studio A1 Architects and situated next to a peaceful lake near Česká Lípa. Another project is a teahouse by David Maštálka, again created by A1 Architects, collaborating with sculptor Vojtěch Bilišič. The house is situated in Prague, and illustrates a minimal place for gatherings, following a Japanese tradition. Situated in a wild garden with several spring apple and cherry blossom trees, the outside is ready to surprise the visitor, while the inside offers a different perspective of the surroundings (Etherington, 2009; Frearson, 2011).

This underlines the importance of teahouses for the Czech tea culture also transferred with modern approaches to open the tradition to younger generations and non-tea related target groups as well as clearly show the social function of teahouses.

Čajomír

According to the words of Petr Zelik (2022), Čajomír is another way to improve and develop the Czech tea culture. Association Čajomír, whose founder is Jaromír Horák, provides tea preparation teaching through the Tea School at Čajomír's in Prague, where he teaches tea lovers and catering workers how to handle tea preparation properly. The school offers various courses which are suitable for both complete beginners and tea professionals (Čajomír, n.d.). The Čajomír Association also organises the annual Čajomír fest – an international tea festival which regularly takes place in Prague in the summer, in the second or third week of August, usually lasting two days. The fourteenth year of Čajomír fest took place in the Exhibition Centre in Holešovice. The festival welcomed tea lovers from different parts of the world. Visitors of the festival could enjoy a great tasting in the so-called "festival teahouses". A rich programme was prepared for both adults and families with children, so everyone could find something for themselves – music and dance performances or educational workshops (Čajomír, n.d.).

Creating tea rituals

Those traditional rituals are difficult to transfer to Central Europe, but our rituals are often associated with some kind of sweet pastry and meeting [. . .] (Zelik, 2022)

In the Czech Republic, the traditional tea rituals that we know from various Asian countries are not quite common and according to Petr Zelik this is due to the difficult transferability to Central Europe. However, it is possible to find some groups of tea lovers who create and perform certain rituals themselves, for example the custom of a family or a community getting together on a Saturday afternoon to prepare tea, which is often accompanied by sweet pastries and a pleasant atmosphere.

Attitude of accommodation and gastronomy establishments towards the development of tea culture

> Both tea and coffee are on the edge of interest, i.e., frequently, the catering industry is satisfied with a basic offer of bagged tea, in the vast majority, only exceptional projects prefer a certain preparation of loose-leaf tea [. . .] (Zelik, 2022).

Accommodation and gastronomy establishments do not focus on offering high quality loose-leaf tea and its preparation. Operators and owners of catering establishments often prefer bagged tea because of the preparing simplicity, lower financial requirements and also the lack of knowledge and skills about tea. If a guest, while ordering a cup of tea, expects loose-leaf tea, it is not a rule but rather an exception based on a specific concept or a desire to provide a higher gastronomy service. There are, however, typical places in the Czech Republic where tea lovers can enjoy loose-leaf tea, such as the above-mentioned teahouses (Zelik, 2019).

Czech Teatenders

Czech Teatenders is an interest group of members within the Czech Bartenders Association (CBA). The Czech Bartenders Association brings together professional bartenders, baristas, beer specialists, teatenders and other professionals in the field of beverage gastronomy in the Czech Republic. The main goal of the Czech Teatenders group is to bring expertise to contemporary gastronomy that focuses on the world of tea. The group specialises in tea and its preparation, organises many professional workshops and seminars on tea every year and also organises competitions for talented young teatenders. According to the official website of the Czech Bartenders Association, the activities of this group are innovative due to the lack of a similar platform in the Western world (Czech Bartenders Association, n. d.). The head of the Czech Teatenders section is Jan Zlámaný. Together with his predecessor, Jiří Boháč, they are the main representatives of this section; they have been working with tea for several years and try to share their knowledge and experience in the form of educating young teatenders and maintaining knowledge about tea within Czech society (Czech Bartenders Association, 2022).

It is also necessary to mention one of the many contributions of the Czech Teatenders group and the Czech Bartenders Association. Since 2022, the profession "teatender" has been officially qualified by the National Institute of Education in the national system of qualifications. Thanks to this qualification, the standards of competences and skills that a professional in this sphere must meet are set. Thanks to this step, the profession of "teatender" has become another professional gastronomic profession and occupation in the Czech Republic, similar to, for example, waiter, chef, sommelier or bartender (Czech Bartenders Association, 2022).

Establishment and development of an important Czech tea company

OXALIS has been operating on the Czech market since 1993. The main focus of the company is the importing, processing and distribution of loose-leaf tea and selected coffee (Zelik, 2019). Annually, the company processes 350 tons of tea and 130 tons of coffee and offers up to 1,450 products. OXALIS employs around 130 people and in 2020 operated 35 of its own stores and 31 franchised stores. Products are imported from a total of 34 countries and exported to 32 countries (OXALIS, 2020). The founder and owner of OXALIS is Petr Zelik, with whom a semi-structured interview was conducted not only about the tea culture in the Czech Republic but also about the tea business.

The first impulse to establish OXALIS was the visit to Sri Lanka and tea gardens in 1992: "You can see the beautiful green fields that stretch beyond the horizon, because the hills are all round, you don't have to see the end, the smell of fresh tea, tea tasted right in those gardens, which was something that really got me [. . .]" (Zelik, 2022).

The biggest problem the company encountered in its early days was the lack of knowledge. It was based on market opportunities and the variety of loose-leaf tea newly offered in that time: "Few people knew what loose-leaf tea was [. . .]. People didn't know what to see in it, they didn't know the difference between green tea and black tea [. . .]" (Zelik, 2022). The form of the loose-leaf tea offer was also an issue. In that time, loose-leaf tea was offered in metal containers that did not allow a visual offering. Therefore, a big step forward was the introduction of glass containers in all OXALIS shops, which helped to bring loose-leaf tea closer to ordinary consumers: "I brought the loose-leaf tea closer to people because I wanted them to see it, to have a chance to smell it [. . .]" (Zelik, 2022).

Petr Zelik considers the biggest opportunity in the tea and coffee trade to be having a chance to cooperate with catering and accommodation establishments, because, according to him, "[. . .] the tea culture has basically not improved at all over the last 30 years [. . .]" (Zelik, 2022). It would be good to raise the Czech tea culture through accommodation and catering facilities, because, according to his statement, the range of hot drinks is largely neglected: "[. . .] The gastronomy sphere simplifies, accelerates and facilitates this culture and there are few passionate individuals who give this part of gastronomy any importance" (Zelik, 2022). The neglect of these products may be related to the hectic nature of catering operations and the desire to simplify processes: "I see some space for revolution [. . .]. It's about education, about convincing those operators and owners that it makes sense, that it's not so hard to prepare those teas" (Zelik, 2022).

As in other countries, the COVID-19 pandemic has had a significant impact on business operations in the Czech Republic. OXALIS records a drop in sales of 3–5% compared to 2019: "the drop of retail was bigger but it was compensated with e-shop. However, when people started purchasing in retail stores again, e-shop sales came back to their previous numbers" (Zelik, 2022). This suggests that e-shops were an important saviour of companies during the pandemic, which only reinforces the importance and relevance of digitalisation in the business environment of today. According to this statement, a significant selling point is the retail tea store, mainly because of the ability to perceive the product with senses.

An interesting trend in the Czech Republic is the increasing demand for the best quality green tea, which has been growing for the last five to eight years: "The trend is also that the consumption of herbal infusions and herbal mixtures is increasing [. . .]". In the world, another trend can be observed with new tea terroirs emerging in places where tea has not been grown in the past: "As climate change progresses, the production probably will be limited in some areas, and perhaps somewhere else it will emerge [. . .]" (Zelik, 2022). The fact is that climate change is affecting all aspects of human life and tea cultivation is not an exception. Another trend in the tea business, which is already typical for coffee, is considered to be "working with a particular family, garden, plantation and telling their story [. . .]" (Zelik, 2022). The tea business has an important social aspect: "[. . .] the more tea grown in the poorer parts of the world we consume, the more, actually indirectly, we help those people to live more decently there [. . .]" (Zelik, 2022).

A significant threat to the tea business is the lack of workforce in the cultivation countries, due to the high intensity of the work and low incomes received for this work. Therefore, it can be assumed that tea may not be as affordable in the future as it is today. Another current economic threat is the rising cost of transport, which is linked to the energy and security crisis (Zelik, 2022). A possible opportunity for tea producers is awareness and education in the field of tea and the promotion of organic tea, which, according to Petr Zelik (2022), is in greater demand in Germany or Austria.

When asked what should be done to develop the Czech tea culture, Petr Zelik suggests several possible activities:

> Certainly, there are some lecture activities that we are trying to do in the Czech Tea Centre [. . .]. Next, there is definitely quality tea literature, which has not been published much in the Czech Republic in recent years [. . .]. We try to publish "Čajový list" (Tea Leaf) twice a year, which is a periodical that popularises tea culture. Last but not least there are beautiful events like the Čajomír etc. (Zelik, 2022)

A few concluding notes

Since 1989, the tea culture in the Czech Republic has been developed and is still changing. The social and cultural role of teahouses as well as the establishment and development of companies engaged in the production and sale of tea, the opening of tourism to countries with a strong tea culture, as well as the emergence and activity of professional and interest groups promoting tea culture in the Czech society show the diversity of tea related activities.

Nevertheless, the level of tea culture, in comparison with some of the more tea developed countries, is still rather lower. It is reflected, for example, in the dominant consumption of tea in the form of teabags, in the lower quality of tea offered in supermarket chains, in the preferences regarding particular types of tea among ordinary consumers, in the lower quality of tea service offered in most catering and accommodation establishments, the level of knowledge and skills of the majority of the population regarding tea, its preparation and service, etc.

In this context, it is necessary to implement further projects and activities that will lead to the strengthening of tea culture in the Czech Republic. Education, tourism and gastronomic practice can be considered as key areas for these activities.

At the formal level of education, tea and tea culture is currently given insignificant emphasis in the Czech Republic, both at the primary, secondary and university levels. Currently, some of the secondary vocational schools have started to realise this deficiency and address it, for example, through supplementary courses and competitions run by leading Czech tea experts (Teatenders). The situation is not much better at the informal education level. Although more and more titles on tea and tea culture are being offered in book sales networks, minimal space is given to the subject in other information channels (e.g., television, radio, etc.). These channels are responding to the low demand from ordinary consumers. The situation regarding the awareness about beverages such as wine, beer and coffee is much better in this way.

One of the ways to strengthen tea culture in Czech society is to include topics related to tea and tea culture during the implementation of educational programmes and other complementary activities in primary and secondary schools. Greater emphasis should also be placed on secondary schools and universities with a relevant vocational focus – hotel, gastronomy and tourism. There, experiences such as visiting tea plantations or tea producers should become a strong source of motivation to further pursue tea, both theoretically and practically. Therefore, the creation of tourism products partly focused on tea areas in tea developed countries and their intensive promotion could be another way to strengthen the tea culture in the Czech Republic.

A major problem of the Czech tea culture is the situation regarding the offer and relevant service of quality tea in most Czech gastronomic establishments. Both the offer and the service can be characterised as low-quality. One of the key reasons for this is the aforementioned low level of theoretical and practical training in the field of tea and tea culture among students of secondary and higher education focused on hospitality and gastronomy. However, the situation in gastronomy is also linked to the lower demand for higher standards from customers. The results of formal and informal training activities are thus complementary. Although Czech society is beginning to place more and more emphasis on the appropriate principles of pairing food with beverages, this phenomenon is mainly evident in alcoholic beverages, mostly in wine. However, the practice in tea-developed countries such as China, Japan or India also confirms the high potential of these activities for tea. Although the first courses and other information materials on the topic of food pairing with tea are beginning to appear in the Czech Republic, this topic is still rarely applied to a sufficient level in gastronomic practice, e.g., even in the group of tea lovers less than 15% of respondents try to follow the principles of pairing dishes with tea. In the case of ordinary consumers, this amount is considerably less (Kratochvílová, 2022).

The strengthening of the tea culture in the Czech Republic can subsequently manifest itself in society on several other levels, for example by increasing the level of mental and physical health of citizens, increasing the level of understanding and therefore openness to other cultures and nations, strengthening social cohesion, etc. The aforementioned survey by M. Kratochvílová (2022) states that almost 30% of the respondents from the group of tea lovers and 22% from the regular consumer group associate tea primarily with peace, well-being and relaxation. Perhaps this is why strengthening tea culture is such a topic and necessary issue in today's European society.

References

Čajomir. (n.d.). Příběh čajové školy [online]. Retrieved January 11, 2023, from https://cajomir.cz/galerie-skola/

Čajomír. (n.d.). Úvodní strana [online]. Retrieved January 11, 2023, from https://www.cajomir.cz/cs/uvodni-strana/

Čajovny V Praze. (n.d.). Seznam čajoven podle částí Prahy [online]. Retrieved January 11, 2023, from http://cajovny.gpage.cz/cajovny/?c=vse

Černý, K. (2020). Ze zámoří do Čech: čokoláda, čaj a káva v raném novověku. Vydání první. Academia.

Czech Bartender Association. (2022). Barista a Teatender jsou konečně na národním seznamu kvalifikací [online]. Retrieved January 17, 2023, from https://www.cbanet.cz/cba_clanek&id=5049

Czech Bartenders Association. (n.d.). Czech Teatenders: O sekci [online]. Retrieved January 17, 2023, from https://www.cbanet.cz/cba_czech_teatenders

Czech Bartenders Association. (2022). Novým vedoucím Czech Teatenders je Honza Zlámaný [online]. Retrieved January 11, 2023, from https://www.cbanet.cz/cba_clanek&id=5118

Dasaev, M. (2021). Konzumace čaje v České republice [online]. Master's Dissertation. University College Prague – Vysoká škola mezinárodních vztahů a Vysoká škola hotelová a ekonomická s.r.o., Vysoká škola hotelová a ekonomická. Retrieved January 10, 2023, from https://is.ucp.cz/th/goiv5/

Etherington, R. (2009, 19 March). Tea house by David Maštálka. Dezeen. Retrieved December 29, 2021, from https://www.dezeen.com/2009/03/19/tea-house-by-david-mastalka/

Frearson, A. (2011, 8 September). Black Teahouse By A1 Architects. Dezeen. Retrieved December 29, 2021, from https://www.dezeen.com/2011/09/08/black-teahouse-by-a1architects/

Hanák, J. (2022). Foursquare City Guide: Čajovny v ČR [online]. Retrieved January 11, 2023, from https://foursquare.com/hukkv/list/%C4%8Dajovny-v-%C4%8Dr

Korosteleva, D. (2021). Analysis of Customer Satisfaction in Czech Teahouses. Bachelor's thesis. University College Prague – Vysoká škola mezinárodních vztahů a Vysoká škola hotelová a ekonomická s.r.o., Vysoká škola hotelová a ekonomická. Retrieved January 10, 2023, from https://is.ucp.cz/th/epv1y/

Kratochvílova, M. (2022). Konzumace čaje v České republice. Master's Dissertation. University College Prague – Vysoká škola mezinárodních vztahů a Vysoká škola hotelová a ekonomická s.r.o., Vysoká škola hotelová a ekonomická. Retrieved January 10, 2023, from https://is.ucp.cz/th/lfjni/

Nielsen Admosphere. (2015). Češi si potrpí na ovocné čaje, nejčastěji je připravují ze sáčku. Retrieved January 7, 2023, from https://www.nielsen-admosphere.cz/news/tz-cesi-si-potrpi-na-ovocne-caje-nejcasteji-je-pripravuji-ze-sacku

Nielsen Admosphere. (2021). Když čaj, tak ovocný a sáčkový. Nejvíce ho Češi pijí na zahřátí a při zdravotních potížích. Retrieved January 7, 2023, from https://www.nielsen-admosphere.cz/news/tz-cesi-si-potrpi-na-ovocne-caje-nejcasteji-je-pripravuji-ze-sacku

Oxalis. (n.d.). CoffeeTearia a Czech Tea Centre [online]. Retrieved January 7, from https://oxalis.cz/cs/coffee-tearia#czech-tea-center

Oxalis. (n.d.). O nás. Retrieved January 9, from https://oxalis.cz/cs/blog/o-nas-49/

Oxalis. (2020). *OXALIS v číslech (za rok 2020)*. Retrieved January 9, https://oxalis.cz/cs/blog/oxalis-cislech-106/

Polák, V. (1936). Lexikální a etymologické drobnosti II. (čaj – thé). *Naše řeč*, pp. 227–230. Retrieved January 14, 2023, from http://nase-rec.ujc.cas.cz/archiv.php?art=3085

Thomová, S., Thoma, M., & Thomas, Z. (2002). *Příběh čaje*. Vyd. Argo.

Vojtechovská, M. (n.d.). Zeměpisec: Čajovnová velmoc Česko? Počet čajoven v ČR a krajíc. Retrieved January 11, 2023, from https://zemepisec.cz/pocet-cajoven-v-cr-a-krajich/

Zelik, P. (2019). *The Oxalis story*. Mlada Fronta.

Zelik, P. (2022, December 21). Interview about the Czech tea company OXALIS.

Hartwig Bohne and Monika Kostera

H.4 Herbata! Polish tea culture and traditions

Introduction

The Polish tea tradition is characterised by a preference for black tea (70% of the sales volume) and blends based on black tea. The Polish term "herbata" includes this black tea as well as the tradition to offer guests, business partners, and family members a glass of tea upon their arrival. As a result, tea is mainly consumed at home and black tea dominates as a daily treat, also ennobled with lemon or sweet additives (Czarniecka-Skubina, 2022) (see Figure H.4.1).

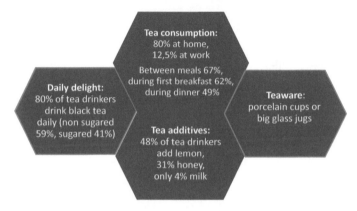

Figure H.4.1: Specifics of Polish tea consumption.
Source: Author, in accordance with Czarniecka-Skubina (2022)

It's all about Herbata

The beverage based on black tea is known as a pure black tea, but also with several flavours, e.g., herbata with lemon, herbata with raspberry syrup (Malinowa) or herbata with quince (Herbata z pigwą) and lemon. In addition, herbata can be served with milk (Bawarka). Until 1790 Bawarka was usually served with half a cup of cream and half a cup of water, but afterwards and until today Bawarka has been served by pouring half a glass of tea into half a glass of hot milk. Taking an alcoholic addition into consideration, the Polish highlander tea (Herbata z prądem), also called "mountain tea," is the black tea version mixed with alcohol, usually vodka. There is also a

https://doi.org/10.1515/9783110758573-036

version containing rum (Herbata z rumem), which was considered to have medicinal properties against the common cold (Klesta, 2020).

The consumption of tea in Poland is an essential part of daily life, and the Polish tea drinkers prefer a long brewing time (up to 5 minutes) with 2-3 grams of tea per cup with 200 ml filtered or tab water (Czarniecka-Skubina, 2022). This relevance of tea imports can also be seen when comparing the figures of tea consumption in Europe (Figure H.4.2). Poland is in the top three tea drinking countries in Europe (World Tea Committee, 2023).

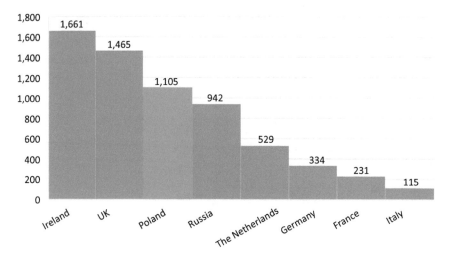

Figure H.4.2: Tea imported for consumption per capita in grams in 2022.
Source: World Tea Committee (2023)

In addition to the figures of tea consumption, the tea brands in Poland are also a sign of modernisation and internationalisation of tea culture. The ranking of popularity is dominated by brands of Lipton Teas and Infusions: 1) Lipton + 3) Tetley + 4) Saga, while on second rank Dilmah Tea is positioned and on fifth position the German brand Teekanne (Czarniecka-Skubina, 2022). In addition, there are smaller companies, e.g., Belin (famous for their pyramid bags), Herbapol (also producing herbal infusions), Bastek (successful tea exports to Western Europe) and Big active (as a part of Herbapol) (Klesta, 2020).

Tea cultures are blended in Poland

Tea came to the court of the Polish king John II Casmir Vasa in the seventeenth century by his French wife Queen Marie Louise. At that time, tea was mostly seen as a medicine with healing effects. While the stimulating effects of tea were still evaluated favourably at the beginning of the eighteenth century, this appreciation had changed to a more negative interpretation, especially by representatives of the Catholic Church. But, simultaneously, people in Poland slowly started to regard drinking tea as a sign of good manners, and also as a contrast to drinking alcoholic beverages. Also, tea porcelain (pots, cups) was imported to Poland. European tea sets appeared much later and, in contrast to coffee, the import of tea didn't actually increase in the second half of the eighteenth century. At that time, official recommendations and advice were given to families, namely how to brew and offer tea properly. In addition, "dancing teas" were held. Tea was an essential part of all social levels; for example, during receptions held at manors, tea and desserts were served while tea replaced champagne at the parties of less affluent families in Warsaw. As tea arrived via Amsterdam and Hamburg in the Polish territories under Austrian and Prussian rule, these households preferred this tea (Assam, Darjeeling) and the usage of teapots and kettles. The households in territories under Russian rule tended to use the samovars and the "caravan tea" which was transported by caravans via Tibet and Russia (Kasprzyk-Chevriaux, 2019).

In the early twentieth century, the preference for tea became stronger than for coffee. This was due to a pragmatic reason, that tea was easier to brew because it was sold ready to brew while coffee still had to be roasted. Therefore, the tea consumption at home was more comfortable, easier and cheaper. In addition, using a samovar was not contemporary any more. Tea became accessible for everybody. The period between the two world wars was very prosperous for the tea culture. The tea trade was developing, with the number of tea shops and teahouses growing. Elsewhere, a special social gathering was invented: the so-called fajfy, or five o'clock – afternoon tea parties similar to the time slot of British afternoon tea, but much more relaxing and like a real party. Also, for politicians at that time, it was a symbol of good manners to organise these "fajfies" (Kasprzyk-Chevriaux, 2019).

In the post-war times before the transformation, the import of tea was coordinated by an expert. From the 1960s until 1990, under the supervision of expert Krystyna Kostera, was directly imported from India, Ceylon (now Sri Lanka), China, and the Soviet Union. It was usually sold under local brands, by Polish retail chains. For example, the more exclusive tea sorts such as Darjeeling and Yunnan were sold by the upmarket chain Delikatesy, but the more popular kinds (lower quality Popularna, good quality Madras and Assam, high quality Cejlon) were sold by the standard chain Społem at an affordable price. Whereas coffee was at times difficult to buy, tea was almost always in good supply and there were several types available, including good quality teas. Green and jasmine tea was available in the 1960s and 1970s in both upmarket stores and in big urban supermarkets. Only in the early 1980s, during the most severe restrictions imposed by the Martial Law, was there a deterioration of the tea supply. The lower quality tea Gruzińska (from Soviet Georgia) and Popularna, as well as the average Jubileuszowa, were most common during that period (Dzbanherbaty, 2019).

After the end of state communism, some new local brands were first developed and entered the market (such as Polindia), but then the global brands and chains took over most of the Polish market. The new brands were marketed as superior to the pre-transformation supply, which was not entirely consistent with the facts. Many big brands are of decidedly lower quality than some of the pre-1989 ones available in popular retail (for example Yunnan) (Dzbanherbaty, 2019).

Conclusion

Tea in Poland is not seen as a special drink, but more as a usual warm beverage after meals or at social gatherings. Loose tea used to be popular, but currently has become much less common mostly due to financial reasons, and teabags are preferred for convenience reasons (Dzbanherbaty, 2019).

Tea came to Poland from both directions, from the West and the East. Therefore, teapots and samowars, teacups from porcelain and tea glasses are used; while some terms are from the "tea"-wording, others are based on the "cay"-wording (Tea in the ancient world, 2018). There is also something of a genuinely Polish tea culture, symbolised by the Polish word for tea – "herbata," meaning herbal infusion.

Tea is a very popular drink in Poland, accompanying social occasions without being a highlighted element, and the tea drinkers are conscious consumers who value quality, pay attention to the price, have their specific habits, as well as brand preferences and sensory knowledge leading to their decision of buying a special sort of tea (Czarniecka-Skubina, 2022).

References

Czarniecka-Skubina, E. et al. (2022). Consumer Choices and Habits Related to Tea Consumption by Poles. Foods 2022/11, article 2873.

Dzbanherbaty. (2019, July 16). Herbata z czasów PRL. Retrieved May 3, 2023, from https://dzbanherbaty.pl/herbata-z-czasow-prl/

Kasprzyk-Chevriaux, M. (2019). Delightful drink or powerful poison: A history of tea in Poland. Retrieved April 23, 2023, from https://culture.pl/en/article/drink-poison-history-tea-poland

Klesta, K. (2020). What is the Polish Tea? The most popular teas in Poland. Retrieved April 23, 2023, from https://polishfoodies.com/polish-tea/#:~:text=In%20Poland%2C%20tea%20is%20as,drink%20of%20choice%20in%20Poland

World Tea Committee. (2023). Report on tea consumption in Europe in 2022. Retrieved April 22, 2023, from www.inttea.com

Gülsün Yildirim and Hartwig Bohne

H.5 Tea culture in Türkiye

Introduction

In Türkiye, which ranks first in tea consumption per capita in the world, tea is consumed more than water. Tea has a very different importance in social and cultural life in Türkiye with its brewing technique, tea materials used and various tea drinking traditions. The special place of tea in Turkish culture led to Turkish tea culture being included in the UNESCO intangible world heritage list in 2022 (UNESCO, 2022).

Consequently, there is a special importance of tea and tea culture for Turks. In addition, details about the historical development process of tea, the brewing of Turkish tea, the manner of service and consumption ritual are essential for understanding the value of tea for the Turkish people.

Historical development of tea in Türkiye

Although tea farming in Türkiye started in 1938 after many attempts (Üstün & Demirci, 2013; Iskender, 2020, p. 5), tea culture in Türkiye dates back to the first century B.C. (Hun Empire). Tea, which was also consumed during the Ottoman Empire, began to be widely consumed in the 1600s (Eröz & Bozok, 2018, p. 1162; Alikılıç, 2016, p. 270). The first tea factory in Türkiye was established in Rize in the Eastern Black Sea Region in 1947, and the tea produced in the country began to meet the demands of consumers in 1963 (Üstün & Demirci, 2013; Mendi, 2018). Organic tea production started in 2009. There are a total of 207 tea factories in Türkiye, 47 of which are Çaykur's factories (a public organisation), with 160 are privately owned.

Tables H.5.1 and H.5.2 show the purchases of fresh tea and dry tea production by Çaykur and the private sector in the Turkish tea industry between 2017 and 2021. These purchases and dry tea production have changed over the years. The biggest reason for the recent increase in fresh tea harvesting is the rapid creation of new tea fields, which is still continuing. This shows us that the increase in harvesting will continue.

Tea cultivation in Türkiye is carried out intensively in the provinces of Rize, Artvin, Giresun and Trabzon (see Figure H.5.1), starting from the Georgian border in the Eastern Black Sea Region, where the climate is favourable, to the province of Ordu. Compared to Asian countries such as China and Sri Lanka, which have equatorial climate characteristics, tea plantations remain fallow for six months of the year as the temperature drops to minus levels in Türkiye. Snowfall on the tea gardens in winter prevents the formation of pests in the tea gardens and there is no spraying against the pests, which ensures that Turkish tea is the most natural among the world's teas (Rize Mercantile Exchange, 2022).

https://doi.org/10.1515/9783110758573-037

Table H.5.1: Five Years Fresh Tea Purchase Amount on the Basis of Provinces and Türkiye.

5 Years Fresh Tea Purchase Amount on the Basis of Provinces and Türkiye (Kg)					
Rize Province	**2017**	**2018**	**2019**	**2020**	**2021**
Private sector	546.266.120	637.038.928	500.328.973	539.996.158	468.619.546
Çaykur	471.158.963	533.823.572	642.451.890	616.115.425	703.732.657
Total	1.017.425.083	1.170.862.500	1.142.780.863	1.156.111.583	1.172.352.203
Trabzon Province	**2017**	**2018**	**2019**	**2020**	**2021**
Private sector	125.254.147	149.182.162	115.864.039	122.445.983	93.135.689
Çaykur	95.232.765	102.541.492	137.635.877	126.713.313	143.121.831
Total	220.486.912	251.723.654	253.499.916	249.159.296	236.257.520
Giresun Province	**2017**	**2018**	**2019**	**2020**	**2021**
Private sector	24.680.037	25.261.469	25.591.493	23.646.765	26.446.116
Çaykur	11.657.178	11.803.714	15.362.302	9.596.024	13.528.880
Total	36.337.215	37.065.183	40.953.795	33.242.789	39.974.996
Samsun Province	**2017**	**2018**	**2019**	**2020**	**2021**
Private sector	–	–	3.284.690	6.666.821	7.247.442
Çaykur	–	–	–	–	–
Total	–	–	3.284.690	6.666.821	7.247.442
Türkiye Total	**2017**	**2018**	**2019**	**2020**	**2021**
Private sector	696.200.304	811.482.559	641.784.505	692.755.727	595.448.793
Çaykur	578.048.906	648.168.778	795.450.069	752.424.762	860.383.368
General Total	1.274.249.210	1.459.651.337	1.437.234.574	1.445.180.489	1.455.832.161

Source: Rize Mercantile Exchange (2022)

Table H.5.2: "Dry" Tea Production in Türkiye for the Last Five Years.

'Dry' Tea Production in Türkiye for the Last Five Years (kg)					
	2017	**2018**	**2019**	**2020**	**2021**
General Total	254.000	297.000	275.000	280.000	287.000

Source: Rize Mercantile Exchange (2022)

Black tea constitutes 97% of tea production in Türkiye and uses the Orthodox System in tea production. Apart from black tea, green tea, oolong and white tea are produced, albeit at low rates. Black tea is classified according to the harvest and in the country there are three harvest times (first, second harvest etc.); the first is in May, second is in July and the last harvest is in September. Black tea is in the powder form in these harvests (Tea Industry Report, 2018). The type of tea predominantly consumed in Türkiye is black tea and is referred to as the national beverage.

Figure H.5.1: A tea garden in Rize.
Source: Gülsün Yildirim

Traditional Turkish tea brewing tea

When it comes to Turkish tea, black tea in powder form should come to mind. When brewing Turkish black tea, water is first placed under the teapot and boiled. The teapot consists of a pot for water at the bottom and a separate pot in which to mix tea and water. Apart from the teapot, tea samovar or big tea boilers are especially used in coffee houses in Türkiye.

While steel or copper teapots are commonly used in houses in Türkiye, electric two-compartment teapots have also been widely used with the development of technology. After the water in the lower pot boils, a little bit of boiling water is poured into the upper empty pot and approximately five tablespoons of tea are slowly poured into this water. Two teaspoons of tea are put into the upper pot for one glass. Two glasses of water are added to one tea glass of tea.

Afterwards, cold water is added to the lower pot once more and this water is left to boil again. Meanwhile, the tea on the top is slowly brewed. Although the brewing time of Turkish tea varies depending on the tea, it is between 10 and 15 minutes on average. If you extend the brewing time too long, the tea will taste bitter. In order to increase the hardness of the tea, it is recommended to increase the amount of tea put in the teapot rather than increasing the brewing time. The brewed tea should be consumed within half an hour. One of the debated issues regarding tea brewing methods is whether the tea leaves should be added to the water in the teapot afterwards or whether the water should be poured directly onto the leaves. Some pour the boiled water directly on the leaves, while others put the water in the teapot first and then add the tea to the water (see Figure H.5.2).

Figure H.5.2: Turkish tea serving.
Source: Gülsün Yildirim

There are some points to be considered while brewing tea. The first of these is the density of the dust in the tea. As the amount of dust in the tea increases, the colour of the brewed tea becomes cloudy and the image quality of the tea decreases. For this reason, teas containing more leaves should be preferred. Those who buy unpacked tea, before putting the tea into the teapot, quickly wash the tea to purify the dust inside. The other issue is that the teapot should not be boiled after the tea is brewed.

To brew a good tea, the water of the tea must be soft and sweet. Care should be taken to ensure that the water is lime-free and chlorine-free. Although the taste and characteristics differ from source to source, the best water for brewing tea is spring water. Tap water generally smells bad and the amount of chlorine in it negatively affects the taste of tea. If tap water is to be used, a good filter should be used. In addition, it is necessary not to brew tea by boiling the previously boiled water again, because as the water boils the oxygen in it is lost, which prevents the tea from giving its essence. While brewing tea, pouring the water in circles from above, not from the side, spreading on the whole surface of the tea causes the water to regain the oxygen it has lost, making the tea more delicious. Finally, while brewing the tea, the water should not be too boiling (Teapotea, 2023).

One of the most important elements when brewing tea is the tea itself. Whether you go to a top quality restaurant, the best hotel in Türkiye, or to an ordinary neighbourhood coffee house, you will drink the same black tea. Drinking tea in a higher quality place does not guarantee an increase in the quality of the tea you drink. In terms of quality, it is generally thought that the first harvest teas are better. The most widely consumed tea brands in Türkiye are Çaykur, Karali, Doğuş, Doğadan, Ofçay and Lipton. These brands have both powder and teabag options. While brewing tea, some in Türkiye add rosebuds, dried tangerines, orange or lemon peels, cinnamon or cloves to the tea.

Traditional manner of tea service in Türkiye

When you go to a cafe or restaurant in Türkiye and you order Turkish tea, you are asked whether you would like to drink weak or strong tea. The tea is poured into a glass in the kitchen and the waiter brings the tea filled glass to the customer. When you say "I would like to drink tea," the tea brought to you will be black tea in the food and beverage businesses in Türkiye. You do not need to say that you would like black tea when ordering. In some food and beverage businesses, you can order a teapot. Optionally, tea is served in the form of a teapot and the waiter brings tea glasses, saucers and sugar on a tray equal to the number of people sitting at the table. Those sitting at the table pour the tea by themselves.

In the teapot used in the presentation of Turkish tea, there are two parts, with the boiled water at the bottom and the brewed tea at the top. In coffee houses common in

Türkiye, samovar and big boilers are used instead of teapots. Traditional Turkish tea is drunk in a slim waisted glass made of glass (which is tulip shaped). While the thin-waisted glass ensures that the tea stays hot for a long time due to its structure, it can be seen how much brewed tea is poured, and, accordingly, the weakness or hardness of the tea can be easily adjusted. Except for the thin-waisted glass, some rarely drink tea in the cup. For Turkish people, tea is drunk in a thin-waisted glass, and the taste of tea in a thin-waisted glass is very special. Alongside the thin-waisted glass, there will definitely be a saucer. Persian saucers, glasses, wooden or porcelain saucers are used in Türkiye. Persian saucers are often used in coffee houses.

In addition to the saucers, a strainer is used to prevent the tea pulp from falling into the glass. However, in some parts of Türkiye, such as the Eastern Black Sea Region, strainers are not used. The reason for not using a strainer is to see if the tea is brewed well. In insufficiently brewed tea, the tea pulps in the glass remain on the surface. In well-brewed tea, the tea pulps sink to the bottom of the glass. In the Eastern Black Sea Region, in the tea service, some businesses ask their customers whether they want tea with pulp, with the expression "whether your tea is with or without garbage." If the customer wants it without tea pulps, they use a strainer to put the tea into the tea glass.

When you order tea in Türkiye, if you do not want to drink your tea with a strong brew, you should specify that you would like to drink weak tea. The darkness of the tea varies according to the amount of tea leaves put in the pot while the tea is brewed and the amount of brewed tea poured from the upper teapot while the tea is being served. In tea presentation, the glasses are first shaken with hot water and the water in the glass is poured. This is done so that the tea glass warms up and does not lose the warmth of the tea put into it. Afterwards, brewed tea is poured from the upper teapot to half of the tea glass, depending on the degree of darkness desired by the person.

In tea brewed in normal standards, half of the tea glass is filled with brewed tea and the other half is filled with boiled water. In order to make tea drinking easier and not burn the hand and mouth, the tea glass is not completely filled and some gap (1–2 cm) is left on top of the tea glass, which is expressed as "a gap for a sip." A saucer is placed under the glass filled with tea and two to three sugar cubes and a teaspoon are placed next to the tea glass. The well-brewed tea in the tea glass is expressed as "rabbit blood" and this colour is a red to claret red colour. People or children, who are not recommended to drink tea due to various health problems, drink weak tea. A little cold water is added to the tea in the tea glass so that young children do not burn their mouths while drinking tea. This warmed weak tea is called "pasha tea."

Tea consumption ritual

Tea is drunk at any time of the day in Türkiye. Tea is essential for breakfast. In addition to breakfast, there is always a boiling teapot in workplaces, homes and traditional coffee houses. Tea is definitely drunk right after lunch and dinner. When a friend is invited as a guest, they are told to "come to us for tea in the evening" rather than "come to me in the evening".

Figure H.5.3: Turkish tea service preparation with tulip-shaped glasses.
Source: Gülsün Yildirim

Before the guest arrives, the tea water is put on the stove to boil. Various treats such as dried fruit, biscuits, nuts (sunflower seeds, roasted chickpeas, hazelnuts, peanuts) and cakes are offered to the guests as tea accompaniments. When the guest is offered tea, if the guest does not want to drink it, this is perceived as rude by the host. While tea is served to the guests who come to the house, the young girl of the house pours the tea into glasses in the kitchen and puts all the tea glasses on a tray. In addition to the tea glasses, tea saucers, teaspoons and sugar are placed on the tray (see Figure H.5.3). The young girl in the house serves tea, starting with the oldest of the guests. The guest first takes the tea glass, then the tea saucer and, if they use it, they take as much sugar in their tea as they want. In the tea service, tea is served in order from the oldest to the youngest guests. As soon as one's glass is empty, the tea is immediately poured into the glass again. Usually, an empty tea glass is taken from the guest; tea is poured in the kitchen, and served to the guest again, without being asked whether they want to drink tea again. If the guest does not want to drink more tea, they leave the tea glass by placing the teaspoon horizontally on the empty tea glass (see Figure H.5.4). This nonverbal communication method, which was widely used in various regions of Türkiye in the past, is not commonly used today. Only in some villages is there a tradition of placing the teaspoon horizontally in the empty tea glass, although it is rare.

Turks use the phrase "Let's take a tea break" instead of "let's take a break" while working at the workplace. Turks believe that tea relieves their tiredness. In Türkiye, tea is an important and special symbol of interpersonal communication. Tea is offered to customers as a sign of hospitality in most of the stores visited for shopping in Türkiye. When people come together, drinking tea makes the environment friendlier and strengthens communication. In Türkiye, there are "coffee houses" which are a private beverage establishment where mainly tea is served. Men come to these coffee houses

Figure H.5.4: Nonverbal communication method with tea.
Source: Gülsün Yildirim

and chat with their friends and play the okey game, backgammon or card games. Although coffee and soft drinks are sold to customers in these coffee houses, mainly tea is consumed here and there are large tea boilers in these teahouses. While the men go to the coffee houses to socialise during the day, the women meet with their female friends at regular intervals and take turns to perform the "Gold Days" event. Only women attend these gold days, where tea is a must. Accompanying the tea, guests are offered various treats carefully prepared the day before. Among these treats, bulgur salad, potato salad, pastry, cake, lentil patties, stuffed leaves, biscuits and desserts are included. After the treats eaten with tea, the women dance and have fun. After this entertainment, the agreed amount of gold or money is given to the host. Each time they gather at the house of another person in the group (Töret, 2012).

There are different traditions in different regions of Türkiye regarding the drinking of Turkish tea. In addition to the tea with pulp in the Black Sea Region, which has been explained previously, the tea sugar used in the Eastern Anatolia Region is different from the other regions, and there is a different tradition for drinking tea with sugar. This sugar, which is called "kitlama sugar", is produced in the Eastern Anatolia Region, especially in Erzurum (see Figure H.5.5). Kitlama sugar, which is a larger and harder sugar compared to the sugar cubes sold in the markets, is first put into the mouth and then a sip of the tea is taken. Some people dip this sugar in tea first, then eat some sugar and drink tea. Some put this sugar under their tongues and take a sip of the tea. Then they take the sugar out from their tongue, circulate it in the mouth for one round and put it under the tongue again. As the tea is sipped, the sugar slowly melts in the mouth. Thanks to the Kitlama sugar, the taste of tea and sugar can be taken separately. This tradition of drinking tea with kitlama sugar, which is unique to

Figure H.5.5: Kitlama Sugar.
Source: Gülsün Yildirim

the Erzurum region, has eliminated the need for a teaspoon when drinking tea. There-fore, teaspoons are not used in this province in the tea service.

Conclusion

While tea brings people together and provides social interaction, it is one of the most important indicators of hospitality. Besides, there are folk songs, poems, idioms and proverbs produced about tea in Türkiye, with some districts having been named about tea. From the traditions in the process of collecting tea to the way tea is poured in a glass and served, tea deeply anchors culture in Türkiye. It is a daily life routine, but also a symbol of pride and comfort for Turks. The Getting offered a typical tulip shaped glass of freshly brewed black tea on the ferries of Istanbul (between the river banks of the Bosporus), making this ritual as well as the hosting character of tea even in public transports visible.

References

Alikılıç, D. (2016). Çay'ın Karadeniz bölgesi için önemi ve tarihi seyri [The importance and historical process of tea for the Black Sea region]. *Journal of Black Sea Studies*, *11*(21), 269–80.

Eröz, S., & Bozok, D. (2018). Çay turizmi ve Rize ili potansiyeli [Tea tourism and potential of Rize province]. *Üçüncü Sektör Sosyal Ekonomi Dergisi*, *53*(3), 1159–176.

İskender, A. (2020). Çay turizmi: Doğu Karadeniz bölgesinde uygulanabilirliği üzerine değerlendirme. [Tea tourism: Evaluation on its applicability in the Eastern Black Sea region]. *Journal of Tourism and Gastronomy Studies*, *8*(3), 1958–971.

Mendi, A. F. (2018). Türkiye çay endüstrisi: Sektörel ve ampirik bir çalışma [Turkish tea industry: A sectoral and empirical study]. *International Journal of Social Sciences and Education Research*, *4*(2), 252–74.

Rize Mercantile Exchange. (2022). Türk Çay Sektörü Güncel Durum Raporu (Turkish Tea Industry Current Status Report) [online]. Retrieved January 1, 2023, from https://www.rtb.org.tr/tr/cay-sektoru-raporlari

Tea Industry Report. (2018). Çay Sektörü Raporu (Tea Industry Report) [online]. Retrieved October 5, 2023, from www.caykur.gov.tr/Pages/Yayinlar/YayinDetay

Teapotea. (2023). Çay Nasıl Bir Suda Çemlenmeli? [What Kind of Water Should Tea Be Stewed in?] Retrieved February 5, 2023, from http://www.teapotea.com/2013/02/27/cay-nasil-bir-suda-demlenmeli/

Töret, A.B. (2012). Geleneksel Altın Günlerine Halkbilimsel Bir Yaklaşım: "Muğla Örneği" [A Folkloristic Approach to the Traditional Golden Days: "The Example of Muğla"]. *Karadeniz Uluslararası Bilimsel Dergi* (14), 117–33.

Üstün, Ç., & Demirci, N. (2013). Çay bitkisinin (Camellia Sinensis L.) Tarihsel gelişimi ve tıbbi açıdan değerlendirilmesi [Historical development and medical evaluation of the tea plant (Camellia Sinensis L.)]. *Lokman Hekim Journal*, *3*(3), 5–12.

UNESCO. (2022). China's, Türkiye's and Azerbaijan's tea culture has been inscribed on the UNESCO World Heritage List. Retrieved March 18, 2023, from https://en.unesco.org/silkroad/content/chinas-Türkiyes -and-azerbaijans-tea-culture-has-been-inscribed-unesco-world-heritage-list

Kateryna Fedosova and Maksym Malyhin

H.6 Ukrainian tea habits and traditions

Introduction

The history and culture of tea consumption in Ukraine dates back several centuries. Ukrainians were familiar with herbal infusions from the Middle Ages. Secrets were known not only by healers, but also by ordinary people, because recipes for making a healing drink were passed down in every family from generation to generation. Peasants in Ukraine, instead of tea, have long brewed mint leaves, strawberries, linden flowers, St. John's wort, rosehip and rose petals, cherry branches, currants, raspberries, etc.

In the seventeenth century, tea from China started to be imported into Ukraine. However, until the eighteenth century, only rich people drank it. Property registers of the church leadership of the Kyiv Metropolitanate representatives in the eighteenth century testify the active consumption of tea. Among private kitchen utensils, one can see almost the entire range of sets for preparing and drinking tea (Yaremenko, 2012).

In 1817, tea bushes from China were first planted on Russian Empire territory in the Imperial Tauride Provincial Botanical Garden in Nikita, Crimea. The tea bushes were ordered multiple times because the natural conditions in Crimea were not favourable for growth. In 1833, Prince Mikhail Semenovich Vorontsov ordered several dozen more tea bushes from China. The director of the Nikitsky Botanical Garden, Nikolaus Ernst Bartholomäus Anhorn von Hartwiss, extensively studied these plants, which bore fruit for the first time in Crimea in 1843. Anhorn von Hartwiss recommended that experiments with the tea be moved to the Caucasian coast of the Black Sea. In 1847, Prince Mikhail Vorontsov ordered tea bushes to be brought from Crimea and, in 1848, these tea saplings were planted in the Sukhumi Botanical Garden and near Ozurgeti, Georgia (George L. van Driem, 2019).

Various tea enthusiasts and merchants established tea plantations in what is now Georgia and engaged in the challenging business of tea production. At the same time, the results of the enthusiasts' experiments showed the impossibility of growing tea north of Abkhazia, which was confirmed by experts' opinions. The first person to prove such a possibility was Judah Antonovich Koshman (1838–1935), a peasant from Ukraine. In the early twentieth century, he grew tea bushes on his small plantations and demonstrated the high quality of the locally sourced tea that was produced. The first experimental tea plantations in the Krasnodar region were established with seeds from Koshman's plantation in Solokh-Aul (Daraseliya et al., 1989).

Among ordinary inhabitants, other drinks were traditional, such as kvass, decoctions of herbs and flowers (for example, linden flowers). Tea became a common drink in the middle of the nineteenth century. Tea merchant Kostiantyn Popov developed tea plantations at the Caucasus and was engaged in the difficult business of tea production. Thus, teahouses began to appear in Ukraine, where samovars with boiling

https://doi.org/10.1515/9783110758573-038

water and teapots with brewed tea were served. They drank tea with milk, cream, lemon, jam, bagels and sugar (Maiboroda & Mazur, 2014).

The tea market is one of the most steadily developing commodity markets in Ukraine today. Every year, experts note an increase of 5–10% in sales. One person in Ukraine consumes on average about 0.5–0.6 kilograms of tea per year. About 70% of Ukrainians drink tea every day (Korchynska, 2018).

According to the branding agency KOLORO, the structure of tea products consumption depends on their types. Some 63% of the Ukrainian population prefer black tea, 16% green tea, 8% flavoured tea, 7% fruit infusion, 4% herbal infusion and 2% specialty teas. The annual volume of the tea market in Ukraine is about 2.225 million tons. A total of 96% of the tea market in Ukraine is import-dependent. Unfortunately, the whole volume of tea made from tea leaves has foreign origins (Kornienko, 2017).

Only fruit and herbal infusions (tisanes) are grown and processed in Ukraine. Such teas are called herbal infusions and are drunk for prevention or treatment of various diseases. Currently, the modern market of Ukraine is witnessing a significant development of the phytotea segment. Phytotea has become a traditional product for consumers who like drinks with an extraordinary taste, having medicinal properties and being simple in preparation. Herbal infusions do not contain black and green tea leaves, but only local herbs, fruits and berries. The high demand for herbal infusions is due to their combination of nutritional, taste and healing properties. Their consumption is associated with a healthy lifestyle. Apothecary plant cultivation is also widespread in Ukraine, and it is developing intensively.

The herbal and fruit infusions segment in Ukraine occupies 4–8% of the tea market. The technology of phytotea production mainly includes drying, crushing of raw plant materials and mechanical mixing (blending). The positioning of herbal infusions in the domestic market is mainly based on their physiological properties and consists of two groups: general health improvement and treatment of certain diseases (Kundius, 2009).

Carpathian tea occupies a special place in the tea market of Ukraine. Almost 7,000 tons of wild fruits and berries, as well as over 5,000 tons of medicinal plants, are harvested in the forests of Ukraine every year. They are good for health and have a distinctive taste and aroma. Clean air and remoteness from big cities make Carpathian products not polluted, extremely nutritious and useful.

Carpathian tea is a combination of various herbs (Ivan tea, linden, chamomile, heather, Echinacea, St. John's wort, calendula, nettle, mint, lemon balm), lingonberry, raspberry and blueberry leaves, elder flowers, cornflower and lavender, as well as berries, mountain ash and rose hips.

Perhaps one of the most famous Carpathian teas is fireweed tea, also known as "Ivan tea" (Chamaenerion angustifolium). Its leaves, dried before and after fermentation, was previously widely used for counterfeiting imported Chinese tea, usually as an adulterant. Fireweed tea (Ivan tea) has antimicrobial and anti-inflammatory, antipyretic and analgesic properties. Tea and mixtures of Ivan tea raw materials are used in traditional medicine for the treatment of gastritis, colitis, gastric ulcer, diarrhoea and other diseases of the gastrointestinal tract, as well as migraines, insomnia and oligo menorrhea (Volochai et al., 2019). Carpathian tea is easy to prepare. It is necessary to pour boiling water over the leaves and wait a few minutes for the tea to brew.

Despite the fact that there has never been any industrial tea cultivation in Ukraine, there is a 1.4-hectare plot of tea plantations in the far west of the country, in the Zakarpattia region, that is more than 70 years old. In 1949, tea researchers from the Research Institute of Tea and Subtropical Agriculture of the Soviet Union in Georgia, having surveyed the territory of Transcarpathia, began work on creating experimental plots for growing tea bushes.

In 1951–52, about 50 hectares of tea plantations were planted in Transcarpathia with Georgian seeds (Tchkhaidze, 1953). In 1954, the size of the experimental and production plots of tea in Transcarpathia reached 75 hectares. Work was carried out on the acclimatisation of the tea plant on these plots (Kislyakov, 1954).

At the main experimental plantation near Mukachevo, 24 studies on agricultural technology and breeding were conducted. Tea was actively cultivated there for four years, reaching a peak harvest of 1.3 tonnes of leaves per hectare. The promising project was finally terminated in 1954–56. Unfortunately, the majority of the original plantation was destroyed and today only a small experimental part under the forest canopy remains (Kundius, 2009).

A Ukrainian enthusiast and Tea Masters Cup Ukraine judge from Kyiv, Maksym Malyhin, started an information project to revive the abandoned plantation in 2015. In 2019, a group of local activists cleared the plantation site, which allowed the revival of the Zhornina plantation to begin in the autumn of that year. Today, the restored area is home to more than 300 tea bushes (Figure H.6.1).

These Ukrainian frost-resistant tea cultivars have survived decades of harsh winters with heavy snow and temperatures as low as 26 degrees below zero (Dan Bolton, 2022). Until 1999, Zhornina was the northernmost tea plantation in Europe. After the emergence of Tschanara Tea Garden in Germany, Jornina lost this status, but remains the most frost-resistant tea crop in the world (Dan Bolton, 2022). Today, the plantation in Mukachevo is a popular tourist attraction. Tourists are told the story of Ukrainian tea and shown the stages of the drink's production, starting with the picking of tea leaves and their hand-twisting (Mukachevo.net, 2017). Despite the war in Ukraine and financial problems, the team led by Maksym Malyhin plans to further develop the project to expand and reopen the Zhornina tea plantation.

As was the case several centuries ago in Ukraine, tea drinking is not just consuming a drink with unique properties, but is a ritual of hospitality and communication. In most restaurants in Ukraine, guests are offered a large tea menu of five to ten items that includes branded teas from different countries and several options of Carpathian herbal infusions. Classic black and green tea as well as herbal infusionsare often served with honey and lemon. Guests are usually offered all kinds of pastries and sweets, such as pancakes with various fillings. The combination of Ukrainian traditional cheesecakes (syrniki) and tea is a very popular breakfast for many Ukrainians (Figure H.6.2).

Figure H.6.1: Horning tea plantation.
Source: Hanna Ponomarenko

Figure H.6.2: Traditional Ukrainian breakfast with tea and syrniki (cheesecakes).
Source: Aleksandra Blinshtein

References

Daraseliya, M. K., Vorontsov, V. V., Gvasaliya, V. P., & Tsanava, V. P. (1989). *Tea culture in the USSR.* Metsniereba.

Kislyakov, V.D. (1954). Ways of developing domestic tea growing. *Bulletin of the Academy of Sciences of the USSR*, no. 4.

Korchynska, O.O. (2018). Characteristics of the tea market in Ukraine. In Zbirnik *naukovih pratz molodih uchenih, aspirantiv ta studentiv* (pp. 160–63). Onaft.

Kornienko, A.A. (2017). Tea market and its development trends in Ukraine. *Informaciyni tehnologii: nauka, tehnika, tehnologiya, osvita, zdorovya*, 4.

Kundius, D. (2009). Assortment of herbal teas on the market of Ukraine. *Tovary i rynki*, *1*, 16–20.

Maiboroda, O., & Mazur, L. (2014). Tea drinking traditions in Ukraine. In Ozdorovchi *harchovi produkty ta dietichni dobavky: tehnologii, yakist ta bezpeka: Materiali Mizhnarodnoi naukovo-praktichnoi konferencii* (pp. 163–65). NUFT.

Mukachevo.net. (2017, January 22). Tea plantation near Mukachevo needs care and could compete with northern teas of the world. Retrieved October 10, 2023, from http://www.mukachevo.net/ua/news/view/185835

STiR Tea & Coffee Industry International. (2022, April 18). Ukraine's frost tolerant tea cultivars by Dan Bolton. Retrieved October 10, 2023, from https://stir-tea-coffee.com/tea-report/ukraine%E2%80%99s-frost-tolerant-tea-cultivars/

Tchkhaidze, I.I. (1953). *Tea culture in Transcarpathia*. Publisher of the Academy of Sciences of the USSR.

Tea Biz. (2022, April 15). Ukraine's cold weather tea by Dan Bolton. Retrieved October 10, 2023, from https://tea-biz.com/2022/04/15/ukraines-cold-weather-tea/?fbclid=IwAR0jozLgXtxU00XEmgzDCVyn

Van Driem, G.L. (2019). *A comprehensive history of tea from prehistoric times to the present day*. Brill.

Volochai, V.I., Mykhaylenko, O.O., Klimovich, N.B., & Romanova, S.V. (2019). Prospects for the use of raw materials of plants of the genus Epilobium L. of the flora of Ukraine for the creation of medicinal products. *Suchasna farmaciya: istoriya, realii ta perspektyvy rozvytku: materiali nauk.-prakt. konf.*, *1*, 275–76.

Yaremenko, M. (2012). Pleasures of the educated in Ukraine of the 18th century (about the culture of tea, coffee and wine consumption by the church elite). *Kyiv Academy*, *10*, 117–82.

I Hospitalitea in Europe: Tea culture and hospitality heritage

European Tea Culture is the holistic enjoyment of tea production on islands or on land, UNESCO listed, traditional tea customs and innovative entrepreneurial spirit as well as a blend of porcelain and glassware, various ceremonial aspects of tea delights, and the unique understanding of tea as a symbol of healthy warmth, security, social anchoring and time shared with nice people.

Hartwig Bohne

I.1 Hospitalitea in Europe: Tea culture and hospitality heritage

Introduction

Europe is diverse. Europe is multi-cultural. And Europe offers many languages to express gratitude and to invite people by showing and creating hospitality. Tea, the simple but elegant beverage, spans Europe from the Azores to Georgia, from Italy to Sweden, and is often used to symbolise a welcoming atmosphere as an invitation to stay in a private environment, hotel or any place (Bohne, 2021; Rohrsen, 2022).

Therefore, tea is more than a beverage and hospitality is more than offering a safe space, food and drinks. Both terms offer a sizable variety of cultural niches, social events, traditions, and habits, developed for hundreds of years. Tea is a symbol of identity and hospitality, and hospitality means understanding and peace (UNESCO, 2022b).

Celebrating tea and hospitality

Tea can be enjoyed in different ways, in classic silver pots, in elegant tea china, and also in tea glasses – pear or tulip shaped. In many regions, tea is the typical and most suitable beverage for business as well as private occasions, in public places or while travelling. This daily character also makes tea relevant for funeral ceremonies or as the official replacement of alcohol in good restaurants. Tea is impressively versatile and therefore a perfect part of daily life (Pettigrew, 2003; Altonaer Museum, 1977; Klauß, 2019).

Tea needs time and needs care to develop the taste, strength, and fragrance. In addition, different sweeteners can support the effects of tea, while in some European regions milk or lemon can be part of the daily enjoyment. While sweet biscuits are preferred in the western part of Europe, salty sweets or vegetables are combined with tea in some eastern regions. Again, the flexibility can create lots of different settings to enjoy tea. Tea is an agile beverage (Rohrsen, 2022; Bohne, 2022b).

Different tea cultures show the unique ability of tea to offer multiple options of gatherings or social events, where the tea and its companions create a space of hospitality and comfort. The warmth of the beverage makes guests feel comfortable and safe, while the easy access to tea, sweeteners and light snacks can create culinary experiences – from the private tea habit to high tea or afternoon tea in a luxury hotel. Tea events and tea ceremonies are impressive symbols of the culture of hospitality (Bohne & Jollliffe, 2021; Bohne, 2022a; Krieger, 2021; Pettigrew, 2001) (see Table I.1).

https://doi.org/10.1515/9783110758573-039

Table I.1: Characteristic European tea consumption habits.

Region/ Country	Typical naming	Drinking pot	Sort(s) of tea	Typical side dishes and supplements	Speciality
Azerbaijan (Caucasus) *UNESCO listed tea culture*	Culture of Cay, tea is served for every guest	"Armudu," a pear-shaped glass	Regional black tea	Cube sugar, fruit dessert or jam, lemon, dried fruits	Tea is served during matchmaking for marriages: non-sugared means no agreement, sugared means successful match
East Frisia (Germany) *UNESCO listed tea culture*	1) Morning tea 2) Elführtje (11:00) 3) Teetied (15:00) 4) Dinner tea 5) Late evening tea before going to bed	(very thin) Porcelain bowl with handle	Original East Frisian Blend (at least 50% Assam + Java or Ceylon)	Typical Frisian biscuit or Frisian tart Rock candy and cream	Tea pot warmer (*Stövchen*) At home up to five times a day
Great Britain	1) Morning tea 2) Elevenses (usually at 11:00) 3) Afternoon Tea, usually served between 14:00 and 18:00	(very thin) Porcelain bowl with handle	Assam + Ceylon + often a sort of black tea from Africa	Scones, tea bread, sandwiches, clotted cream, strawberry jam/ lemon curd Milk + white Sugar	Milk jug and sugar pot made from silver Two rhythms: "Mif" ("Milk in first") or "Tif" ("Tea in first")
Russia	Zavarka	Small glass mug without handle	Oolong (Russian Caravan) or Russian Blend (Darjeeling + Kemun + Assam)	Rich sweet dishes, syrup, biscuits, jam, cakes, slices of lemon + white lump sugar	Samovar and Podstakannik (gilded glass holders)
Türkiye *UNESCO listed tea culture*	Acik cay – light infusion Koyu cay – strong infusion	Tulip-shaped glass mug without handle	Ceylon	One piece of white lump sugar, placed under the lip before drinking – never with milk Additional offer: "Un Kurabiyesi" (flour biscuits made from butter, flour, sunflower oil, vanilla extract)	Semawer/ "Caydanlik" (boiling method with two pots) Typical tea garden "Cay Bahceşi"

Source: Author, based on Bohne (2022a); Bohne (2022b); Klöver (2018); Krieger (2021); Yurtoglu (2018); UNESCO (2022b)

As a promising theme, tea traditions represent a mixture of historical developments and social commitment, loyalty and pride of populations as well as of guests. By including different sorts of tea and supplements, the authenticity can be evaluated by the guests in all steps of the consuming process. Regional habits and local specifications underline the role of hospitality as well as the potential to be seen as an anchor for sustainable traditions strengthening the satisfaction of inhabitants as well as of regional hospitality stakeholders (Hjalager & Richards, 2002).

The time to consume the food and beverage offers in hotels is also the possibility to enjoy the atmosphere and the generosity of hotels. Therefore, tea service is a challenge and an opportunity to bind and impress guests, to sell more than "only" tea and to make the teatime an unforgettable, quiet, and relaxing moment.

The establishment and development of tea events show a special European approach to use the procedure of brewing and consuming of tea for private, social, and business gatherings or as a simple occasion to meet for networking. The culture of afternoon tea, but also the establishment of tea gardens (not plantations) in Great Britain, The Netherlands, Türkiye, and Georgia as well as the teahouses or salon de thé primarily in Great Britain and France are testimonials of a tea-based understanding of hospitality. These tea spaces and also tea parties, e.g., in Poland, complete the impression of tea as a comfortable instrument for hospitable moments and occasions. Also, the connection with culinary arts, the transfer of special recipes and ingredients or the decoration of dedicated rooms, e.g., in hotels, for the tea related events, are also symbols of pride and the appreciation of tea for these initiatives (Bohne & Jolliffe, 2021; Kasprzyk-Chevriaux, 2019; Pettigrew, 2003; Rohrsen, 2022)

In addition to the tea space and its decoration, tea caddies as well as hotel branded tea blends are advantageous opportunities to combine special flavours and materials with the tea experience in a hotel. Primarily luxury hotels, e.g., Hotel Sacher Wien, Rocco Forte Hotels, Mandarin Oriental Hotels, St. Regis Hotels, The Claridges London, Grand Hotel Stockholm (made by the Tea Centre of Stockholm), offer these unique tea selling propositions in order to give guests the opportunity also to take this tea moment to their homes. In addition, JING Tea is creating a special blend for Savoy London and, The Lowry Hotel Manchester offers a special arrangement, guests can create their own tea – for drinking in the hotel and to take the individualised tea blend at home. Such a tea experience becomes a remembering element of the stay in hospitality (Carter, 1996; Ford, 2022; Lewis, 2022).

Tea as a destination

Apart from consuming tea and enjoying hospitality in hotels, gardens, or tea rooms, tea can also be seen as vital for traveling or focusing on regional culture. For this, UNESCO listed, first in 2016, the East Frisian Tea Culture, the first tea related intangible cultural heritage worldwide. Additionally, in 2022, the Turkish and the Azerbaijanian Tea Culture have been acknowledged for the same reason. While in East Frisia the focus is on the ceremonial consuming tradition bringing people together (using a specially decorated porcelain, rock candy and cream, adding sweet biscuits or cakes), Türkiye and Azerbaidjan represent tea producing and consuming countries, craftmanship and a different set of consumption, e.g., glass-based, using samovars, white sugar and, adding also salty snacks. But, these three tea related cultural heritages underline the mainly social function of tea culture, the deep relation of tea and the local/regional society, seeing and using tea as a symbol of hospitality in its very bride interpretation (Vink, Kappert-White & Bohne, 2022; UNESCO, 2022a; UNESCO, 2022b; UNESCO Germany, 2016).

Also, tea plantations are more and more becoming an interesting part of the European tea culture. Due to climate changes, but also entrepreneurial courage, tea plantations in Germany, Sweden, Ukraine, Scotland, and also in France, The Netherlands, and Switzerland can be found. The longest tradition of tea production in Europe have the plantations on the Azores (Portugal), in Georgia and in Türkiye. The hospitable approach of the tea plantation is very divers, e.g., from a private visit by prior call to guided tours of tour groups and professionally arranged tea tastings. Tea from the plantations on the Azores, in Georgia, Scotland or Türkiye, can also be found in hotels or gastronomic establishments in their region, but most of the plantations are small and exclusive or experimental, so that the touristic aspect is not the first priority. These plantations could also be an essential element of upcoming cultural routes, which are initiated by European tea entrepreneurs and academics in order to get support from the Council of Europe.

As the tea culture in Europe can be seen as a transnational heritage, it would be a sustainable approach linking all tea plantations, entrepreneurs, centres of consumption traditions and cultural attractions in order to make the European tea culture and its hospitable elements more visible and easier accessible.

Conclusion

Tea is a holistic delight. The colour of the plant, the fragrance of dried tea leaves, the brewed beverage; all these options make tea an universal product, a superb ingredient or an enjoyable drink in a class of its own. Consequently, tea is used for decoration and design, to differentiate F&B services and to create memorable teatime experiences, and also to initiate parties and gatherings based on non-alcoholic enjoyment. The colonial background and the perspective on cultural transfer from Asia to Europe, and the entrepreneurial spirit for importing, exporting and plantations, as well as for porcelain or other tableware, create a clear view on the vast range of business opportunities based on tea (see Table I.2).

Table I.2: Tea as a holistic delight.

Welcome and warmth for everybody	
Culinary:	Visible:
– Only drinks or full meal	– Design and decoration
– Pairing or replacement	– Arts and culture
– Tea infused products or pure tea	– Tea museums, festivals, and exhibitions
Social:	Usable:
– Private gatherings	– Samovars and spirit kettles
– Business occasions	– Teapots and porcelain
– Daily use or unique events	– Glass (tulip/pear shaped) or silver
Traditional:	Explorable:
Entrepreneurship and European heritage	Tea plantations, gardens, and teahouses
Sustainable and conscious enjoyment	

Source: Author

The social role of tea showing political developments, influences from other countries or simply the results of trade routes also makes tea a symbol of historic dependencies and a piece of evidence of creational processes inspired by tea, to be seen in the likes of teahouses or on tea plantations, but also documented properly in the European tea museums, e.g., in East Frisia.

As a final picture of tea culture in Europe, the following table shows the diverse impacts on tea culture and hospitality as well as their connections in Europe (see Table I.3).

Table I.3: Development of tea culture in Europe.

Arrival to Europe		
	– Mid of 16th century: Trade of tea between Portugal and Macao	– 1638: Tea arrived by caravans via Mongolia in Russia as a gift to the Russian Tsar, afterwards available in all parts of Russia
	– Tea imported to Italy (Venice), also transported to the region of today's Austria/Hungary and Czech Republic	– The tea tade by caravans remain the most important means till 1916 (completition of Transsibirian railway)
	– 1610: First ship with tea arrived in Europe (port of Amsterdam)	
	– Shipping from China to Western Europe via Cape of Good hope, dominated by Tea Clippers (fast merchant sailing vessel) between 1843 and 1869 (opening Suez Canal)	– Within the first half of 17th century tea arrived in Türkiye by caravans via Tibet/Afghanistan (Old Silk Road)
	– 1635: Tea trade is verified in France	– Mid of 17th century: tea was introduced at the Polish court by Queen Louise (French origin), imported from the West (via Hamburg) and the East (by caravans via Russia)
	– 1637: First mention of tea in Germany, initially as medicine, later as a luxury good	
	– 1644: First direct tea import to Great Britain	– Mid of 19th century: First tea bushes planted in Georgia, in 1893 industrialised tea production started
	– 1668: First arrival of tea in Denmark via Amsterdam	
	– 1685: First tea import to Sweden via Amsterdam and Hamburg	– Late 19th century: Tea cultivation and production started in Azerbaijan
	– 1820: Tea cultivation on the Azores started	– 1920: Start of tea agriculture in Türkiye based on Georgian tea plants, in 1938 first tea factory opened
	– 1835: First direct tea import from China to Ireland by Samuel Bewley	

Table I.3 (continued)

Tea consumption habits and tableware	– Early 17th century: East Frisian Tea Culture, and also the import of tea porcelain from China to Europe evolves – 1662: Wedding of Catherine de Braganza (Origin Portuguese) and the British King Charles II = Tea consumption got promoted by the new queen by transferring her tea related preferences from Portugal to Great Britain – 1670: First British silver teapot presented by Lord Berkley to East Indian Company – Due to the preference for Chinese decor, the „Chinoiserie" porcelain became famous in Europe as of late 17th century – Around 1730: Establishment of tea (pleasure) gardens in Great Britain – 1759: Josiah Wedgwood started producing tea porcelain in Stoke-on-Trent – Late 1830s/early 1840s: Raising popularity of the (British) Afternoon tea as a light meal initiated to bridge between lunch and late dinner, based on experiences in Prussia, France and English SPA towns	– 1710: Foundation of Meissen porcelain manufactory in Germany – Around 1730: First Samovar developed and used in Suksun/Russia – 1744: Establishment of Imperial porcelain company in St. Petersburg – 1764: Foundation of Wallendorf porcelain company in Germany, famous for East Frisian tea china „Dresmer teegood" – 1826: Foundation of Herend porcelain in Herend/Hungary – Second half of 19th century: Establishment of mass production of tulip shaped glass for tea consumption in Beykoz/Türkiye – 1870: Sweet tea break at five o'clock introduced in Russia – 1882: Foundation of Bauscher Hospitality Porcelain company by August & Conrad Bauscher in Germany – 1920s: In Poland, a social gathering was invented: fajfy, or five o'clocki – as afternoon tea parties

Table I.3 (continued)

European tea entrepreneurs	– 1692: First proof of tea trade by Francois Damame, later Dammann Frères/Paris – 1706: Thomas Twining opened first tearoom in London – 1840: Foundation of Bewley's Tea Company in Dublin – 1854: Foundation of tea company Mariage Frères in Paris – 1860: Parisian Compagnie Coloniale (Compagnie & Co.) started tea business	– 1806: East Frisian tea entrepreneur Johann Bünting founded his company and blended the first "Original East Frisian Tea Blend" in the city of Leer – 1823: Johann Tobias Ronnefeldt started his tea business in Frankfurt/Main – 1835: A.C. Perch's Thehandel founded in Copenhagen – 1852: Eduard Messmer started his tea business in Baden-Baden – 1862: Julius Meinl I started his tea and coffee business in Vienna – 1867: Tea company Kousmichoff (later Kusmi tea) founded in St. Petersburg
Awards	– 2016: East Frisian Tea Culture listed as UNESCO intangible heritage – 2021: East Frisians awarded world record of tea drinking (300l per capita per year)	– 1900: World's Exhibition Paris Award: Caucasian Tea is the Best in the World – 2022: Turkish and Azerbaijani Tea Cultures listed as UNESCO intangible heritage

Sources: Author, based on Haddinga (1977); Hincheldey (2009); Krieger (2021); Rohrsen (2022); Schäfer (2003); UNESCO (2022); Öğüt (2009); Altonaer Museum (1977); Kasprzyk-Chevriaux (2019); Yurtoglu (2018); UNESCO (2022a); Öğüt (2009)

References

Altonaer Museum. (1977). Tee-Kulturgeschichte. Eigenverlag.

Bohne, H. (2022a). Tea ceremonies. In D. Buhalis (Ed.), *Encyclopedia of tourism management and marketing*, pp. 331–35. Edward Elgar Publishing Ltd.

Bohne, H. (2022b). Tea consumption heritage. In D. Buhalis (Ed.), *Encyclopedia of tourism management and marketing*, pp. 335–37. Edward Elgar Publishing Ltd.

Bohne, H., & Jolliffe, L. (2021). Embracing tea culture in hotel experiences. *Journal of Gastronomy and Tourism*, 6(1–2), 13–24.

Bohne, H. (2021). Uniqueness of tea traditions and impacts on tourism: The East Frisian Tea Culture. *International Journal of Culture, Tourism, and Hospitality Research*, special issue: *Opportunities and Challenges at the Connection of Coffee, Tea, and Tourism*, 15(3), 371–83.

Carter, M. (1996). *Teapots*. Apple press.

Ford, S. (2022). Tea and the tea caddy. A brief story of the early history of tea and ist containers. Retrieved April 23, 2023, from https://colnestour.org/magazine_article/tea-tea-caddy-brief-study-early-history-tea-containers/

Gaylard, L. (2021). *Das Teebuch*. DK Penguin Random House.

Hjalager, A.-M., & Richards, G. (2002). *Tourism and gastronomy*. Routledge.

Kasprzyk-Chevriaux, M. (2019, December 10). Delightful drink or powerful poison: A history of tea in Poland. Retrieved April 23, 2023, https://culture.pl/en/article/drink-poison-history-tea-poland

Lewis, S. (2022). Tin of tea: A history of loose leaf tea storage. Retrieved April 23, 2023, from https://www.plumdeluxe.com/blogs/blog/tin-of-tea

Klauß, N. (2019). *Die neue Trinkkultur*. Piper.

Klöver, H. (2008). *Tee in Ostfriesland*. Sambucus Verlag.

Krieger, M. (2021). Geschichte des Tees. Anbau, Handel und globale Genusskulturen. Böhlau Verlag.

Öğüt, Ş.T. (2009). Material culture of tea in Türkiye: Transformations of design through tradition, modernity and identity. *The Design Journal*, *12*(3), 339–63.

Pettigrew, J. (2001). *A social history of tea*. National Trust.

Pettigrew, J. (2003). *Design for tea*. Sutton Publishing.

Rohrsen, P. (2022). *Das Buch zum Tee*. C.H. Beck Verlag.

Schäfer, D. (2003). *Samowar*. Verlag für die Frau.

UNESCO. (2022a). Cultural selection: The diffusion of tea and tea culture along the silk roads. Retrieved April 2, 2023, from https://en.unesco.org/silkroad/content/cultural-selection-diffusion-tea-and-tea-culture-along-silk-roads

UNESCO. (2022b). Decision of the Intergovernmental Committee: 17.COM 7.B.44 about the inscription of Culture of Çay (tea), a symbol of identity, hospitality and social interaction on the Representative List of the Intangible Cultural Heritage of Humanity. Rabat, November 30, 2022. Retrieved July 5, 2023, from https://ich.unesco.org/en/RL/culture-of-ay-tea-a-symbol-of-identity-hospitality-and-social-interaction-01685

UNESCO Germany. (2016). Nationwide inventory of intangible cultural heritage.

East Frisian tea culture. Retrieved January 3, 2023, from https://www.unesco.de/en/east-frisian-tea-culture

Vink, L., Kappert-White, A., & Bohne, H. (2022). Cultural heritage and tourism: Friesland tea. In L. Jolliffe (Ed.), *Routledge handbook of tea tourism* (pp. 58–66). Routledge.

Yurtoglu, N. (2018). Tea cultivation and tea policies in the Republic of Türkiye (1923–1960). *History Studies – International Journal of History*, *10*(8), 209–32.

Epilogue

Hospitable establishments in Europe are perfect spaces for celebrating tea cultures of Europe, showing the heritage and excellence of welcoming gastronomy – in private or business environments.

Tea culture in Europe is full of opportunities, creativity and coziness, as well as entrepreneurial spirit. Either in the north or in the west, in the south or in the east, there are different preferences in terms of sorts of tea, brewing methods, porcelain or glass or silver utensils as well as different sweeteners and cakes/biscuits – all these choices make each of the different cultures very unique.

Tea in the arts shows that the situations in which people are enjoying tea mostly symbolise moments of calmness and quietness, surrounded by comfort and refinement. Tea is important and also used to create special afternoon tea events, such as through tea pairing arrangements and alongside mixing beverages.

In addition, teahouses invite people to see the useful joint architecture of tea and design, presenting a lifestyle for many decades, which is also transferred to contemporary challenges. Finally, three UNESCO listed tea cultures in Europe are clear signals for the value of tea cultures, showing daily routine as well as special occasions.

Meanwhile, for every consumer, tea has its very own significance in his or her life, but above all there is probably the enjoyment, the ritual of preparation and the appreciation of the moment. In this sense, I would like to thank you for your appreciation and the time you have spent reading this book and hope that it has inspired you on your own personal journey of discovery.

"No matter where you are in the world, you are at home when tea is served."
(Earlene Grey)

May 2024
Prof. Dr. Hartwig Bohne

https://doi.org/10.1515/9783110758573-040

Index

https://doi.org/10.1515/9783110758573-041